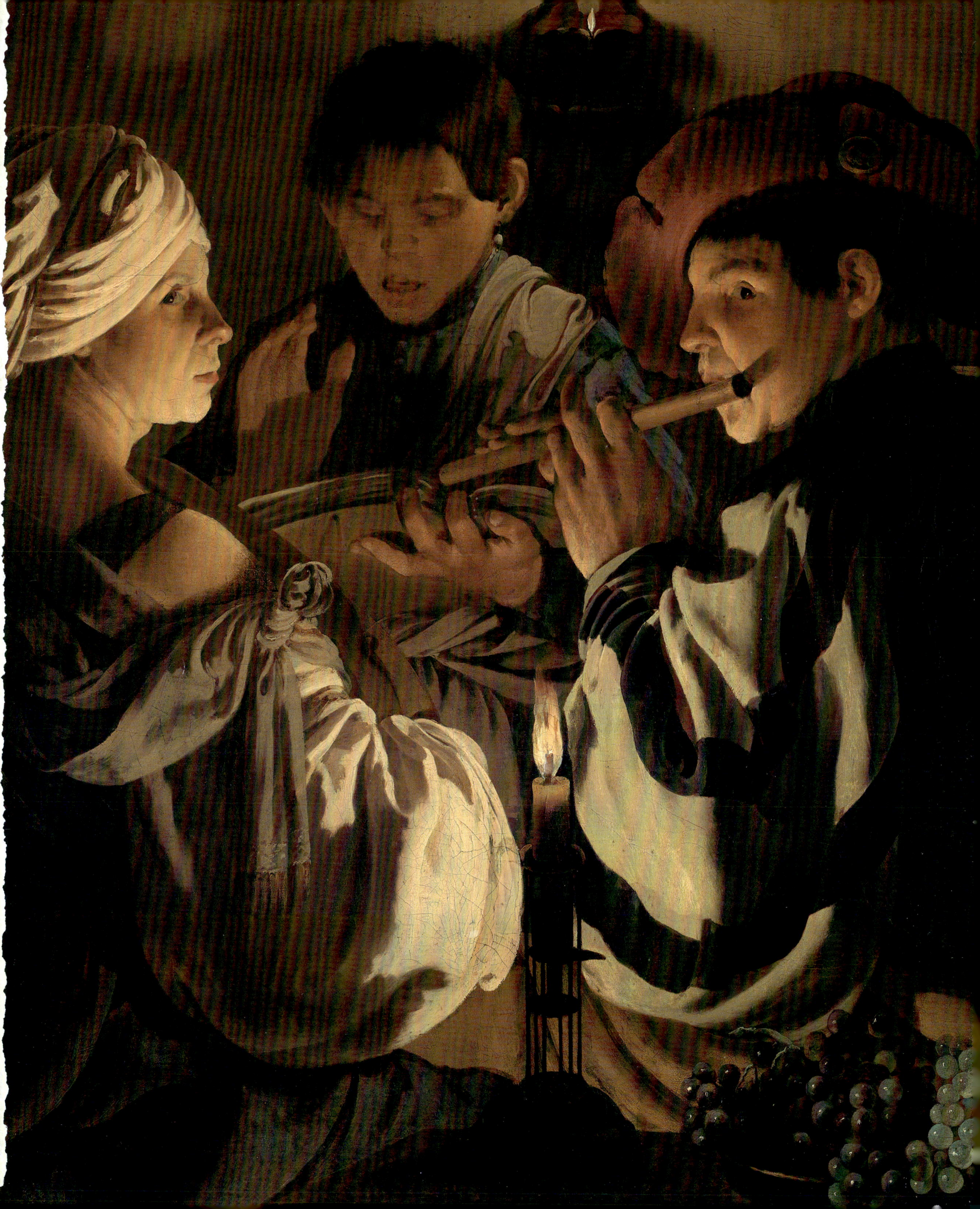

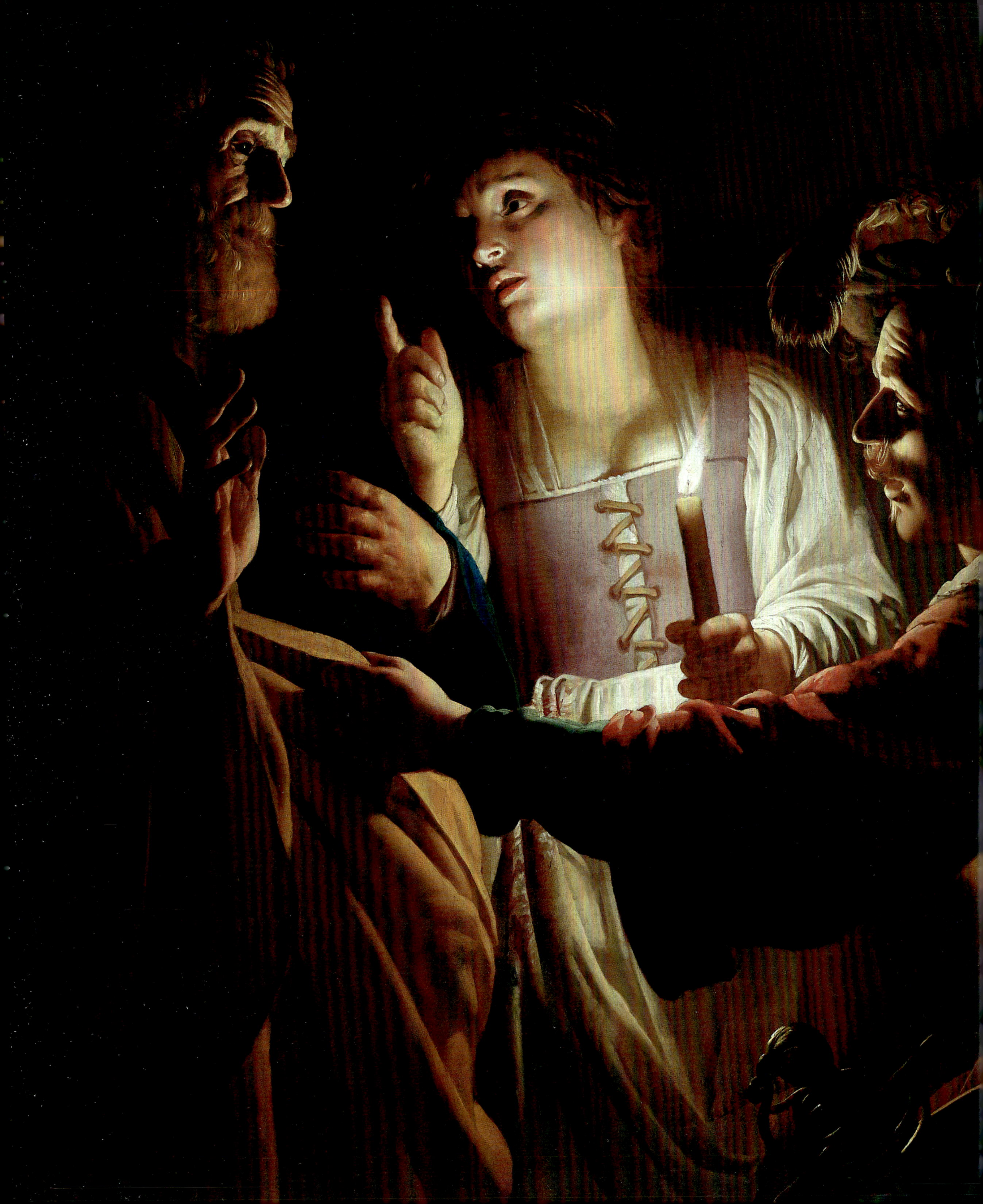

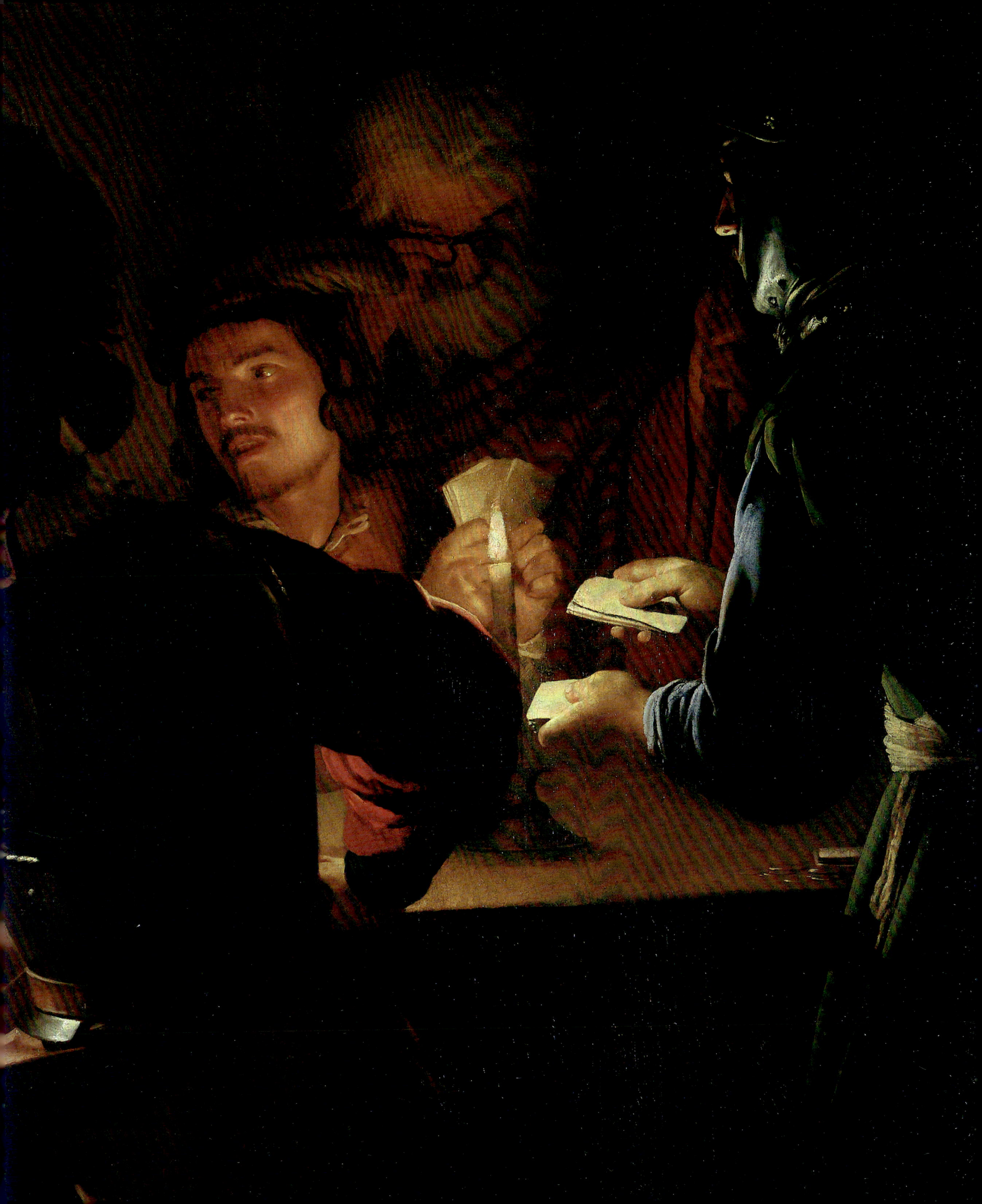

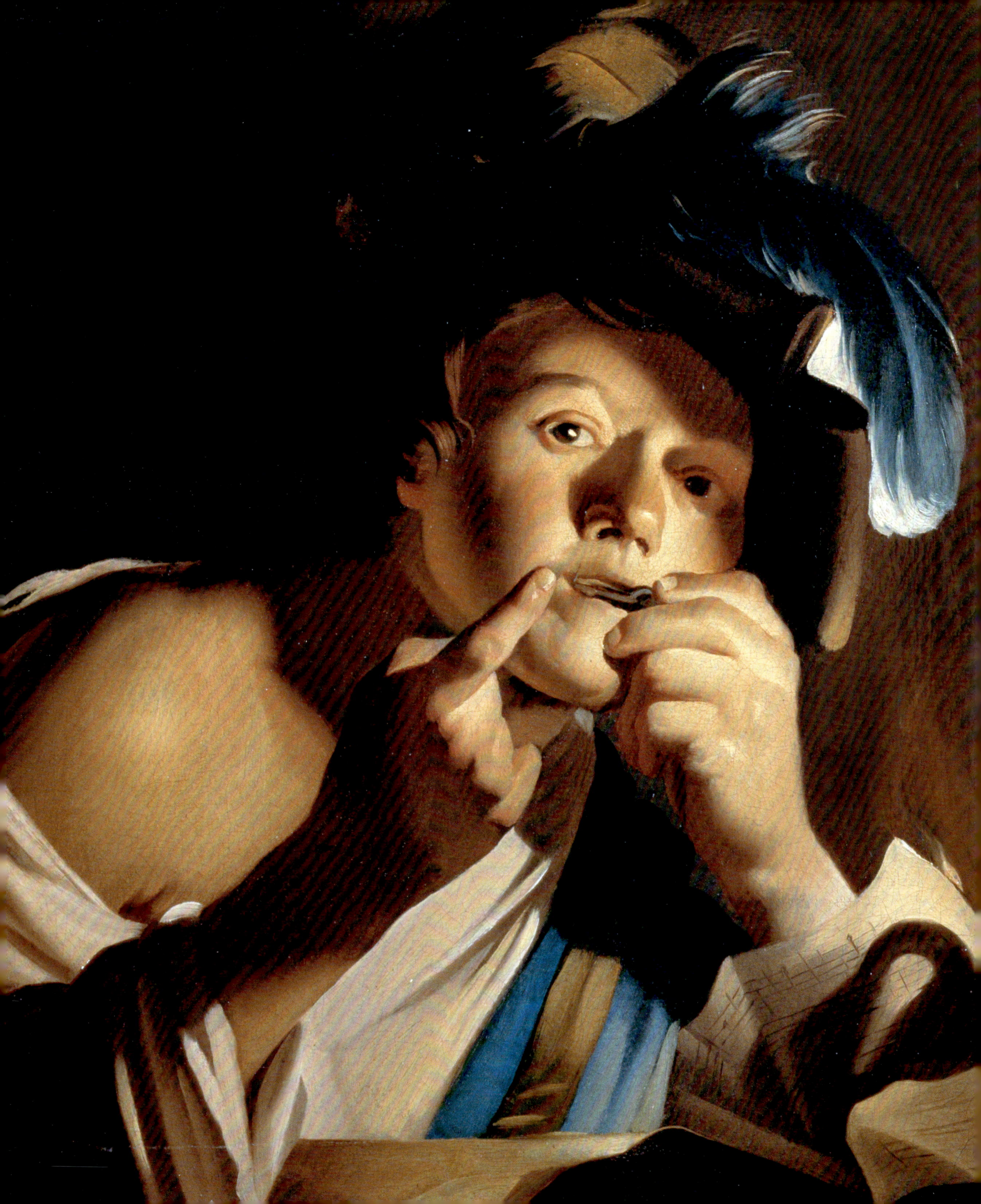

UTRECHT, CARAVAGGIO AND EUROPE

Edited by
Bernd Ebert and Liesbeth M. Helmus

With contributions by
Marten Jan Bok, Bernd Ebert, Liesbeth M. Helmus,
Susanne Hoppe, Helen Langdon, Volker Manuth, Ashok Roy

HIRMER

CENTRAAL MUSEUM

ALTE PINAKOTHEK

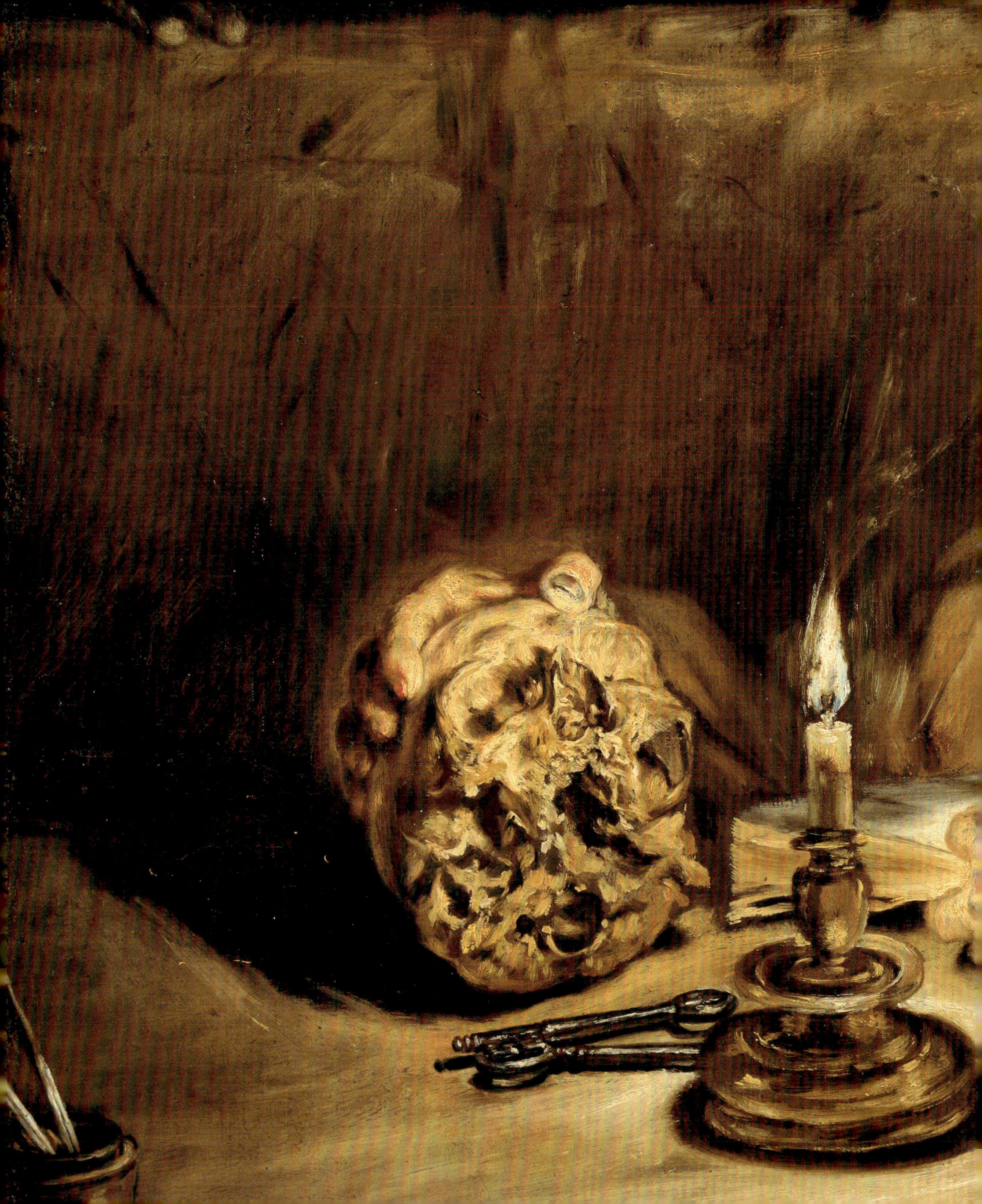

Acknowledgements by the Centraal Museum

The exhibition at the Centraal Museum in Utrecht would not have been possible without the Gieskes-Strijbis Fonds, which provided us with essential financial support during the preparations. The exhibition is also supported by the Dutch government in the form of an indemnity guarantee from the Cultural Heritage Agency on behalf of the Minister of Education, Culture and Science.

Many other funds and companies are sponsoring this special and ambitious exhibition. The Blockbusterfonds stimulates cultural entrepreneurship and supports the realisation of prominent exhibitions such as this one by offering a credit facility and support in the form of ticket purchases. This support also serves as an important stamp of approval.

The Mondriaan Fonds enabled us to research the feasibility of international loan pieces, as a result of which many works never seen before in the Netherlands are now on display in Utrecht. Their contribution also facilitated an intensive exchange with our partner the Alte Pinakothek in Munich.

The Van Baaren Stichting is not just an important lender of art, but also contributes significantly to our activities. The foundation immediately recognised the importance of this exhibition and provided very generous backing. The K.F. Heinfonds likewise contributed generously to the realisation of this exhibition.

We are very grateful for the trust shown by the Turing Foundation, for it also encouraged other partners to support us. Thanks to the contribution by the Fentener van Vlissingen Fonds, we were able to place the Utrecht artists in an international perspective.

Finally, we thank the Prins Bernhard Cultuurfonds for awarding us the Curatorial Stipend in 2015, which enabled us to appoint a junior curator. This enabled the curator responsible for the exhibition, Liesbeth Helmus, to devote more time to the preparations.

Our close collaboration with Philips Lighting and its lighting experts has ensured the unique illumination of the exhibition and the individual works. The company M4Four helped enhance the allure of the exhibition with their unique floors, specially created under the instruction of the museum.

We also thank Siemens Netherlands and the province of Utrecht. The city and province of Utrecht have enabled us to promote this exhibition both domestically and internationally. Their contribution has furthermore stimulated collaboration with various other cultural institutes in the city and province, in particular with Kunsthal KAdE in the city of Amersfoort.

To conclude, we thank our constant partners, the city of Utrecht and the participants in the BankGiro Loterij for their continued support of our museum. This allows us to offer new and returning visitors a remarkable cultural experience, year after year.

Marco Grob and Bart Rutten
Directors
Centraal Museum

Foreword by the Sponsors of the Munich Exhibition

Without patronage, generous sponsors and affluent clients and buyers, Caravaggism would probably never have existed. It was the wealthy and influential families of Rome who patronised the young, impecunious painter Michelangelo Merisi from the town of Caravaggio in Lombardy, who acquired his early, extraordinary works, and who welcomed him as a guest in their palaces. They did the same for his followers, the young painters who had undertaken perilous journeys across Europe to complete their training in Rome, study the works of classical antiquity and the Renaissance and interact with their contemporaries. Not all of the *oltramontani*, as foreigners coming from beyond the Alps were called, achieved fame and some soon fell into oblivion. Yet a few of them, demonstrating great talent and skill and taking advantage of a network of social contacts, can today be found in the world's major museums. Of the numerous artists who are ranked among the so-called Caravaggisti, those famous masters who achieved their breakthrough as artists have been selected for the exhibition.

An international exhibition project, whose scholarly and organisational aspects have been prepared transnationally over the years by a large team in a cooperation between two important museums, which was able to obtain over 70 large-scale paintings from museums, churches and private collections throughout the world, requires extensive support. The Ernst von Siemens Kunststiftung and the Sparkassen-Finanzgruppe are very happy to be associated with this project in Munich as partners and main sponsors. They are united in their aim of paving the way for this extraordinary survey of exhibits, of exciting as many visitors as possible about them, and of making the scholarly work accessible in the shape of an exquisite catalogue and innovative digital formats. Both partners operate nationwide in Germany and are constantly involved in facilitating acquisitions for museums and collections and supporting restoration works or outstanding exhibition projects.

When he established his foundations, the music lover Ernst von Siemens' central concern was to support projects and institutions that promised to make a significant cultural contribution. In addition to the visual arts, this also included music and the theatre. The dramatic, almost stage-managed compositions of the Caravaggisti provide the basis for allowing those sister disciplines to enter into a unique kind of dialogue. With their creative means of brush and paint, the artists sought to capture on canvas emotions, affects and movements, in order to generate empathy and captivate the viewers of their works. The composer, musician or actor probably aims to achieve much the same. But what creative means would they use? How would a composer, a stage director, a dramaturge or even a young painter render Caravaggesque pictorial themes today? These, too, are questions addressed by *Utrecht, Caravaggio and Europe*, along with the project's partners, the Opera Studio of the Bavarian State Opera, the University of Music and Performing Arts and the Academy of Fine Arts in Munich. Ernst von Siemens would have been delighted with the extensive programme of events accompanying this exhibition. Encouraging such an involvement with different art forms and promoting intercultural dialogue is also an essential aspect of the Sparkassen-Finanzgruppe's social responsibility. Support for the *Utrecht, Caravaggio and Europe* project became possible when three of its organisations joined forces: the Deutscher Sparkassen und Giroverband, the Bayerische Sparkassenstiftung and Stadtsparkasse München. All three parties made substantial contributions to fund the presentation and communication of the exhibition.

The Sparkassen-Finanzgruppe supports particularly innovative formats that also appeal to a younger public. The artists included in this exhibition were themselves just young adults when they created the works that still fascinate us today. As partners, we hope that the many visitors to the exhibition and readers of this catalogue will be filled with enthusiasm about their art which was, in its time, contemporary, novel and bold.

Dr. Martin Hoernes
Secretary-General
Ernst von Siemens
Kunststiftung

Helmut Schleweis
President
Deutscher Sparkassen-
und Giroverband

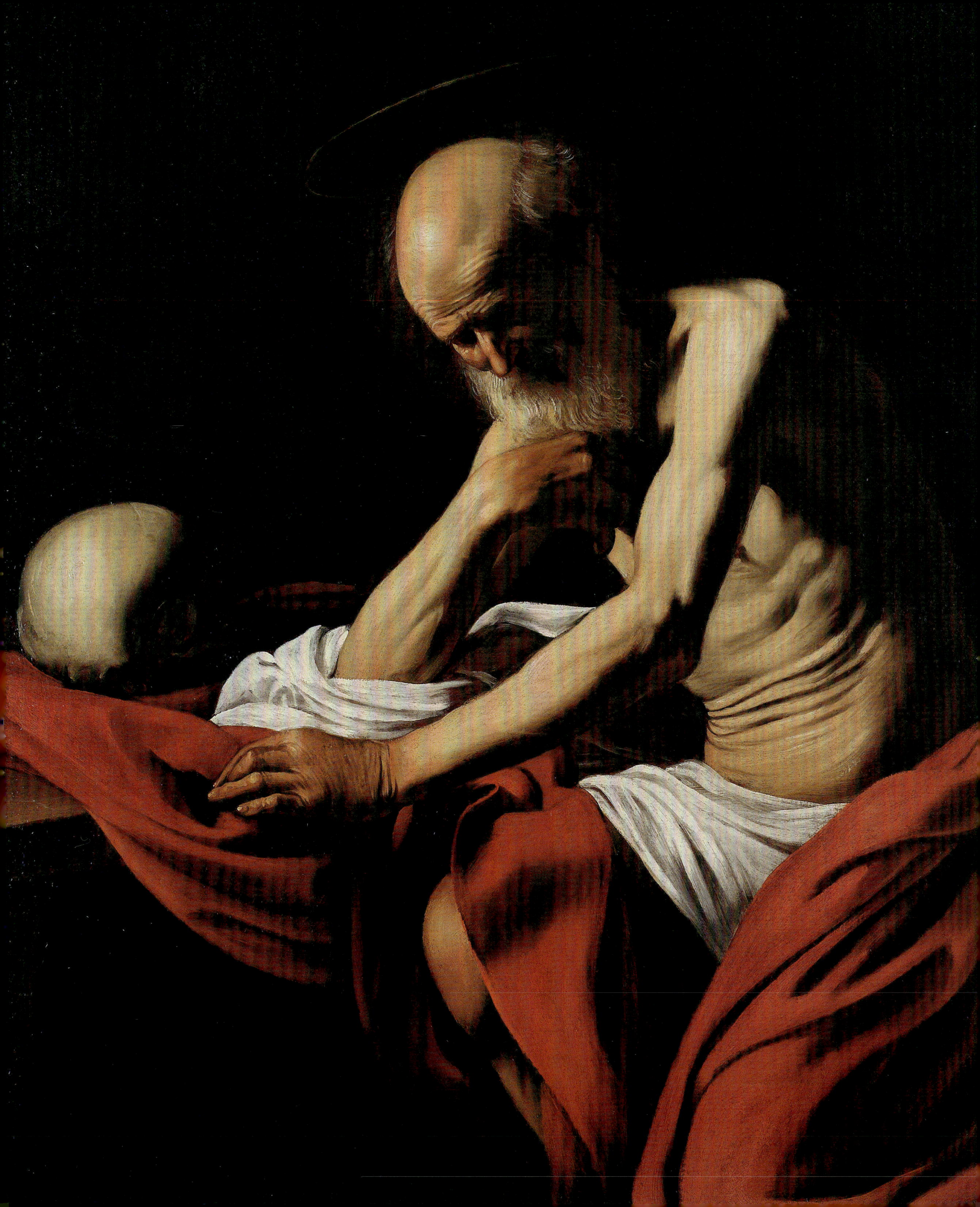

Lenders

This exhibition would not have been possible without the unwavering support of both public and private lenders, for whose generosity we are very grateful.

Amsterdam, Rijksmuseum
Antwerpen, Koninklijk Museum voor Schone Kunsten
Berlin, Staatliche Museen zu Berlin – Gemäldegalerie
Braunschweig, Herzog Anton Ulrich-Museum
Budapest, Szépművészeti Múzeum
Diest, Stadsmuseum De Hofstadt
Dresden, Staatliche Kunstsammlungen Dresden, Gemäldegalerie Alte Meister
Dublin, National Gallery of Ireland
Florence, Galleria degli Uffizi
Florence, Museo della Misericordia
Genoa, Musei di Strada Nuova – Palazzo Bianco
Hartford (Connecticut), Wadsworth Atheneum Museum of Art
Kassel, Museumslandschaft Hessen Kassel, Gemäldegalerie Alte Meister
Langres, Musée d'Art et d'Histoire de Langres
London, The Schorr Collection
London, The National Gallery
Los Angeles (California), Los Angeles County Museum of Art
Madrid, Museo Nacional Thyssen-Bornemisza
Madrid, Real Academia de Bellas Artes de San Fernando
Minneapolis (Minnesota), Minneapolis Institute of Art
Montserrat, Museu de Montserrat
Munich, Bayerische Staatsgemäldesammlungen
Naples, Quadreria dei Girolamini
New York (New York), The Metropolitan Museum of Art
Norfolk (Virginia), Chrysler Museum of Art
Oberlin (Ohio), Allen Memorial Art Museum, Oberlin College
Oslo, Nasjonalmuseet for kunst, arkitektur og design
Paris, Musée de l'Assistance Publique – Hôpitaux de Paris
Paris, Musée du Louvre
Perth and Kinross Council Scotland, Perth Museum and Art Gallery
Raleigh (North Carolina), North Carolina Museum of Art
Rancate (Mendrisio), Pinacoteca cantonale Giovanni Züst
Rennes, Musée des Beaux-Arts de Rennes
Rome, Gallerie Nazionali di Arte Antica di Roma (Palazzo Barberini, Galleria Corsini)
Rome, Musei Capitolini, Pinacoteca Capitolina
Rome, Santa Maria della Scala
Schwerin, Staatliches Museum Schwerin
The Hague, Mauritshuis
Toulouse, Musée des Augustins
Utrecht, Museum Catharijneconvent
Utrecht, Centraal Museum
Valencia, Museo del Patriarca, Real Colegio Seminario de Corpus Christi
Vatican City, Musei Vaticani, Pinacoteca Vaticana
Washington, D.C., National Gallery of Art

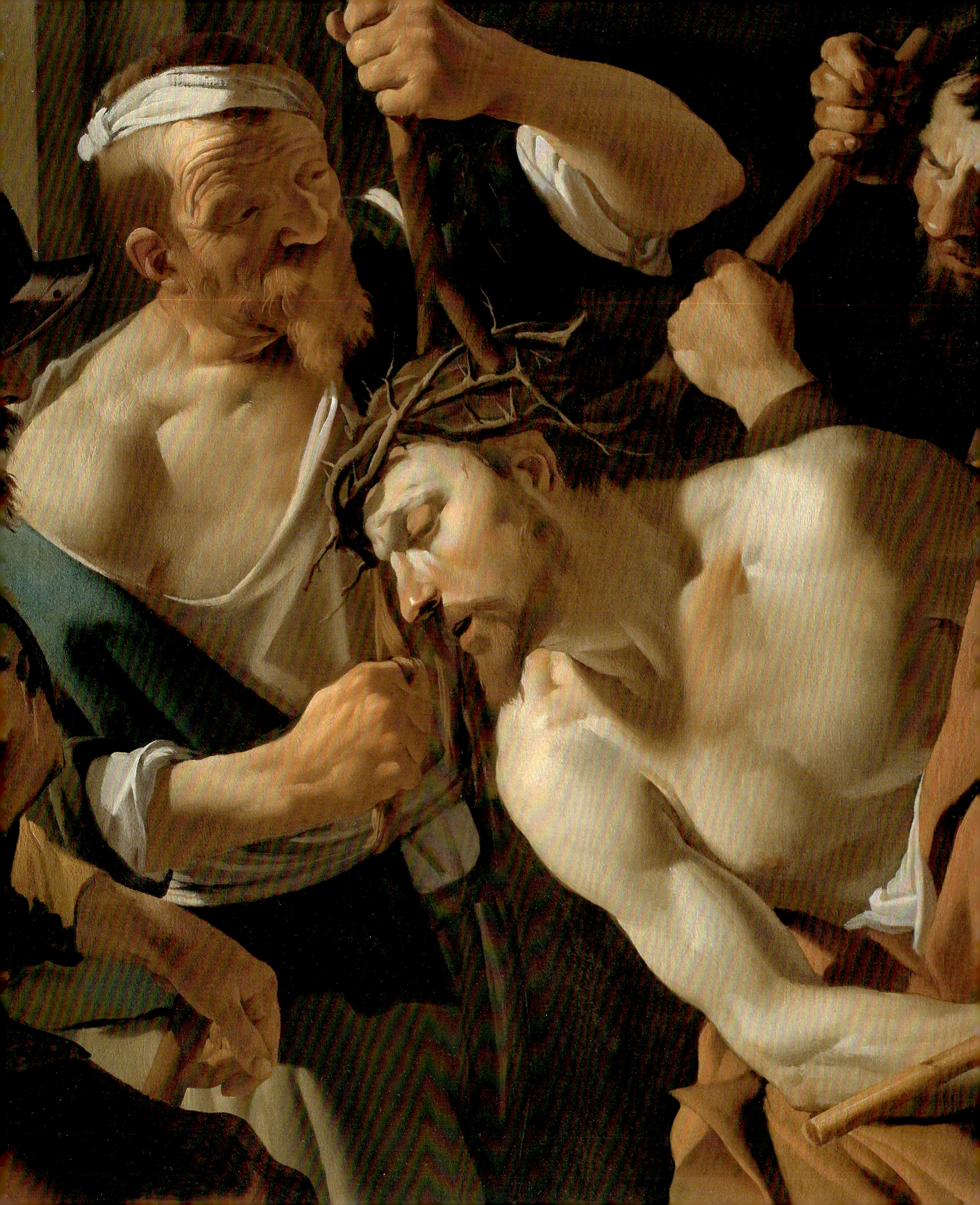

CONTENTS

Directors' Foreword

In devoting an exhibition to the Utrecht Caravaggisti, our museums have undertaken to look at an era when Europe was characterised by lively international exchanges and intense artistic productivity, and to impress upon our present-day public why works created four centuries ago still arouse our fascination and empathy. The artists who moved to Rome and, while there, appropriated the legacy of Caravaggio (only a few of them met him in person) were young – very young – with some barely 20 years old. So young and already so creative – what does that have to do with us? It shows the power of audacious, inventive artists and of young people in general, which is why we are also very keen to draw youthful visitors into our exhibitions.

These young artists followed their dream and took great risks to make them come true. They wanted to get closer to the source and see for themselves how they could improve their own works. Even today, their ambition and courage is an inspiration, opening our eyes to all those young people who follow their hearts to go in quest of a better future for their abilities. Those risks feed the energy that can still be experienced in the masterpieces by the Utrecht Caravaggisti.

Utrecht is the first location to host this exhibition that assembles works from many countries and collections. The cooperation agreement was signed two years ago in Munich. Present on this occasion, and illustrating the importance of the project, were not just the Directors of both institutions but, moreover, the Dutch royal couple. This moment has not been forgotten, and finds its continuation at the second venue in Munich starting in April 2019, where the exhibition, while differing in a few isolated instances from its first incarnation, will still be based on a large number of shared loans.

Why do the works of the followers of Michelangelo Merisi, called Caravaggio, appeal to us in such a striking and intense way? There are probably multiple partial answers to that question. A key factor is surely that they are works of great power and brilliance; that they are captivating in their compositional clarity, painterly finesse, and artistic and technical perfection. This is why they are appreciated by a wide public. Even today, the biographical details of Caravaggio's life as a quite pugnacious, freely creative painter contribute to a veritable fascination with his life's journey between creativity and anarchy. A third aspect is, perhaps, particularly notable for the understanding of our time, as Caravaggio, like his pupils and followers, turned to subjects that could be described as fundamental human issues. People cheat at card games; in subjects such as Judith, people murder on behalf of third parties; defending himself successfully against Goliath, David pits the weak against the reputedly stronger. In other words, it is about violence, strength, deception and lies, about anthropologically timeless themes of human relationships, contemporary versions of which we can see today in films and high-quality TV series. This results in the most thrilling constellations of figures in a particular painting, allowing us to tell curious museum visitors, both young and adult, the liveliest stories – stories that are very much of today. Hence, art education in many ways also plays an important role in making the subject matter of these works accessible.

The exhibition brings together paintings and artists from many countries; for this, we are very grateful to all our lenders. The European idea is central to the project both in its development and realisation, and in the wealth of works and the almost pan-European origin of the artists. We want to express our heartfelt gratitude to all those who have been involved in preparing this exhibition project and making it happen. The European project is lived and remembered in an ideal manner here: around 1610, these young men travelled across the Alps, bringing the inspirations they had found in the Eternal City back to the North – an interplay of creativity!

For the Centraal Museum in Utrecht, it is therefore particularly pleasing to see the return of so many works by young pioneers in Rome, flanked splendidly by artists who shared their adventurous spirits from so many other parts of Europe. Occupying an impressive position in Europe at the end of the 16th and beginning of the 17th century, Rome had a lively cultural climate, blazing a trail for what would later be celebrated as the Dutch Golden Age.

Assembling such a large number of major Caravaggesque paintings of such high quality in an exhibition shown in two locations would not be possible without the extraordinary generosity of the lenders. A large number of people have been involved and instrumental in the negotiations over the years, most notably the respective curators and decision makers of the lending museums, as well as private owners. Important assistance has been provided not only by the diplomatic missions, but also by Willem Jacobus Kardinal Eijk, Archbishop of Utrecht und Cardinal Reinhard Marx, Archbishop of Munich and Freising, whose advocacy was recognised by the lenders in particular.

For the two responsible museum partners, this project, which was possible only with the substantial involvement of additional institutions, is unusual in its scale. The Gieskes-Strijbis Fonds played a vital role for Utrecht by providing the financial basis for the exhibition at a critical point in the preparations. It financed the lion's share of the transport costs in order to bring these first-rate works to Utrecht. The exhibition was also made possible in part by the Dutch government, as the Cultural Heritage Agency of the Netherlands provided state liability for the loans on behalf of the Minister of Education, Culture and Science. Many other funds are supporting this exhibition, which is remarkably ambitious for the Centraal Museum, and in some cases they even went beyond their own subsidy ceilings. This strengthened us in our conviction that we were undertaking something exceptional. Such generous support was a stimulus that transcended the financial input alone. We are deeply indebted to the City of Utrecht, the Prins Bernhard Cultuurfonds, the Mondriaan Fonds, the Van Baaren Stichting, the K.F. Heinfonds, the Turing Foundation, the Fentener van Vlissingen Fonds, the Blockbusterfonds and Siemens Netherlands for helping to make this exhibition possible, and we thank them for the trust they placed in us. The contribution by Philips Ligthing enabled us to light the works in a professional manner.

From the very beginning, for the exhibition in Munich, the Bayerische Staatsgemäldesammlungen was able to build on the support of the Ernst von Siemens Kunststiftung and the affiliated partners of the Sparkassen-Finanzgruppe, including the Deutscher Sparkassen und Giroverband, the Bayerische Sparkassenstiftung and the Stadtsparkasse München, as well as the Kulturstiftung der Länder. We are extremely grateful to them all.

We would like to express our heartfelt thanks to all the other participants who have organised and created this exhibition project in many different ways.

Marco Grob
Managing Director
Centraal Museum,
Utrecht

Bernhard Maaz
General Director
Bayerische Staatsgemälde-
sammlungen, Munich

Bart Rutten
Artistic Director
Centraal Museum,
Utrecht

Utrecht, Caravaggio and Europe

BERND EBERT AND LIESBETH M. HELMUS

Caravaggio's (1571–1610) huge popularity, which has risen to great heights in the past quarter of a century, has led to heated discussions about attributions, countless 'discoveries' and to a host of exhibitions. The focus is not only on the paintings by the master himself, but also by extension on the works of his supposed followers. They include the Utrecht Caravaggisti, who have been the subject of three previous exhibitions, in 1952, 1986/87 and 2009.[1] It is time for a revision.

Utrecht, Caravaggio and Europe gathers together work by the three leading Utrecht Caravaggisti: Hendrick ter Brugghen (1588–1629), Gerard van Honthorst (1592–1656) and Dirck van Baburen (c. 1592/93–1624). They, like their colleagues, were certainly influenced by Caravaggio himself, but they were also indebted to Caravaggesque painters in Italy, Spain, France and Flanders. All three were independent, self-willed artists with outspoken characters of their own. New, highly detailed monographs have been published on Honthorst, ter Brugghen and Baburen in the past few decades.[2] The *Utrecht, Caravaggio and Europe* exhibition sets out to acquaint the general public with the content of the many art-historical studies that have revised and refined our view of the position and achievements of these three artists.

Like their colleagues from Flanders, France and Spain, the three Utrecht painters travelled to Rome independently of each other in the early decades of the 17th century. They went there to see the art of classical antiquity at first hand, to study the masterpieces of the Italian Renaissance, and above all to learn about the revolutionary innovations introduced by Caravaggio. They wanted to see for themselves the 'extraordinary things' that the painter and art historian Karel van Mander said that he had done.

Rome was the cultural centre of Europe at the beginning of the 17th century. There were no fewer than 2,700 artists registered in the city in the period 1600–1630, among them 572 foreigners. They lived in the same districts, and many of them shared the same lodgings. These young men, some of them little more than youths, came from the four corners of the world but all saw the same things: Caravaggio's paintings, as well as those by his predecessors and contemporaries. Together these younger artists formed what Benedict Nicolson called the 'International Caravaggesque Movement', yet they were all very different, depending on their origins. They brought their own cultures with them, spoke different languages, had followed various traditions of artistic training, and would have had a variety of reasons for coming. Their pictures show that they interpreted and translated all their impressions and experiences differently. That is what distinguishes this exhibition from the previous ones. It is about the differences, not the similarities. The aim has been to highlight the specific features and quality of the works by the Utrecht artists. The central questions are how they distinguished themselves from their contemporaries, and whether they are recognisable as an independent and typically Dutch element within the larger Caravaggesque movement.

The point of departure each time is a work by one of these Utrecht followers. The chronology of their paintings governs the sequence of the catalogue sections. Honthorst's Oslo drawing, which is signed and dated 1616, is the earliest evidence of his presence in Rome, and Hendrick ter Brugghen's *Penitent St Peter* signed and dated 1616 from the Centraal Museum in Utrecht is the earliest known work by the artist. The latest painting is ter Brugghen's *Annunciation* of 1629 in Diest, which was painted in 1629, the year of his death. Baburen had already died in 1624, and Honthorst had moved increasingly towards a Classicist style. The 78 works in the exhibition, all but one dating from between 1600 and 1630, are the core period of Caravaggism, thus providing a very sharply defined focus on what was made in those three decades.

Themes have been chosen within this chronology. The paintings by Caravaggio and 16 contemporaries and followers are all by the first generation of travellers to Rome. Exhibiting them alongside the works by the Utrecht artists shows at a glance what was happening, what is different. It is also clear that Jusepe de Ribera (1591–1652), in addition to Caravaggio and Bartolomeo Manfredi (1582–1622), played a key role for Baburen and ter Brugghen. The reciprocal influence of these artists who were working simultaneously in Rome is evident in their art. Studying together and discussing paintings by different artists was their great pleasure. That was the discourse then, and still is today.

We are very grateful to all the lenders to the exhibition and the authors of the catalogue, and are also indebted to the following individuals for sharing their thoughts with us, lending their support, and for their critical reading of this publication: Jan Baptist Bedaux, Lisanne Bedaux, Giovanna Capitelli, Marco Cardinali, Keith Christiansen, Roberto Contini, Adam Eaker, Simone Ebert, Sybille Ebert-Schifferer Gabriele Finaldi, Wayne Franits, Frances Gage, Axel Hémery, Nicolas Joly, Guillaume Kazerouni, Guillaume Kientz, Annick Lemoine, Volker Manuth, Patrice Marandel, Patrick Matthiesen, Arnold Nesselrath, Gianni Papi, Sebastian Schütze, Nicola Spinosa, Letizia Treves and Gregor Weber.

1 Utrecht/Antwerp 1952; Utrecht/Braunschweig 1986/87 and Frankfurt 2009. In 2015, the Uffizi organised the first monographic exhibition on Gerard van Honthorst: Exh. cat. Florence 2015.
2 Judson/Ekkart 1999; Papi 1999, and Exh. cat Florence 2015; Slatkes/Franits 2007 and Franits 2013a.

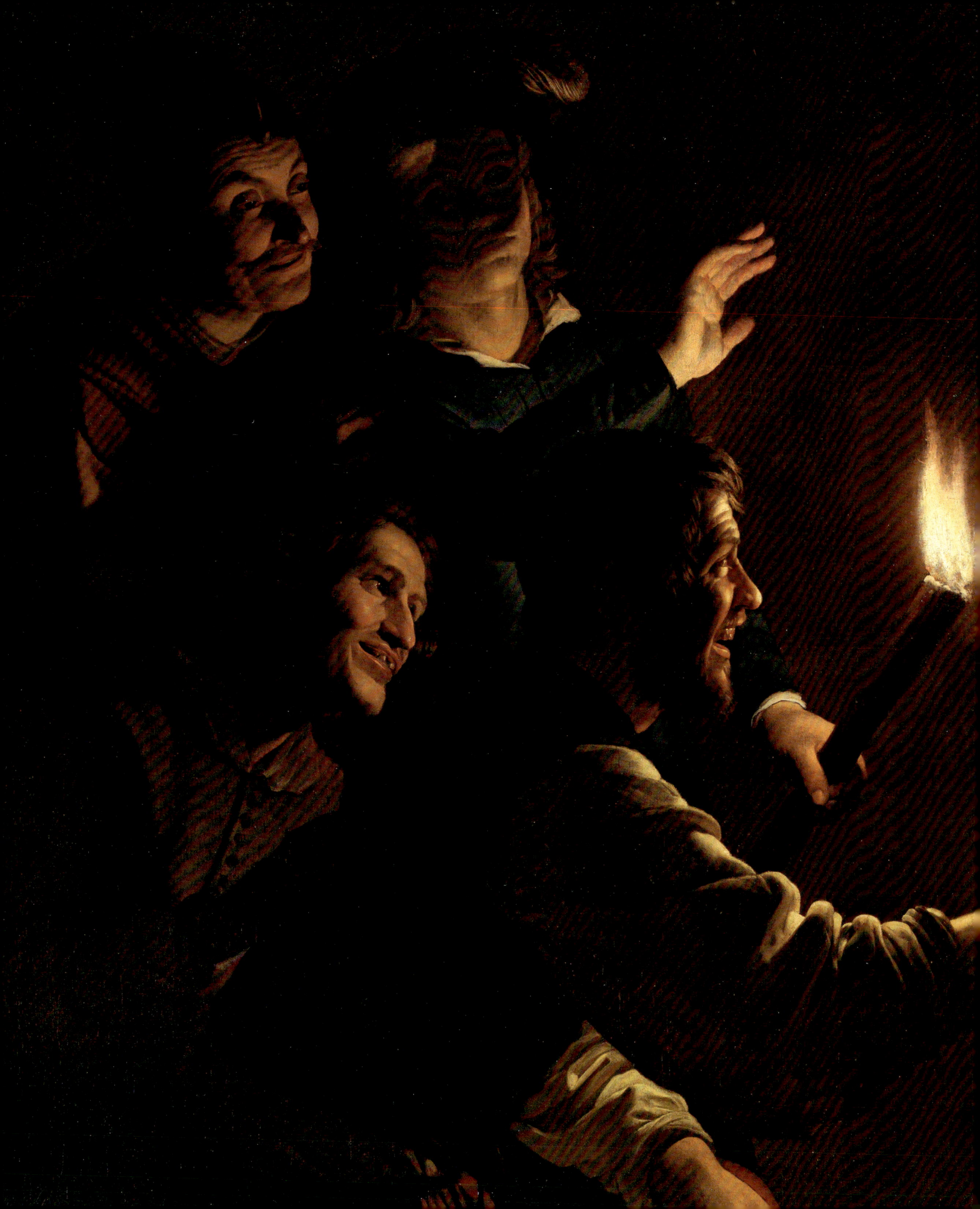

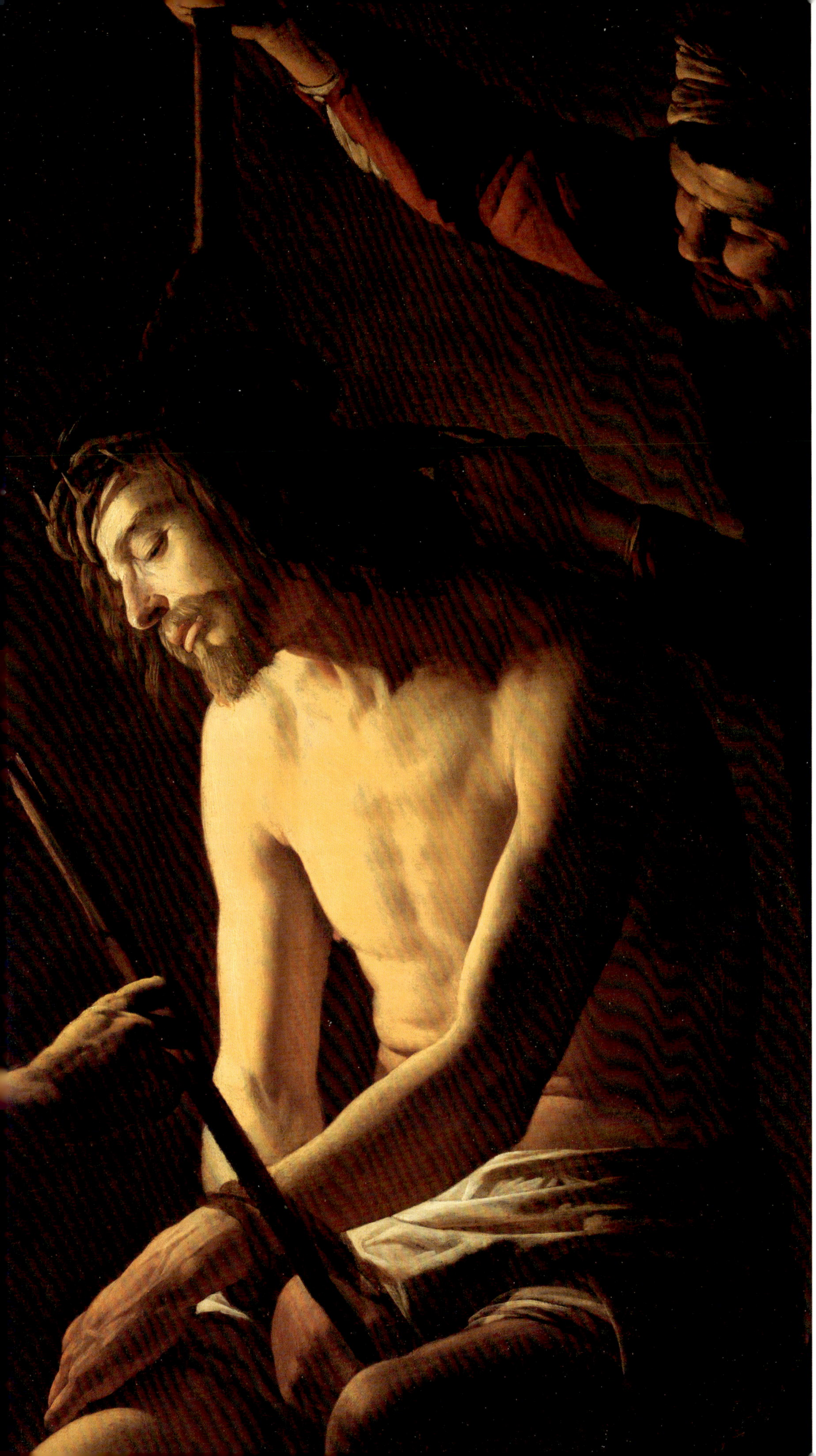

Essays

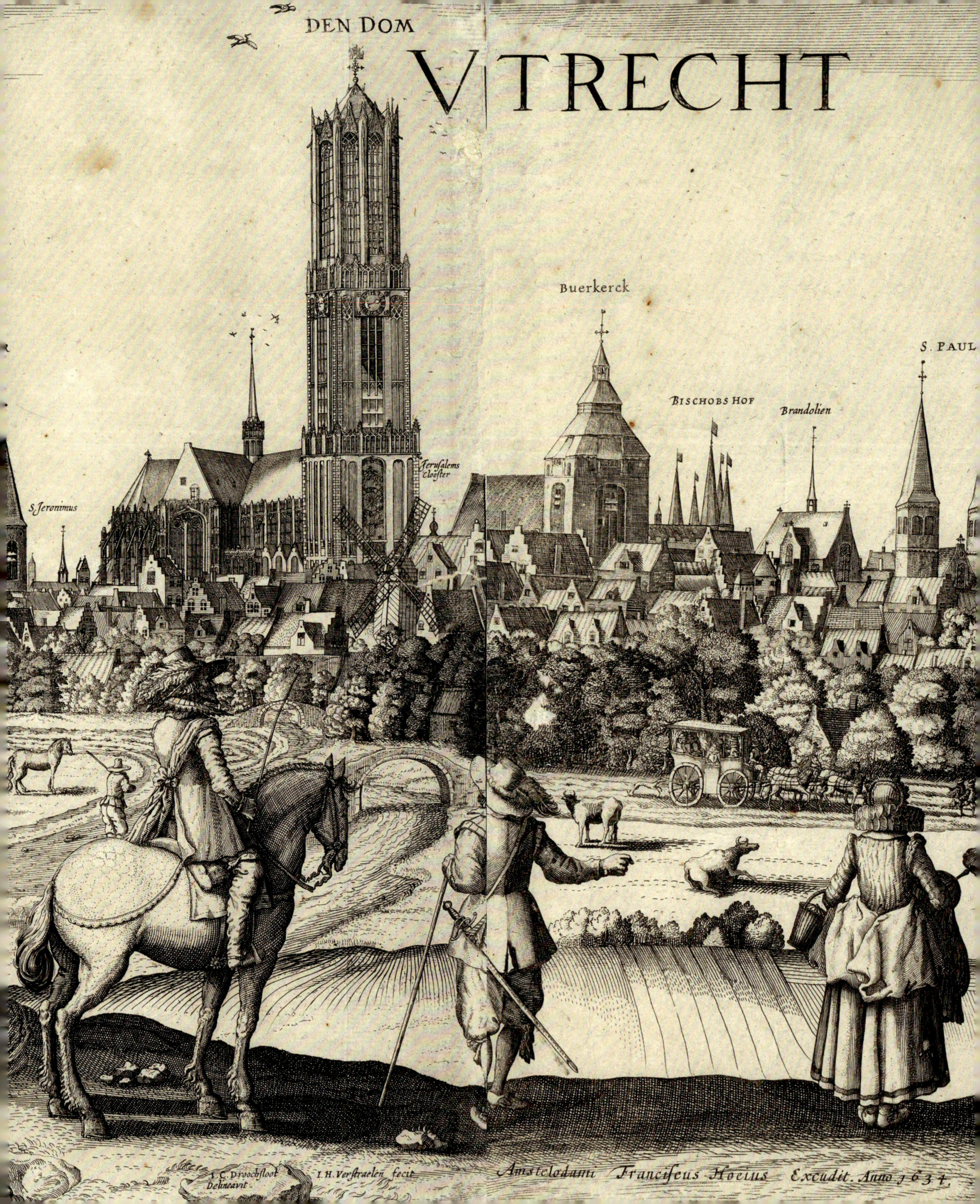
DEN DOM
VTRECHT
Buerkerck
S. PAUL
BISCHOBS HOF
Brandolien
Jerusalems Cloester
S. Jeronimus
I. C. Droochsloot Delineavit
I. H. Verstraelen fecit
Amstelodami Franciscus Hoeius Excudit. Anno 1634.

Utrecht, a Libertine City[1]

MARTEN JAN BOK

Utrecht is treated in the art-historical literature as a Catholic, rather old-fashioned, introverted, medieval city and province that was overshadowed by the dynamic province of Holland in the early decades of the 17th century. It is said that in that period, which coincided with the flowering of Caravaggism, Utrecht preferred to treasure its traditional ecclesiastical ties with Rome rather than play a part in the worldwide expansion of the young Dutch Republic,[2] with the result that the important innovations in art that ushered in the 'typically Dutch' Golden Age passed the city by. It is this 19th-century, nationalistic myth of the typically 'bourgeois' and Calvinist nature of the Netherlands that distorted the image of Utrecht, and still does. However, that view of the character of Utrecht has been overtaken by the findings of recent research into Church history.[3] In reality it turns out that the leading Utrecht Caravaggisti – Hendrick ter Brugghen, Gerard van Honthorst and Dirck van Baburen – were trained in a city that had already been governed for quite a while by a moderate Protestant elite. They grew up in a world no longer dominated by the Catholic Church, but one in which the orthodox Calvinist Protestants did not prevail either. The Reformed Church in Utrecht was liberal and libertine. So it was not the Catholics who dictated the mood of the city. The central thesis of this essay is that Utrecht, above all, was able to become a breeding ground for the international Caravaggist style because its aristocratic and patrician elite with its libertine mindset took its lead from international cultural developments. In this it was closer to The Hague, the court city, than to the port city of Amsterdam.

On the artistic front a direct line of descent can be traced from the most important pre-Reformation Utrecht masters to the teachers of the Utrecht Caravaggisti. All of them specialised in the depiction of the human figure. That skill, so essential for biblical and mythological history painting, was passed on from one generation to the next, even after the Reformation.

Utrecht as a Religious and Economic Centre

On a summer day in July 1620, the young painter Gerard van Honthorst returned from Rome to his native Utrecht.[4] On the final leg of his journey he would have had the cathedral tower, 112 metres high, as a beacon to guide him (fig. 1). On a clear day it can still be seen on the horizon from dozens of kilometres away. The cathedral, the nave of which was to be destroyed in 1674 in a 'terrible tempest', stands on the spot where the small fortress of Trajectum once guarded the northern frontier of the Roman Empire on the River Rhine. In the Middle Ages, the city was the largest and mightiest in the northern Netherlands. It was the religious and administrative centre of an extensive prince bishopric within the Holy Roman Empire, and in the course of centuries dozens of collegiate churches, abbeys, monasteries, convents, parish churches, hospitals and chapels were built there. Lying within the city

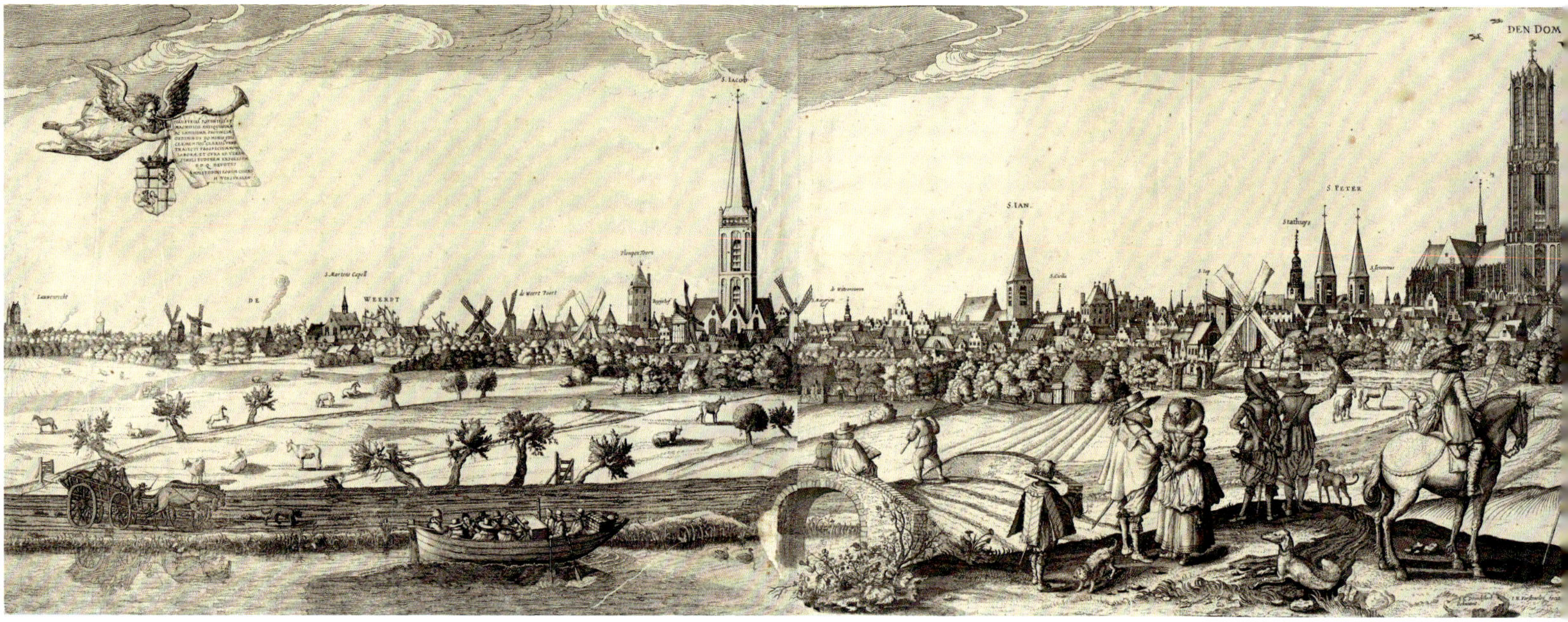

Fig. 1 Jan Hendricksz. Verstraelen (after Joost Cornelisz. Droochsloot), *Profile View of Utrecht from the West*, 1624/25, Het Utrechts Archief, Utrecht

walls was Oudegracht [Old Canal], the lifeline linking Utrecht by water with the cities of Holland and the German hinterland. The houses of the merchants and craftsmen, with their cellars running beneath the streets, had direct access to the wharves lining the canal. Between those houses were the tower houses that stood as mementos of the political conflicts of the medieval nobility (fig. 2). In the heart of the city, by a bridge over Oudegracht, was the city hall, to the left of which was the City Weigh-House, and to the right the city crane. Behind the crane in a drawing by Pieter Jansz. Saenredam (fig. 3),[5] on the west side of the canal, one can just see the corner house on Snippevlucht, the busy alleyway where Honthorst had his first studio, and where Hendrick ter Brugghen came to live a few years later. To the left of Saenredam's vantage point lay the Ganzemarkt (Goose Market) with the inn where Honthorst was welcomed home by his friends and colleagues.

Faith

The Utrecht to which Honthorst returned had shrugged off its image of an archetypal Catholic city decades earlier. The see of Utrecht had lost its political independence to Emperor Charles V in 1528. It is true that the bishopric had been elevated to an archbishopric under his successor, the Spanish King Philip II, but that did not last long. In 1579, Utrecht sided with the rebellious provinces. A year later it forbade the practice of Catholicism in public, and the archbishop died soon afterwards. The Reformation was a fact. With some 30,000 inhabitants, Utrecht was no longer the largest city in the northern Netherlands. It continued to serve as the regional marketplace for the entire province and as the transit port between the cities of Holland and the more distant Dutch and German hinterland, but the port city of Amsterdam and the industrial city of Haarlem would outstrip it. Those two cities profited from the stream of immigrants coming from the southern Netherlands, which became more like a flood after 1585, when the Spanish king regained control of Antwerp.

The most influential Protestant cleric in Utrecht was Hubert Duifhuis (c. 1515–1581). He started out as a Catholic priest, but openly joined the Reformation in 1578.[6] As preacher of the St James congregation he proclaimed the equality of all

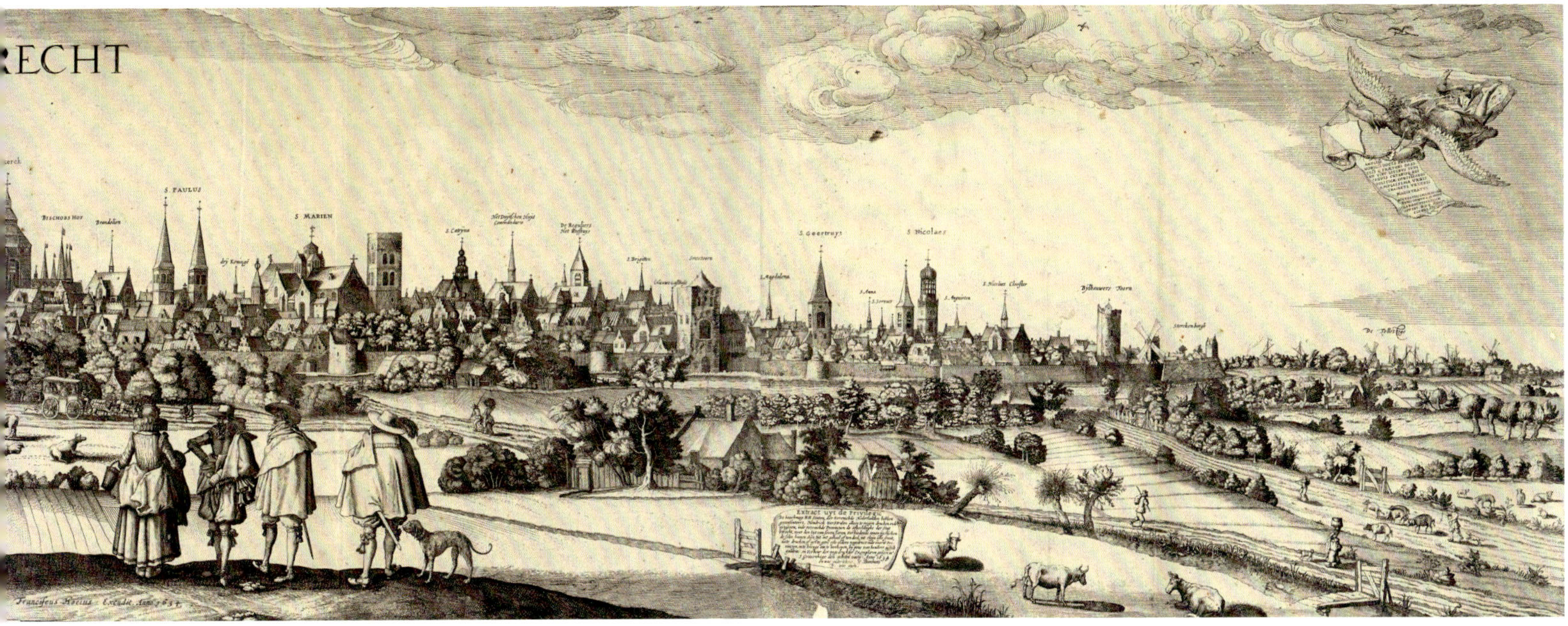

the faithful, of the poor, the rich, the illiterate and the scholar. He rejected all forms of ecclesiastical hierarchy, and felt that it was not up to the clergy or elders to test the conscience or orthodoxy of individual believers. According to him, everyone was duty bound to study the Bible, to examine his or her own conscience, and to enter into a conversation with God. Such an attitude was unacceptable to the Catholic Church, and the followers of Calvin, who set great store by Church discipline, also opposed him fiercely. And it was the latter, above all, who created tension in Utrecht. Duifhuis only wanted to speak of practical matters in the Church council, and certainly not of individual believers, controversial theological questions or political matters.[7]

Duifhuis's spirit lived on after his death in 1581. With the exception of a short-lived, radical Calvinist intermezzo in 1586–1588, Utrecht was to have a largely libertine Protestant Church for several decades. The Duifhuis congregation was under the political supervision of a city government consisting of a majority of equally libertine patricians who supported a broad people's Church.[8] The city appointed preachers with whom Duifhuis's supporters felt at ease.[9] Their radical opponents, most of whom came from the southern Netherlands, contemptuously called them 'libertines', those who knew neither God nor Commandment. The opponents were a minority who continued to stir up trouble.[10] In the 1590s, the most radical among them refused to listen to sermons in the churches but gathered instead in open fields outside the city.[11] Partly under pressure from the other provinces, the Utrecht authorities were forced to make concessions in the years that followed, but it was not until 1609 that the conflict reached a pitch in the struggle between supporters of the theologian Jacobus Arminius (Remonstrants) and Franciscus Gomarus (Counter-Remonstrants).

In 1592, Rome had declared the northern Netherlands to be a missionary territory because of the dysfunction of the bishoprics. Catholics had great difficulty in regrouping after the transfer of their churches to the Protestants. Catholic priests worked in private homes and in the chapels of nunneries that had not yet been secularised and of hospitals. Catholics were distrusted by their fellow citizens as long as the war

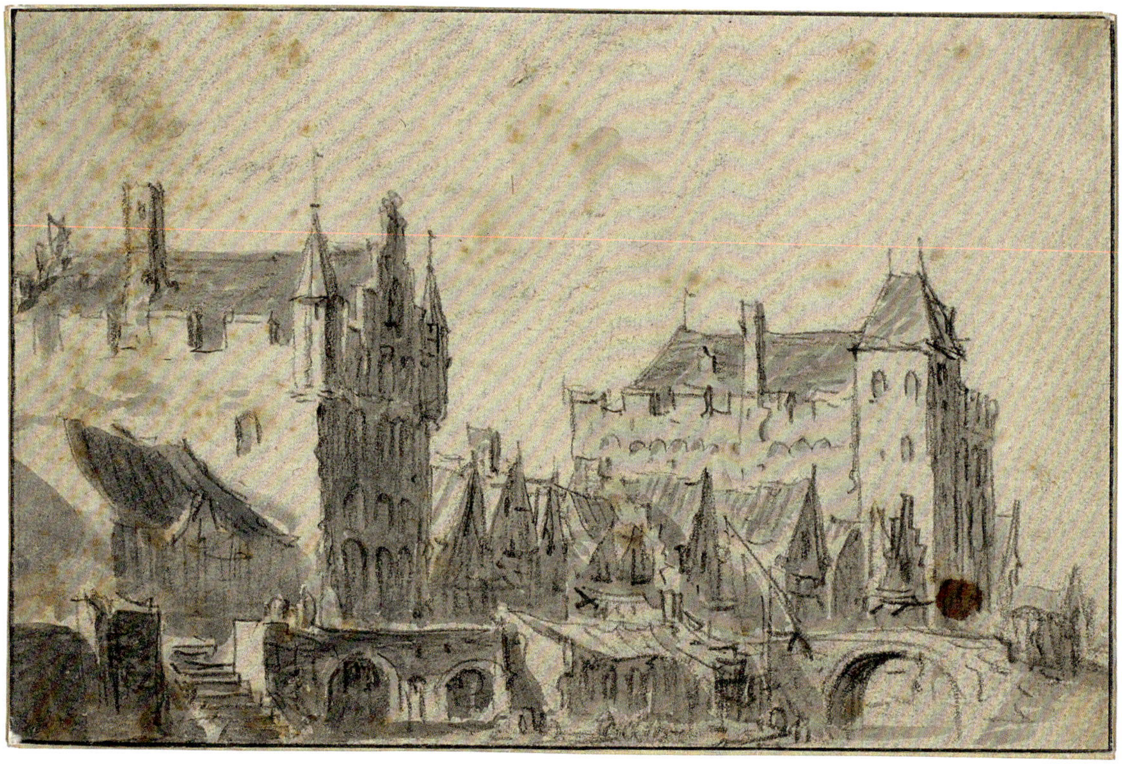

Fig. 2 Jan van Goyen, *The Buildings on the North Side of Oudegracht, with the Tower Houses of Fresenborch on the Left and Oudaen on the Right*, c. 1650, Museum Boijmans Van Beuningen, Prentenkabinet, Rotterdam

with Spain continued. It was only when it became clear in 1608 that Spain and the Republic were going to declare a truce (1609–1621) that they regained some self-confidence and the government increasingly found it necessary to take action against them.[12] It did so by breaking up their meetings, confiscating Eucharistic objects and altarpieces, and levying fines. One victim of this harassment in 1596, 1609 and 1615 was the priest Victor van Scorel, son of the famous painter and canon Jan van Scorel.[13] The Italian biographer of artists Filippo Baldinucci later heard from the engraver Cornelis Bloemaert, who was working in Rome, that similar action had apparently been taken in Utrecht against his father, the painter Abraham Bloemaert.[14]

Peace for a While

The Twelve Years' Truce began in 1609. The war was over, the borders were opened and trade began to flourish again. A period of great economic progress followed. Utrecht recovered due to growing immigration from the southern Netherlands and Germany, as opposed to the population decline of the preceding years.[15] The new residents had to be housed, and former monastic sites were used for the purpose.[16] Monasteries and chapels were given a new public function or were rented out as business premises. The divisions that had been masked during the war years now became apparent again, leading to fierce internal political and ecclesiastical conflicts. As early as January 1610, there was a coup in Utrecht when the guilds supported the civic guard in installing a more democratic city government at the expense of the nobles and the patriciate.[17] Both orthodox Calvinists and Catholics hoped that it would improve their position. The painter Joachim Wtewael, who now took a seat in the city council, was one of the rebels.[18] The States of the Province of Utrecht, in which the representatives were mainly drawn from the ranks of the nobility and the patriciate, refused to recognise the new council. When the political turmoil threatened to spill over into other provinces, the States General (the Representation of the Province of Utrecht) sent an arbitration commission to Utrecht, one of whose members was Stadholder Maurits, Count of Nassau. The commission abandoned its work at the beginning of March with nothing to show for its efforts, whereupon the States General resorted to force. Maurits sent his half-brother Frederik Hendrik to Utrecht with an army in order to reinstall the old city council. After four months Wtewael was a private citizen once more.

How did these developments affect the ordinary citizen's practice of religion? Every choice was risky as long as the war lasted and internal strife was at its bitterest. In matters of faith it was safer to keep one's options open. 'The single most significant fact for the religious history of the Netherlands c. 1578–1620 is the extraordinary number of people who belonged to no church at all', according to the historian Benjamin Kaplan.[19] That was not just the case in Utrecht but in other Dutch cities too. In Haarlem around 1620, fewer than half the population were officially members of a congregation.[20] Most people considered themselves to be believers, but they only went to church as members of an audience (*liefhebbers*). Others were simply not interested at all. After Duifhuis, the Reformed Church in Utrecht was a home for anyone who walked into a church, with no questions asked. Until 1618, there was no register of members. Anyone who came forward could partake in the Lord's Supper, all children were baptised and all couples were married. Consequently, we do not know whether the painters Dirck van Baburen and Hendrick ter Brugghen formally belonged to any church. Gerard van Honthorst was a Catholic.

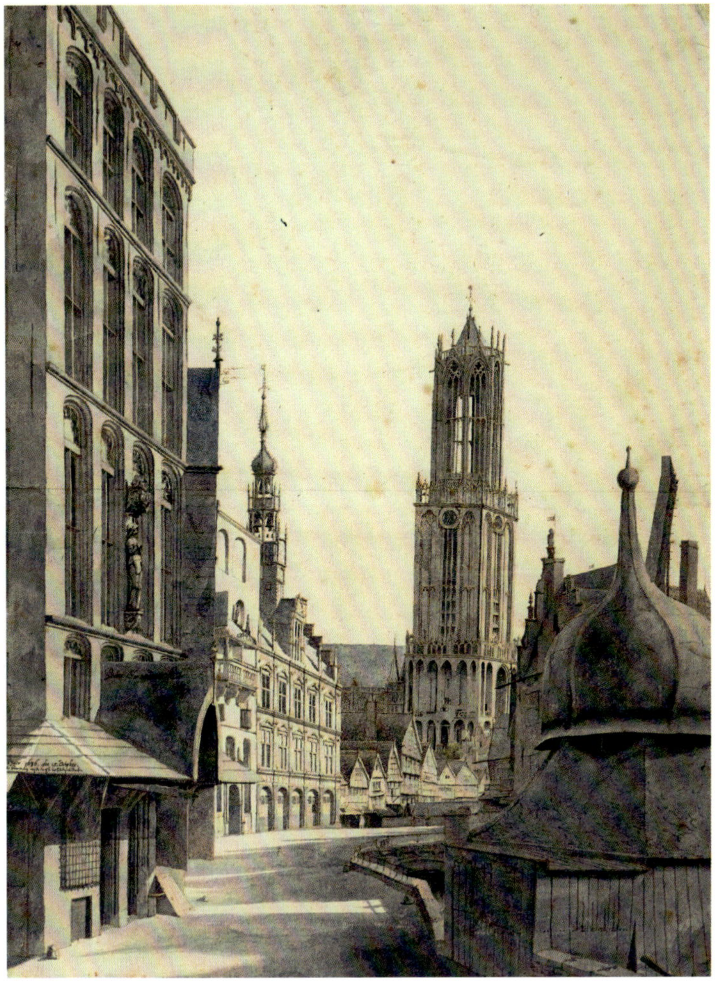

Fig. 3 Pieter Jansz. Saenredam, *View of the Stadhuisbrug in Utrecht, with the Cathedral Tower and Utrecht City Hall*, 15 October 1636, Het Utrechts Archief, Utrecht

Cultural Life

The nobles and the local patricians, who dominated cultural life in Utrecht, owed their wealth to their landholdings and to their incomes from the public offices they held. As the province's administrative and welfare centre, Utrecht had a large service sector embracing the administration of justice, the legal profession, public notaries and medical care. Many of the inhabitants had a university education, and as a result of that and the city's large Latin School, Utrecht was a centre of Neo-Latin poetry.[21] During the war with Spain the city also housed a large garrison of mostly English, Scottish and French soldiers,[22] who just like the other immigrants were allocated churches of their own. The presence of these foreign soldiers and their officers, many of whom were aristocrats, gave the city an international, cosmopolitan flavour.[23] The English Humanist Henry Peacham, who lodged with the governor in Utrecht around 1614, wrote: 'When I was in Utrecht and lived at the table of that honorable gentleman, Sir John Ogle, lord governer, whither resorted many great scholars and captains, English, Scottish, French, and Dutch, it had been enough to have made a scholar or soldier to have observed the several disputations and discourses among many strangers, one while of sundry forms of battles, sometime of fortification, of fireworks, history, antiquities, heraldry, pronunciation of languages, etc., that his table seemed many times a little academy'.[24] It is against this backdrop that we have to view

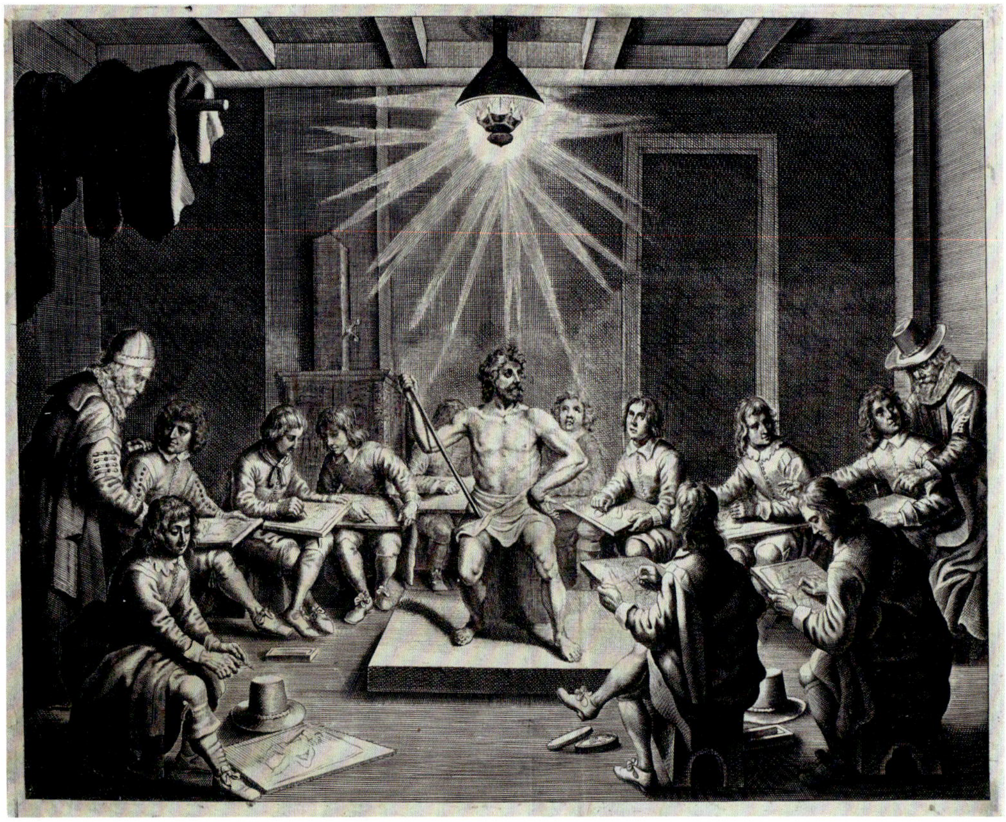

Fig. 4 Crispijn van de Passe, *A Drawing Academy (Abraham Bloemaert and Paulus Moreelse Giving Drawing Lessons from the Male Nude to a Group of Young Pupils)*, Het Utrechts Archief, Utrecht

the development of the Utrecht school of painting in the first quarter of the 17th century.

In his *Schilder-boeck* of 1604, Karel van Mander dwells at length on the two talented Mannerist artists Abraham Bloemaert and Joachim Wtewael, who turned Utrecht into a major artistic centre, together with Paulus Moreelse, whom van Mander only included in his book because he was a young, rising talent at the time. Bloemaert and Moreelse trained a large number of young artists, Hendrick ter Brugghen, Gerard van Honthorst and Dirck van Baburen among them. In Utrecht since time immemorial, painters had been members of the Saddlers' Guild, which represented many crafts. They now found it stifling, however, so in 1611 several artists, including Moreelse and Wtewael, submitted a request to the city council to be allowed to set up their own artists' guild.[25] It was granted and they founded the Guild of St Luke, membership of which was restricted to painters and sculptors. That was followed a little later by the establishment of a drawing academy.[26] There is a print of a group of young artists practising drawing from the male nude under the supervision of Bloemaert and Moreelse (fig. 4).[27] The arrival of the engraver Crispijn van de Passe from Cologne in 1611 enriched Utrecht with a leading producer of graphic art and reproductive printmaking for the first time in its history.[28] Van de Passe specialised in portrait prints of aristocrats and other prominent figures, from whom he expected to find a clientele in the provincial capital, dominated as it was by the nobility and the patriciate.[29]

The Utrecht art market thus profited from the Republic's economic revival during the Twelve Years' Truce. The new institutional infrastructure reflected the artists' ambitions, and in the space of ten years the number of active artists in the city doubled to almost 40.[30]

Bloemaert's pupil Hendrick ter Brugghen did not witness all these innovations, for he must have left for Italy before the

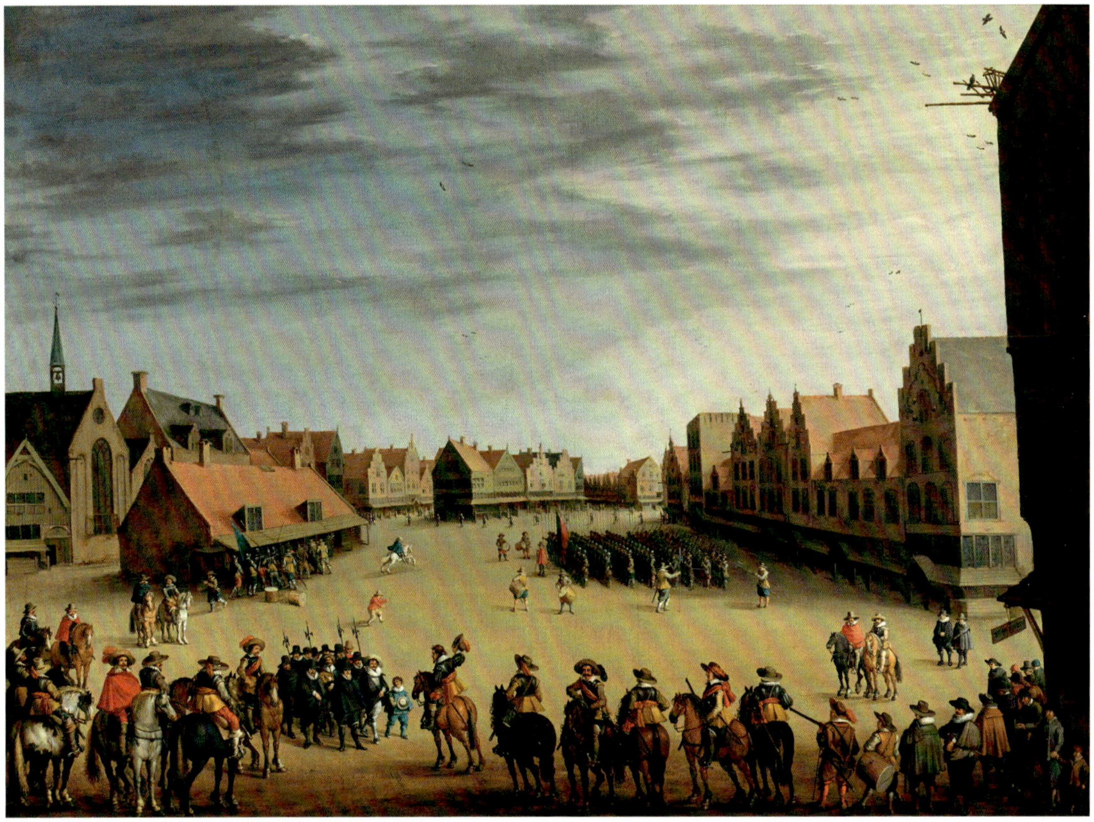

Fig. 5 Joost Cornelisz. Droochsloot, *Prince Maurits Disbanding the Waardgelders on the Neude in Utrecht on 31 July 1618*, dated 1629, Centraal Museum, Utrecht

start of the truce and the associated boom. Gerard van Honthorst, who was also taught by Bloemaert, and Dirck van Baburen, who became a pupil of Moreelse in 1611, did see the beginnings of this revival. It was during their absence abroad that the political and religious discord reached a fever pitch.

A Troubled Truce

The theological conflict between the followers of the two Leiden professors, Jacobus Arminius and Franciscus Gomarus, brought the Republic to the brink of civil war during the truce with Spain. The difference of opinion centred around the doctrine of predestination. Gomarus believed that God decided in advance whom he would select for salvation and eternal life and whom he would not. Arminius, on the other hand, believed that people could choose to be believers out of their free will. It would be on the basis of that choice, a person's conduct in life and the charitable works they did, that God would decide to forgive sins or not. After Arminius's death in 1609, his followers enshrined their views in what was called a Remonstrance, from which they took their name as Remonstrants. Their opponents are referred to as Counter-Remonstrants. All the preachers in Utrecht were adherents of Arminius, and there was little support for the Counter-Remonstrants.[31]

The ecclesiastical and associated political differences led to a power struggle in the young Republic. Tensions reached such a pitch that some cities, including Utrecht, hired mercenaries (so-called *waardgelders*) in order to maintain order, because the populace distrusted its own civic guard. The two most powerful men in the Republic, Stadholder Count Maurits and Johan van Oldenbarnevelt, the pensionary of the States of Holland, who originally came from the province of Utrecht, found themselves in total opposition to each other. The explosion came when Maurits sided with the Counter-Remonstrants in 1617. Remonstrant politicians were thrown out of office and

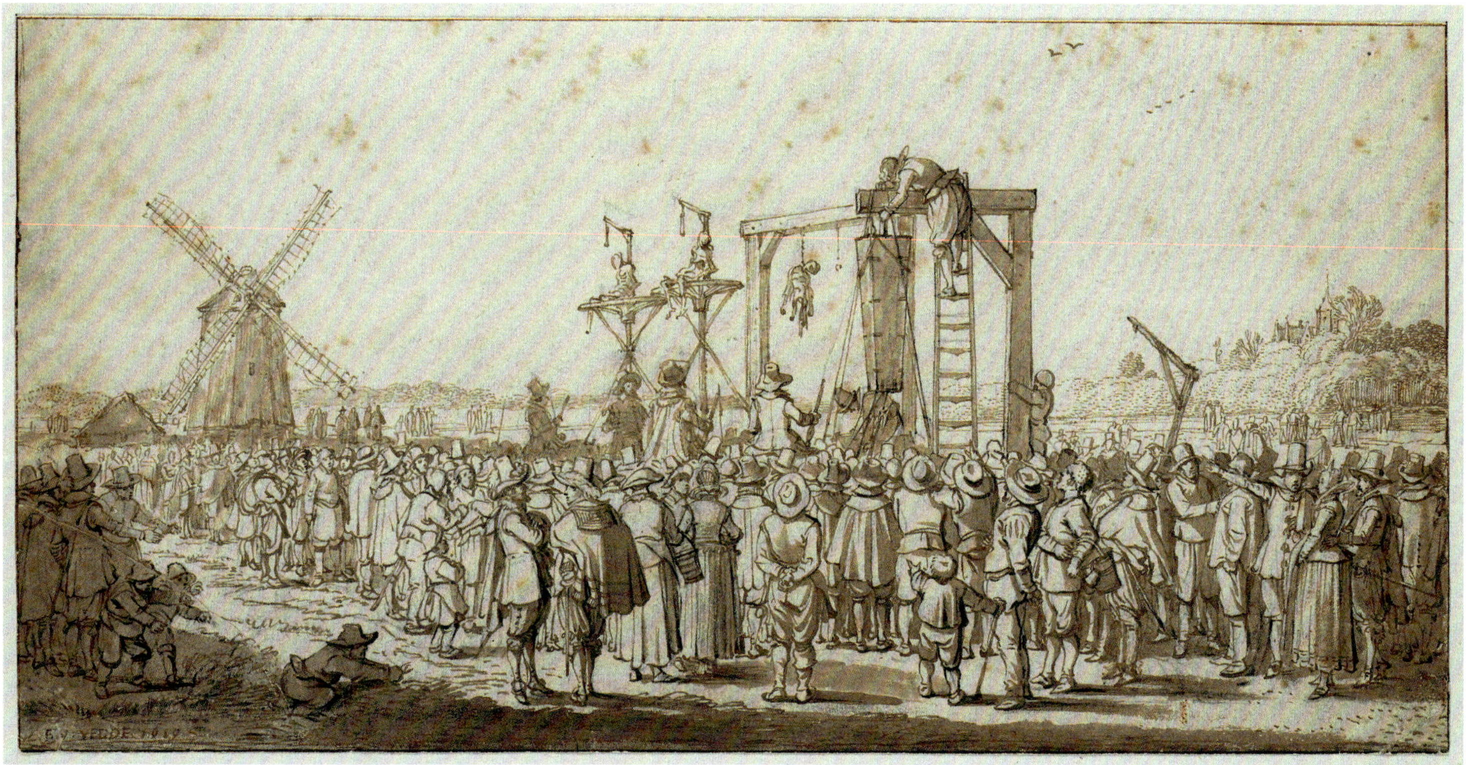

Fig. 6 Esaias van de Velde, *Hanging Gilles van Ledenberch's Coffin on the Gallows outside The Hague*, 1619, Teylers Museum, Haarlem

replaced. Maurits, who was now Prince of Orange, disbanded the *waardgelders* on 31 July 1618, while he was in Utrecht with his troops (fig. 5). He replaced the city council, the members of which had been elected each year, with a corporation of councillors appointed for life, known as the *Vroedschap*. He also made radical changes to the provincial government. Sir John Ogle was replaced as governor of the garrison by Ernst Casimir, Count of Nassau, a cousin of the stadholder. All of this greatly restricted the relative independence of the province of Utrecht within the Republic. Oldenbarnevelt's supporters, who included the famous jurist Hugo Grotius, were accused of high treason and arrested. Another detainee was Gilles van Ledenberch, secretary to the States of Utrecht, who committed suicide in The Hague. He was sentenced to death posthumously on 12 May 1619, and his coffin was hanged on the gallows (fig. 6). The next day Oldenbarnevelt was beheaded on the Binnenhof in The Hague.

In Utrecht this political upheaval was followed by a religious one. Church buildings were again put at the disposal of the Counter-Remonstrants. In 1618, when they held their first religious service in public, it turned out that only 3,000 people attended, one-tenth of the city's population.[32] The number of genuine members proved to be no more than around 2,000 in 1620, when the first membership register was drawn up. That was after the Synod of Dordrecht, at which the Counter-Remonstrants succeeded in expelling their Remonstrant colleagues from the Church throughout the Republic. From then on sermons in Reformed churches could only be delivered by preachers who endorsed the doctrines laid down in Dordrecht. All the Remonstrant preachers in the province of Utrecht were dismissed, as well as a lot of schoolmasters and sextons. Many of the preachers went into exile. Remonstrant meetings were disrupted, as had previously happened with gatherings of Catholics and Counter-Remonstrants.

Art and Politics

The surviving archives of the Utrecht Guild of St Luke show that the political and religious strife had little if any effect on it, even if some members were definitely active in politics.[33] Joachim Wtewael, for instance, who had taken part in the coup of 1610, was once again in on the act in 1618, this time in the company of Paulus Moreelse, who was appointed to the new *Vroedschap* by the stadholder.[34] Wtewael did not follow him until 1632, after the death of his brother Johan, who also achieved office in 1618.[35] The names of Moreelse and Wtewael appear in the first, 1620 register of professing Counter-Remonstrant members,[36] and starting in 1619 they filled several official functions in the guild.[37] The Catholic Abraham Bloemaert was still a member of the board in 1618, but from then on the city council bypassed him in favour of more politically reliable (Counter-Remonstrant) members of the Reformed Church, such as Moreelse. Their names are also mentioned as filling other offices, such as governors of charitable institutions. The guild made an exception for the Catholic Gerard van Honthorst, for in January 1625 he was appointed dean of the guild. In his case, his great fame and his good contacts at court would have been sufficient recommendation for the council to entrust him with the office. In that period, according to his pupil Joachim von Sandrart, he had as many as 25 pupils.

Aristocrats of an internationalist bent were a breeding ground for a flourishing cultural life and a large luxury goods sector.[38] Painting was part of it, as was the silversmithing trade, the leading exponent of which was Adam van Vianen, whose brother Paulus worked as an imperial court goldsmith in Prague. In 1618, the landscape and animal painter Roelant Savery moved from Prague to Utrecht. He, too, had been a court painter, and he advertised the fact by hanging the imperial coat of arms on the front of his workshop. Utrecht's cultural offerings expanded further in 1618 with the foundation of a chamber of rhetoric under the motto 'Wt rechte liefde' [Out of true love].[39] The members of such rhetorical societies practised the arts of poetry, amateur dramatics and song. The chamber put on its first performance on 3 January 1619. A few months later, French actors were given permission to perform in St Paul's Abbey.[40] The pupils of the French schoolmaster Vincent Stalpaert staged French tragedies in the great hall of the Catharijneconvent throughout the July fair,[41] and English actors also performed regularly in Utrecht.[42] New life was also breathed into the old tradition of putting on classical plays in Latin and contemporary drama in Neo-Latin by the students of the Latin School. The chamber of rhetoric was a great success. Much of its audience must have consisted of officers and their entourage. In 1620, no less a person than Duchess Sophia Hedwig of Braunschweig-Wolfenbüttel, wife of governor Ernst Casimir, recommended a troupe of French actors to the States of Utrecht.[43] During the 1621 fair, the entire company of rhetoricians rode through the city in two open carriages, 'finely attired, with pipes and drum, and with a new banner', and were given a civic welcome by the sheriff and burgomasters.[44] On 6 May that year, they performed Adriaen van den Bergh's *Ieronimo*, a translation and adaptation of Thomas Kyd's play *The Spanish Tragedy*, the central character of which is Hieronimo.[45] The script was immediately published by the book printer and engraver Jan Amelisz. (van Paddenburch), who had joined the Guild of St Luke in 1616. In 1622, there was a performance of van den Bergh's tragedy *Polidoor*, and it too was published by Jan Amelisz. Both plays were spectacular showpieces, with plenty of murder and mayhem. In between the acts of the plays ditties were sung, such as 'Little frozen soul', 'My prudish wife is startled' and 'Behold the whoreson standing there'. Texts of that kind recall the licentious culture of the Roman underworld described by Helen Langdon in this catalogue, which the Utrecht Caravaggisti knew at first hand. The often scabrous inscriptions on the prints after their genre scenes leave nothing to the imagination in that respect.[46] They are of a piece with the wine-soaked gatherings of the young Dutch painters in Rome, the Bentvueghels. The written sources on the Bentvueghel society are replete with all the elements of youth culture and student life (taverns, drinking, brawling and lewdness). The eroticism, carefree mood and 'rakish looseness' that Baburen, ter Brugghen and Honthorst depicted in dozens of single-figure paintings of musicians in the years 1621–1624 are an echo of their Italian years.[47] We know little about the first owners of those pictures, but we can cautiously assume that they were to be found in the milieu that was famed for its unbridled eroticism: the nobility and the officer corps of the States army. They were also the buyers and people who commissioned the pastoral paintings of shepherds and shepherdesses in a carefree Arcadian setting that also evolved in Utrecht in the 1620s.[48] The Utrecht nobleman and pro-Remonstrant politician Peter van Hardenbroeck had himself portrayed by Baburen in 1623 as the lovelorn shepherd Daifilo, with his later wife Agnes van Hanxelaer as the king's daughter in the pastoral play of 1605 by Pieter Cornelisz. Hooft (1581–1647) (fig. 7).[49] Agnes was a nun who fled the convent that year, and reportedly eloped with van Hardenbroeck.

The painters themselves would have settled down after sowing their wild oats in Rome. There are few tales of licentiousness in Utrecht, let alone of them resorting to fisticuffs. Most of them married, started families and tried to live from their brush. They became respected citizens.

After returning home, though, they did continue their artistic rivalry, which in Utrecht as in Rome ensured a rapid development of the arts. Every artist who introduced a new subject saw it picked up and improved upon by other painters. Wayne Franits has called this 'emulative artistic environment' the 'Utrecht laboratory'.[50]

Caravaggism in Wartime

A new episode in Utrecht's history was ushered in by Prince Maurits's seizure of power in 1618, the inauguration of a city council with members appointed for life, and the recognition of the Counter-Remonstrant strand as the only permitted public Church. The Twelve Years' Truce ended on 9 April 1621 and the Republic went to war again. It is in that light that we should view the return of Gerard van Honthorst, followed a few months later by Dirck van Baburen. Both of them wanted to get home before it became too dangerous to travel. The Utrecht Humanist and art lover Arnoldus Buchelius wrote in his diary that a welcoming party was held for Honthorst in the Poortgen inn on 26 July 1620.[51] He also noted the names of those who were present. Some of them were people who have already been mentioned above: the painters Paulus Moreelse and Abraham Bloemaert, the engraver Crispijn van de Passe and the goldsmith Adam van Vianen.[52] Adam's brother Gijsbrecht van Vianen, former governor of the Moluccas in the Dutch East Indies and an early collector of Chinese porcelain, was also there. They were joined by the painter and art dealer Herman van Vollenhoven, who in 1623 handled a *Flute Player* that was attributed to Correggio (1489–1534), and who five years later tried to export twelve paintings with Caravaggesque subjects to Asia.[53] And finally there were a few relatives of Honthorst's travelling companion, Jacob Willemsz. Colijn de Nole, who came from a family of sculptors. Those present were there mainly to see and hear how Honthorst had got on in Italy. The conversation then turned to the art of Rubens and his successful sales, which were put down to the reproductive prints by Lucas Vorsterman, which were said to be too expensive. That was a subject of particular interest to Bloemaert and van de Passe: Bloemaert because he had published much of his oeuvre in printed form down the years, and van de Passe because he was a print publisher and would have seen Honthorst as a potential supplier of designs. Everyone in the inn would have hoped that Honthorst would inject even more life into the Utrecht school of painting. But, as has been said, the mood had changed. The city that Honthorst had left as a young man and to which he returned as a fully fledged master painter turned out no longer to be the libertine city he had known. Hendrick ter Brugghen alone, who had come back from Italy in 1614, had been a witness to the recent upheaval. Baburen and Honthorst in Rome would have been kept abreast of what was going on through letters and the tales of travellers, but the personal experience of the changes was undoubtedly different. Moreover, they had to go in search of clients at a time when war threatened, which always made the art market nervous. It was not without reason that Karel van Mander had spoken in 1604 of 'our peace and prosperity loving art of painting'.[54] According to him, the 'art-destroying, heinous Mars' was painting's greatest enemy.[55] The economy stagnated when the truce ended, and there was indeed a crisis in the market for paintings.

With the disappearance of the libertines from the city government, the artists found themselves confronted by a local government that had to implement a Counter-Remonstrant programme. That was coupled with renewed disruption of the meeting places of religious minorities. At the insistence of the Church council, a cultural offensive was set in motion that reached its peak in the 1620s, in the very period when Caravaggism was the dominant style in Utrecht.[56] Sunday rest was enforced more strictly, and the public celebration of traditional Catholic feast days was banned. The authorities also interfered in the private lives of their citizens. Dancing and loud music were curbed not only in taverns but in the home as well. Active steps were taken against debauchery during communal meals with neighbours, excessive drinking, gambling, playing sports and games in public, or light-hearted gatherings

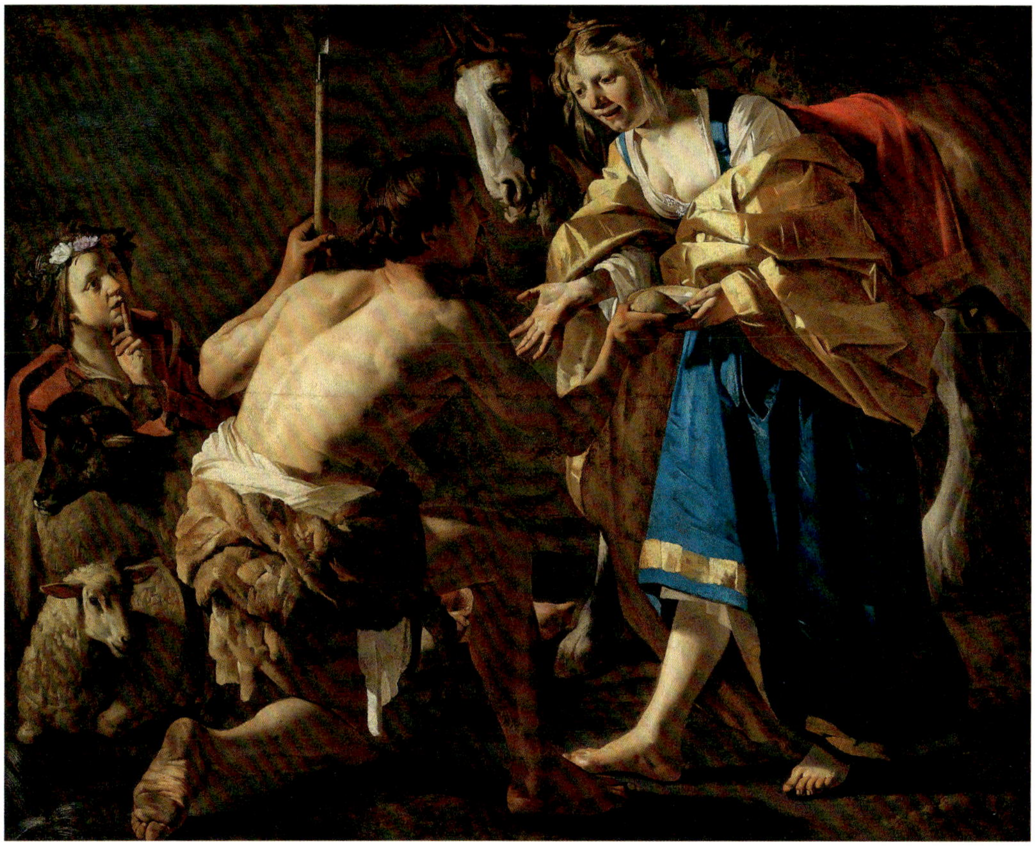

Fig. 7 Dirck van Baburen, *Granida and Daifilo* (Portrait historié of Peter van Hardenbroek and Agnes van Hanxelaer), 1623, private collection

of unmarried young men and women, which were referred to as 'merry companies' ('*jongspelen*'). We do not hear much more about the chamber of rhetoric. More restrained forms of entertainment were permitted, such as listening to organ music and serenades by the city musicians. Even the Counter-Remonstrant artists clashed with the enforcers of Church discipline. In 1627, for instance, Joachim Wtewael was prohibited from attending the Lord's Supper because people had danced at his daughter's wedding.[57] And in 1618, Paulus Moreelse was already reproached by a political opponent, who said that he 'is unworthy of any position, having himself consorted greatly with whores'.[58] It is true that Moreelse was a member of the congregation, possibly out of political opportunism, but his wife and children were not, and one of his sons, the painter Johannes Moreelse, later returned from Rome with a papal knighthood.

War was ever-present in the 1620s due to the ceaseless troop movements through the city and the province. New companies of soldiers were forever being mustered One week after Honthorst's return, the States army marched from Utrecht to Germany in a vain attempt to prevent the Palatinate from falling into the hands of the imperial troops. The Republic wanted to fight the war as far away as possible from its own territory, which is why it financed the armies of the Protestant warlords Christian, Duke of Braunschweig, and Ernst, Count of Mansvelt, who sowed death and destruction in Germany. It was a strategy that did not always work. In February 1624, for instance, Spanish troops crossed the frozen River IJssel from the east and invaded the Veluwe region. They came so close to the provinces of Utrecht and Holland that panic broke out. On top of that, for the first time in more than a century, drift ice broke through the Lek Dike near Vreeswijk (fig. 8). All the

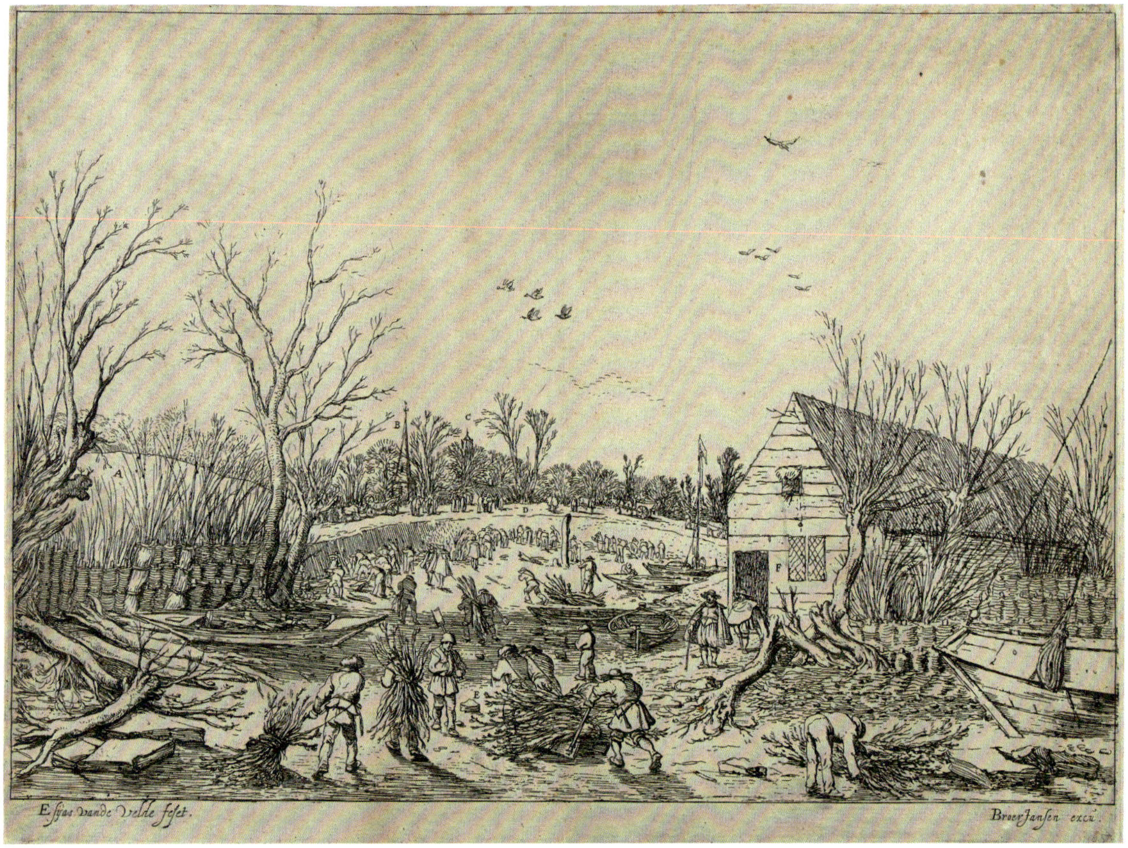

Fig. 8 Esaias van de Velde (Broer Jansz. excud.), *Repairing the Lek Dike near 't Waal, South-East of Vreeswijk, after its Collapse on 16 January 1624*, 1624/40, Rijksprentenkabinet, Amsterdam

land between Utrecht, Rotterdam, Delft, Leiden and Amsterdam was inundated, so that 'houses float away and people and cattle drown'.[59] In the city of Utrecht, the water reached inside the city gates, and most of the cellars were flooded. As a result, on 9 February (according to the chronicler Cornelis Cornelisz.), 'the entire province [had] fled, taking their belongings and children with them'.[60] Prince Maurits brought a large army to defend the city, accompanied by thousands of peasants from Holland to cut the frozen rivers open. He inspected the city walls jointly with his cousin Frederick V of the Palatinate, the exiled King of Bohemia (the so-called 'Winter King'), Duke Christian of Braunschweig, and the Landgrave of Hessen, and gave instructions for the defence of the city. A week later, though, the thaw set in and the Spanish troops had to retreat hurriedly over the river in order not to be hemmed in. By 15 February, the danger had passed. Prince Maurits and his half-brother Frederik Hendrik went to church in the cathedral to give thanks for the happy outcome. The army left Utrecht a few days later.[61]

It was in the aftermath of these dramatic events, on 21 February, that Dirck van Baburen died, aged around 30 and unmarried. Although it has always been assumed that he was a victim of the plague, which was raging in 1624, it is just as possible that he had fallen ill in the bitter winter. As an able-bodied man he would certainly have served in one of the civic guard companies that were called up to defend the city.[62] Until shortly before his death he was working on a monumental canvas of a subject from Homer's *Iliad*, *Achilles before the Dead Body of Patroclus* (fig. 9).[63] It may have been commissioned by one of the senior military officers who was in Utrecht in the last days of Baburen's life.[64]

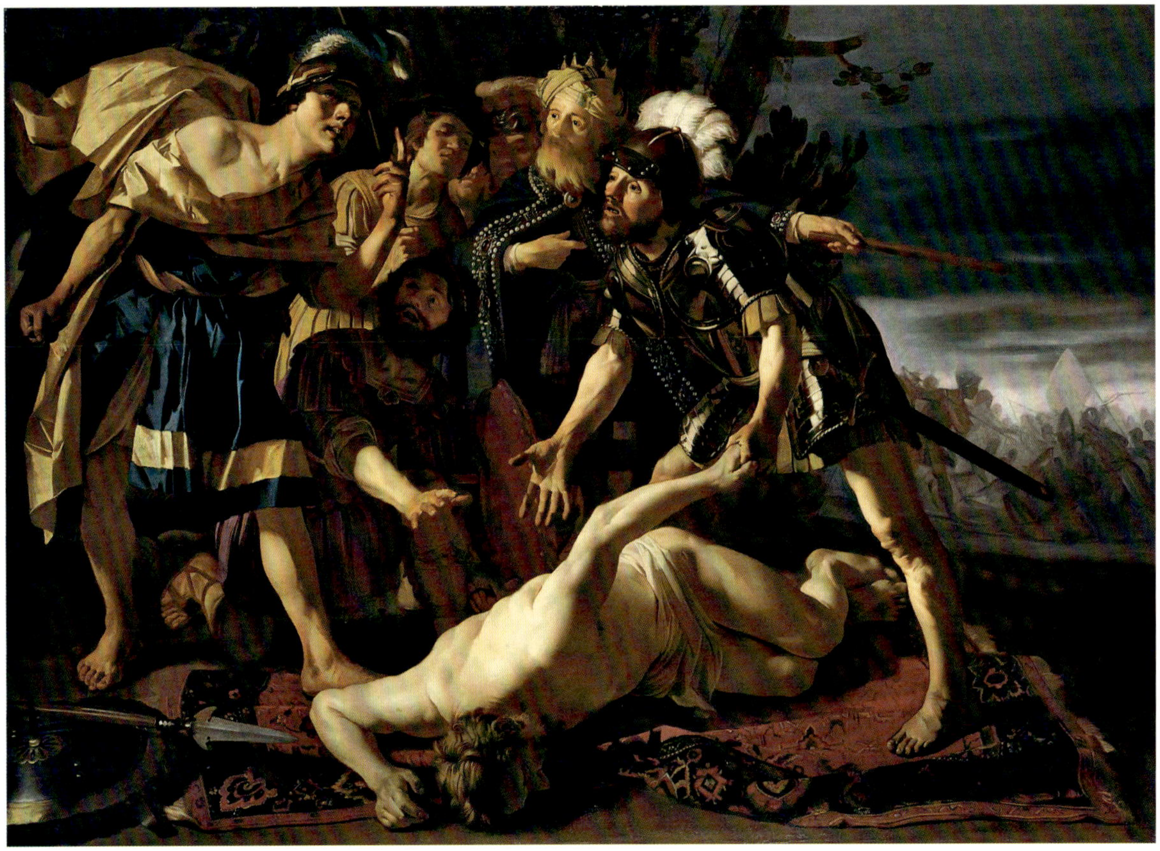

Fig. 9 Dirck van Baburen, *Achilles before the Dead Body of Patroclus*, 1624, Museumslandschaft Hessen Kassel, Gemäldegalerie Alte Meister, Kassel

Most of Hendrick ter Brugghen's artistic career took place after the resumption of the war. If the genealogical notes of his grandson Hendrick Richardsz. ter Brugghen are to be believed, the painter had five brothers who were soldiers.[65] They are said to have served the King of Bohemia, two as captains of horse under the Duke of Braunschweig, the two others as captains under the Count of Mansvelt. Nothing more is known about them, but it stands to reason that, if they did indeed exist, they perished in battle somewhere in Germany in the 1620s. Ter Brugghen's *Sleeping Mars* of 1629 was perhaps an expression of a longing for an end to the war (fig. 10).[66] Ter Brugghen himself, though, never lived to see the peace. In the late summer of 1629, Spanish and imperial troops once again marched to the west. They occupied Amersfoort, near Utrecht, and plundered the countryside to within a few kilometres of the city. In order to calm the panic among the inhabitants the States General moved their meeting from The Hague to Utrecht. Although the invasion was brief, it caused great damage and desperation. There was also the plague to contend with. Ter Brugghen died in early November 1629. According to Joachim von Sandrart, 'a hostile fate pursued his good fortune to the grave'.[67] His pregnant wife was left behind with five young children. On Christmas Eve, she made her confession of faith in the Counter-Remonstrant congregation, which her dead husband had never done. One wonders whether it was out of conviction or in the hope of receiving support from the parish.[68]

Gerard van Honthorst, finally, did live to see the Peace of Münster in 1648. He was the most successful of the Utrecht Caravaggisti. Thanks to his good contacts at the Hague courts

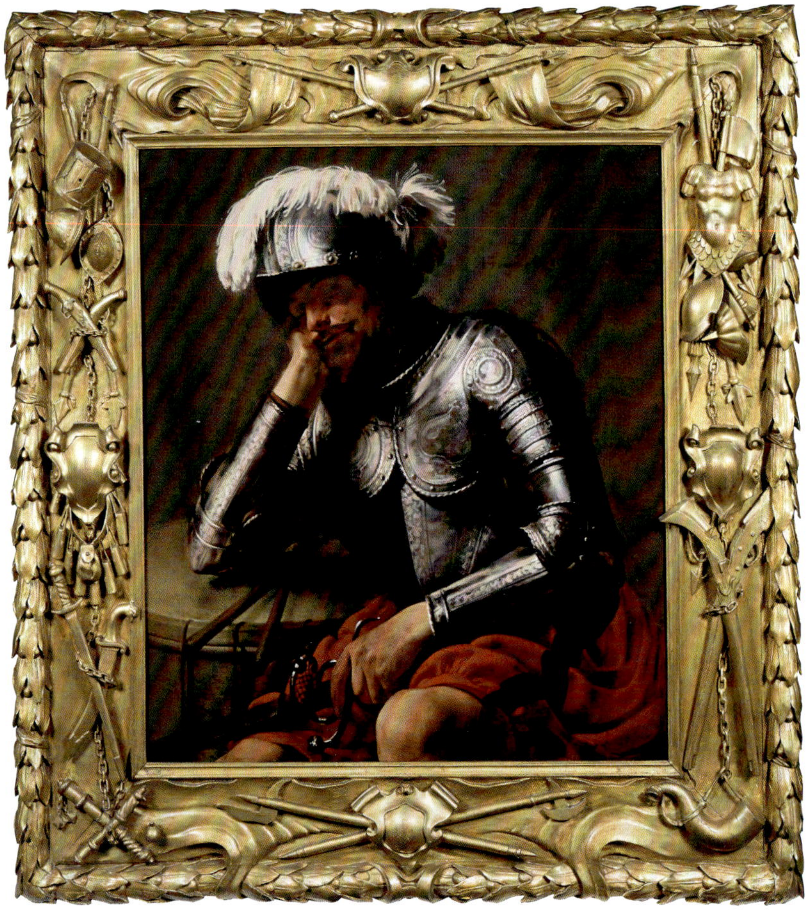

Fig. 10 Hendrick ter Brugghen, *Sleeping Mars*, 1629, Centraal Museum, Utrecht

of Frederik Hendrik and the Winter King and the latter's wife Elisabeth Stuart, he was flooded with commissions. He opened a second studio in The Hague, where he gave painting lessons to aristocratic ladies from the court circles. Although he had long ago abandoned the Caravaggist style, he remained a painter from libertine Utrecht. His later work displays nothing of the bourgeois and Calvinist character that was regarded as typically Dutch for far too long.

1 Parts of this essay previously appeared in Bok 1997/98. Biographical data are drawn in part from pp. 370–393 of that publication. The 'libertines' formed an ecclesiastically unattached group that had split from Catholicism but which did not espouse a reformed creed. See Von Rosen 2015, p. 2016. In this essay, 'libertine' used to designate this denominational independence.
2 See, for example, Federle Orr 1997/98, pp. 100–101.
3 See especially Kaplan 1995.
4 Van Campen 1940, pp. 1–2.
5 *View of the City Hall Bridge in Utrecht, with the Cathedral Tower and Utrecht City Hall*, 15 October 1636, pen in brown, black chalk, washed with grey and coloured with pink, green and brown watercolour, 512 × 385 mm, Het Utrechts Archief, Utrecht, cat. 28593.
6 Van Bueren/Van Dijk 2017, pp. 168–175.
7 Van Schaik 2000, p. 237.
8 Kaplan 1995; Van Schaik 2000, pp. 234–240.
9 Van Schaik 2000, p. 237.
10 Kaplan 1995, pp. 138–148.
11 Van Schaik 2000, pp. 237–240.
12 Ibid., pp. 240–241.
13 Leeuwenberg 2008, pp. 23–24.
14 Roethlisberger 1993, pp. 47, 569.
15 Rommes 1998, pp. 23–24. The population started growing again around 1590.
16 Temminck Groll et al. 1972.
17 For the events of 1610, see Kaplan 1995, pp. 240–244.
18 Van de Water 1729, vol. 3, p. 180.
19 Kaplan 1995, p. 68.
20 Spaans 1989, pp. 104–105.

21 See Bloemendal 2003.
22 Rommes 1998, pp. 22, 199.
23 This passage comes from Bok 2000, p. 22.
24 Peacham 1622 (1962), p. 154.
25 Muller 1880, pp. 63, 92, 95. The painters De Goyer and Segerman already had long careers in local politics behind them. For Marten de Goyer, see Bok 2014, pp. 75, and for the sculptor and co-founder Adriaen Fredericksz. van Oudendyck, see Neurdenburg 1951.
26 Bok 1994, pp. 178–183.
27 Crispijn van de Passe the Younger, *A Drawing Academy*, engraving, 299 × 380 mm (image), Het Utrechts Archief, Utrecht, cat. 31422.
28 Veldman 2001, pp. 175–178. There may even be a connection between de Passe settling in Utrecht and the drive to establish the guild. He must have left Cologne in early August 1611. The guild received its statutes from the city on 13 September (Muller 1880, p. 86).
29 Veldman 2001, p. 175.
30 Bok 1994, p. 168. See also Marten Jan Bok, Judith Brouwer and Harms Nijboer (eds.), 'The ECARTICO database' [www.vondel.humanities.uva.nl/ecartico].
31 Kaplan 1995, p. 246. See ibid., pp. 229–260, for the sequel to the conflict in Utrecht.
32 Ibid., pp. 254–255.
33 Van de Water 1729, vol. 3, p. 180.
34 Ibid., p. 183.
35 Ibid., p. 185.
36 Het Utrechts Archief (HUA), Nederlands hervormde gemeente Utrecht, kerkenraad [746], 205.
37 Muller 1880, pp. 127–128.
38 See, for example, Olde Meierink/Bakker 1997; Geraerts 2015; Reinders 2017.
39 'Utrechtsch kronijkjen', p. 91. See also HUA, Stadsbestuur van Utrecht 1577–1795 [702], 121, Vroedschapsresoluties, 12 April 1619.
40 HUA, Staten van Utrecht [33], 264-24, Resoluties van Gedeputeerde Staten, 16 July 1619.
41 HUA, Staten van Utrecht [33], 264-24, Resoluties van Gedeputeerde Staten, 22 April 1619, 23 April 1619. HUA, Stadsbestuur van Utrecht 1577–1795 [702], 121, Vroedschapsresoluties, 19 April 1619, 26 April 1619.
42 Albach 1977, p. 21.
43 HUA, Staten van Utrecht [33], 264-25, Resoluties van Gedeputeerde Staten, 25 January 1620.
44 'Utrechtsch kronijkjen', p. 108: '[...] schoon in de kleer, met pypen ende trom, ende een nieu vendel'.
45 For the actor Adriaen van den Bergh, who later became famous, see Albach 1977, pp. 21–22. His daughter Adriana went on to become the first Dutch actress.
46 On this, see Exh. cat. Utrecht 2017.
47 Hillegers 2017, pp. 16–17.
48 Kettering 1983, pp. 13–16.
49 Canvas, 165.7 × 211.5 cm3, private collection; Franits 2013a, pp. 154–156, cat. A31.
50 Franits 2009.
51 Van Campen 1940, pp. 1–2.
52 Bok 1997/98, pp. 86–87. Buchelius merely speaks of 'Adamo', so he could also have been referring to the painter Adam Willaerts, who was dean of the Guild of St Luke that year, together with the sculptor Willem Colijn de Nole, who was the father of Honthorst's travelling companion, Jacob Colijn de Nole.
53 Bok 1988.
54 Van Mander 1604, fol. 299v.
55 Ibid.
56 Bogaers 1985, *passim.*
57 Pollmann 2000, p. 184.
58 Bezemer 1896, pp. 85–86: '[...] hij allen staet onweerdich is, als sich selven oock met hoeren seer verloopen hebbende'. His opponent would have been a Remonstrant.
59 Quoted from Buisman 2000, p. 355: '[...] husen wechdryven, menschen ende vee verdrincken'. For the flooding, see also pp. 355–363.
60 'Utrechtsch kronijkjen', pp. 118–122: '[...] het heele Sticht [was] gevlucht, met haer goet ende kinderen'.
61 Ibid., p. 117.
62 Ibid., p. 113.
63 Dirck van Baburen, *Achilles before the Dead Body of Patroclus*, 1624, canvas, 204 × 287 cm, Museumslandschaft Hessen Kassel, Gemäldegalerie Alte Meister, Kassel, inv. M2008/1, GK 1238.
64 Gregor Weber has cautiously identified the patron as the Utrecht governor Daniel de Hertaing, Lord of Marquette, Lieutenant General of Cavalry. On this, see Franits 2013a, pp. 166-168, cat. A36.
65 Arnhem, Gelders Archief, archief familie Van Rhemen, handschriften (0908), inv. 7B1 (genealogies of family names beginning with B), fol. 111a (online: scan no. 269). Detailed information about the ter Brugghen family will be found on fols. 110a–122v (online: scans nos. 251–305).
66 Slatkes/Franits 2007, pp. 144–147, cat. A44.
67 Sandrart 1675, vol. 2, bk. 3, p. 308: 'hat...ein unfreundliches Glück seine Wolfahrt biß ins Grab zu seinem Schaden verfolgt'.
68 Soon afterwards, the States of Utrecht awarded her son Richard ter Brugghen a scholarship at the Collegium Paulini from the property of the secularised Abbey of St Paul, and the city gave her daughter Elisabeth an allowance from the property of the secularised St Cecilia Convent. HUA, Paulusabdij te Utrecht [85-1], 525, list of stipendiaries in the Seminarium Paulinum, 24 August 1632. HUA, Bewaarde archieven I [708], 892-17, accounts of the steward of the Convent of St Cecilia between 1631 and 1632, fol. 29v, 1 October 1631.

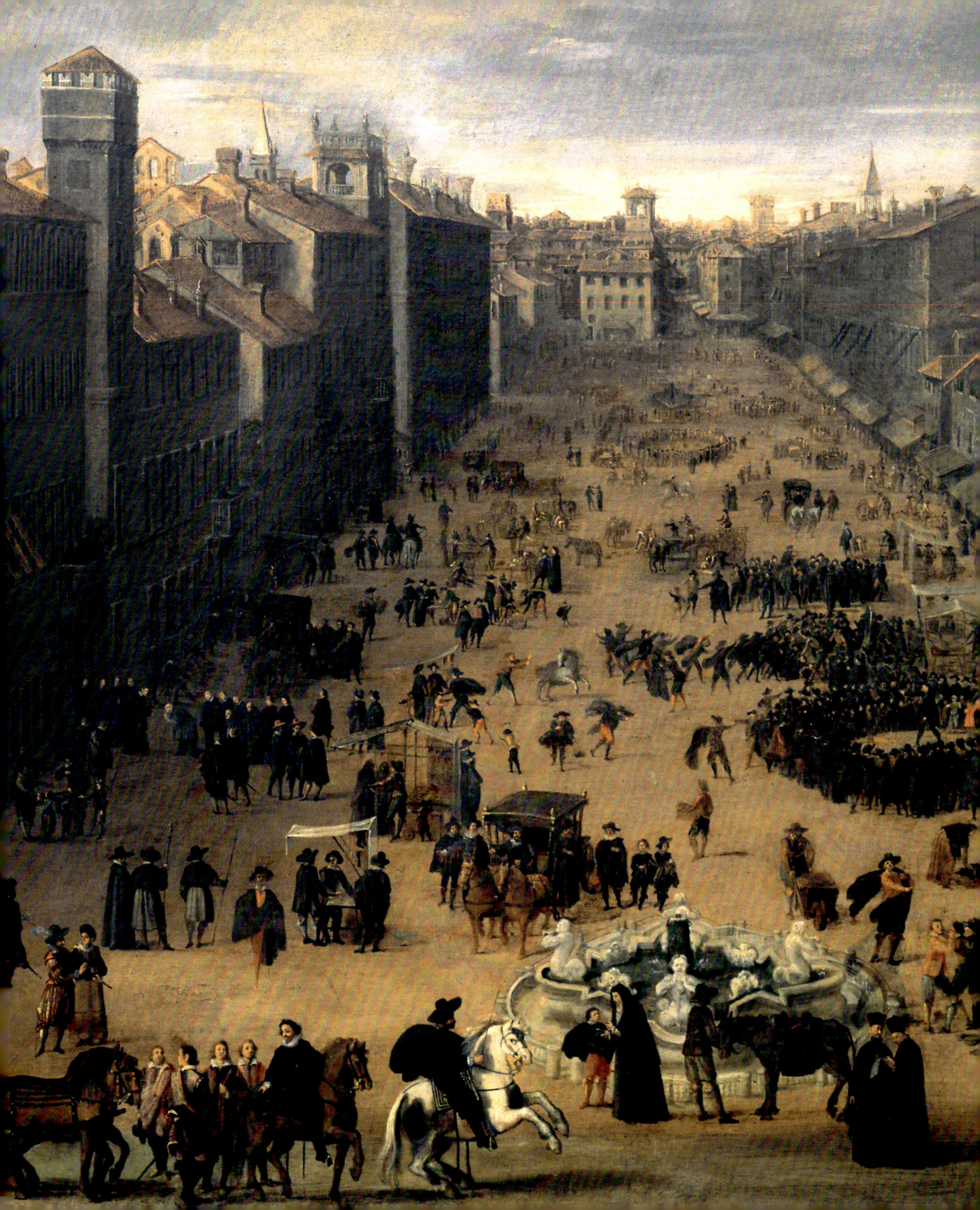

Rome, 1600–1630

HELEN LANGDON

The City
In the early years of the 17th century, the traveller arriving in Rome from northern Europe crossed the ancient Ponte Milvio to journey down the Via Flaminia, and, passing through the great archway of the Piazza del Popolo, entered one of the most spectacular urban spaces of Rome. The archway framed an ancient Egyptian obelisk, surmounted by a cross, which drew the eye from afar and created a dramatic prelude to the grandeur of the city. For a visitor from the entirely medieval Utrecht, the piazza would have been an astonishing introduction to the marvels of both ancient and Christian Rome (fig. 11).

Rome, the *caput mundi*, was again the grandest city in Europe. No other Italian city challenged its primacy, for the Pope was both spiritual leader and absolutist ruler; his Christian city appropriated the centrality of ancient Rome, and had considerable impact on the international scene. Throughout the 16th century, as the papacy fought the dangers of Protestantism, visitors had lamented its desolation, the hilly parts almost uninhabited, and the famed monuments engulfed by weeds and mounds of earth. But as the threat of Protestantism waned, the phenomenally energetic building Pope, Sixtus V (r. 1585–1590), envisaged a new city, *Roma Sancta*, which richly symbolised the triumph of faith, and attracted pilgrims from throughout Europe. Wide, straight avenues, clear routes for procession, linked the seven pilgrimage churches of Rome. The city boasted the largest number of churches anywhere in the world, and across the changing skyline there threaded obelisks, creating focal points and evoking the splendour of an ancient world which now paid tribute to a newly confident Catholicism. In the Jubilee Year of 1600, hundreds of thousands of pilgrims, outnumbering the permanent population, came to wonder at its rebirth.[1] Antonio Tempesta's *Map of Rome* (1593, fig. 12) shows this modern city, within whose walls there lived around 100,000 people, most densely in the low-lying areas around the bend of the Tiber.[2] Tempesta emphasises the street networks and expansion of Sistine Rome, but he also shows how rural was the landscape beyond the Aurelian walls. His map seems neatly packaged, but in reality Rome was unruly and exuberant, a vast building site, where streets remained unpaved, and buildings were left half finished for many years. And everywhere the life of the countryside invaded the city. Oxen drank at the fountain by the Arch of Titus, now englobed by houses and stalls; the Forum, renamed the Campo Vaccino, had become the site of a cattle market; sheep and pigs wandered in the streets. Vineyards and orchards spread to the walls, and the gardens of the great villas entranced the visitor with a paradisial beauty. Roman sculptures added the lustre of a classical past, and the facades of the Villa Celimontana and the Villa Medici on the Pincio were encrusted with ancient reliefs, creating an open-air museum. The gardens were open to the public, and northern artists drew amongst the ruins, and exploited the odd contrasts of ancient fragments and contemporary reality.

Rome lies before the viewer like a great world stage, forming the magnificent backdrop to the festivals and rituals of the secular and religious worlds, performed by an unusually fluid and highly cosmopolitan population. At the apex of power and society was the papal court, and around it the many courts of nobles, cardinals and ambassadors, whose magnificence astonished.[3] Their ostentatious coaches, and numerous retainers, crowded the streets; their spectacular entries and departures created a constant sense of drama. Equally resplendent were displays of intense religious passion, and the city was, above all, a 'spectacle of fayth and good works'.[4] In its centre the new orders were prominent, the Jesuits at the great isola of the Gesù, the Oratorians at the Chiesa Nuova, and the Theatines at Sant'Andrea della Valle. Both Jesuits and Oratorians were involved in the restoration of early Christian churches, with their relics and martyrs' tombs, and their fragments of mosaic. They sought to create a sense of continuity with the primitive church, and to evoke the eternal presence of the early saints at the side of the modern worshipper. The medieval St Francis was a favourite. Pilgrims visited his cell at San Francesco a Ripa, and his successor, the Capuchin friar, with threadbare habit and baskets for offerings, was, like the black-robed Jesuit, a prominent figure in the streets of Rome.[5] Across the river, the complex around San Pietro in Montorio, high on the Gianiculum Hill, played a major role in this spiritual and artistic theatre; here, it was believed, St Peter had been crucified, and his martyrdom was likened to that of Christ, and the Gianiculum to Jerusalem.[6] Close by, at the Carmelite church of Santa Maria della Scala, there gathered a group of Spanish intellectuals, trained in oratory and steeped in the contemplative traditions and poetry of St Theresa and St John of the Cross. Their church, freshly embellished, created a new focus in this poorest and most marginal area for pilgrims journeying between Trastevere and the Vatican.[7]

Rome's was a processional culture. In 1597, on 18 October, the Feast Day of St Luke, Caravaggio himself took part, with 104 artists, in the Devotion of the Forty Hours, a form of continuous prayer accompanied by dazzling effects of light and dark.[8] The streets were alive with the penitential processions of lay confraternities, magically enhanced by flaming torches, and by the joyful translation of relics, and canonizations.[9] The military victories of the Catholic world were celebrated. In 1622, an image of the Madonna, to whose intercession the Habsburg victory at the Battle of the White Mountain (1620), was attributed, was carried to the Carmelite church of San Paolo a Termini, later Santa Maria della Vittoria, accompanied by a lavishly orchestrated cortège, of music, priests and churchmen, lighted torches, the spoils of war and many captured flags, some torn and bloody.[10] Capital executions were fear-inspiring spectacles. The condemned man was accompanied by large crowds from the prison gate to the place of execution. Heads were put in baskets and left at the scene to terrify the crowd.[11] Other ceremonies were ritual displays of humility. The pilgrim was greeted at the gates of Rome by the charitable Archconfraternity of the Trinità dei Pellegrini. Its members, even those of high rank, would wash his feet in memory of Christ at the Last Supper. Several in the circle of Caravaggio were members of this confraternity, and bare feet are prominent in Caravaggesque painting. Close to the confraternity's hospice is the church of Sant'Agostino, with Caravaggio's altarpiece of the *Madonna of Loreto* (fig. 13);[12] here two pilgrims, their feet dirty, kneel before the Madonna in a dark Roman *vicolo*. They seem emblems of this vividly Catholic Reformation city in the early years of the 17th century.

The courts of Pope and cardinals also attracted scholars, scientists, poets, musicians and men of letters from all over Europe. The new science, based on observation, was shifting medieval notions, and in 1603 the *Accademia dei Lincei*, the first scientific institution in Europe, was founded by Federico Cesi (1586–1630); Galileo Galilei (1564–1642) was a member, as was Cardinal Francesco Barberini (1597–1679). The household of the German Johannes Faber, physician and botanist to the Pope, suggests a multi-disciplinary breadth of learning; Faber held gatherings at his house near the Pantheon, where scientists and artists, amongst them the German Adam Elsheimer, enjoyed the study of both antiquity and science, particularly of astronomy and the study of light.[13] A new literary world took shape at the academies. Poets and *letterati*, cultivated *gentiluomini* and *dilettanti* gathered and enjoyed a moment of exceptional closeness between the arts of poetry and painting. Literary men were fascinated by Caravaggio, and at this moment the most celebrated poet of the age, Giambattista Marino, a friend of the artist, was creating a poetics of the

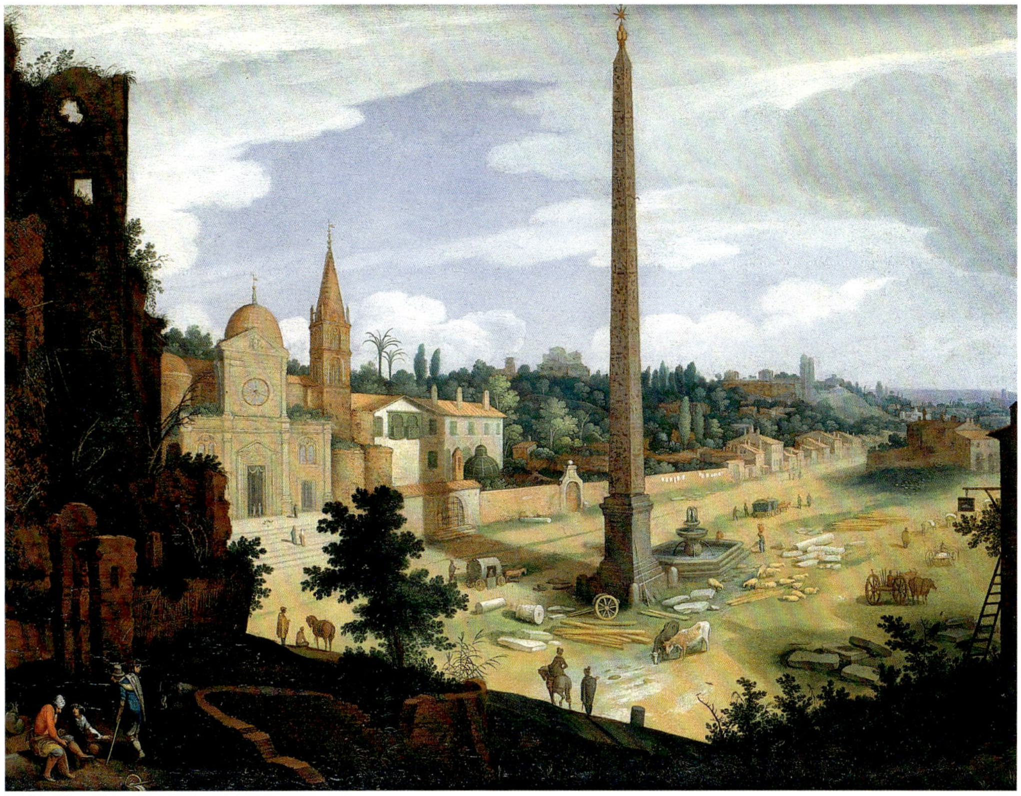

Fig. 11 Willem van Nieulandt, *View of the Piazza del Popolo*, 1600/25, Museo di Roma, Palazzo Braschi, Rome

Fig. 12 Antonio Tempesta, *Map of Rome*, 1593, The Metropolitan Museum of Art, New York, Edward Pearce Casey Fund, 1983 *(see following page)*

marvellous, which enthralled with its *novità*. The Perugian *Accademia degli Insensati*, which had close connections with Rome, met at the Casa Grande in the Via dei Giubbonari, home to Maffeo Barberini, patron of scholars and literary men. Here poets explored a fresh aesthetic, moving from the earthly world to a contemplation of the divine. In 1603, the famous *Accademia degli Umoristi* was founded, and many supporters and contacts of Caravaggio became members.

Music, too, was immensely important. The city delighted visitors with the variety and beauty of sacred music, of which the Oratory of San Filippo Neri was an important centre. A gentleman aspired to be an accomplished musician and many of the nobles and cardinals were extremely learned and discriminating musical connoisseurs. Popular and élite music were unusually close; nobles enjoyed the new style of song for the solo voice, which had such power to convey passionate emotion; streets and taverns were filled with music making, drinking concerts, workmen's songs and amorous serenades.[14] A similar fluidity characterised the world of the theatre. In Roman palaces temporary stages were set up for the actors of the *commedia dell'arte*, but they also performed in the piazza and on processional carts, often showing night-time scenes, with effects of candlelight.[15] Gypsies and card players were everywhere, in everyday life and as popular theatrical characters. Gypsies brought with them the glamour of exotic countries and the charm of folk songs, or *zingaresche*, often sung at street corners. Music and theatre were to colour every aspect of the Caravaggesque world.

But beneath the extraordinary splendour and cultural subtlety of the upper reaches of society there threatened another world, of the dispossessed and the marginal, the 'gran Teatro delle umane miserie'[16] Because of the special position in the city of a church with a celibate priesthood, and the existence of so many courts that each employed its band of retainers, as well as the growing need for builders, bureaucrats and lawyers, the population was heavily skewed towards the male.

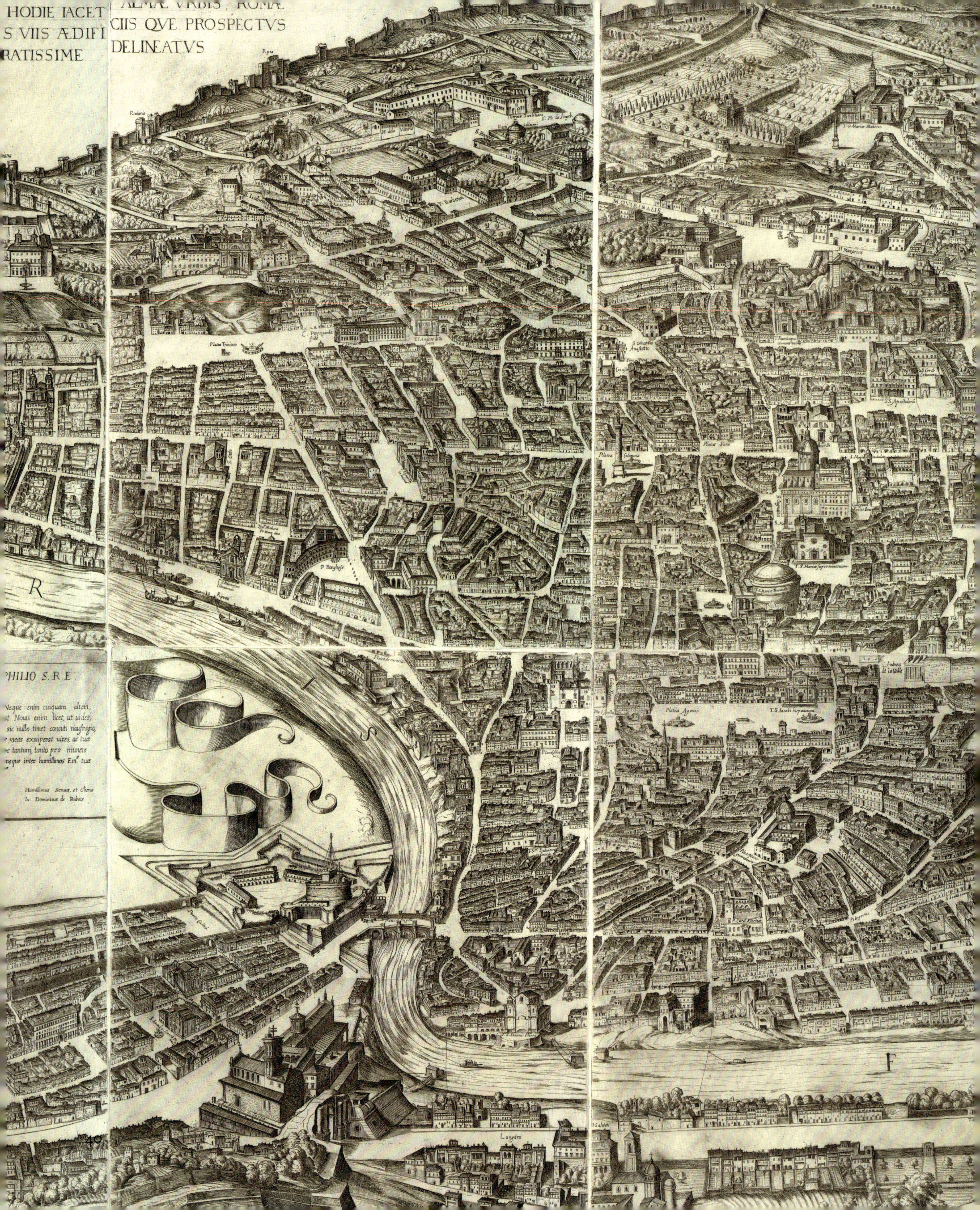

HODIE IACET
S VIIS ÆDIFI
RATISSIME
ALMÆ VRBIS ROMÆ
CIIS QVE PROSPECTVS
DELINEATVS
PHILIO S.R.E
Neque enim cuiquam alteri,
st. Nouis enim licet, ut uides,
sic nullo timet concuti naufragio,
meas exsuperat uires, ac tuæ
oc tantum, tanto pro munere
neque inter humillimos Em.ª tuæ
Humillimus Seruus, et Cliens
Io: Dominicus de Rubeis

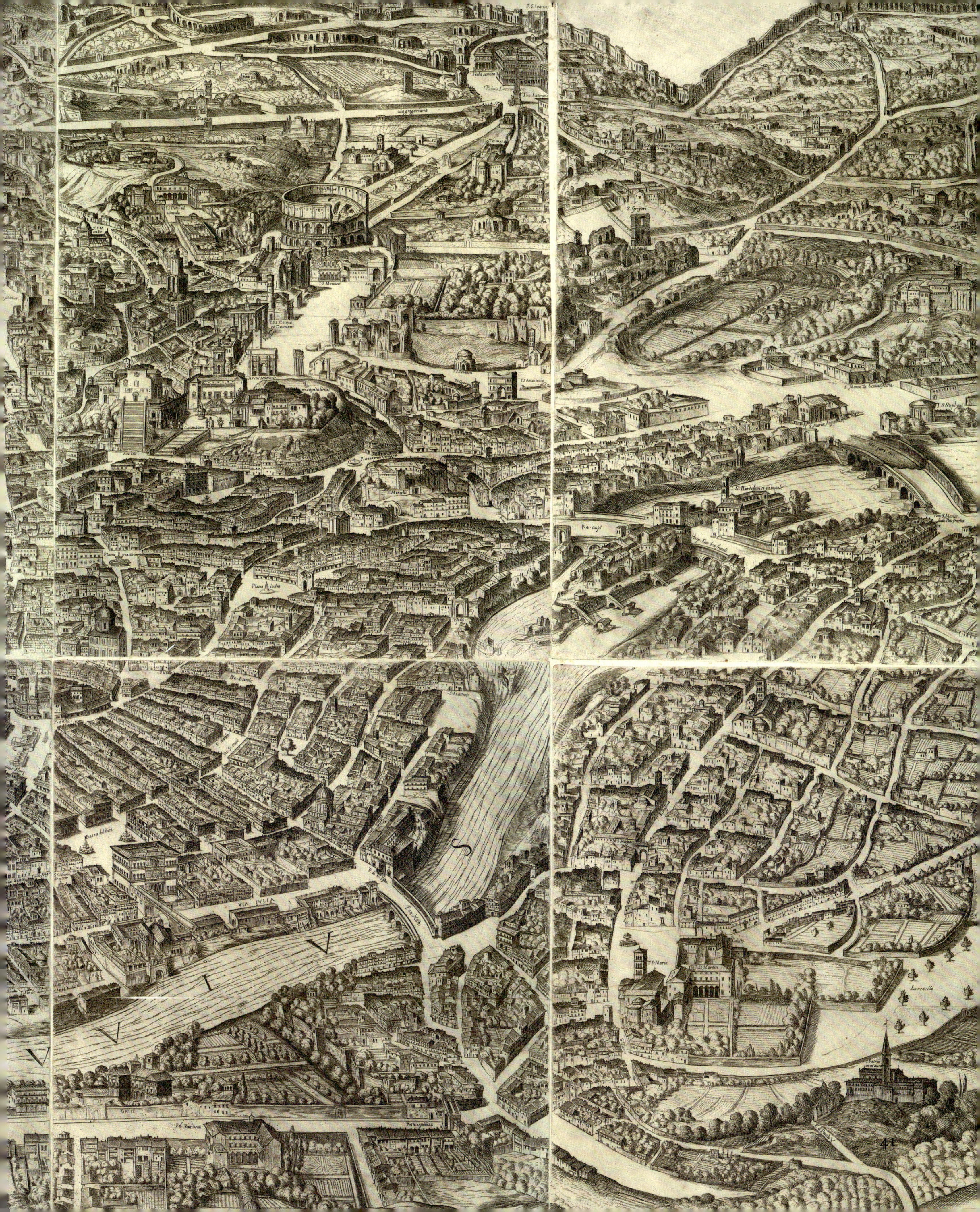
VIA IVLIA
Pon. Xisto
41

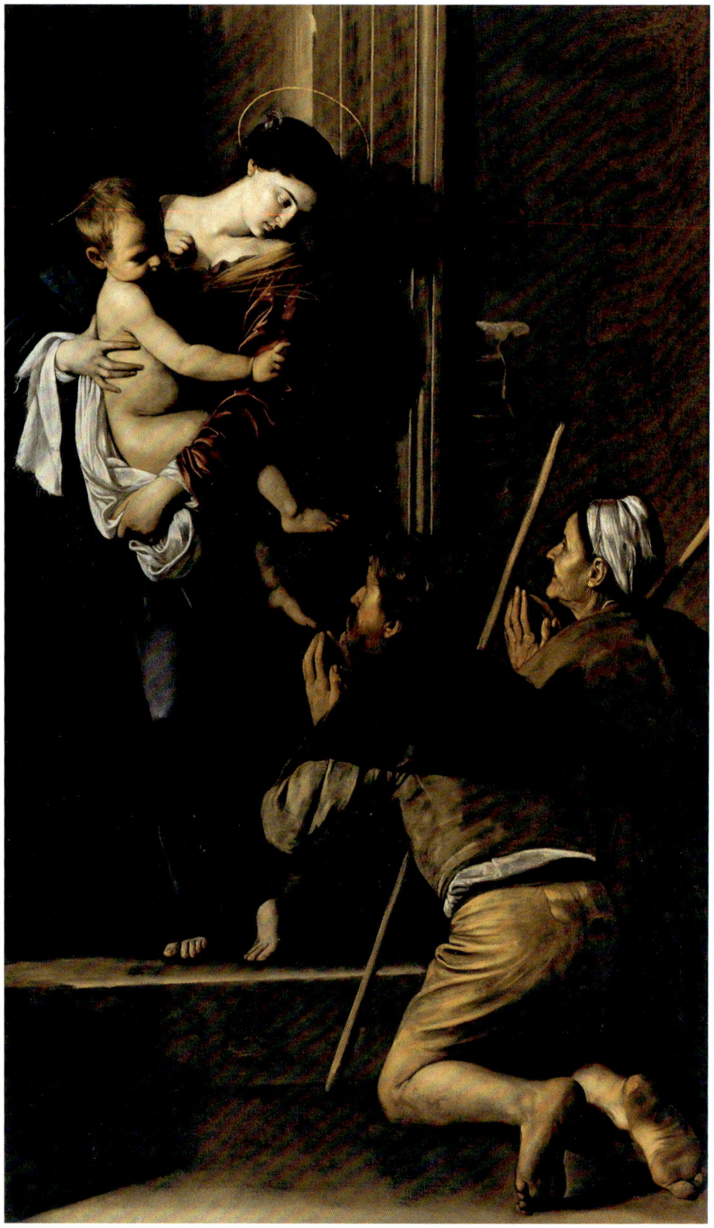

Fig. 13 Michelangelo Merisi, called Caravaggio, *Madonna di Loreto*, 1603/05, Sant'Agostino, Cappella Cavalletti, Rome

This led to an extraordinarily high population of prostitutes.[17] The city's charitable institutions attracted the poor, and a flood of beggars, roaming vagrants, gypsies, thieves and charlatans, mingling with mercenaries freshly returned from the wars of religion, filled the streets, creating fear and even hatred. Gaming was forbidden, and the city was plastered with edicts denouncing it; yet all over Rome men gamed, from every class of society, in the taverns and guardhouses, in the gardens and palaces of great cardinals and princes, in the Vatican itself. The end result of all this was predictable: early 17th-century Rome was an extremely violent place. It was forbidden to carry a sword, but many did, and the *avvisi*, or Roman newspapers, record an uninterrupted flow of assaults and brawls. Some fights were between the retainers of different houses, but many were between belligerent young men, inflamed by drink and cards, who indulged in rituals of affronted honour, throwing stones at the windows of prostitutes, or fouling their doors with excrement.[18]

The streets and *piazze*, and the individual characters of Rome's thronged streets and taverns, spring to vivid life in art. The Piazza Navona (fig. 14), displays, in an extended space, all the diversity of Rome, with its coaches and street performers, its healers, transient sellers and stalls. Sly and crafty, Jacques Callot's *Captain of the Rogues* (fig. 15),[19] entices the spectator, an emblem of Rome's underworld, whose legendary tricks obsessed the authorities. From a more elegant sphere comes Franceso Villamena's *Giovanni Alto* (fig. 16),[20] so brightly dandified, with his neat lace collar and bizarre feathers, standing before the Quirinal, with all the contrast of Rome behind him; its priests, soldiers and retainers, carriages, beggars and animals. His dainty, bowed shoe is set against an antique foot, and a skeletal dog and snake add a sinister note of transience.

This, then, was Rome in the early years of the century: rich, cultured and innovatory and socially full of contrasts. It acted as a magnet to artists from all over Italy and northern Europe; they were attracted by the freedom from guild restrictions, by the opportunities created by the great building works, and by the growing appetite, in every strata of society, from the great households to the most modest, for every imaginable kind of art. Religious art dominated, ranging from the great pictorial cycles commissioned by the popes, to the exhilarating and confident imagery that enriched the churches, oratorios and confraternities. Small images of the Virgin and saints

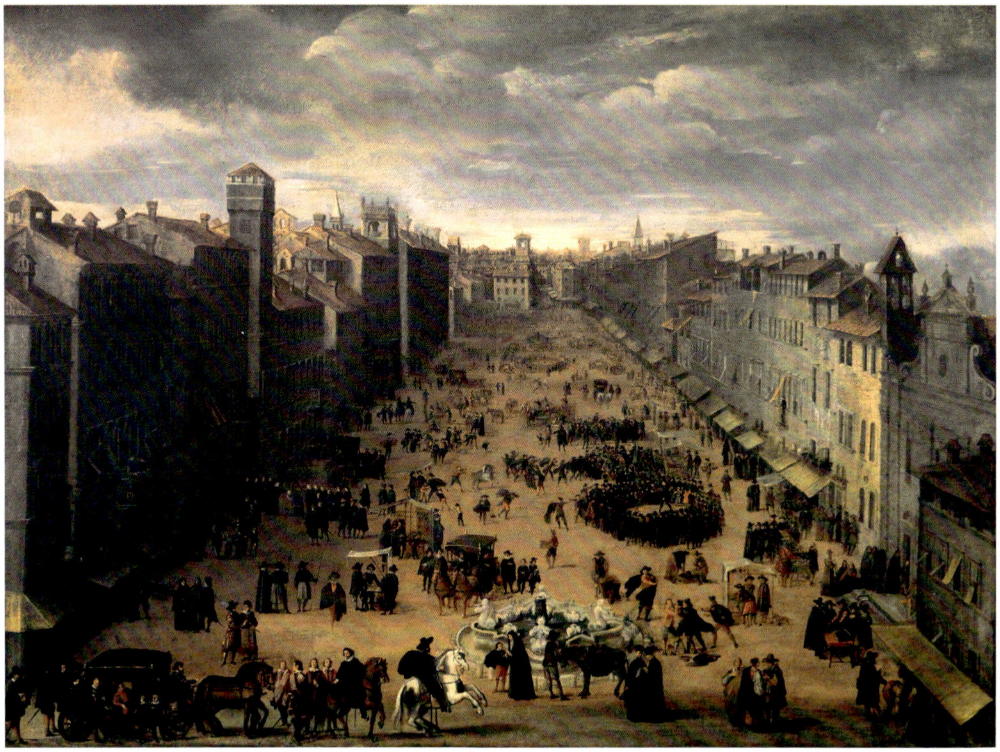

Fig. 14 Anonymous, *Piazza Navona with Market*, 1625/44, Museo di Roma, Palazzo Braschi, Rome

hung in simple households, whilst more sophisticated private individuals bought very many devotional paintings. Individual saints, above all St Mary Magdalene and St Francis, were popular subjects.

The Artists

Rome regained its role as the artistic centre of Europe, made glorious by the splendour of an ancient civilisation, and renowned for the celebrated works of Michelangelo and Raphael. But the city also boasted an exciting contemporary scene. The decade from 1610 to 1620 was dominated by the Bolognese followers of Annibale Carracci, but very many artists from France and the Netherlands, and some from Spain, were drawn by the fame of Caravaggio. Amongst them were the three artists from Utrecht, Hendrick ter Brugghen, Gerard van Honthorst, and Dirck van Baburen; as many as 25 out of a possible 48 Utrecht painters went to Italy.[21]

To these artists the great altarpieces of Caravaggio were an astonishing break with the tired traditions of the late 16th century. In the Cerasi Chapel of Santa Maria del Popolo, in the Piazza del Popolo, Caravaggio's lateral paintings, *The Crucifixion of St Peter* and the *Conversion of St Paul* (figs. 49, 50), hauntingly dark and challengingly realistic, framed Annibale's *Assumption of the Virgin*, with its light, clear colours and monumental, idealised figures. They would immediately have introduced foreign artists to the subtlety of aesthetic debate in Rome. In San Luigi dei Francesi were Caravaggio's *Calling of St Matthew* and his *Martyrdom of St Matthew* (fig. 17), amongst the most famous paintings in Europe. Their illusionism and drama of light and shade was astonishing. No earlier artist had painted, in oils on canvas, scenes from contemporary reality that seem to take place in the chapel before our very eyes. Many French and Flemish artists were to echo their colourful figures and their evocation of the perils of dark Roman streets and courtyards. They would have been aware, in the fleeing group of young swordsmen in the *Martyrdom*, of Caravaggio himself, looking back in pride at the world that he had created, and calling on young artists to follow him. In the Chiesa Nuova, where the spirit of San Filippo Neri lived on, Caravaggio's unusually classical *Entombment of Christ* (cat. 22) was one of a

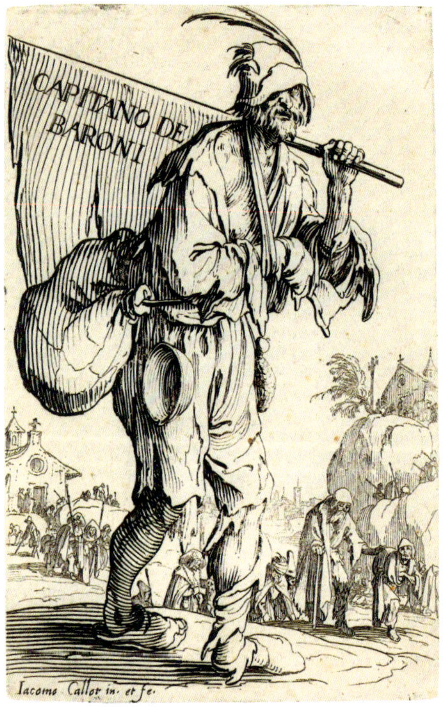

Fig. 15 Jacques Callot, *Captain of the Rogues*, c. 1622, National Gallery of Art, Rosenwald Collection, Washington

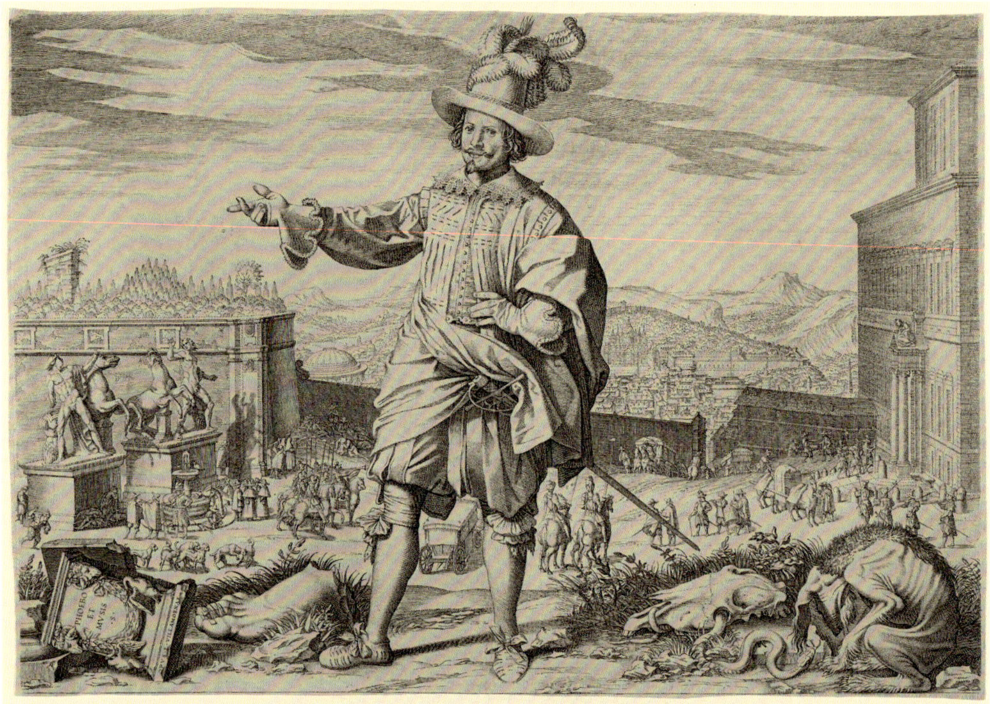

Fig. 16 Francesco Villamena, *Giovanni Alto standing by the Quirinal*, 1623, The Metropolitan Museum of Art, New York, bequest of Phyllis Masser, 2011

series of altarpieces dedicated to the mysteries of the Virgin, which together brilliantly conveyed the new richness and emotionalism of religious art in Catholic Rome.

In Caravaggio's first years in the city he was relatively poor and obliged to hawk his talents from studio to studio, moving from room to room, often undertaking quite menial jobs. He was supported by a dealer, Costantino Spata, and by an older painter, Prospero Orsi. His lucky break came when he caught the attention of Cardinal Francesco Maria del Monte and won an honoured place in his household.[22] Such a position, as part of the *famiglia* of a Cardinal or secular grandee, ensured food and lodging, and the coveted privilege of bearing arms. Caravaggio probably lived for some time with Del Monte in the Palazzo Madama, just across the road from San Luigi dei Francesi. His neighbourhood remained the southernmost part of Campo Marzio.

A little later, the artists' centre moved further north, and the foreign followers of Caravaggio flocked to the parishes of Santa Maria del Popolo, San Lorenzo in Lucina, and Sant'Andrea della Fratte.[23] Tax exemptions in the Via Sistina, the Via del Babuino, and the Via Margutta were an attraction,[24] while the hilltop light made the Via Sistina and the Scesa di Capo le Case popular. Directed lighting was important to Caravaggesque painters; Ribera, in 1612, won permission to construct an overhead light in the studio of his house.[25] It became common for these youthful foreign artists to set up households together; Dirk van Baburen and David de Haen lived in a house on the Piazza Trinità dei Monti in 1619 and were joined by Nicolas Régnier and a servant in 1620.[26] Rent was high, and often they were obliged to paint in their living spaces. Their closeness encouraged a constant exchange of ideas, and was the spur to an extraordinary flowering of creativity.[27] The streets and merchants' shops, where paintings were displayed and sold, and the printsellers and bookshops around the Piazza Navona became lively centres of talk about art.[28]

At the centre of these artists' fascination with Caravaggio was his practice of painting 'dal naturale', or from life, which

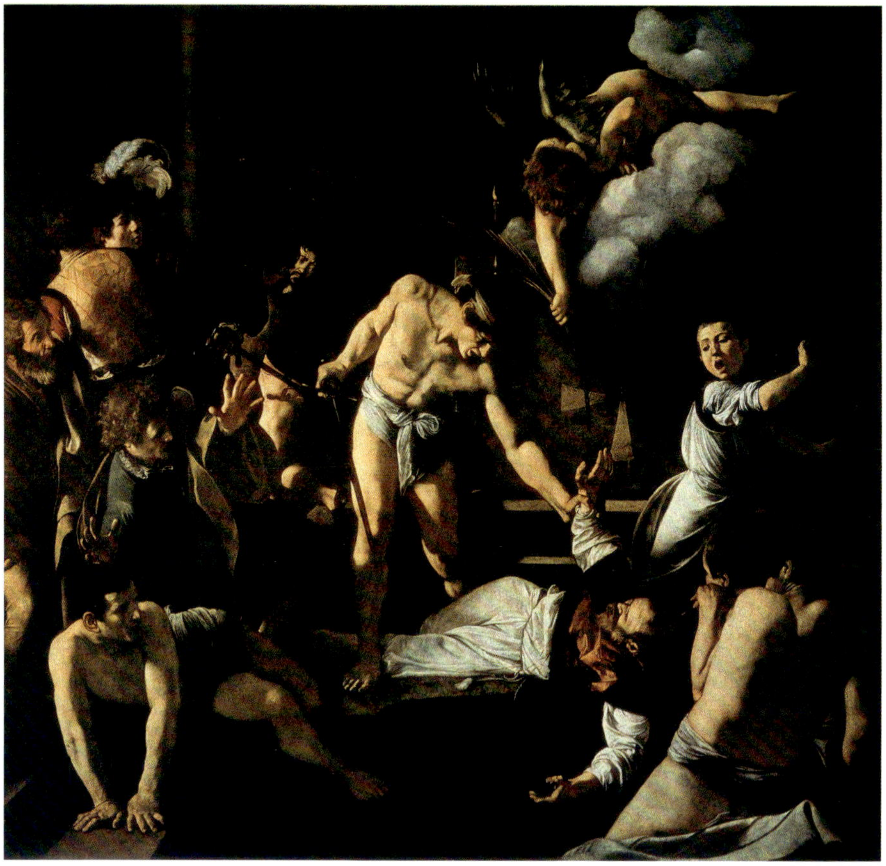

Fig. 17 Michelangelo Merisi, called Caravaggio, *Martyrdom of St Matthew*, 1599/1600, San Luigi dei Francesi, Contarelli Chapel, Rome

gave to his art such an astonishing intensity of presence. Caravaggio, Bellori tells us, rejected the superb statuary of antiquity and the famous paintings of Raphael; 'the young ones particularly gathered around him, praised him as the unique imitator of nature' each finding 'in the piazza and in the street their masters and the models for imitating nature'.[29] The pictures themselves suggest their closeness; they shared models and studio props, maybe pieces of armour, or Capuchin habits, or fragments of classical cornices or bas-reliefs. The lively account of Orazio Gentileschi's barber gives us a glimpse of their world; Orazio, he tells us, employed an elderly pilgrim from Palermo, 'handsome in appearance, with a face like that of St Paul, bald-headed, with white hair, and with a fine, full beard that is as heavy on the cheeks as in the beard itself'.[30] Naturalist artists took pleasure in ageing faces, with furrowed brows and wrinkled necks, full of expression and character. Guido Reni, who in his early Roman years engaged with Caravaggio's naturalism, modelled a famous terracotta head from a striking local character who frequented the Ripa.[31] This head, with scraggy neck and bizarrely protruding ears, recurs in works by Ribera and by Cecco del Caravaggio.[32] Painting from the model seemed dangerously easy to classicist critics, but these artists did not renounce drawing. It is striking that Giulio Mancini's first comment on Honthorst, in his vivid description of the artist, is that he was a good draughtsman, and frequented the *accademie del vivo*, several of which were flourishing in Rome at this date. Many foreign artists participated in the activities of the Accademia di San Luca, an official and papally sanctioned institution, where artists and men of letters together promoted the visual arts. Amongst the amateurs was Asdrubale Mattei, later a fervent supporter of Caravaggism.[33]

Caravaggio's charismatically dark presence, – he had 'a dark complexion and dark eyes, and his eyebrows and hair were black'[34] – and his disordered way of life exerted an almost equal fascination. Gaspare Celio's biography of 1614 launches this myth. Prospero Orsi, Celio tells us, looked all day for Caravaggio to introduce him to Cardinal del Monte. He found him raggedly clad, asleep, close to the famed Pasquino, a sculpture renowned throughout Europe for the scurrilous verses attached to it.[35] Later we hear of Caravaggio, unwashed, but dressed in princely velvets, which he let fall into contemptuous rags.[36] His disorder was rivalled by that of Ribera, who lived in colourful and picaresque squalor, surrounded by ugly, undressed girls, sprawling on a single mattress, and was often involved in night-time scuffles with the police.[37] But not all artists were tempted by the low life; some had houses, often in the same area as Caravaggesque painters, and aspired to gentlemanly behaviour. Honthorst, elegantly dressed, melancholy and restrained in manner, and unusually trustworthy, knew how to show his work to prospective patrons and was happy to paint before them.[38]

Nonetheless, most northern artists, unlike the Bolognese, shared Caravaggio's passion for the rowdy life of street and tavern, where Caravaggio himself, 'excessively fearless' and quarrelsome, roamed the streets, looking for a 'chance to break his neck or jeopardise the life of another'.[39] He was accompanied, Sandrart tells us, 'by his young friends, mainly lustyfellows, painters and swordsmen'[40] in search of sex and adventure, of tennis and similar ball games. The taverns of Rome were legendary, and the Osteria del Moro, in Via del Babuino, and the Osteria della Lupa, both in the Campo Marzio, near to the artists' quarter, were favourites; the Osteria del Sole, on the Via di Ripetta, was a haunt of dice players.[41] In these inns young artists regularly ate, enjoyed a pie and a sausage, were entertained by popular musicians and lute players, and mingled with courtesans, *bravi* and unoccupied soldiers. Above all they gambled, braving the perils of notorious cheats and the seductive wiles of gypsies; some *locande* were set up with a number of tables, offering a variety of games, some permitted, others forbidden. Most foreign artists spoke Italian well, perhaps having made a start with the Dutch–Italian lessons reminiscent of the modern phrase book, which were included in the guidebook, *Delitiae Italiae*, published in 1602.[42] Playing cards and mixing with prostitutes honed their skills. Jean Ducamps, arrested for playing *riffa* in a barber's shop close to the Osteria del Moro, amusingly protested that he was playing *toccatiglia*, a permitted game, and that he went to the shop every day to improve his Italian.[43]

Prostitutes were a colourful part of this unruly street life. Most famous was Fillide Melandroni, whom Caravaggio knew and painted. She was a pugnacious street fighter, viciously threatening to scar rivals with a knife; but she was comfortably off, delighting in luxury, and owning many splendid dresses and jewels. It seems that both artists and courtesans moved easily between two worlds, and the refined Honthorst spent a night in prison in 1619, arrested for having carried a sword in the house of the prostitute Vittoria da Rieti, whom he had known for ten months.[44] It was forbidden to carry a sword, but many did and violence was endemic. In 1606, after a series of skirmishes with the police, Caravaggio killed a man, and was forced to flee Rome.[45] Violence amongst his followers escalated in the 1620s: David de la Riche, for example, Valentin's room-mate, was murdered in 1626, one of several such disastrous events.[46] The foundation of the Bentvueghels between 1617 and 1620, an eccentric society of mainly northern artists, who were dedicated to Bacchus and sought inspiration in heavy drinking, exacerbated this aggression. Pieter van Laer's *Carnival Revellers in a Tavern*[47] (fig. 18), with masked actors entertaining a colourfully dressed assembly suggests their high spirits.[48] But theirs was a different world, and they did not seek to join the Accademia di San Luca; only Dirck van Baburen, from the Utrecht painters, was a member of this society.

This shady urban underworld is presented in a wealth of tavern scenes, initially inspired by the novelty of Caravaggio's iconic *The Gypsy Fortune Teller* (cat. 73) and the *Cardsharps* (fig. 89). And swords and daggers gleam threateningly in many religious works suggesting sudden brawls in dark Roman streets, whilst grisly decapitations evoke the horrors of public spectacles of violence.

Caravaggio and many of his northern followers lived violent lives among violent people, but their studios clustered around the palazzi of the Medici, the Giustiniani, the Aldobrandini, the Crescenzi, whose cortiles and great staircases were opening out from the narrow medieval streets. The Roman palazzo was truly resplendent; their imposing facades jostled for attention, and within high churchmen and aristocrats

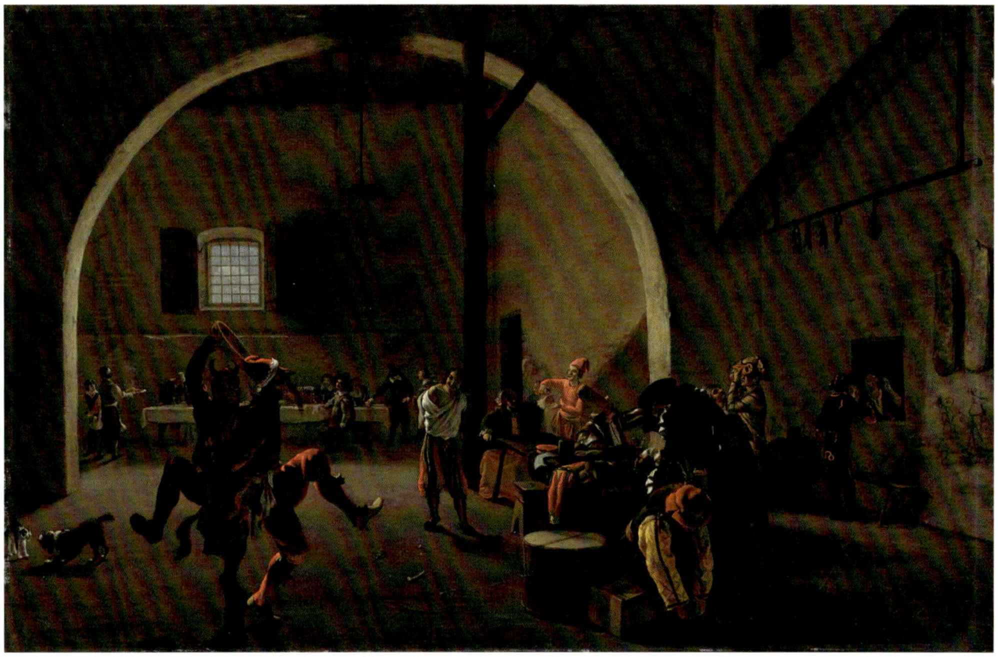

Fig. 18 Pieter van Laer, *Carnival Revellers in a Tavern*, c. 1635, Bayerische Staatsgemäldesammlungen, Alte Pinakothek, Munich

displayed status and wealth through lavish displays of art, of textiles, paintings and ancient sculptures, of long galleries gleaming with *stucchi*, gilt furniture and mirrors (fig. 19). A striking feature at this moment was the development of the picture gallery, and the rapid growth of demand for a new kind of easel painting, which was tailor-made for this kind of display. These galleries were intensely sociable, and easily accessible to high-ranking visitors. The cultivated viewer enjoyed the pleasures of *conversazione*, and the displays of art were themselves witty, encouraging unusual juxtapositions and *paragone*.[49]

Two households stand out: those of Cardinal Francesco Maria del Monte, at the Palazzo Madama, and that of Cardinal Benedetto Giustiniani and his brother, Vincenzo, just across the road in the magnificent Palazzo Giustiniani, where there hung 15 Caravaggios and 13 works by Ribera. These distinguished connoisseurs and patrons shared an unusual breadth of learning and interests, and their palazzi were important centres of an interdisciplinary culture. In this small neighbourhood, where French and Flemish artists mingled, was an astonishing concentration of the new naturalistic art, and we may imagine them moving easily between the collections of the Palazzo Giustiniani, and the church of San Luigi, just across the road, with its celebrated Caravaggios. After Caravaggio and Ribera had left Rome, Vincenzo continued to patronise Caravaggesque painters. In 1621, David de Haen had moved into the palazzo of Pietro Cussida, the Spanish patron of the chapel in San Pietro in Montorio, on the Via del Corso but later he, Honthorst and Nicolas Régnier lived in the Palazzo Giustiniani. Vincenzo's artists had privileged access to his collections, while Inigo Jones and Rubens visited in the entourage of noble patrons. Del Monte meanwhile guarded his paintings jealously, and Giulio Mancini was reduced to bribing a servant to admit a copyist.[50] Other nobles enjoyed showing their pictures to painters; Prince Paolo Savelli was happy to invite a friend of Orazio Gentileschi (perhaps Honthorst) to see his paintings in the palazzo at Monte Savello, which included, amongst works by Elsheimer, Rubens and Saraceni, Caravaggio's famous and immensely influential *The Denial of St Peter*.[51]

This painting, *The Denial of St Peter*, is a half-length narrative, intended for close viewing, and conveying intense emotion, a type favoured as a gallery painting. Caravaggio's most famous works of this kind, such as the *Crowning with Thorns*

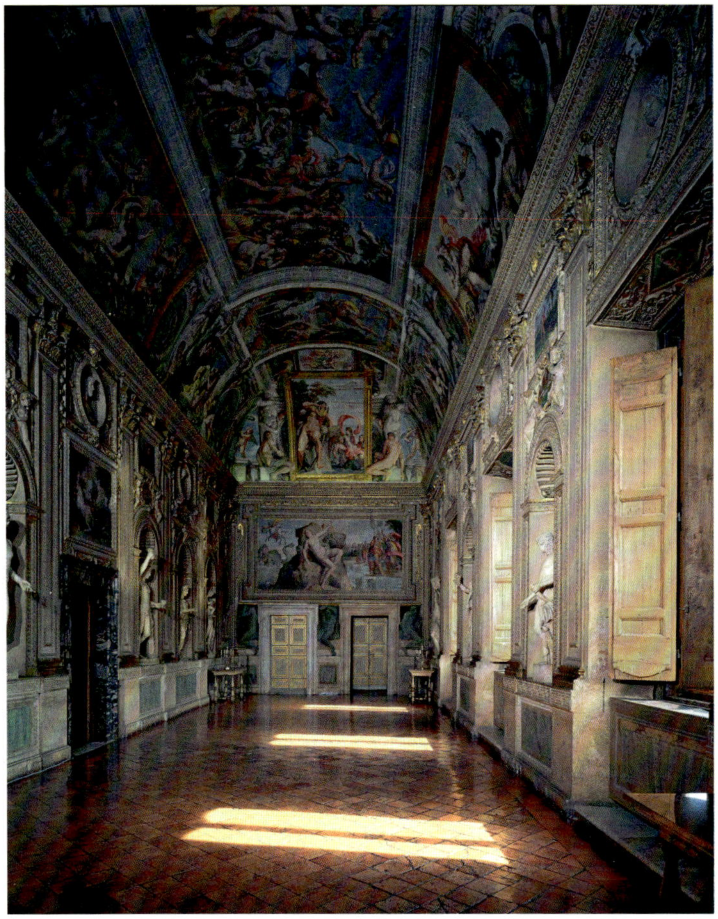

Fig. 19 Galleria Farnese, Palazzo Farnese, Rome

(fig. 84), *David with the Head of Goliath* (fig. 93) and *The Taking of Christ*,[52] inspired immensely rich chains of reaction and response; his followers both paid homage to him and sought to surpass his astonishing innovatory power.

Many Caravaggesque painters specialised in gallery paintings. It was harder for both Italian Caravaggisti and foreigners to compete in the violently competitive world of public commissions; even as late as Paul V the official world favoured the late Mannerist painters. Artistic rivalries often erupted into violence. Cristoforo Roncalli, for instance, was attacked over the commission for the mosaics in St Peter's;[53] intemperate verbal attacks, were common, and the volley of astonishingly obscene verses which greeted Giovanni Baglione's *Resurrection of Christ* for the Gesù, resulted in Caravaggio's notorious trial for libel. Patrons of private chapels, bankers, lawyers and newly rich officials at the papal court sought to impress with their altarpieces, tombs and coats of arms; they made precise aesthetic choices and sought the reflected glory of Caravaggio, 'among the most famous modern masters in Rome'.[54] Sometimes the interests of patrons conflicted with those of the church, and Caravaggio's *Death of the Virgin*[55] was rejected by the Barefoot Carmelites of Santa Maria della Scala, but put on public display in Rome and passionately admired by the art world. In this decade naturalistic paintings began to enter private chapels. Carlo Saraceni ran a large workshop producing dark and realistic works for Roman churches; between 1615 and 1620 Dirk van Baburen, David de Haen and Honthorst won outstandingly important commissions for Roman churches. Night scenes were popular, and these artists explored different types of dramatic luminism.

With the pontificate of Gregory XV (1621–1623), a Bolognese pope who favoured his compatriots, the Roman art world changed and the Utrecht painters left Rome. But under Urban VIII (1623–1644) powerful voices remained. Two unusual, and very different, commissions suggest the variety of a late flowering of Caravaggism. Asdrubale Mattei, well aware of the prestige endowed by art, commissioned a series of Caravaggesque paintings for his gallery in the Palazzo Mattei. He privileged the works of Giovanni Serodine, which, so freely painted, so emotionally expressive, stood on the threshold of a new and powerful naturalism. In contrast, the three paintings of the Cappella della Passione in Santa Maria in Aquiro are backward looking, recalling the contemplative candlelight effects of Honthorst, and seem touchingly old-fashioned additions to the Church's series of Caravaggesque commissions.[56]

1 Delumeau 1975, p. 44, gives their number as 536,000, and the residents as 100,000.
2 Robertson 2015, p. 10.
3 Delumeau 1975, p. 108. Delumeau quotes St Charles Borromeo's words: 'To succeed in Rome one must love God, and own a coach'. On luxury see Petrocchi 1970, p. 55.
4 Martin 1969, p. 8.
5 Panciroli 1600, p. 318.
6 Zuccari 2004.
7 Sturm 2015, pp. 9–27.
8 Pampalone, 2012, pp. 213–235.
9 San Juan 2001, pp. 95–99. San Juan cites Montaigne, who described how 'the whole city appeared to be in flames'.
10 Labrot 1987, pp. 250–253; Gigli 1994, vol. 1, pp. 102–106.
11 On Caravaggio and violence, see Varriano 2006, chapter 5.
12 1603/05, canvas, 260 × 150 cm, Sant'Agostino, Cappella Cavalletti, Rome.
13 Huemer 1996, pp. 4–10.
14 Ebert-Schifferer 2012, p. 36.
15 Bonfait 2012, p. 137.
16 Pestilli 2017, p. 109.
17 Delumeau 1975, p. 102, estimates that there were 17 prostitutes per 1,000 females between 1599 and 1605.
18 Cohen 1992.
19 c. 1622, etching, 14.4 × 9.3 cm, National Gallery of Art, Rosenwald Collection, Washington, inv. 1949.5.282.
20 1623, etching, 35.5 x 52.5 cm, The Metropolitan Museum of Art, New York, bequest of Phyllis Massar, 2011, accession no. 2012.136.919.
21 Bok 1994, p. 5, as quoted in Franits 2013a, pp. 189–194.
22 Gandolfi/Zuccari 2017/18, p. 251.
23 The *stati delle anime*, the Easter censuses undertaken by parish priests, have provided a wealth of information on Rome's population, though many Protestants left Rome for this counting. See Vodret 2011; Amadio 2005 and Zicarelli 2005, pp. 33; Fosi 2011, pp. 9–11.
24 Bodart 1970, vol. 1, p. 106.
25 Danesi Squarzina 2006. This article traces Ribera's frequent changes of residence in Rome.
26 Franits 2013a, p. 7.
27 Bonfait 2012, pp. 69–77.
28 For the growth of the art market, and the variety of types of painting, see Cavazzini 2008.
29 Mancini/Baglione/Bellori 2016, p. 72.
30 Exh. cat. Rome/New York/St. Louis 2001/02, p. 94.
31 Malvasia 1678, vol. 2, p. 59.
32 For the influence of this head, see Farina 2014, pp. 70–75.
33 For the role of amateurs and informal academies, see Gage 2009.
34 Mancini/Baglione/Bellori 2016, p. 102.
35 Gandolfi/Zuccari 2017/18, p. 253.
36 Mancini/Baglione/Bellori 2016, p.104
37 Mancini 1956, p. 249. For the text of Mancini's letter of 7 April 1617, see Farina 2014 p. 222, note 47.
38 Mancini 1956, p. 258.
39 Mancini/Baglione/Bellori 2016, p. 56.
40 Sandrart 1675 (1925), p. 277.
41 For the precise location and present-day appearance of the Osteria della Lupa, see Verdi 2011, p. 42.
42 Ens 1602.
43 Cavazzini 2014/15, p. 60.
44 For the trial documents, see Exh. cat. Florence 2015, p. 258.
45 Lorizzo 2015a, p. 97.
46 Cavazzini 2014/15, p. 62.
47 c. 1635, canvas, 53.6 × 82.3 cm, Bayerische Staatsgemäldesammlungen, Alte Pinakothek, Munich, inv. 4834.
48 Bonfait 2012, pp. 79–80, discussed how different are the colourful dress and feathered hats of the Bentvueghels from the black and sombre raiment of the Bolognese.
49 Ago 2006, pp. 134–136; Feigenbaum 2014.
50 Langdon 2012, p. 45–46.
51 Lorizzo 2015a, p. 96. The painting was in the Savelli collection by 1624; from 1613 it had been in the collection of Guido Reni.
52 1602, canvas, 133.5 × 169.5 cm, National Gallery of Ireland, Dublin, inv. L.1470.
53 Robertson 2015, p. 284. For the rivalries over the altarpieces in St Peter's, see Robertson 2015, pp. 29–34.
54 Giovanni Magni, 17.01.1607, quoted in Schütze 2009, p. 271.
55 1601–1605/06, canvas, 3.69 × 2.45 cm, Musée du Louvre, Paris, inv. 54.
56 The attribution of these paintings remains puzzling. For a summary of the arguments, see Papi 2015, pp. 79–80.

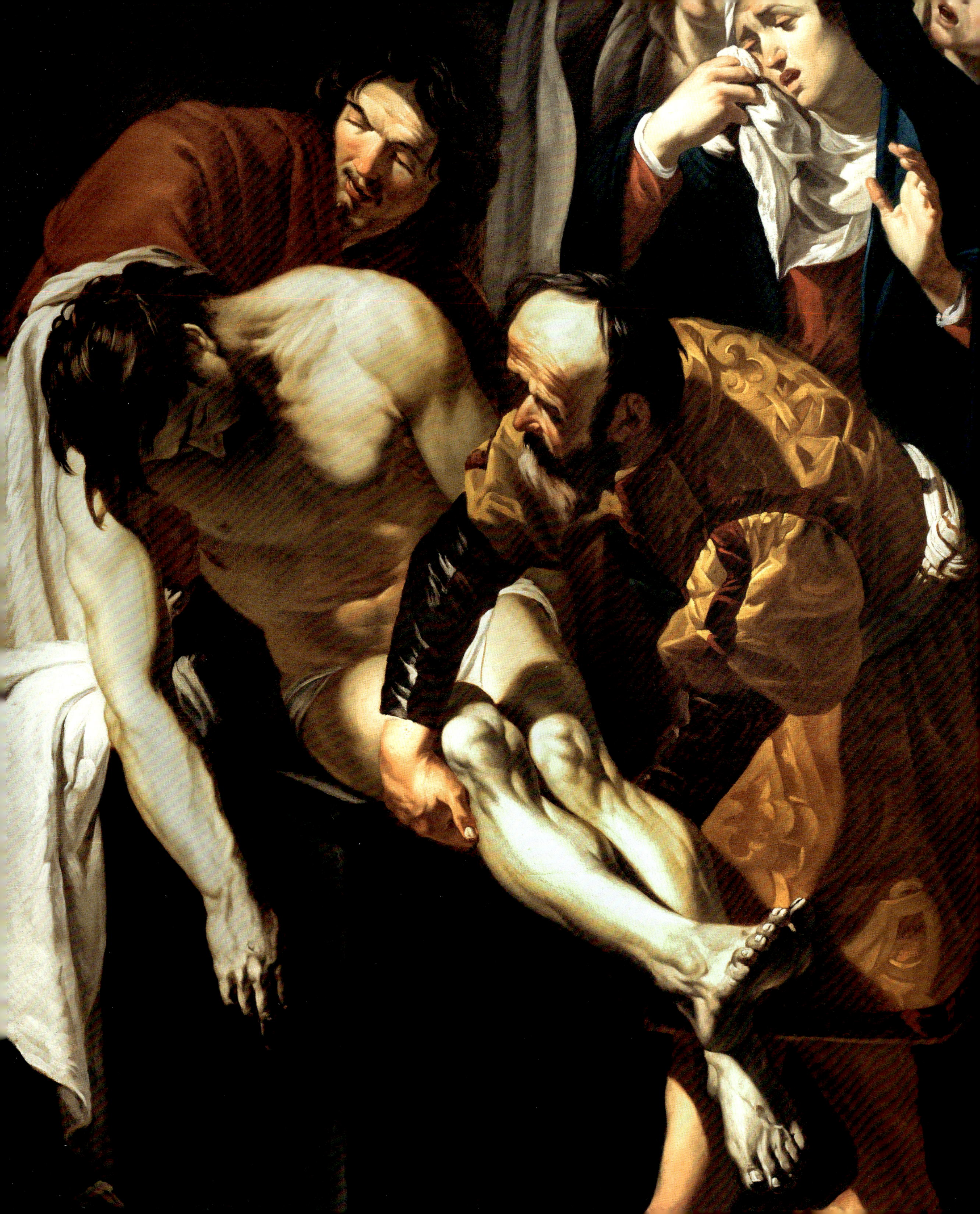

The Utrecht Caravaggisti: Imitation and Improvement

LIESBETH M. HELMUS

The Discalced Carmelites live and work deep in the Trastevere neighbourhood on the right bank of the Tiber. Their complex consists of a friary, church and pharmacy (fig. 43). Here, at the foot of the steps of one of the houses, a mother knelt each day before an image of the Virgin and Jesus, praying for a cure for her deformed child. Miraculously, her prayers were heard, leading in 1593 to the building of the Chiesa di Santa Maria della Scala, the church of 'St Mary of the Steps'. That house of God, a cruciform basilica with six side chapels, was completed in 1610. In 1617, the Utrecht artist Gerard van Honthorst was commissioned to paint an altarpiece for its mortuary chapel of Giovanni Battista Longhi (cat. 20). At the same time, his fellow townsman and colleague Dirck van Baburen was also at work not eight hundred metres away. High up on Mount Janiculum, with a panoramic view of Trastevere, he and his Amsterdam colleague, friend and assistant David de Haen were decorating the Pietà Chapel in the church of San Pietro in Montorio (fig. 21, cat. 21). By then, their older colleague Hendrick ter Brugghen had already completed his Italian adventure.

Three young man at work abroad – expats who had travelled south to Rome on the advice of the art theorist and biographer Karel van Mander, who noted in his *Schilder-boeck* of 1604 that 'Michael Agnolo da Caravaggio' was doing 'extraordinary things' in Rome. According to van Mander he had 'already acquired a great reputation, honour and name with his works'. He then urges young painters to follow Caravaggio. 'As regards his technique, it is such that it is very pleasing, and a wondrously beautiful manner, to be emulated by young painters'.[1] By 'technique' van Mander was referring to the Italian *maniera* and *pratica*, the technical skills of the painter that were acquired through practice.[2] A good 'technique' or a 'wondrously beautiful manner' denotes the way of working: handling of line, hatching, the effects of light and shade, and so on.[3] Time and again, van Mander stresses how important it is for apprentices to study and copy good works of art by other artists. He calls that 'stealing' or 'harvesting'.[4] Learning by looking and copying.[5] The *translatio*, or copying a work of art, is followed by the *imitatio* of the great master, imitating his style. The highest achievement is *aemulatio*, or surpassing that model.[6]

In order to round off their training, Baburen, Honthorst and ter Brugghen went to Rome to study under a master painter, as van Mander had advised them to do. However, they did not find Caravaggio there. When ter Brugghen set off for Italy in the second half of 1607, Caravaggio had already left Rome, and he died in 1610, several years before the arrival of Baburen and Honthorst. What they did see were Caravaggio's many altarpieces and other paintings, but not only his, also those of his predecessors and contemporaries. They looked, studied and improved – not with the idea of surpassing the art of Caravaggio and his followers, but with the possibly almost unconscious tendency to modify it to suit their personal preferences.

The fact that the three young Utrecht artists travelled to Italy was not just due to van Mander: it was a tradition. The previous two generations of Utrecht artists also undertook a journey southwards, not only to complete their training but also, as in the case of Jan van Scorel (1495–1562), because of close ties to the Roman Catholic Church. Up until the Reformation, the cathedral city of Utrecht was the most important religious centre in the northern Netherlands. Abraham Bloemaert (1566–1651), Joachim Wtewael (1566–1638) and Paulus Moreelse (1571–1638) dominated the artistic life of Utrecht after Scorel's death, and they too all travelled south. Bloemaert went to Paris at an early age, and Wtewael went to Padua and Saint-Malo.[7] It is known that Moreelse went to Italy before 1596, and probably to Rome, but there is nothing to show that he was truly influenced by what he saw there.[8] All three began their careers when Mannerism was at its height in the Low Countries. It was a style characterised by the depiction of an idealised nature. The normal proportions of the human body were replaced by the supranormal. The neck, limbs, fingers and toes are elongated, as is the entire length of the figure, while the head and feet are made smaller. The shoulders of the male figures are considerably wider relative to the waist. In addition, the torso is often twisted to such an extent that it is forced into an unnatural pose. The painter's palette consisted of pastel tints that were placed next to each other as complementary areas of colour: lemon yellow beside lilac beside pink and light blue. Wtewael continued painting in the Mannerist style his whole life long (fig. 22).[9] Starting in the 1620s, Bloemaert's style evolved towards Classicism, although certain Mannerist traits never disappeared altogether. Paulus Moreelse was the leading portrait painter in Utrecht, and he also played a prominent role in the development of pastoral painting.

Moreelse and Bloemaert were the most important instructors from whom rising young painters could learn their craft. Moreelse had at least 28 pupils and Bloemaert around 100.[10] Both of them gave drawing lessons in the Utrecht Drawing Academy, which was founded soon after 1611. Drawing from the life model or copying examples were extremely important parts of the training: 'nulla dies sine linea', the elder Pliny's 'no day without a line'.[11] Practising drawing every day was considered to be essential for attaining perfection. Bloemaert was a gifted and very virtuoso draughtsman, and there are around 1,700 of his sheets still in existence.[12] Only a dozen of Moreelse's drawings are known.[13] The fact that there are so few may have had something to do with his speciality as a portrait painter.

Baburen was trained in Moreelse's workshop, and ter Brugghen and Honthorst were taught by Bloemaert. Whatever the three Utrecht artists learned from their teachers, it was not a preference for drawing. There is not a single sheet that can be convincingly attributed to Baburen or ter Brugghen. Of the three, only Gerard van Honthorst left a drawn oeuvre that now amounts to some 85 known works.[14] The physician, art collector and artists' biographer Giulio Mancini states in his *Considerazioni sulla pittura* that Honthorst in Rome attended the 'Accademie del vivo', where he drew 'from life', meaning from the life model, and that he also displayed a 'buonissimo gusto del disegno', literally an excellent taste for drawing.[15]

The journey to Italy was long and dangerous. If ter Brugghen, Honthorst and Baburen had read van Mander's words of encouragement, and there is a fair chance that they had, then they would also have taken his fatherly admonitions to heart. 'I would like to encourage you most earnestly to travel, were it not that I fear that you could take the wrong path, for Rome, more than other places, is the city that is often the goal of the painter's journey, being the head of the schools of painting, but it is also the ideal place for wastrels and prodigal sons to spend all that they have. One shrinks from permitting one's child to make that journey.'[16] So be careful, for Rome is the place where you risk losing everything. 'But if you nevertheless do go on your travels, do not do so unless you yourself wish to and your parents give their permission. Avoid small inns and bad company, do not show that you have much money with you. Do not reveal that you are on a long journey, Be respectable and polite, do not get into arguments, always have a goodly amount of money, but at the same time take care not to loan much to your own unfortunate fellow countrymen. Learn the local customs everywhere, follow the good ones and avoid the bad. Leave early and also seek lodgings early, and inspect the beds and sheets closely in order to avoid sickness and vermin. But above all, never have anything to do with light women, for leaving aside the sin they could damage you for life.'[17] Van Mander, who had himself travelled to Rome, was speaking from experience.[18]

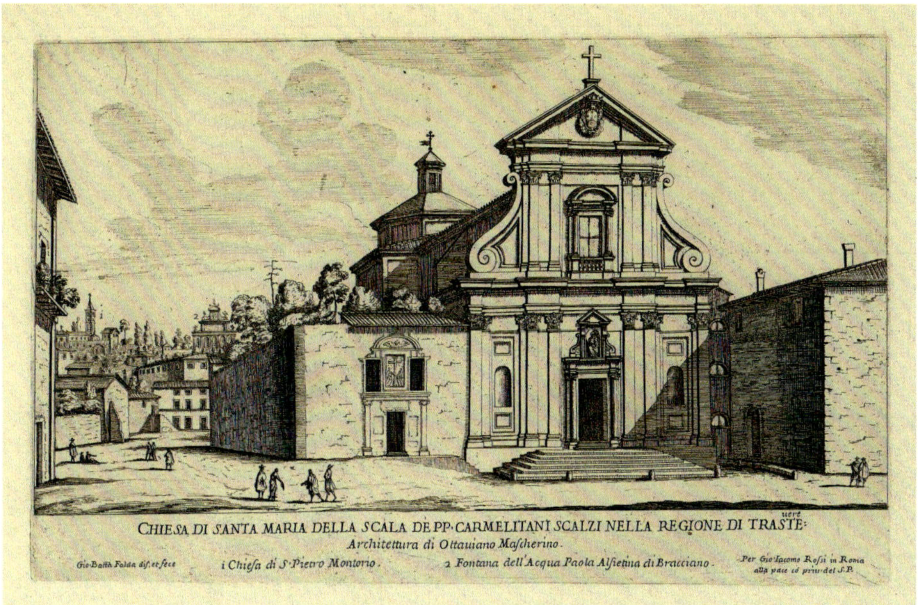

Fig. 20 Giovanni Battista Falda (1643–1678), *The Santa Maria della Scala, with the Friary to the left of the Church and the Pharmacy to the right*, German Archaeological Institute, Rome

Many travel tips, a description of the cities of Italy and their distances apart, the coinage and above all an Italian language course were all available in the Netherlands in 1602. That was the year in which the Arnhem printer Jan Jansz. issued a translation of the *Delitiae Italia*, a travel guide that had been written by Georg Kranitz von Wertheim for the Holy Year of 1600. It was printed in Cologne and translated into Dutch by the writer and translator Caspar Ens (c. 1570–1650), who lived there. The language course was extremely handy. Divided into eight chapters, it deals with many practical situations, such as asking the way, ordering a meal and visiting inns. It took the form of short dialogues in two columns, Dutch and Italian, giving possible answers and questions.[19]

Hendrick ter Brugghen was the first of the trio to go to Italy (fig. 23).[20] The date of his departure is not known, but it must have been after 23 April 1607, because the records place him in Utrecht on that day.[21] There are no primary sources on his stay in Rome, but it is almost certain that he was there. The direct evidence of Caravaggio's influence is evident in his work, and he himself spoke of his Italian sojourn after his return. On that occasion, he also said that he had been in Milan in 1614.[22] He was back in Utrecht in the autumn of that year.[23]

Baburen and Honthorst travelled at around the same time, but separately. It is assumed that Baburen left after finishing his apprenticeship to Paulus Moreelse, which means that he arrived in Italy in the autumn of 1612, or early 1613 at the latest.[24] Honthorst probably also arrived around 1613.[25] In 1615, Baburen painted an altarpiece of the martyrdom of St Sebastian for a church in Parma.[26] In 1619, he was living with David de Haen in Rome in a house belonging to the parish of Sant'Andrea delle Fratte. In the summer of 1620, it turns out that they moved to the Piazza Trinità dei Monti, where they shared a house with Nicolas Régnier, a painter born in Maubeuge.[27] According to Joachim von Sandrart, his later pupil, Honthorst lived for a long time in Palazzo Giustiniani.[28] It is known that the two Utrecht artists were in touch in Rome from a series of ten drawings, six of which are portraits of artists. They are of Honthorst and Baburen, his housemates de Haen and Régnier, and Claude Lorrain and Artemisia Gentileschi (fig. 24).[29] The drawings are attributed to Leonaert Bramer and date from around 1620, when his artist sitters were all still in Rome. Honthorst arrived back in Utrecht on 26 July 1620, where a welcoming party was organised for him.[30] Baburen must have embarked on his return journey in the summer or autumn of the same year.[31]

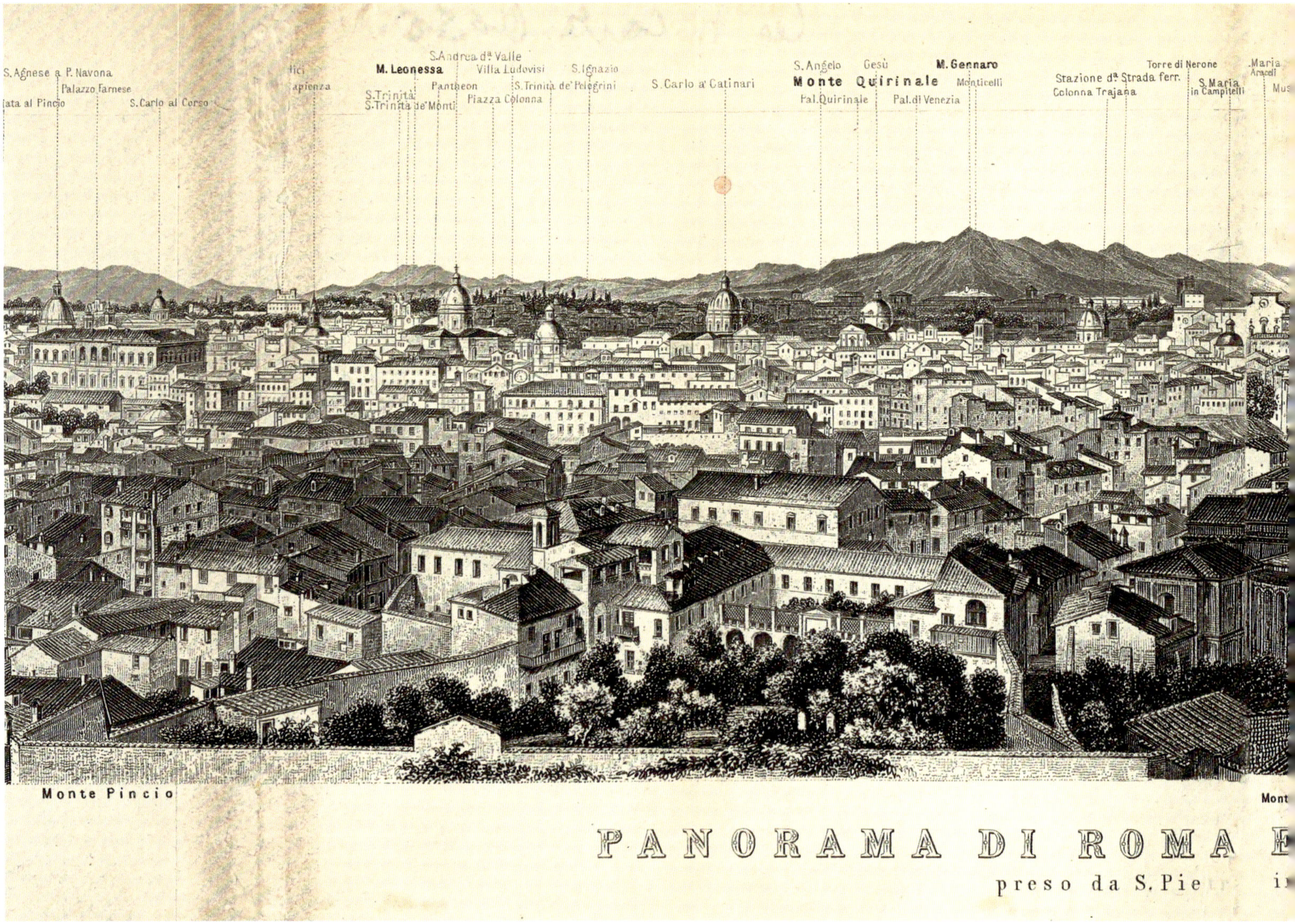

Fig. 21 *Panorama of Rome and its Surroundings seen from the San Pietro in Montorio,* 1870. Bibliothèque nationale de France, Paris

The information about Baburen's whereabouts in 1619 and 1620 is from the *Stati delle Anime*, the registers drawn up annually before Easter by the priests of the 70 parishes of Rome. They recorded their forename and family name, age, place of origin, profession, kinship, and the baptismal, burial and marriage registers. This source is a treasure trove of information about the demographic, social and economic history of Rome, which had a population of around 100,000 at that time. More than 2,700 names of artists are listed in the period 1600–1630, 572 of whom were foreigners. The 'fiamminghi' made up 298, or 52% of this group. They came from Flanders, Wallonia, Brabant, the North Pas-de-Calais, and the northern Netherlands. Those from the southern regions were in Rome throughout the period examined here, and were the most prosperous group, with workshops employing the largest number of assistants. The artists from the northern Netherlands arrived in the second and third decades of the 17th century. Their workshops were smaller, with just two to

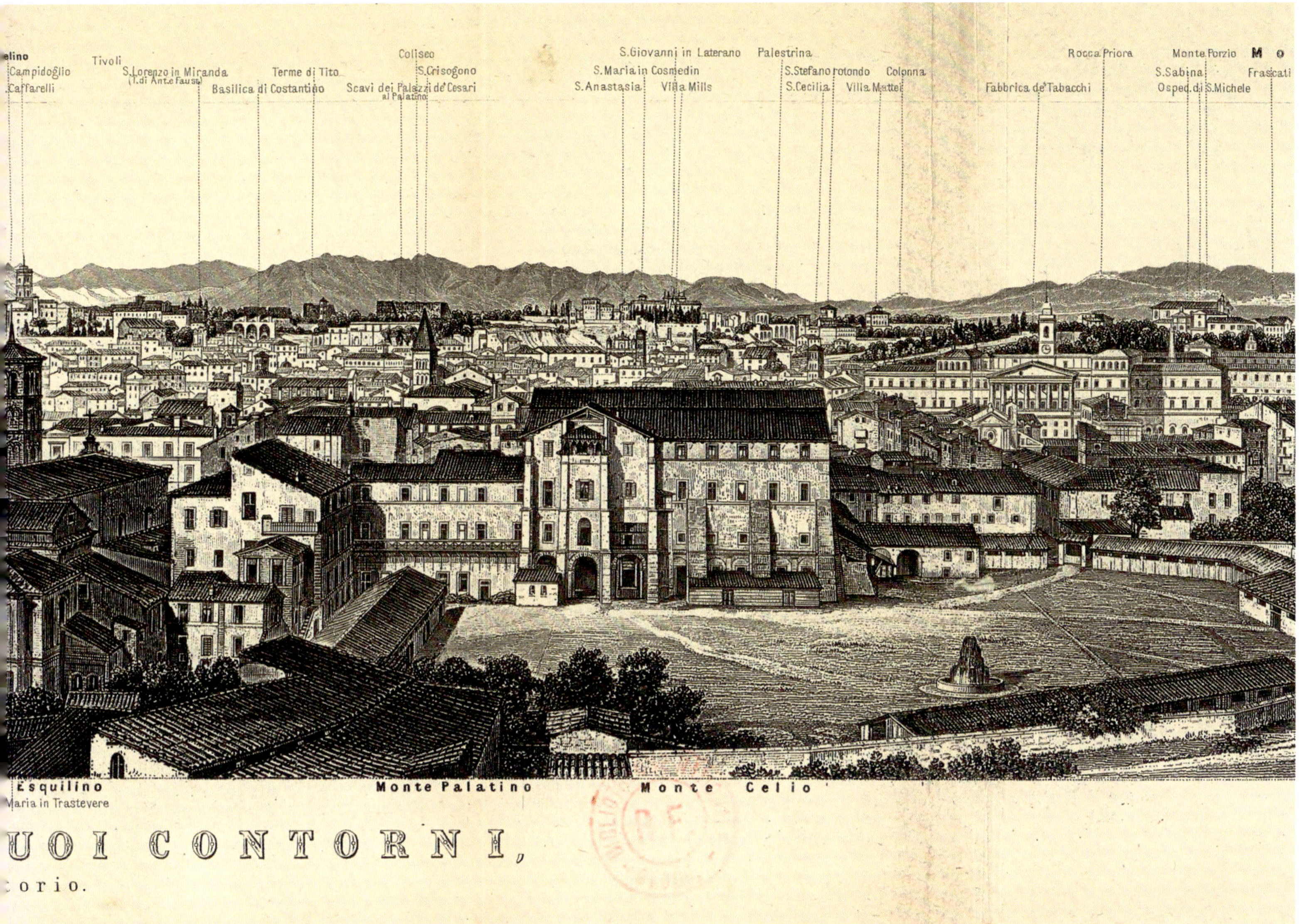

six members.[32] Baburen and Honthorst, in other words, belonged to a large group of artists who had made the journey to Rome. It is clear not only from the portrait series by Leonaert Bramer that they had fallen on their feet as foreigners in a strange city.

Giulio Mancini (1559–1630) describes Honthorst in his *Considerazioni sulla pittura* of 1617–1621 as courteous and hospitable, but also as a rather withdrawn and melancholy man.[33] However, his evidently shy nature did not prevent him from embarking on a lengthy relationship with a prostitute. On 12 June 1619, a year before his return to Utrecht, he stated that the night before, between four and five in the morning, he had been arrested in the house of Vittoria da Rieti. He said that he had known her for nine or ten months, and that they had 'carnal knowledge' of each other. The problem was not that he visited a prostitute but that he wore his sword when he did so. He had official permission to wear it in public, but not in 'casa di puttan', brothels, or 'luoghi prohibiti', forbidden

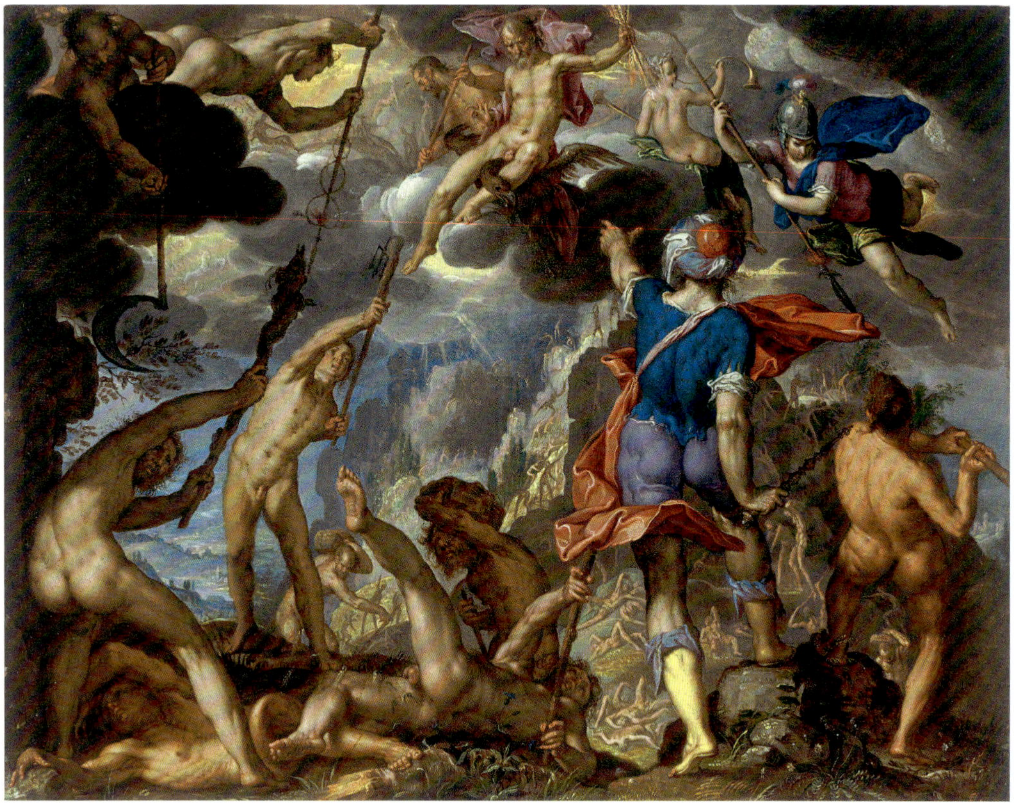

Fig. 22 Joachim Wtewael, *The Battle between the Gods and the Giants*, c. 1608. The Art Institute, Chicago, IL, USA, through prior acquisition of the George F. Harding Fund

establishments.[34] It emerges from this declaration that the 29-year-old Honthorst was assimilated, spoke Italian, walked around with a sword like every man in Rome, and had a regular lover. Baburen is known to have been a member of the Bentvueghel, the Dutch–Flemish artists' society in Rome that was founded in 1620. It is not known whether Honthorst was as well, but de Haen and Régnier certainly were. As if it was a student club, new members had to undergo an initiation ceremony, and were given a nickname. Baburen's was 'Bier vliech' (Beer Fly), so he may have been a heavy drinker.[35]

The two Utrecht artists were quite clearly at home in Rome, and had succeeded in attracting the attention of important patrons. Their paintings could be seen on altars that were accessible to the public, in the churches of Santa Maria della Scala and San Pietro in Montorio, and were also in the homes of collectors. The charismatic and fabulously wealthy banker Vincenzo Giustiniani (1564–1637) was one of their clients. He and his ten-year-older brother Benedetto (1554–1621) had been living in Palazzo Giustiniani since their father's death in 1600. Vincenzo died on 28 December 1637. His collection was recorded in the probate inventory of the palazzo drawn up on 9 February 1638 on the orders of the heirs. Most of the 600 or so paintings were in the three 'stanze de' quadri antichi' and the Galleria on the 'piano nobile'.[36] The most valuable ones were protected behind coloured 'bandinelle', curtains that could be opened and closed with tasselled cords. Benedetto, as a cardinal, had a preference for religious paintings, which he grouped thematically as far as possible. As a connoisseur, Vincenzo was more interested in the painter's artistic personality. He considered that the autograph nature of a work was important, so was very reluctant to make his pictures available to copyists.[37] The collection also comprised more than 1,200 statues, contemporary as well as antique, furniture, ivories, silver and gold objects, and everything that was expensive.

It was not only the scale of the collection that was unrivalled, its variety and high quality were too. The palazzo served as a cultural centre where connoisseurs, artists (who like Honthorst sometimes lived there for longer periods) and scholars under the leadership of Vincenzo, who acted as the host, studied and discussed the works of art.[38] The subject of the debate was the *paragone*, the comparison between the arts of painting and sculpture, their differences (two versus three dimensions, coloured versus uncoloured), and the superiority of the one over the other. Comparisons between the paintings themselves, the quality and the technique were also discussed, which in the Renaissance focussed on the superiority of *disegno* (drawing) over *colore* (colour), or vice versa. Traditionally, those two key aspects of the art of painting, drawing and colouring were centred on Rome (which had supplanted Florence around 1600) and Venice respectively.[39] In essence they are the two different ways in which a painting can be made. By drawing and sketching before starting to paint, the idea or invention first forms in the artist's mind. The artist who skips that process and immediately starts painting, as was done in Venice, works in a totally different way, with the result looking less thought-out, more spontaneous.

All of this emerges from the *Discorso sopra la pittura*, or 'Discourse on the art of painting', in which Vincenzo gave a summary of the results of the discussions in 1617/18.[40] The text is one of a series that Anna Banti has called *Discorsi sulle arti e sui mestiere*.[41] Those on the figurative arts deal not only with painting, but with sculpture and architecture too. All these *discorsi*, also called *lettere* (letters), were addressed to Teodoro Ameyden (1586–1656), who hailed from Den Bosch in the northern Netherlands and had settled in Rome in the Holy Year of 1600, where he lived for the rest of his life. Ameyden was a historian and poet as well as a lawyer, and one can assume that he took part in the discussions in Giustiniani's house.[42]

Vincenzo's letter about painting consists of twelve articles.[43] The first three deal with the practice of copying. They are followed by six articles in which he discusses the various genres of painting, such as portraits, flowers and other small objects, perspectives, landscapes, grotesques and military battles, and hunting, in short scenes in which people and animals are in motion. The final three articles are the most interesting, because in them Vincenzo discusses the three manners of painting, namely painting entirely from the imagination ('come si dice, di maniera'), painting directly from nature ('dipingere con avere gli oggetti naturali d'avanti'), and a combination of the two.[44] That last, twelfth method, in which painters are able to paint both from the imagination and from life, was the most perfect, in Vincenzo's opinion. The artists he ranked in that top category were the Carracci, Guido Reni and Caravaggio. Those in the eleventh, second highest group, were 'Gherardo', 'Enrico' 'Teodoro', Rubens and Jusepe de Ribera. So it emerges from Vincenzo's discourse that he considered that the three men from Utrecht, Gerard van Honthorst, Hendrick ter Brugghen and Dirck van Baburen were not only of the same calibre as Rubens and Ribera but also had a manner that Vincenzo regarded as being on the second highest level.

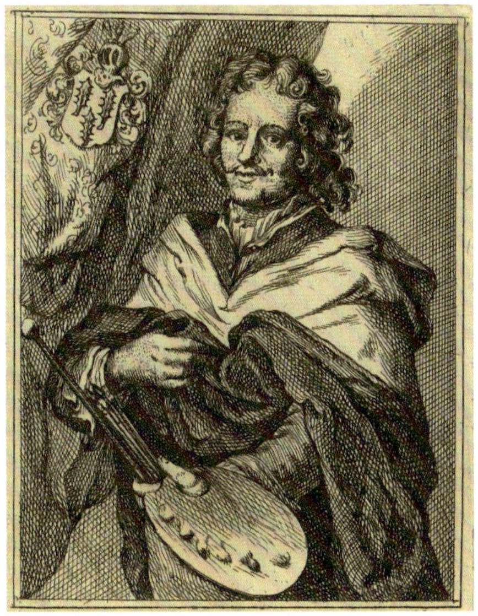

Fig. 23 Pieter Bodart after Gerard Hoet, *Portrait of Hendrick ter Brugghen*, c. 1708, Rijksprentenkabinet, Amsterdam

It is logical to assume that when building up his collection Vincenzo tried to acquire paintings by the artists whom he put in the very highest category, and it is clear from the inventory of 1638 that he and his brother Benedetto certainly succeeded in doing so. It lists 15 paintings by Caravaggio, 18 by the brothers Agostino and Annibale and their cousin Ludovico Carracci, and five by Guido Reni. The situation is different in the eleventh category. Jusepe de Ribera is very well represented with 13 paintings, and there were three pictures by Gerard van Honthorst. The 1621 inventory identifies Benedetto as the owner of *The Liberation of St Peter* (cat. 12).[45] Around 1617 Honthorst painted *Christ before the High Priest* on commission for Vincenzo (cat. 19). A third picture, which may

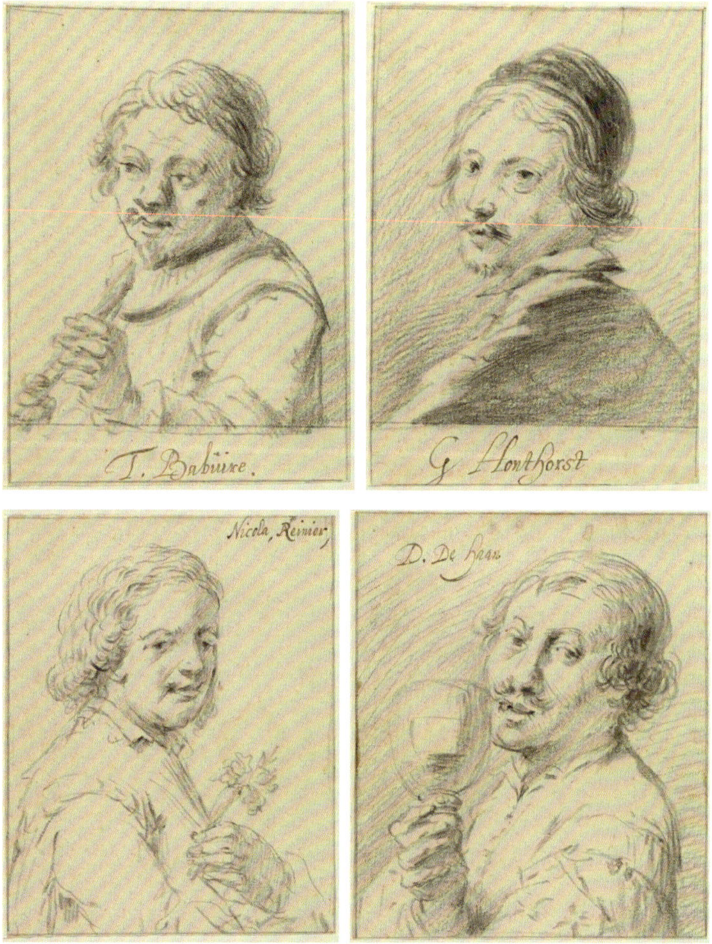

Fig. 24 Leonaert Bramer (attr.), *Dirck van Baburen, Gerard van Honthorst, Nicolas Régnier and David de Haen*, c. 1620. Royal Museums of Fine Arts of Belgium, Brussels

have been an allegory of painting, is lost.[46] Vincenzo ordered a large overdoor of *Christ Washing the Apostles' Feet* almost two metres wide from 'Theodoro fiamengo', Dirck van Baburen (fig. 32).[47]

There were no works by Hendrick ter Brugghen or Rubens in the brothers' collection. Oddly enough, there are no known paintings by ter Brugghen prior to his return to Utrecht. Vincenzo and Benedetto must have known Rubens well, for he paid three visits to Rome (1601–02, 1605–06 and 1607–08) at a time when he was already a very prominent figure. They would also have undoubtedly been aware of his negotiations for Duke Vincenzo Gonzaga of Mantua for the purchase of Caravaggio's altarpiece with *The Death of the Virgin* that had been rejected by the Discalced Carmelites for their church of Santa Maria della Scala. Rubens (1577–1645) was a good deal older than Honthorst and Baburen, and had left Rome before they arrived there. Theoretically he could have met ter Brugghen during his last stay in the city. Around 1612/14, back in Antwerp, Rubens painted what appears at first sight to be a fairly faithful copy after Caravaggio's famous *Entombment of Christ*, probably on the basis of a drawing (fig. 25).[48] That altarpiece was in the family chapel of Girolamo Vittrice in the Chiesa Nuova in Rome (fig. 26, cat. 22). In 1642, it was called his very finest work by the Roman painter and artists' biographer Giovanni Baglione (1566–1643), and again in 1672 by Giovanni Pietro Bellori (1613–1696).[49] The altarpiece encapsulated everything to which Caravaggio owed his great fame as a painter. It is a monumental depiction of a poignant moment in the story of Christ's suffering. The undisguised realism, the frozen dramatisation, and the pronounced chiaroscuro that highlights Christ's pale, dead body make this one of the crowning achievements in Western art history.

Rubens had every opportunity to study the masterpiece closely, for in 1606 he had received the commission for the high altarpiece in that church.[50] It is immediately obvious that Rubens based his *Entombment* directly on Caravaggio's composition, but the changes shift the emphasis.[51] Instead of the theatricality of Caravaggio's display of Christ's body to the viewer, Rubens treated the event as a burial. The empty tomb is visible below the heavy capstone off which John is stepping, supporting Christ's body while he and Nicodemus lower it down into the tomb. The three women are no longer individual figures but are portrayed by Rubens as a single group of mourners. He also added an arched niche to define the space in which the action is taking place. On the right side there is an old man with a stick who is absent in Caravaggio's version. It is not clear who he is meant to be.[52] The Flemish painter's autonomous position in Western art history rules him out as a Caravaggist, yet his *Entombment* is a more faithful imitation of Caravaggio than any painting by Baburen, ter Brugghen or Honthorst. Rubens studies Caravaggio, borrows, and then modifies the entire concept as he sees fit, choosing a far smaller size and panel instead of canvas.

Dirck Baburen did the same in his *Entombment of Christ* (cat. 21, fig. 66) for the San Pietro in Montorio. He, too, took Caravaggio's altarpiece as his point of departure and altered

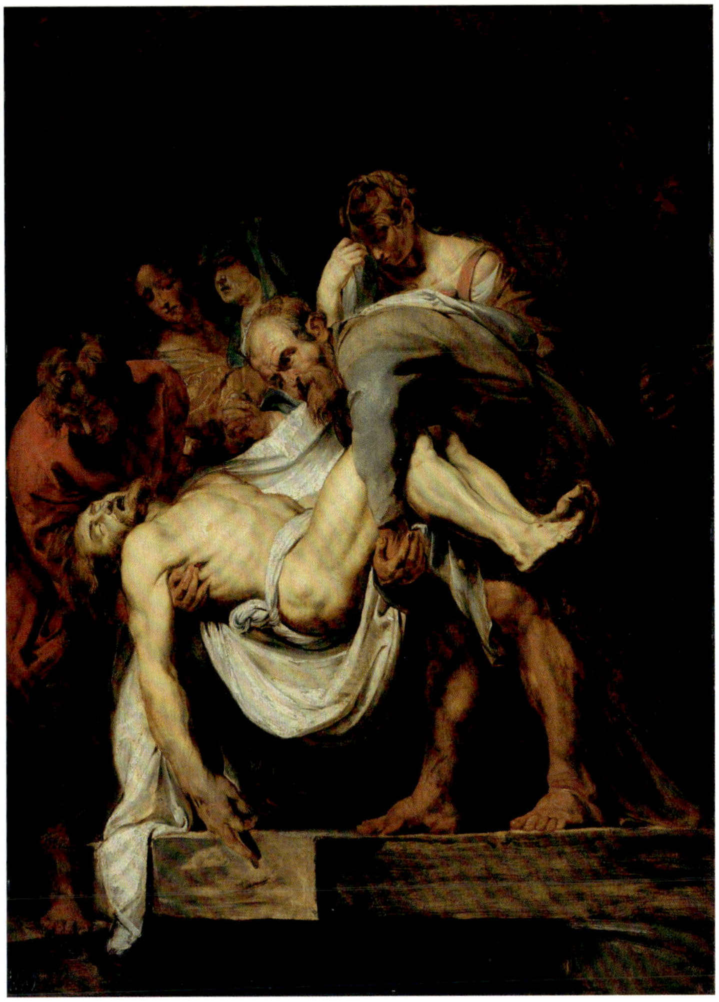

Fig. 25 Peter Paul Rubens, *The Entombment of Christ*, c. 1612/14. National Gallery of Canada, Ottawa

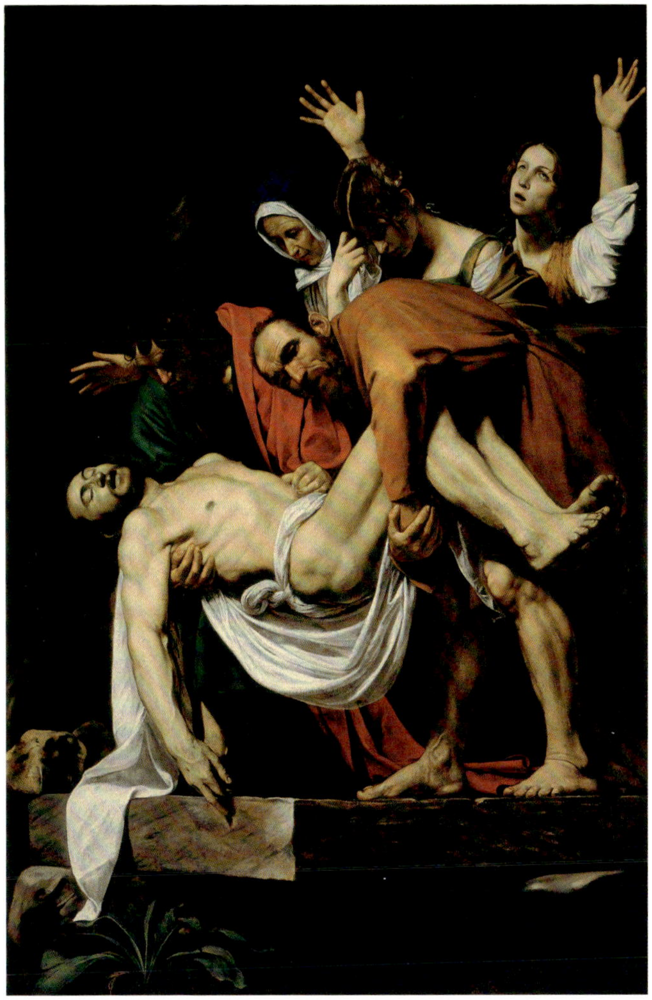

Fig. 26 Michelangelo Merisi, called Caravaggio, *The Entombment of Christ*, 1602/03 (cat. 22)

the content by making changes. His composition is also different, making it far less of a direct borrowing than Rubens's version. He grouped the figures around the tomb on ground level instead of high up on the capping slab, considerably shortening the distance to the viewer. Christ's body is resting on the corner of the tomb. John and Nicodemus are holding on to him as if they are pausing for a moment before lowering him into the tomb. Baburen, like Rubens, is depicting the act of burial. But there is more to it than that. Baburen is far more rigorous in his naturalism than Caravaggio. Nicodemus makes an uncomfortable impression with his distorted, elongated head with its high hairline. The faces of the three women are harshly distorted by their despair and sorrow.

These are not the only unattractive figures in Baburen's oeuvre. His wise old scribes whom Christ visited in the temple have dirty feet with ugly, knobbly toes and filthy long toenails (cat. 45). Prometheus, who stole fire from the gods so as to give it to mortals, is punished by being chained to a rock in the Caucasus by Vulcan, the god of fire (cat. 54). It was there that he was tortured every day for centuries by an eagle pecking away at his liver, which was renewed each night. Prometheus's forehead is deeply furrowed as he screams, his nose and ears

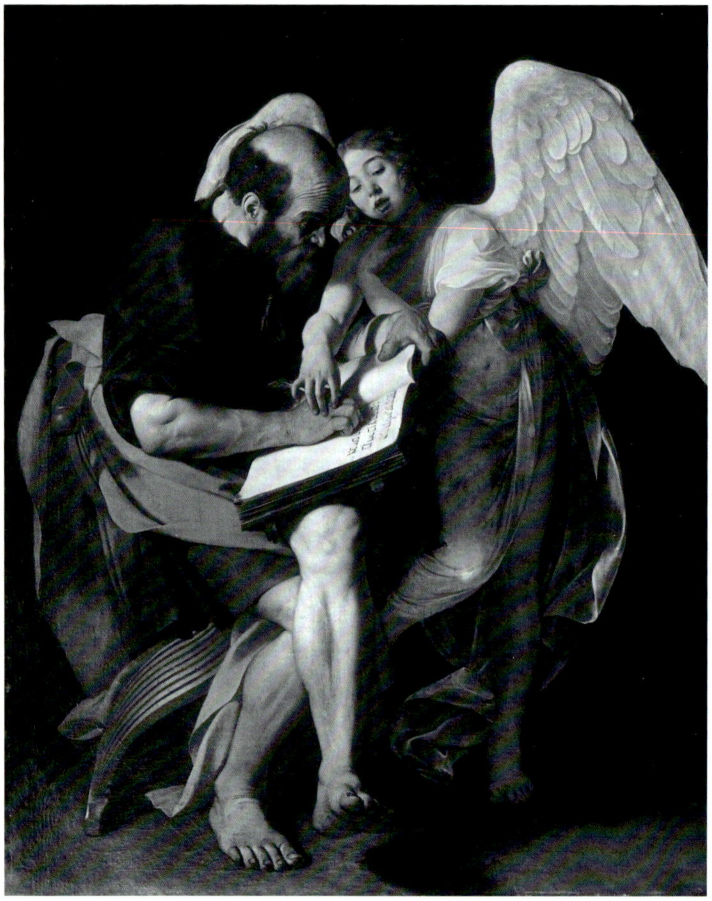

Fig. 27 Michelangelo Merisi, called Caravaggio, *St Matthew the Evangelist with the Angel*, formerly Kaiser Friedrich Museum, Berlin

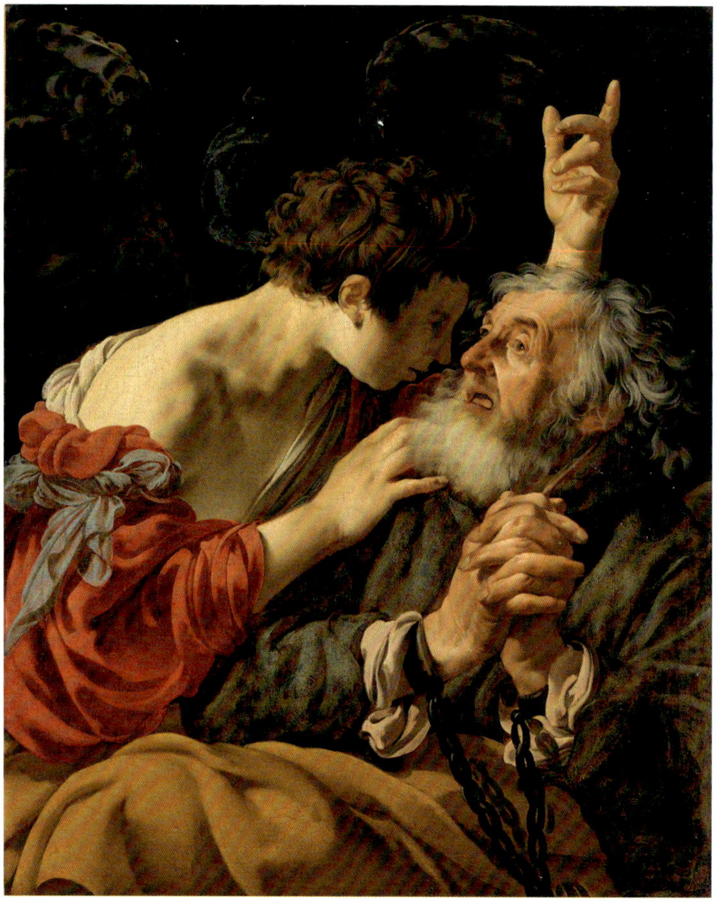

Fig. 28 Hendrick ter Brugghen, *The Liberation of St Peter*, 1624 (cat. 13)

are red and, although his hands appear to be reddened from the pressure of the manacles, that is not the case for his feet too are a darker colour. Reference has often been made to this literal copying after the model, whose clothed skin is usually white, whereas the parts of the body that are exposed to the sun each day, such as the face and hands, are a sunburned brown. A good example of this is *The Merry Drinker*, with his pale, bared shoulder and brown neck and face (cat. 30). The drunkard has a nose inflamed by alcohol, his gaze is unfocussed, and since he is laughing drowsily with his mouth open we can see his ruined teeth.

Ter Brugghen worked as Baburen did. He took not the second but the first, rejected version of Caravaggio's *St Matthew the Evangelist with the Angel* (figs. 27, 28, cat. 13) as the point of departure for his *St Peter Released from Prison* in the Mauritshuis.[53] The subject of the altarpiece was St Matthew writing his gospel under the inspiration of an angel. Caravaggio painted a beautiful young angel pressing up close against the aged evangelist and whispering the words he was to write. His right hand is literally guiding St Matthew's writing hand. Baglione reports that the altarpiece was installed in the church of San Luigi dei Francesi in 1602, but attracted such devastating criticism that it was removed.[54] The biographer Giovanni Pietro Bellori explains why. The priests felt that the figure, with his legs crossed and his feet sticking out so inelegantly towards the public had neither the decorum nor the look of a saint. It was Caravaggio's first public commission, and he was desperate and deeply offended by the rejection. Vincenzo

Giustiniani intervened. He took the painting for his own collection and had Caravaggio make another one.[55] That second version, with the angel hovering over St Matthew, is still there on the altar of the Contarelli Chapel. The rejected work was moved to the Palazzo Giustiniani and, according to the 1638 inventory of Vincenzo's collection, it hung together with other pictures by Caravaggio in the 'stanza grande de' quadri antichi', which is where ter Brugghen would have seen it.[56]

In ter Brugghen's *Liberation of St Peter*, the angel has crept far closer to the saint than in Caravaggio's first composition. Their noses are not quite touching, but because the angel is resting his hand on Peter's shoulder he is ruffling his tangled beard. The shabby fisherman is bewildered by what is going on, and appears to be shrinking back from his miraculous liberation from prison. His toothless mouth is open in astonishment, and his deep-set eyes are gazing wildly past the angel. Ter Brugghen makes no allowance for the fact that Peter is a saint. He paints him as an old, confused man in a perilous position. As Joachim von Sandrart said: 'He followed nature and its uncharitable imperfections aptly but unpleasantly in his work'.[57] Ter Brugghen, and Baburen too, accept 'ugliness' as part of the setting. They paint ugliness and beauty as the subject demands. That is a totally different approach from Caravaggio's, who according to Bellori only takes nature as the subject for his brush.[58] His verisimilitude was praised, but there were also critics who felt that he occasionally took his 'slavish imitation of nature' too far, so much so that his work displayed a lack of decorum. Baburen and ter Brugghen go much further than Caravaggio, and it is that sometimes excessive faithfulness to nature that typifies their work.

Gerard van Honthorst was far closer to Caravaggio in the degree of his faithfulness to nature than his two Utrecht colleagues. He was also, as Giulio Mancini rightly remarked, clearly influenced by the work of Correggio (1489–1534) and Annibale Carracci (1560–1609).[59] Gherardo delle Notti – 'Gerard of the Nights' – became famous during his time in Rome for his use of an artificial light source such as a candle or torch placed behind an object or figure.[60] As a result, the flame itself is no longer the brightest part of the composition but the space around it, creating an evenly lit, intimate picture surface. Honthorst's figures are more aesthetic than Baburen's and ter Brugghen's, his manner is far smoother and more delicate, and his compositions roomier. Baburen and ter Brugghen cramped their scenes and figures so tightly within the available picture surface that strips of canvas or planks were later added to their works (cats. 45, 75).[61]

Honthorst's career gathered pace after his return home in July 1620. It is true that at first he continued producing the kind of works with which he had made his name in Italy. *The Adoration of the Shepherds*, *The Tooth-Puller* and the *Merry Company* (fig. 40) are three large nocturnes of 1622, the year in which he joined the Utrecht Guild of St Luke.[62] By the time Rubens came visiting on the morning of 28 July 1627 he already had a large and flourishing studio of some 25 pupils and had been dean of the guild for some years.[63] His idealised, smooth Classicist figures were very much to the taste of the aristocracy. He travelled to London in the spring of 1628, where he received commissions from the English court, and after 1630 he carved out another place for himself at the Hague court of Stadholder Frederik Hendrik and Amalia van Solms. He could also count the King of Denmark and the Elector Brandenburg among his clients.[64] When he died in Utrecht in 1656, he left a vast oeuvre of more than 500 paintings, which included around 200 portraits.[65] The fame he had enjoyed in his youth had evaporated long since, as can be seen from the remark made about him in 1678 by the painter and art theorist Samuel van Hoogstraaten (1627–1678). He said that Honthorst had wielded a 'vigorous brush' in his heyday, but lapsed 'into a stiff glibness, [...] either to please the ladies or because profit had lulled him to sleep'.[66]

Baburen also returned to Utrecht in 1620, or 1621 at the latest. He died an early death in 1624, when he was around 30 years old. He was a bachelor, and lived in Utrecht with his mother and sister.[67] His oeuvre, which is regularly added to, consists of 36 paintings, according to the 2013 catalogue.[68] His paintings are so closely related to those of ter Brugghen that there is a persistent but totally unsubstantiated theory that they shared a studio in Utrecht.[69] There are certainly similarities in their work, but they can just as well be explained by the fact that both were influenced in Rome not only by Caravaggio but also by the Spaniard Jusepe de Ribera. Pietro Cuside, who commissioned Baburen to paint *The Entombment*, also collected pictures by Ribera. It is perfectly conceivable that Baburen was commissioned to paint the altarpiece because his rival had left for Naples in 1616.[70] It elicited a great compliment in 1661 from Cornelis de Bie (1627–1712/15), biographer of artists, when he wrote that 'Theodore Baburen painted fine and vigorous things in a chapel in the Church of St Peter in Montorio in Rome, worthy never to fade from the memory of enthusiasts, but on the contrary worth seeing and being drawn by all young visitors travelling to Rome'. Just as Karel van Mander had encouraged young painters in 1604 to go to Rome to see and imitate the work of Caravaggio, so de Bie urged them half a century later to study and draw Baburen's altarpiece in the same city.[71]

Ter Brugghen died in 1629. His earliest known painting dates from 1616, two years after his return to Utrecht, the last one from the year of his death. His oeuvre of 89 known pictures, some of them replicas, consists mainly of large, monumental, religious history pieces and half-lengths, of musicians in many cases.[72]

The new idiom that ter Brugghen, Baburen and Honthorst introduced after their return from Italy set the tone for young artists who specialised in figured works.[73] One was Rembrandt, who broke with a long tradition when he decided to take his inspiration from the work of the returned Utrecht artists rather than go to Italy himself. His two teachers had travelled there, and his first patron, Constantijn Huygens, had urged him to undertake the journey as well. Rembrandt, though, did not want to interrupt his career and, more importantly, evidently felt no need to go there. There was a new self-confidence in the air, an honest feeling of independence.[74] It was thanks to the Utrecht artists that the new-fashioned, modern Dutch painting bore the traces of the revolutionary upheaval that Caravaggio had caused around 1600 in Rome. The new beginning around 1630 marked the end of the flowering of Utrecht Caravaggism.

1 »alree met zijn wercken groot gherucht, eere, en naam gecreghen«. »Sooveel zijn handelinghe belangt, die is sulcx, dat se seer bevallijck is, und een wonder fraey maniere, om de Schilder-jeught nae te volgen«. Van Mander 1604, fol. 191.
2 Van Mander 1604 (1973), vol. 2, p. 435, no. II 12m, and Miedema 1994–1999, vol. 2, p. 268.
3 Van Mander 1604 (1973), vol. 2, p. 430, no. II 9b.
4 Van Mander 1604 (1973), vol. 1, p. 86, article 46. See also Sluijter 2005.
5 Van Mander 1604 (1973), vol. 2, p. 389.
6 See Sluijter 2005 for the concept of imitation and emulation in 17th-century Dutch art theory.
7 Roethlisberger 1993, vol. 1, p. 17, Lowenthal 1986, pp. 27–28; Helmus 2015/16, p. xxi.
8 Domela Nieuwenhuis 2001, pp. 20–21.
9 Joachim Wtewael, *The Battle between the Gods and the Giants*, c. 1608, copper, 15.6 × 20.3 cm, The Art Institute, Chicago, through prior acquisition of the George F. Harding Fund, 1986.426.
10 Domela Nieuwenhuis 2001, pp. 251–265. The names of 33 of Bloemaert's pupils are known, but it is estimated that at least 100 started their careers in his workshop. See M.J. Bok in Roethlisberger 1993, vol. 1, pp. 645–651.
11 Pliny the Elder, *Natural History*, book 35, On Painting. See Bok 1990 for the drawing lessons followed by the Utrecht painters.
12 Bolten 2007.
13 De Jonge 1938, pp. 9–13.
14 See Exh. cat. Paris 2014 and Van der Sman 2015.
15 Mancini 1956, p. 258: 'Et andando per le accademie del vivo, mostrò buonissimo gusto nel disegno'. The 'accademie' referred to by Mancini were not official organisations with rules and a curriculum but studio gatherings of painters who drew from a model they hired among themselves, among other activities. See Řezníček 1972, p. 186.
16 Van Mander 1604 (1973), vol. 1, p. 93, article 66.
17 Ibid., p. 94, article 69–70.
18 See also Cohen-Willner 2014, pp. 349–355.
19 See also Van der Helm 2014. The full text of the book in the collection of the Biblioteca Nazionale Centrale di Rome is online at http://books.google.com/books?id=Q2GTKPMS4PQC&hl=&source=gbs_api
20 Pieter Bodart after Gerard Hoet, *Portrait of Hendrick ter Brugghen*, c. 1708, etching, 131 × 109 mm.
21 On 23 April 1607, a 'Henrick ter Brugge' is referred to as a soldier. For this and the reference to M.J. Bok see Slatkes/Franits 2007, p. 4.
22 On 1 April 1615, ter Brugghen declared before a notary that he 'practised art in Italy for some years', and that he was in Milan in the summer of 1614. See Houck 1899, p. 356.
23 Slatkes/Franits 2007, pp. 4–7.
24 Franits 2013a, pp. 4–5.
25 Judson/Ekkart 1999, pp. 5–6.
26 The painting, which was in the Chiesa di Santa Maria dei Servi in Parma at that time, is mentioned around 1780 in a travel journal. Not a trace of it has been found since then. See Franits 2013, p. 6.

27 Vodret 2011, Dirck van Baburen: p. 514, no. 2088, and David de Haen: p. 272, no. 460. See also Franits 2013a, p. 7.
28 Judson/Ekkart 1999, p. 6. Vodret 2011 mentions on p. 326, no. 838 a 'Gherardo fiammingo pittore' who was recorded in 1610 and 1611 when he was 25 and 26 years old. Since Honthorst was born in 1592, that painter cannot be the one from Utrecht.
29 Leonaert Bramer (attr.), *Dirck van Baburen, Gerard van Honthorst, Nicolas Régnier* and *David de Haen*, c. 1620, pen in black, 137 × 102 mm, 137 × 98 mm, 138 × 111 mm, and 130 × 112 mm, Royal Museums of Fine Arts of Belgium, Brussels, inv. 4060/3124, 4060/3127, 4060/3122 and 4060/3130 respectively. See Suzanne Baverez in Exh. cat. Rome/Paris 2014/15, pp. 154–157, cat. 10.
30 Judson/Ekkart 1999, pp. 5–14.
31 Franits 2013a, p. 34.
32 Vodret 2011, pp. 169–170.
33 Mancini 1956, p. 258.
34 Cavazzini 2005, pp. 43 and 48 (note 36).
35 Four members of the Bentvueghels are depicted with their attributes in an anonymous drawing in Museum Boijmans Van Beuningen, Rotterdam, black and red chalk, 280 × 418 mm, inv. MB 292. It is assumed that the figure on the far right, 'Den Berbier / alias biervliech', is Dirck van Baburen. See Janssens 2001, pp. 75–76, and Gert Jan van der Sman in Exh. cat. Rome/Paris 2014/15, pp. 148–153, cat. 9.
36 See Salerno 1960b and Salerno 1960c for Vincenzo Giustiniani's inventory of 9 February 1638.
37 Salerno 1960a.
38 See Cappelletti 2016 for the northern artists who lived in Palazzo Giustiniani.
39 Van Mander 1604 (1973), vol. 2, pp. 415 and note 426.
40 See Danesi Squarzina 1998, p. 112, for the dating of the letter.
41 Banti 1981.
42 See Hendrix 2005 for a brief biography of Ameyden.
43 See Banti 1981, pp. 41–45, for the full text.
44 This is a fundamentally different interpretation of the text from the one in Salerno 1960a, p. 25. He refers to the contrast between Mannerism, 'di maniera', and naturalism, 'dal naturale'. His explanation of the text is invalidated by the simple fact that the painters whom Giustiniani assigned to the tenth category (Federico Barocci, Giovanni Francesco Romanelli, Domenico Passignano and Giuseppe Cesari, called Cavaliere d'Arpino) did not all paint in the style known as Mannerism in art history.
45 Danesi Squarzina 1997, p. 786, no. 97.
46 Danesi Squarzina 2003, vol. 1, pp. 458–459. For the patronage of the Giustiniani brothers see the essay by Bernd Ebert in this publication, pp. 69–72.
47 Salerno 1960b, p. 95, no. 45, and p. 98, no. 125.
48 Peter Paul Rubens, *The Entombment of Christ*, c. 1612/14, panel, 88.3 × 66.5 cm, National Gallery of Canada, Ottawa, inv. 6431.
49 Baglione 1642, p. 137, and Bellori 1672 (2005), p. 182. See also Alessandra Rodolfo in Vodret et al. 2016, pp. 398–401.
50 Peter Paul Rubens, *The Ecstasy of St Gregory the Great*, 1606/07, canvas, 477 × 288 cm, Musée de Grenoble, Grenoble, inv. MG97. The painting was rejected, so Rubens took it back to Antwerp and placed it over his mother's grave in St Michael's Abbey.
51 See also Judson 2000, pp. 243–245, cat. 75.
52 Judson 2000, p. 244, identified this figure as Nicodemus, which would make the bearded man Joseph of Arimathea, who is holding Christ's body together with John the Evangelist.
53 Blankert 1990, pp. 21–22.
54 Baglione 1642, pp. 137-138.
55 Bellori 1672 (2005), p. 181. See Lavin 1974 on Caravaggio's two versions of the altarpiece.
56 Salerno 1960c, p. 135, no. 1.
57 Sandrart 1675, II, bk. 3, p. 308: '[...] in seinen Werke, die Natur und derselben unfreundlichen Mängel sehr wol, aber unangenehm gefolgt'.
58 Bellori 1672 (2005), p. 180.
59 Mancini 1956, p. 258.
60 The earliest mention of 'Gherardo delle Notti' comes in 1709/10. See Lincoln 2016, p. 246.
61 Domela Nieuwenhuis 2007, pp. 88–95.
62 Judson/Ekkart 1999, p. XXXIII. *The Adoration of the Shepherds*, Wallraf-Richartz Museum, Cologne, inv. WRM 2122 (Judson/Ekkart 1999, pp. 63–64, cat. 23); *The Tooth-Puller*, Staatliche Kunstsammlungen, Gemäldegalerie Alte Meister, Dresden, Gal-Nr. 1251 (Judson/Ekkart 1999, pp. 210–211, cat. 275); *Merry Company*, Bayerische Staatgemäldesammlungen, Alte Pinakothek, Munich, inv. 1312 (Judson/Ekkart 1999, pp. 219–220, cat. 283).
63 See Swillens 1945/46 for Rubens's visit to Utrecht. Honthorst was dean in 1625, 1626, 1628 and 1629. See Judson/Ekkart 1999, p. XXXIII.
64 See Judson/Ekkart 1999, pp. XXXIII–XXXIV, for the biographical data.
65 Judson/Ekkart 1999.
66 Van Hoogstraaten 1678, p. 234.
67 Franits 2013a, p. 58.
68 Franits 2013a.
69 Slatkes 1965, pp. 94–98, and Slatkes 1996, pp. 199–200.
70 Macro 2003, p. 75, Papi 2006, p. 47, and Porzio/D'Alessandro 2015.
71 Schuckman 1986, p. 19.
72 That is the number given in the Slatkes/Franits 2007 oeuvre catalogue.
73 See Blankert 1997/98, pp. 33–34.
74 See Brown 2002, pp. 9 and 26–28.

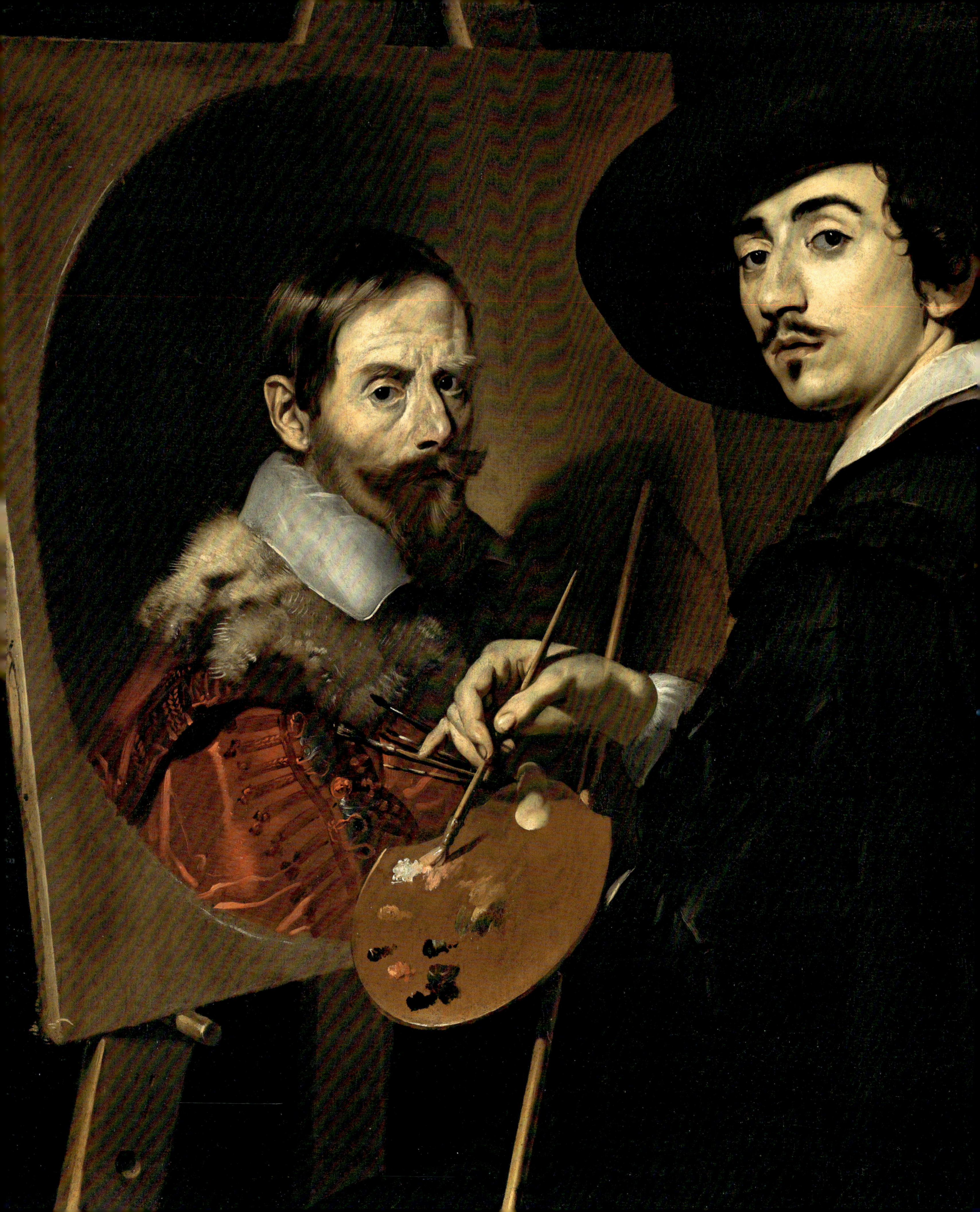

The Utrecht Caravaggisti in the Interplay between Clients, the Art Market and Collectors

BERND EBERT AND SUSANNE HOPPE

From the beginning of the 16th century, numerous Dutch artists were drawn to Italy where, especially in Rome, they had the opportunity to study ancient architecture and sculpture, artworks by famous masters such as Raphael and Michelangelo, and the latest trends in painting. 'Rome is, before other cities, the place where painters' travels tend to head; it is the principal of painting schools.'[1] While staying abroad, usually for several years, they sought to win private commissions, yet only a few managed to gain access to the particularly competitive market in the Eternal City and build up a reputation as successful artists. Generally referred to uniformly as 'fiamminghi' (Flemings), the painters from both the southern and northern provinces of the Netherlands were competing with their local Roman counterparts and a variety of artists who streamed into the city from other parts of Italy, France and Spain. Among the 'fiamminghi' were Hendrick ter Brugghen, Gerard van Honthorst and Dirck van Baburen who, at the beginning of the 17th century, were still young when they set off on the journey from Utrecht to Rome.

Besides the altarpieces, which are still on display at the original locations they were intended for, the foundations for research in recent decades have included numerous contemporary documents and sources, for example account books, inventories and written records providing information about the production and the clients or owners of paintings.

In Utrecht, the research situation is very different. Only few records are known and it is no longer possible to document in detail the originating contexts of the works ter Brugghen, Honthorst and Baburen created after their return home, even though the number of surviving paintings there is significantly higher. Of the some 40 extant paintings considered to be by the hand of Baburen, 14 were created in Italy[2] and about 30 in Utrecht.[3] While he focused exclusively on religious subjects in Italy, the share of secular images from his Utrecht period is about three times that of the religious ones. Honthorst likewise created seven to eight times as many secular as religious works in the 1620s. This suggests that the increased production of secular imagery in Utrecht was related to the tastes and preferences of clients and collectors.

Rome

At the beginning of the 17th century, Rome was only the fourth largest city in Italy, but with its population of over 100,000 it was many times larger than Utrecht with roughly 30,000 inhabitants.[4] Yet above all, Rome was a modern metropolis and the seat of the pope as the head of the Catholic Church. Large-scale construction projects initiated at the end of the 16th century still dominate today's cityscape.[5] The reputation of the vibrant metropolis on the Tiber as one of the most important art centres of Europe and the increasing building activity in the context of the Counter-Reformation attracted a stream of artists and craftsmen into the city. The ecclesio-political situation and changing pontificates led

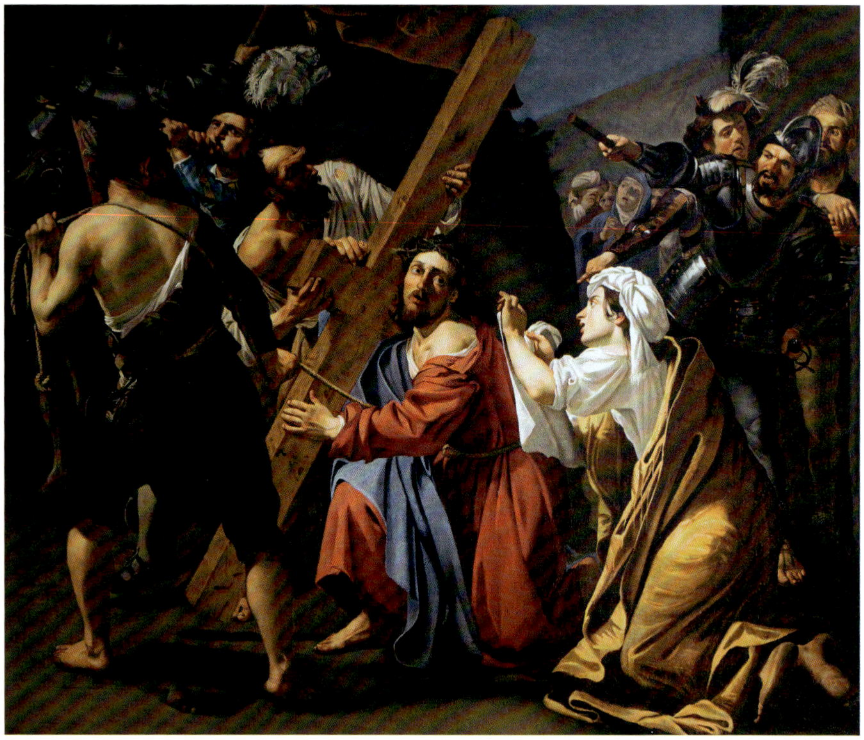

Fig. 29 Dirck van Baburen,
The Carrying of the Cross, 1617/18,
San Pietro in Montorio, Rome,
Capella della Pietà

numerous influential bankers, wealthy nobility, envoys and members of the papal family to settle in the vicinity of the Roman Curia. The members of the ruling elite commissioned the decoration of their palaces and summer residences, and altarpieces for newly established family chapels. With regard to the many church buildings, this was not just a matter of piety but specifically one of image cultivation by individual families. The same aspirations of influential patrons to political power, moreover, led to the creation of large art collections and galleries in their palaces.[6] Art patronage was often a means to an end. While aimed at promoting the visual arts, literature and music, it also served as a 'purposefully deployed instrument of legitimation and representation of social status and political power'.[7]

In spite of the tremendous construction activity in Rome and the relatively large number of art-loving patrons and collectors, there was 'cut-throat business'[8] among the many artists, even those of renown.[9] The main thing was to be favoured by the commissioners for prestigious altarpieces and easel paintings for their galleries.[10] Over the course of the 16th and, especially, the 17th century, oil paintings became increasingly important in the decoration of palaces, while the importance of frescoes diminished.[11] Yet the production of paintings in Rome boomed not just because of the many commissions for churches and private individuals, but also because of the growing demand in the free market.[12] Even artists who were in the service of a patron and lived in his household were at the same time active for other clients and the art trade to secure an adequate income.[13] Works were often sold, or at least brokered, through intermediaries. Hence, some artists acted themselves as art dealers and also exhibited the work of fellow painters in their workshops. But in many cases, it was paint sellers, gilders, barbers, tailors or even physicians who used their premises for the trade in paintings.[14] Another common way in which artworks were disseminated far beyond the city limits was as gifts by the patron to family members or diplomatic gifts to political allies. Not only originals were given as presents but also copies, replicas and different versions of a painting. The large number of contemporary copies attests to the popularity of certain works, because the main point was to own the invention (*invenzione*) of a particular painter. Unless copies were already produced in the artist's workshop, you needed the owner's authorisation to produce them. Copying was often explicitly prohibited, so as not to reduce the value of the original,[15] though commissioned works without proper authorisation are known as well.[16] Copyists worked in the large workshops of the masters and the private academies run by collectors, and at the Accademia di San Luca – for training purposes or to produce commissioned pieces or works for the art trade.[17]

Clients and Collectors

Rome was home to a large number of art-loving, Humanist-educated and well-read patrons and collectors who exchanged views not only on religious discourse but also on poetry, literature, theatre, music and the sciences at academies, in private circles and in their galleries.

A correlation that is in some cases very close can be seen between the interests of clients and the subjects of the paintings which were produced for them or which they collected. The collection of the music, literature and theatre enthusiast Cardinal Francesco Maria Bourbon del Monte (1549–1627), for example, included the *Lute Player* (fig. 74), the *Musicians* (fig. 96), the *Fortune Teller* (cat. 73) and the *Cardsharps* (fig. 89) by Caravaggio.[18] Del Monte also took an interest in the sciences,[19] which begs the question whether investigations of optical phenomena, such as the effect of strong light and shade contrasts or reflections and refractions of light on rounded surfaces – for instance, a glass vase filled with water, as in the painting *Boy Bitten by a Lizard*[20] – had inspired their pictorial realisation. Among the followers of Caravaggio, it was above all Gerard van Honthorst who, very much in line with the Dutch tradition, gave light a special role in his paintings. As early as 1604, in his didactic poem *Den grondt der edel vry schilder-const* (The Foundations of the Noble and Free Art of Painting), Karel van Mander had devoted a special chapter under the heading *Van de Reflecty, Reverberaty, teghen-glans oft weerschijn* (On Reflection, Reverberation or Reflex) to the depiction of optical phenomena, light reflexes and reflections.[21] Honthorst gained great fame and commanded high prices for his paintings, especially because of his night scenes with visible artificial light sources, mostly candles, whose natural-looking light spreads atmospherically in the space. The large number of copies of the compositions he created in Italy,

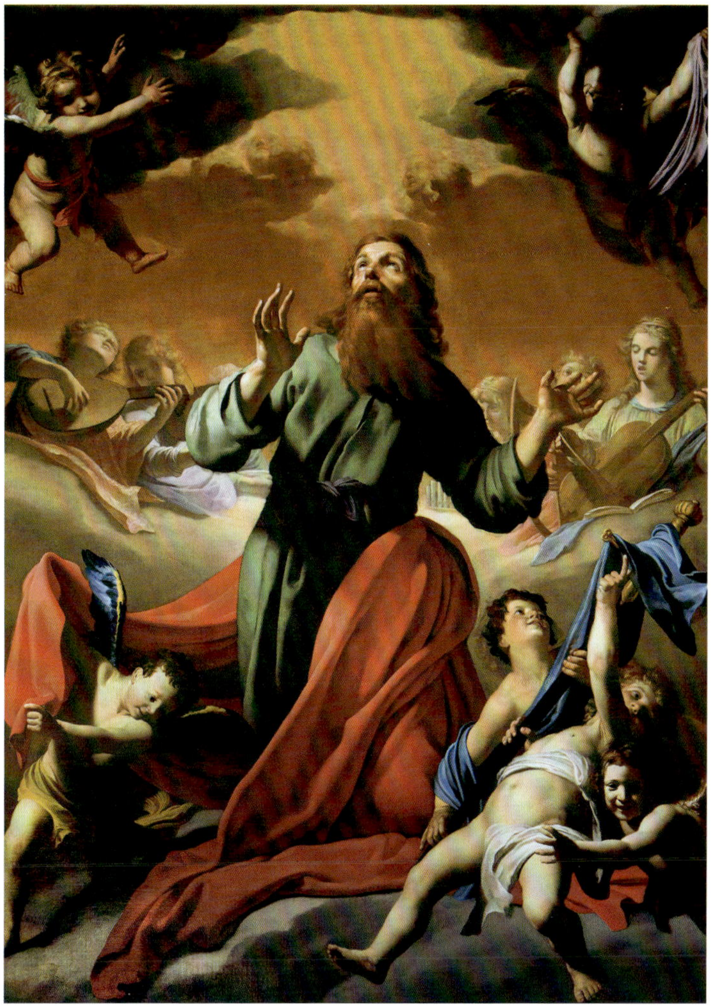

Fig. 30 Gerard van Honthorst, *St Paul Caught up into the Third Heaven*, 1617, Santa Maria della Vittoria, Rome, vestry

such as *Christ before the High Priest* (cat. 19) or *The Liberation of St Peter* (cat. 12) are evidence of his popularity.[22]

But how did the young foreign artists secure major, prestigious commissions for gallery paintings and altarpieces after their arrival in Rome? A painter's success depended, in addition to his skills, on a social network that was as large as possible and on contact to members of wealthy and influential families who, as buyers and patrons, had their own extensive connections and were able to broker additional commissions.[23] It is well known that Caravaggio owed his success not least to his well-connected and influential patrons.[24] In recent

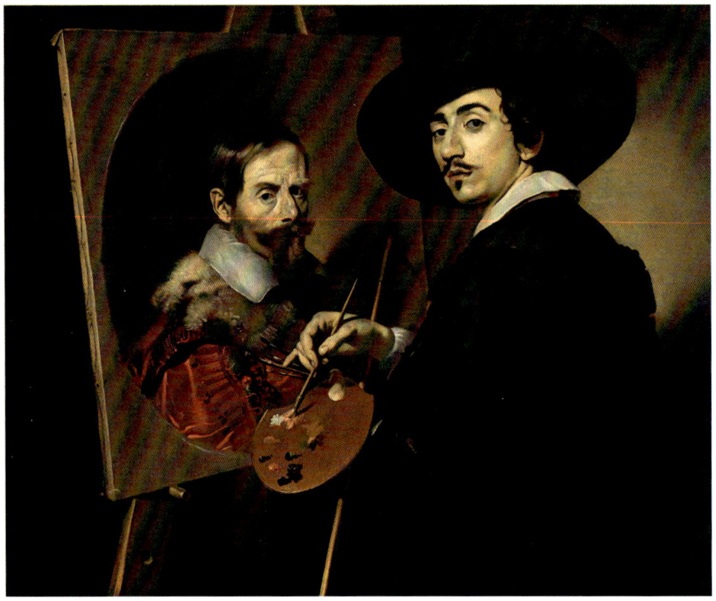

Fig. 31 Nicolas Régnier, *Double Portrait of Nicolas Régnier and Vincenzo Giustiniani*, c. 1623/25, Harvard Art Museums / Fogg Museum, Cambridge, MA, gift of Mrs. Eric Schroeder, 1982

decades, numerous individual studies on collection inventories and the social and economic connections of clients, middlemen and buyers have contributed to a more detailed picture of the network to which Caravaggio and his followers had recourse.[25]

The first verifiable commission for one of the Utrecht Caravaggisti in Italy is documented for the year 1615. It went to Dirck van Baburen who had probably come to Italy around 1613 when he was almost twenty. For the Church of Santa Maria dei Servi in Parma he painted a depiction of the martyrdom of St Sebastian that is now lost.[26] Another two years passed before he received his first commission in Rome where, together with his fellow countryman David de Haen, he decorated the Pietà Chapel in San Pietro in Montorio, the church of the Spanish community. The decorative programme of the chapel which, in addition to the *Entombment of Christ*, also included the *Carrying of the Cross* (fig. 29), the *Raising of the Cross*, the *Mocking of Christ* and the *Prayer in the Garden of Gethsemane*, was probably due to the Spanish client, Pietro Cussida (or Pedro Cossida, d. 1622), the representative of the Spanish king in Rome.[27] Through references to Titian, an artist known to be favoured by the Spanish court, Baburen was able to establish a connection between the status of his client and the artwork in his altarpiece, *The Entombment of Christ* (cat. 21).[28]

Honthorst was already in his mid-twenties when he made his debut in Rome and received his first documented commission.[29] This was in 1617, when the Discalced Carmelites commissioned him to create the main altarpiece for the church of San Paolo a Termini (from 1622 on, Santa Maria della Vittoria) (fig. 30).[30] A first payment for the painting was received as a charitable donation made by Michele Peretti (1577–1631), the brother of Cardinal Alessandro Peretti di Montalto (1571–1623), at the time one of the most important men in Rome. Loredana Lorizzo interprets the neo-Classicist tendencies of the painting, which gravitate towards the style of the Carracci pupils Domenichino and Lanfranco, as a possible response to the taste of the Peretti di Montalto who were not particularly partial to Caravaggesque painting.[31]

Honthorst's next commission was the 1617/18 *Beheading of John the Baptist* for the Longhi Chapel at Santa Maria della Scala (cat. 20). Both these commissions for altarpieces are directly or indirectly linked to Padre Domenico di Gesù e Maria (1559–1630) who, from 1614 on, was prior of Santa Maria della Scala and, starting in 1617, *preposito generale* of the order's Italian congregation which had its seat in San Paolo a Termini. Padre Domenico was not only closely connected to the Borghese, Peretti di Montalto, Savelli and Giustiniani families in Rome, but also had extensive international political ties.[32] The padre often visited the monastery of San Silvestro in Monte Compatri, about 30 kilometres south-east of Rome, where a cell was permanently reserved for him. It may not be a coincidence that another painting by Honthorst was located in this monastery until it was stolen in 1976.[33]

In 1618, Principessa Flaminia Colonna Gonzaga had Honthorst prominently depict her as donor next to Sts Francis and Bonaventure above the main altar of the church of Santi Francesco e Bonaventura in Albano Laziale.[34] At the behest of her nephew, Principe Paolo Savelli (1586–1632), the church and the adjacent monastery were built in 1618–1619. Evidence shows that Savelli, who, from 1620 on, served as envoy of Emperor Ferdinand II to the Holy See, had connections to Padre Domenico di Gesù e Maria as well.[35] Paolo Savelli also notably patronised Orazio Gentileschi who lived in his household for a while.[36] He commissioned him around 1616/20 to

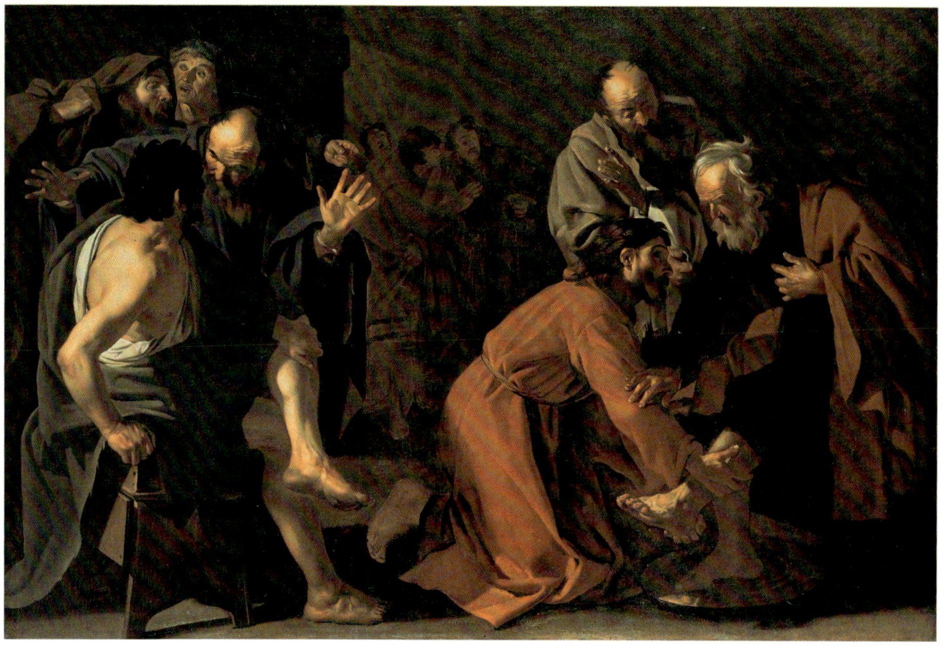

Fig. 32 Dirck van Baburen, *Christ Washing the Apostles' Feet*, c. 1617/18, Staatliche Museen zu Berlin, Gemäldegalerie, Berlin

paint the altarpiece for his family chapel in San Silvestro in Capite.[37] The most important patron of Valentin de Boulogne, on the other hand, was Cardinal Francesco Barberini (1597–1679), who in 1629 commissioned the Frenchman to paint an altarpiece for St Peter's.[38] Simon Vouet is also known to have created an altarpiece for St Peter's, which was commissioned by Urban VIII but is now lost.[39]

The early commissions for altarpieces helped Dirck van Baburen and Gerard van Honthorst achieve a certain level of renown within Rome, for the works were accessible to the public and could be seen by potential clients and discussed among fellow painters. Other artists such as Jusepe de Ribera, Bartolomeo Manfredi, Nicolas Régnier and Valentin de Boulogne, by contrast, created their paintings increasingly, it seems, for the palaces and mansions of their respective clients or for the free market. The former offered the opportunity to find a patron, which meant a stable income. Painting for the free market, in turn, provided the artists with greater freedom in choosing their subjects. This may also explain the rapid rise in popularity of secular subjects (companies grouped around tables, musicians, gamblers), which are particularly prominent, for instance, in the work of Régnier and Valentin and on which Honthorst also focused in Rome (cat. 28). But this does not mean that the artists abandoned religious painting, for at the beginning of the 17th century, paintings of biblical scenes, saints and, in particular, the Passion of Christ were part and parcel of the decoration not just of private palaces but of every household in Rome.

The Giustiniani family from Genoa were among the most important clients and collectors of Caravaggio and his followers.[40] In addition to the Italian Caravaggisti Bartolomeo Manfredi, Orazio Borgianni, Lo Spadarino and Cecco del Caravaggio (cat. 39), the Frenchmen Valentin de Boulogne, Simon Vouet and Nicolas Régnier and the Spaniard Jusepe de Ribera, their collection also included works by Honthorst, Baburen and de Haen.

After the death of Giuseppe, the father, his sons Cardinal Benedetto (1554–1621) and Vincenzo (1564–1637, from 1604 the Marchese di Bassano di Sutri) lived from 1600 on at the Palazzo Giustiniani, which was located between the Pantheon and San Luigi dei Francesi. Benedetto had been appointed cardinal by Pope Sixtus V in 1586 and had close connections with the cardinals and art patrons Del Monte and Peretti di Montalto. Vincenzo was one of the wealthiest men in Rome and continued the role of his father as financier to Pope Clement VIII.[41]

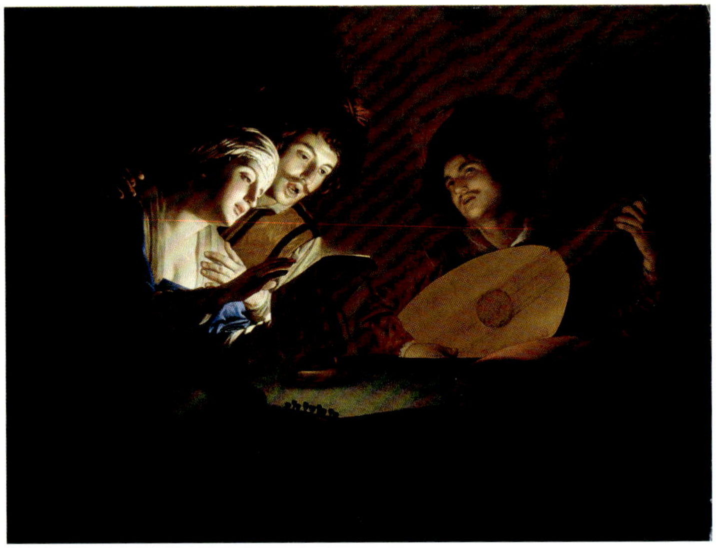

Fig. 33 Gerard van Honthorst, *Concert with Three Musicians*, c. 1616/18, National Gallery of Ireland, Dublin

The brothers compiled one of the most extensive art collections in Rome, as is impressively documented by the inventories of Benedetto and Vincenzo's household. A list drawn up in 1600–1611 of art objects in the possession of Benedetto itemises 108 paintings;[42] in the 1621 inventory of his estate, this number was already 283, and in the following period until Vincenzo's death in late 1637 the collection eventually grew to 632 paintings.[43] Apart from the collection of paintings, the extensive holdings of ancient sculptures are particularly noteworthy; in 1636/37, they were published in a two-volume catalogue entitled *Galleria Giustiniana* featuring copperplate engravings by, among others, Cornelis Bloemaert (1603–1692), Theodore Matham (1589/1606–1676) and Michel Natalis (1610–1668).[44] This project was coordinated by Joachim von Sandrart who, after his apprenticeship with Gerard van Honthorst, entered into the service of Vincenzo Giustiniani around 1629.

The inventories of the Giustiniani brothers document their preference for ancient and contemporary art, including works by the Bolognese School and Caravaggio. The inventories of Benedetto, for example, who was legate in Bologna between 1606 and 1611, mention eleven paintings by Annibale Carracci and four by Caravaggio. Both lists are organised by room and thus provide a good overview of where and in what context the paintings were displayed.[45] Vincenzo showed them arranged by artists and styles, while his brother Benedetto had organised them according to subject matter.[46] Vincenzo's inventory specifies that 13 canvases by Caravaggio were hanging in the 'Stanza grande de' quadri antichi'. With a total of 15 paintings, his was by far the largest collection of Caravaggios at the time.

Undoubtedly one of the most knowledgeable connoisseurs in Rome, Vincenzo Giustiniani wrote a series of essays on various subjects such as music, hunting, budget management and etiquette as well as on art. His friend, Teodoro (Dirck van) Ameyden (1586–1656), a jurist from the Dutch city of 's-Hertogenbosch living in Rome, described him as follows: 'Vincenzo, the Marchese of Bassano, was of unrivalled virtue and merit and known throughout the world, in particular to me.... Never before had the world seen such a mind. He talked about everything and was proficient in everything, even the most bizarre sciences'.[47] Ameyden was also the addressee of Vincenzo's treatises on painting (*Discorso sopra la pittura*), sculpture (*Discorso sopra la scultura*) and architecture (*Discorso sopra l'architettura*), which he wrote around 1618 in the form of letters.[48] Some ten years later, he also wrote his treatise on music titled *Discorso sopra la musica*. In 1606, Vincenzo Giustiniani had travelled Northern Italy and Central Europe together with the painter Cristoforo Roncalli (c. 1552–1626), visiting, among other countries, Germany and the Netherlands and stopping over in Maastricht, Leuven, Brussels, Antwerp and Ghent.[49] Thus, he was familiar with and appreciative of northern European painting and the main art centres and schools.[50] Yet Vincenzo was not just a collector but also a patron and, besides high-ranking guests, would occasionally accommodate artists at the Palazzo Giustiniani in Rome as well, among them Gerard van Honthorst (probably until his departure in the summer of 1620), David de Haen (1621–1622) and Nicolas Régnier (1622–1623).[51] His high regard for Gerard van Honthorst in particular is also apparent in his *Discorso sopra la pittura*, in which he divides painting into twelve categories, with the last one representing to Giustiniani that art of painting for which he has the greatest praise.[52] Honthorst ('Gherardo') is mentioned together with 'Enrico e Teodoro', most likely Hendrick ter Brugghen and Dirck van Baburen, and listed in the penultimate category, for 'the majority of the *Fiamminghi* who have practiced in Rome were adept at colouring'.[53] In this category, the art connoisseur appreciates above all the 'skilled use of

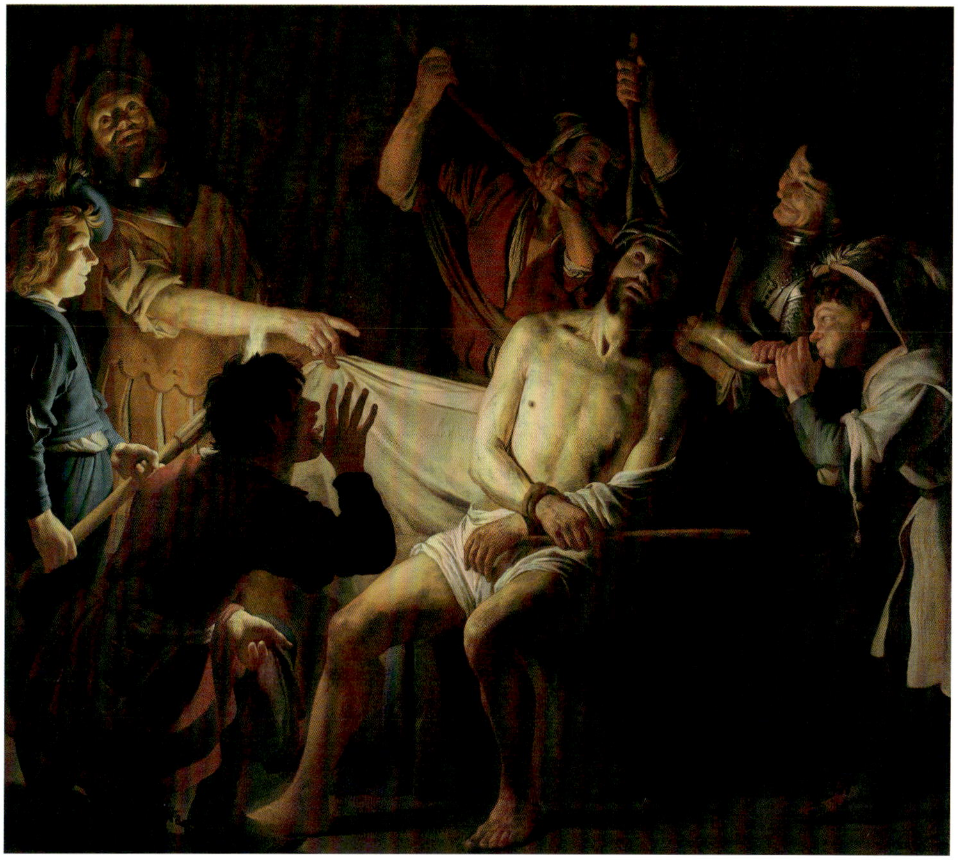

Fig. 34 Gerard van Honthorst, *The Crowning with Thorns*, c. 1622, Rijksmuseum, Amsterdam, purchased with support from the Rembrandt Association, the Stichting Jubileumfonds Rijksmuseum and the Rijksmuseum-Stichting

colours…, especially the expertise to give colours in all areas appropriate light…so that the eye is satisfied about the interplay of light and shade without any change to the intrinsic colour…'.[54]

It may be assumed that Honthorst created his painting *Christ before the High Priest* in close coordination with the Giustiniani brothers, in whose household he was living at the time (cat. 19). In addition to the choice of subject, they probably also discussed formal and stylistic similarities and differences compared to Luca Cambiaso's version of the subject, which was already part of the collection. Honthorst painted the *Liberation of St Peter* c. 1616/18 (cat. 12).[55] Judson suggests that there was an intense exchange of views between Honthorst and Benedetto, in whose inventory the painting was listed, regarding the composition and style of the work and that the two men agreed that the composition should closely follow that of Caravaggio's *Calling of St Matthew* (fig. 78) which was on display in the Contarelli Chapel of San Luigi dei Francesi opposite the Palazzo Giustiniani.

Another painting by Honthorst from the Giustiniani collection is considered lost. Today, it is interpreted as an allegory of painting: it showed a woman crushing pigments and, next to her, a head probably representing the artist.[56] Self-portraits by Orazio Borgianni and Nicolas Régnier are also mentioned in the inventories. They were part of the large collection of portraits the Giustiniani had compiled of deceased and contemporary artists and architects. Portrait galleries were not uncommon in Roman collections. But the many artists' portraits in Vincenzo's collection attest to the great store he set by the artists in his role as a patron.[57] This is also suggested by the *Double Portrait of Nicolas Régnier and Vincenzo Giustiniani* (fig. 31), which shows Régnier painting his patron.[58] Along with three portraits of the men of the house, Benedetto, Vincenzo and Giuseppe Giustiniani, Dirck van

Baburen's *Christ Washing the Apostles' Feet* (fig. 32) and Ribera's *Christ among the Doctors* (cat. 25) were on display in a room on the ground floor.[59] Gianni Papi points to the stylistic affinity of Baburen with the early work of Ribera.[60] Their juxtaposition in a room of the Palazzo Giustiniani once again shows the criteria by which Vincenzo arranged his paintings. All in all, 13 canvases by Ribera are listed in the Giustiniani collection.[61]

Large parts of Italy were under Spanish rule and, as a result, Spaniards also played a major role in Roman society and the network of art patrons.[62] As representative of the Spanish king in Rome, Pietro Cussida is particularly noteworthy as one of the most influential individuals who acted as art agent for Philip III and Philip IV.[63] Through him, Dirck van Baburen quickly gained recognition in Rome, for it was Cussida who commissioned Baburen and de Haen with the decoration of his chapel in San Pietro in Montorio.[64] Among the works in the collection of the Spanish representative were Baburen's *The Capture of Christ* with the Malchus Episode (c. 1615/16) (fig. 91), and a painting depicting Archimedes.[65] Jusepe de Ribera, known as Lo Spagnoletto (the little Spaniard), who – as documents show – was previously in Parma like Baburen, was also among the artists patronised by Cussida, and several of his works were in the latter's collection. In addition to the *Denial of St Peter* of c. 1615/16 (cat. 10), Cussida owned an apostle series by the Spaniard as well as a series of the Five Senses and the *Raising of Lazarus*, which today is on display at the Prado.[66] Ribera's departure for Naples in 1616 may have been the reason why Cussida commissioned Baburen rather than his fellow countryman to paint the altarpieces for San Pietro in Montorio.

Juan de Lezcano (1567–1634), secretary of the Spanish ambassador, Francisco Ruiz de Castro (1579–1637), also actively commissioned and collected artworks. His 1631 will, which lists about 140 paintings, mentions twelve canvases by Orazio Borgianni, including two on the subject of Christ among the Doctors, one of which is probably identical to the c. 1609 painting now on display at the Rijksmuseum in Amsterdam (cat. 27).[67]

Cardinal Francesco Maria del Monte lived in the immediate vicinity of the Giustiniani brothers. He resided at the Palazzo Madama, which Grand Duke Ferdinando I de' Medici (1549–1609), the friend and protector whose interests he represented at the Papal Court, had made available to him.[68] Del Monte is considered one of the earliest and most important patrons of Caravaggio. He owned eight works by him and helped the artist obtain additional commissions by introducing him to prominent members of society. After all, Caravaggio did not yet have a network of buyers on which he could draw when he arrived in Rome in the early 1590s. Following the pictorial tradition of his native Lombardy, he created genre-like single figures which he initially sold exclusively on the free market. This strategy, relatively well researched in the case of Caravaggio compared with his followers,[69] was probably pursued in much the same way by other young artists. Although Del Monte did not act as one of the patrons of the Utrecht Caravaggisti, evidence shows that he did own a work by Honthorst. In addition to numerous art treasures, the 1627 inventory of his estate comprises, 599 paintings, musical instruments and a very well-stocked library.[70] Among the paintings is a musical group by Honthorst, which after Del Monte's death passed on to Cardinal Francesco Barberini.[71] According to the inventory, this work hung along with Caravaggio's *Lute Player* (fig. 74) and two other paintings referred to as 'Una Musica' and a depiction of Mount Parnassus, in a room otherwise exclusively decorated with portraits of women. Most recently, Loredana Lorizzo has linked the painting to Honthorst's *Concert with Three Musicians* in Dublin (fig. 33).[72]

Probably through Del Monte, the first works by Caravaggio also found their way to Florence. Today, the Uffizi Gallery still holds, among other works, a *Bacchus*, a copy of *The Incredulity of St Thomas* (cat. 48), and a painted shield with the head of Medusa. The shield was probably a gift Del Monte presented to Ferdinando I in 1598. Paintings by Caravaggio's followers, including Manfredi and Honthorst, also entered the Medici collection through Cosimo II de' Medici (1590–1621), the Grand Duke of Tuscany. Cosimo acquired some of these works, verifiably those by Honthorst, on the Roman art market and it is assumed that, in selecting them he relied on consultants such as Del Monte, Mancini and Piero Guicciardini (1560–1626), the Grand Duke's ambassador in Rome.[73] Three paintings by the Utrecht artist appear as early as 1623 in an inventory which presumably lists the possessions of Cosimo II, including the *Merry Company with a Lute Player* (cat. 28). The canvases probably came to Florence together with the *Adoration of the Shepherds*. Piero Guicciardini had commissioned Honthorst in 1619 to paint this work for his family chapel in the church of Santa Felicita, and the latter completed it, possibly as his last work in Italy, in 1620.[74] Honthorst was paid a total of 250 scudi, which was, as far as we know, the highest remuneration he received for any of his works during his time in Italy.

Another document providing insight into the considerable appreciation of Honthorst's night scenes towards the end of his stay in Rome is the inventory of Paolo Mercati, a jurist who dabbled in poetry and, in 1628, joined the Franciscan order.[75] Compiled for this purpose in May 1628, the inventory lists artists, painting formats, hanging, and estimated prices. Apparently, entering the order was a move planned well in advance, since Mercati had already sought to sell his collection in 1622, albeit unsuccessfully. Showing the collector's high regard for the followers of Caravaggio, the lists mention canvases by the Utrecht artists in addition to works by the Italian painters Antiveduto della Grammatica, Orazio Riminaldi and Bartolomeo Manfredi. As early as 1622, Mercati owned two ovals by Baburen depicting the philosophers Democritus and Heraclitus and, hanging right next to them, a *Denial of St Peter* by Gerard van Honthorst. With an estimate of 150 scudi, the latter painting, linked by Sickel to a privately owned canvas in England (fig. 54), is one of the most expensive works in the collection.[76]

Honthorst left Rome in 1620 as a renowned and esteemed artist. He drew on the experiences and successes he had gained in Italy, and on the international contacts he had forged there, to run a successful workshop at home. Baburen probably pursued similar goals when he returned – possibly at the same time or the following year – to Utrecht. The fame both had achieved in Rome and their specific skills and innovative pictorial ideas all excellent features that enabled them to prevail in the flourishing and competitive Dutch art market.

Utrecht

In the roughly ten years Honthorst and Baburen spent in Italy, the economic situation of their home country had improved significantly as a result of the truce with Spain (1609–1621). The republic's northern provinces saw a rapid increase in international trade, the population benefitting thereby directly or indirectly. An influential and affluent burgher class formed, and it invested its wealth in the construction and refurbishment of fashionable canal-side houses and country estates,

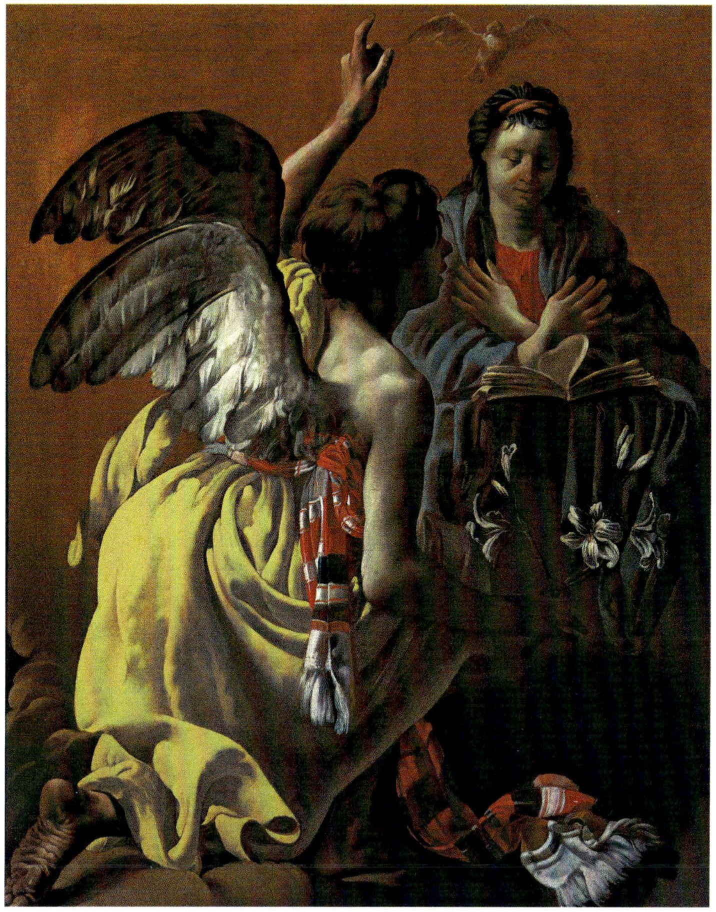

Fig. 35 Hendrick ter Brugghen, *The Annunciation*, c. 1624/25, Kunsthaus Zürich, Zürich, gift of Dr Joseph Scholz Stiftung and René Wehli, 2009

which were furnished with valuable leather wall coverings, the finest silk fabrics, luxurious furniture made of exotic woods, Chinese porcelain and artworks (fig. 82). Looking back, the Dutch painter and art theoretician Samuel van Hoogstraten (1627–1678) took stock in 1678: 'At the beginning of the century, the walls in Holland were not yet as densely hung with paintings as they are today. But this custom crept in more and more each day and soon led some painters to take to painting quickly, indeed, to producing a piece, whether small or large, a day'.[77]

With the growing demand for paintings, the number of painters grew as well. In 1620, there were 350 painters in the northern provinces, compared to 280 in 1610.[78] In Utrecht, there were about 40 painters by that time, and the production and trade in art and in painters' essentials developed into an industry of its own.[79] After a period in which the number of commissions dropped in the context of the Reformation movements, Utrecht once again developed into an art centre towards the end of the 16th century. This was accompanied by the establishment of large master workshops with numerous assistants and pupils, including those of Joachim Wtewael (1566–1638), Abraham Bloemaert (1566–1651) and Paulus Moreelse (1571–1638), and the founding of the Guild of St Luke and the drawing academy in the years 1611/12.[80]

Even though individual commissions were still awarded directly to the artists, they were by now clearly outweighed by the share of paintings sold through the art market.[81] The large supply of paintings on the market, which, due to the painters' specialisation and improved production conditions, could be offered at quite affordable prices, allowed a broad segment of the population to acquire original works. Painters sold their canvases to clients who visited their workshops, offered them for sale at the annual fair or submitted them to one of the many charitable lotteries or auctions.[82] Less valuable works even served as a means of payment at taverns or in games of dice. Before 1630, there were still relatively few art dealers in the Netherlands. Usually, artists themselves dealt in works of fellow painters, being allowed to do so as masters by the rules of the guild.[83]

Although history painting was generally regarded as the highest art form, requiring particular skill and experience from the artist and, in the case of major commissions, also promising to enhance his reputation, its share in the overall production of paintings declined. As contemporary inventories show, there was now a greater preference for landscapes, genre paintings, still lifes and portraits. Biblical subjects with scenes from the Old and New Testaments, which at the beginning of the 17th century had amounted to a third of all paintings in private collections, began to lose their importance in most collections.[84]

After returning from Rome, the three Utrecht Caravaggisti adapted to these conditions and, at the beginning of the 1620s, developed distinct pictorial forms adapted to the Dutch market, such as half-length, single-figure portrayals and merry companies with musicians, gamblers and prostitutes. These images were very popular, be it to satisfy the voyeuristic desires of viewers or to offer them a range of partly moralistic interpretations.[85] Although the painters drew noticeably on Italian models in stylistic and formal terms, at the same time they built on Dutch pictorial traditions (cat. 50). In addition to paintings for the free market, the workshops of the Utrecht Caravaggisti also produced works for both public and private clients and collectors.

Clients and Collectors

As an analysis of contemporary inventories in the Netherlands shows, works of the Utrecht Caravaggisti were to be found in many private collections.[86] Yet only in isolated cases can early provenances be linked to a specific commission. In Utrecht, it was probably above all the landed gentry and families from the former clerical elite who, together with the internationally minded members of the high nobility, acted as patrons.[87] Some of the artists themselves belonged to this elite, such as Joachim Wtewael and Paulus Moreelse, or had close family ties to members of the Utrecht city council, such as Gerard van Honthorst.[88]

For several years now, research has focused on the question of which faith clients and buyers belonged to, and whether this affected the awarding of commissions.[89] The results show that the denomination of painters and clients or buyers played only a limited role. It is now believed that the Dutch artists worked for a wide range of customers of different faiths.[90] While the Calvinists preferred stories from the Old Testament for religious pictures, Roman Catholic customers favoured subjects for private devotional use from the New Testament, especially crucifixion scenes with the Carrying of the Cross and the Deposition, episodes from the life of Christ and the Virgin Mary, and depictions of saints.[91]

Subjects that were particularly popular in the context of the Counter-Reformation included the Supper at Emmaus and depictions of the Incredulity of St Thomas and the Liberation of St Peter.[92] Honthorst painted the Liberation of St Peter in three versions. Ter Brugghen's *Incredulity of St Thomas* in Amsterdam (cat. 47) and his *Liberation of St Peter* in Schwerin (cat. 14) are also thought to have been commissioned by a Catholic client.[93] Thus, the focus turned to the Catholic communities in the search for possible patrons.[94] Even though freedom of religion was guaranteed and other religious groups were tolerated in the young, predominantly Calvinist republic, public practice of the Catholic faith had been outlawed since 1580. Church services of other faiths were held in clandestine, hidden, house churches called *huiskerken* or *kapellen*. Having typical house façades, they could not be identified as churches

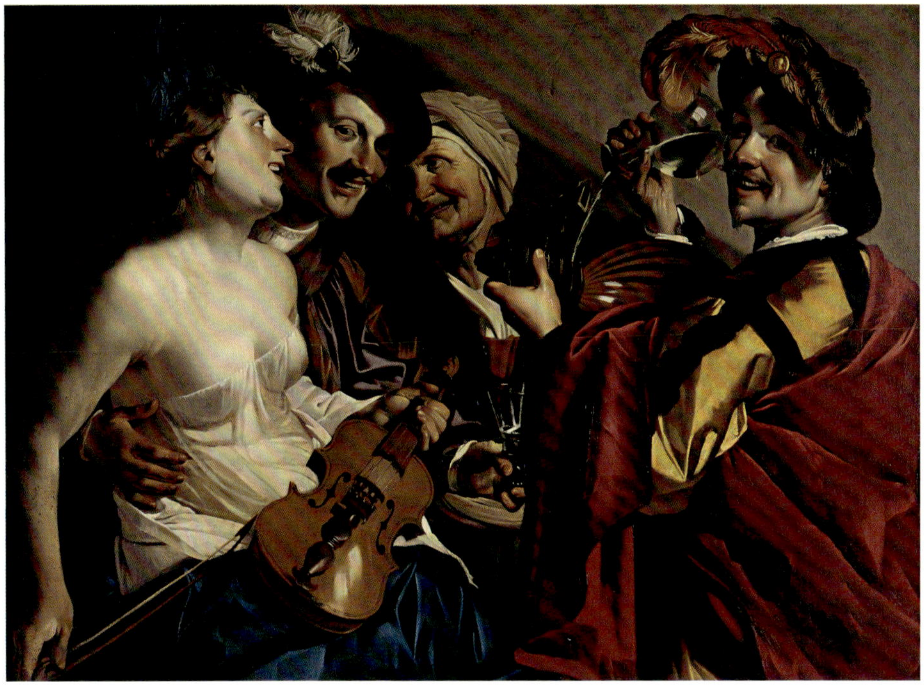

Fig. 36 Dirck van Baburen, *Loose Company*, 1623, Landesmuseum Mainz, Mainz

from the outside, but inside they were often richly decorated. In many places, the former bishop's see of Utrecht among them, the growing number of priests led to a growth in the Catholic population and the establishment of numerous hidden churches. In 14 Catholic parishes, about 40 Catholic priests – that is, a quarter of all active clergy in the Netherlands – worked in Utrecht.[95] As Xander van Eck, among others, has been able to establish, numerous Caravaggesque religious history paintings were found in hidden churches, including works by Gerard van Honthorst, Dirck van Baburen, Jan van Bijlert (1597/98–1671), Wouter (Pietersz.) Crabeth II (1593/94–1644) and Hendrick Bloemaert (1601–1672).[96] At the time of the Counter-Reformation, those striking depictions of the Passion of Christ or of saints with their approximately life-size, three-quarter or full-length figures placed close to the front of the painting and dramatically illuminated by the glow of artificial light sources, would have been particularly well suited to making a deep impression on churchgoers. At least one work that may have been commissioned for a hidden church, the Dominican church 'Het Stadhuis van Hoorn' in Amsterdam, survives: the *Crowning with Thorns* of c. 1622 by Honthorst at the Rijksmuseum in Amsterdam (fig. 34).[97] But for Hendrick ter Brugghen, no paintings for hidden churches are documented, even though his oeuvre includes a relatively large number of religious images.[98] Leonard J. Slatkes and Wayne Edward J. Franits suggest that his *King David Playing the Harp Surrounded by Angels* of 1628 (fig. 97) may have been created for a church gallery with an organ, which was not unusual for depictions of this subject especially in Utrecht.[99] In the case of ter Brugghen's composition *The Rich Man and the Poor Lazarus* (cat. 75), completed in 1625, evidence also points to a commission by a public institution. The choice of this unusual subject, the size of the canvas and its finely woven structure all suggest a commissioned work, possibly for the 'Melatenhuis' in Utrecht, a facility for lepers.[100]

In 1629, the last year of his life, Hendrick ter Brugghen signed and dated his second version of *The Annunciation* (cat. 78), which he is thought to have created as an altarpiece for the church of the beguinage in Diest.[101] This commission was probably related to a refurbishment of St Catherine's Church, in which, besides Hendrick ter Brugghen, Frans Francken the Younger (1581–1642) and Theodoor van Loon (1581/82–1649)

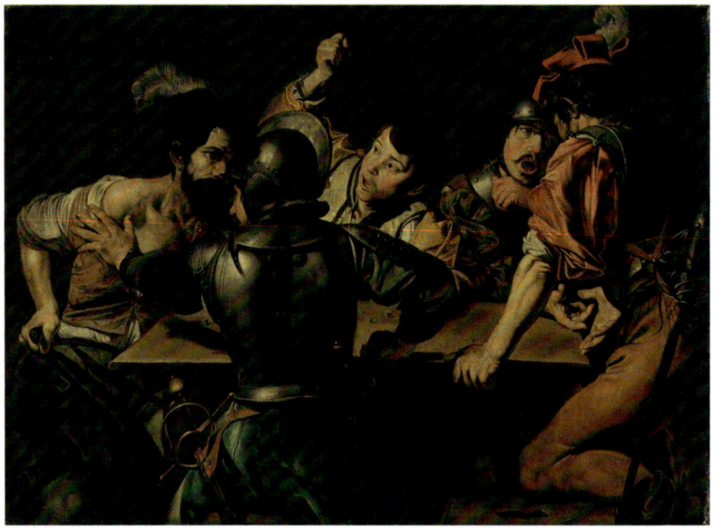

Fig. 37 Valentin de Boulogne (copy), *Soldiers Playing Dice*, 17th century, Bayerische Staatsgemäldesammlungen, Alte Pinakothek, Munich

were also involved. Whether ter Brugghen was commissioned because his Flemish fellow painter van Loon, who had previously received commissions from the Beguines, was in Rome from 1628 on and therefore unavailable, remains an open question. A connection to ter Brugghen may have existed through the Dutch royal court, as the city of Diest, which was located in Brabant, had been a possession and royal capital of the House of Orange-Nassau since the late 15th century.[102] A first version of he *Annunciation* was created around 1624/25, probably for the Deventer-based van Ryssen family, and is today held at the Kunsthaus Zürich (fig. 35).[103]

Unlike Rome, the Netherlands had no prominent art collectors or patrons in whose inventories Caravaggesque paintings constituted a particularly large proportion. At the same time, however, there was clearly a growing interest in Italian painting among individual collectors.[104] If we are to believe the statement made around 1630 by Rembrandt and Jan Lievens (1607–1674) that it was easier to see Italian paintings north of the Alps than in Italy, painters and people interested in art would have been able to study the style-defining Italian models in the original, and in considerable breadth.[105] Among the most prominent collections featuring works by Italian masters were those of the Amsterdam merchant, art dealer and patron Marten Kretzer (c. 1598–1670),[106] the Amsterdam and Delft-based art dealer Johannes de Renialme (c. 1600–1657) and the brothers Gerard (1599–1658) and Jan Reynst (1601–1646) in Amsterdam,[107] whose collection with more than 200 Italian paintings was one of the most important of all. According to Karel van Mander, one of the finest works of Jacopo da Bassano, an *Adoration of the Shepherds*, was in the collection of the merchant Jacques Niquet (c. 1571–1642) who was active in Amsterdam and Venice.[108] In 1617, two paintings by Caravaggio are documented in the possession of the Flemish painters Louis Finson (1580–1617) and Abraham Vinck (1580–1621) in Amsterdam, including the *Our Lady of the Rosary* in Vienna.[109]

Besides Italian paintings, Marten Kretzer also owned the *Sleeping Mars* by Hendrick ter Brugghen (fig. 10). The de Renialme collection included, in addition to a painting by Orazio Borgianni that may be identical to his *Christ on the Mount of Olives* in Braunschweig,[110] two canvases by Baburen[111] and a *Crucifixion* by ter Brugghen.[112]

While it is possible to reconstruct early provenances for some of the works exhibited, the inventories are generally from the second half of the century, making it impossible to differentiate between the awarding of a commission and some other form of acquisition. Strikingly, the paintings were found primarily in collections outside the Province of Utrecht: Hendrick ter Brugghen's *Flute Player* (cats. 32, 33) was in the collection of the Leiden-based philologist, historian and writer Petrus Scriverius (1576–1660) before 1663. His *St Sebastian* (cat. 69) was inventoried in the possession of the Amsterdam painter and art dealer Pieter Fris (1627/28–1706), who was forced to pawn his art collection in 1668. Ter Brugghen's *Incredulity of St Thomas* (cat. 47) and his depiction of a Crowning with Thorns and Mocking of Christ, which can possibly be identified with one of the versions in Rennes (cat. 17) or Sydney (fig. 62), were – together with his *Beheading of St John* and a *Bacchanal* by Baburen – in the possession of the silk merchant and collector Abraham Peronneau and his wife, Maria Poniche, in Amsterdam before 1687.[113] Baburen's *Christ among the Doctors* (cat. 45) and one of his brothel scenes are recorded as early as 1644 in the collection of Boudewijn de Man in Delft.[114] The latter is possibly identical to Baburen's *Loose Company* at the Landesmuseum Mainz (fig. 36).[115] His *Prometheus Being Chained by Vulcan* (cat. 54) was in the possession of Isaak van den Blooken in Amsterdam before 1706.

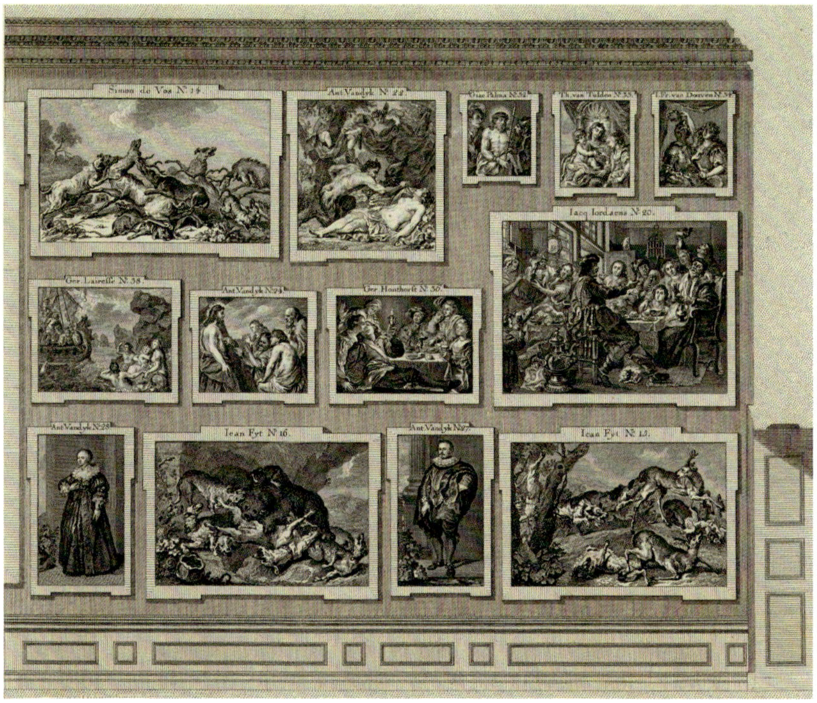

Fig. 38 Nicolas de Pigage, the Düsseldorf Gallery, room 1, left-hand side (from *La Galerie Électorale de Dusseldorff*), 1778

Members of the royal court in The Hague, rather than acquiring Italian or French paintings, favoured above all Flemish masters.[116] The works of the Utrecht Caravaggisti mentioned in the inventories of the stadtholder, which can supposedly be linked to paintings surviving to this day, are not characterised by a dramatic orchestration of light and shade, being instead uniformly bright, richly coloured and painted in a neo-Classicist, idealising manner. Works by ter Brugghen[117] and Honthorst for the Noordeinde Palace of the stadtholder's court in The Hague and the palace in Honselaarsdijk have come down to us.[118] These include Honthorst's 1625 *Granida and Daifilo* in Utrecht,[119] his 1624 *Lute Player* and *Woman Playing the Guitar* in Paris[120] and possibly also his *Concert* of the same year in Paris[121] or the 1623 version in Washington (cat. 66).

It was the art collector and ambassador of the English court, Sir Dudley Carleton (1573–1632), who paved the way for extensive contacts to England.[122] Carleton also introduced Honthorst to Frederick V of the Palatinate, the Wittelsbach 'Winter King' of Bohemia who had been living in exile since 1620, and his wife, Elizabeth Stuart, who temporarily resided in The Hague or at their summer residence, the Palazzo Renesse in Rhenen in the Province of Utrecht. Recorded in the inventory of the Rhenen palace is also a mantelpiece painting by Hendrick ter Brugghen, which today is no longer identifiable.[123]

One of the few documented commissions by a private client went to Baburen in 1623. The Utrecht nobleman Peter van Hardenbroek (1593–1658) and his wife, Agnes van Hanxelaer (d. 1659) had themselves portrayed as Princess Granida and the shepherd Daifilo (fig. 7).[124]

Even during their lifetime, the paintings of the Utrecht Caravaggisti were already included in major collections in both Italy and the Netherlands. Although no collector or patron emerged in the Netherlands, who explicitly patronised a Utrecht painter through commissions or acquisitions of his works, the number of canvases they produced and the prices they obtained for them in the market, and their assessments in 17th-century collection inventories attest to the appreciation their artworks garnered. The revenue a single painting by ter Brugghen generated in the 1620s, during his lifetime, equalled twice the monthly income of a member of the middle class, thus demonstrating the high status of the artist.[125] The large number of workshop replicas and copies produced into the 18th century is indicative of a strong demand for the works of the Caravaggisti, which were to be found in numerous major European collections. Among the latter was the collection of the Wittelsbach Elector Palatinate, Johann Wilhelm (1658–1716), which was world famous in its day and whose main works are now part of the holdings of the Alte Pinakothek in Munich.[126] In the Elector's picture gallery in Düsseldorf, Gerard van Honthorst's *Merry Company* of 1622 (fig. 40) was placed centrally in the first large room and contrasted with Valentin de Boulogne's *Soldiers Playing Dice*[127] (figs. 37, 38).

1 Van Mander 1604, fol. 6v, verse 66: 'Want Room is de Stadt, daer voor ander plecken / Der Schilders reyse haer veel toe wil strecken / Wesende het hooft der Picturae Scholen'.
2 Franits 2013a, cats. A1–A14, also documented in writing: ibid., cats. L3, L7. Also workshop creations: ibid., cats. A3BW1, A7BW1, A10W1, A13W1.
3 According to Franits 2013a, 29 works by the artist's hand can be dated between 1620 and 1624. Two paintings datable to c. 1622 are lost, so the total number of works from the Utrecht years is 31.
4 For the population of Rome, see Eugenio Sonnino in Van Kessel/Schulte 1997, pp. 50–70.
5 See, for Rome, also the essay by Helen Langdon in this volume, p. 37.
6 Ago 2006, esp. pp. 121–136; for the relationship between political developments and art production in Rome, see Karsten 2003.
7 Karsten 2003, p. 7.
8 Cavazzini 2016.
9 Brown 2001; Sickel 2001; Curti 2017/18.
10 For the relationship between commissioners and painters in the Baroque age in Rome and Venice, see Haskell 1963.
11 Robertson 2015, p. 127.
12 For the Roman art market: Fantoni/Matthews/Matthews-Grieco 2003; Cavazzini 2004; De Marchi/Van Miegroet 2006; Cavazzini 2008, pp. 123–126; Von Bernstorff 2010, p. 128. The passion for collecting paintings took hold of almost all social classes, see Cavazzini 2004; Fratarcangeli 2008; Nicolai 2008, esp. pp. 157–162.
13 Cavazzini 2016/17, p. 25. For the earnings of an artist in Rome, see Spear 2003; Spear/Sohm 2010 and Spear 2012.
14 Cavazzini 2004, pp. 363–367; Savina 2013, pp. 22–29.
15 For the copies after paintings by Caravaggio, see Moir 1976; Exh. cat. Düsseldorf 2006/07 and Savina 2013.
16 Richards 2011/12, p. 65, and the essay by Helen Langdon in this volume, p. 48.
17 Savina 2013, pp. 16, 48–49, 194.
18 Frommel 1971; Ebert-Schifferer 2009, pp. 90–117.
19 Ebert-Schifferer 2018, esp. pp. 48–53.
20 c. 1593–1594, canvas, 65.8 × 52.3 cm, Fondazione Longhi, Florence.
21 Among the Northern European paintings who explored optical phenomena in Rome around 1600 was, notably, Adam Elsheimer (1578–1610). For the history of optics and painting, see Thielemann 2018.
22 Judson/Ekkart 1999, pp. 80–81, 94–95.
23 See, among others, Reinhard 1979.
24 See, for example, Sickel 2003.
25 For recent research, see Ebert-Schifferer 2017/18.
26 Exh. cat. Utrecht/Braunschweig 1986/87, p. 175, note 25; Slatkes/Franits 2007, p. 5, 135, note 9; Franits 2013a, pp. 6, 238, cat. L7.
27 Gigli/Marchetti/Simonetta 2013.
28 Fukaya 2016, pp. 115–119.
29 Judson/Ekkart 1999, pp. 6, 10–13.
30 *St Paul Caught up into the Third Heaven*, 1617, canvas, 400 × 250 cm, Santa Maria della Vittoria, Rome. Judson/Ekkart 1999, pp. 92–93, cat. 72; Megna 2003, pp. 89–91; Lorizzo 1995, pp. 163–165; Lorizzo 2015a, p. 92.
31 Lorizzo 2015a, p. 92.
32 For Padre Domenico di Gesù e Maria: Lorizzo 1995; Mazzetti di Pietralata 2012, pp. 1268–1273; Lorizzo 2015a, pp. 92–94.
33 *Jesus in St Joseph's Workshop*, c. 1617, canvas, 142 × 118 cm; Lorizzo 1995, pp. 162–163; Judson/Ekkart 1999, pp. 67–68, cat. 36; Lorizzo 2015a, p. 94. It is worth noting here that the painting collection of the monastery was almost exclusively Caravaggesque; see Mazzetti di Pietralata 2012, pp. 1246–1247.
34 To this day as main altarpiece in the church: *Madonna in Glory with Saints Francis of Assisi and Bonaventure and Princess Colonna Gonzaga*, 1618, canvas, 370 × 233 cm; Judson/Ekkart 1999, pp. 96–97, cat 76; Gianni Papi in Exh. cat. Florence 2015, pp. 176–177, cat. 25; Lorizzo 2015a, pp. 95–96.
35 Mazzetti di Pietralata 2012, pp. 1270–1271.
36 Christiansen 2001/02, pp. 15–19; Mazzetti di Pietralata 2014. See also cat. 43.
37 *The Stigmatisation of Saint Francis*, canvas, 284 × 173 cm, Ministero dell'Interno, Direzione Generale per gli Affari dei Culti, Rome. The church already had two altarpieces by Gentileschi, both from 1609: *The Calling of St Sylvester* and *The Martyrdom of St Stephen*. Created at the same time, a *Holy Family with St Elisabeth, the Infant St John and an Angel* by Orazio Borgianni was also on display in San Silvestro in Capite. See for this and additional examples, see Mazzetti di Pietralata 2012, p. 1250.
38 *The Martyrdom of Sts Processus and Martinianus*, 1629–1630, canvas, 302 × 192 cm, Musei Vaticani, Pinacoteca Vaticana, Vatican City, inv. 40381. See also cat. 44.
39 In 1624/25, Vouet created two paintings depicting the life of St Francis for the family chapel of Paolo Alaleone, Master of Ceremonies of Urban VIII, in San Lorenzo in Lucina.
40 Salerno 1960a–c; Danesi Squarzina 1997; Danesi Squarzina 1998; Exh. cat. Rome/Berlin 2001; Danesi Squarzina 2003; Lorizzo 2009.
41 Robertson 2015, p. 135.
42 Danesi Squarzina 2003, vol. 1, pp. 5–31.
43 Danesi Squarzina 2001, p. 20; Robertson 2015, pp. 139–140.
44 Danesi Squarzina 2003, vol. 1, pp. LXXV–LXXVIII.
45 For a description of the rooms of Benedetto and Vincenzo at the Palazzo Giustiniani and their uses, see Danesi Squarzina 2003, vol. 1, pp. LXXXIX–XCVI; Robertson 2015, pp. 138–140.
46 Danesi Squarzina 2003, vol. 1, pp. LXXXIX–XCVI.
47 '[C]avaliere di virtù e meriti incomparabili noti a tutto il mondo, ma particolarmente a me [...] Non viddi mai tal ingenio al mondo. Di tutto s'intendeva, di tutto discorreva, anche delle scienze più ricondite [...].' See Gedova 2017, p. 329, note 136.
48 See Banti 1981.
49 His secretary, Bernardo Bizoni, wrote a travelogue entitled *Diario di viaggio di Vincenzo Giustiniani*. See Bizoni 1995.
50 Sanvito 2001.
51 The Dutch painters Cornelis Bloemaert, Theodor Matham and Reinier van Persijn also lived at the Palazzo Giustiniani. Gerson 1983, pp. 143–144; Danesi Squarzina 2003, vol. 1, pp. LXXV–LXXVI.
52 In addition to Carracci and Guido Reni, Caravaggio is mentioned here too. Banti 1981, p. 44. See also the essay by Liesbeth M. Helmus, p. 57.
53 'La maggior parte dei Fiamminghi esercitati in Roma, che hanno saputo ben colorire.' Ibid., p. 44.
54 'Di sapere maneggiare i colori,...e soprattutto con sapere dare il lume conveniente al colore di ciascheduna parte..., in modo che l'occhio resti sodisfatto dell'unione del chiaro e scuro senza alterazione del proprio colore....' Ibid., p. 44.
55 Judson/Ekkart 1999, p. 12.
56 'Un quadro con il ritratto d'una Donna che macina colori con una Testa [ritratto di Gherardo pittore fiammengo] dipinto in tela alta palmi 5. larga 4. in circa [di mano del medesimo Gherardi] senza cornice.' Danesi Squarzina 2003, vol. 1, pp. 458–459.
57 See Ibid., p. C.

58 c. 1623–1625, canvas, 111 × 138 cm, Harvard Art Museums / Fogg Museum, Cambridge MA, inv. 1982.116; Lemoine 2007, p. 239, cat. 37; Annick Lemoine in Exh. cat. Nantes 2017/18, pp. 111–113, cat. 9. Giustiniani owned a total of nine paintings by the Frenchman, see also Lemoine 2000.
59 Danesi Squarzina 2003, vol. 1, pp. 280–281.
60 Papi 2002, esp. p. 27–31.
61 Danesi Squarzina 2003, vol. 1, pp. 255–256.
62 Dandelet 1997; Dandelet 2001; Dandelet/Marino 2007.
63 For Cussida and his inventories see Grilli 1994; Grilli 2005/06; Franits 2013a, p. 8.
64 See cat. 21.
65 *Archimedes*, c. 1616–1617, canvas, 100.5 × 81 cm, private collection; Franits 2013a, pp. 76–78, cat. A2.
66 Papi 2002, p. 34. *The Raising of Lazarus*, c. 1616, canvas, 171 × 289 cm, Museo Nacional del Prado, Madrid, inv. P007768.
67 Gallo 2015. Also Vannugli 1998; Vannugli 2009.
68 See Borsi/Del Gaizo 1984.
69 For example, Sickel 2003; Ebert-Schifferer 2009.
70 Frommel 1971.
71 Today presumed lost; see Judson/Ekkart 1999, pp. 216–217, cat. 280; also Frommel 1971, p. 36.
72 Lorizzo 2015a, pp. 97–98; previously already in Papi 1999, pp. 162–163; Judson/Ekkart 1999, pp. 224–225, cat. 287 (dated c. 1623).
73 Fabbri 2005, p. LXXII.
74 Canvas, 338.5 × 198.5 cm, Galleria degli Uffizi, Florence, inv. 1890, no. 772; Judson/Ekkart 1999, pp. 10, 13, 61–63, cat. 22. Commissions for two additional altarpieces in the chapel went to Cecco del Caravaggio and Lo Spadarino. Gianni Papi in Exh. cat. Florence 2015, p. 190, cat. 32.
75 Sickel 2006.
76 Ibid., p. 208: the prices probably reflect the purchase value. By comparion, an *Apollo and Marsyas* by Manfredi is estimated at 70 scudi, while most other estimates give prices between 10 and 30 scudi. Baburen's ovals, for instance, were listed at 12 scudi.
77 'In 't begin deezer eeuw waeren de wanden in Holland noch zoo dicht niet met Schilderyen behangen, alsze tans wel zijn. Echter kroop dit gebruik dagelijx meer en meer in, 't welk zommige Schilders dapper aenporde om zich tot ras schilderen te gewennen, jae om alle daeg een stuk, 't zy kleyn of groot, te vervaerdigen.' Van Hoogstraten 1678, p. 91.
78 Rasterhoff 2017, p. 169.
79 Bok 1997/98, p. 93, mentioned another 50 to 60 or so, which he currently reduces to just under 40. See the essay by Marten Jan Bok in this volume, p. 27.
80 Bièvre 2015, p. 381; see Bok 1990; Bok 1994.
81 For the art market in the northern Netherlands in the first half of the 17th century, see Boers 2012 with further references to older literature, as well as Bok 2008. For commissioners, buyers and collectors see, among others, Kempers 1991; Schwartz 2002.
82 North 1992, p. 107; Bok 1997/98, p. 97; North 2017, p. 10. For a comparison with the lotteries in Rome, see Lorizzo 2011. First documentary evidence of a sale of a painting by ter Brugghen at an auction in Amsterdam dates from 19 March 1625, when 'Marcus Mutius Romeyn' was sold for 44 guilders. Exh. cat. Utrecht/Braunschweig 1986/87, pp. 71, 74; Slatkes/Franits 2007, pp. 142–144, cat. A43.
83 Montias 1988, p. 245.
84 North 1992, pp. 131, 138, 154.
85 Cf. the studies by Wayne Franits on genre paintings and by Eric Jan Sluijter on history paintings: Sluijter 1992; Franits 1997, pp. 114–120; Franits 2004.
86 Slatkes/Franits 2007, pp. 29–32.
87 Olde Meierink/Bakker 1997/98. For the relationship between patron and artist, see Hendrix 1996.
88 Olde Meierink/Bakker 1997/98, p. 72.
89 See, among others, Van Eck 1999; Van Eck 2008; Seaman 2012; Von Rosen 2015.
90 Manuth 1993/94, pp. 240–241; Slatkes/Franits 2007, ch. 2.
91 See North 1992, p. 137; Kaplan 2002.
92 Van Eck 1993/94, pp. 226, 230.
93 Ibid.
94 See, among others, Exh. cat. Utrecht 1991; Schillemans 1992; Van Eck 1993/94; Van Eck 1999.
95 Bièvre 2015, p. 392.
96 Van Thiel 1990/91, p. 54; Schillemans 1992, p. 45–47; Van Eck 1993/94; Van Eck 1999; Van Eck 2008; Seaman 2012; Von Rosen 2015, p. 202.
97 Canvas, 192.4 × 221.5 cm, Rijksmuseum, Amsterdam, inv. SK-A-4837; see also Judson/Ekkart 1999, pp. 85–86, cat. 60; Seaman 2012, p. 67, note 42.
98 Olde Meierink/Bakker 1997/98, p. 85; Van Eck 1999, p. 73.
99 Slatkes/Franits 2007, p. 85, cat. A7.
100 Blankert 1982, p. 53; Slatkes/Franits 2007, pp. 23, 93–94, cat. A11.
101 Slatkes/Franits 2007, pp. 89–91, cat. A9.
102 This information was kindly provided by Marten Jan Bok, Amsterdam.
103 Canvas, 104 × 84 cm, Kunsthaus Zürich, Zürich, inv. 2010/1; Slatkes/Franits 2007, pp. 88–89, cat. A8; Klemm 2010.
104 Lugt 1936; Van Veen 1992; Mijnlieff 1993; Meijer 2000; Hall 2001; Van der Veen 2002, pp. 78–81.
105 According to Constantijn Huygens c. 1630. Strauss/Van der Meulen 1979, p. 69.
106 For Kretzer see Exh. cat. Utrecht 1980, pp. 10, 27–28, and the ECARTICO database: URL: http://www.vondel.humanities.uva.nl/ecartico/persons/16465 (accessed 10 September 2018).
107 Logan 1979; Bok 1988; Lammertse/Van der Veen 2017. Also see Cohen-Willner 1999 and the ECARTICO database: URL: http://www.vondel.humanities.uva.nl/ecartico/persons/28053 (accessed 10 September 2018).
108 Van Mander 1604, fol. 180v.
109 c. 1601, canvas, 364.5 × 249.5 cm, Kunsthistorisches Museum, Gemäldegalerie, Vienna, inv. GG 147; Prohaska 1980; Meijer 2000, pp. 377–379.
110 c. 1610, canvas, 100 × 123, Herzog Anton Ulrich-Museum, Braunschweig, inv. 475.
111 Slatkes/Franits 2007, p. 243, cat. L17.
112 Lammertse/Van der Veen 2017, p. 175.
113 Slatkes/Franits 2007, p. 104, cat. A18, and pp. 121–122, cat. A32; Franits 2013a, p. 238, cat. L8. On 6 January 1692, ter Brugghen's works are estimated by Johan Rosa and Jan Pietersz Zomer at 40 and 60 guilders, respectively. Baburen's *Bacchanal* is estimated at 150 guilders.
114 Franits 2013a, pp. 119–122, cat. A22, as well as pp. 158–160, cat. A31. The two paintings by Baburen which were inventoried on 15 March 1644 were estimated at 655 and 155 guilders respectively.
115 1623, canvas, 108 × 153 cm, Landesmuseum Mainz, Mainz, inv. 108; Franits 2013a, pp. 158–160, cat. A31.
116 Fock 1979, pp. 469–470.; Sluijter 2015/16, p. 92.
117 Slatkes/Franits 2007, pp. 31, 140–141, cat. A42.
118 Sluijter 2015/16, p. 95, nos. 33, 36, 40, with further references; Drossaers/Lunsingh Scheurleer 1974–1976, vol. 1, p. 183, nos. 44, 50, 51; p. 184, no. 66; p. 186, nos. 101, 102; p. 207, no. 611.
119 Canvas, 145.2 × 179.3 cm, Centraal Museum, Utrecht, inv. 5571; Judson/Ekkart 1999, pp. 159–161, cat. 189; Cat. Utrecht 1999, vol. 2, pp. 971–974, no. 292.
120 Canvas, 83 × 67 cm, Musée du Louvre, Paris, inv. 1368, Judson/Ekkart 1999, pp. 176–177, cat. 222; canvas, 82 × 68 cm, Musée du Louvre, Paris, inv. 1369, ibid., p. 175, cat. 220.
121 Canvas, 168 × 178 cm, Musée du Louvre, Paris, inv. 1364; Judson/Ekkart 1999, pp. 207–209, cat. 273.
122 Ibid., pp. 19–23.
123 Bok/Kobayashi 1985, pp. 14, 18; Slatkes/Franits 2007, pp. 273–274, cat. L32.
124 Olde Meierink/Bakker 1997/98, p. 72; Franits 2013a, pp. 154–156, cat. A31. See the essay by Marten Jan Bok in this volume, p. 30.
125 For ter Brugghen, see Slatkes/Franits 2007, p. 29.
126 Exh. cat. Munich 2009.
127 At the time as an original by Valentin, now as a 'copy after', 17th century, canvas, 124 × 172.5 cm, Bayerische Staatsgemäldesammlungen, Alte Pinakothek, Munich, inv. 2233.

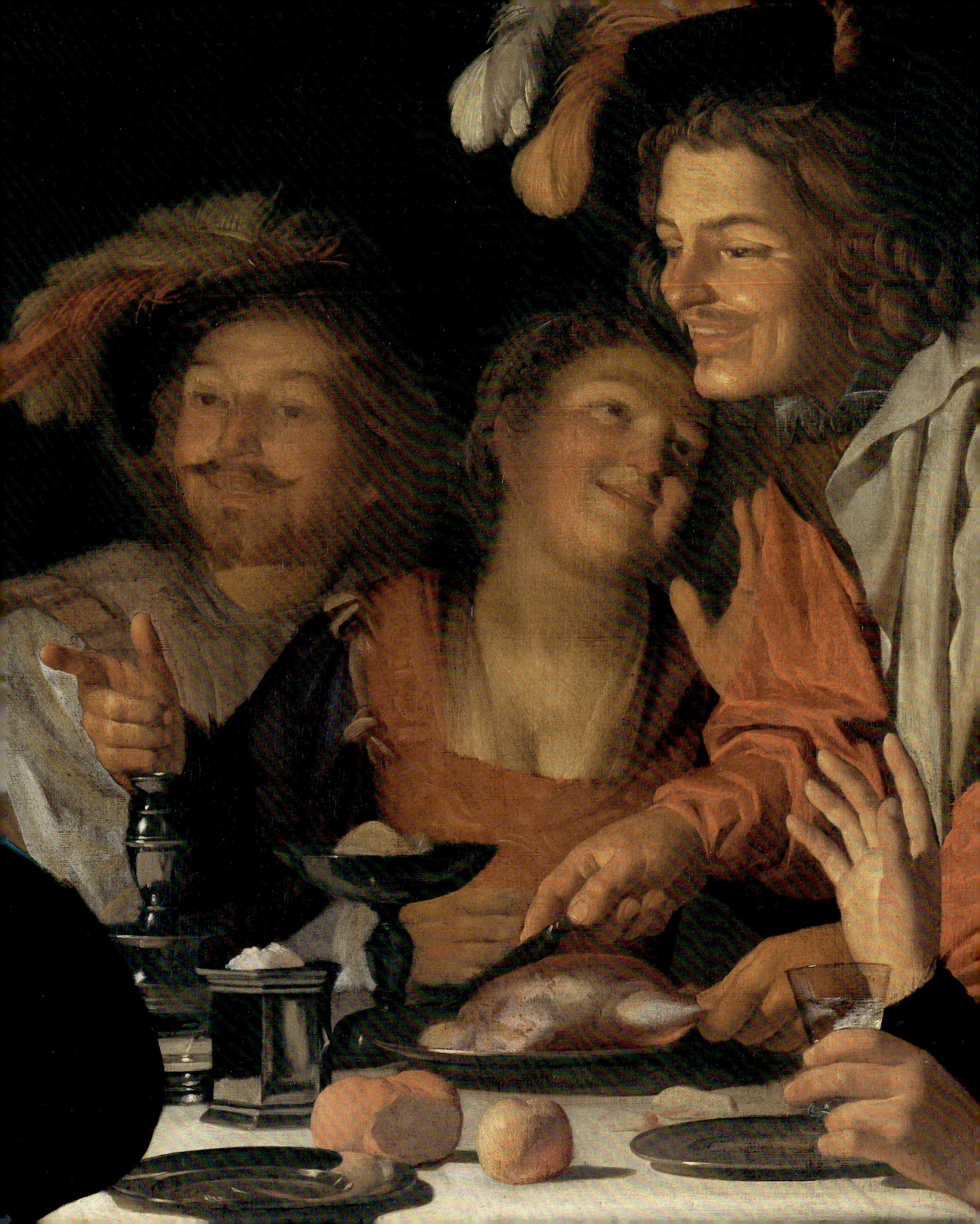

The Utrecht Painters: Caravaggism, Technique and Expression

ASHOK ROY

In 1607, when, it has been speculated, Hendrik ter Brugghen, painter of Utrecht and former pupil of the locally influential Mannerist painter Abraham Bloemaert first arrived in Rome, that city's most explosively recent creative force in painting, Caravaggio, had already departed for Naples in 1606. Neither ter Brugghen nor his fellow countrymen, Dirck van Baburen or Gerard van Honthorst, who also travelled to Rome in the second decade of the 17th century, could have met Caravaggio in person since Baburen was in the city from some time between 1612 and 1615 and Honthorst perhaps from the beginning of the second decade of the century. What is important, however, is that they would all have encountered his reputation, knowing of it in advance, and were able to see some of the works the creation of which had been causing unusually great excitement in public and private circles in Rome and beyond at just this time.

It is easy to imagine young painters from northern Europe who were serious about their craft wishing to expand their exposure to new and revolutionary ways of creating paintings, and to see at first hand a volume of new art in the largest, richest and most competitively diverse art market in the world. This was in spite of the difficulties of settling in Rome even temporarily among so many other migrant, aspirant painters from other parts of Italy and elsewhere in Europe. The existing community of foreign painters in the city offered advantages to incomers since they were largely located in one part of the city, and that would have offered a practical infrastructure for the studio and workshop-based production of paintings for the market. Strictly speaking, there were several markets since there were extensive potential opportunities for both public and private commissions in Rome, although success in the former could be seen as more important and valuable since it almost certainly guaranteed steady income from the latter, as Caravaggio himself some years before had enjoyed. The atmosphere must have been one of the most intense and sometimes acrimonious competition between groups and individuals anxious to succeed in attracting commissions from the Church and the coterie of collectors and connoisseurs who had the influence required to establish reputations through their patronage.

The aim in a competitive market was to rise above others through artistic and painterly accomplishment. The means was a blend of emulation of works by already established, successful artists, combined with a level of originality that might attract the attention of either the cognoscenti or those responsible for ensuring the Church continued to inspire faith through the installation of new works of art of high public impact. A new arrival's emulation of highly successful and influential ways of painting, as established by Caravaggio for example, required at least two essential accomplishments: a thorough understanding of the practical means by which these types of compositions were devised and laid down, par-

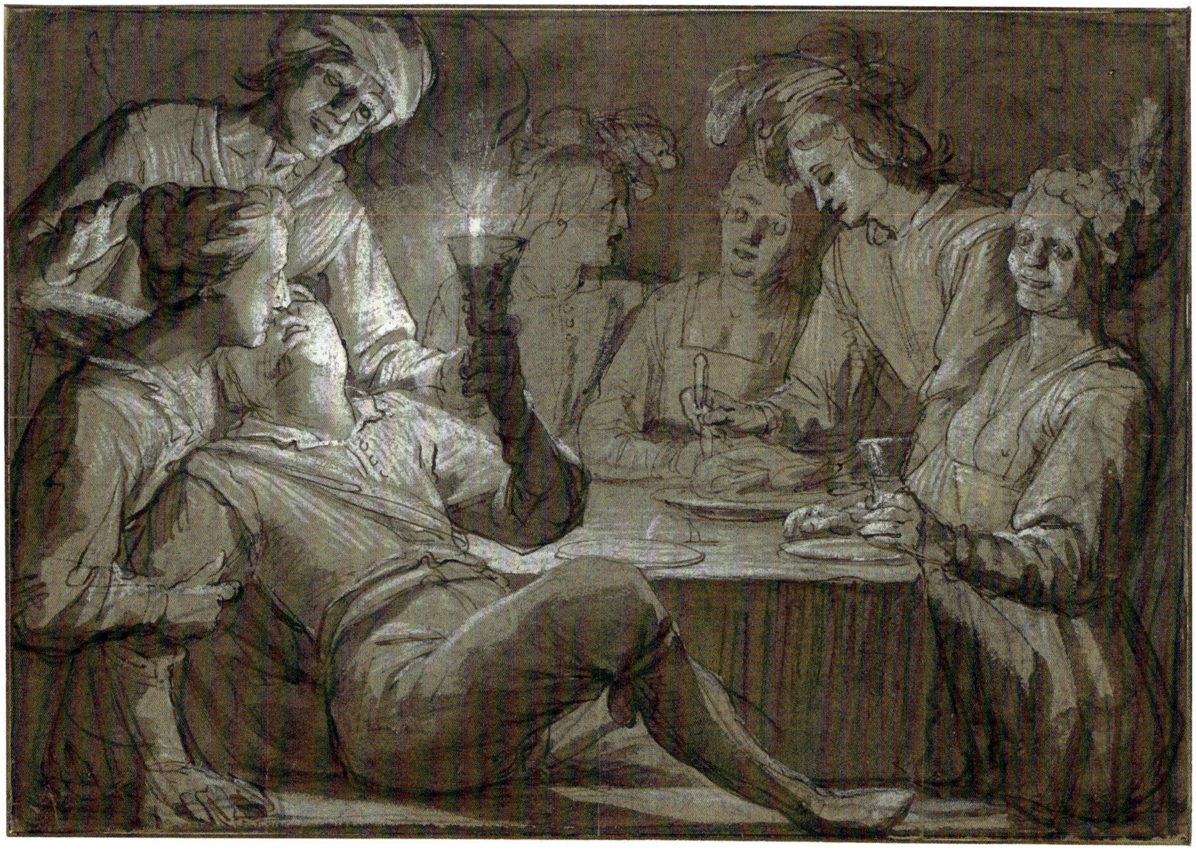

Fig. 39 Gerard van Honthorst, *The Prodigal Son* (*Merry Company with Candlelight*), c. 1622, Albertina Museum, Vienna

ticularly where they were to be fairly large-scale, multi-figure designs; and a means of painting in the modelling and disposition of figures that aligned sufficiently recognisably with one of the new trends of the Baroque style. Caravaggio gave the impression of managing this almost without effort. This was his superficial impact, however, since a number of Caravaggio's works show evidence in their X-radiographic images of radical changes made during the course of painting. In both his commissions for the Contarelli and Cerasi Chapels, completely new replacements were made for parts of each scheme.[1]

It is important to ask whether those painters resident in Rome, or who had come to the city to absorb and exploit what was new there, strove to re-create what was known or supposed of Caravaggio's compositional and technical methods in order to produce pictures for the market. For potential commissions, one line would be to satisfy a need for the look of Caravaggio's autograph works, which were in short supply, or to provide some strong reference to them so as to be recognised as clearly in their debt, and thus desirable to collectors. The alternative is that what might be termed first-generation Caravaggism was the result of painters such as Baburen and Honthorst consciously producing paintings that had a recognisable set of characteristics associated with Caravaggio's range of interests and mode of expression, but which were made using more idiosyncratic materials and techniques that had the convincing look of their influential models. This question applies equally to those roughly contemporary painters in Rome, for example Manfredi, Ribera, Valentin, Régnier, Saraceni and others, who explicitly followed the Caravaggio model sufficiently closely for many of their works to be attributed to him during the 19th century and after.[2]

In a technical sense, it is likely that pictures owing this relatively early debt to Caravaggio were made using techniques

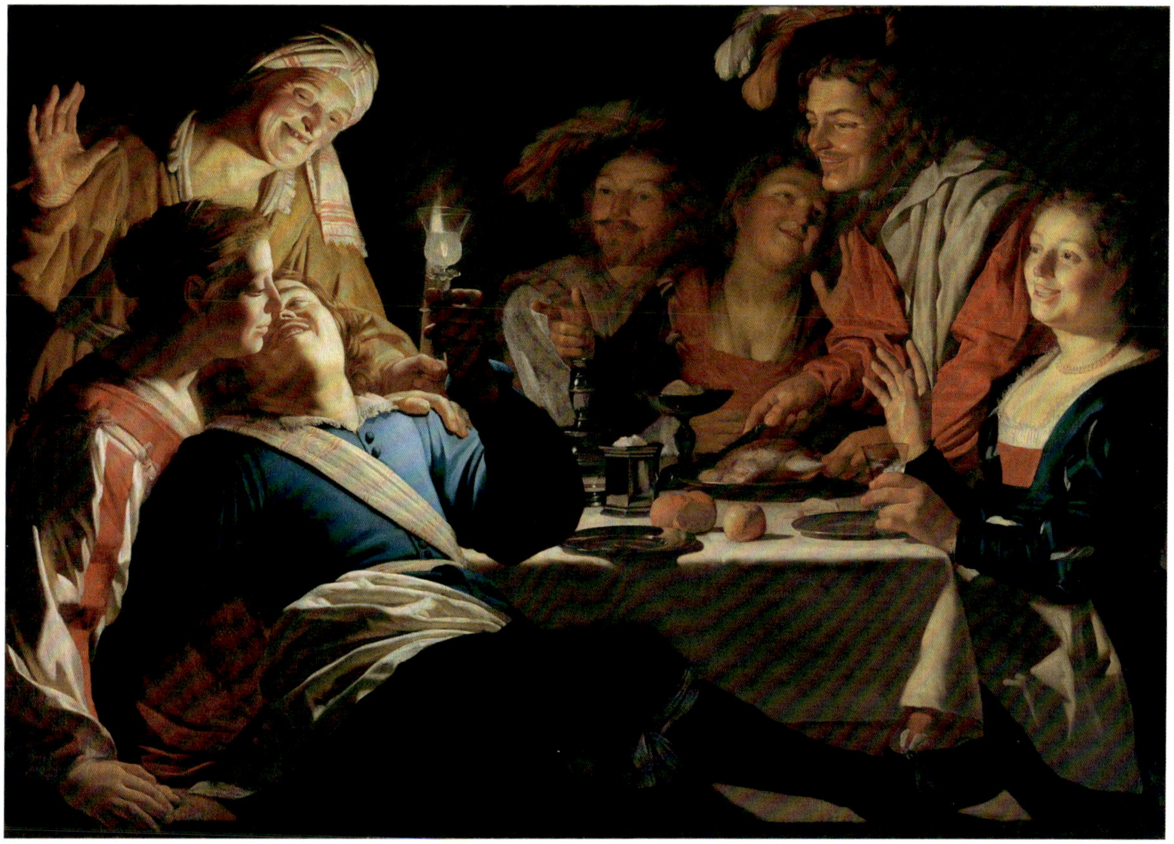

Fig. 40 Gerard van Honthorst, *Merry Company*, 1622, Bayerische Staatsgemäldesammlungen, Alte Pinakothek, Munich

both learned and developed individually, combined with methods that followed beliefs circulating about Caravaggio's technical innovations. Some preliminary work on ter Brugghen and Honthorst directed at this broad question has been carried out at the National Gallery in London in recent years.[3] This found the preponderance of individualistic techniques devoted to achieving the look of the Caravaggesque, but no clearly identifiable role for Caravaggio's most idiosyncratic practices, at least not for these Utrecht followers. As study of these pictures has progressed, it has become clearer that Baburen, Honthorst and ter Brugghen each developed very different technical approaches in their response to Caravaggio's innovations.

The last decade or so has seen considerable progress in understanding Caravaggio's technical practices more fully using modern scientific methods of examination. Perhaps the most significant and surprising new revelation has been the detection and recording of underdrawings in the works of Caravaggio using advanced methods of digital infrared imaging.[4] This discovery has given a dramatic new insight into Caravaggio's method of composition, but does not conflict with his well-known innovation, recorded in Giulio Mancini's early account in his *Considerazioni sulla pittura*, of using posed, living models in a darkened studio. This was the wider practice that came to be promoted in private 'Accademie dal naturale', described by Giovanni Baglione, where some form of directional natural illumination was used to create artificially stark enhanced light-and-shadow transitions on a model posing before aspirant painters.[5] Keith Christiansen has described recently a deconstruction of Caravaggio's process of creating a multi-figure composition using, at least partially, posed models in an evaluation of the painting practices of his dedicated and highly original French follower, Valentin de Boulogne.[6] Christiansen reinforces the valid point, first commented upon by Mancini, that both the individual, sometimes outrageously contorted poses of the models in Caravaggio and the additive process that must have been employed to bring together a complete tableau often resulted in an 'inevitable effect of frozen action and the appearance of piecemeal construction'.[7] This is a striking feature of the *Martyrdom of St Matthew* (fig. 17), the success and grandeur of which is not, however, undermined by its statically composed moment.

According to Bellori's comments, of those later followers of Caravaggio in Rome it was the dedication of the group of younger painters to his principles of composition that attracted veiled criticism; they regarded him as 'the only true imitator of nature [...]' and 'looking upon his works as miracles, they outdid each other in following his method, undressing their models and placing their lights high'.[8] This arrangement is just as Ribera, for example, is recorded to have sought for his rented studio and it is reasonable to suppose that the piecemeal result of combining several figural images into a whole would always produce a frozen tableau look, and might be used as evidence of the practice.

Do we then see visual evidence of this kind in the identified Roman works of either Honthorst or Baburen? The lack of paintings from the hand of ter Brugghen from his time there argues against a meaningful discussion in his case. By the time he returned to Utrecht, his pictures seem not to have required the live model in quite that sense, and ter Brugghen's widespread deployment of underdrawing, often with corrections, indicates a more conventional approach.[9]

Equally, for Honthorst there is no obvious design for a picture that could not have been composed by conventional means, that is via the procedures the painter would have acquired as part of his training in the studio of Abraham Blomaert, or some individual adaptation of this. It is perhaps most significant that in the trio of Utrecht painters considered here, it is Honthorst most particularly for whom a number of detailed preliminary drawings for painted compositions are known. These are more than just linear graphic works, but are also often worked up to express volume in values of light and shade in preparation for a painted work. Some of Honthorst's drawings seem as much about a proposed disposition of light in a picture, worked out in washes representing light and shade, as in the planned relationship of figures (fig. 39).[10] At least one Honthorst drawing exists which has around its periphery the markings applied for a squared grid, presumably for the purposes of scaling up to a large compositional cartoon, or other means of creating a full-size painting.[11] The lack of complete correspondence in the design of Honthorst's compositional drawings with paintings that derive directly from these, for example *Merry Company* in Munich,[12] reinforces rather than detracts from the identification of the drawing as a direct source for the painting (fig. 40), and follows a way of using and adapting compositional drawings that was common from the early 16th century.

It is perhaps also relevant that Baburen's earlier training was in the workshop of Paulus Moreelse, a Blomaert competitor in Utrecht, and a painter more associated with portraiture than other types of picture. It was common in the 16th and 17th centuries for portrait painters to make preliminary sketches of sitters and their settings, although not all did so consistently. The function of these drawings of a likeness was quite different from compositional drawings for multi-figure religious, history or genre scenes, where the relationships in space and the interactions of figures are usually the essential elements to explore. Linear designs were sometimes also completed in washes and white highlights to plan the intended play of light in the composition.

On his arrival in Rome, Baburen, perhaps not even 20 years old, might well have felt ill-equipped to join the crowd of creators of new Baroque pictures, large in scale, and populated with many figures. Baburen was clearly an accomplished painter, however, since with his countryman David de Haen, who had also been in Rome from an early age, the two received a significant commission finished in 1617 to paint a scheme of several works for the Pietà Chapel of San Pietro in Montorio of which his *Entombment* (fig. 66) was both the centrepiece and subsequently the best known. This picture derives partly, but definitively, from Caravaggio's *Entombment of Christ* (cat. 22), originally in the Chiesa Nuova and therefore publicly available. Based on the design of certain of Baburen's autograph works, we can conjecture that he among the Utrecht painters in Rome was necessarily most compelled by Caravaggio's use of life models to hold poses that were otherwise difficult to capture. The figure of the partly slumped body of Christ in the San Pietro in Montorio *Entombment* would surely have been created in this way, with the place of the stone block on which

Christ rests taken by a studio prop acting as support for the model. In the same way, the collapsing body of the wounded saint in the Thyssen composition of *St Sebastian attended by St Irene and her Maid* (fig. 41)[13] has the appearance of a real model in the studio represented virtually life-size, with diffuse directional lighting from the left. In this picture there is a reserve in the composition for the figure of the saint, most evident at the junction of his loincloth with the background, a feature also indicative of the use of a live model at the centre.

In Baburen's large-scale *Chaining of Prometheus* (cat. 54), produced after his return to Utrecht, from their disposition it seems reasonable to propose that the two main life-size figures of Vulcan and Prometheus were very likely posed by models. These poses hark back to Caravaggio more strongly than in other works by Baburen, and the supine figure of Prometheus was recycled by him in a depiction of a *Flaying of Marsyas* (fig. 92).[14] This latter picture departs from an entirely Caravaggesque concept through the use of a strong Mannerist mauve colour for Apollo's drapery and a directional, somewhat flattened lighting scheme. In the *Chaining of Prometheus*, fluid outlines of both black and dark brown, which can be interpreted as underdrawing, are easily visible at the surface, and mark out Prometheus's limbs, his proper right wrist and upper torso, and the front edge of Vulcan's proper left leg particularly below the knee where the paint may also have been scored, emphasising the line.[15]

It was discovered by Matteo Marangoni in 1922 that an essential part of Caravaggio's method of composing a group scene was to make a series of visible incisions in the ground or paint layers of the developing composition,[16] the function of which may well have been for the painter to record or adjust the positions of his models, their heads, limbs and so on, between sittings. These incisions were also used to indicate the intended placing of other features of a complex arrangement for the painting, and have now been documented comprehensively for a number of his works.[17] It is known for other Baroque painters to inscribe into wet paint to produce various effects: Rembrandt was the most prolific, but neither Rembrandt nor Caravaggio's Utrecht followers used incisions for the purposes of devising a composition.

We have little reliable information on ter Brugghen's output during his stay in Rome. The most important recent advance is Liesbeth Helmus's identification of the *Penitent St Peter* (cat. 3) as ter Brugghen's earliest autograph work,[18] and one for which technical study confirms an early 17th-century origin, whether it was produced in Rome or fairly immediately on his return to the North.[19] Through the observations that have been made on this picture, there is a chance that other unidentified early works may come to light in future. In the absence of others of his pictures from the period to study at present, a broader assessment of technique can be gained for ter Brugghen's somewhat later production sometime after his return to Utrecht by 1615.

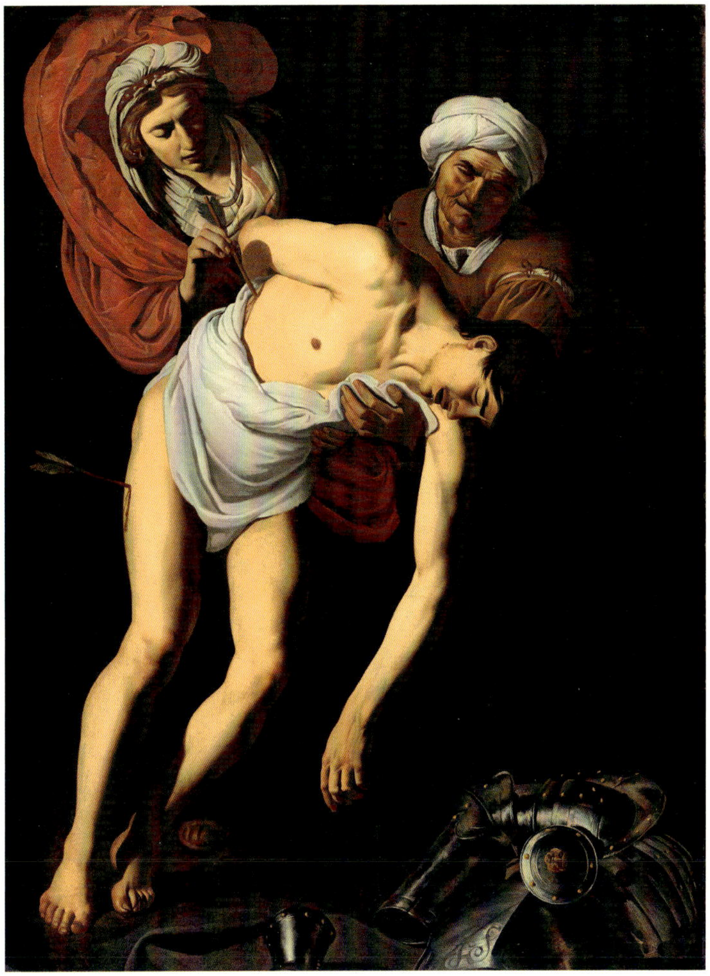

Fig. 41 Dirck van Baburen or David de Haen, *St Sebastian attended by St Irene and her Maid*, c. 1615/21, Museo Nacional Thyssen-Bornemisza, Madrid

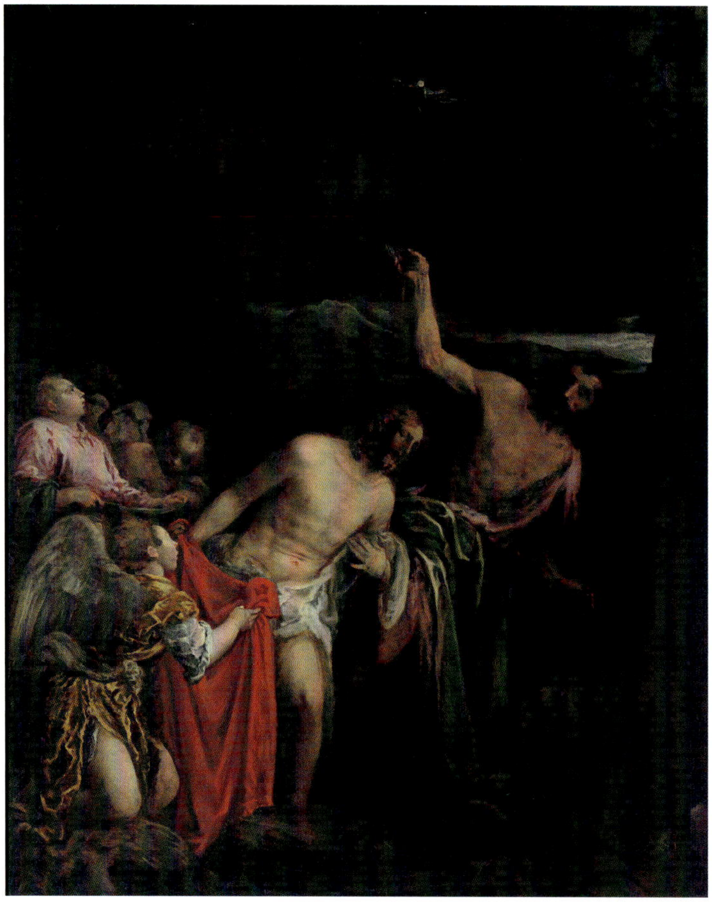

Fig. 42 Jacopo da Ponte, called Bassano, *The Baptism of Christ*, c. 1590, The Metropolitan Museum of Art, New York. Partial and Promised Gift of Mr. and Mrs. Mark Fisch, 2012

The more complex, multi-figure compositions in ter Brugghen's work do not hint at the use of posed models, neither does his approach to lighting their action. With the exception of candle-lit scenes or the few late, more explicitly Caravaggesque pictures such as *The Denial of St Peter* in Chicago[20] and the London *Concert* of c. 1626/27 (cat. 67), the adoption of an un-Caravaggesque, softer, more Mannerist colour requires for its decorative effects a less stark transition in light and shade. This can be seen in the two versions of *The Calling of St Matthew* now in Le Havre (fig. 79) and Utrecht (cat. 36). *The Incredulity of St Thomas* (cat. 47) lies squarely between these two divergent tendencies in ter Brugghen's art, and in its planning shows features such as outline dark underdrawing, for example for Christ's head, shoulder and hands, and the edges of draperies. The overall palette of the picture, with yellows made by combining ochre and yellow lake, and a strong dark green drapery incorporating deep green earth pigment, is both muted and full of contrast, corresponding to the almost frontal direction of light in the picture.[21]

At this time, the older practice of using large multi-member wood panels for paintings was rapidly diminishing in favour of the more versatile and ultimately more durable canvas supports. Canvases were also considerably cheaper to construct, transport and adapt to particular contexts of display, especially where architectural settings were the intended destination. Caravaggio's Contarelli Chapel paintings are a good case in point, both in terms of scale and of the relationship to the decorative, coloured marble framing arrangement in each of the three walls of the ensemble into which they fit rather imprecisely. Baburen's *Entombment* in San Pietro in Montorio is a smaller-scale example.

This is not to say that wood panels were ruled out entirely, and there were important, widely known earlier works available for painters to study, including for example Raphael's monumental 'Transfiguration' altarpiece on cherry-wood planks,[22] over four metres tall as the high altar of San Pietro in Montorio. Caravaggio had worked on panel on a very few occasions, although apparently unsuccessfully in the case of the Cerasi Chapel paintings for which cypress wood panels had been supplied for his use in the first versions and were part of the contract; these were later substituted by canvas.[23] His one surviving panel is the *David with the Head of Goliath* now in Vienna.[24] No autograph painting by Baburen on panel has been identified, and only two by ter Brugghen are known, of which the *Sleeping Mars* (fig. 10) in Utrecht[25] is the most iconic.

By roughly the third decade of the 16th century, particularly for canvas painting, but also for other surfaces, it was increasingly common to apply a coloured or tinted ground to the support, usually of some shade of grey or greyish brown, becoming somewhat darker as the century progressed. The tendency towards darker grounds as time passed can be seen in the work of Titian and Tintoretto, who is known to have applied 'palette scraping' mixtures to canvases. Jacopo Bassano, painting in the Veneto, had notably developed some profoundly dark oil grounds to provide a basis for the nocturnal scenes of the type culminating in the late *Baptism of Christ* in the Metropolitan Museum (fig. 42), for which the Bassani had become popular and influential exponents.[26]

One strong influence in the development of coloured and darker grounds for easel painting arose from the Carracci, 'Accademia degli Incamminati' in Bologna, in which the new basis for theoretical teaching in art was to overturn what was perceived as the dead-end of Mannerist thinking and expression.[27] In this case, the use of red-brown and darker grounds owed its origin to an improved, that is to say more naturalistic, method of constructing thc illusion of volume in space, particularly when applied to the human figure. It understood that the appearance of three-dimensionality was as much to do with absorption of light creating shadow on the painted surface as with the reflection of light functioning to project forwards an object or an element of the human figure. To appreciate the kind of colour and tonality recommended for the ground on canvas, Annibale Carracci's *Boy Drinking*, where a dark brown ground is exposed in several parts of the picture, or his unfinished *Self-portrait* in the Uffizi (fig. 43), are interesting examples.[28] In the *Self-portrait*, much of the background is simply the unpainted, brownish-red ground layer.

To start on a dark ground and develop lighter paints on top could be said to be a fundamental tenet of the Baroque method, since in its expression at the limits to which it could be pushed it created the most dramatic impressions Caravaggio's paintings made on their beholders from the mid-1590s. This was almost certainly the underlying visual message that so influenced those painters who came to Rome in Caravaggio's wake, and who must have immediately known an importantly radical invention when they saw it. If that is correct, it was the appearance of the paintings, rather than their intrinsic technique, that was the significant aspect a painter should seek to emulate, and this would explain why the painting techniques as developed in Rome by Baburen, Honthorst and, we might presume, ter Brugghen, are essentially their own and adapted to their particular ends. As an example of this, ter Brugghen's *Penitent St Peter* (cat. 3) is painted on a double ground, the upper layer of which is a light brownish-grey tone. This method of grounding a canvas may well hark back to the technique of his earlier training in the North.

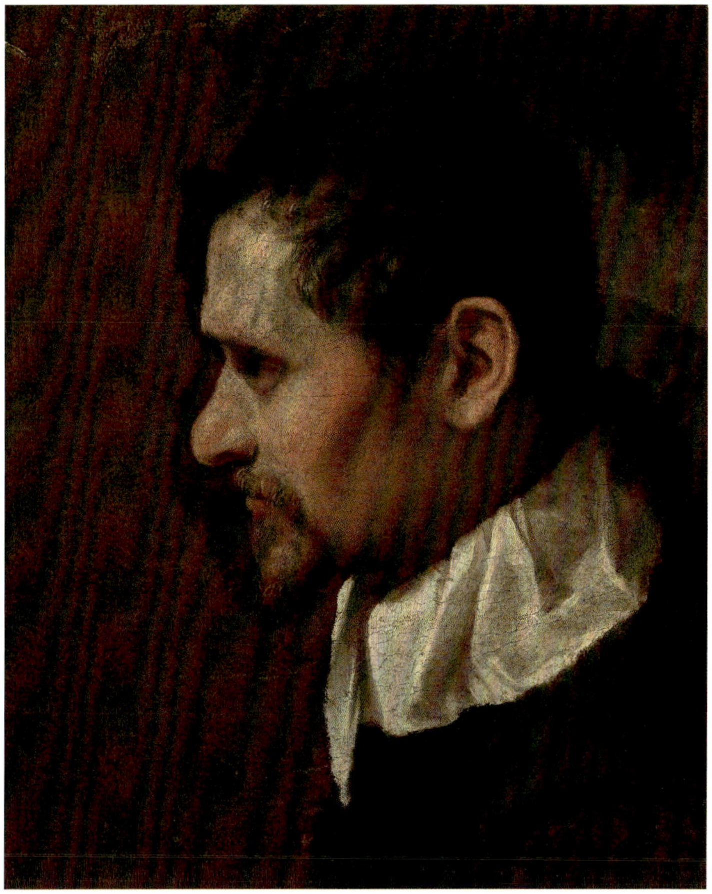

Fig. 43 Annibale Carracci, *Self-Portrait*, c. 1590, Galleria degli Uffizi, Florence

In Caravaggio's own practice, his exposure before Rome to Lombard traditions had resulted in the adoption of light-grey or mid-grey grounds on canvas, composed largely of lead white and charcoal. One example is the *Boy Peeling Fruit* in the Royal Collection in Britain,[29] of c. 1592/1593, now identified by many art historians as Caravaggio's earliest work, which has a middle-tone, brownish-grey ground. Other works from the first half of the 1590s, *The Fortune Teller* (cat. 73) and *The Cardsharps* (fig. 89), are similar.[30] These are all pictures in which the use of light is relatively diffuse and frontal – 'tempered shadows' in Bellori's words[31] – although generally with a bias from the left. No part of any figure is cast into the deepest kind of contrasting shadow. By the time Caravaggio came to paint the London *Boy Bitten by a Lizard*,[32]

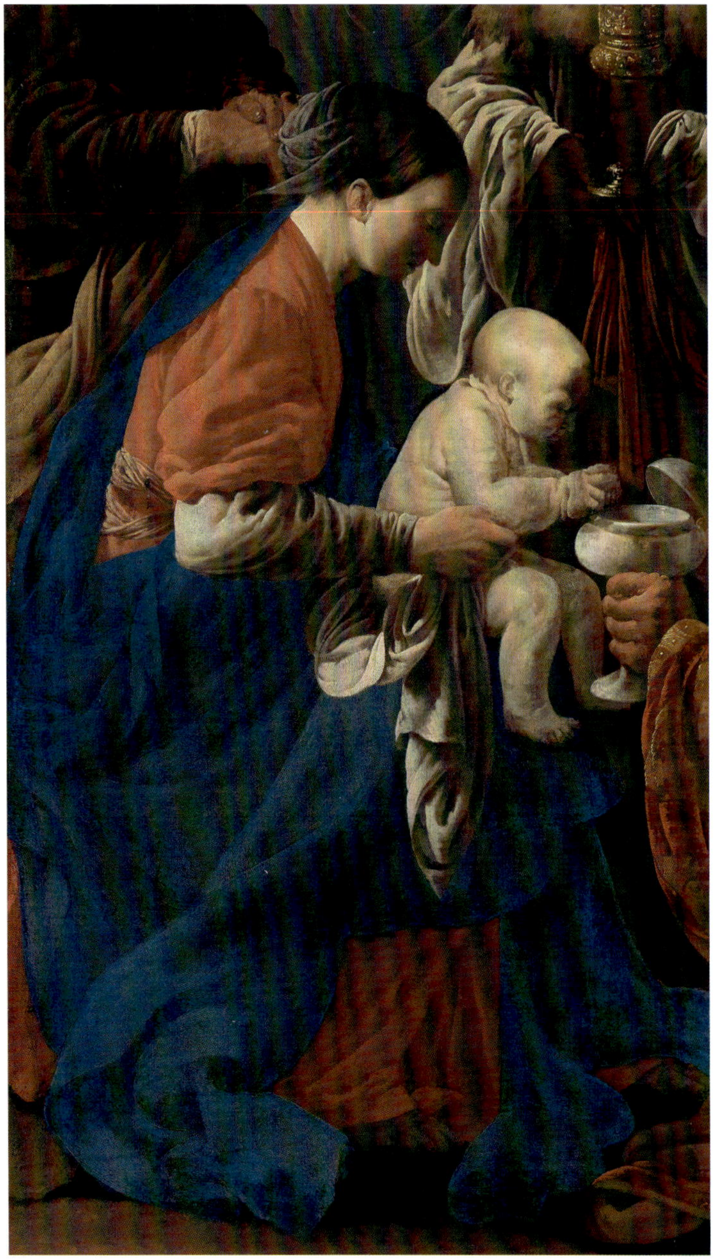

Fig. 44 Hendrick ter Brugghen, *The Adoration of the Kings* (detail), 1619, Rijksmuseum, Amsterdam

he primed the canvas with a mid-brownish, single ground composed of natural earth pigments with calcite and silica and a small amount of white.[33] It is this layer (and colour) that, with great economy of technique, is left uncovered to represent the mid-tones and shadows of the flesh paint, and became a key method Caravaggio continued to use in the development of much larger compositions with multiple figures. It is a way of painting that can be used to create the strongest contrasts of light and shade with scarcely any reliance on gradual transitions, and works equally well for other compositional elements such as light and shadow values in draperies, interior architectural details, still life and so on.

Caravaggio's later canvas grounds were often very dark and cool in tone, and even after he left Rome this seems to have become a consistent method, although the precise constitutions, thicknesses and textures were very varied. In some cases, the upper layer of two dark brown applications was rendered even darker by a finishing layer containing much black pigment, a method used as early as the Contarelli Chapel commission.[34] When we consider the equivalent grounding procedures chosen by the Utrecht Caravaggists in Rome and some of their Italian and French contemporaries, methods and colours as variable as Caravaggio's are found. But a great difference is an apparent reluctance among those directly influenced by Caravaggio boldly to leave uncovered areas of brown or grey-brown ground as he had done, without surface modification provided by any superimposed thin layer of paint. Among those who came closest to Caravaggio's radical and simplified method were Manfredi, Valentin and Ribera, who in their different ways understood and sought to continue the core of Caravaggio's innovations into the 1620s. For Valentin and Ribera, and also in works by Manfredi, where the dark grounds are used as a conscious element of the intended colour composition, they are almost always modified by a final thin scumble of grey, brown or black paint. Stronger colours in areas of drapery painting are used, through which the ground colour remains discernible.[35] There may well have been concerns in the minds of these painters that they would face criticism for producing works unflatteringly categorised as *non finito*, and that this would detract from their intended high reputations and professional standing on which they hoped to trade.

It was more common to cover the ground completely with the design layers of paint, while making important use of the colour of the canvas priming to influence the overall tone of the picture and its lighting effect. A good case is Honthorst's *Christ before the High Priest* (cat. 19), which has a single, thick, red-brown ground of earth pigments providing depth and warmth to the whole composition, whose colour is modified by thin layers of semi-translucent and more opaque paints, but is nowhere fully exposed.[36]

Hendrik ter Brugghen is known to have returned from Italy to Utrecht by 1615, and although the first secure picture attributed to him has been traditionally the *Adoration of the Magi* signed and dated 1619 (fig. 44),[37] the *Penitent St Peter* (cat. 3) is earlier and can be related in the manner of painting of the saint's head to that of the kneeling king of the larger, later work.[38] This *Adoration* shows a decisive break and obvious shift in interest from the artist's Roman exposure, and is remarkable not for its return to Mannerism but for its archaic appearance, which owes more to the 16th century than to the 17th and includes the traditional use of a strong, bright blue for the Virgin's drapery. It has been discovered by technical study that the canvas was prepared with a double ground consisting first of a layer of dark brown containing brown and black pigments followed a layer of red iron oxide with chalk.[39]

The majority of ter Brugghen's paintings that have been examined, and indeed other paintings in Utrecht from the 1620s, have canvases primed with a general form of double ground in which the exact constituents and colour of each layer varied. This relatively consistent priming system was common in the Netherlands and elsewhere in Northern Europe, including in France and England. Current thinking is that this practice may well relate to the availability to the studios of ready-grounded canvases, with both layers in place, produced by professional primers as commercial artists' suppliers. The method must have been widely known and no doubt was also adopted within the workshop by apprentices and assistants.

For ter Brugghen's canvases, the double ground system is common until the end of his career, including in the very late *Liberation of St Peter* in Schwerin (cat. 14).[40] The lower ground layer is usually some combination of red or red-brown ochreous mixture, while the upper layer is generally lighter in colour although often varied in tone from warm dull reds and mid-browns to shades of mid-grey and greyish brown. We may assume that the upper ground, the actual colour onto which ter Brugghen laid his compositions, was chosen to influence the finished appearance of the picture, its tonality, mood and lighting. As examples, the upper ground layer is brownish grey in *The Calling of St Matthew* (cat. 36), a mid-grey colour, with a second warm imprimatura on top in *A Man Playing a Lute*,[41] a mid- to dark brown colour in *The Rich Man and the Poor Lazarus* (cat. 75) and a strong greenish-brown tone in *Jacob Reproaching Laban*.[42]

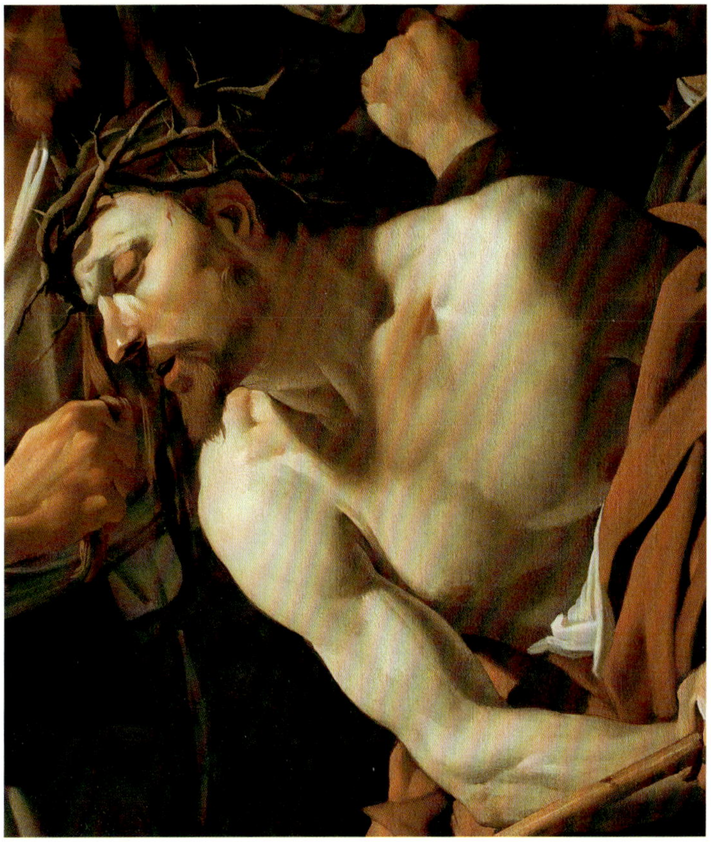

Fig. 45 Dirck van Baburen, *Crowning with Thorns* (detail), c. 1621/22, Museum Catharijneconvent, Utrecht (cat. 41)

From close assessment of Caravaggio's painting practice, it is evident that his manner of painting figures, particularly the depiction of uncovered human flesh, was unusually straightforward, assured and unlaboured. His characteristic method of working up highlight values directly over a dark brown canvas priming, where relatively exposed ground was left to stand

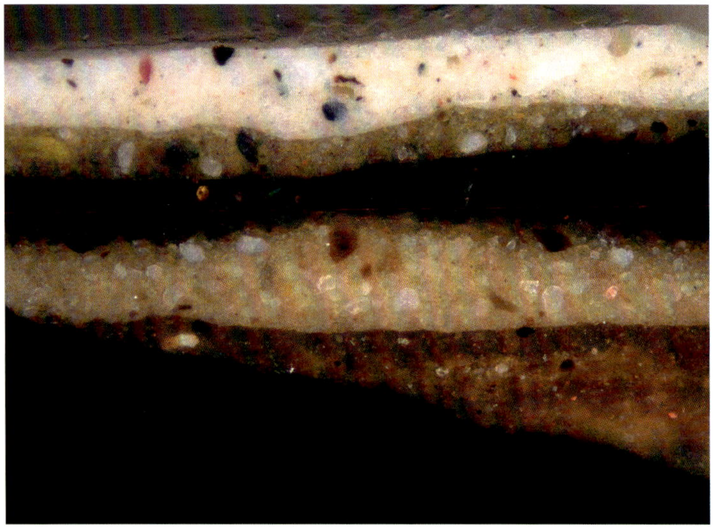

Fig. 46 Gerard van Honthorst, *St Sebastian* (cat. 68), paint cross-section showing dark underlayers for the saint's light-coloured surface flesh paint

for the deepest shadows, was both a highly effective and economical method. It required though a rare bravura confidence. The sharp contrasts between light and deepest shadow in the painting of the heads of his figures and in their bodies was used to strikingly recognisable effect throughout Caravaggio's career. Late large pictures such as the *The Raising of Lazarus*,[43] exemplify this flesh painting technique at its most fully developed, but it occurs in smaller earlier works, including those of single figures from around the mid-1590s such as the *Boy Bitten by a Lizard* in London.

Even for their Roman works, Caravaggio's followers tended to employ different methods of painting flesh; that is certainly the case for the Utrecht painters. Theirs must have been conscious planning, since it would have been fairly straightforward for a trained painter to understand Caravaggio's core method by direct scrutiny of his pictures, without explanatory instruction or written guidance. The choice of a more individualistic approach to depicting figures, their flesh particularly, must lie in a differing concept and formula of the lighting in paintings, flowing from an interest in portraying interior scenes distinctively. This most often involved a number of figures illuminated by artificial light. Neither Baburen nor Honthorst attempted in their painting of heads and figures to exploit so starkly Caravaggio's theatrically overemphasised deep shadow set against projected highlight, where there was barely any transitional mid-tone; instead their modelling was rather softer, and in general became more distinctive as their painterly individuality developed away from Rome. That is, their approach was always more Leonardesque, or Giorgionesque in concept, even early on, as in St Peter's head and beard in ter Brugghen's *Penitent St Peter* (cat. 3). In Baburen's *Christ Crowned with Thorns* of 1621/22 (cat. 41), for example, there is strong treatment of light and shadow in the figures, but the solidly painted highlighted and mid-tones predominate and, crucially, the shadow areas can be seen as worked over lighter flesh paints (fig. 45). These paints are dense and smoothly brushed out, a way of working that is confirmed in X-ray images, where these have been recorded.[44]

In contradistinction to Caravaggio's inventive method for flesh paint, his near contemporaries, seeking a tempered Caravaggesque effect, often seem to have applied a separate device to create solidity and modelling for figures. This involved underpainting areas of flesh with a cool dark greyish or brownish-grey paint over a dark ground, which lent a cool tone and darkened the lighter flesh tones on top. It seems likely also, that this underlayer may have been a modelled semi-monochrome layer, according to the procedure of creating a 'dead-coloured' stage of underpainting as described in treatises somewhat later – by Sandrart, for example.[45] The technique is effective and convincing for portraying a living being, but works with particularly gruesome effect when the body of the dead Christ or that of a martyred saint is represented. An additional technique to suggest morbidity was ter Brugghen's incorporation of green pigment into the flesh tones of the crucified Christ[46] or the dead body of St Sebastian. In his early work, interestingly, the saint's head in ter Brugghen's *Penitent St Peter* employs some green undermodelling in the shadows.[47] Honthorst's rather solidly modelled, evenly lit *St Sebastian* in London (cat. 68) has an extensive very dark brown underpaint beneath the flesh of the slumped body (fig. 46), and both Ribera and Valentin used similar techniques for their depictions of flesh, as in Ribera's early *St Jerome writing*,[48] a technique he continued to use over the next two decades. Dark underlayers for flesh paint are present in the two versions of Valentin's *Christ Crowned with Thorns* in Munich (cat. 44, fig. 47).[49]

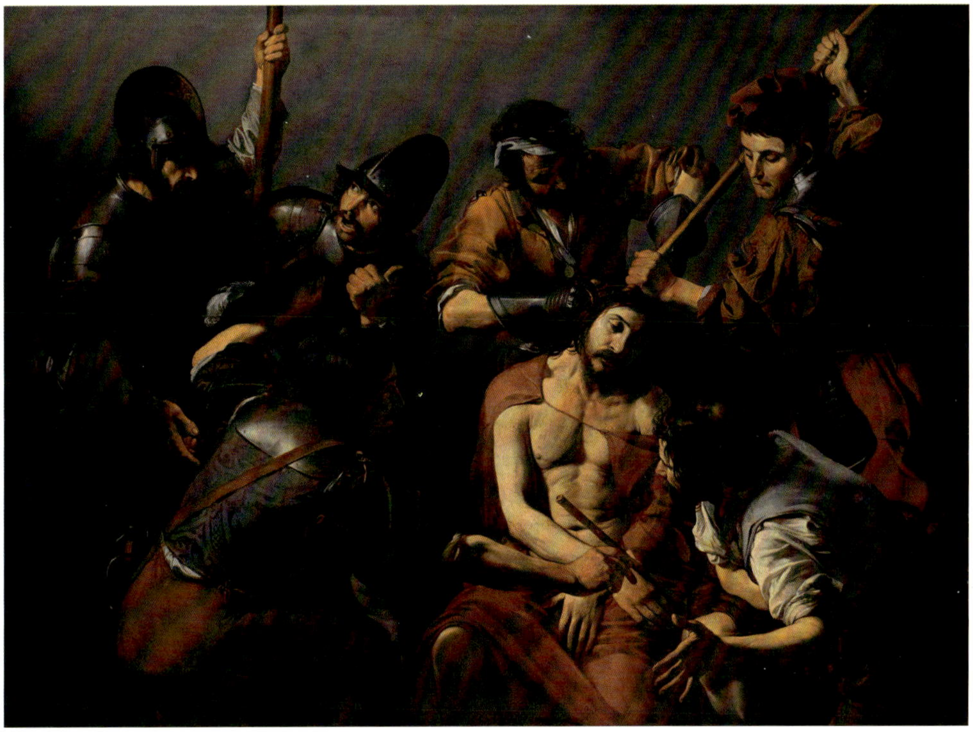

Fig. 47 Valentin de Boulogne, *The Crowning with Thorns*, c. 1627/28, Bayerische Staatsgemäldesammlungen, Alte Pinakothek, Munich

No picture by Caravaggio involves an artificial light source such as a candle or flare. For Honthorst and the others by contrast, candlelight or sometimes a flaming torch was a characterising compositional tool often used to illuminate the scene. Usually the source of light was explicit to the viewer, although sometimes it was implied as an effulgence from a flame, hidden in some way by a participant in the action or by an object. The choice of an artificial light source or sources has two fundamental consequences for the painter: representation in paint of the play of this type of light, less directional and less diffuse than daylight, over the faces and bodies of those depicted, and the way in which strong colour in draperies, for example, responds to candlelight, the actual physics and optics of which is unforgiving for any fully decorative effect. Few painters bothered with physical reality in this latter regard, generally suggesting that candlelight can illuminate and therefore represent effectively the very rich colours of dyed and patterned fabrics of draperies.[50] Ter Brugghen's *Esau Selling His Birthright* (cat. 77) lit by a single central candle flame is a good example.

Colour was more important to the Utrecht painters than it had ever been to Caravaggio after certain of his earlier works painted before about 1598; and later in their careers it became even more so. In some isolated pictures, such as the London *Supper at Emmaus* (fig. 69) and the *Madonna of the Rosary* in Vienna,[51] he made use of a wider palette than is generally associated with the post-1598 paintings. Caravaggio's restricted palette, however, can have had nothing to do with a lack in availability of a great range of artists' materials in 17th-century Rome (or elsewhere in Italy) since, as might be expected for any major centre for the production of art, the trade in materials was well established there. With certain exceptions involving local production, supply or specific tradition, the range of the artists' palette for easel painting had been largely standardised by the 17th century through pan-European trade, and few genuinely new colour materials had been introduced in the previous 200 years. An exception was the growing popularity of smalt (a blue cobalt glass pigment) both north and south of the Alps. The use of natural ultramarine was in decline (except for its valuable role in the skies of southern

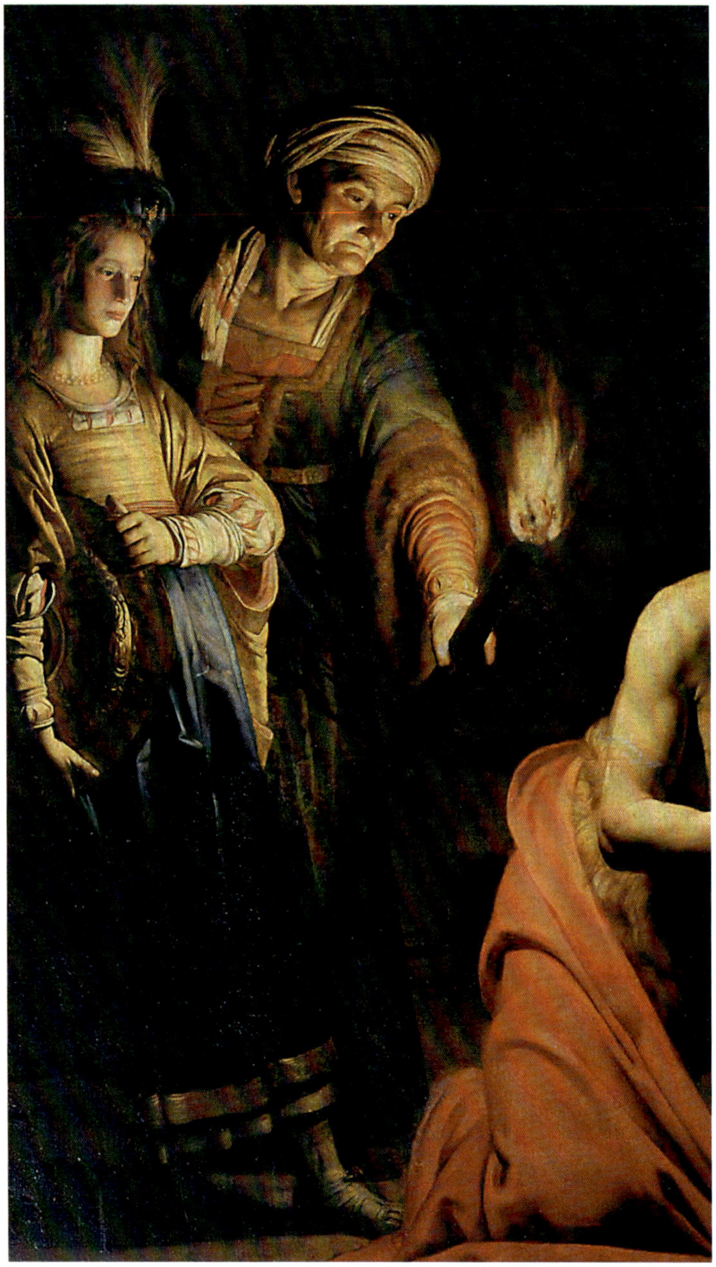

Fig. 48 Gerard van Honthorst, *Beheading of John the Baptist* (detail), 1617/18, Santa Maria della Scala, Rome (cat. 20)

landscapes), probably as much for its unfashionably vivid colour as its high cost, but it was clearly available in Rome, if the extensive use of ultramarine in Guercino's vast canvas painting of the *Burial of St Petronilla* for St Peter's is anything to go by.[52] On a smaller scale, in a Caravaggesque picture, Simon Vouet's portrayal of *Judith* (cat. 64) shows her in a rich blue elaborate satin dress, painted in natural ultramarine, the colour of which is accentuated in the shadows by an underpaint of black.[53] In more conventional mode, for Honthorst's *Beheading of John the Baptist* ultramarine was used for Salome's blue dress (cat. 20, fig. 48).[54]

Apart from smalt, the other common blue in Baroque easel painting continued to be natural mineral azurite, certainly used by Caravaggio in that smaller proportion of his pictures that contains blue of any kind. In these examples, the pigment often becomes very dark in tone, as it was known to do when used relatively pure in an oil binder. A good example is the darkened greenish tone developed by St Peter's azurite cloak in ter Brugghen's *Penitent St Peter* (cat. 3).[55]

For the majority of Caravaggio's works his palette is dominated by rather few colours, and therefore seems to consist of a fairly selective range of materials: black pigments, lead white, the brilliant strident opaque red of vermilion (a favourite of this painter), and a variety of natural earth colours of yellow, brown, dull red and dull orange, these last being important staples for any type of dark passage in a painting. In that context, a picture such as Honthorst's *Christ before the High Priest* (cat. 19) typifies just this form of palette over a warm dark ground.[56] Where a greater range of colour or a higher key was required, painters had access to, and could rely on, manufactured types of lead-tin yellow or lead-tin-antimony yellow (each probably by-products of the ceramics industry),[57] green earth, natural malachite and manufactured copper-based greens such as verdigris.[58]

In addition, there were available a considerable variety of so-called 'lake pigments', natural dyestuff-based pigments most commonly of red, but also yellow intense colours for glazing and mixing.[59] The natural translucency of red lakes in oil is very evident, for example, in the deep red sleeve of the angel in ter Brugghen's *Liberation of St Peter* in The Hague (cat. 13).[60] As a standard part of the palette there are many other cases, and red lakes in particular were commonly used to form the delicate pinks and mauves favoured by ter Brugghen and Honthorst in their rather later works from Utrecht, for example ter Brugghen's *Calling of St Matthew* (cat. 36), in which red lakes are present in tint with white pigment (and blue) for its distinctive pastel tones. Similar effects can be seen in Honthorst's *Concert* of 1623 (cat. 66), which employs bright nearly frontal general illumination, of no explicit source, to emphasise the wide range of clear decorative and contrasting colour which is such a strikingly un-Caravaggesque element of the picture and equally very different from Honthorst's manner of painting of this type of scene in his Roman years. The Washington painting has a warm brown ground, but the overlying paint is so substantial, including the majority of the passages of flesh painting, that the influence of the ground colour is greatly subdued to the point of near invisibility.[61]

It is worth noting that the Baroque palette just described contains pigments that can be unstable. Lake pigments, whether red or yellow, are subject to fading under the influence of light,[62] but where thickly applied as a glaze the reds can hold up extremely well, as in the red velvet doublet of the central male figure in Honthorst's *Procuress* of 1625 (cat. 72). Blues are vulnerable too: azurite can become discoloured and blackish in the oil medium, while smalt can lose its blue colour sometimes substantially, or cause paint films containing the pigment to become brownish or greyish.[63] An extreme case recently discovered is of the formerly blue stripes (now virtually pale grey-green) on the sleeve of ter Brugghen's late image of a *Man with a Tankard* in Munich.[64] Natural ultramarine, prized for its immutability, can lose its colour almost entirely in particular circumstances, a phenomenon known as ultramarine sickness.[65] Other pigments in regular use in this period, including lead white, all of the black pigments,[66] natural earths, vermilion and lead-tin yellow, are generally stable in oil medium, and so the relative colour shifts that can take place over time are between the appearance of these stable materials and the lakes and certain blues. It is always essential, therefore, to bear in mind the possibility of colour change when assessing or interpreting any easel picture of the period, and that applies as much to Caravaggio as to his followers.

Although the work of ter Brugghen, Baburen and Honthorst diverged further in many ways on their return to Utrecht, each of the painters developed the theme of single half-length figure canvases of musicians, drinkers, philosophers and so on. By the time they painted this form of picture, ter Brugghen, Baburen and Honthorst had abandoned the Roman Baroque method of painting over a single dark ground, and instead generally prepared their canvases with double grounds in a way that had become standard in the Netherlands. This was a radical change of technique. The influence of the upper ground layer colour is often evident in the backgrounds of the paintings warming up the general tone, as in for example the London *Lute Player* by ter Brugghen.[67]

It remains a commonplace in collections around the world that where the works of ter Brugghen, Honthorst and Baburen are on display, the picture labels invariably mention their singular debt to Caravaggio, or their description as examples of Caravaggism. This may be historically unavoidable, but for all those who would wish to appreciate the more distinctive achievements of these significant and creative painters, it is always worthwhile putting to one side for a moment what is usually expected from Caravaggio's revolutionary genius. We can then assess more coolly and fairly the very different and original works the Utrecht painters created, not least in the undeniably advanced technical skills they developed to achieve their desired and varied visions.

Acknowledgements
I would like to express particular thanks to the following colleagues, each leading experts in the technical study of paintings, for their most generous and unstinting help in providing information on, and interpretation of, works included in the essay: Gwen Tauber of the Rijksmuseum, Amsterdam; Heike Stege at the Doerner Institut, Munich; and Melanie Gifford at the National Gallery of Art, Washington D.C.

1 X-radiographs of paintings by Caravaggio frequently show major changes of composition during the course of painting, one of the most dramatic of which is the double reworking of earlier compositions for the *Martyrdom of St Matthew* for the right-hand wall of the Contarelli Chapel (fig. 17). See Zuccari 2016.
2 Some sense of the widely inclusive nature of early Caravaggio attributions can be gained from Witting 1916.
3 Roy 2012.
4 Some first results of the examination of paintings by Caravaggio using multispectral IR-reflectography (NIR multispectral imaging) were published in 2012. See Bellucci/Frosinini 2012. Conventional infrared images have been published by Vodret et al. 2016, vol. 1, as 'Comparative Plates: Diagrams of Incisions, IR-Reflectograms and X-Radiographs', pp. 248–253.
5 Baglione 1642, p. 164.
6 Christiansen 2016/17. Christiansen also clarifies the meaning of the contemporary term 'dal naturale', see note 6, p. 244.
7 '[...] since it is impossible to put in one room a multitude of people acting out a story, with that light coming in from a single window [...]. As a result the figures, though they look forceful, lack movement, expression and grace'. Translated from G. Mancini, 'Considerazioni sulla pittura' (c. 1617–21) in Hibbard 1983, p. 350.
8 'Tanto che li pittori all'hora, [...] e particolarmente li giovini [...] celebravano lui solo, come unico imitatore della natura, e come miracoli, mirando l'opere sue, lo seguitavano à gara, spogliando modelli, & alzando lumi...' Bellori 1672, p. 205.
9 Underdrawing with IRR or the naked eye has been detected in a number of Ter Brugghen's works such as *The Incredulity of St Thomas* (cat. 47), *The Calling of St Matthew* (cat. 36), *The Rich Man and Poor Lazarus* (cat. 75), and *The Concert* (cat. 67). Melanie Gifford, Research Conservator for Painting Technology, and Douglas Lachance, Paintings Conservation Technician, National Gallery of Art in Washington, kindly supplied information on underdrawing and an unpublished IRR image for *The Bagpipe Player* (1624, canvas, 100.7 × 82.9 cm, National Gallery of Art, Washington, D.C., inv. 2009.24.1).
10 A number of examples are reproduced in van der Sman 2015.
11 See van der Sman 2015, p. 105, fig. 3, for a drawing squared around the periphery.
12 1622, canvas, 132.8 × 196.5 cm, Bayerische Staatsgemäldesammlungen, Alte Pinakothek, Munich, inv. 1312.
13 c. 1615/21, canvas, 169 × 128 cm, Museo Nacional Thyssen-Bornemisza, Madrid, inv. 347 (1986.4).
14 See Franits 2013a, pp. 162–164, cat. A34.
15 Faint or stronger underdrawing in dark paint outlining the edges of figures is found in several works by Baburen. I am most grateful to Gwen Tauber, Senior Painting Conservator, Rijksmuseum, for her generous sharing of unpublished technical information on a number of relevant paintings in the Rijksmuseum Collection. Incisions in surface paint are far less common, although these have been noted in neck of the violin and elsewhere on Baburen's Caravaggesque *Concert* (1623, canvas, 105.4 × 133.3, Detroit Institute of Arts, Detroit, inv. 2017). See Franits 2013a, pp. 164–165, cat. A35; p. 165, no. 3; p. 267, pl. XV.
16 See Marangoni 1922.
17 Clear schematic diagrams of Caravaggio's compositional incisions for 17 Roman paintings, and four others are available in Vodret et al. 2016, vol. 1, as 'Comparative Plates: Diagrams of Incisions', pp. 248–253.
18 Helmus 2009; Helmus 2004.
19 Laurent Sozzani and Eneida C. Parreira, 'Examination and Treatment Report', 1 June 2004, Centraal Museum archives, unpublished. The use of a double ground on the canvas was shown to consist first of a reddish (ochreous layer), with a warm tone of grey over this. Azurite was found to be the main pigment of Saint Peter's cloak.
20 c. 1626/29, canvas, 132.3 × 178 cm, The Art Institute, Chicago, inv. 1969.3.
21 A short description of the palette of the picture is included in Cat. Amsterdam 2007, vol. 1, p. 92.
22 1516/20, panel, 410 × 279 cm, Pinacoteca Vaticana, Vatican City, inv. 40333.
23 The earlier version of *The Conversion of St Paul* (now Rome, Odescalchi Collection) was on cypress wood; see Robertson 2015, p. 272. An X-radiograph shows the structure of this panel as made up of a number of horizontal boards; see Vodret et al. 2016, p. 258, fig. LXII.
24 c. 1606/07, panel, 91.2 × 116.2 cm, Kunsthistorisches Museum, Vienna, inv. Gemäldegalerie 125.
25 1629, panel, 106.5 × 92.8 cm, Centraal Museum, Utrecht, inv. 5460.
26 The development of Titian's grounds is discussed in Dunkerton et al. 2015, pp. 6–39. The discovery of dark grounds composed of recycled paint mixed with further drying oil in works by Tintoretto is noted in Plesters 1980, pp. 36–37, 39. The Jacopo Bassano, *Baptism of Christ*, c. 1590, canvas, 191 × 160.3 cm, Metropolitan Museum of Art, New York, Acc. Nr. 2012.99, is regarded as unfinished, which emphasises the influence of the dark ground even more strongly.
27 Initially called 'Accademia delli Desiderosi', the name was changed to 'Incamminati' in the 1590s. See Robertson 2008, pp. 68–96.
28 *Self-Portrait in Profile*, c. 1590, canvas, 45.4 × 37.9 cm, Galleria degli Uffizi, Florence, inv. 1890, no. 1797. *Boy Drinking*, c. 1583, canvas, 75.5 × 64 cm, Christ Church Picture Gallery, University of Oxford, Oxford, inv. JBS180.
29 c. 1592/93, canvas, 63 × 53 cm, Royal Collection Trust, inv. RCIN 402612.
30 De Ruggieri 2016, pp. 107–111.
31 '[...] maniera di Giorgione, con oscuri temperati', Bellori 1672, p. 204.
32 c. 1595/96, canvas, 66 × 49.5 cm, The National Gallery, London, inv. NG6504.
33 Keith 2012, pp. 24–25.
34 It has been shown for the later paintings that the ground preparations became quite varied in constitution and texture, but remained largely in shades of dark brown. Their precise constitution was varied in their components, thickness and texture. See for example Falcucci 2012, p. 32, 36; Ciatti/Lalli 2012, pp. 15–16.
35 For example, Valentin's *Christ Crowned with Thorns* (cat. 44) and *Christ Driving the Money Changers from the Temple* (cat. 38).
36 See Roy 2012, pp. 87–88.
37 Canvas, 132.5 × 160.5 cm, Rijksmuseum, Amsterdam, inv. SK-A-4188.
38 Helmus 2009, pp. 58–61.
39 A double ground on canvas (and other painting materials) are described in Cat. Amsterdam 2007, vol. 1, p. 90. The Virgin's cloak is evidently intended to give the impression of a passage in natural ultramarine, in keeping with aspects of its archaic look. In this case the pigment is smalt and since it is mixed with lead white, it has kept its colour well.
40 Castro et al. 2009, pp. 183–184.
41 1624, canvas, 100.5 × 78.7 cm, The National Gallery, London, inv. NG6347.
42 *Jacob Reproaching Laban*, 1627, canvas, 97.5 × 114.3 cm, The National Gallery, London, inv. NG4164. Roy 2012, pp. 91–93. Samples from *The Rich Man and the Poor Lazarus* (cat. 75) were supplied by Laurent Sozzani, private restorer, Amsterdam; analysed by the present author.
43 c. 1609, canvas, 380 × 275 cm, Museo Regionale, Messina, inv. 984.
44 The X-radiograph of the *Christ among the Doctors* (cat. 45), for example, shows Baburen's later tendency to work his flesh tones containing much lead white quite evenly and solidly, particularly in those paintings with relatively frontal lighting, see Plahter/Plahter 1999, p. 46, fig. 6, pp. 50–51.
45 Sandrart 1675, vol. 1, book 3, p. 72.
46 Samples from ter Brugghen's *The Crucifixion of Christ with the Virgin and St John* (cat. 76) containing green pigment were taken by the late Joyce Plesters in 1980 and analysed by the present author in the Scientific Department of the National Gallery (unpublished).
47 Laurent Sozzani and Eneida C. Parreira, p. 4 (see note 19 above).
48 c. 1615, canvas, 131.5 × 98 cm, Museo del Prado, Madrid, inv. P005201.
49 For Honthorst's *St Sebastian* (cat. 68), see Roy 2012, pp. 88–89. Direct observations under the stereomicroscope by the present author and Jan Schmidt, Head of Conservation, Alte Pinakothek, Doerner Institut, Munich, of the 1627/28 upright version of Valentin's *Crowning with Thorns* revealed a dark underlayer, virtually uncovered, for Christ's flesh, which was also used consistently by the artist to emphasise the dark contours of Christ's limbs and body.
50 The burning flame of a wax candle or oil-lamp shows very little spectral

colour content below about 520 nm. There is a steadily rising curve peaking in the red part of the visible spectrum at 700 nm. Therefore, these artificial sources of illumination can only show, in physical reality, the warm colours of yellow, orange and red.
51 c. 1601, canvas, 364.5 × 249.5 cm, Kunsthistorisches Museum, Vienna, inv. GG 147.
52 1623, canvas, 720 × 423 cm, Pinacoteca Capitolina, Rome, inv. PC 140. Large areas of ultramarine are used in the blue draperies and sky of the picture.
53 Personal communication, Dr Elisabeth Hipp, Head of French and Spanish Painting, Alte Pinakothek, Munich.
54 It is evident from a 1617 document and payment relating to the commission that Honthorst used ultramarine in the drapery. Judson/Ekkart 1999, p. 71; catalogue entry by Liesbeth Helmus, *The Beheading of John the Baptist*, p. 144, note 4.
55 Laurent Sozzani and Eneida C. Parreira, p. 6 (see note 19 above).
56 Roy 2012, pp. 86–88.
57 Kühn 1993. See also Roy/Berrie 1998.
58 As an example of this general range of the Baroque palette, the following have been identified in Baburen's *Christ among the Doctors* (cat. 45): azurite, smalt, malachite(?), lead-tin yellow, vermilion, organic red (a lake), red and yellow ochres, lead white. See Plahter/Plahter 1999, pp. 47–48.
59 Kirby/van Bommel/Verhecken 2014.
60 A beautifully well-preserved passage of painting in red lake pigment for a contemporary picture may be found in the deep red *mozzetta* of *St Gregory the Great* by Ribera, c. 1612/15, canvas, 102 × 73 cm, Galleria Nazionale d'arte antica di Roma, Palazzo Barberini, Rome, inv. 0908 (F.N. 1217).
61 Unpublished information on the nature of the ground. Personal communication, Melanie Gifford, Research Conservator for Paintings Technology, National Gallery of Art, Washington, D.C.
62 Two types of red lake, based on cochineal and madder, have been identified in Christ's red drapery in Manfredi's *Crowning with Thorns* (cat. 42). Before the recent restoration, it appeared pale brownish due to severe fading. Personal communication, Dr Heike Stege, Head of Scientific Department, Doerner Institut, Munich, and Dr David Peggie, Scientific Department, The National Gallery, London. An example of fading of a yellow lake is provided by ter Brugghen's *Liberation of St Peter* (cat. 14). See Castro et al. 2009, pp. 11, 13.
63 Mühlethaler/Thissen 1993; Robinet et al. 2011.
64 1627, canvas, 71.3 × 60 cm, Bayerische Staatsgemäldesammlungen, Alte Pinakothek, Munich, inv. 4845. Smalt identified by XRF by Dr Heike Stege, Head of Scientific Department, Doerner Institut, Munich.
65 Klaas 2011. As an example, Valentin's *Christ Crowned with Thorns* (cat. 44) shows significant deterioration of ultramarine in the grey-blue sleeves of Christ's tormentor.
66 Sulphur-rich coal as a black pigment was identified in Manfredi's *Christ Crowned with Thorns* (cat. 42) by Dr Heike Stege, Head of Scientific Department, Doerner Institut, Munich.
67 See Roy 2012, pp. 91–93.

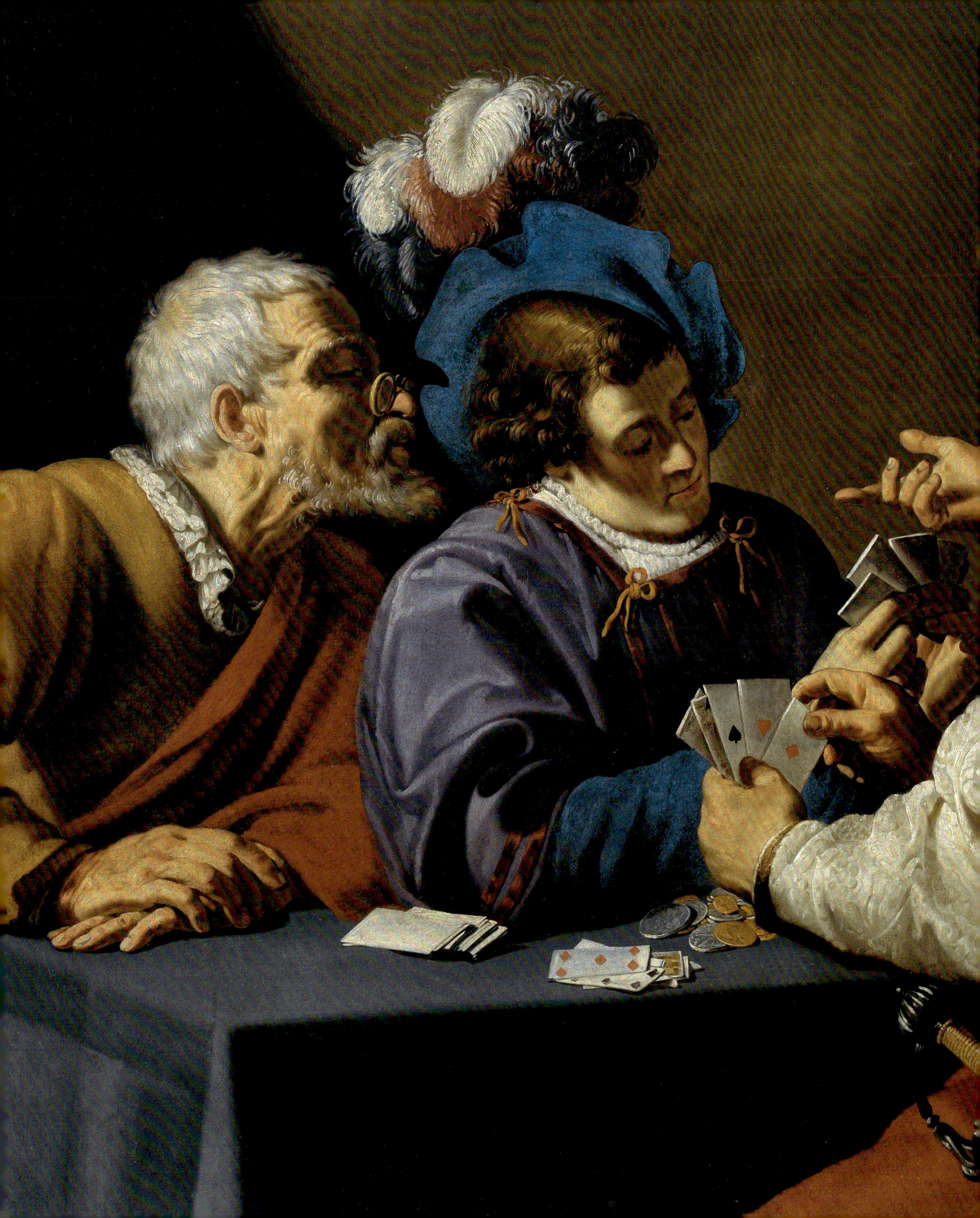

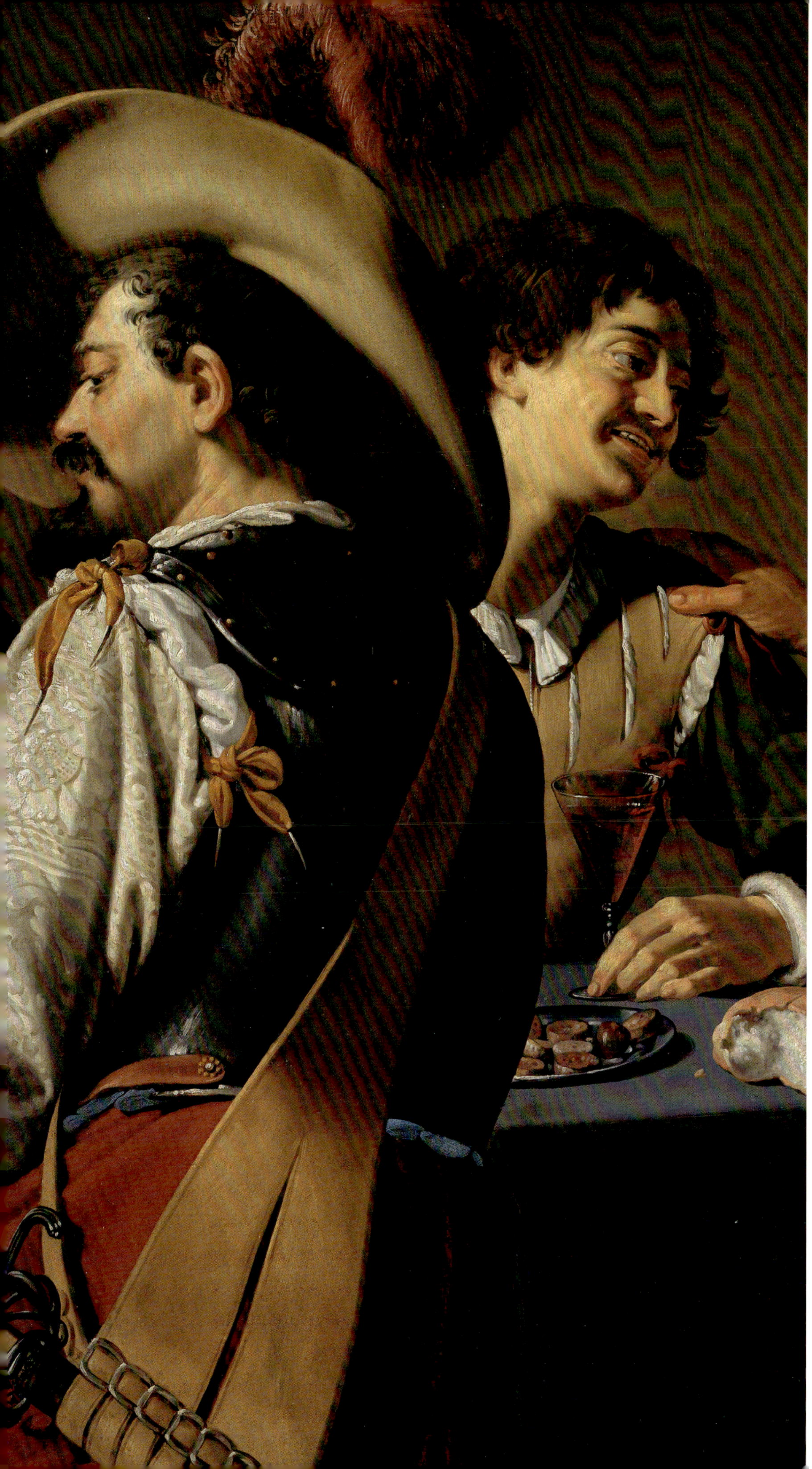

Catalogue

1616

The Crucifixion of St Peter

1

Gerard van Honthorst
The Crucifixion of St Peter, 1616
Pen on paper, brown wash, 378 × 265 mm
Signed and dated bottom left: 1616 honthorst
Nasjonalmuseet for kunst, arkitektur og design, Oslo, inv. NG.K&K.H.B.015597

2

Michelangelo Merisi, called Caravaggio (copy after)
The Crucifixion of St Peter, 1602/05
Canvas, 230 × 170 cm
Museo del Patriarca, Real Colegio Seminario de Corpus Christi, Valencia, inv. P 027

The drawing of *The Crucifixion of St Peter* (cat. 1), signed and dated 1616, is the earliest known evidence of Gerard van Honthorst's presence in Rome. It was the year he visited Santa Maria del Popolo on the Piazza del Popolo beside the northern gate into the city, which would have been the first impression of Rome for travellers from the north such as Honthorst.

Santa Maria del Popolo has a nave and two aisles, with two chapels flanking the choir. Honthorst took his pen, brushes and inkpot into the small chapel adjoining the north side of the choir. Its patronage rights were acquired by Tiberio Cerasi (1544–1601) in 1600, and he immediately commissioned Rome's three best-known artists to refurbish his future funerary chapel. Carlo Maderno was responsible for its reconfiguration and architectural design, while Annibale Carracci painted the *Assumption of the Virgin* altarpiece for the altar. Caravaggio was asked to paint the side walls or *laterali* with *The Crucifixion of St Peter* and *The Conversion of St Paul*, the joint founders of the Christ Church. The apostle Peter, who was Christ's deputy on earth and the patron saint of Rome, was crucified upside down at his own request, because he did not consider himself worthy to die as Christ had done. The Roman Saul, who changed his name to Paul after his conversion, became a Christian after seeing a vision on the road to Damascus in which Jesus urged him to become his disciple.

The contract between Tiberio Cerasi and Caravaggio for painting the two panels was signed on 24 September 1600. The artist agreed to make two paintings of the above-mentioned scenes on panels of cypress wood measuring ten palms high and eight palms wide for the sum of 400 *scudi*. He would deliver them within eight months, that is to say by 24 May 1601. Drawn designs had to be submitted for the client's prior approval.[1] Cerasi died on 3 May 1601, three weeks before the deadline. He had added a codicil to his will the previous day in which he made his heirs, the brothers of the Ospedale della Consolazione, responsible for completing the chapel.[2]

There has been a great deal of speculation about what happened next. Giovanni Baglione wrote in 1642 that Caravaggio made two new paintings, because his patron had not approved of the first two, which were then acquired by Cardinal Giacomo Sannesio (1560–1621).[3] Caravaggio did indeed paint two new compositions, but this time on canvas, for which he was paid the final

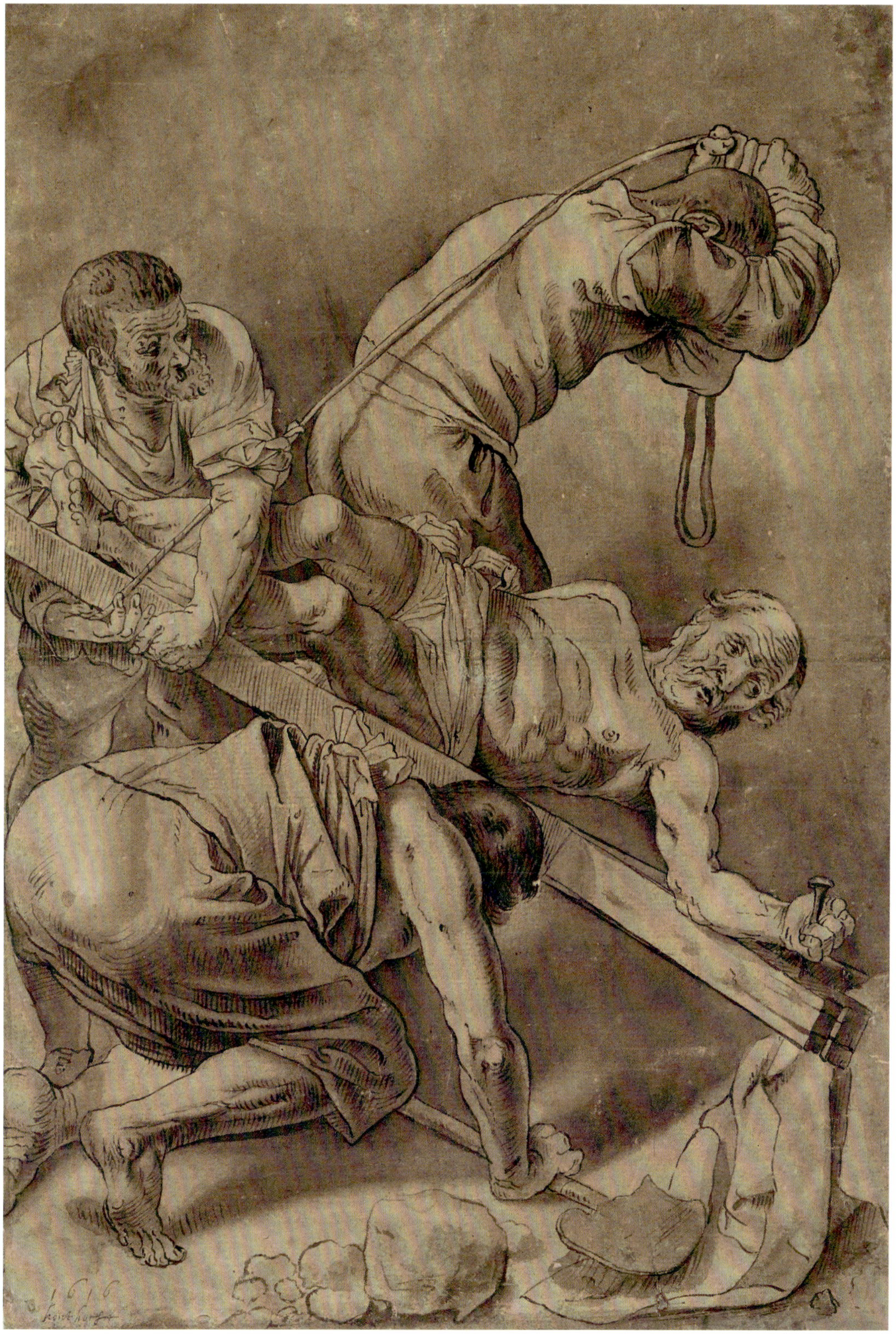

1

Gerard van Honthorst
The Crucifixion of St Peter, 1616
Nasjonalmuseet for kunst,
arkitektur og design, Oslo

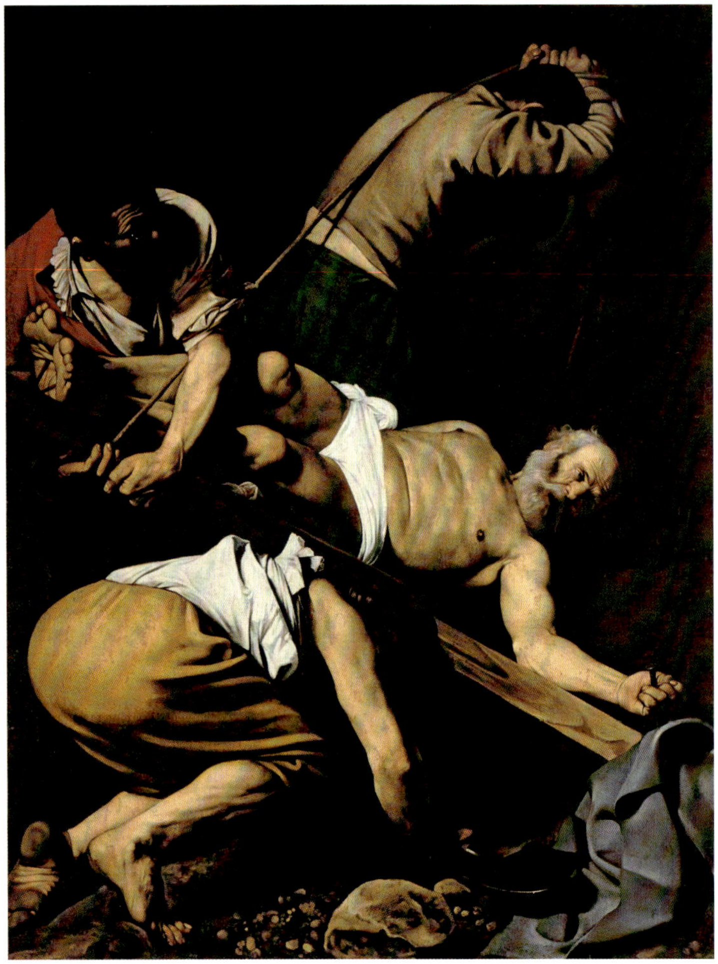

Fig. 49 Michelangelo Merisi, called Caravaggio, *The Crucifixion of St Peter*, 1602, Santa Maria del Popolo, Cerasi Chapel, Rome

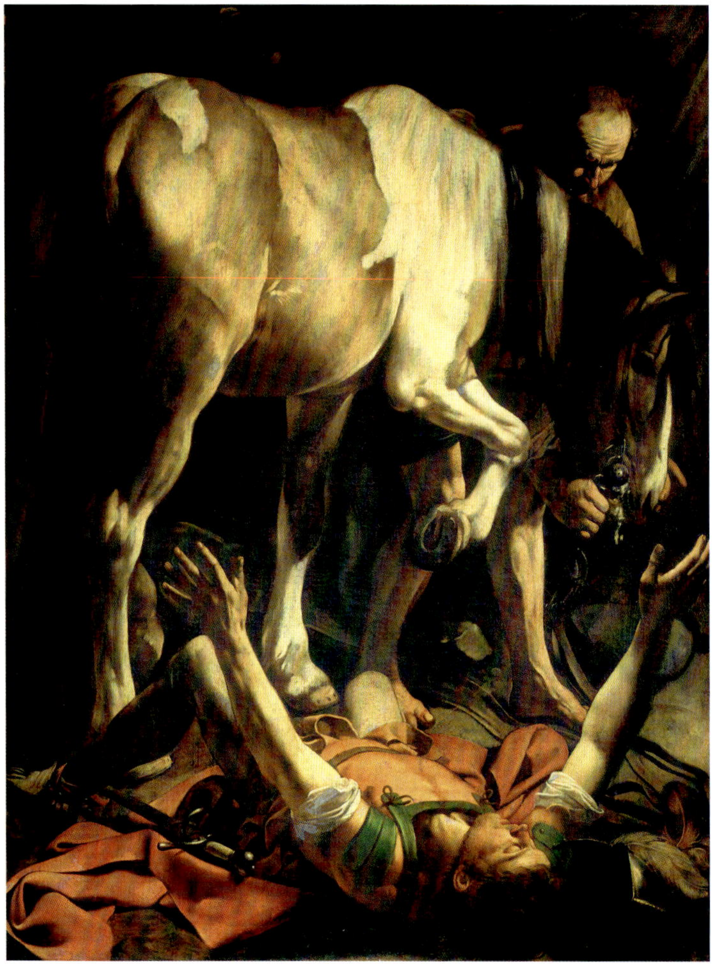

Fig. 50 Michelangelo Merisi, called Caravaggio, *The Conversion of St Paul*, 1602, Santa Maria del Popolo, Cerasi Chapel, Rome

instalment of his fee on 10 November 1601 (figs. 49, 50). However, he did not receive the full 400 *scudi* specified in the contract but only 300 *scudi*. The brothers arranged that he would keep the paintings in his workshop until the chapel was finished.[4] They were installed there on 1 May 1605.[5]

Art historians have come up with all kinds of arguments for the rejection of the panel paintings by Cerasi, or by Caravaggio himself, some of them more convincing than others.[6] It is unlikely, though, that Cerasi turned them down so close to the delivery date, for it had been stipulated in the contract that Caravaggio had to submit the designs to him for approval. In addition, no payments would have been made if Caravaggio had been in breach of contract, so there is probably another reason why the two panels were not accepted.[7]

The fraternity of the Ospedale della Consolazione did not honour Cerasi's last wish, or at any rate not completely. For example, it cut costs by replacing the polychrome marble panels on the walls of the presbytery with much cheaper ones with painted marbling.[8] It is also possible that the brothers and Caravaggio disagreed about the amount of the final instalment, whereupon the artist decided to sell the panels to Sannesio instead. That enabled him to adopt a more radical approach to the form and content of the scenes and to come up with a more original and unconventional design. In that case he would have agreed to supply two new paintings on canvas

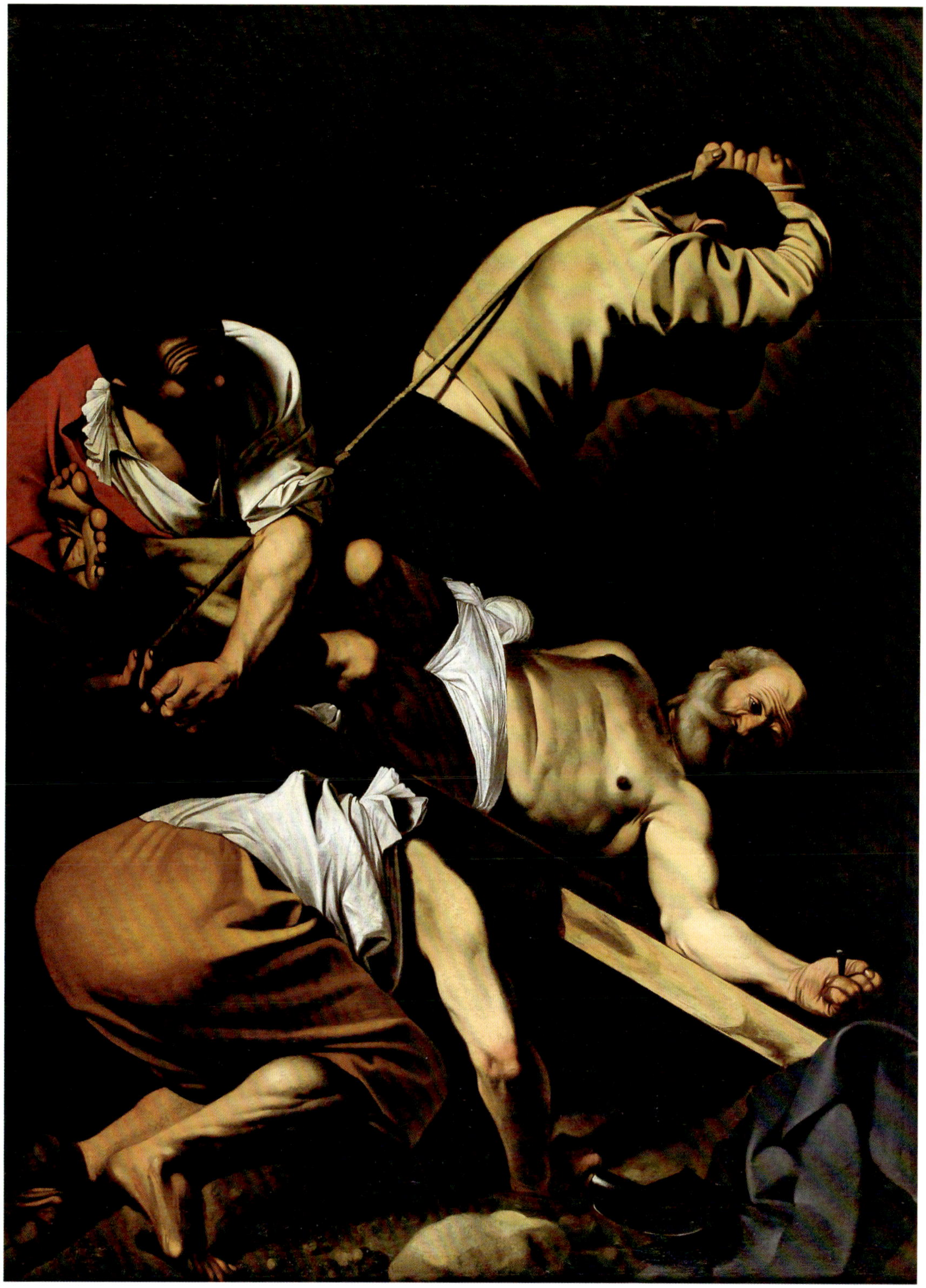

2
Michelangelo Merisi, called Caravaggio (copy after)
The Crucifixion of St Peter, 1602/05
Museo del Patriarca, Real Colegio Seminario
de Corpus Christi, Valencia

within six months (as against the eight months for the panel versions) for a lower fee, due to the simpler composition with fewer figures. Delivery and payment of the final instalment took place as agreed on 10 November 1601.

The two canvases remained in Caravaggio's workshop until their installation four-and-a-half years later, and it would have been in that period that an assistant or other member of the shop made the excellent copy after *The Crucifixion of St Peter*, which was in the collection of Archbishop Juan de Ribera (1532–1611) in Valencia in 1611 (cat. 2). That first version was done by an experienced copyist working directly from the original. Many of the smaller copies were made as exercises by young, anonymous pupils.[9] Ribera was the founder of the Real Colegio Seminario del Corpus Christi in Valencia, where priests were trained in accordance with the spirit and views of the Council of Trent. On his death his collection passed to the Colegio, the present-day Museo del Patriarca.[10]

The painted copy of *The Crucifixion of St Peter* was already in Valencia when Honthorst made his drawing in 1616, so he would have worked from the original in the Cerasi Chapel. It is not at all unusual that he used ink rather than chalk,[11] for there are contemporary drawings and prints of artists working outside their shop, even in the open air, with a pen, brush and inkpot.[12] And it was only logical that Honthorst made a drawing. He was merely doing what he had been taught by Abraham Bloemaert back in Utrecht. His entire training was based on drawing.[13]

Up until now this drawing, which is the only known study that Honthorst made after an original by Caravaggio, has been dismissed in the literature as a slavish copy. Jay Richard Judson writes in his Honthorst monograph that the sheet clearly shows that the Utrecht artist was not yet able to give a credible rendering of human anatomy in 1616. Nor did he succeed in placing the light and dark passages so as to heighten the realism of the scene. Judson's final conclusion is that Honthorst had not, or not yet, understood the revolutionary message of Caravaggio's technique.[14] He bases his comments on a critical analysis of the object itself, the actual drawing. In doing so he overlooks the why, the question of what Honthorst was trying to achieve with his drawing, his motivation, in other words. For there is not the slightest reason to assume that he intended to capture the chiaroscuro. The sheet looks more like a figure study. That also explains Honthorst's choice of *The Crucifixion of Peter* (fig. 49) rather than *The Conversion of St Paul* on the facing wall (fig. 50). The main subject of the *Crucifixion* is an almost nude figure in an unusual pose, whereas Paul in the *Conversion* is clothed, while his horse takes up much of the composition.[15]

One major change that Honthorst introduced shows that he was far from making a slavish imitation but had thought long and hard about what he was doing. Peter is looking at his left hand, which has been nailed to the wood of the cross. Caravaggio had covered the end of the crossbeam with a cloth that mirrors Paul's cloak on the opposite wall. Honthorst very deliberately made a different choice by leaving the end of the beam uncovered. What we see instead is how the nail had been driven in with such force that it had split the wood. Honthorst must have thought of this when he made his alteration. LMH

1 Spezzaferro/Mignosi Tantillo 2001, p. 110, no. 3; Macioce 2003, pp. 91–92, I doc 94. See also Marini 2001, pp. 446–452.
2 Spezzaferro/Mignosi Tantillo 2001, pp. 110–111, no. 4; Macioce 2003, p. 103, I doc 11, and p. 104, I doc 112.
3 Baglione 1642, p. 130. The paintings are listed in Sannesio's inventory of 2 April 1644. Spezzaferro/Mignosi Tantillo 2001, p. 118. *The Conversion of Paul,* 1600/01, panel, 237 × 198 cm, Collezione Odescalchi, Rome. The whereabouts of *The Crucifixion of Peter* are not known.
4 Spezzaferro/Mignosi Tantillo 2001, p. 111, no. 7; Macioce 2003, p. 106, I doc 116.
5 The dedication took place on 11 November 1606. Spezzaferro/Mignosi Tantillo 2001, p. 111, nos. 8 and 9; Macioce 2003, pp. 161–162, I doc 189, and p. 213, II doc 319/a.
6 See Friedlænder 1945; Mahon 1951, p. 227; Nolin 2008, p. 41; Belinda Granata, 'Conversion of St Paul' in Vodret et al. 2016, vol. 2, pp. 305–307.
7 See also Spezzaferro 2001.
8 Ibid., p. 17.
9 The Valencia version is the only one that is the same size as the original, with almost all the details matching, and is executed with comparable colours and technique. Moir 1976, pp. 93–94, mentions 17 painted copies (no. 240 is identical with 24k or 24l), seven of which are in Spanish collections and six may have been lost. See also Moir 1972, pp. 136–137, no. 6.
10 See also Nicole Hartje in Exh. cat. Düsseldorf 2006/07, pp. 240–241, cat. 31. In addition, see Benito Domenech 1980, p. 254, cat. 27.
11 There are no traces of chalk on the drawing, nor is there a known chalk drawing of the subject by Honthorst. With thanks to Tina Grette Poulsson (Nasjonalmuseet for kunst, arkitektur og design, Oslo), who examined the drawing under the microscope on 3 February 2016.
12 For depictions of artists working outdoors with inkpots see Exh. cat. Berlin 2007/08, pp. 156–157, cat. 43, and pp. 180–181, cat. 53. With thanks to Paul van den Akker.
13 Bok 1990; Exh. cat. Utrecht/Schwerin 2011/12, p. 58, cat. 2.
14 Judson 1986/87, pp. 55–56, fig. 48; Judson/Ekkart 1999, pp. 331–332, cat. D16.
15 Both works: 1602, canvas, 230 × 175 cm, Santa Maria del Popolo, Cerasi Chapel, Rome. There are only two known copies after *The Conversion of St Paul*: an anonymous drawing and a small painting by Vincenzo Camuccini. Moir 1976, p. 92, nos. 23a and b.

1616

Saints

3
Hendrick ter Brugghen
The Penitent St Peter, 1616
Signed and dated bottom left:
HT Brugghen.fecit.161[6]
Canvas, 67.7 × 85.8 cm
Centraal Museum, Utrecht, inv. 15762

4
Jusepe de Ribera
St Peter, 1616/20
Canvas, 78 × 65 cm
Quadreria dei Girolamini, Naples,
inv. Pf. 272

5
Jusepe de Ribera
St Andrew, 1615/20
Canvas, 136 × 112 cm
Quadreria dei Girolamini,
Naples, inv. Pf. 285

6
Nicolas Tournier
St Andrew, c. 1616
Canvas, 115 × 85 cm
Private collection

7
Michelangelo Merisi, called Caravaggio
St Jerome Meditating, 1605/06
Canvas, 145.5 × 101.5 cm
Museu de Montserrat, Montserrat,
inv. R.N. 200.165

8
Giovanni Serodine
St Peter Reading, c. 1628/30
Canvas, 91 × 133.5 cm
Pinacoteca cantonale Giovanni Züst,
Rancate (Mendrisio), inv. PZ 25

Hendrick ter Brugghen, whom many regard as the most talented of the Utrecht Caravaggisti, is a puzzling painter. It is only when he was 28 years old that one can start to get an idea of his talent, his idiosyncratic choices and his painterly nature. He is very individualistic and recognisable in his translation of traditional subjects, and impulsive in his treatment of them. He starts painting as if unprepared to do so, restarts, turns the entire canvas around if needs be, lays in a new composition and then alters what he had begun.[1] This and his supposedly melancholic nature undoubtedly contribute to the myth-making that surrounds him.[2]

In 1619, at the age of 31, ter Brugghen signs and dates the *Adoration of the Magi* that is now in the Rijksmuseum in Amsterdam (fig. 44). It is generally accepted as his earliest dated, autograph painting. The museum's purchase of it in 1970 prompted Pieter van Thiel, chief curator of paintings there at the time, to investigate the early oeuvre once more. This led him to examine *The Penitent St Peter* (cat. 3), the authenticity of which was widely disputed, and to publish his findings in the *Bulletin van het Rijksmuseum* in 1971. He says of it that 'Although the painting has suffered a bit here and there, ter Brugghen's facture is nevertheless clearly visible, above all in the keys, which a copyist would never have depicted with such freedom and assurance, and then in the hands and the passage around the nose and eye. The thick edges rimming the brushstrokes, the distinctive way in which the cheek is placed against the nose, the shape of the ear, the rendering of the hair and the beautiful outline of the skull correspond in every respect to the execution of the head of the kneeling king in *The Adoration of the Magi* of 1619'.[3] X-radiographs show that the density and structure of the canvas of *The Penitent St Peter*, irregular with small knots, is comparable to that of *The Adoration of the Magi*. The same applies to the painting technique.[4]

Van Thiel's observations were never able to convince Benedict Nicolson, Leonard J. Slatkes or Albert Blankert, although they were always of the opinion that the subject and composition of *The Penitent St Peter* were impressive, and characteristic of ter Brugghen. Nicolson, who wrote the first monograph on the artist, repeatedly calls it a copy.[5] Slatkes and Blankert, the organisers of the exhibition *Nieuw licht op de Gouden Eeuw: Hendrick ter Brugghen en tijdgenoten* of 1986/87, also regarded it as a copy, but one done after a lost original

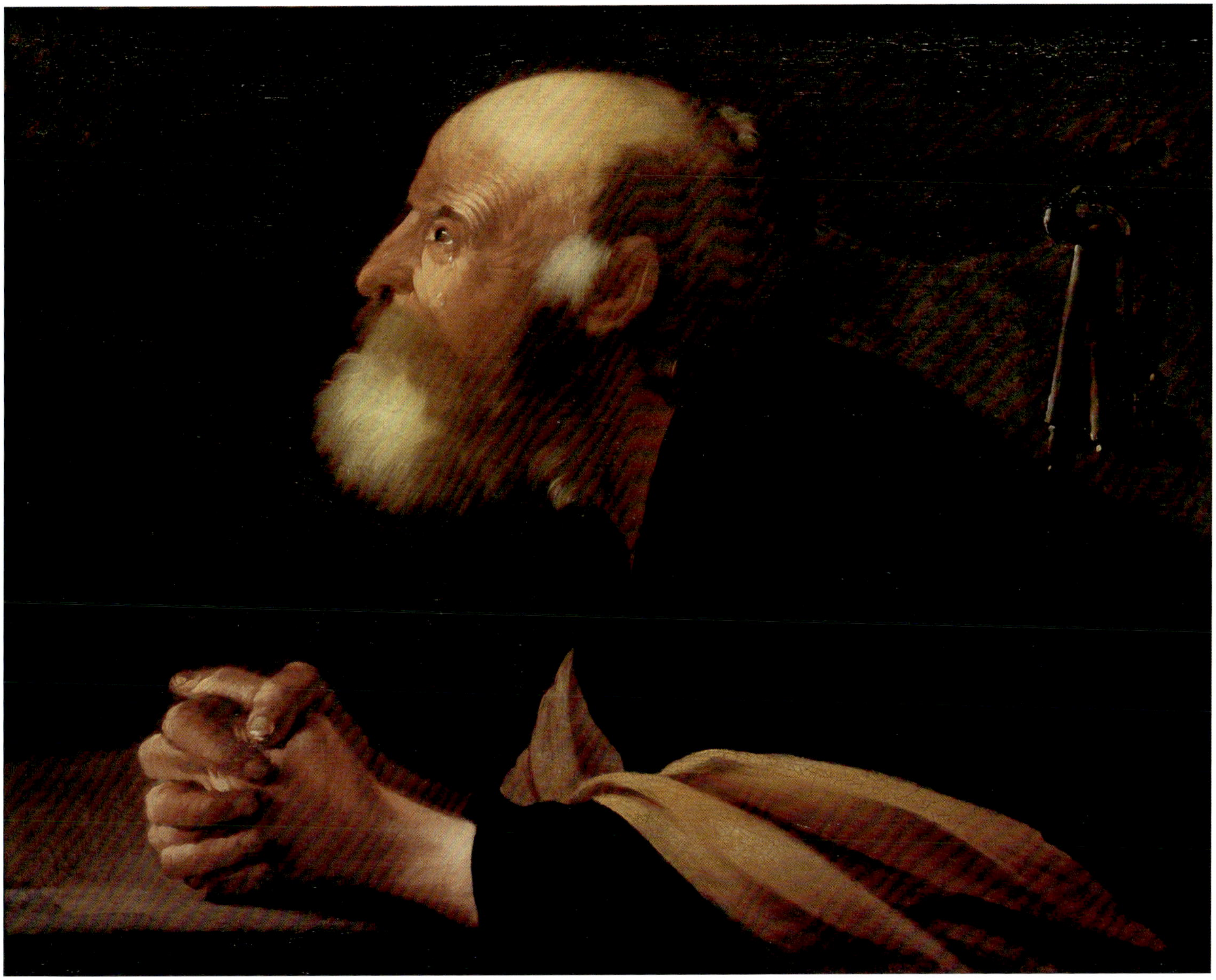

3
Hendrick ter Brugghen
The Penitent St Peter, 1616
Centraal Museum, Utrecht

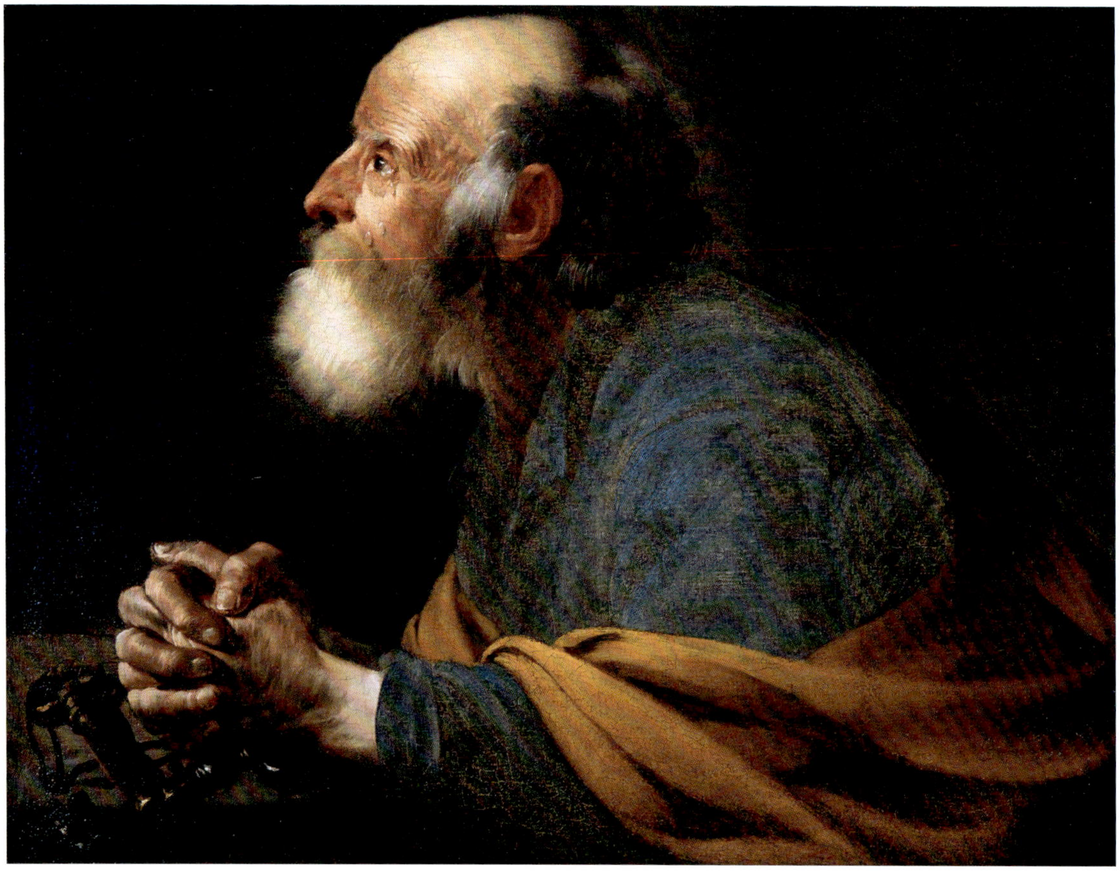

Fig. 51 Hendrick ter Brugghen (workshop), *The Penitent St Peter,* 1616/25, private collection

(from which the signature and date were borrowed), or in Slatkes's view a workshop copy at best.[6]

The discovery in 1992 of a previously unknown and unsigned version of *The Penitent St Peter* in a private collection (fig. 51) was a reason for the Centraal Museum to restore its painting in 2003 and investigate it anew.[7] The most striking feature of the two versions is the different position of the keys to 'the kingdom of heaven', which the apostle had received from Jesus. There are two of them, one to open the gates of heaven and the other to open the world. They are lying just in front of him in the rediscovered version instead of hanging from a nail in the wall behind him. Peter's pose is also different. In the Utrecht picture he is leaning forward in the direction of the light, with his hands and wrists resting on the table in front of him.

The painting in the private collection, the canvas of which is relatively coarse and loosely woven,[8] is better preserved, and partly for that reason looks far stronger than the one in Utrecht. Since the saint's cloak has remained blue, the tone of the picture is also much more colourful. During the restoration of the Utrecht version it was discovered that the background, the sleeve and shoulder of Peter's greenish robe and the darker passages of the gold-coloured cloak were all overpaintings. After their removal, the figure gained more volume and the illusion of three-dimensionality was heightened. The rays of light from a window outside the composition became visible. They are iconographically inseparable from the scene, but are missing in the other version. They also accentuate the contrast between the background, the saint and the table, as well as the *trompe-l'oeil* effect of the keys on the wall, establishing their place in the space. The signature and date, finally, are original: 'HT Brugghen. fecit.161[6]'. The lower part of the last digit is a lowercase 'o', so that number should very probably be read as a '6'. In a nutshell, there is no longer the slightest reason to doubt the attribution to ter Brugghen.[9]

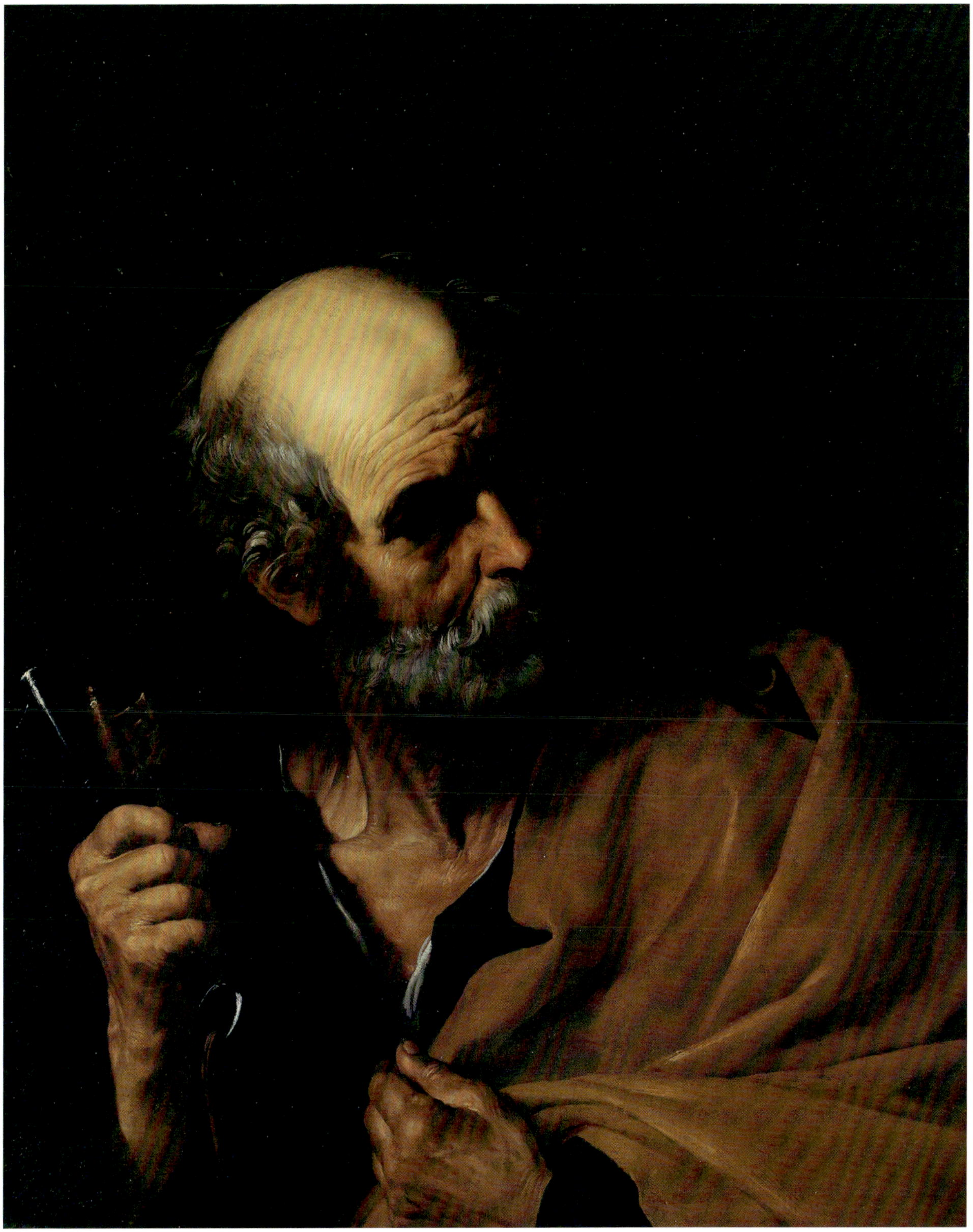

4
Jusepe de Ribera
St Peter, 1616/20
Quadreria dei Girolamini, Naples

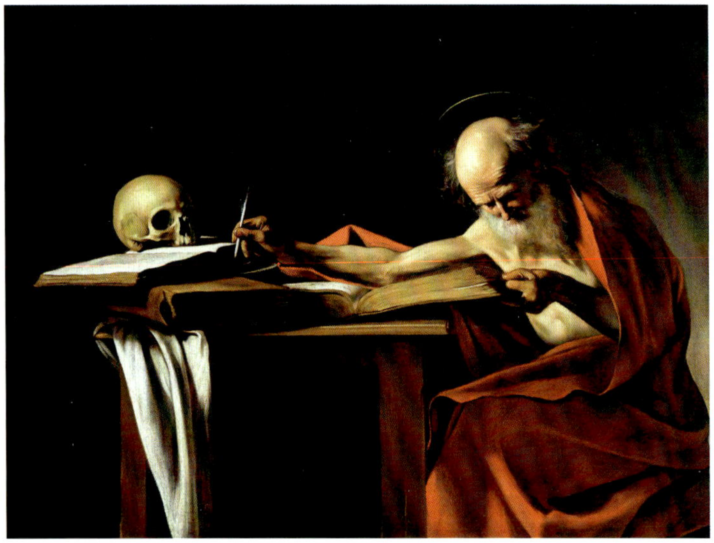

Fig. 52 Michelangelo Merisi, called Caravaggio, *St Jerome*, 1605/06, Galleria Borghese, Rome

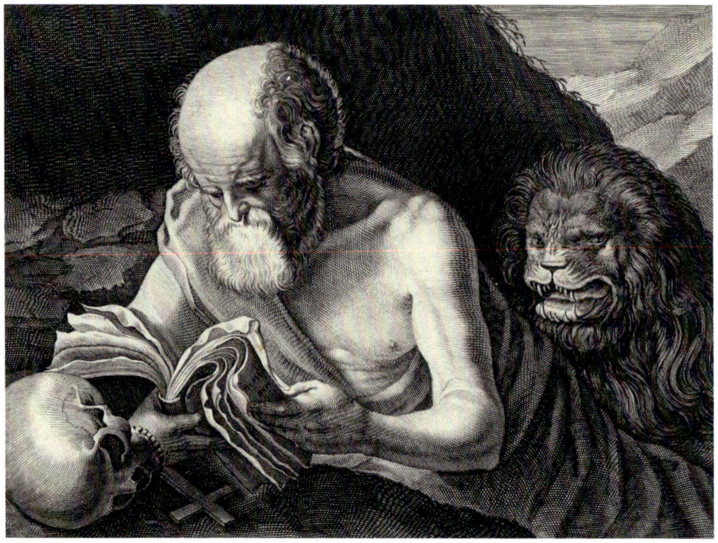

Fig. 53 Willem van de Passe after Hendrick ter Brugghen, *St Jerome in a Landscape with a Lion*, c. 1618/19, Rijksprentenkabinet, Amsterdam

Peter, Andrew and Jerome are among the half-length saints depicted most often by the Caravaggisti. Peter's repentance as depicted by ter Brugghen was due to his denial of Christ when he was arrested. Earlier in the evening he had told Peter that he would deny knowing him three times before the cock crowed twice.[10] It is only when Peter hears the cock crow three times that he realises that Jesus had told the truth, whereupon he wept bitter tears. Peter owes his great importance to the fact that he is the first apostle and Christ's deputy on earth. According to John 21:15–18 Christ charged him to act as the shepherd of his flock after his death. He is portrayed with keys, as in ter Brugghen's picture, or with a cross. At his own request Peter was crucified upside down, because out of respect he did not wish to die as Jesus had done (cat. 1, 2). His brother Andrew also chose another form of crucifixion on an X-shaped cross, which is nowadays known as a St Andrew's cross.

The apostles Peter and Andrew do not appear as single figures in Caravaggio's oeuvre. Since Gianni Papi convincingly identified the Master of the Judgement of Solomon with the young Spanish painter Jusepe de Ribera, it has become clear how not only Dirck van Baburen (cat. 24) but also the French painter Nicolas Tournier were influenced by the Spaniard.[11] The latter, who was working in Rome at the same time as ter Brugghen (1611/12–1616), became one of the most influential painters in the city after Caravaggio's departure for Naples in 1606. His looser way of painting, direct, almost aggressive figurative vocabulary, and figures with a distinctive physiognomy had a great impact on his colleagues in the city. He is probably the missing link in the search for ter Brugghen's early work.[12]

Several apostles feature repeatedly in Ribera's early oeuvre, either in a so-called *Apostolato* (a series of Christ the Saviour and the twelve apostles), to which his *St Peter* (cat. 4) could have belonged, or in paintings that were intended to be separate works in their own right.[13] Most of them are single half-lengths with an intense, direct gaze in a cramped position in the foreground of the picture plane. Ribera's *St Peter* may not have been a direct influence on ter Brugghen. It is more a question of the type of scene.

St Andrew (cat. 5) is an example of Ribera's large canvases. It had an immediate influence on Nicolas Tournier, who, as we now know, is documented in Rome in 1616.[14] His impressive *St Andrew* (cat. 6) is regarded as his greatest achievement.[15] Tournier translates Ribera's *St Andrew* into a more elegant image. He places the cross in front of the saint, thus imposing a strict geometry on the composition. The gracefully spread, long fingers and the effect of seemingly delayed action are typical of the French painter. The same applies to the underdrawing showing through the top paint

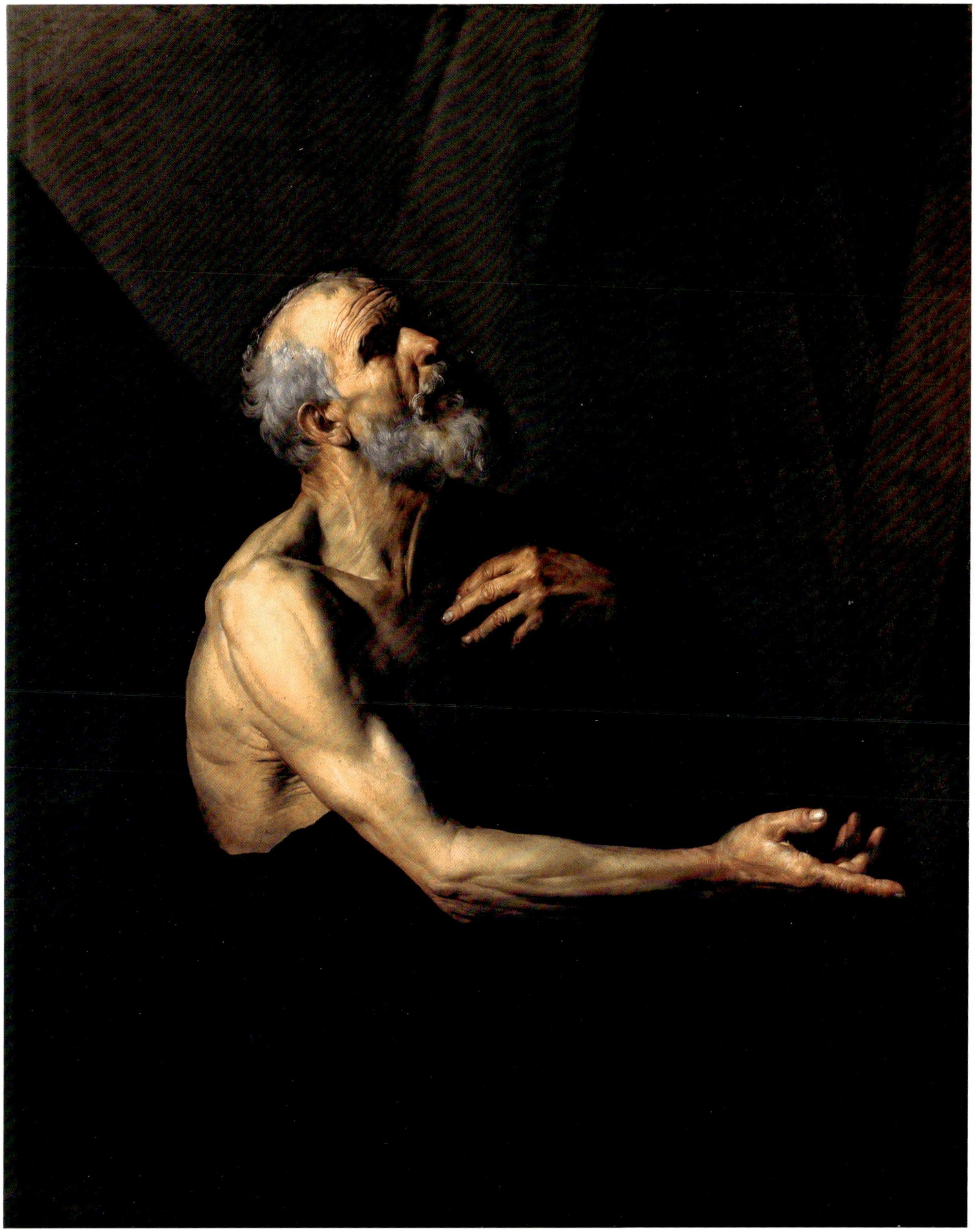

5
Jusepe de Ribera
St Andrew, 1615/20
Quadreria dei Girolamini, Naples

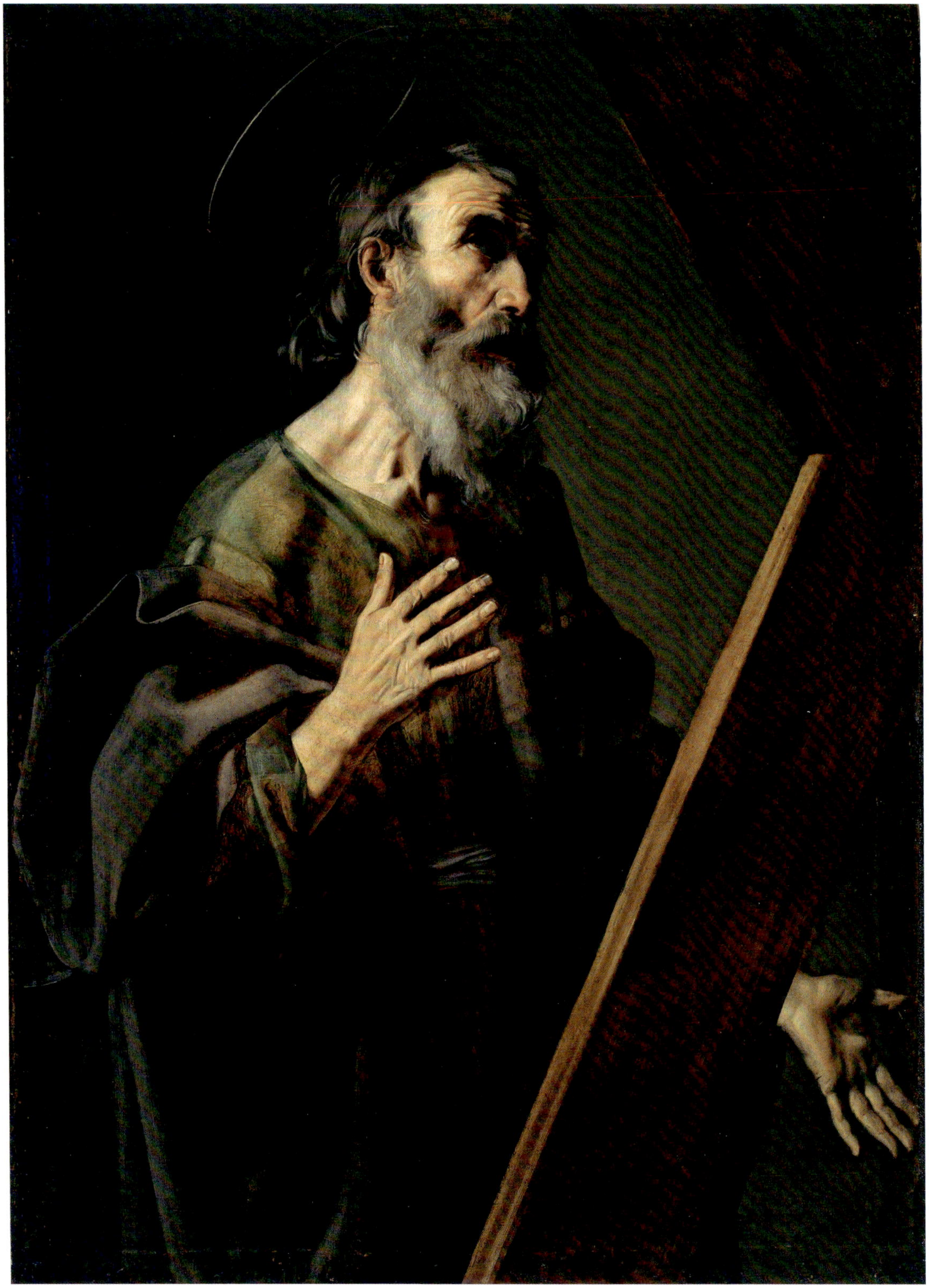

6
Nicolas Tournier
St Andrew, c. 1616
Private collection

layer, and the many pentimenti that Tournier made during the painting process.

One saint who is often depicted with a physiognomy closely related to Peter's is Jerome. Caravaggio depicted him as an old man with a worn-out body that has suffered from the many self-chastisements to which it was subjected. Meditating, reading and writing, he passes his days in total solitude, a skull as a *memento mori* within easy reach. His red garment, slung loosely around his shoulders or allowed to slide down to around his loins, is an allusion to his time as a cardinal. There is no longer any doubt about the autograph nature of Caravaggio's *St Jerome Meditating* in Montserrat (cat. 7), which was once attributed to Ribera.[16] Although it is known that the *St Jerome* in the Galleria Borghese (fig. 52) was either commissioned by Cardinal Scipione Borghese or was given to him by Caravaggio, it too, remarkably, was also attributed to Ribera at one time.[17] It emerges from an engraving after a lost painting by Hendrick ter Brugghen that he too painted the Church Father (fig. 53).[18] His composition and approach, though, were completely different. He added the lion, from whose paw, according to legend, St Jerome pulled a thorn, and situated the saint in a landscape.

Occupying a lonely peak is Giovanni Serodine, who painted a canvas of St Peter with extraordinary daring and virtuosity in almost monochrome tones (cat. 8). The composition has something of Caravaggio's *St Jerome* in the Galleria Borghese.[19] Peter is identified by the keys on the table. He is reading. With his right hand he is clasping the skull that is on its side, presenting the bottom of it to the viewer. Balanced between the index and middle fingers of his left hand is the opened book that rests on his left arm. The candle illuminating the sketchily indicated space really does appear to be flickering. Another spectacular detail is the open drawer below the table with a book sticking out of it. This is a painting by an independent painter who ploughed his own furrow. It is Rembrandt *avant la lettre*. LMH

1 Ter Brugghen started by painting a subject resembling *The Calling of St Matthew*, c. 1620, canvas, 152 × 195 cm, Le Havre, Musée d'art moderne André Malraux, inv. 77-7 (fig. 79), but turned the canvas around and then painted *Liberation of St Peter* (cat. 14). With thanks to Gero Seelig of the Staatliches Museum Schwerin, who shared this information with me on 8 September 2016 and is preparing a publication on the subject. See too, for example, Van Suchtelen 1991.
2 Bok 2009.
3 Van Thiel 1971, p. 107.
4 Van Thiel 1988, Helmus 2007b, pp. 27–37; Helmus 2009.
5 Nicolson 1958, pp. 116–117, cat. D 90; Nicolson 1960, p. 470; Nicolson 1973, p. 238.
6 Slatkes 1981/82, p. 183; Slatkes 1988, pp. 80, 81; Slatkes/Franits 2007, pp. 223–225, cat. W9. Blankert 1986/87, p. 41, note 24; Blankert 1991, p. 39, note 9. See also Helmus 2009, pp. 30–31.
7 Exh. cat. Paris 1992, pp. 28–32, cat. 7; Helmus 2007b; Helmus 2009.
8 Canvas, 67.5 × 85.6 cm.
9 Franits in Slatkes/Franits 2007, p. 225, cat. W9, note 1: 'I [WF] am inclined to consider this picture as possibly having been executed by ter Brugghen with assistance from his workshop'. Gert Jan van der Sman is one of the very few people who still believe that *The Supper at Emmaus*, 1616, canvas, 160.3 × 188.3 cm, Toledo Museum of Art, Toledo, inv. 1983.1, is a signed work dated 1616 by ter Brugghen. See Exh. cat. Madrid 2016, p. 138, cat. 28.
10 Matthew 26:31–35, Mark 14:27–31, Luke 22:54–62 and John 18:25–27.
11 Papi 2002; Papi 2003a; Papi 2004; Papi 2005/06; Papi 2011. The identification has been accepted almost universally since the publication of Exh. cat. Madrid 2011, but there is discussion about the chronology of Ribera's early work. See, for example, Gash 2010; Salomon 2011; Lange 2013, pp. 17–18. For Ribera's influence on Tournier see Hémery 2015.
12 For Ribera's influence on ter Brugghen see also Weber 2015/16, pp. 254–255.
13 Nicola Spinosa in Exh. cat. Madrid 2011, p. 158, cat. 24; Exh. cat. Lecce 2013/14, pp. 66–67, cat. 10. See also Gallo 2010b and Lange 2013, p. 215, cat. A-32. For examples of Ribera's *Apostolato* see Exh. cat. Madrid 2011, pp. 104–115; Exh. cat. Rennes/Strasbourg 2014/15, pp. 82–91, cats. 8–12.
14 Cavazzini 2016/17, p. 21.
15 Hémery 2015.
16 See, *inter alia*, Mina Gregori in Exh. cat. New York/Naples 1985, pp. 298–300, cat. 84; Nicole Hartje in Exh. cat. Düsseldorf 2006/07, p. 226, cat. 18; Schütze 2009, p. 270, cat. 39; Ramon 2014, pp. 59–79.
17 *St Jerome*, 1606, canvas, 112 × 157 cm, Galleria Borghese, Rome. Giorgio Leone in Vodret et al. 2016, vol. 2, pp. 593–597.
18 Willem van de Passe after Hendrick ter Brugghen, *St Jerome in a Landscape with a Lion*, c. 1618/19, engraving, Rijksprentenkabinet, Amsterdam, inv. RP-P-OB-2226.
19 See Exh. cat. Rancate 2015, pp. 102–111, cat. 9.

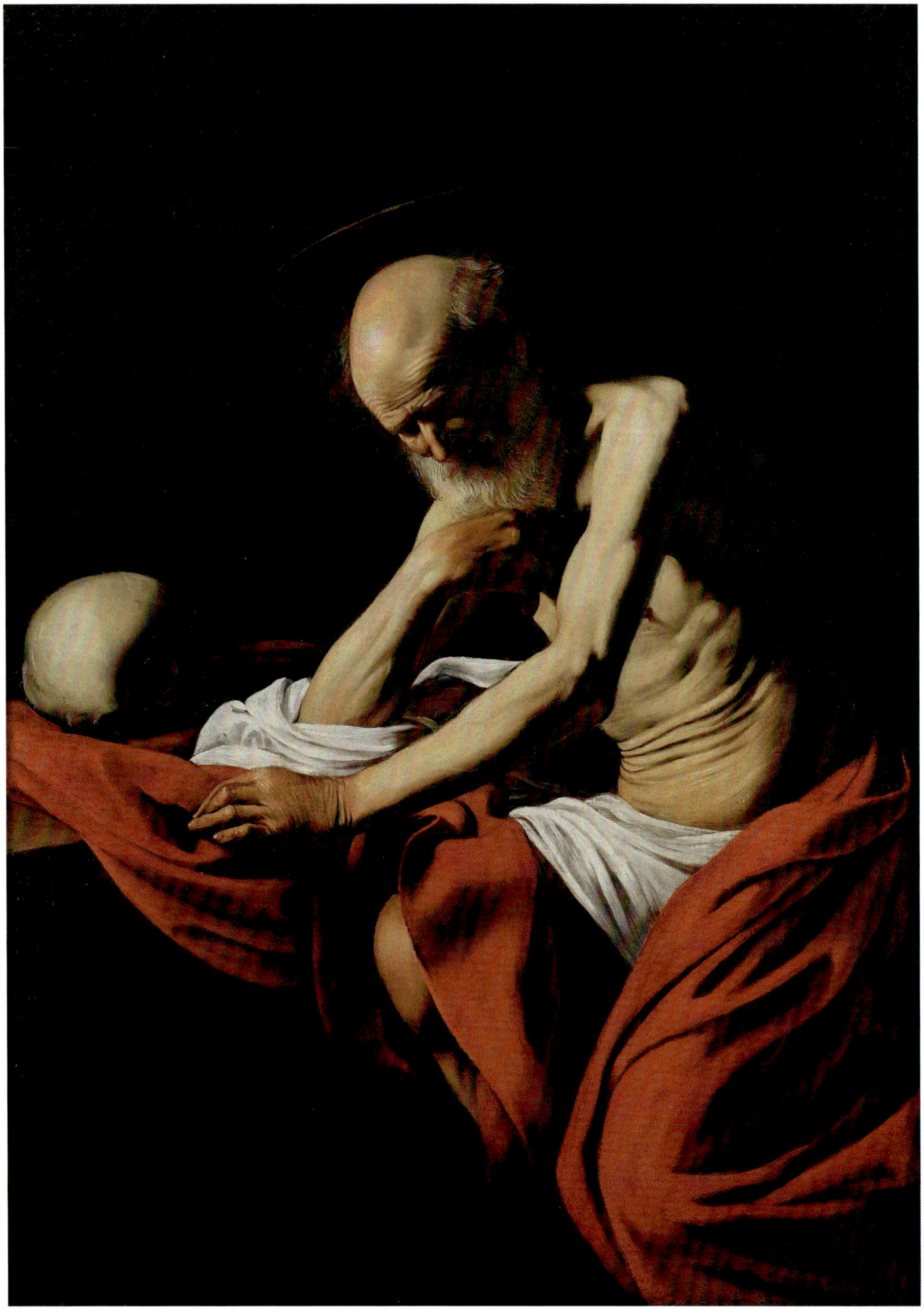

7
Michelangelo Merisi, called Caravaggio
St Jerome Meditating, 1605/06
Museu de Montserrat, Montserrat

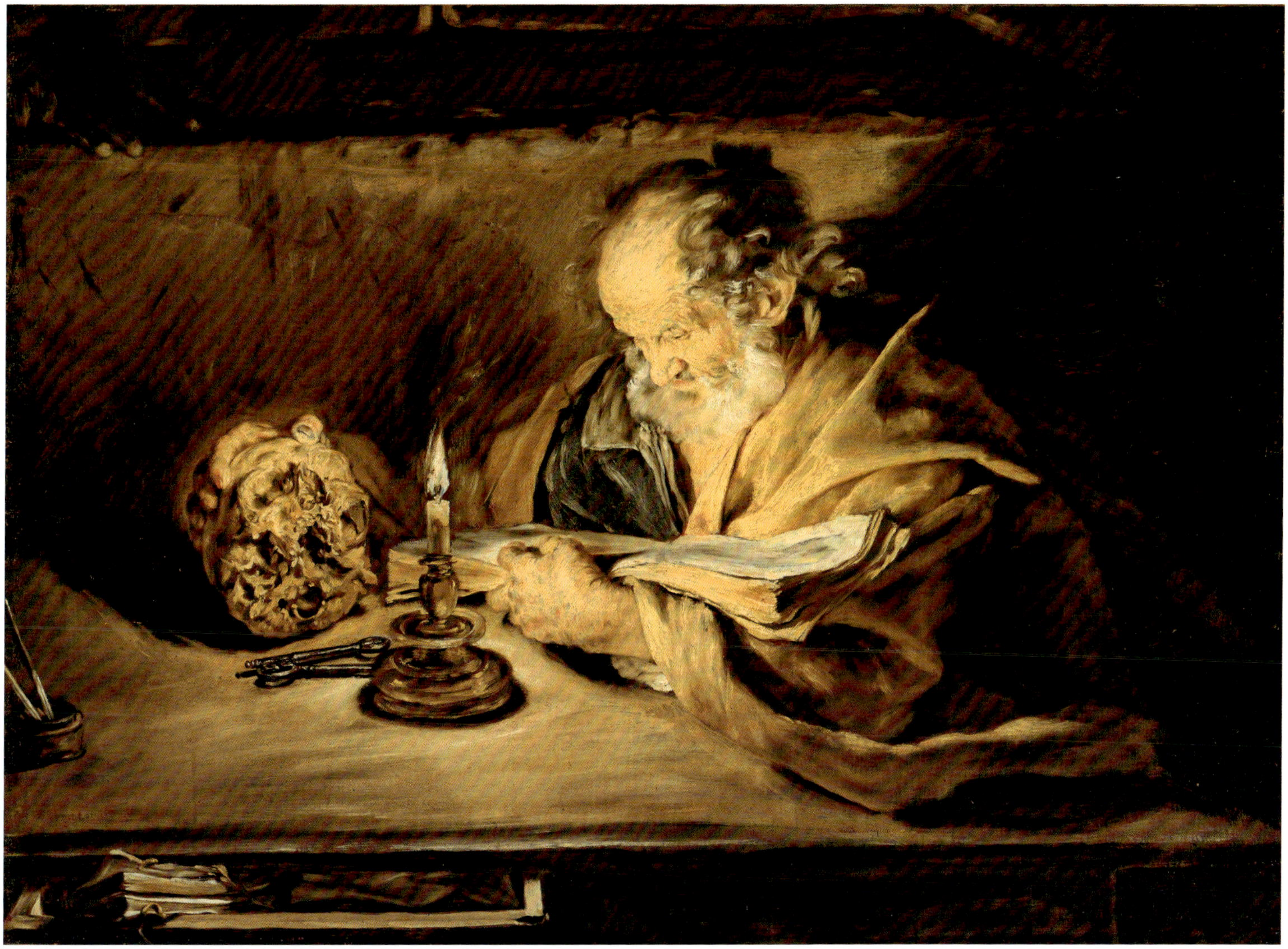

8
Giovanni Serodine
St Peter Reading, c. 1628/30
Pinacoteca cantonale Giovanni Züst,
Rancate (Mendrisio)

c. 1616/17

The Denial of St Peter

9
Gerard van Honthorst
The Denial of St Peter, c. 1616/17
Canvas, 150 × 197 cm
Musée des Beaux-Arts de Rennes,
Rennes, inv. DT.876.1.1

10
Jusepe de Ribera
The Denial of St Peter, c. 1615/16
Canvas, 163 × 233 cm
Gallerie Nazionali di Arte Antica di Roma,
Galleria Corsini, Rome, inv. 438
Munich only

11
Gerard Seghers
The Denial of St Peter, c. 1620/25
Canvas, 157.5 × 227.3 cm
North Carolina Museum of Art, Raleigh,
purchased with funds from the State of North
Carolina, inv. 52.9.112

In their accounts of the Passion of Christ, the Evangelists pay particular attention to the denial of the Apostle Peter.[1] At the Last Supper, Christ had predicted that one of his disciples would disown him three times before the rooster crows. Peter had denied this and sworn allegiance to his lord. When the soldiers arrested Jesus and took him to Caiaphas (cat. 19), Peter followed them to the house of the high priest. In the courtyard, a maid accused him of being a follower of Jesus, which he denied. As predicted, Peter denied his lord twice more before the break of day.

Since the beginning of the 17th century, the Denial of St Peter ranked among the more popular and common pictorial subjects.[2] For the Caravaggisti, it offered an opportunity to depict the episode, which according to the biblical account occurred at night, in an impressive, genre-like manner with lighting effects, and use a powerfully expressive visual language to convey the emotions of the accusers and the accused apostle, his horror, his rejections and his shame.

Honthorst painted the subject at least three times. The likely earliest version in Rennes (cat. 9) has been dated c. 1616/17.[3] In his horizontal, six-figure composition, Honthorst compares the denial scene on the left with a group of card-playing soldiers sitting around a table on the right. An old, bearded man wearing a pince-nez and holding a cane peeks from behind at the cards in the hand of the distracted player. The rear figure of a soldier in the foreground, who grabs the apostle by the cloak with his outstretched arm, acts as an intermediary between the two groups of figures. The maid standing next to the apostle and turning towards him holds a candle in her left hand, while accusing him with a raised hand and admonishing index finger. Peter dismisses the accusation by placing one hand reassuringly against his chest and raising the other in a defensive and denying gesture.

The large-scale, multi-figure version in an English private collection (fig. 54) was probably created around the same time in Italy. In it, Honthorst depicts the denial scene in mirror image, increases the number of staffage figures, and centres the lighting on the apostle's gesture of denial.[4] In his third composition, which he ended up painting around 1622/24 in Utrecht, Honthorst reduces the number of figures again and focuses fully on the biblical story (fig. 55).[5]

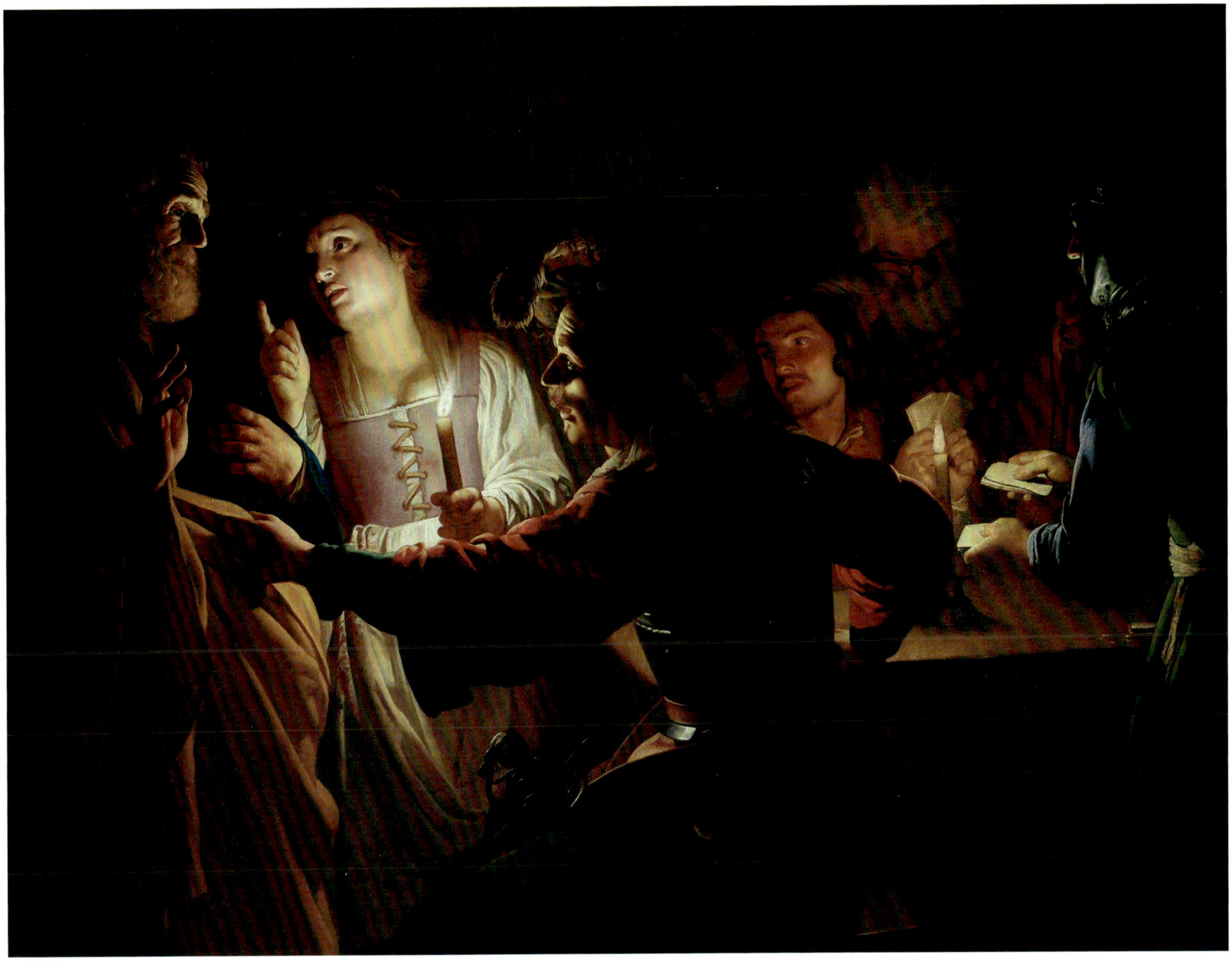

9
Gerard van Honthorst
The Denial of St Peter, c. 1616/17
Musée des Beaux-Arts de Rennes, Rennes

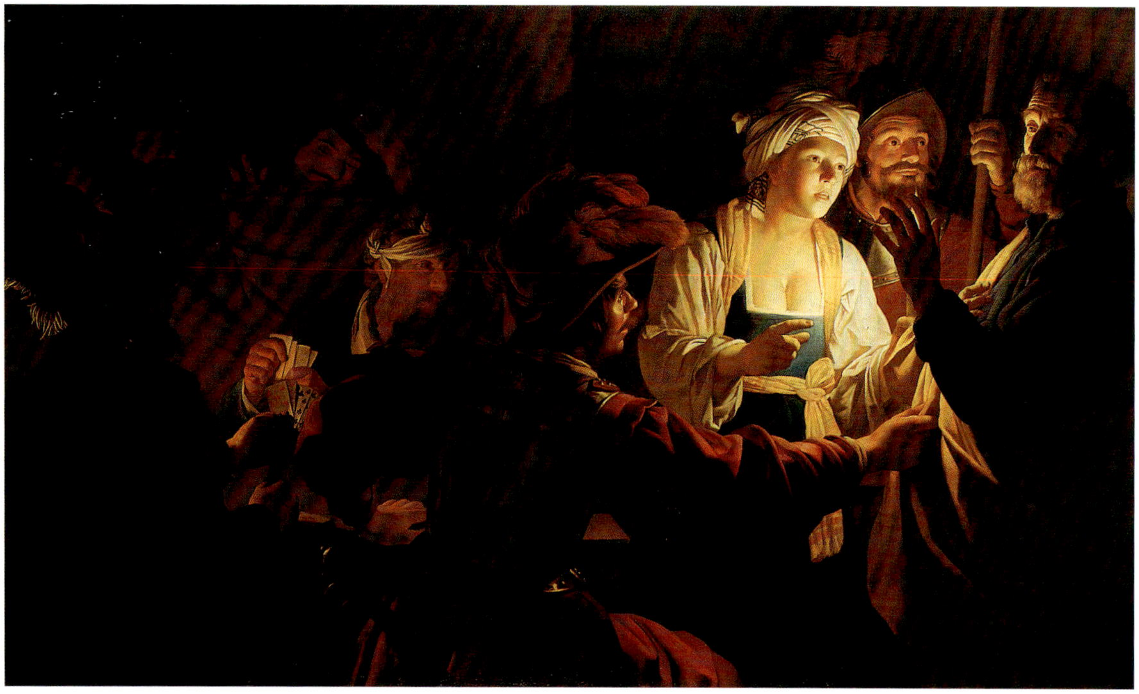

Fig. 54 Gerard van Honthorst, *The Denial of St Peter*, c. 1618, private collection

During his time in Rome, Honthorst likely studied a number of denial scenes by other contemporary artists, which influenced his own depiction of the subject. We can distinguish three types of compositions among the works of Caravaggio and his followers: denial scenes featuring standing figures only (figs. 55, 57); compositions including soldiers sitting on the ground;[6] and, as a third variation, compositions including soldiers sitting at a table and placing dice or cards. In the latter most common type of composition with a group of figures around a table, the actual Denial of St Peter is usually marginalised both visually and thematically.[7] This depiction was new and did not draw on any existing pictorial tradition.

For a long time, it was assumed that Bartolomeo Manfredi first had the idea of adding a dice-playing scene to the biblical story.[8] His painting in Braunschweig (fig. 56) was considered a benchmark work which subsequently served as a basis for other Caravaggisti.[9] In 2002, when Gianni Papi recognised the previously unidentified Master of the Judgment of Solomon as Jusepe de Ribera and later ascribed the denial scene at the Galleria Corsini to the Spanish artist as well (cat. 10), the prevailing scholarly consensus started to unravel.[10] According to Papi, Ribera most likely painted the work around 1615/16 in Rome before settling in Naples.[11] By now, the assumption is that this composition preceded Manfredi's painting.[12]

Unlike Honthorst, Manfredi, Seghers, and the Frenchmen Valentin de Boulogne and Tournier, Ribera places St Peter and the maid on the right-hand side of his painting. The soldier in the foreground, who is turning to the left and leaning on the table, turns his back on the denial scene and focuses his full attention on his opponent's last dice roll. It is the figure of the bald-headed old man standing behind the table who accuses Peter with outstretched arm.

The combination of the denial scene and the group of playing soldiers dressed in fancifully coloured attire around a table in half- or three-quarter-length may derive from Caravaggio's *Calling of St Matthew* in the Contarelli chapel of San Luigi dei Francesi in Rome, which was painted around 1599/1600 (fig. 78). Even if this work depicts a different episode from the New Testament and has publicans rather than soldiers sitting at the table, there are obvious similarities, for example, in the arrangement of the two standing figures

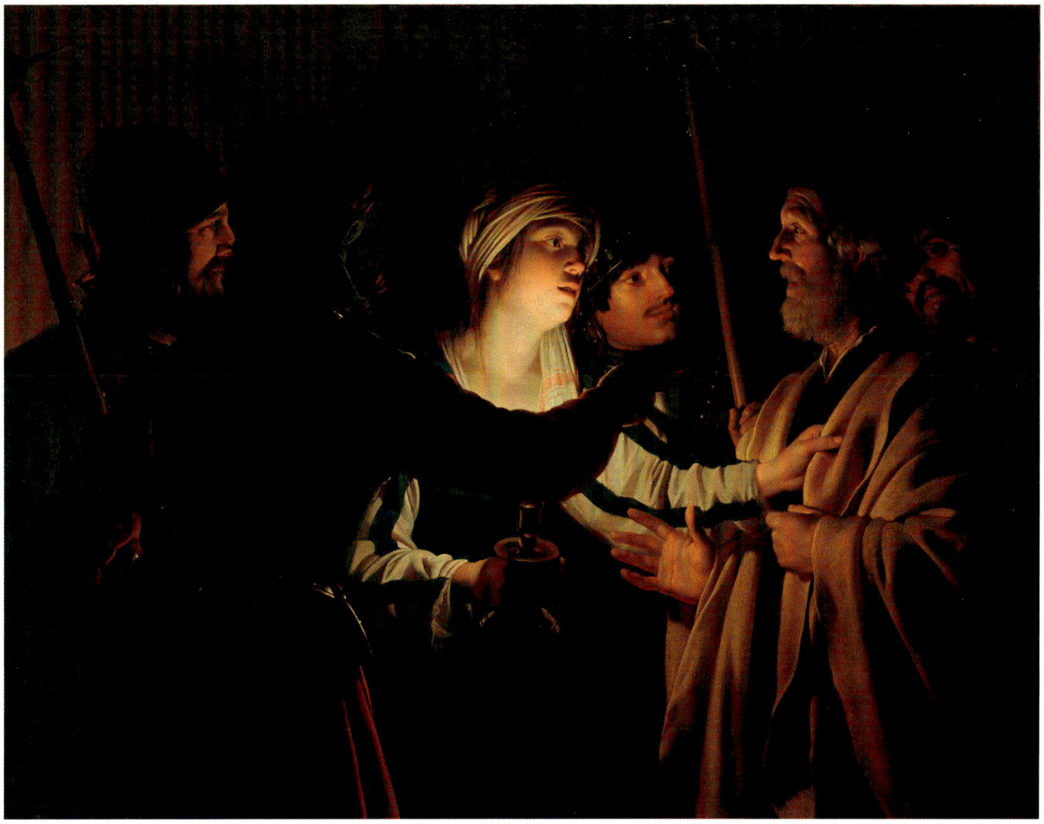

Fig. 55 Gerard van Honthorst, *The Denial of St Peter*, c. 1622/24, Minneapolis Institute of Art, Minneapolis, The Putnam Dana McMillan Fund

to the right of the table and the expressive gestures of the main protagonists. The rear figure sitting at the table in Caravaggio's painting becomes an important *repoussoir* motif in the subsequent depictions of the Denial of St Peter.

Caravaggio's *Calling of St Matthew* was well known and much discussed among artists of the time.[13] It likely made a profound impression on the Caravaggisti, impacting their compositional schemes directly, rather than by way of Ribera or Manfredi – including on the young Gerard van Honthorst, who lived across the street from San Luigi dei Francesi at the Palazzo Giustiniani.

Yet unlike Caravaggio, Ribera, Manfredi and his followers, Honthorst did not rely on the even illumination of pictorial space by an undetermined light source located outside the picture and, instead, opted to remain faithful to the bible in his depiction of the nocturnal scenes. Using candles as light sources, he illuminates each scene to great effect. Visible in one case and hidden in the other, the candle flames highlight the action in different ways.[14] Honthorst stands out among the Caravaggisti for his ability to capture the moment of greatest tension by moving his figures extremely close to the viewer and presenting them in dramatic candlelight. For example, her index finger raised in admonition, the brightly lit maid accuses the apostle who – only in Honthorst's depiction – is simultaneously harassed, and grabbed by the coat, by the darkly silhouetted rear figure of the soldier.

The Antwerp-born Gerard Seghers created yet another impressive interpretation of the subject (cat. 11).[15] He, too, depicts the biblical story as a night scene featuring a total of eight figures which are dramatically lit by two candles. The lighting effects of the genre-like soldier scene dominate the first impression, and the actual religious subject reveals itself only at second glance. Seghers shows the moment when St Peter rejects the accusations by pointing at himself, while the figures gathered around the table follow the dispute with amazement and gesture as they join in.

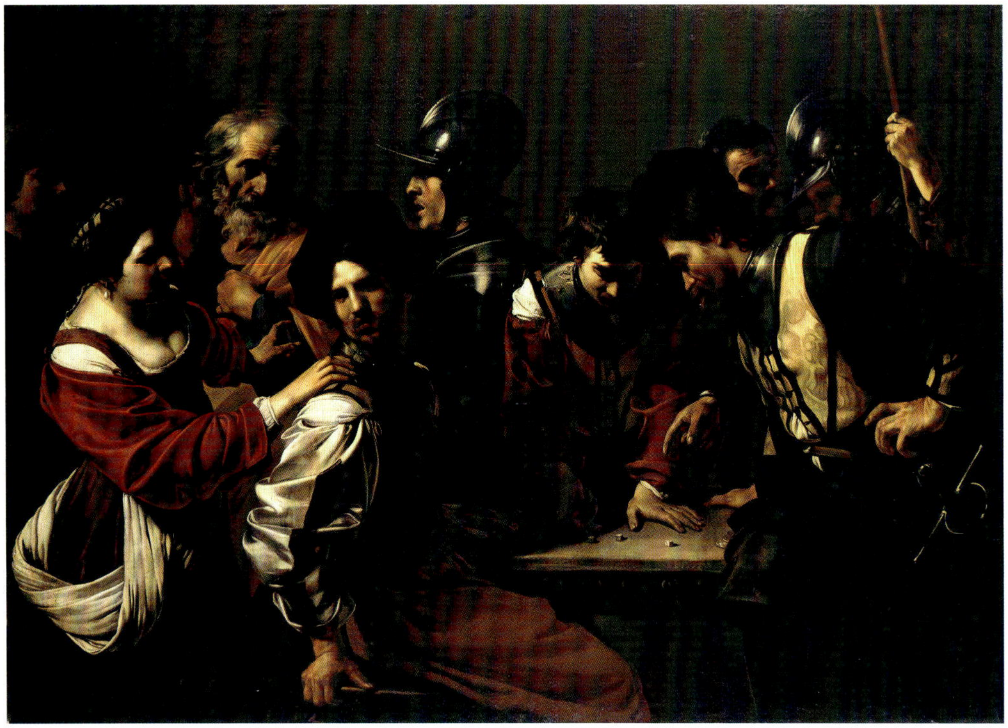

Fig. 56 Bartolomeo Manfredi, *The Denial of St Peter*, c. 1616/18, Herzog Anton Ulrich-Museum, Braunschweig

Stylistically, Seghers drew especially on Gerard van Honthorst, aside from the great masters Caravaggio and Bartolomeo, for his lively narrative style and dramatic lighting.[16] The similarities with Honthorst's works in Rennes, England and Minneapolis lie above all in the rendering of varying light intensities produced by the candle in the maid's hand and the candle with hidden flame standing on the table.

Seghers had specialised in the depiction of the Denial of St Peter in his work. Numerous versions and copies after paintings attributed to him attest to the popularity of the subject and the success he had with it.[17] Technical analysis of the *Denial of St Peter* in Raleigh, which revealed numerous pentimenti, suggests that this painting was the earliest version.[18] Seghers created this interpretation of the subject during the first half of the 1620s when he had risen to become a successful artist and, through marriage, a wealthy burgher in Antwerp. Another version of the subject in Saint Petersburg (fig. 57),[19] which focuses on the biblical story, also indicates that Seghers initially stuck to his Caravaggesque style, until the influence of Rubens came to be formative in the second half of the 1620s.

Although Honthorst's composition with visible artificial light sources also remains indebted to the Dutch tradition, the dramatic, narrative-enhancing illumination of the close-up figures in candlelight, combined with elements of the Caravaggesque repertoire, should still be seen as a novel and independent achievement by the Utrecht master.[20] Unlike the chiaroscuro that is prevalent in the works of Caravaggio, Manfredi and the French Caravaggisti, the principle of lighting in Honthorst conforms to light and shade phenomena that are immediately comprehensible to the viewer, making his paintings appear natural and less stagey. It is those qualities which the roughly same-aged Fleming Gerard Seghers sought to incorporate into his style. BE

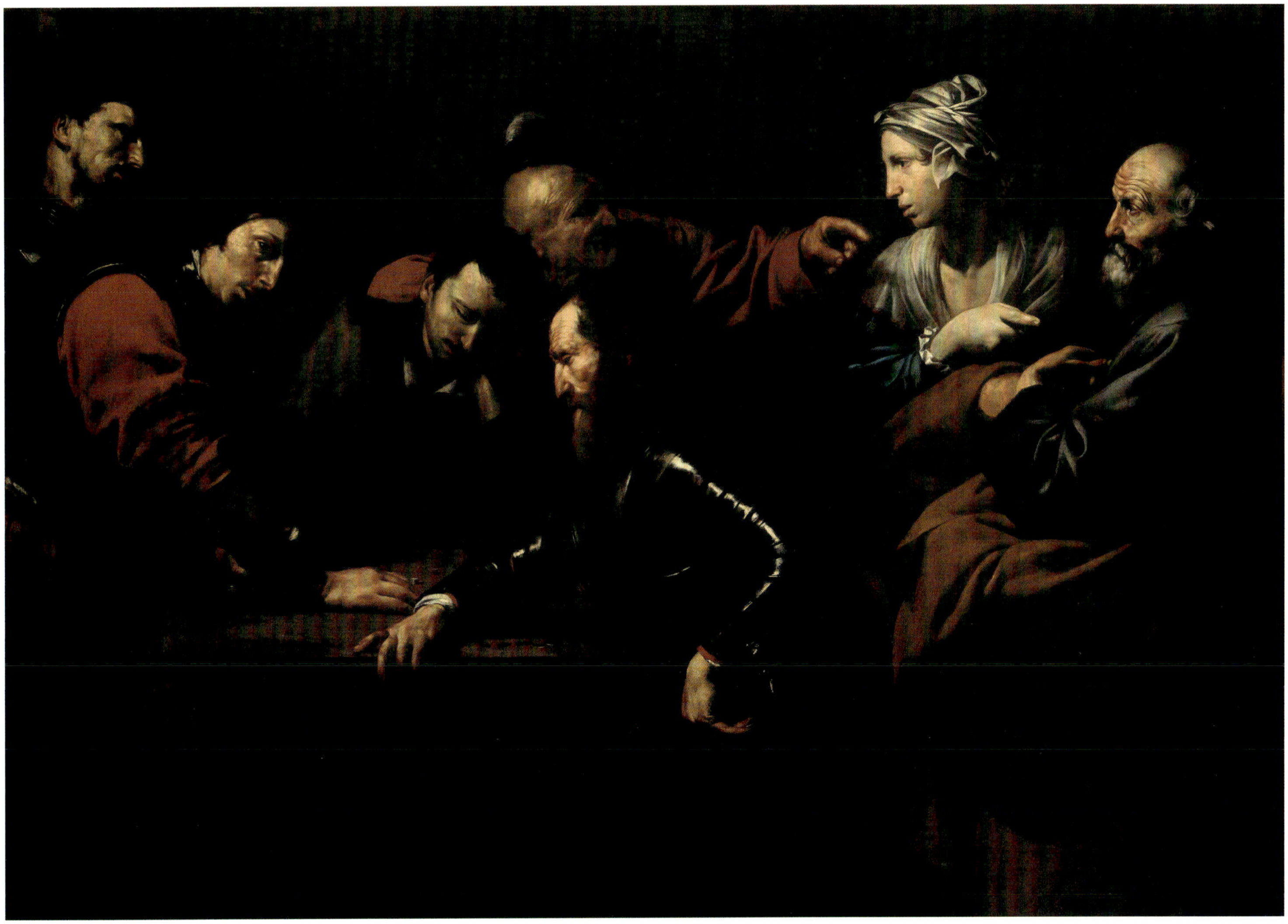

10
Jusepe de Ribera
The Denial of St Peter, c. 1615/16
Gallerie Nazionali di Arte Antica di Roma,
Galleria Corsini, Rome

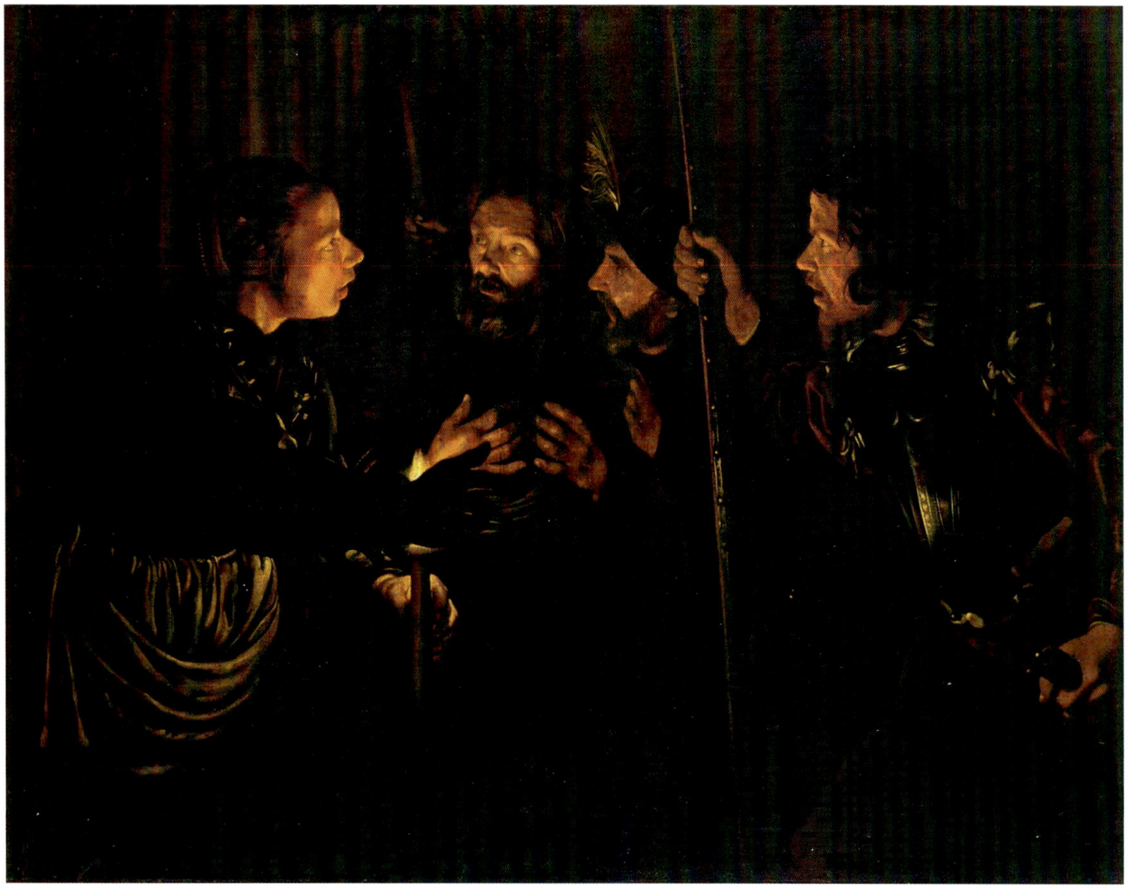

Fig. 57 Gerard Seghers, *The Denial of St Peter*, c. 1620/24, State Hermitage Museum, Saint Petersburg

1 Matthew 26:69–75; Mark 14:66–72; Luke 22:55–60; John 18:16–17, 18:25–27.
2 Hahn 1977, pp. 113–114.
3 Judson 1959, p. 163 (as a possible workshop copy after a lost original); Ramade 1988 (c. 1612/20); Judson/Ekkart 1999, pp. 75–77, cat. 54 (c. 1618/20); Papi 1999, p. 138 (1615/16); Loredana Lorizzo in Exh. cat. Florence 2015, pp. 162–163, cat. 18 (c. 1616/17).
4 *The Denial of St Peter*, c. 1618, canvas, 137 × 244 cm, private collection; Judson/Ekkart 1999, p. 77, cat. 55 (c. 1618); listed in the 1622 inventory of Paolo Mercati as 'una Negatione di S. Pietro grande, opera di Gherardo fiammengo di notte con 7 mezze figure', Sickel 2006, p. 208.
5 *The Denial of St Peter*, c. 1622/24, canvas, 110.5 × 144.8 cm, Minneapolis Institute of Art, inv. 71.78; Judson/Ekkart 1999, pp. 78–79, cat. 56 (c. 1622/24); Gianni Papi in Exh. cat. Florence 2015, pp. 198–199, cat. 35 (c. 1620–1622).
6 For example, Hendrick ter Brugghen, *The Denial of St Peter*, c. 1626/29, canvas, 132.3 × 178 cm, The Art Institute, Chicago, inv. 1969.3.
7 Hahn 1977, p. 116.
8 Ibid., p. 136; Hartje 2004, p. 268.
9 *The Denial of St Peter*, c. 1616/18, canvas, 166 × 232, Herzog Anton Ulrich-Museum, Braunschweig, inv. GG 495. For its dating, see: Cuzin 1980, p. 22 (c. 1615/20); Leonard J. Slatkes in Exh. cat. Utrecht/Braunschweig 1986/87, pp. 313–314, cat. 70 (c. 1615); Merlo 1987, p. 74 (late work); Hartje 2004, pp. 259, 339–341, cat. A23 (c. 1616–18); Papi 2013, pp. 175–176, cat. 39 (1616/18).
10 Papi 2002, pp. 22, 35, 37.
11 Nicolaci/Gandolfi 2011, pp. 53–54 (c. 1614/15); Gianni Papi in Exh. cat. Madrid 2011, p. 130, cat. 13 (c. 1615/16); Salomon 2011, p. 476 (c. 1613/14); Gianni Papi in Exh. cat. Rome 2011/12, p. 254, cat. IX. 5 (c. 1615); Guillaume Kientz in Exh. cat. Rennes/Strasbourg 2014/15, pp. 20, 33 (c. 1615); Keith Christiansen in Exh. cat. New York/Paris 2016/17, pp. 83–85, cat. 3 (c. 1615).
12 Leonard J. Slatkes in Exh. cat. Utrecht/Braunschweig 1986/87, p. 314 (c. 1615); for its dating, see also Maccherini 1999, pp. 133–135, 137; Hartje 2004, pp. 339–341, cat. A23; Gianni Papi in Exh. cat. Rome 2011/12, p. 254; Papi 2013, pp. 175–176.
13 Pericolo 2011, pp. 211–241.
14 Hahn 1977, pp. 122–123b.
15 Bieneck 1992, pp. 140–141, cat. A12.
16 Nicolson 1971, pp. 304–308; Judson/Ekkart 1999, p. 76.
17 Nicolson 1971, pp. 304–305.
18 Bieneck 1992, p. 140, cat. A12; Cat. Raleigh 2009, p. 318. For versions and copies, see Bieneck 1992, cat. A10, A11, A13–A17, B120; Nicolson 1971.
19 *The Denial of St Peter*, c. 1620/24, panel, 122.5 × 160.5 cm, State Hermitage Museum, Saint Petersburg, inv.00-3058; Bieneck 1992, p. 139, cat. A11.
20 Neumeister 2003, p. 160.

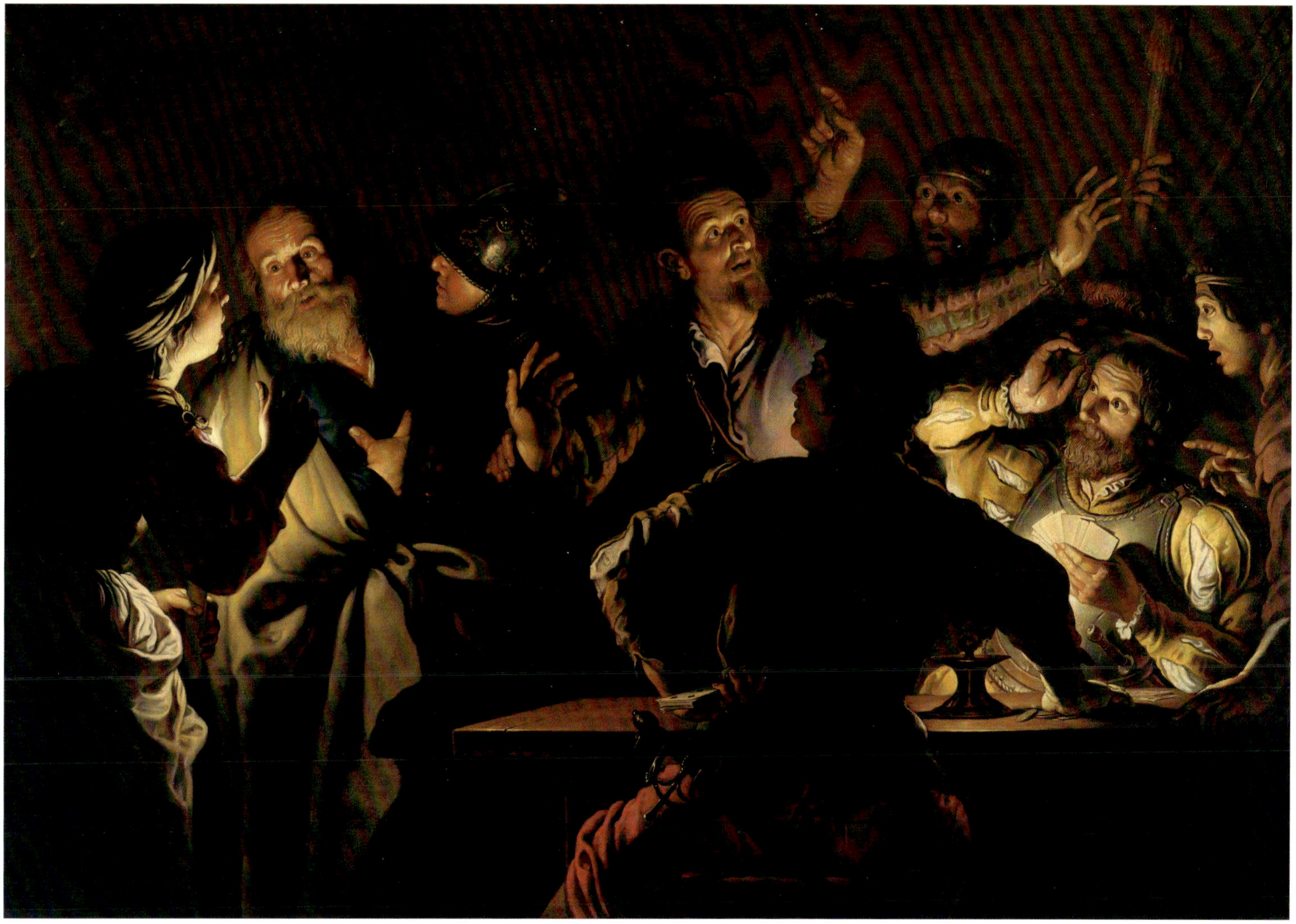

11

Gerard Seghers
The Denial of St Peter, c. 1620/25
North Carolina Museum of Art, Raleigh, purchased with funds from the State of North Carolina

c. 1616/18

The Liberation of St Peter

12
Gerard van Honthorst
The Liberation of St Peter, c. 1616/18
Canvas, 129 × 179 cm
Staatliche Museen zu Berlin,
Gemäldegalerie, Berlin, Kat. Nr. 431

13
Hendrick ter Brugghen
The Liberation of St Peter, 1624
Signed and dated on the left near the angel's shoulder: HTBrugghe[n]/[16]24 [HTB ligatured]
Canvas, 104.5 × 86.5 cm
Mauritshuis, The Hague, inv. 966

14
Hendrick ter Brugghen
The Liberation of St Peter, 1629
Signed and dated bottom left on the stone slab: HTBrugghen fecit 1629 [HTB ligatured]
Canvas, 152 × 210 cm
Staatliches Museum Schwerin, Schwerin, inv. 913

15
Simon Vouet
St Jerome and the Angel, c. 1620/21
Canvas, 144.8 × 179.8 cm
National Gallery of Art, Washington, D.C.,
Samuel H. Kress Collection, inv. 1961.9.52

Honthorst's painting in Berlin is the earliest of these three thematically related pictures and, unlike the two works by ter Brugghen, it was painted in Italy (cat. 12).[1] At least this is suggested by the mention of a picture which, listed as no. 97 in the inventory of Benedetto Giustiniani that was compiled on 31 March 1621, is described as 'a painting showing Saint Peter in prison being awakened by an angel'.[2] This work is likely identical with the *supraporte* (overdoor) mentioned in February 1638 in the inventory of Marchese Vincenzo Giustiniani, the brother and heir of Benedetto, which is said to depict 'Saint Peter in prison with the angel who comes to liberate him, artificial night [...], allegedly by the hand of Gerard'.[3]

Honthorst's dramatically lit scene is crucially indebted to Caravaggio's *Calling of St Matthew* at the Contarelli Chapel in San Luigi dei Francesi (fig. 78). The angel entering the prison cell from the right and extending its left arm towards Saint Peter is reminiscent of Caravaggio's figure of Christ. Caravaggio's Christ, however, points towards Matthew with his right hand, which is slightly bent at the wrist, a gesture famously adopted in mirror image from the outstretched arm of Adam in Michelangelo Buonarroti's depiction of God the Father breathing life into Adam in the Sistine Chapel. Richard J. Judson views a drawing of the Liberation of St Peter ascribed to Honthorst as a study for the painting in Berlin, even though it depicts the subject in much greater detail and the differences between the two are substantial (fig. 58).[4] Judson argues that, in the drawing, Honthorst had sought to combine the more classicist maniera of Annibale Carracci with the naturalism of Caravaggio. He cites the Liberation of St Peter by Domenico Zampieri, called Domenichino, a student and assistant of Annibale Carracci, created in 1604 for the Roman church of San Pietro in Vincoli as a direct source.[5] In his Berlin painting, Honthorst emphasises the dramatic effect of the light which bursts into the dark confines of the dungeon when the angel opens the heavy door and turns to the surprised St Peter. The soldiers seen in the drawing are omitted in the painting.

Hendrick ter Brugghen's depiction of the same subject, painted in 1624 in The Hague (cat. 13), shows the scene in a vertical format against a dark backdrop with half-length figures appearing in the very front of the painting where they take up almost the entire space.[6] Unlike in Honthorst's *Liberation of St Peter* in Berlin, the

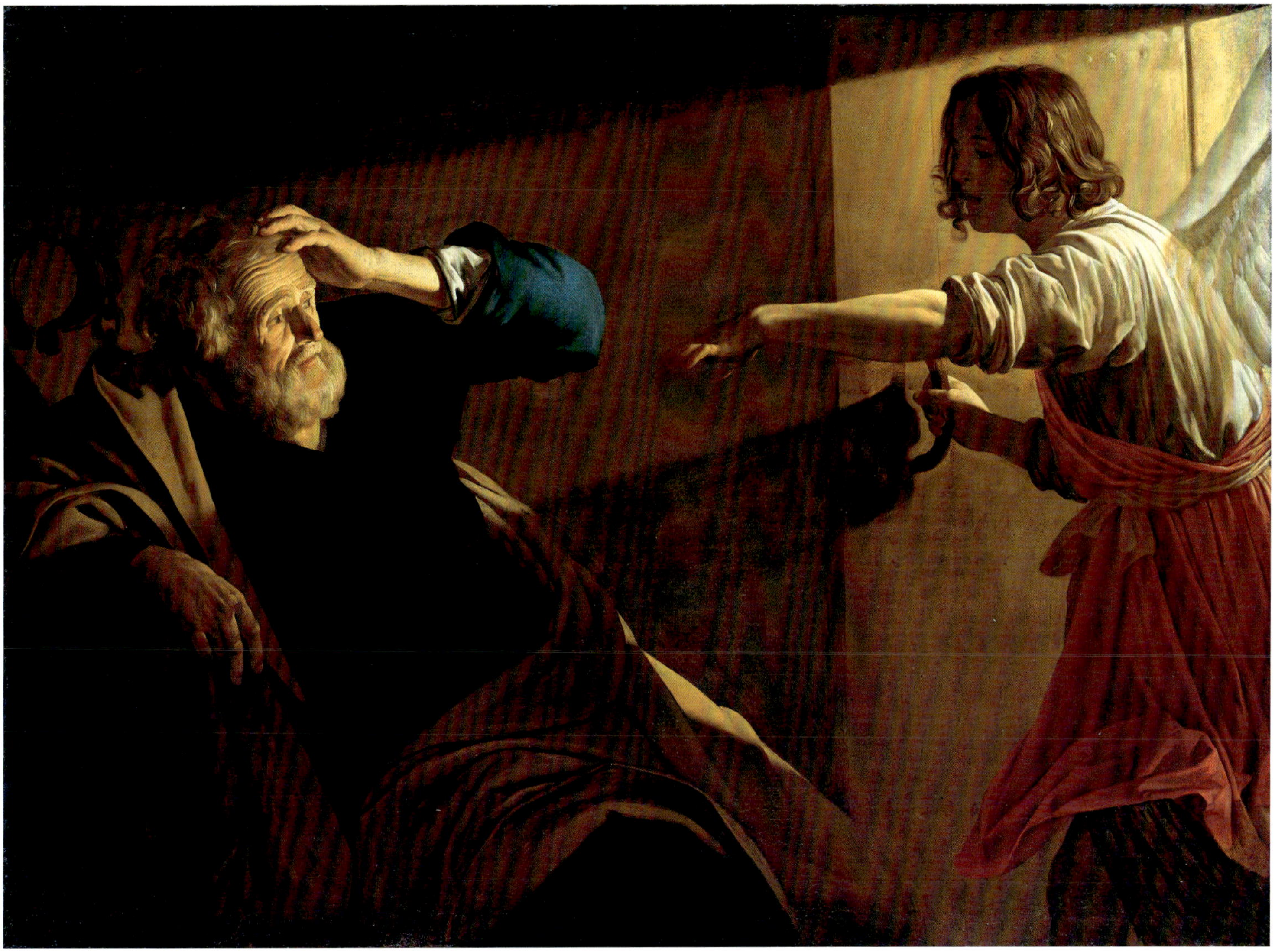

12
Gerard van Honthorst
The Liberation of St Peter, c. 1616/18
Staatliche Museen zu Berlin,
Gemäldegalerie, Berlin

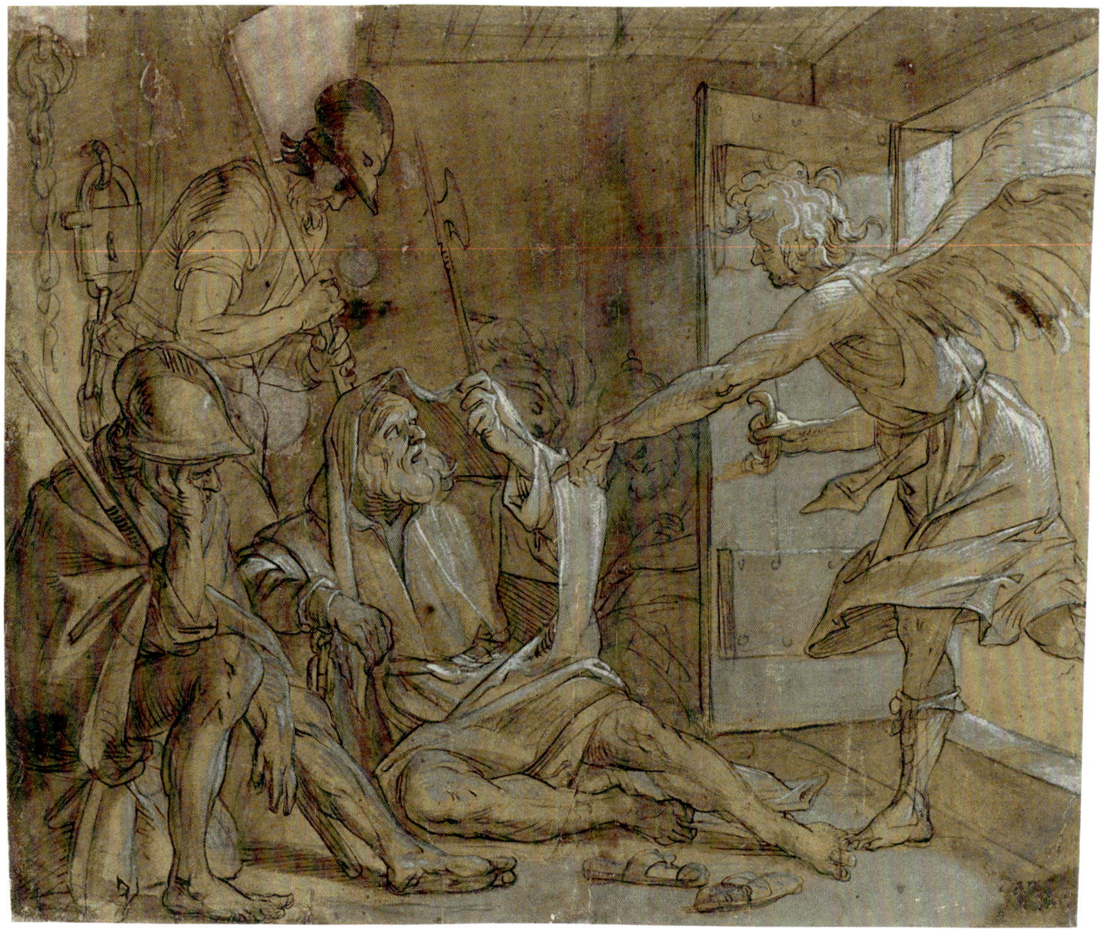

Fig. 58 Gerard van Honthorst, *The Liberation of St Peter*, c. 1615, Staatliche Kunstsammlungen Dresden, Kupferstichkabinett, Dresden

light enters the painting from the upper left and heightens the contrast between the figures and the background. St Peter's clasped hands are still chained. Wide-eyed and his toothless mouth open, he gapes at the youthful angel who touches his shoulder with its right hand while pointing upward with its left to stress the divine intervention. Like Honthorst's, ter Brugghen's depiction is brought alive by the contrast between the two protagonists, the confrontation between the aged apostle with his weather-beaten face and coarse hands, on the one hand, and the boyish-looking angel with its pale skin and slimmer fingers, on the other. Benedict Nicolson regarded the painting as a late work of the painter, as there are obvious connections to some works ter Brugghen created in 1628/29.[7] The figure of St Peter, for example, seems to be based on the same model as the harp-playing King David in the painting in Warsaw (fig. 97), which is dated to 1628.[8] And the angel putting one hand on the apostle's shoulder while pointing upward with the other looks like a reversed half-length version of the figure in the 1629 *Liberation of St Peter* in Schwerin (cat. 14). Another related figure is the Archangel Gabriel in the *Annunciation* in Diest (cat. 78), also painted in 1629. The signature and the date 1624 on the painting in The Hague were uncovered only in 1963 when it underwent restoration. This suggests that, in his late works of 1628/29, ter Brugghen drew on certain types of figures and gestures he had developed years earlier.[9] The gestures of the angel in the 1624 *Liberation of St Peter* also prove that – long before his *Annunciation* in Diest – the painter had studied the c. 1623 *Annunciation* by Dirck van Baburen, a work now lost which has come down to us only in a copy by Jan Janssens (fig. 108).

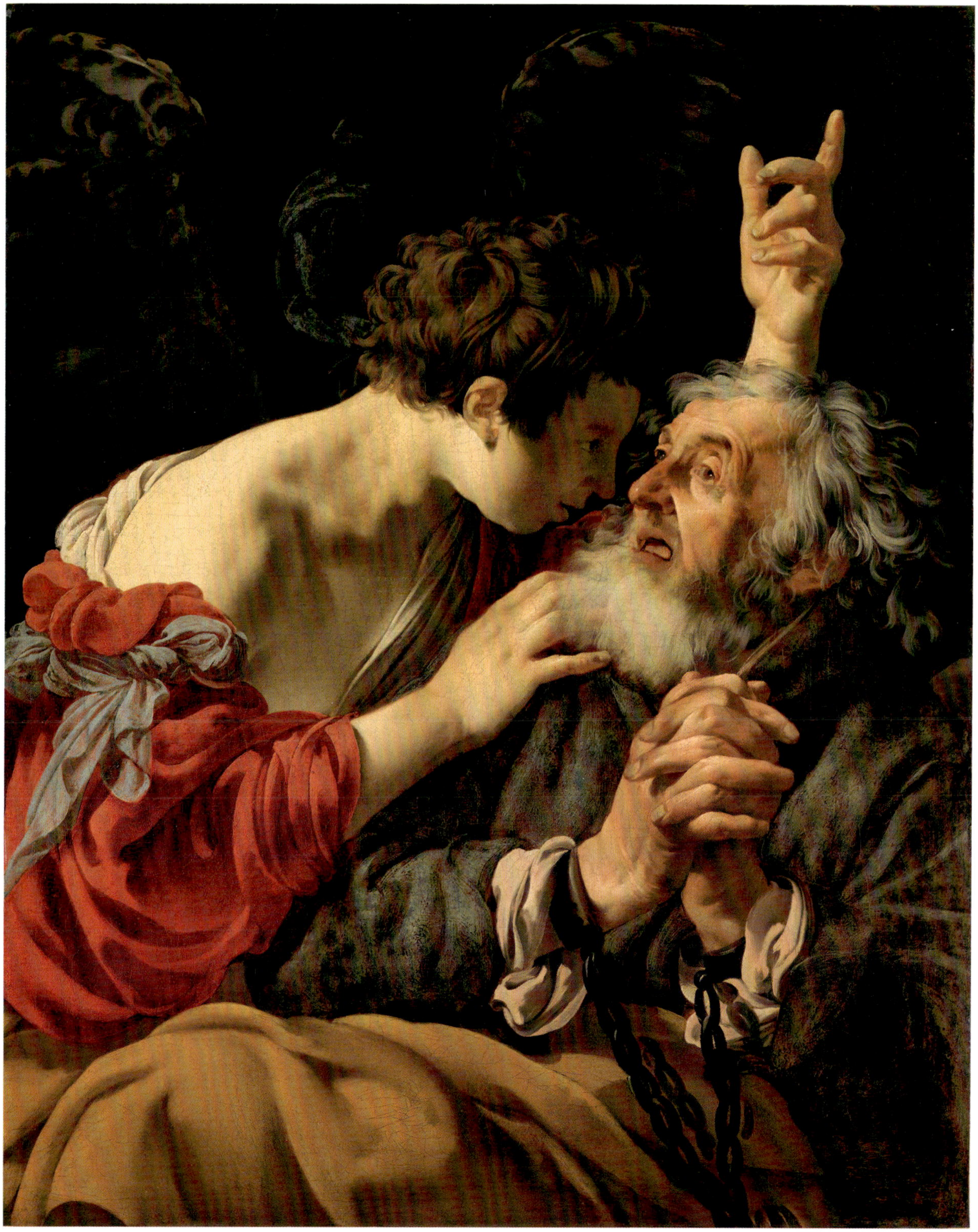

13
Hendrick ter Brugghen
The Liberation of St Peter, 1624
Mauritshuis, The Hague

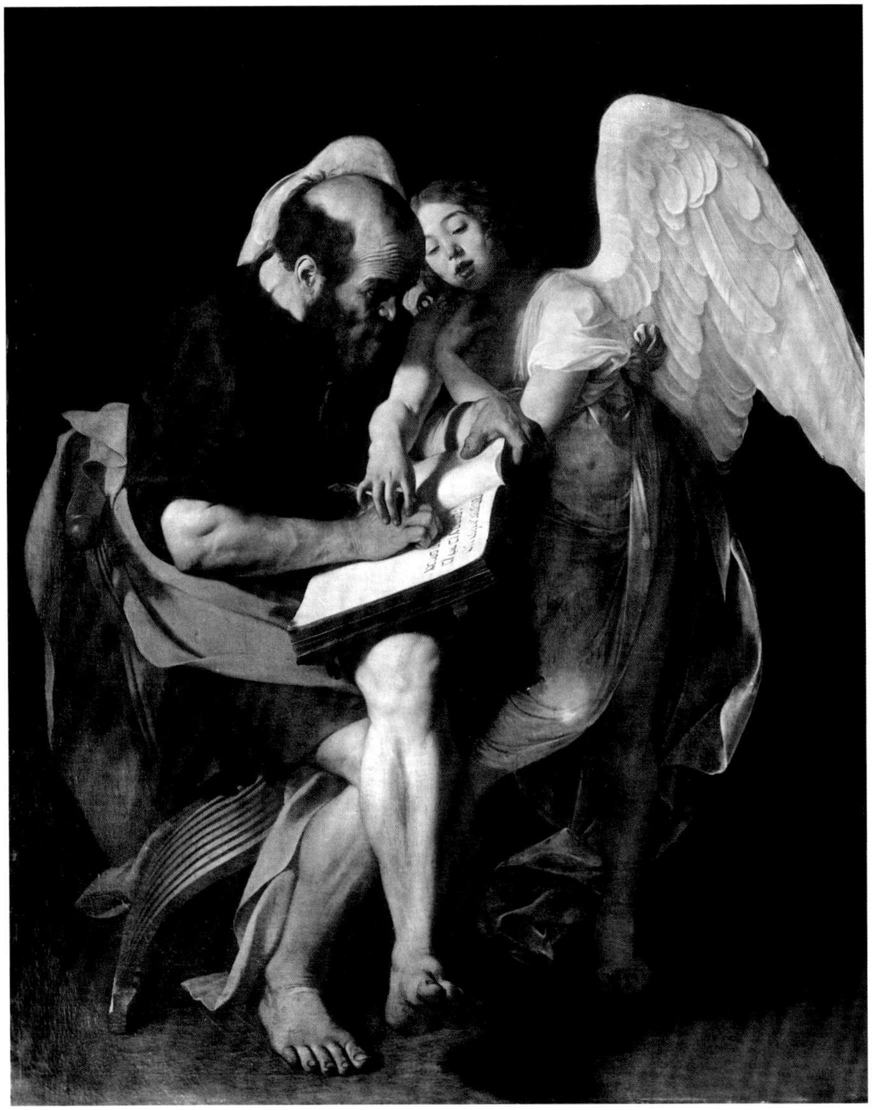

Fig. 59 Michelangelo Merisi, called Caravaggio, *St Matthew and the Angel*, formerly Kaiser Friedrich Museum, Berlin

In his 1629 *Liberation of St Peter* in Schwerin, ter Brugghen depicts the scene using full-length figures.[10] By touching his shoulder, the angel approaching from the right has roused St Peter from his sleep and he turns to the celestial being, startled. We can see the chains around his wrists and the ankle shackles lying next to him. By depicting the attributes of the prince of the apostles – the two keys are lying to his left on the floor in the foreground – ter Brugghen obviously wanted to ensure the readability of the scene, which is also aided by the traditional colours of the apostle's robes, blue and yellow. The extremely foreshortened depiction of the recumbent figure of St Peter compels us to look at the dirty soles of his feet, an image found repeatedly in Caravaggio's paintings. A comparison of the two angels in ter Brugghen's The Hague and Schwerin versions of the *Liberation of St Peter* with the corresponding figure in the work of Honthorst reveals that ter Brugghen departs from the iconographic tradition. His two angels have unusually short hair rather than the mid-length curls which were common around 1600, as exemplified by the angel in Caravaggio's *Stigmatisation of St Francis*.[11]

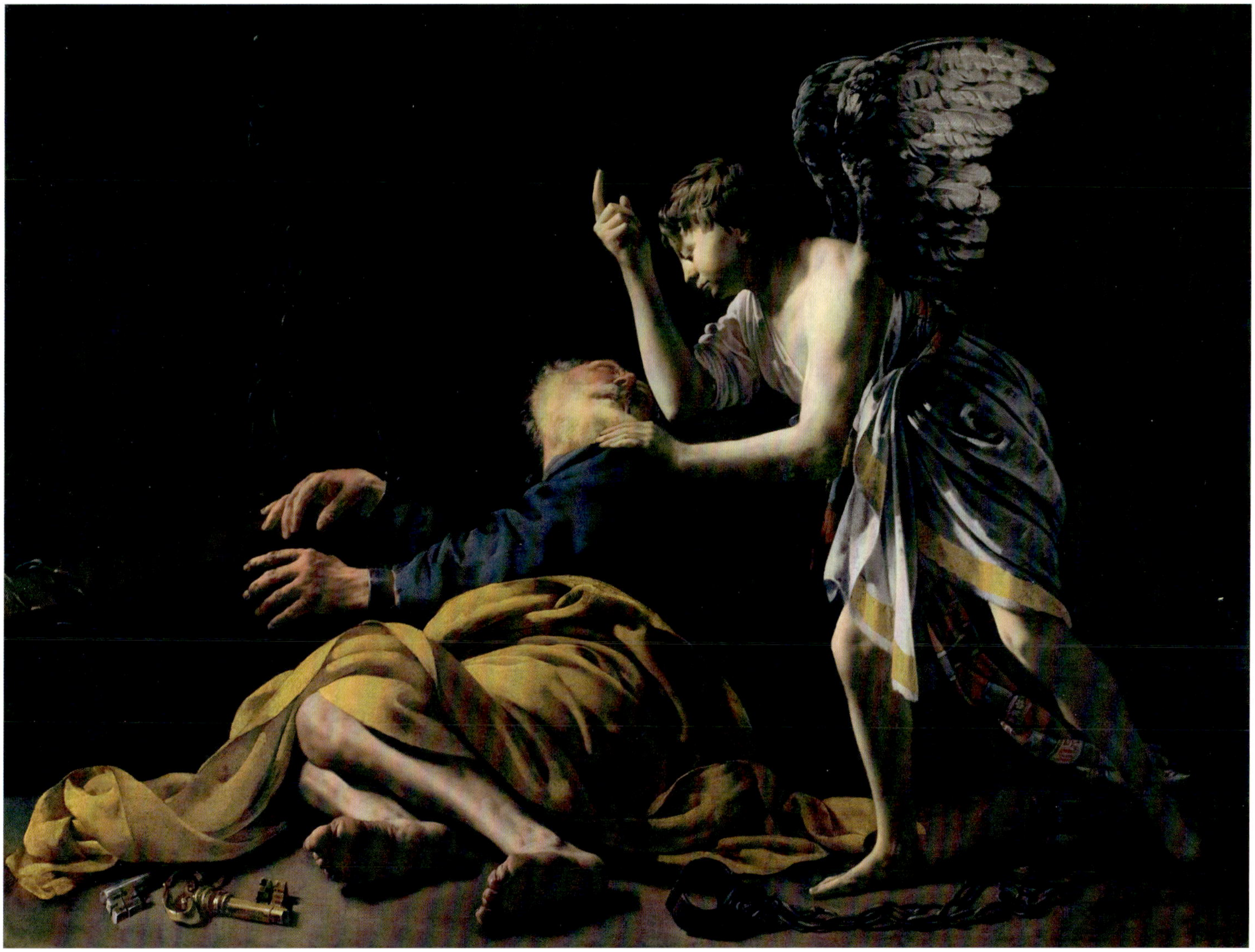

14
Hendrick ter Brugghen
The Liberation of St Peter, 1629
Staatliches Museum Schwerin, Schwerin

The encounter between a youthful angel and an old man is also the theme of Simon Vouet's *St Jerome and the Angel* (cat. 15).[12] The nocturnal scene is set in the study of the Church Father who has been interrupted in his writing by an angel approaching from behind, a trumpet in his left hand. The translator of the Latin bible (Vulgate) is identified as a cardinal by the red mantle draped in front of his bare torso. On the table in front of him are writing utensils as well as a skull and an hourglass which allude to the finiteness and transience of man's earthly existence. The angel's trumpet may also been seen in this context, as it refers to the Last Judgement and, by extension, to the return of Jesus Christ as a judge deciding on salvation and damnation: 'Indeed, that trumpet will sound, and then the dead will be raised never to decay, and we will be changed'.[13] The scene where the Church Father hears the trumpets of the Last Judgement, a subject especially popular in the 17th century, probably had its source in several passages in the 1429 Regula Monachorum, which are linked to the writings of St Jerome. There we read, for example: 'Always the terrible trumpets sound in your ears, saying "Arise, ye dead, and come to your judgment!"'[14]

Simon Vouet undoubtedly was also familiar with the first version (lost since 1945) of Caravaggio's altarpiece for the Contarelli chapel featuring St Matthew and the angel, a depiction similarly characterised by the particularly close proximity of the two figures (fig. 59). During Vouet's time in Rome, this work was in the Giustiniani collection where numerous painters could study it. The head of the Church Father with furrowed brow and suntanned face is reminiscent of Caravaggio's 1605/06 *St Jerome* in the Galleria Borghese in Rome (fig. 52).[15] Yet unlike Caravaggio and ter Brugghen, Vouet favoured a much less rugged type of figure and the encounter of the young, almost classical-looking angel with the weather-beaten Church Father unfolds less dramatically – not least because of the different subject. VM

1 Judson/Ekkart 1999, pp. 93–95, cat. 74; see also Loredana Lorizzo in Exh. cat. Rome/Berlin 2001, pp. 312–313, cat. D14.
2 'Un quadro di San Pietro in prigione destato dall'angelo ...', quoted by Judson/Ekkart 1999, p. 94.
3 'Un quadro sopraporto di San Pietro Carcere con l'angelo, che lo viene a liberare finto di notte ..., si crede di mano di Gherardi ...', quoted by Judson/Ekkart 1999, p. 94.
4 c. 1615, pen and black ink, heightened with white, over pencil, 302 × 368 mm, Staatliche Kunstsammlungen Dresden, Kupferstichkabinett, Dresden, inv. C 909; Judson/Ekkart 1999, pp. 330–331, cat. D15. The attribution was made by Von Schneider 1928, pp. 113–115. See Judson 1986/87, p. 111.
5 Canvas, 119.5 × 147 cm. In 1761, the original work by Domenichino found its way to Potsdam (Sanssouci) and it has been lost since 1945. The version surviving in the vestry of San Pietro in Vincoli is apparently a copy; see Spear 1982, vol. 1, pp. 133–134, cat. 11, incl. fig. 14.
6 Slatkes/Franits 2007, pp. 128–129, cat. A36.
7 Nicolson 1958, p. 60; see also Broos 1993, pp. 97–102.
8 Slatkes/Franits 2007, pp. 84–86, cat. A7.
9 See Leonard J. Slatkes in Exh. cat. Utrecht/Braunschweig 1986/87, p. 164.
10 Slatkes/Franits 2007, pp. 130–132, cat. A37. A second full-length version which is dated c. 1625/26 and ascribed to ter Brugghen and his workshop is in National Museum of Western Art, Tokyo, canvas, 137.5 × 172 cm, inv. P.1980-0001; see Slatkes/Franits 2007, pp. 215–216, cat. TW5. Its problematic state of preservation complicates an assessment of the painting.
11 c. 1595/96, canvas, 92.5 × 127.8 cm, Wadsworth Atheneum, Hartford, inv. 1943222.
12 Dominique Jacquot in Exh. cat. Nantes/Besançon 2008/09, p. 124, cat. 21. There, Taddeo Barberini (1603–1647), Prince of Palestrina, is erroneously referred to as its first owner. More likely, the painting was first mentioned in two inventories of Cardinal Carlo Barberini (1630–1704), which were drawn up in Rome in 1692 and 1704, respectively. See the information on its provenance provided by Aronberg Lavin 1975, p. 441, VI. inv. 92–04, no. 337. It is not known when the painting found its way into the Barberini collection.
13 1 Corinthians 15:52.
14 Quoted from PL, vol. 30, col. 387.
15 Canvas, 112 × 157 cm, inv. 56; see Schütze 2009, p. 271, cat. 41.

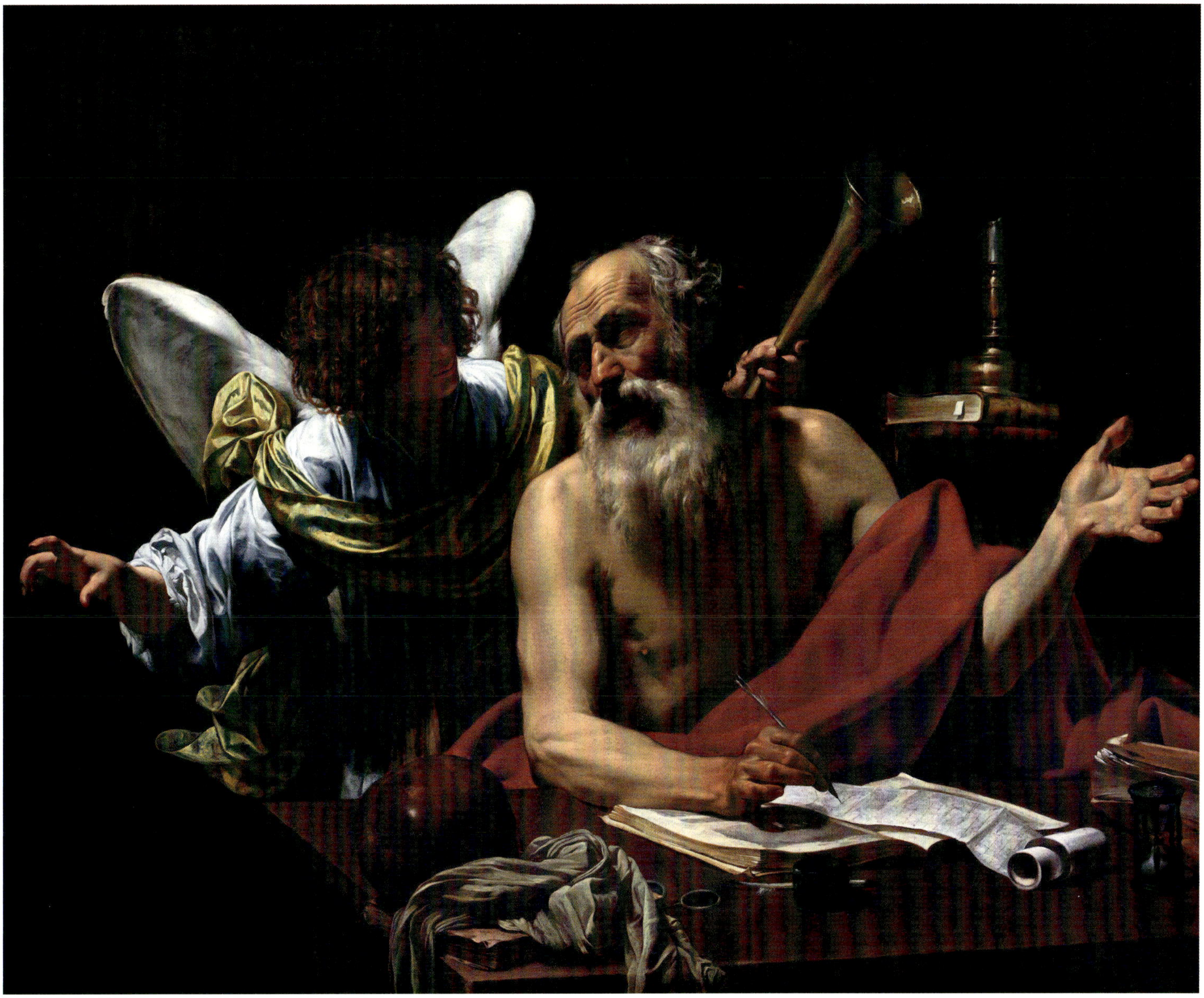

15
Simon Vouet
St Jerome and the Angel, c. 1620/21
National Gallery of Art, Washington, D.C.,
Samuel H. Kress Collection

c. 1617

The Mocking of Christ

16

Gerard van Honthorst
The Mocking of Christ, c. 1617
Canvas, 146.1 × 207 cm
Los Angeles County Museum of Art, Los Angeles, gift of The Ahmanson Foundation, inv. AC1999.92.1

17

Hendrick ter Brugghen
The Mocking of Christ, c. 1625
Canvas, 157 × 118.5 cm
Musée des Beaux-Arts de Rennes, Rennes, on loan from the Musée de l'Assistance Publique, Paris, inv. AP 1760

18

Giovanni Serodine
The Mocking of Christ, c. 1626
Canvas, 113 × 152 cm
Pinacoteca cantonale Giovanni Züst, Rancate (Mendrisio), inv. PZ 461

Depictions of scenes from the final days in the life of Christ are a fixture of the pictorial canon of the Counter-Reformation. In order to strengthen the faith, it was important to strike the deepest chords in viewers and move them to compassion, indeed, to have them partake, in their devotion, in the physical suffering and the humiliation of the Redeemer. In early Christian representations of the Passion, the focus was still on the triumph over death through the Resurrection. While scenes of the Mocking of Christ were depicted only sporadically in the Middle Ages, they have become more frequent since the Renaissance. Often, the subjects of the Crowning with Thorns and the Mocking are conflated into one image.

According to the biblical account, Christ was arrested by soldiers after the Last Supper and the betrayal by Judas and taken to the house of the high priest Annas. There he was interrogated by the high priest Caiaphas and accused of blasphemy (cat. 19). After this interrogation Christ was mocked by supporters and servants of the high priest, who spat him on the face and beat him.[1] The next day, a second mocking took place following the interrogation by Pilate, when the soldiers crowned him with a crown of thorns and mocked him as 'King of the Jews'.[2]

Datable to c. 1617, Gerard van Honthorst's painting at the Los Angeles County Museum of Art (cat. 16) is one of several works in which Honthorst depicts the Mocking and the Crowning with Thorns as a night scene by candle or torchlight.[3] These paintings, whose dimensions and number of figures vary, were created in the period between 1614 and 1617 in Italy.[4] The *Crowning with Thorns* at the J. Paul Getty Museum in Los Angeles (fig. 60) as well as the Mocking scenes in the Church of Santa Maria Immacolata in Rome and the Spier Collection in London (fig. 61) are considered to be the earliest ones and may be dated to c. 1614.[5]

Even though the scene discussed here combines the Crowning with Thorns and the Mocking in a single image, Honthorst paid particular attention to the four men who mock Christ in the left half of the painting. The henchman on the right who uses a forked branch to press the spiky crown of thorns onto the captive's head while pulling his hair in mockery, is relegated to the background in terms of both composition and narrative. The men on the left are presented in more dramatic fashion

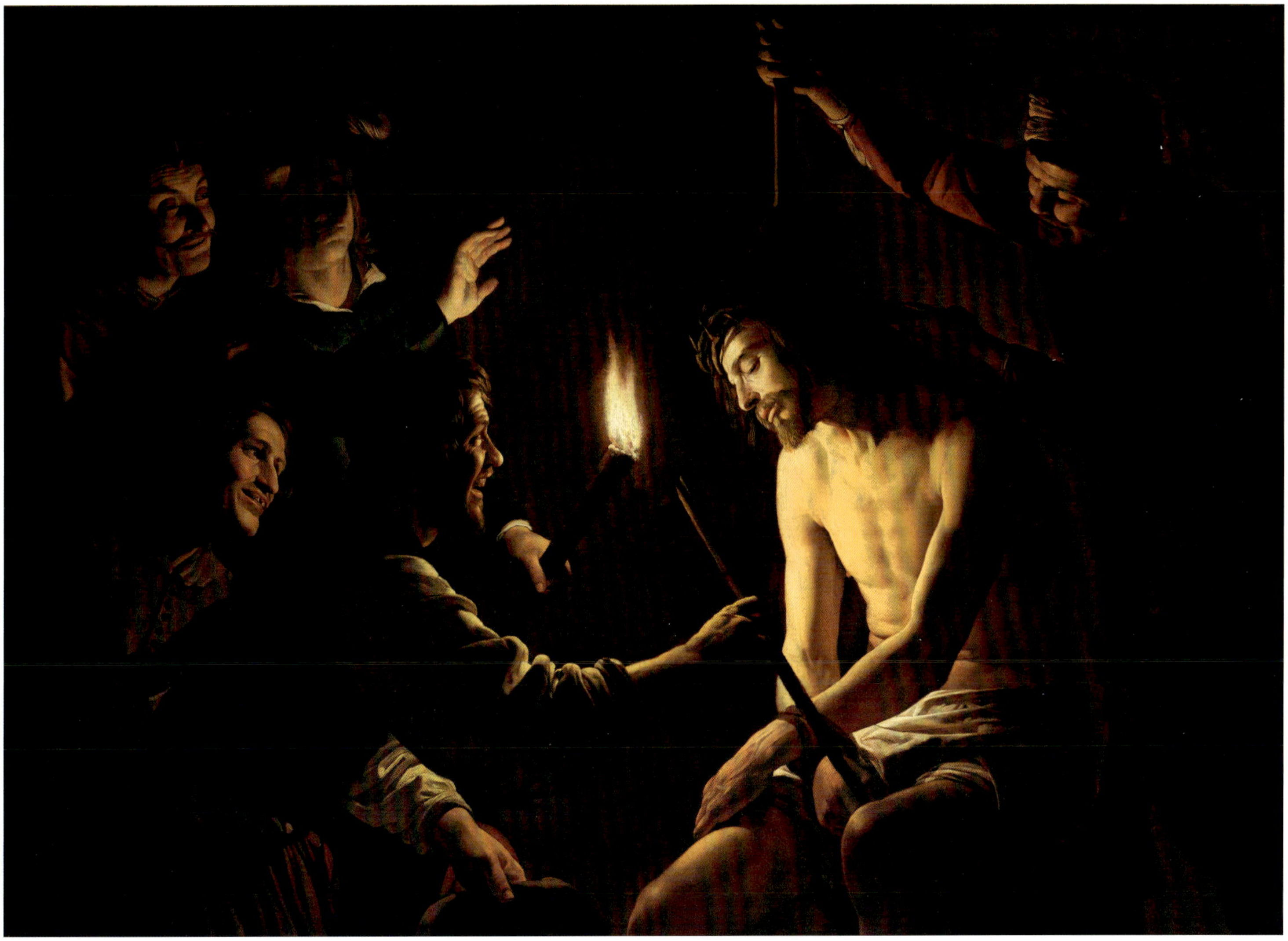

16
Gerard van Honthorst
The Mocking of Christ, c. 1617
Los Angeles County Museum of Art, Los Angeles,
gift of The Ahmanson Foundation

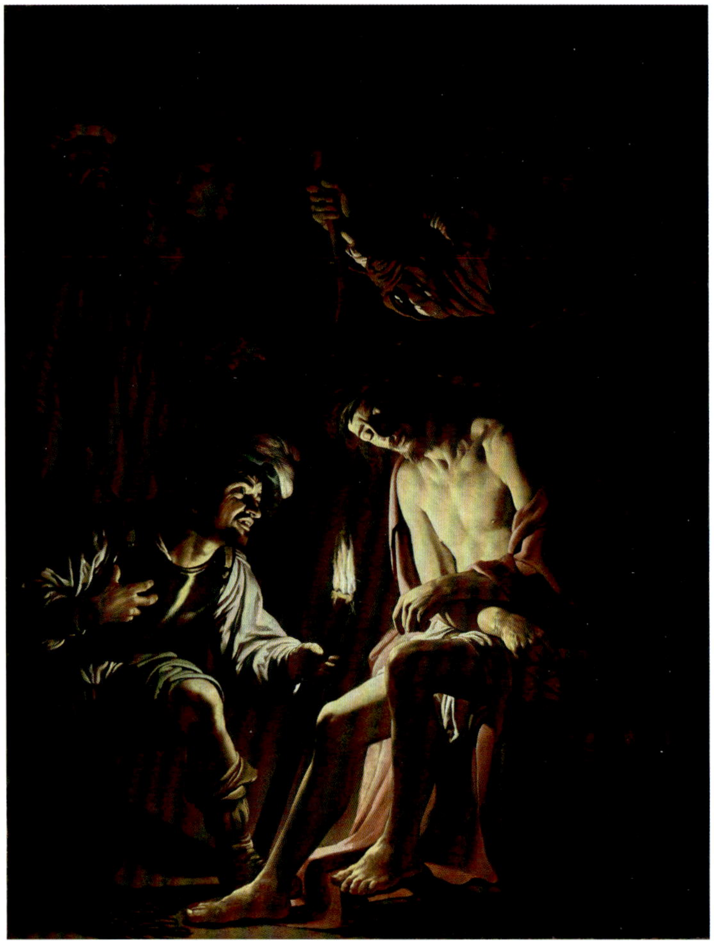

Fig. 60 Gerard van Honthorst, *Christ Crowned with Thorns*, c. 1614, The J. Paul Getty Museum, Los Angeles

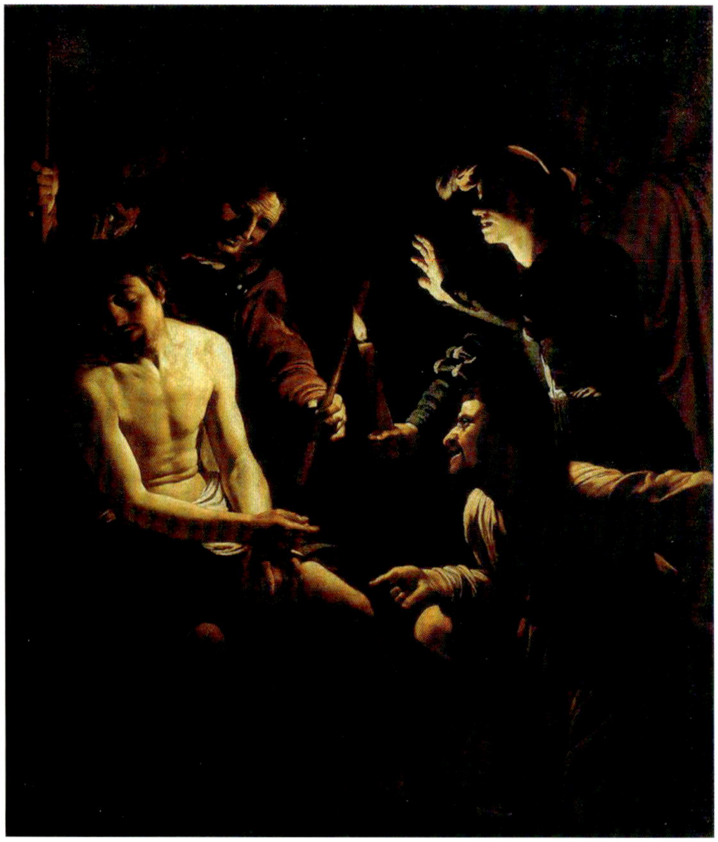

Fig. 61 Gerard van Honthorst, *The Mocking of Christ*, c. 1614, The Spier Collection, London

through the play of light and shade; the light of the torch is reflected to great effect on their grinning and laughing faces. Honthorst shows particular skill in depicting the interaction of light and shade in skin wrinkles and garment folds. A feature typical of him is the face shaded by a raised hand with which one of the mockers tries to shield himself from the bright torchlight and, at the same time, the 'enlightening' reflection of the body of Christ. Honthorst already introduced this motif in his Mocking scene in the Spier Collection, which may be dated to c. 1614 (fig. 61). He contrasts the humbly forward-leaning, exposed body, which stoically endures torment, pain and humiliation, with the foolish conduct of the tormentors, and goes so far as to symbolically dress the mocker on the far left in a red and yellow jester's costume and gugel-like jester's hood with little bells hanging from its peaks.

Hendrick ter Brugghen, Honthorst's fellow countryman, also explored the subject multiple times, with his compositions drawing primarily on examples of 16th-century northern European art.[6] To a much greater extent than any of the other Caravaggisti, ter Brugghen continued to draw on the pictorial forms of the Dürer period in his paintings, combining them in distinct ways with Caravaggesque stylistic elements. Aside from the large-scale, multi-figure version from the year 1620 at the Statens Museum for Kunst in Copenhagen[7] and the version datable to c. 1625, which was formerly in Sydney (fig. 62),[8] this is impressively evident in the painting in the collection of the Musée de

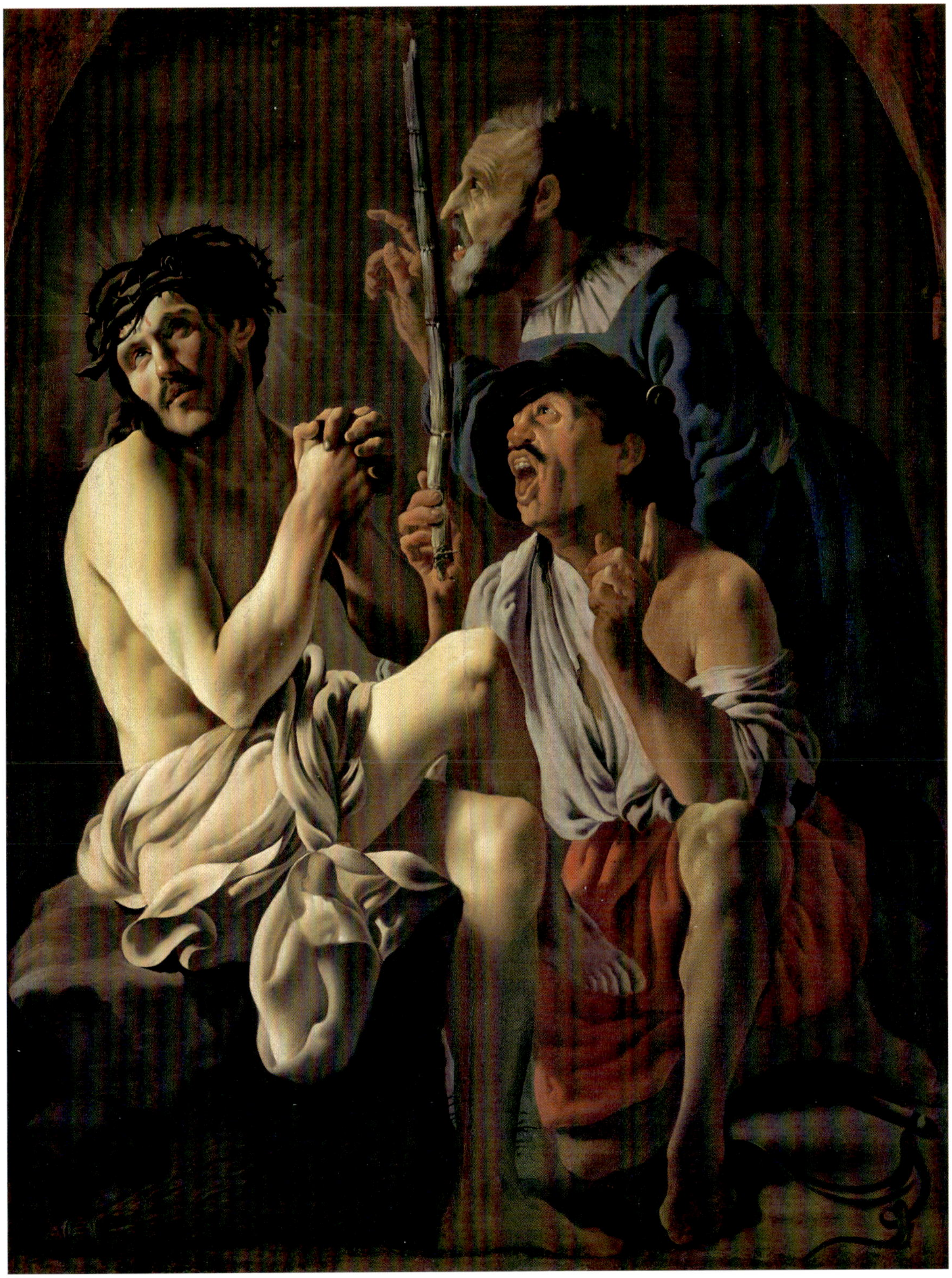

17
Hendrick ter Brugghen
The Mocking of Christ, c. 1625
Musée des Beaux-Arts de Rennes, Rennes,
on loan from the Musée de l'Assistance Publique, Paris

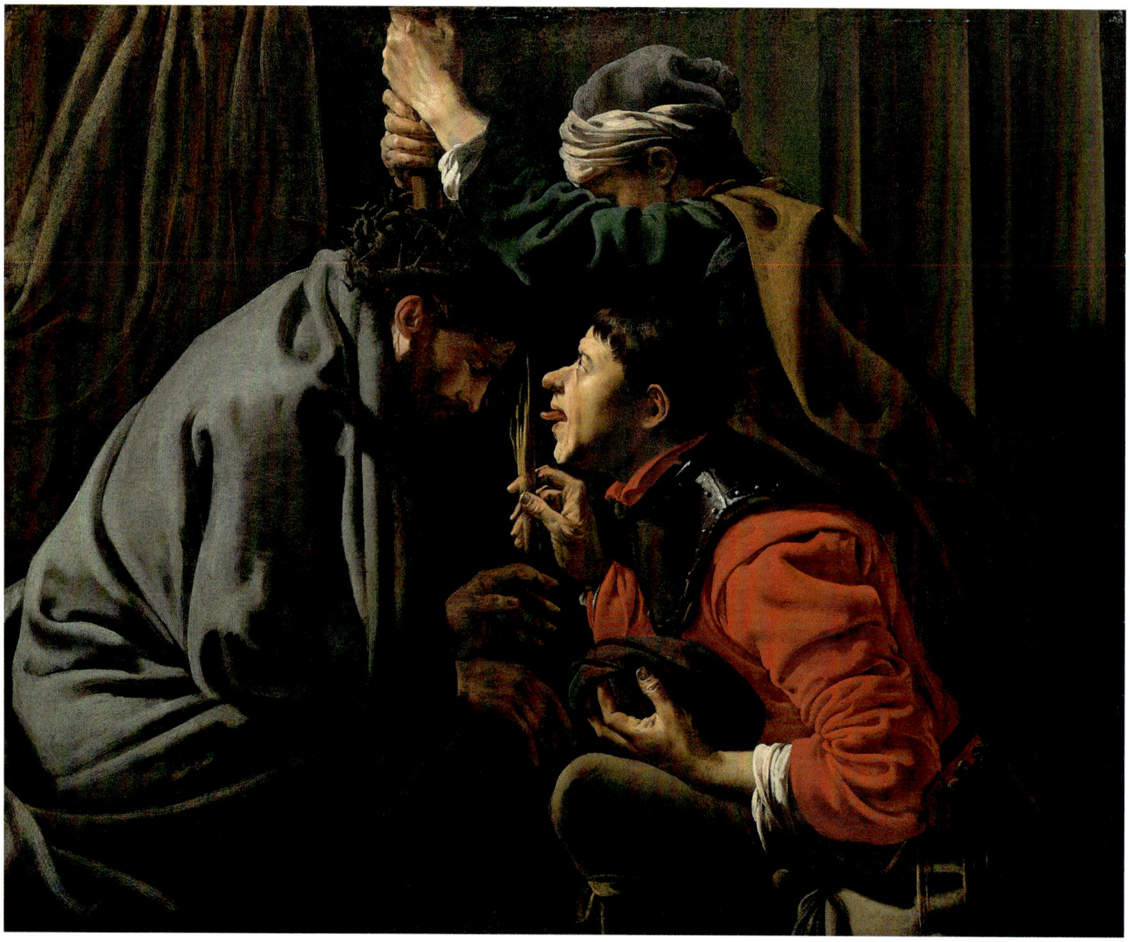

Fig. 62 Hendrick ter Brugghen, *The Crowning with Thorns and the Mocking of Christ*, c. 1625, formerly The James Fairfax Collection, Sydney

l'Assistance Publique in Paris (cat. 7).[9] Wearing only a cloth around the hip and the crown of thorns on his head while sitting with crossed legs, folded hands and lowered head on a stone bench and praying, the figure of Christ derives from a woodcut by Albrecht Dürer, which served as frontispiece to the *Large Passion* of 1511 (fig. 63).[10]

Ter Brugghen's Christ conforms for the most part to Dürer's model; he even adopts the halo that surrounds the head of Christ. Differences in the details, such as the large, pearl-shaped tears running down the face of the captive and the less elegant position of the awkward foot, attest to ter Brugghen's aspiration to give Dürer's model a distinct twist. The idealised, brightly illuminated figure of the Saviour offers a stark contrast to the ugly, grimacing henchmen. In the way the limbs overlap, this painting shows striking similarities to the *St Sebastian* ter Brugghen painted in 1625 (cat. 69). The posture of adoration struck by the man kneeling to the right of Christ is expressive of the mocking of the 'King of the Jews' with symbolically added 'regalia' such as the wooden stick as sceptre and the wreath of thorns as crown.

Aside from Dürer, sources may be found in two prints created around 1509 and 1519 by Lucas van Leyden as well as in a similar composition by Maarten van Heemskerck in Pommersfelden (fig. 64), which is dated c. 1545.[11] Particularly the dramatic gestures and caricature-like distorted faces of the henchman draw on Late Gothic models; their malicious behaviour is reflected in their savage-looking appearance. Noticeable to viewers at the time, these borrowings in combination with a Caravaggesque colour scheme

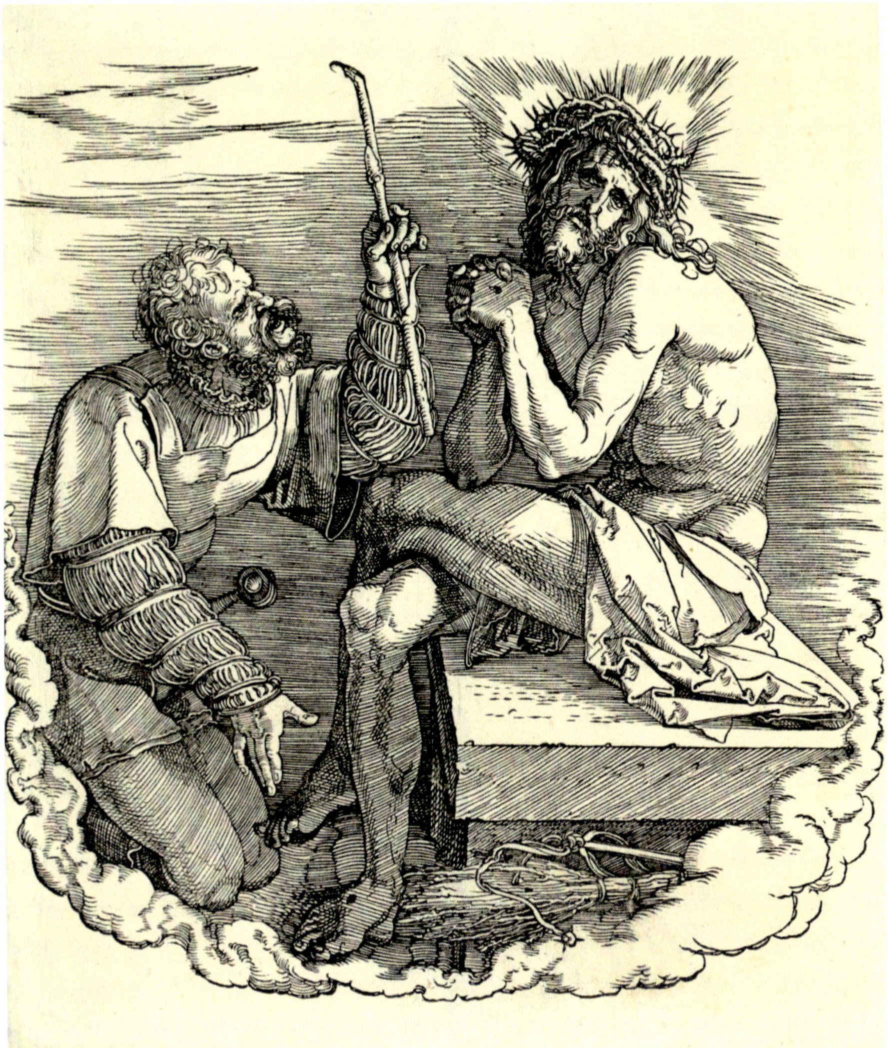

Fig. 63 Albrecht Dürer, *The Mocking of Christ*, frontispiece to the *Large Passion*, 1511, Albertina Museum, Vienna

and light arrangement, a reduction to essential pictorial elements, and the almost life-size figures add up to a very distinct and recognisable style typical of ter Brugghen. Compared to the atmospheric chiaroscuro compositions of Honthorst with idealised-looking figures, the paintings of ter Brugghen are characterised by a radical, sometimes exaggerated realism which openly showed the ugliness of human nature.

Giovanni Serodine, an artist from the region around Lake Maggiore, created another expressive depiction of the subject of the Mocking of Christ (cat. 18). For the candle prominently placed between the figures and dramatically illuminating the protagonists in otherwise dark surroundings, Serodine drew on a style-defining device developed by his Dutch fellow painter Honthorst to whom a copy of this painting was, in fact, at some point ascribed.[12] It may be a coincidence that the rare motif of the hat taken in mockery from the man in front and presented with the open underside already appears in Honthorst's Mocking scene (cat. 16). The *fica* gesture of the henchmen with the thumb thrust between the index and middle fingers was a familiar obscene gesture both south and north of the Alps, as examples in the work of Dürer show.[13] However, it is not just an expression of disdain, mockery and blasphemy, but must also

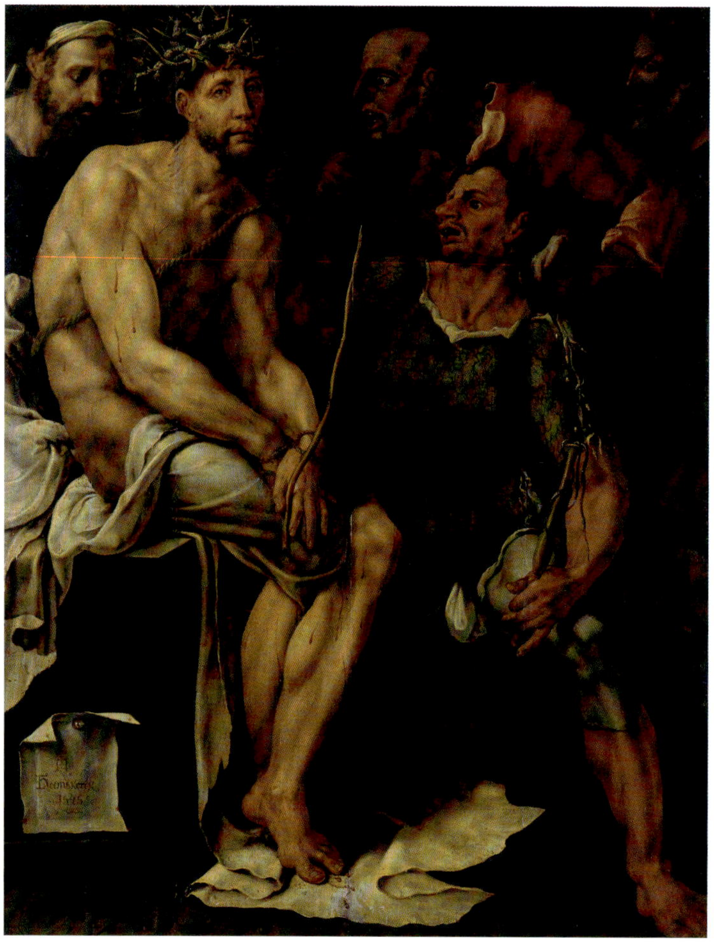

Fig. 64 Maarten van Heemskerck, *The Mocking of Christ*, c. 1545, Kunstsammlungen Graf von Schönborn, Pommersfelden

be seen as an apotropaic gesture intended to ward off evil. Serodine's painterly execution with the lively brushwork is closer to Upper Italian painting, especially the work of Jacopo da Ponte, called Bassano (c. 1510/15–1592), and the Venetian school than to the style of Caravaggio or the Utrecht Caravaggisti. In the paintings of Honthorst and ter Brugghen, the colour and surface of the complexion and body of Christ resemble an ivory figure and contrast strongly with the figures of the mockers. In Serodine's painting, on the other hand, the tanned skin of the Saviour is close to that of his tormentors. Accordingly, the brightest spot in the image is not Christ but rather the stretched neck of the mocking young man on the left. The emphasis on 'this-worldliness' and human nature is in stark contrast with Christ's 'otherworldliness'. BE

1 Matthew 26:67–68; Mark 14:65; Luke 22:63–65. See Poeschel 2014, p. 172.
2 Matthew 27:27–30.
3 Judson/Ekkart 1999, pp. 351–352 (addendum).
4 None of the paintings is dated; the precise dating and sequence is disputed. Judson/Ekkart 1999, pp. 83–88, cats. 59–62.
5 *Christ Crowned with Thorns*, canvas, 222.3 × 173.4 cm, The J. Paul Getty Museum, Los Angeles, inv. 90.PA.26; Judson/Ekkart 1999, pp. 10, 83–85, cat. 59. *The Mocking of Christ*, canvas, 179 × 210, Santa Maria Immacolata, Rome; Judson/Ekkart 1999, pp. 87–88, cat. 62. *The Mocking of Christ*, canvas, 197.5 × 170.5 cm, The Spier Collection, London; Judson/Ekkart 1999, pp. 349–350 (addendum). Gianni Papi dates the works earlier in Exh. cat. Florence 2015, pp. 138–139, cat. 6 (c. 1610–1615); Gianni Papi in Exh. cat. Rome 2011/12, pp. 132–133, cat. V. 9 (c. 1612/13); see also Vodret/Leone 2008. Honthorst's *Crowning with Thorns* at the Rijksmuseum in Amsterdam (inv. SK-A-4837) (fig. 34) was painted only upon the artist's return to Utrecht c. 1622; Judson/Ekkart 1999, pp. 85–86, cat. 60.
6 Slatkes/Franits 2007, S. 99.
7 *The Crowning with Thorns*, signed and dated 1620, canvas, 207 × 240 cm, Statens Museum for Kunst, Copenhagen, inv. kmssp365; Slatkes/Franits 2007, pp. 98–99, cat. A13.
8 *The Crowning with Thorns and the Mocking of Christ*, canvas, c. 1625, 108.5 × 133 cm, formerly The James Fairfax Collection, Sydney; Slatkes/Franits 2007, pp. 104–105, cat. A18.
9 Ibid., pp. 101–102, cat. A17.
10 Véronique Noël-Bouton in Exh. cat. Paris 1970/71, p. 33, cat. 32.
11 *The Mocking of Christ*, c. 1545, panel, 73 × 101 cm, Kunstsammlungen Graf von Schönborn, Pommersfelden, inv. 231; for van Leyden, see Van Kooij 1987.
12 Exh. cat. Rancate 2012/13, pp. 150–152.
13 Annick Lemoine in Exh. cat. Rome/Paris 2014/15, pp. 29–33, and Lemoine 2015, pp. 55–67.

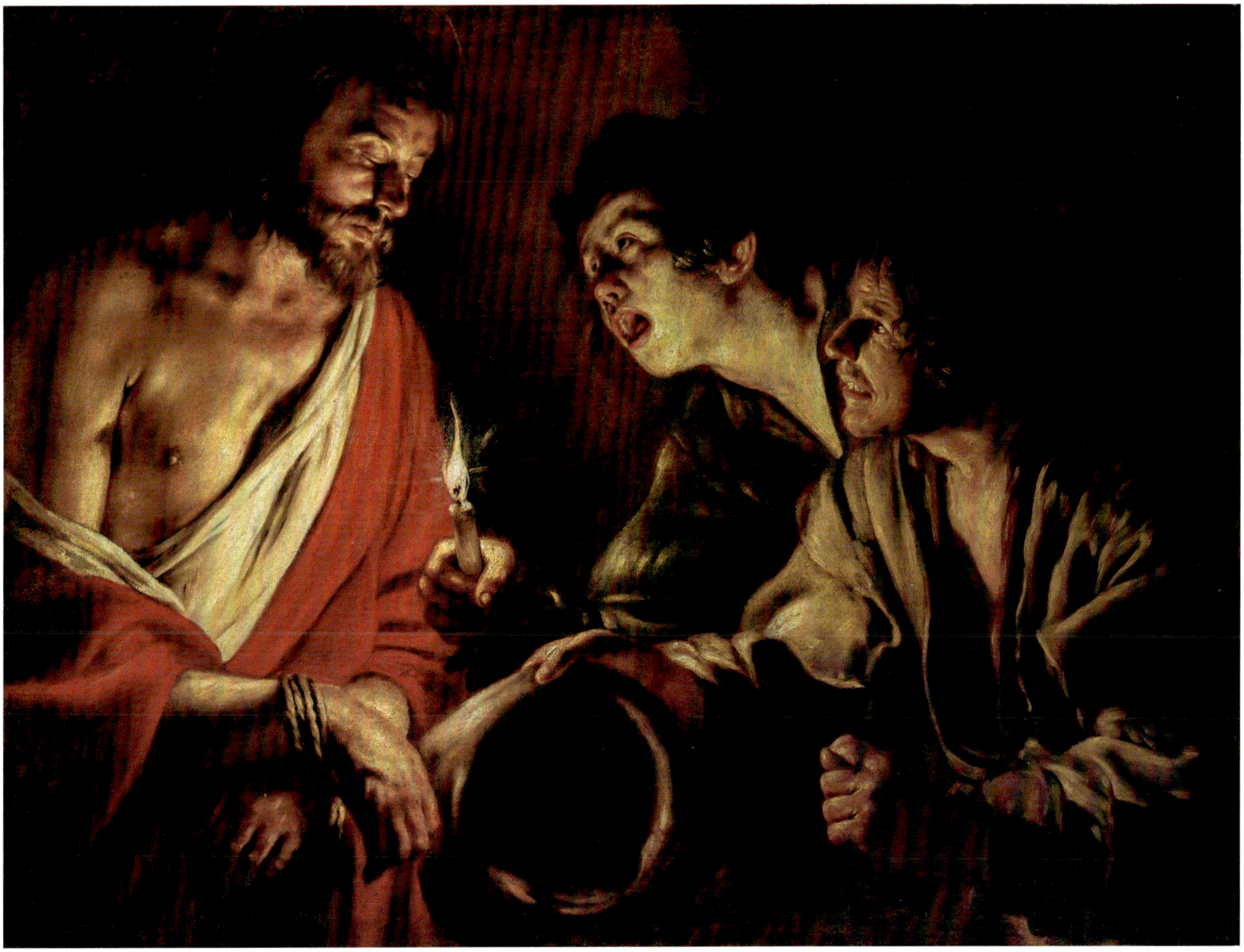

18
Giovanni Serodine
The Mocking of Christ, c. 1626
Pinacoteca cantonale Giovanni Züst,
Rancate (Mendrisio)

c. 1617

Christ before the High Priest

19
Gerard van Honthorst
Christ before the High Priest, c. 1617
Canvas, 272 × 183 cm
The National Gallery, London, inv. NG3679

The depiction of *Christ before the High Priest* (cat. 19) holds a special place in the oeuvre of Gerard van Honthorst on account of its unusual subject, format and composition.[1] The painting was created around 1617 in Rome when Honthorst was in the service of the two brothers Cardinal Benedetto and Marchese Vincenzo Giustiniani, in whose household he lived.[2] In the 1638 inventory of the estate of Vincenzo, the younger brother, the painting is listed as 'Christ before Caiaphas'.[3] Joachim von Sandrart, who worked in the workshop of Honthorst in Utrecht from 1625 on, had seen the painting in 1628 at the Palazzo Giustiniani and described it in his *Teutsche Academie* of 1675 as 'Christ before Pilate'.[4] Justus Müller Hofstede, on the other hand, proposed an identification as 'Christ before Annas', the father-in-law of Caiaphas.[5]

The time of day shown in the scene provides a hint as to which interrogation is depicted. Honthorst's choice of a night scene rules out the identification as Pilate, for the Gospels tell us that the encounter with the prefect Pontius Pilate took place during the day, whereas Christ was interrogated in the house of the high priest Annas at night. The two men depicted to the side of the high priest are most likely the two false witnesses mentioned by Matthew in his account of the interrogation by Caiaphas.[6] Hence an identification as the high priest Caiaphas is the most plausible.[7]

The scene is set in a dark room where the only light is provided by a single candle. It illuminates the two protagonists of the story, while leaving the men on the left and the soldiers in the background in semi-darkness.[8] Honthorst shows the moment when the high priest implores Jesus to say whether he is the Son of God. Behind Christ, several soldiers in Roman dress and armed with lances stand in front of an open door, ready to take the accused away. The candle lights the raised hand of Caiaphas, whose index finger points upwards, towards heaven. The judge's face and the book with the Commandments of Mosaic law lying in front of him are also brightly lit by the candlelight. The most highlighted is the figure of the humble Christ whose flesh tones and white robe outshine the entire scene.

The painting's format is unusual, for as a large, vertical-format work with a religious subject it suggests an altarpiece rather than a commissioned piece for a private gallery. But it was especially because of the unique composition concentrating on the essentials and the orchestration of light using just a single light source

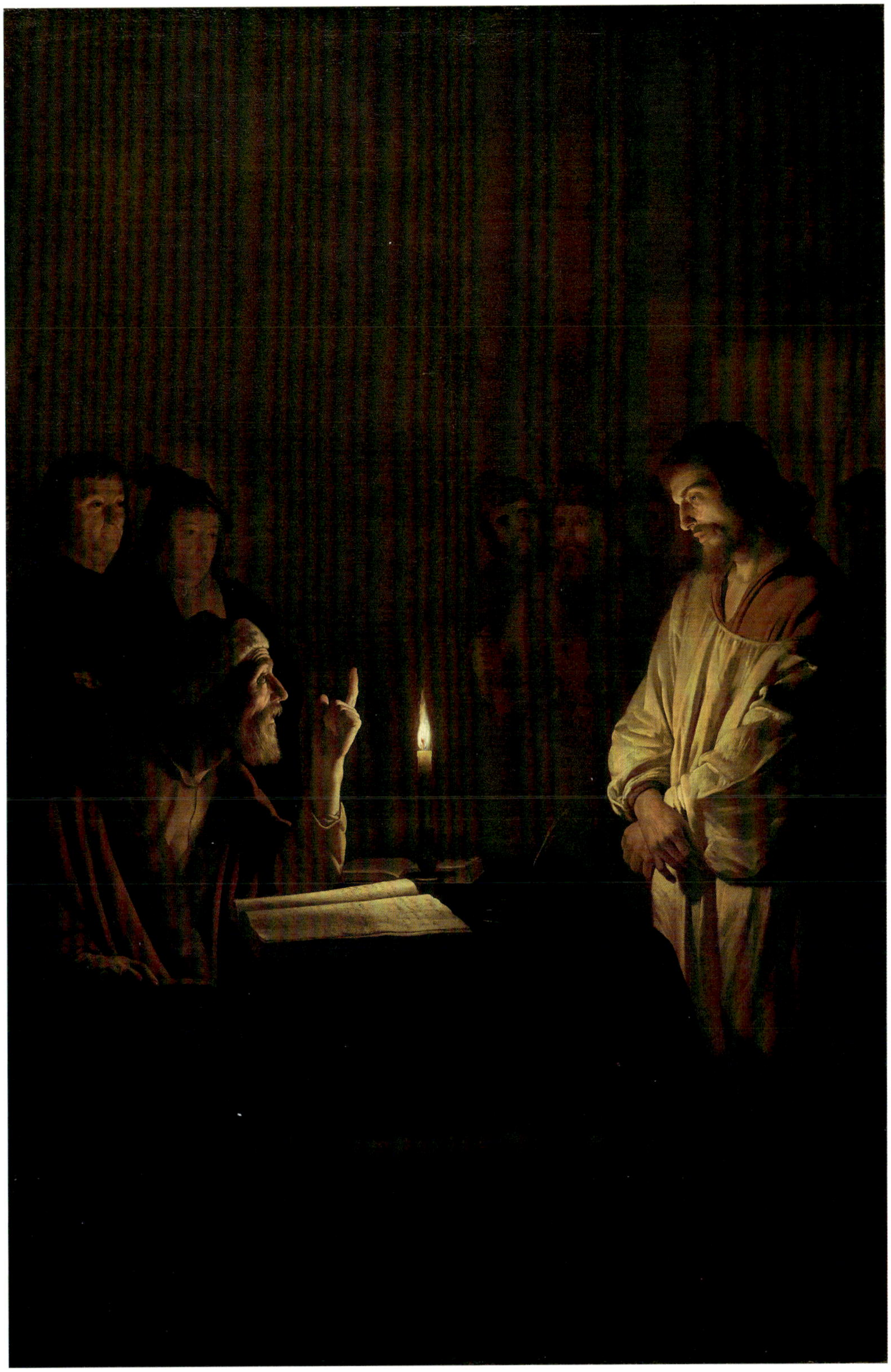

19
Gerard van Honthorst
Christ before the High Priest, c. 1617
The National Gallery, London

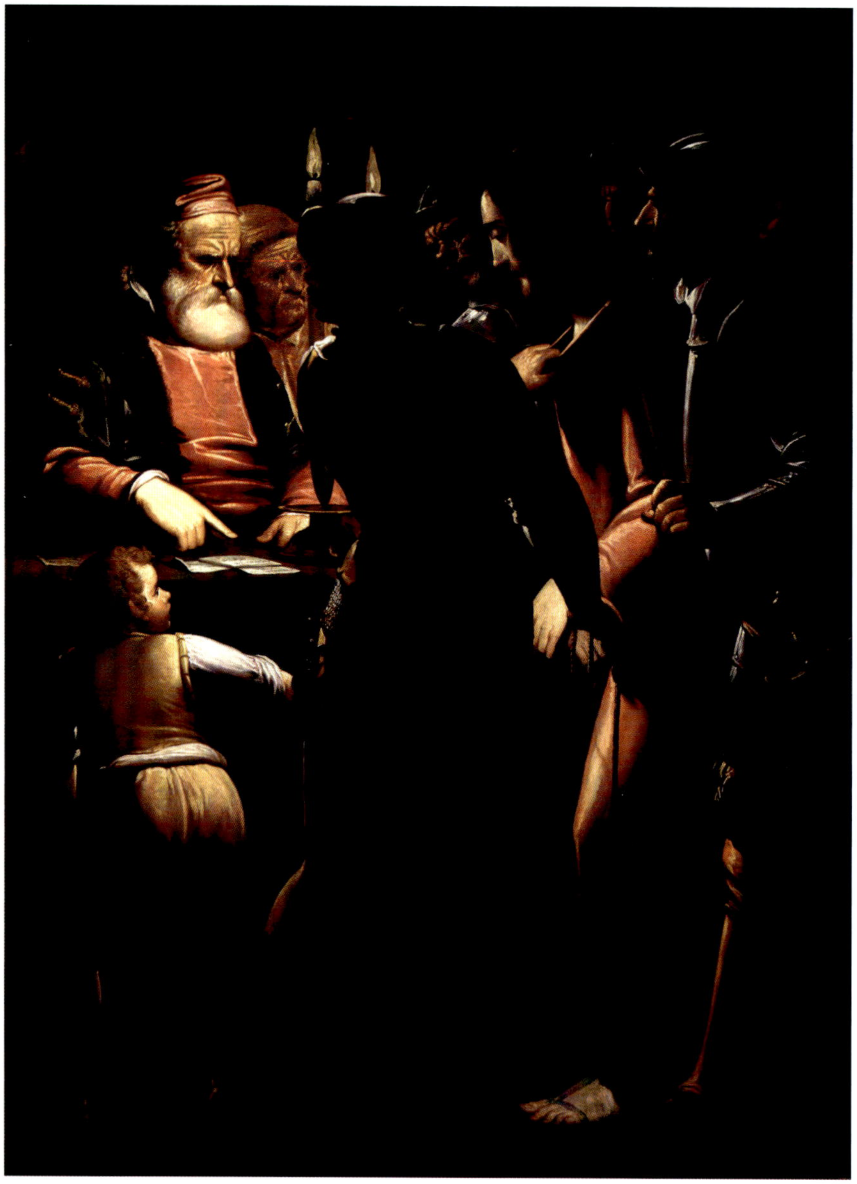

Fig. 65 Luca Cambiaso, *Christ before Caiaphas*, after 1570, Museo dell'Accademia Ligustica di Belle Arti, Genoa

that the painting was already highly praised and much-copied even during the artist's lifetime.[9] Hence it is surprising that none of his fellow painters took up the subject.

Night scenes had already become established as a new genre during the second half of the Cinquecento in Italy. The Giustiniani brothers were particularly fond of *pintura tenebrosa* as well, and their collection included numerous examples of nocturnal scenes lit by candle or torchlight by the likes of Francesco Bassano the Elder, Alessandro Turchi, Annibale Carracci and Joachim von Sandrart. In inventories, these works are described as 'lumi di candela', 'facelle', 'finiti di notte', 'torce' and 'candelieri'.[10] The collection at the Palazzo Giustiniani also included a night scene by the Genovese painter Luca Cambiaso (1527–1585), which can be dated after 1570 and shows Christ before Caiaphas (fig. 65).[11]

Honthorst's decision to depict this unusual subject as a night scene with candlelight suggests that the young Dutch painter regarded it as a challenge to compete with the Italian source. Cambiaso's depiction appears artificial, as the candle flames stand out unnaturally like light points against the almost black background, and their light falls only on the active figures which appear even brighter than the flames themselves. Honthorst, by contrast, uses the candle flame to subtly illuminate the entire pictorial space, which he opens far upwards. The pictorial realisation in the tradition of Adam Elsheimer of the latest scientific understanding of optics with regard to the diffusion of light in space was likely of topical interest to both the client and Honthorst.[12] In Honthorst's visualisation, Cambiaso's 'artificiality' is converted into a naturalistic depiction of the behaviour of light without any loss of intimacy or expressivity. BE

1 Judson/Ekkart 1999, pp. 80–83, cat. 58.
2 Papi dates the painting as early as 1615/16: Papi 1999, p. 136, and Gianni Papi in Exh. cat. Florence 2015, p. 158, cat. 16.
3 'Un quadro di Christo avanti Caifas di notte dipinto in tela alta palmi 13. Larga 8. [si crede di mano di Gherado] senza cornice.' ASR, Notai del Tribunale dell'A.C., prot. 1377, ff. 744r–1045v, notaio Domenico Buratti, quoted by Danesi Squarzina 2003, vol. 1, p. 312; see also Silvia Danesi Squarzina in Exh. cat. Rome/Berlin 2001, p. 314.
4 Sandrart 1675 (1925), pp. 172–173: 'as could then be seen in many palaces, especially that of Marchese Gustiniani where he had lived for a long time and created many highly laudable works, including a large night-scene showing our Redeemer bound, dressed in a white shirt, standing before Pilate who interrogates him, as the glow of candles and lights illuminates everything in true naturalness, with such verisimilitude as is unsurpassed in art'.
5 Justus Müller Hofstede in Exh. cat. Utrecht/Braunschweig 1986/87, p. 16; Müller Hofstede 1988, p. 15.
6 Matthew 26:57–66.
7 Cat. London 1991, vol. 1, pp. 190–192, no. 3679.
8 In the *Liberation of St Peter* (cat. 12) Honthorst goes a step further, as he omits the soldiers, who were still depicted but not highlighted in the preliminary drawing (fig. 58), from the painting, thereby increasing the focus.
9 Judson 1959, pp. 27, 30, pp. 164–165, cat. 44. Overall, some 30 copies of the painting are known, six of which were created during Honthorst's lifetime. See Braun 1966, pp. 135–136, cat. 13; Cat. London 1991, vol. 1, p. 191; Judson/Ekkart 1999, pp. 80–81; Prohaska/Swoboda/Cardinali 2010, pp. 214–215.
10 Irene Baldriga and Silvia Danesi Squarzina in Exh. cat. Rome/Berlin 2001, p. 220.
11 *Christ before Caiaphas*, canvas, 188 × 138 cm, Museo dell'Accademia Ligustica di Belle Arti, Genoa, inv. 66. Silvia Danesi Squarzina in Exh. cat. Rome/Berlin 2001, p. 314; Danesi Squarzina 2003, vol. 1, p. 428.
12 In Rome, Honthorst had, as Sandrart writes, 'just as Adam Elzheimer with small-scale, [...] risen to prominence with large-scale life-size night-scenes and gained a great reputation'. Sandrart 1675 (1925), p. 172.

1617/18

The Beheading of John the Baptist

20

Gerard van Honthorst
The Beheading of John the Baptist, 1617/18
Canvas, 345 × 215 cm
Chiesa di Santa Maria della Scala, Rome

The commission to paint *The Beheading of John the Baptist* (cat. 20) came at the beginning of Gerard van Honthorst's most successful period in Italy. In the space of three years he painted a dozen canvases as well as four very large altarpieces with a total surface area of no less than some 35 square metres.[1] He had succeeded in becoming one of the most sought-after artists in Rome and thereabouts in a very short time. The major public commission for the altarpiece with *The Beheading of John the Baptist* would certainly have contributed to that.

The painting is still *in situ* on the altar of the most south-western chapel of Santa Maria della Scala in Rome. Giovanni Battista Longhi, major-domo of Cardinal Tolomeo Gallio, stipulated in his will that the chapel that had been allocated to him was to be dedicated to his name saint, John the Baptist. It was not Longhi himself who decided to award the commission for the altarpiece to Honthorst. After Longhi's funeral on 20 December 1610 it was Maurizio Sanzio, the executor, who had the chapel completed in accordance with Longhi's wishes.[2] Sanzio provided extra funds, because there was not enough money to pay for the altarpiece.[3] That may have been why seven years elapsed before the commission was awarded. In any event, the delay allowed Honthorst to be considered as a candidate, for he was not yet in Rome in 1610. Sanzio himself commissioned the Dutchman, or perhaps he allowed the Discalced Carmelites to choose the artist they considered the most suitable. In any event, Honthorst only received a final bonus from them, although they did pay for the expensive ultramarine.[4]

A papal bull of 20 March 1597 allocated Santa Maria della Scala, which was still under construction, to the Discalced Carmelites as their church. They had been operating as a separate group in the mendicant order since their recognition by Pope Clement VIII four years previously, so at the time of Honthorst's commission they were a relatively young community with a modern, newly built complex in the Trastevere neighbourhood. The allocation of their chapels to private individuals and the right to be buried there fell directly under their jurisdiction. It was they who had the last word. The brothers were careful and critical about the furnishing of their church, not so much about the choice of artists but certainly as far as the iconography was concerned.

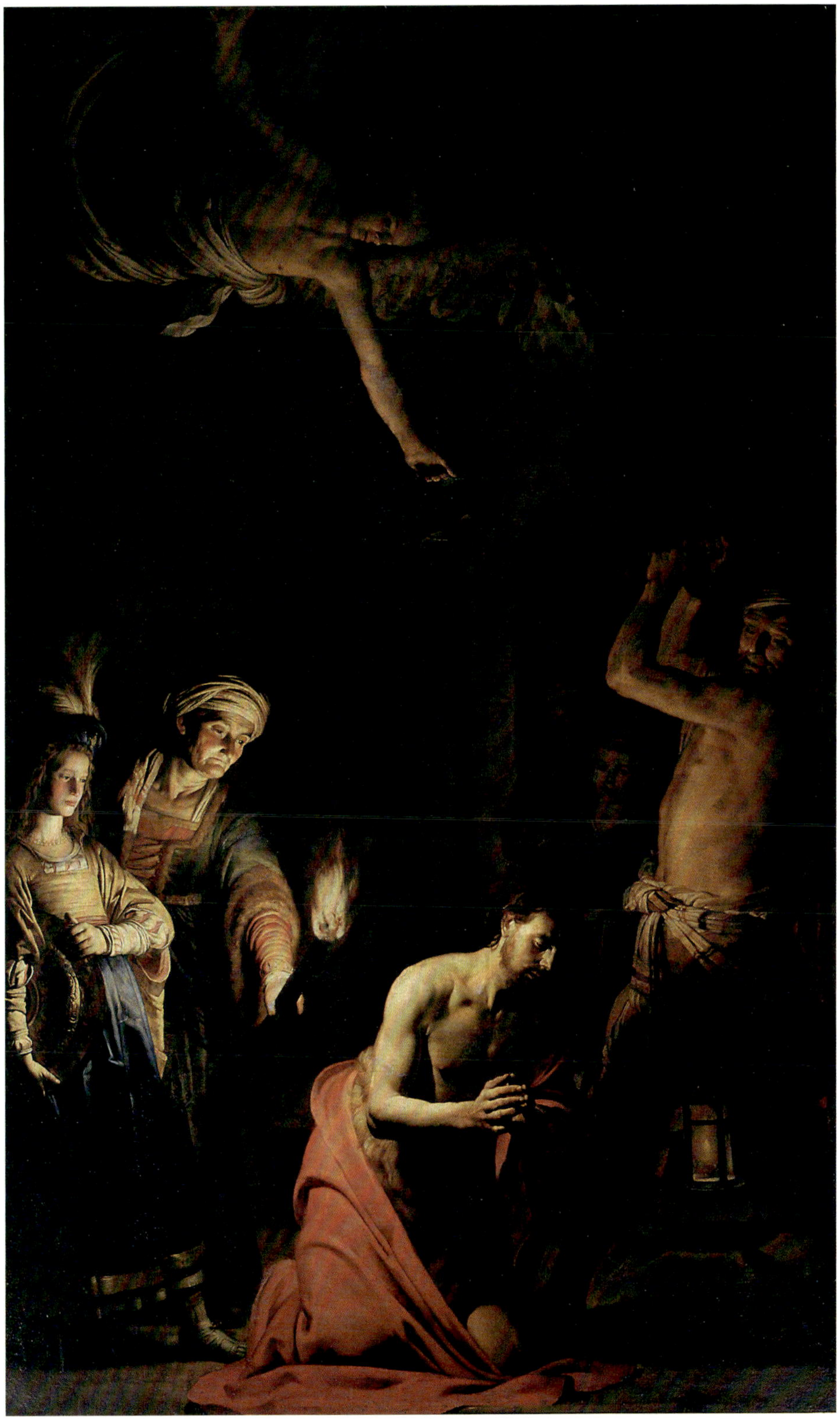

20
Gerard van Honthorst
The Beheading of John the Baptist, 1617/18
Chiesa di Santa Maria della Scala, Rome

It is significant that they rejected Caravaggio's altarpiece with *The Death of the Virgin* that is now in the Louvre.[5] It was intended for the second chapel from the entrance on the north side of the church, which was the largest and most important one, and the first one to be decorated. The right to use it was allocated to the lawyer Laerzio Cherubini (c. 1550–1626), who was buried there on 2 May 1626. The subject, dimensions, price and delivery date of the altarpiece were laid down in the contract that both parties signed on 1 June 1601.[6] Caravaggio completed the commission in 1605/06. However, the brothers had it removed because of a supposed lack of decorum. Rubens finally mediated in its purchase in 1607 by Vincenzo I Gonzaga, Duke of Mantua, whose court painter he was. The sum of 280 *scudi* was paid for the painting, which was already famous. It was put on display in Rome in April 1607, a week before it left for Mantua, in order to give connoisseurs and art lovers a chance to study it.[7] Carlo Saraceni painted a new altarpiece with *The Death of the Virgin* for the chapel, but it too was refused, before the brothers accepted his second altarpiece with *The Assumption*.

Honthorst would have been aware of these ups and down when he accepted the commission in 1617. The scene that he painted was peaceful and respectful, despite the grisly subject. The event is described in Matthew 14:1–13, Mark 6:14–29 and Luke 9:7–9. The Baptist had criticised the marriage of King Herod Antipas to his sister-in-law Herodias, the wife of his brother Herodes Philippus. This was the reason for throwing him into prison. The dance that Salome, the king's step-daughter, performed at a banquet was so impressive that he promised to give her whatever she desired, even if it was half of his kingdom. On the insistence of her mother Herodias, out of whose first marriage she was born, Salome asked for the head of John the Baptist, which she received.

The girl has just finished her dance. Beautiful and dressed in her party best, with a red blush on her cheeks, she is holding the large dish on which the Baptist's head will be placed after his beheading. She is looking at the executioner, who has raised his sword high in order to deliver the fatal blow. There are other bystanders. An old woman is holding a large burning torch to give the executioner a better view, and in the shadows on the right a man and a woman are acting as silent witnesses. The Baptist is kneeling with his eyes closed, his hands joined in prayer. Hovering above him is an angel with the victory wreath of holy martyrs with which John will be crowned in heaven. LMH

1 Judson/Ekkart 1999, pp. 54–55, cat. 10; pp. 59–60, cat. 20; pp. 67–68, cat. 36; pp. 69–70, cat. 37; pp. 73–74, cat. 50; pp. 75–77, cat. 54; p. 77, cat. 55; pp. 79–80, cat. 57; pp. 80–83, cat. 58; pp. 83–85, cat. 59; pp. 87–88, cat. 62; pp. 93–95, cat. 74; pp. 217–218, cat. 281, and addendum pp. 349–352. Several of those paintings may have been made as altarpieces.
2 Megna 2003, pp. 92–94.
3 Marcucci 2012, p. 85, note 50; Bilancia 2012, p. 100, docs. 12–14.
4 On 7 July 1618, they paid 4.50 *scudi* for ultramarine and on 1 January 1619 4 *scudi* as a bonus for completing the altarpiece. See Megna 2003, p. 90; Exh. cat. Florence 2015, p. 174, cat. 24; Lorizzo 2015b, p. 257, with corrections to Borsook 1954, p. 271; Judson/Ekkart 1999, p. 71.
5 1601/06, canvas, 369 × 245 cm, Musée du Louvre, Paris, inv. 54. See Parks 1985; Gage 2012; Gage 2014.
6 Macioce 2003, p. 105, I doc 114; Bilancia 2012, p. 98, docs. 3–5.
7 Marcucci 2012, p. 75, and p. 85, note 49.

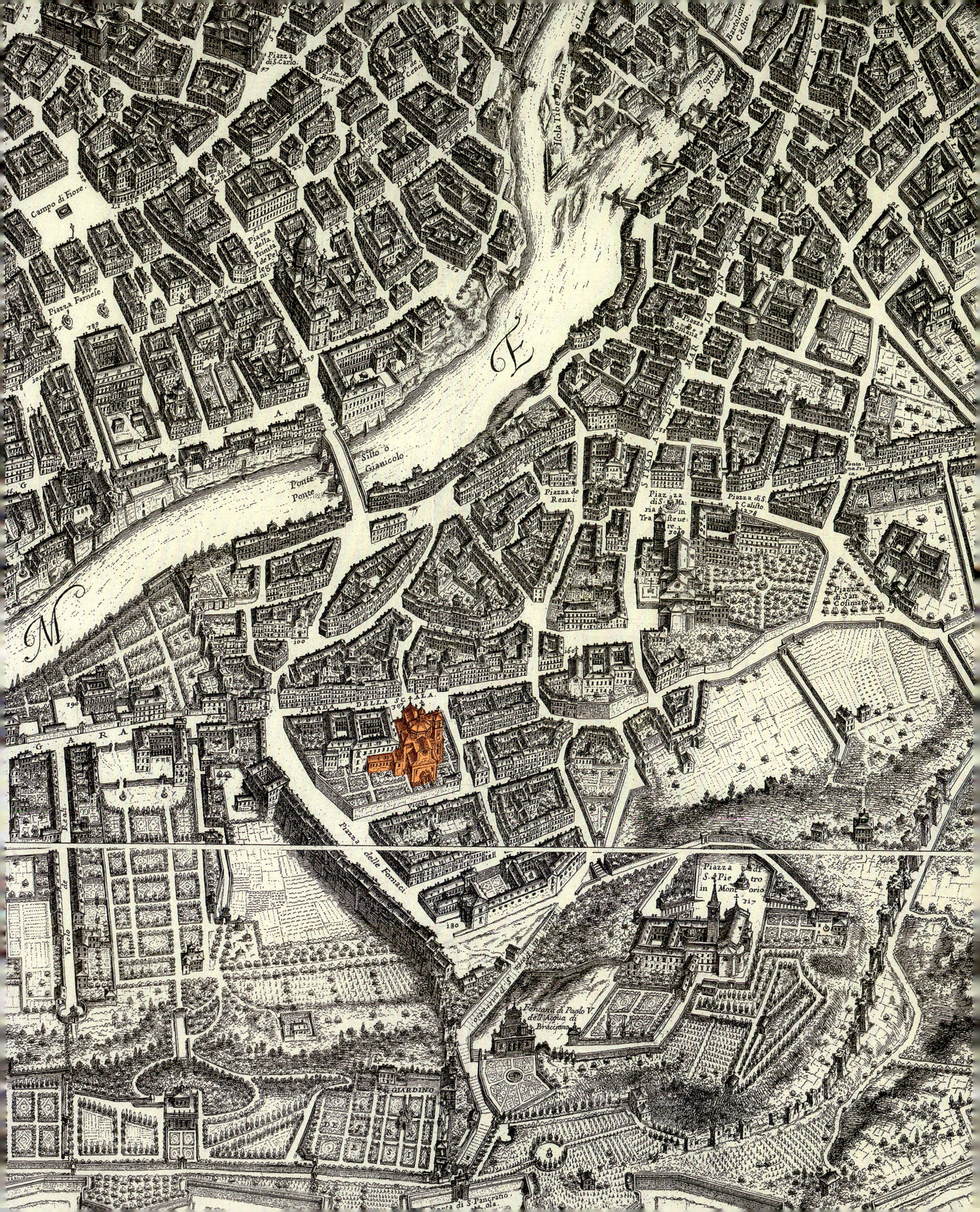
Campo di Fiore
Piazza Farnese
Piazza di S. Carlo
E
M
Piazza de Renzi
Piazza di S. Calisto
Piazza di S. Cosimato
Piazza delle Fornaci
Piazza S. Pietro in Montorio
Fontana di Paolo V dell'Acqua di Bracciano
GIARDINO

1617/18

The Entombment of Christ

21
Dirck van Baburen
The Entombment of Christ, 1617/18
Canvas, 219.4 × 139.5 cm
Centraal Museum, Utrecht, inv. 8233

22
Michelangelo Merisi, called Caravaggio
The Entombment of Christ, 1602/03
Canvas, 300 × 203 cm
Musei Vaticani, Pinacoteca Vaticana,
Città del Vaticano, inv. 40386

23
Nicolas Tournier
The Entombment of Christ, 1635/38
Canvas, 314 × 166 cm
Musée des Augustins, Toulouse, inv. Ro 284

To modern eyes, the distorted proportions of the face of Nicodemus in the right foreground may make it hard to understand why this *Entombment of Christ* by Dirck van Baburen was so extraordinarily popular in the 17th and 18th centuries (cat. 21). There are no fewer than 29 painted copies, three engravings and eight drawings after the original.[1] Even today it is regarded by specialists as the high point in the painter's oeuvre.[2] So it is not Nicodemus's high forehead and receding hairline that make it a masterpiece, it is the composition as a whole. This painting from the collection of the Centraal Museum is the only known version that Baburen painted himself after the original work, possibly with the aid of assistants in his Roman workshop.[3] The altarpiece of which this is a repetition is *in situ* on the altar of the lavishly decorated Pietà Chapel in San Pietro in Montorio in Rome. It is the fourth and largest chapel on the left from the entrance, and is also the most attractive because of the dome and its location on the sunny side of the church.

The altarpiece was commissioned by Pietro Cussida (?–1622), a rich Spanish diplomat who served Philip III and IV of Spain. When he arrived in Rome in 1602, Cussida went to live in the palazzo on the corner of Via del Corso and Via Frattina. The building was renovated by Carlo Maderno (1556–1629) and housed Cussida's costly painting collection. In 1600, Maderno had been responsible for the renovation of the Cerasi Chapel in Santa Maria del Popolo, for which Caravaggio painted *The Crucifixion of St Peter* and *The Conversion of St Paul* (figs. 49, 50). Around 1603, Pope Paul V appointed him chief architect of St Peter's. He was, in brief, the best known and most influential architect of the day, and it is almost certain that Cussida commissioned him around 1615 to design his chapel in San Pietro in Montorio as well. The result is a remarkably lavish and colourful space executed in a pre-Baroque style in which the decorative programme around Christ's Passion is carried out consistently and ingeniously.[4] At the age of 22 or 23, Dirck van Baburen received the prestigious commission from Cussida to paint the high altarpiece (fig. 66), and he and David de Haen (c. 1585–1622), his later housemate, were also asked to make four paintings for the walls flanking the altar.[5] There is indirect evidence that Cussida planned to house an art collection in his native Zaragoza, part of which would consist of replicas of the paintings for the chapel. The *Entombment* displayed here is one of them.[6]

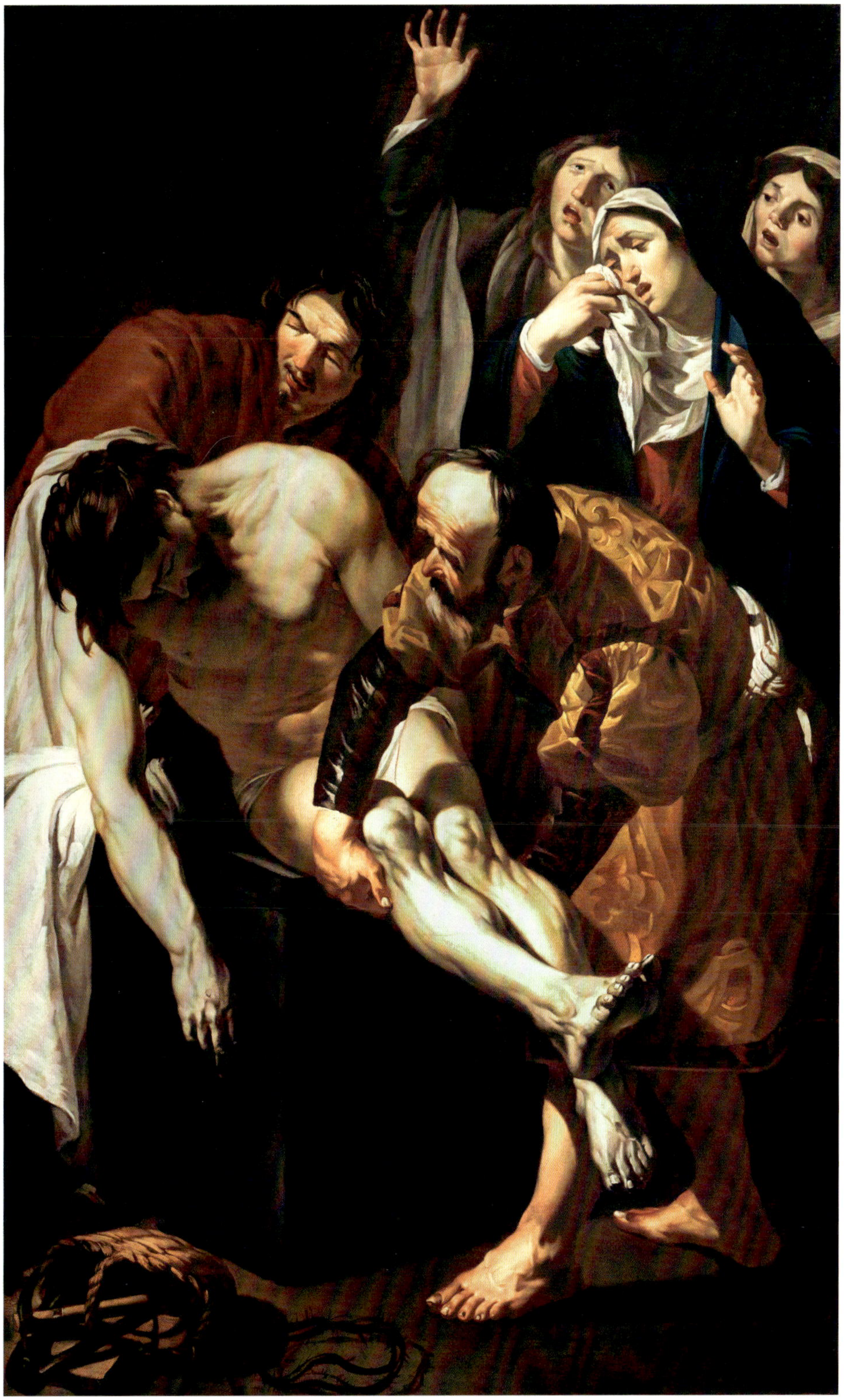

21
Dirck van Baburen
The Entombment of Christ, 1617/18
Centraal Museum, Utrecht

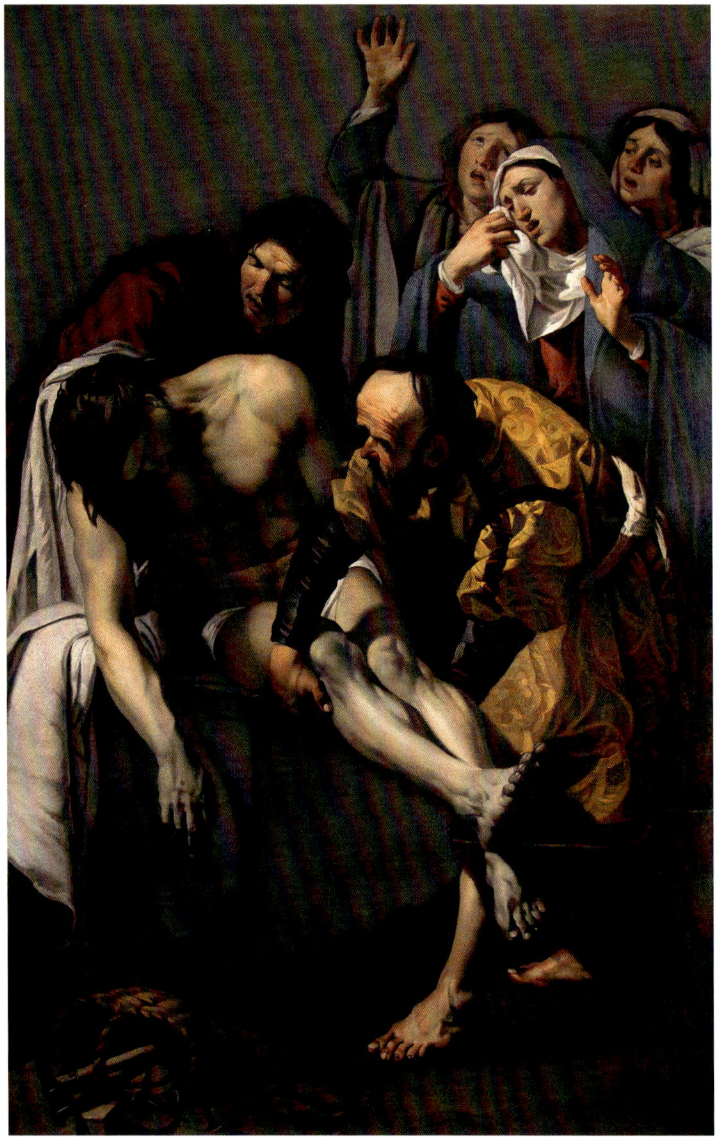

Fig. 66 Dirck van Baburen, *The Entombment of Christ*, 1617, San Pietro in Montorio, Cappella della Pietà, Rome

Both the monumental composition and the pronounced chiaroscuro of Baburen's *Entombment* are based on Caravaggio's painting of the subject that he made around 1602/03 for the family chapel of Girolamo Vittrice in the Chiesa Nuova in Rome, which was also dedicated to the Pietà (cat. 22).[7] According to the Roman painter and artists' biographer Giovanni Baglione (1566–1643), this majestic painting was regarded by contemporaries as the artist's finest work.[8] Christ's body gleams against the dark background, in which the entrance to the tomb can just be made out. His upper body is supported by the right arm of John the Evangelist. Nicodemus has lifted up the lower body with both arms wrapped around Christ's knees, his hands clasped to get a firmer grip. Behind this central group are the three Marys. The sorrowing Mother of God is gazing down, worn out, at her dead son. The beautiful Mary Magdalene is dabbing her eyes to dry her tears. The third woman must be Mary of Cleophas, who is gazing upwards as she raises her outstretched arms to the skies in despair and has opened her mouth to scream. Raised high up on the slab covering the tomb they show us, the spectators, the dead Christ, who is the Saviour for every believer.

Although the borrowing from Caravaggio's *Entombment* is unmistakable, Baburen does something that is essentially different.[9] The tomb slab has been transformed into a tomb.[10] John is preventing Christ from falling forward by holding him up by the armpits, while Nicodemus is once again holding the legs, but the burden is not so great. It is as if they have just paused for a moment before lowering the heavy body into the tomb. This position, with Christ leaning forward, places part of his body in shadow. His head is hanging down, so his face, which is also shadowed, is no longer plainly visible. Now it is a young Virgin Mary who is dabbing her eyes, with Mary of Cleophas and Mary Magdalene immediately behind her.[11] The figures are not only closer together, they have also been moved nearer to us, grouped on the ground around the tomb. The body is not being displayed to us, as it is in the Caravaggio. This is far more a question of a dramatic event to which we are the accidental witnesses.

Nicolas Tournier painted his *Entombment* around 1635/38 (cat. 23), after his return to Languedoc. An important difference from Caravaggio and Baburen is that his interpretation is not a separate painting but was part of a trilogy of works made for the high altar of the Église des Pénitents Noirs (Church of the Black Penitents) in Toulouse. Hanging to the left of a *Crucifixion* was *The Carrying of the Cross* (fig. 67) and to the right this *Entombment*.[12] Viewed thus from left to right they showed the most important moments in the Passion in chronological order.[13] One major difference between Tournier's *Entombment* and those of Caravaggio and Baburen is the composition. The French painter's figures are all on the same level, which eliminates the tension from the scene. What is even more important is that Tournier sacrifices any trace of realism to elegance. Calmly and seemingly without effort, Nicodemus and John carry Christ's body to what they believe will be his last resting place – the opened tomb on the right.

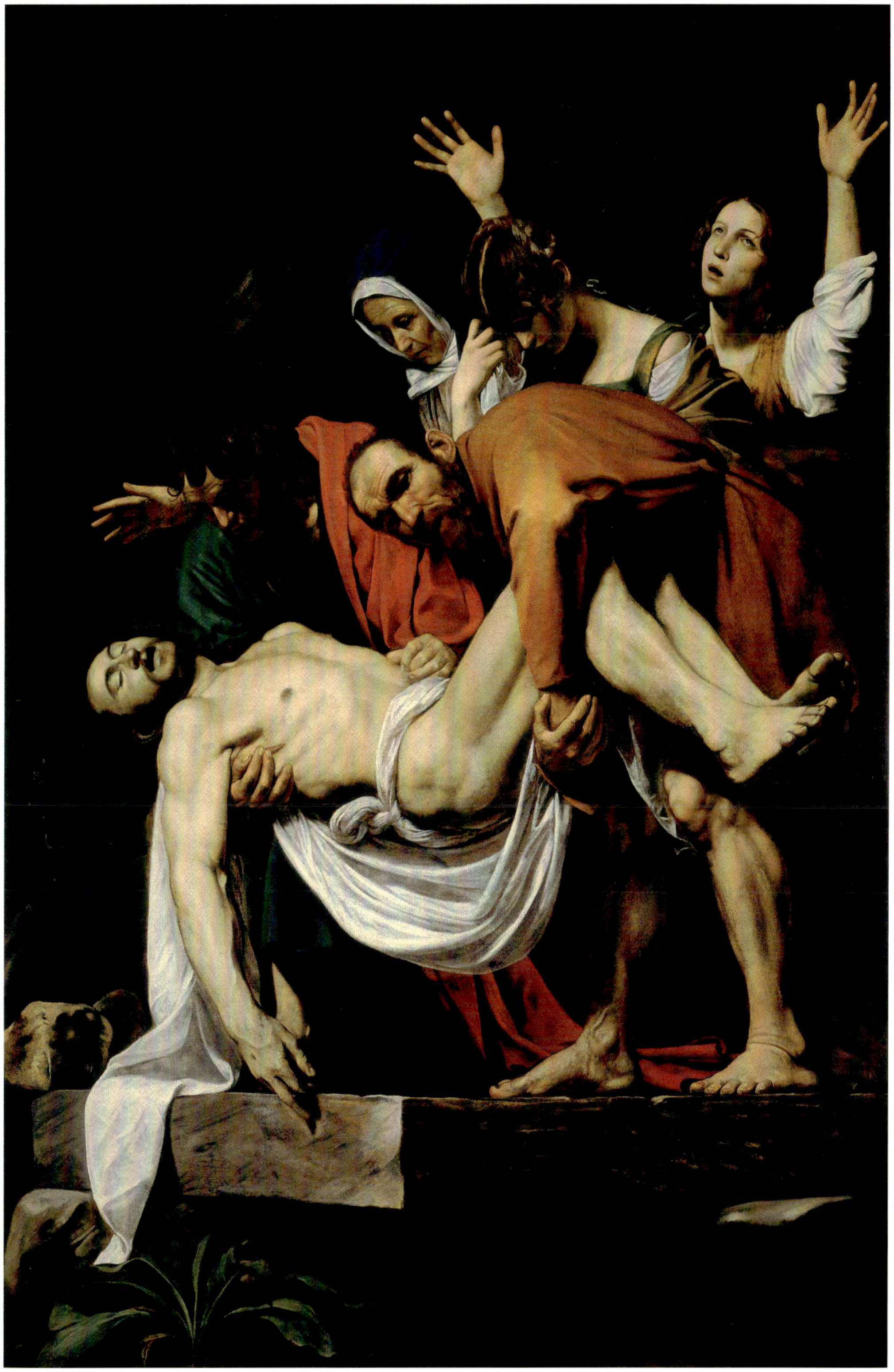

22
Michelangelo Merisi, called Caravaggio
The Entombment of Christ, 1602/03
Musei Vaticani, Pinacoteca Vaticana, Città del Vaticano

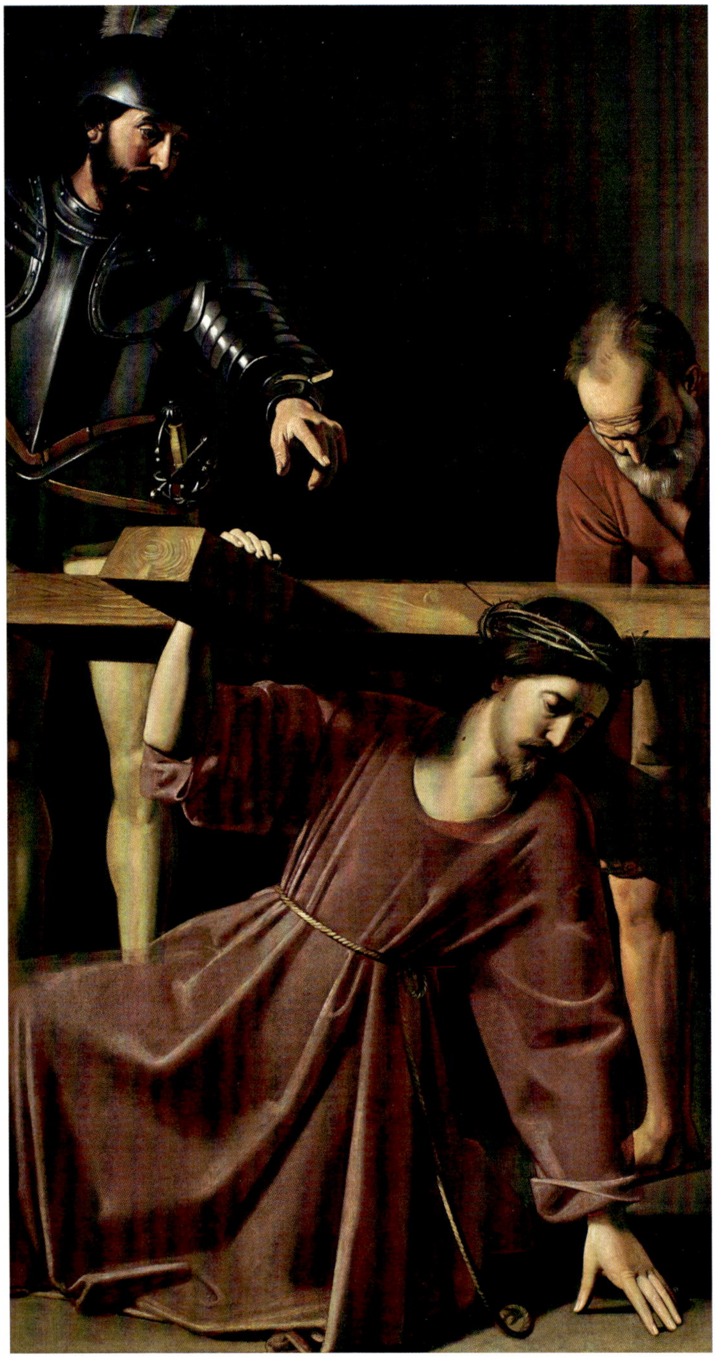

Fig. 67 Nicolas Tournier, *The Carrying of the Cross*, 1632/35, Musée des Augustins, Toulouse

The same lack of realism can be seen in Tournier's *Carrying of the Cross* (fig. 67). The cross itself is so light that Christ only needs the fingertips of his right hand to prevent himself from falling down. The pathos that is so marked in the versions by Caravaggio and Baburen has disappeared altogether. LMH

1 Franits 2013a, pp. 82–92, cat. A3.
2 See, for example, Exh. cat. Madrid 2016, p. 128, cat. 25.
3 Cat. Utrecht 1999, vol. 2, pp. 579–580, cat. 8; Franits 2013a, pp. 82–83, cat. A3BW1.
4 Gigli/Marchetti/Simonetta 2013.
5 Dirck van Baburen, *The Entombment of Christ*, 1617, canvas, 222 × 142 cm. At the bottom of the right-hand wall is Dirck van Baburen, *The Carrying of the Cross*, 1617/19, canvas, 199.4 × 248.9 cm, with above it David de Haen, *The Mocking of Christ*, 1617/19, canvas, 155 × 330 cm (lunette). At the bottom of the left wall (until 1757, when it was lost) was *The Raising of the Cross*, 1617/19, and above it David de Haen, *The Prayer in the Garden of Gethsemane*, 1617/19, canvas, 155 × 330 cm (lunette). All in Rome, Chiesa di San Pietro in Montorio, Cappella della Pietà. The composition of *The Raising of the Cross* is known from a drawing of 1750 by Charles-Nicolas Cochin. See Franits 2013a, pp. 235–236, cat. L3 and fig. 2. I find the attribution of the two lunettes to David de Haen convincing. See Valentina White in Exh. cat. Rome 2011/12, vol. 2, p. 192, cat. VII.5; Franits 2013a, p. 16, and p. 98, cat. A7; Exh. cat. Madrid 2016, pp. 130–131, cat. 26. Grilli 2005/06, p. 58, fig. 2, believes that *The Prayer in the Garden of Gethsemane* is by Baburen. In 1619 and 1620 Baburen and De Haen lived in a house on the Piazza Trinità dei Monti in the parish of Sant'Andrea delle Fratte; Vodret 2011, p. 514, no. 2088. On Baburen in Rome see, among others, White 1995; Treffers 2010; Franits 2013a, pp. 6–25.
6 Franits 2013a, pp. 78–81, cat. A3. Replicas and/or copies have also survived of four other paintings in the chapel, but there is not a trace of a second version of *The Raising of the Cross*. See Grilli 2005/06, pp. 59–62; Franits 2013a, pp. 16–18.
7 Alessandra Rodolfo in Vodret et al. 2016, vol. 2, pp. 398–401, cat. XIII.
8 Baglione 1642, p. 137. See also Alessandra Rodolfo in Vodret et al. 2016, pp. 398–401.
9 See also Exh. cat. Madrid 2016, pp. 128–130, cat. 25.
10 For a similar pose of Christ's body by Angelo Caroselli, Pietà, c. 1611/12, fresco, Chiesa Nova, Vittrice Chapel, Rome, see Franits 2013a, p. 81; Franits 2013b. For more possible pictorial sources see Fukaya 2016.
11 It is not possible to distinguish between the two individual Marys standing behind the Virgin. See also Exh. cat. Madrid 2016, p. 128, cat. 25.
12 *The Crucifixion*, 1632/35, canvas, 220 × 121 cm, Musée des Augustins, Toulouse.
13 Exh. cat. Toulouse 2001, pp. 152–154, cat. 35. The three paintings were confiscated after the French Revolution and transferred to the Augustinian convent, which was turned into a museum in 1793. *The Carrying of the Cross*, which vanished without trace in 1828, was rediscovered in Italy in 2009 and bought by the Weiss Gallery, London, which offered it for sale at TEFAF in 2010 and Paris Tableau in 2011. The French state confiscated the picture, which had been trimmed on both sides, and returned it to the Musée des Augustins. Not a trace of The Crucifixion has ever been found. See BBC News, 7 November 2011, and franceinfo: culturebox, 18 May 2017.

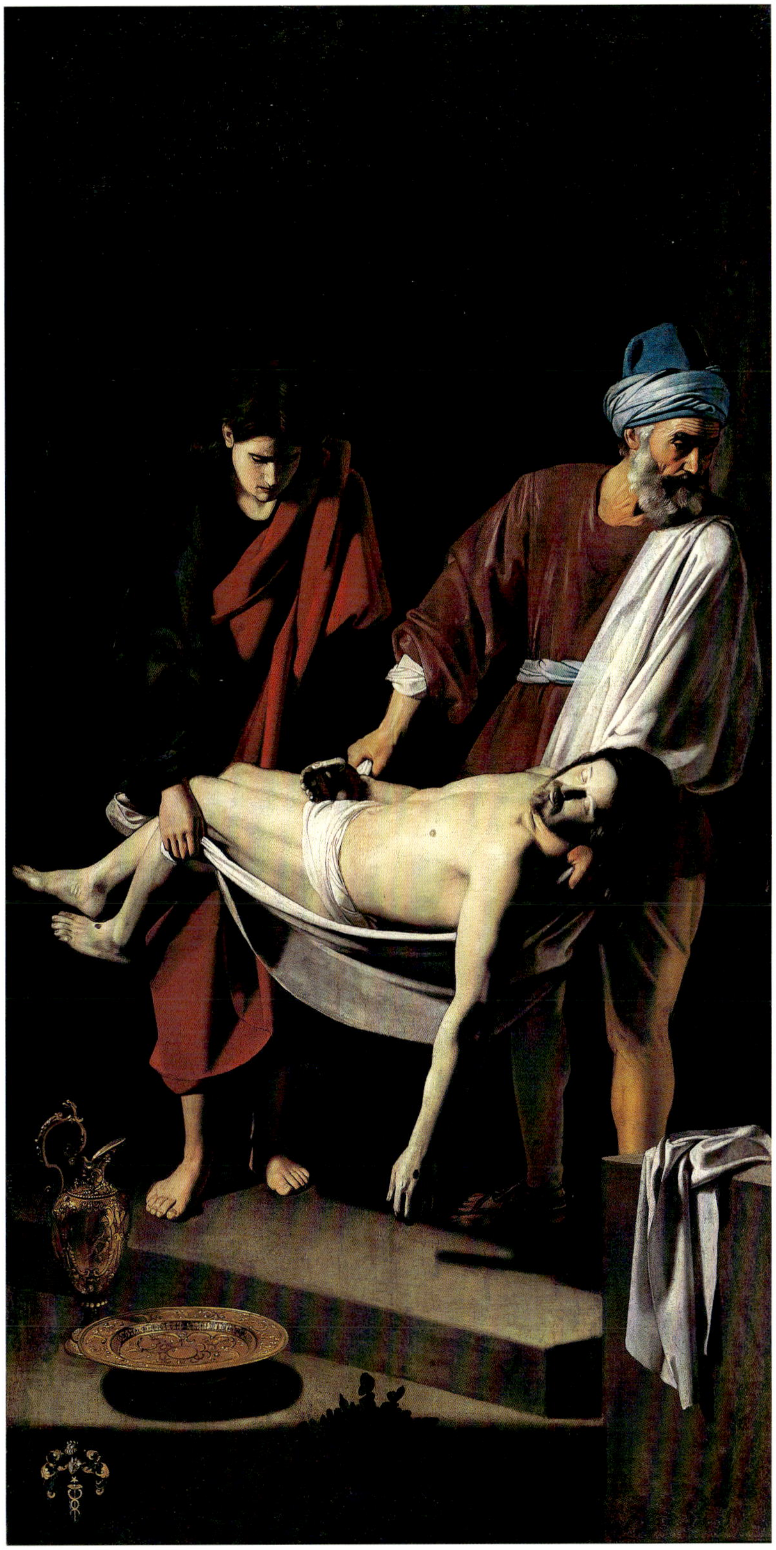

23
Nicolas Tournier
The Entombment of Christ, 1635/38
Musée des Augustins, Toulouse

c. 1618

Christ among the Doctors

24
Dirck van Baburen
Christ among the Doctors, c. 1618
Canvas, 135 × 202 cm
Museo della Misericordia, Florence,
(founded 1244), inv. 1973 n. 65[0]

25
Jusepe de Ribera
Christ among the Doctors, 1612/13
Canvas, 188 × 270 cm
Musée d'Art et d'Histoire de Langres,
Langres, inv. d.2011.1.1

26
Bartolomeo Manfredi
Christ among the Doctors, c. 1618
Canvas, 130 × 190 cm
Galleria degli Uffizi, Florence,
inv. 1890, no. 767

27
Orazio Borgianni
Christ among the Doctors, c. 1609
Canvas, 78.2 × 104.6 cm
Rijksmuseum, Amsterdam (on loan
from the Broere Charitable Foundation),
inv. SK-C-1709

Dirck van Baburen died young, and left only a small oeuvre. When the American art historian Leonard J. Slatkes received his doctorate in Utrecht in 1962 for his work on Baburen he knew of 28 surviving autograph paintings.[1] A dozen have been added since then, some of which were already known from photographs.[2] It was not just paintings that were rediscovered, but new photographs were also published that led to new attributions. In 1981/82, Slatkes recognised *Christ among the Doctors* as a Baburen from a black-and-white photograph (cat. 24).[3] Although the picture is unsigned, there has never been any doubt about its authorship. It is related to the paintings of the same subject by Bartolomeo Manfredi and Jusepe de Ribera, painters who both influenced Baburen. It is well known that all three artists influenced each other, working as they were in Rome in the second decade of the 17th century. The question is: who influenced whom? Lacking dates and for want of archival sources pinning down the year of execution, every answer is hypothetical. The case of *Christ among the Doctors* shows yet again how complex it is to unravel the interactions involved.

Slatkes dates the Baburen he discovered to around 1618 on the basis of a stylistic analysis.[4] Wayne Franits concurs in his monograph of 2013.[5] Gianni Papi dates it a later earlier, in 1616/17.[6] The picture's provenance goes back no further than the second half of the 18th century.[7]

Papi believes that Jusepe de Ribera's *Christ among the Doctors* (cat. 25) was painted around 1612/13.[8] Baburen knew that painting. It and twelve other works by the Spanish painter were in the collection of the banker and art collector Marchese Vincenzo Giustiniani (1564–1637). His inventory of 1638 lists it as a work by 'Spagnoletti', Ribera's nickname.[9] It is also known from the same inventory that Giustiniani collected pictures by Baburen. His *Christ Washing the Apostles' Feet* (fig. 32), which is now in the Gemäldegalerie in Berlin, was together with Ribera's painting in one of the rooms of his palazzo.[10] For a long time Ribera's *Christ among the Doctors* in Langres, its present location, was attributed to the Master of the Judgement of Solomon. Gianni Papi's identification of that anonymous artist with the young Ribera ensured that the picture was restored to the Spaniard.[11] But it was being associated with Baburen even before then. Slatkes, in his publication of 1981/82, draws attention to the points of similarity

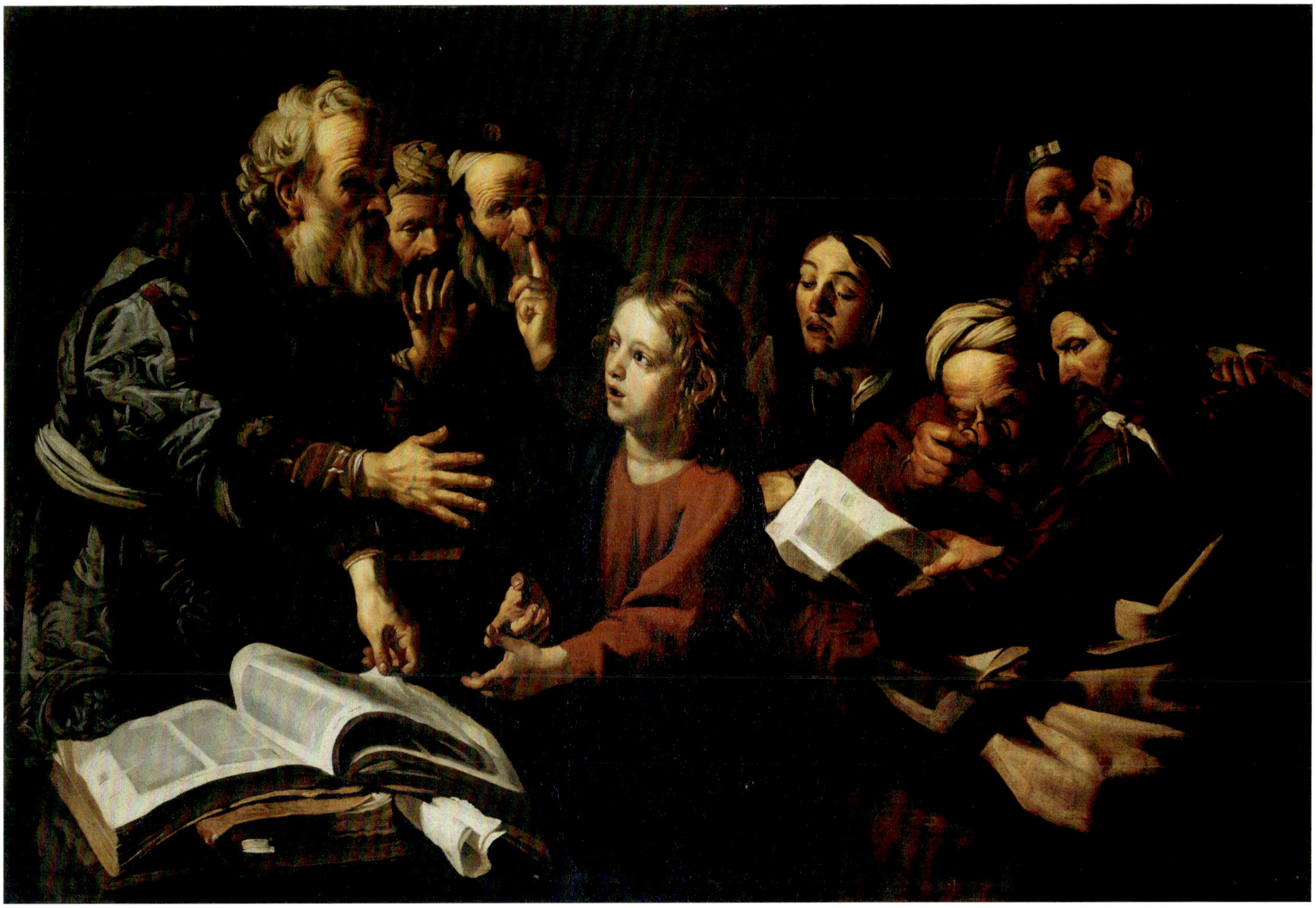

24
Dirck van Baburen
Christ among the Doctors, c. 1618
Museo della Venerabile Arciconfraternita
della Misericordia, Florence

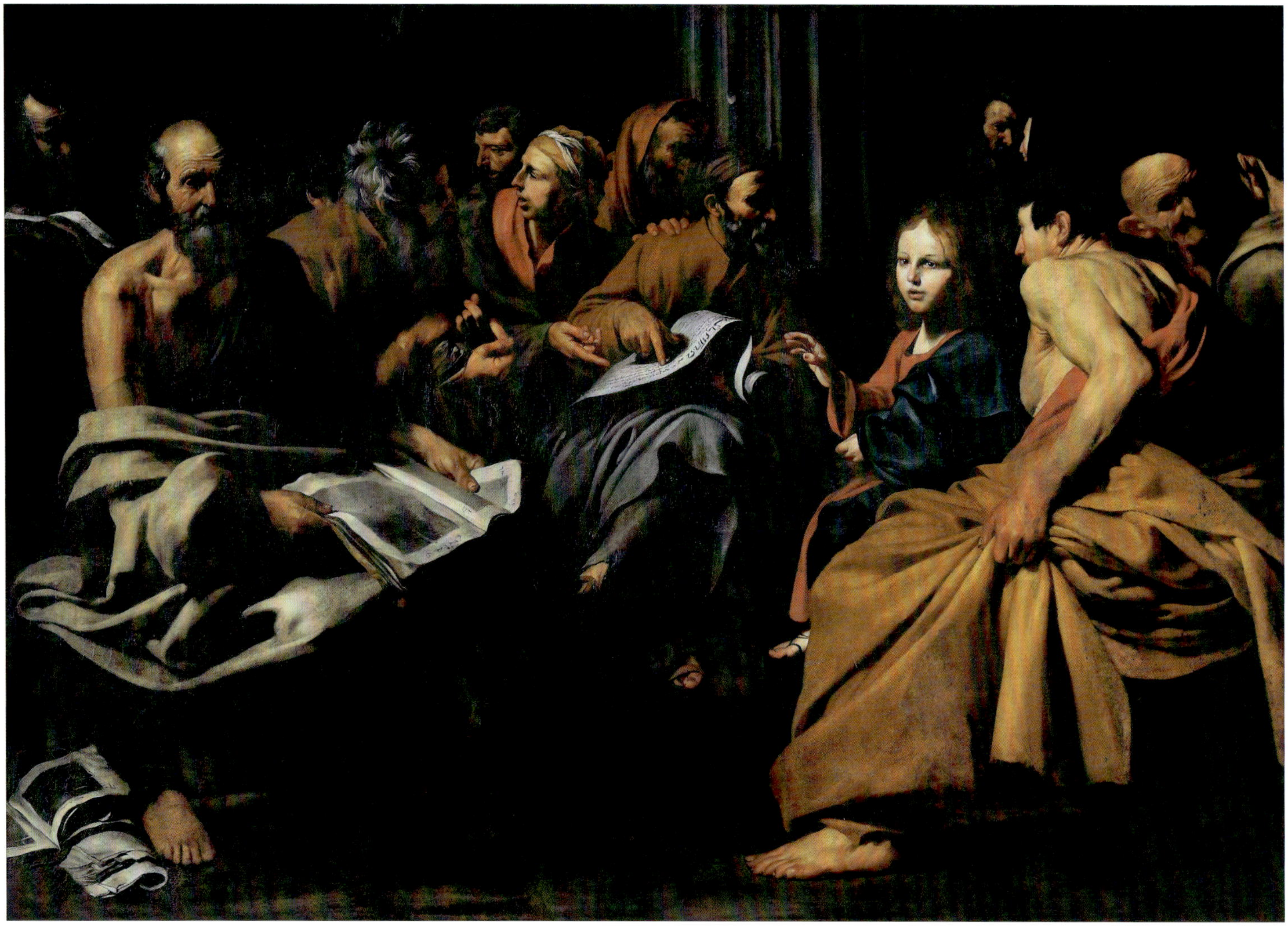

25
Jusepe de Ribera
Christ among the Doctors, 1612/13
Musée d'Art et d'Histoire de Langres, Langres

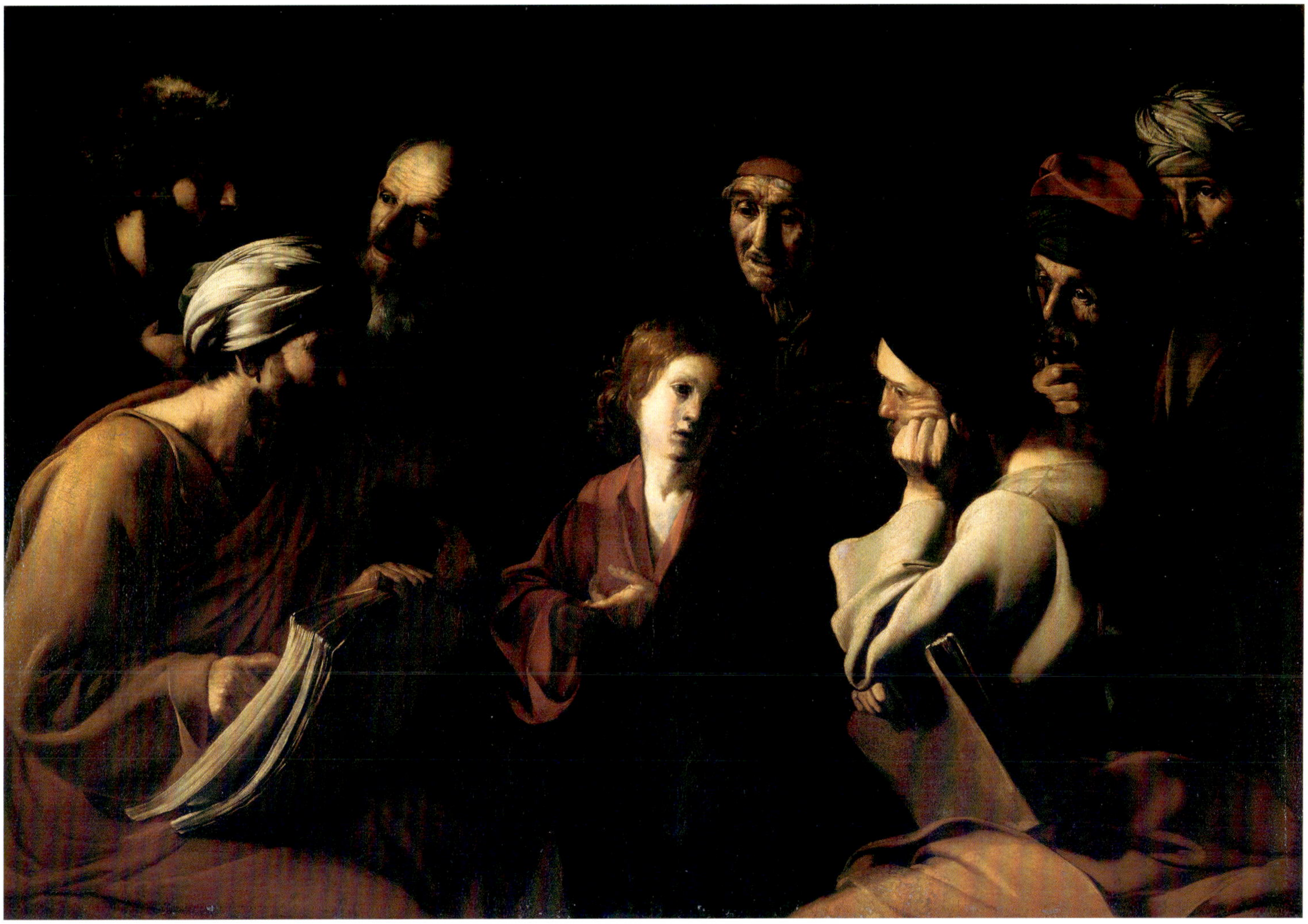

26
Bartolomeo Manfredi
Christ among the Doctors, c. 1618
Galleria degli Uffizi, Florence

between the painting in Langres and his newly discovered Baburen, which according to him preceded Ribera's version of the Bible story.[12] Slatkes therefore believed that Baburen had influenced Ribera, and not the other way round.

The earliest mention of Bartolomeo Manfredi's *Christ among the Doctors* (cat. 26) dates from 1666, when it and its companion piece, *The Tribute Money*, were listed in the inventory of Cardinal Carlo de' Medici (1595–1666) of that year.[13] Franits dates that painting to around 1618, which would permit a direct borrowing by Baburen. Nicole Hartje, in her monograph on Manfredi, is more elastic in her dating of 1617/19.[14] Gianni Papi, on the other hand, dates it much later, around 1620/21, which rules out any influence of the Italian on his colleague from Utrecht.[15]

Compositionally the paintings by Baburen and Manfredi are the most closely related. Both place the young Christ in the centre of the picture, with the doctors around him. One major difference, though, is that Baburen's old men are actively engaged in the dispute, whereas they are simply listening in the Manfredi.[16] That interaction in the Baburen with the sweet young Christ, ticking off his arguments on his fingers, makes this the tensest and most convincing image. Ribera moves Christ from the centre to the right, and since there are far more figures on the left, whose poses and varied gazes make them look inattentive and certainly unconcentrated, his composition falls to pieces.

Orazio Borgianni came from a very different tradition. Born in Rome, he worked mainly in Spain between roughly 1600 and 1606, but then returned to Rome for good.[17] Only his later work was influenced by Caravaggism. His *Christ among the Doctors* (cat. 27) may have been painted for Juan de Lezcano, secretary to Francisco Ruiz de Castro, the Spanish ambassador in Rome from 1609 to 1616. Borgianni knew both men very well. Lezcano's inventory of 1631 lists no fewer than twelve paintings by Borgianni, who appointed Lezcano one of his executors in his will of 10 November 1615 and bequeathed him a sword and a small painting of *The Crucifixion*. Borgianni left De Castro several portraits and a tondo with the head of Medusa.[18] Harold E. Wethey dates *Christ among the Doctors* c. 1605/10 in his 1964 article on Borgianni.[19] Marco Gallo opts for c. 1610/16, Gianni Papi the beginning of the second decade of the century, while the Rijksmuseum, where the picture has been on permanent loan since 2012, prefers c. 1609.[20]

Borgianni's figures are half-lengths crowded together on the picture surface. The old men are jostling around the child, hemming him in as they bend their heads towards him. Since Christ is pointing at the book held by the scholar to his left but has turned his head towards the men on his right, there is a kind of gracefulness that is missing in the works by Baburen, Ribera and Manfredi. Christ's face and gesturing hands are in the centre of the scene.[21] As far as the composition is concerned, Borgianni made a different but very powerful choice. According to Luke 2:42–51, the parents of the 12-year-old Jesus had come to Jerusalem to celebrate Passover when they lost sight of their child. They eventually found him, three days later, in the Temple, where he was in a discussion with learned Jewish theologians about Holy Scripture. It is a story about youth and old age, about charisma and amazement, but also about surprise, bewilderment and dismay.

In all four paintings the young Christ is wearing a red robe with a blue cloak on top. Those colours have a universal meaning. Red is an allusion to love, to the future suffering of the Passion, and to the blood of the sacrifice that Christ is to make on the cross. Blue stands for chastity, innocence, sincerity and hope.[22] Nothing is known for certain about Christ's appearance or the colour of his hair, so it is all the more surprising that he is red-haired in all four pictures. Although one would have expected blond, red could refer to the gold-coloured haloes around the heads of Christ, saints and angels. When Pope Gregory the Great (c. 540–604) saw a group of white, blond-haired boys in the slave market in Rome he asked where they had come from. Upon hearing that they were 'Angles' [English] he uttered the immortal words 'Non angli sed Angeli' ['Not English, but angels'].[23] LMH

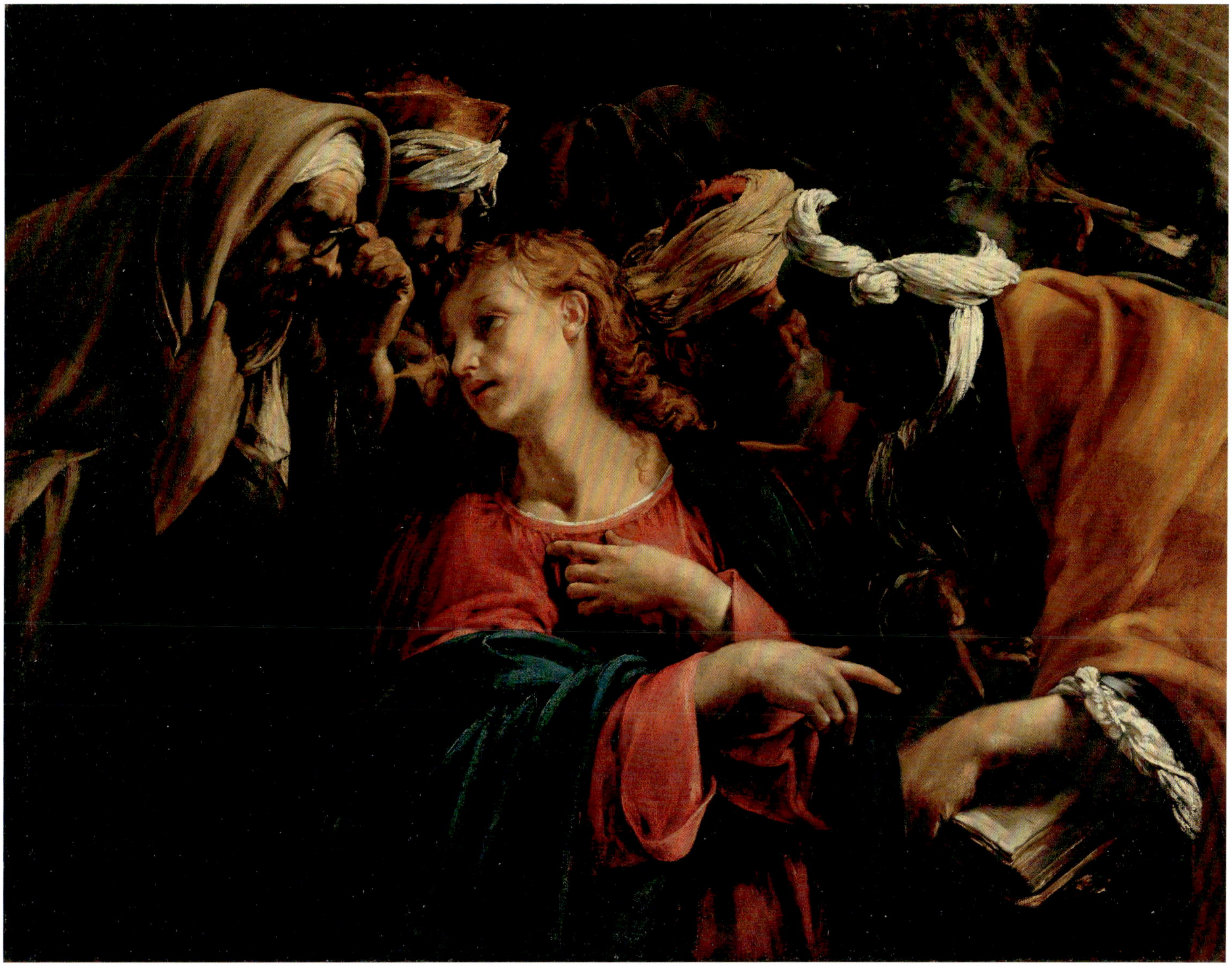

27
Orazio Borgianni
Christ among the Doctors, c. 1609
Rijksmuseum, Amsterdam (on loan
from the Broere Charitable Foundation)

1 Slatkes 1962, pp. 101–102, cats. A1–A28.
2 Franits 2013a, pp. 75–168, cats. A1–A36. Dirck van Baburen, *Apollo Flaying Marsyas*, c. 1623, canvas, 192 × 160 cm, Sarah Campbell Blaffer Foundation, Houston, inv. BF.2015.1, (fig. 92) was put on the art market in 2014/15 by Otto Naumann in New York.
3 Slatkes 1981/82, p. 181, presumed at the time that the picture had been lost.
4 Slatkes 1981/82, p. 181.
5 Franits 2013a, pp. 96–97, cat. A6.
6 Exh. cat. Florence 2010, p. 130, cat. 10; Exh. cat. Florence 2015, p. 212, cat. 41.
7 Franits 2013a, p. 96, cat. A6.
8 Gianni Papi in Exh. cat. Florence 2010, p. 215, cats. 40–50 dates it 1611/12.
9 Salerno 1960b, p. 96, no. 46 (*Christ among the Doctors*), p. 96, no. 76, p. 101, nos. 141–148, and p. 103, nos. 199–200.
10 Dirck van Baburen, *Christ Washing the Apostles' Feet*, c. 1617/18, canvas, 199 × 297 cm, Staatliche Museen zu Berlin, Gemäldegalerie, Berlin, inv. 462. For the mention in the inventory, see Salerno 1960b, p. 95, no. 45. Franits 2013a, pp. 92–94, cat. A4. For Vincenzo Giustiniani's entire inventory, see Salerno 1960a–c.
11 Gianni Papi in Exh. cat. Madrid 2011, pp. 116–118, cat. 7; Exh. cat. Rennes/Strasbourg 2014/15, pp. 58–61, cat. 3; Gianni Papi in Exh. cat. Milan/Vienna 2005/06, p. 254, cat. III.3.
12 Slatkes 1981/82, p. 181. Needless to say, Papi 2002, p. 30, and Papi in Exh. cat. Milan/Vienna 2005/06, p. 47, does not agree.
13 Bartolomeo Manfredi, *The Tribute Money*, c. 1618, canvas, 130 × 190 cm, Galleria degli Uffizi, Florence, inv. 1890, no. 778. Hartje 2004, pp. 350–356, cats. A28 and A29.
14 Hartje 2004, pp. 353–356, cat. A29.
15 Exh. cat. Florence 2010, pp. 214–215, cats. 49–50. Rossella Vodret also places the picture late in Manfredi's career in Strinati/Zuccari 2010, vol. 2, p. 97. Giuseppe Merlo dated it 1610/20 in Exh. cat. Cremona 1987, p. 72, cat. 8.
16 See also Franits 2013a, pp. 96–97, cat. A6.
17 Gallo 2010a, p. 336.
18 Gallo 1997, pp. 116–119, and p. 131, note 91; Vannugli 1998; Vannugli 2009; Gallo 2015, pp. 185–186, no. 4.
19 Wethey 1964, p. 154.
20 Gallo 2010a, p. 340, fig. 5; Papi 1993, pp. 117–118, cat. 28; Bull et al. 2013, p. 295.
21 Borgianni may have known Albrecht Dürer's painting of *Christ among the Doctors*, 1506, panel, 64.3 × 80.3 cm, Museo Nacional Thyssen-Bornemisza, Madrid, inv. 134(1934.38). There, too, the doctors are half-lengths crowded around the young man, who once again has red hair.
22 For the meaning of these colours see Timmers 1947, p. 824.
23 With thanks to Daniel Benito of the Museo del Patriarca, Real Colegio y Seminario de Corpus Christi, Valencia, who sent me this information by e-mail on 5 April 2017.

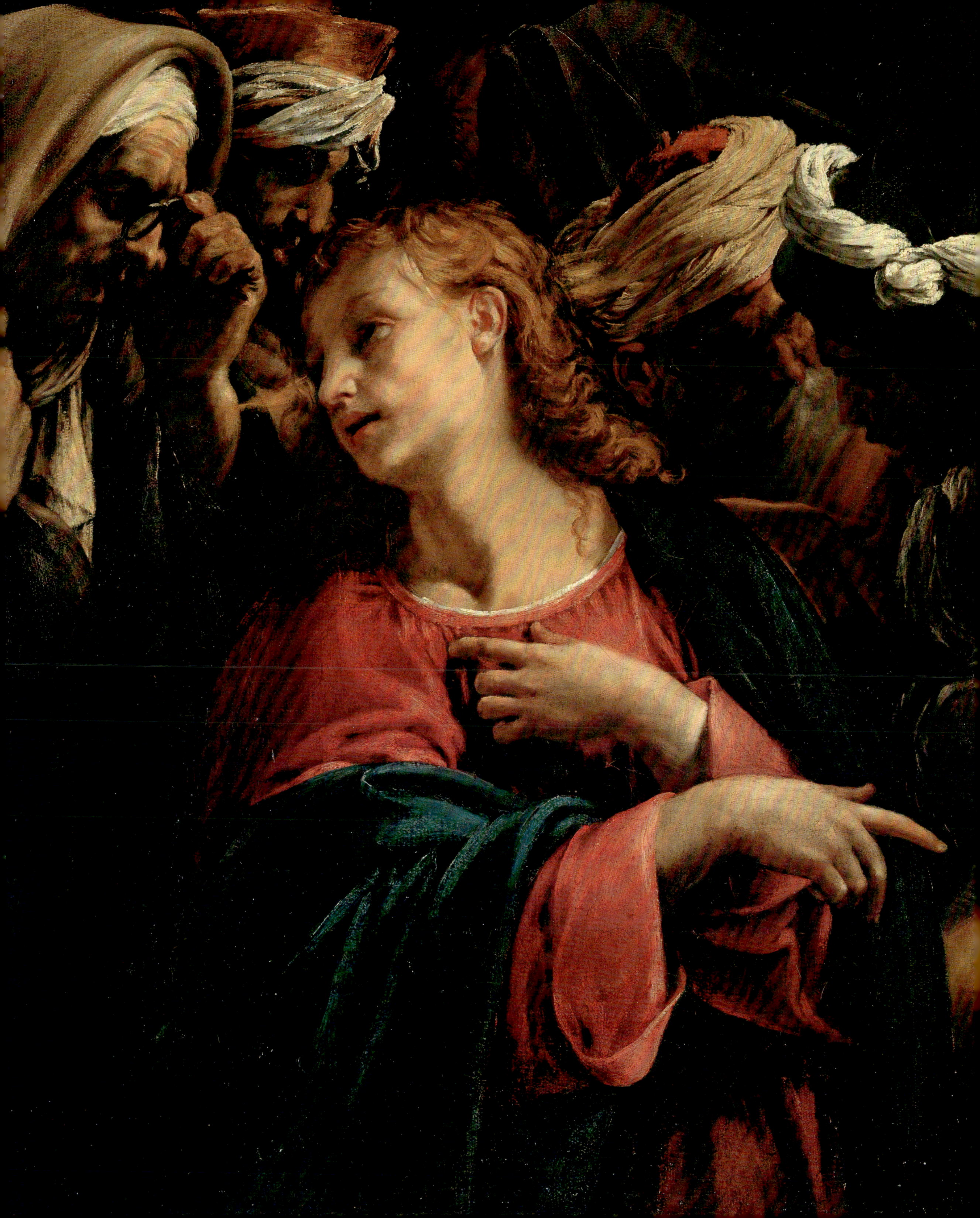

c. 1619/20

Merry Companies

28
Gerard van Honthorst
Merry Company with a Lute Player, c. 1619/20
Canvas, 144 × 212 cm
Galleria degli Uffizi, Florence, inv. 730

29
Gerard van Honthorst
The Debauched Student, 1625
Signed and dated in the open folio on the left below the illustration: Gart van Honthorst fecit 1625
Canvas, 125 × 157 cm
Bayerische Staatsgemäldesammlungen, Alte Pinakothek, Munich, inv. 391

30
Hendrick ter Brugghen
The Merry Drinker, c. 1625
Inscribed top right: HTB 16[...] [HTB ligatured]
Canvas, 71.4 × 59.8 cm
Centraal Museum, Utrecht, acquired in 1955 with the support of the Rembrandt Association, inv. 11480

In Rome in the first quarter of the 17th century, multi-figure groups of merrily music-making, gambling, and carousing soldiers or elegantly dressed cavaliers and courtesans established an extraordinarily popular form of genre painting and were among the main subjects of Caravaggesque art. The approximately life-size, half- or three-quarter-length figures are usually shown at night, grouped around a stone or wooden table placed parallel to the lower edge of the picture. The female figures wear colourful, wide dresses with open necklines and often have ostrich feathers in their hair. The men are often shown in armour or in colourfully striped costumes with slashed sleeves and feathered berets.[1] Sometimes they are joined by a toothless old woman with a turban-like headdress or a gypsy woman. Even though the surrounding pictorial space is rarely defined in greater detail, the stage-like and relatively sparely lit scenes seem to be set in a tavern or brothel. Yet rather than actual tavern scenes, they are fictional scenes featuring fictional figures.

Before his return to Utrecht in 1620, Gerard van Honthorst painted a *Merry Company with a Lute Player* (cat. 28) which is very likely identical with a painting the art critic Giulio Mancini describes as 'una Cena di Buffonarie' [a Meal of Buffoons] in the treatise on painting he wrote in 1620/21.[2] Mancini particularly praises the lighting of the scene by means of two artificial light sources and the resulting reflections and shadows. He tells us that Honthorst had produced the painting for the Grand Duke of Tuscany, Cosimo II de' Medici (1590–1621), in whose 1623 inventory it is mentioned.[3] This inventory lists two other genre paintings by Honthorst, which likewise arrived in Florence on 16 February 1620.[4]

It is possible to see that Manfredi served as a model, yet Honthorst arrived at solutions that are very much his own due to a combination with the Dutch pictorial tradition.[5] By using spotty illumination, he manages to highlight individual areas of the image and draw the viewer's attention to particular figures and actions. A preliminary drawing shows how Honthorst experimented with the exposed candlelight (fig. 68). In the painting he then introduced a second, hidden light source on the right, which illuminates a man being fed by a whore to great effect. During his apprenticeship with Abraham Bloemaert, he had been able to study Karel van Mander's *Schilder-boeck*, published in

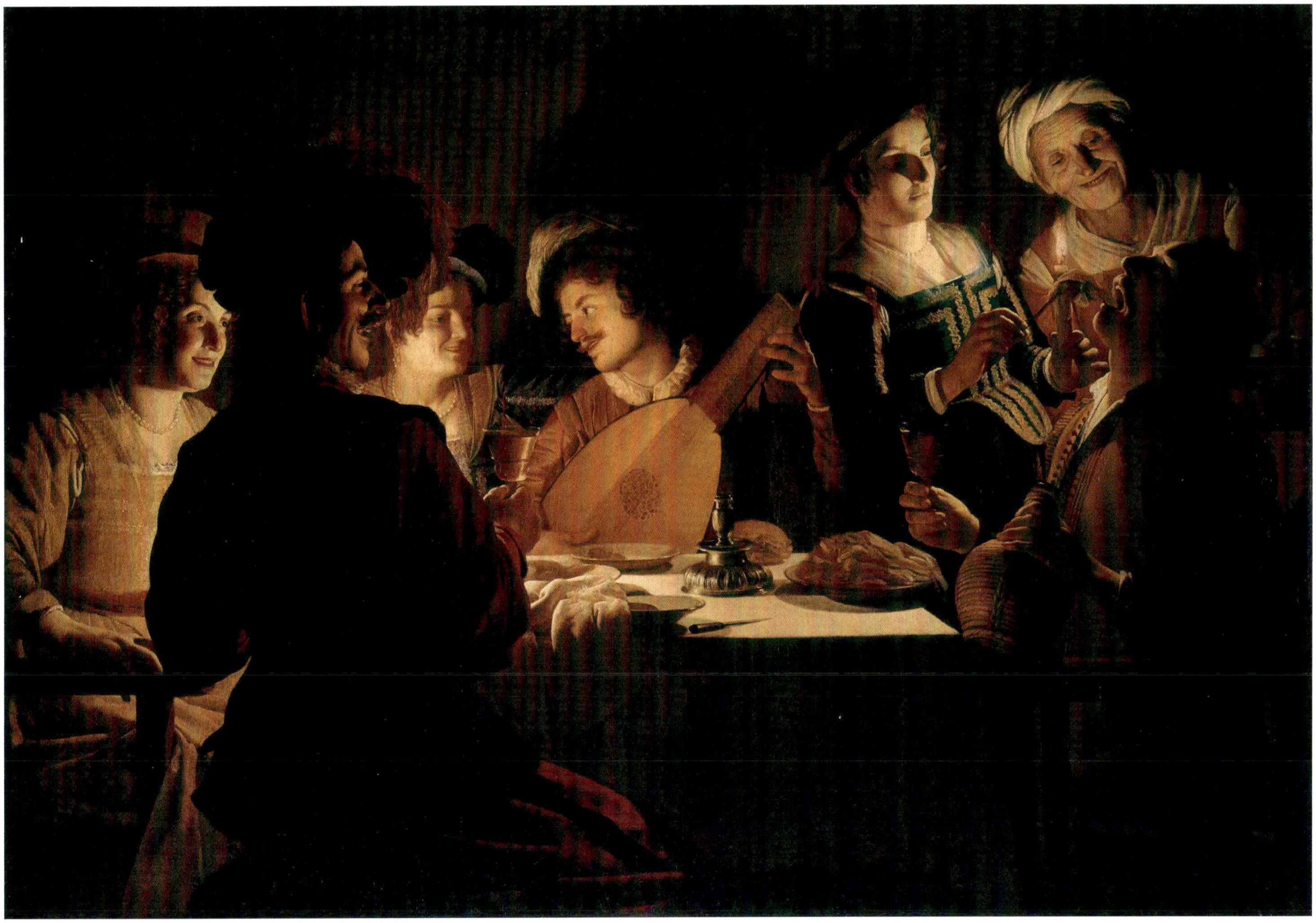

28
Gerard van Honthorst
Merry Company with a Lute Player, c. 1619/20
Galleria degli Uffizi, Florence

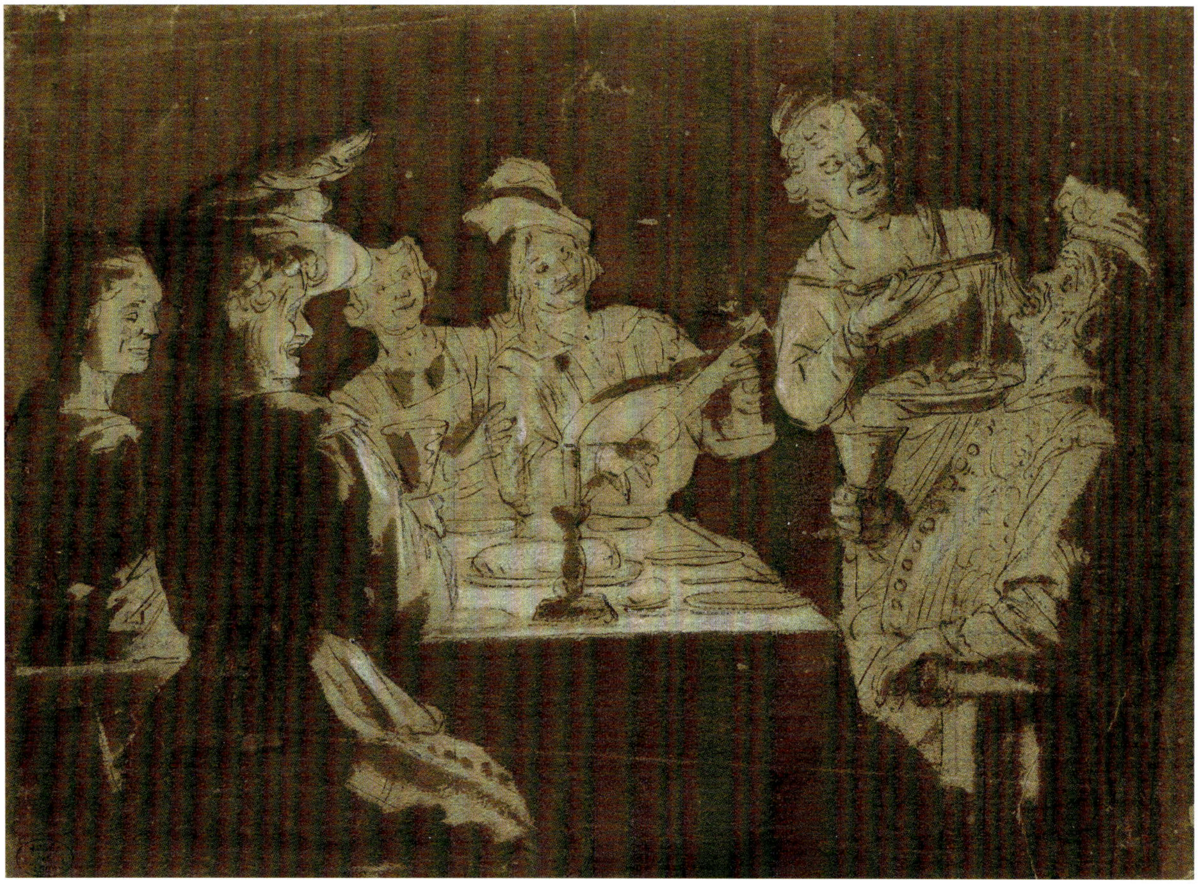

Fig. 68 Gerard van Honthorst, *Merry Group with a Lute Player*, c. 1619/20, Musée de Grenoble, Grenoble

1604, which includes the following passage: 'Candles as source of light, which is after all not such an everyday subject, are difficult and it is an art to paint them. But it is a good idea to have a figure in the dark in front, shaded from top to toe and the light only allowed to touch the contour of naked flesh, hair, or clothing. Also, taking the light source as a mid- or starting, the shadow has to seek its direction everywhere away from that point'.[6] Honthorst followed the advice of van Mander and placed the figure of the young man with feathered beret in the foreground right in front of the left candle flame. Unlike in the preliminary drawing, Honthorst's realised painting includes a large shadow being cast on the rear wall. This adoption of a detail from Caravaggio's *Supper at Emmaus* in London (fig. 69) remains unique among the Caravaggisti. The figure of the old woman on the right, still missing in the study, is likewise featured in Caravaggio's *Supper at Emmaus* in Milan (fig. 70).[7]

It was Bartolomeo Manfredi who, in Rome at the beginning of the second decade, introduced the type of the merry company grouped around a table as a distinct genre. One of his earliest examples is *A Drinking and Musical Party* (fig. 71), which was possibly created as early as 1612/14.[8] Formally, he draws on Caravaggio's compositions in the *Supper at Emmaus* (figs. 69, 70) and the group of publicans placed around a table in the *Calling of St Matthew* (fig. 78), datable to 1599/1600. Manfredi's compositions became prototypes which were subsequently adapted and developed further by his Dutch, Flemish and French fellow painters.[9] Numerous copies and variations document the popularity of the subject. They have come down to us especially from the French Caravaggisti, such as Tournier and Régnier who temporarily worked in Manfredi's workshop during their time in Rome.[10]

In the Netherlands, merry companies gathered at a table were already a popular subject in the 16th century. It was derived from

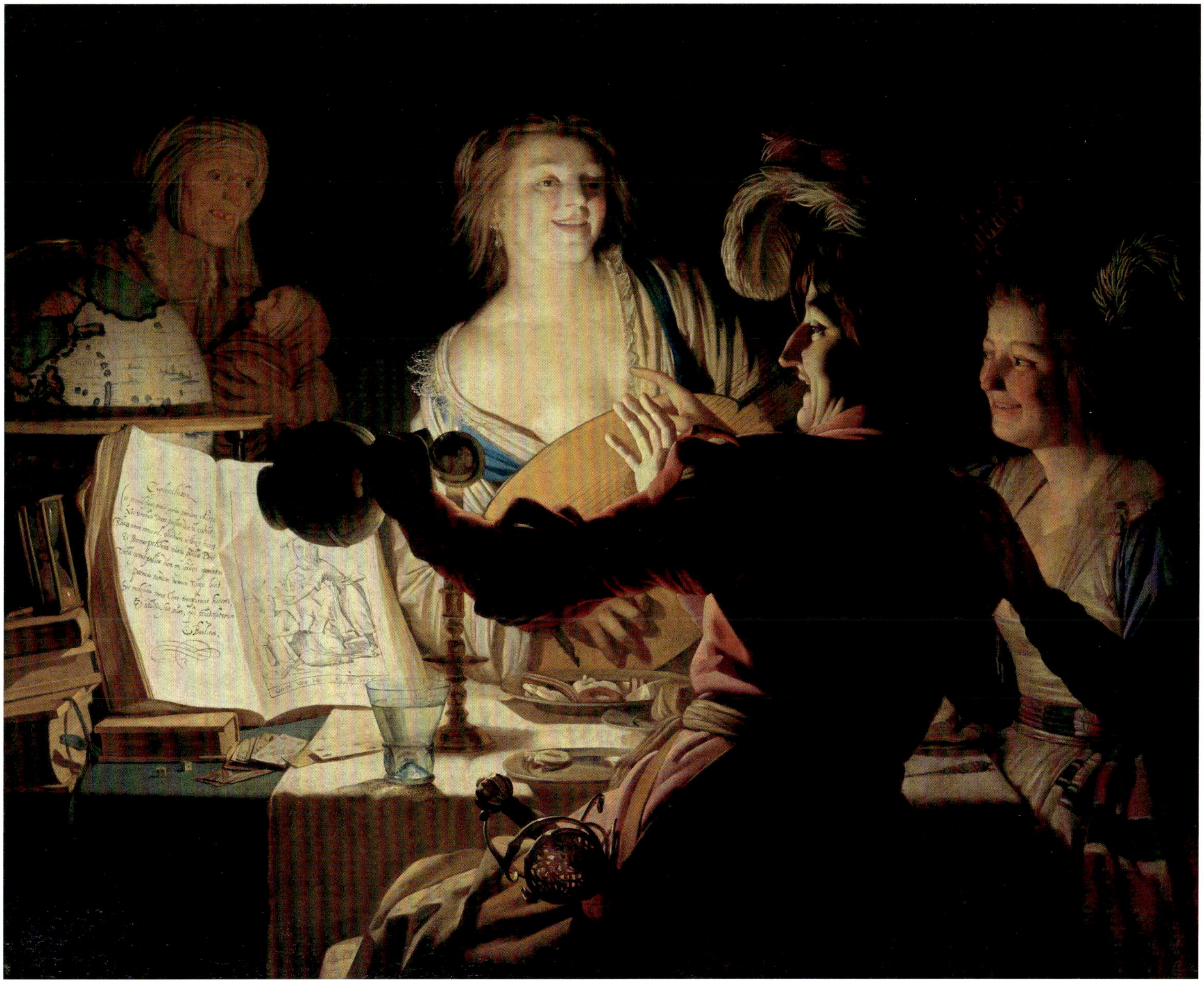

29
Gerard van Honthorst
The Debauched Student, 1625
Bayerische Staatsgemäldesammlungen,
Alte Pinakothek, Munich

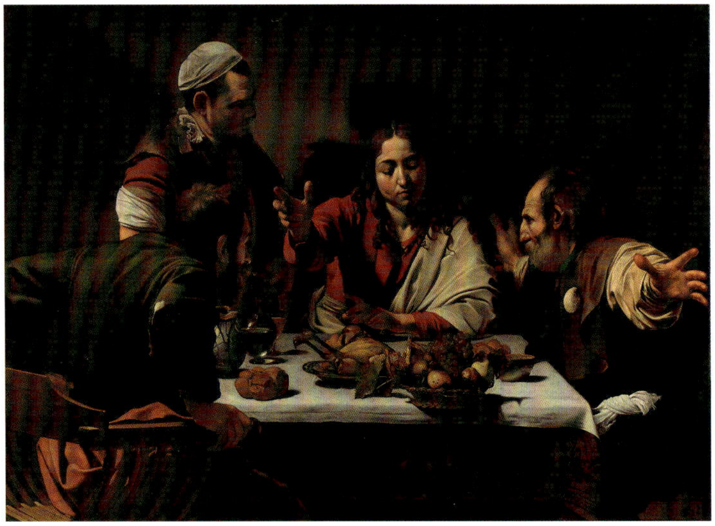

Fig. 69 Michelangelo Merisi, called Caravaggio, *The Supper at Emmaus*, 1601/02, The National Gallery, London

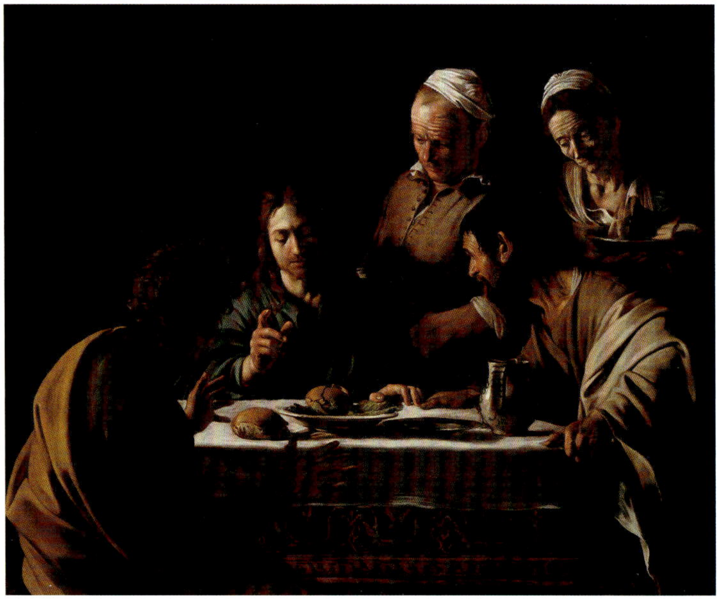

Fig. 70 Michelangelo Merisi, called Caravaggio, *The Supper at Emmaus*, 1606, Pinacoteca di Brera, Milan

the biblical parable of the prodigal son who had squandered his goods and chattels among prostitutes (Luke 15:11–32).[11] While Manfredi's companies consist almost exclusively of younger and middle-aged male genre figures, the men in Honthorst's paintings are joined by mostly young and elegantly dressed ladies following the Dutch tradition. Though the Utrecht painter's allusion to the biblical parable was probably just subliminal, it must be assumed that the merry company did convey a moral message. With the rest of the group laughing, the man on the right is being fed by the whore standing next to him. While he leans his head back and opens his mouth wide, he is still holding a wine glass and carafe in his hands.[12] This gesture may very well allude to the consequences of intemperance and the deadly sin of *gula*, or gluttony.

Honthorst develops the subject further in his composition known as *The Debauched Student*, which he dated and signed in 1625 (cat. 29).[13] An elegantly dressed young man with feathered beret and officer's sword as well as two tarted-up young ladies are grouped around a table. On the right side, the table is richly set with a white cloth and dishes. On the left, numerous objects are arranged which have led to the identification of the young man as a student: a globe, stacked books, an hourglass, as well as a large, open tome. Apparently, we are in the study of the young man whose desk has been unceremoniously covered with a green velvet cloth for a game of dice or cards and for the meal afterwards. The student turns his back to us and he raises a wine jug with his left hand; holding it horizontally with the lid open, he peers into it. With his right hand he tries to reflect the light of the candle in such a way that it lights the inside of the apparently empty jug.[14] The figure of the *kannekijker* who peers deeply into a jug traditionally represented a drunkard of the kind presented even more radically, and blatantly up close, by ter Brugghen in his *The Merry Drinker* of c. 1625 (cat. 30).[15] The glassy eyes and spaced-out gaze, the lasciviously bared shoulder, the red drinker's nose, and the salty herring he is grabbing are all clear indications of the carouser's inebriated state. Tournier had previously conceived thematically similar individual figures of drinking men in Rome (fig. 72).[16] Yet his elegantly dressed and self-confidently posing soldiers are not at all like the coarse, burlesque and 'off-the-rails' type of men by ter Brugghen.

Yet Honthorst not only denounces the excessive consumption of alcohol in his painting. The young ladies who, based on their headdresses and their colourful clothing, can be identified as prostitutes, at the same time distract the young man from his studies. The epigram and the illustration in the open tome provide

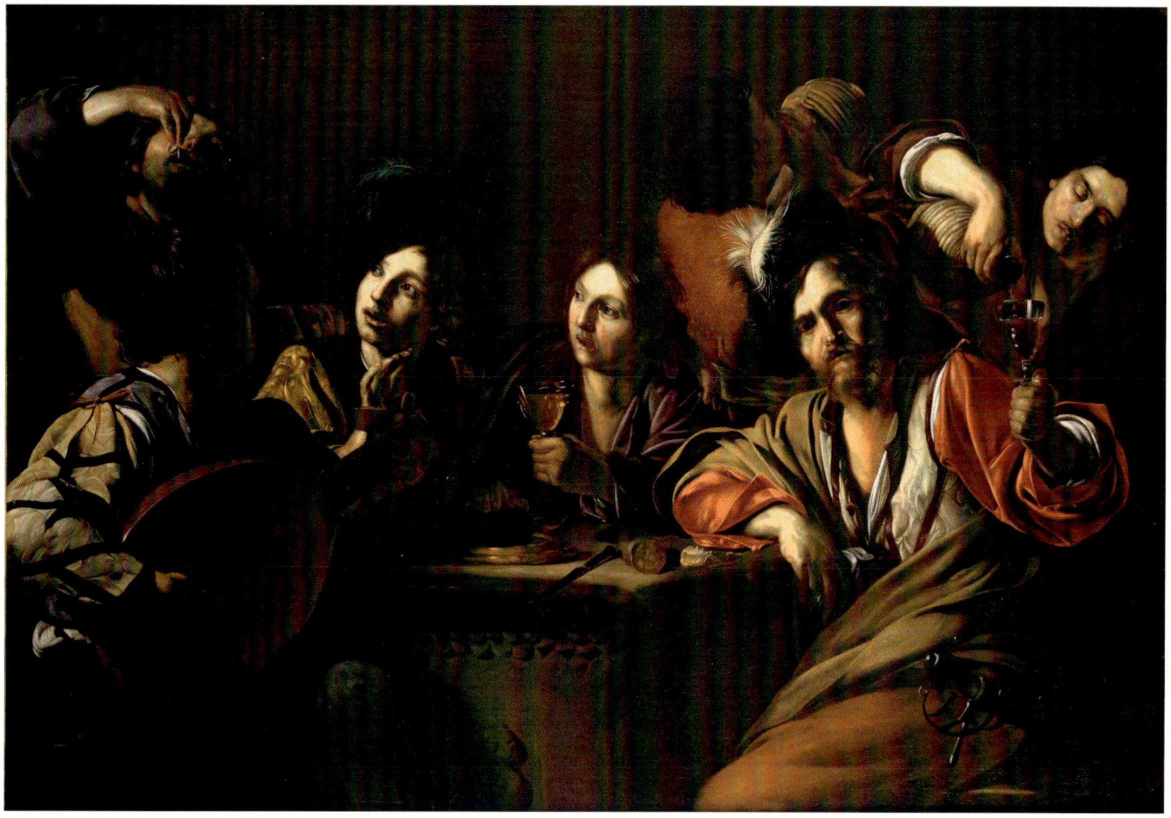

Fig. 71 Bartolomeo Manfredi, *A Drinking and Musical Party*, c. 1612/14, private collection

the key to the interpretation of the painting: Pallas Athena, the goddess of science and wisdom, is pressed down and subdued by Bacchus and Amor. Similar to the depictions of the prodigal son, the student has strayed from the right path. Usually representing the procuress, the toothless old woman emerging from the background on the left probably also points to the consequences of his licentious and profligate way of life. In her arms she carries an infant to which the whore sitting next to the student points. Not coincidentally, the outsized nose of the child is reminiscent of the student's physiognomy.

Honthorst's night-time companies are characterised by a particularly atmospheric treatment of light in which individual areas of the image are deliberately illuminated for the purpose of condensing narrative moments. His manner of choreographed darkness draws on the composition of Manfredi, but the high-contrast effects of light and shade in details such as the objects on the table, the hands, and cloth folds are closer still to the dramatic visual language of Caravaggio. Honthorst's candlelit groups gathered around tables visibly differ from the style of the French Caravaggisti, such as Tournier, Valentin de Boulogne and Régnier (cat. 52). It was the Dutchman's ability to depict in a natural way the effect of warm light breaking through the darkness which was appreciated internationally and later earned him the sobriquet 'Gherardo delle Notti'. BE

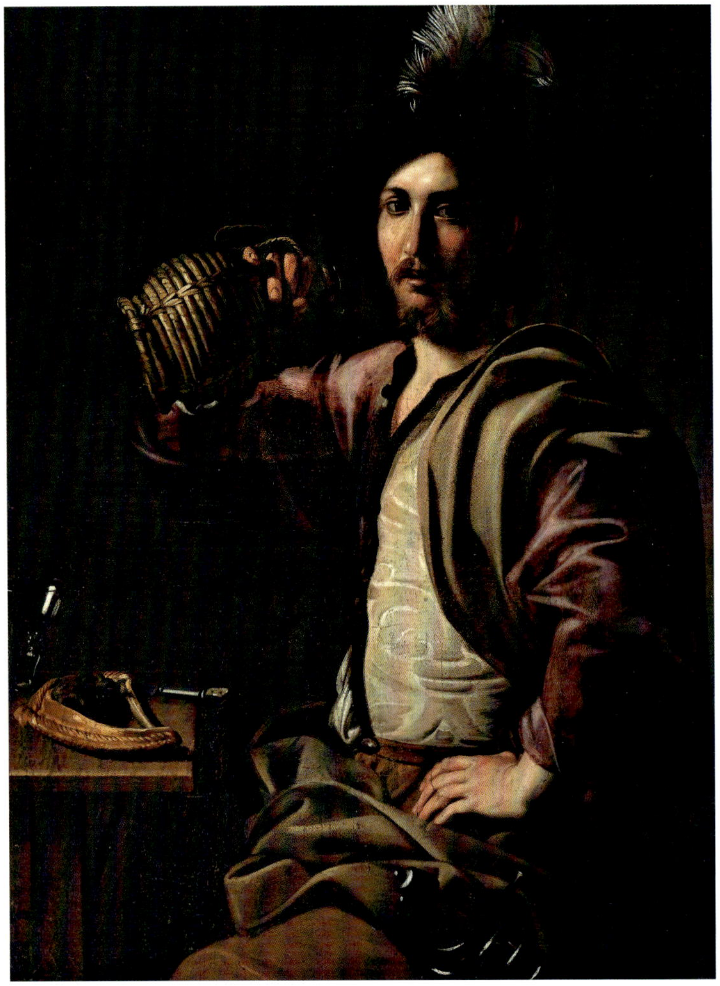

Fig. 72 Nicolas Tournier, *Young Man with a Demijohn*, before 1620, Galleria Estense, Modena

1 These clothes are not consistent with the fashion of the time, but rather inspired by 16th-century clothing and the German *landsknecht* costumes; see, among others, Hartje 2004, p. 227; Dekiert 2003, pp. 261–272.
2 Mancini 1956, p. 258. For the painting see, among others, Albert Blankert in Exh. cat. Utrecht/Braunschweig 1986/87, pp. 31–32; Papi 1999, pp. 159–160, cat. 31; Judson/Ekkart 1999, pp. 217–218, cat. 281; Gianni Papi in Exh. cat. Florence 2015, pp. 188–189, cat. 31.
3 Nadia Bastogi in Exh. cat. Florenz 2010, p. 355, no. 26.
4 Both Florence, Galleria degli Uffizi: *Merry Company ('Wedding Feast')*, c. 1617, 138 × 203 cm, inv. 735; *Fortune Teller*, c. 1620, canvas, 137 × 204 cm, inv. 734 (see fig. 102); Judson/Ekkart 1999, pp. 214–216, cat. 278, 279.
5 For the use of light in the work of Honthorst and the Dutch tradition, see, among others, Müller Hofstede 1988, pp. 13–34, and Neumeister 2003, esp. pp. 146–218.
6 Van Mander 1604, ch. VII, par. 34; quoted in English in Ernst van de Wetering, *Rembrandt: The Painter Thinking* (University of California Press, 2016), p. 150.
7 1601/02, canvas, 141 × 196.2 cm, The National Gallery, London, inv. NG172; 1606, canvas, 141 × 175 cm, Pinacoteca di Brera, Milan, inv. 966.
8 Canvas, 129.5 × 190.5 cm, private collection; Hartje 2004, pp. 212–214, 218, 312–315, cat. A11 (c. 1612/14); Gianni Papi in Exh. cat. Rome/Paris 2014/15, pp. 172–173, cat. 15 (c. 1619/20); Letizia Trevis in Exh. cat. London/Dublin/Edinburgh 2016/17, pp. 78–79, cat. 12, p. 179 (c. 1615/20).
9 Hartje 2004, p. 128, 218. Joachim von Sandrart already pointed to this influence in his biographies and coined the term 'Manfredi Manier'; Sandrart 1675 (1925), p. 170.
10 Cuzin 1987; Letizia Trevis in Exh. cat. London/Dublin/Edinburgh 2016/17, p. 78.
11 See Renger 1970 and Boyd Morris 2011. For the possible influence of the Dutch genre paintings on Caravaggio see Friedlaender 1955, pp. 81–82.
12 For the identification of the young ladies as prostitutes, see cat. 72.
13 For in-depth discussions of this painting, see Dekiert 1999; Judson/Ekkart 1999, pp. 220–222, cat. 284; Dekiert 2003, pp. 272–285. The German title, Liederlicher Student, may derive from the description of the painting by Johann Christian von Mannlich who refers to the figure as a 'lüderlicher Student'; Mannlich 1805, vol. 2, p. 207.
14 Albert Henry Payne accordingly gave the painting the title *Empty Jug*, Payne 1849–1852, vol. 2, p. III.
15 Cat. Utrecht 1999, vol. 1, pp. 162–164, vol. 2, pp. 759–760, cat. 124 (c. 1625); Slatkes/Franits 2007, pp. 162–164, cat. A52 (c. 1623/24).
16 *Young Man with a Demijohn*, before 1620, canvas, 124 × 93 cm, Galleria Estense, Modena, inv. 41.

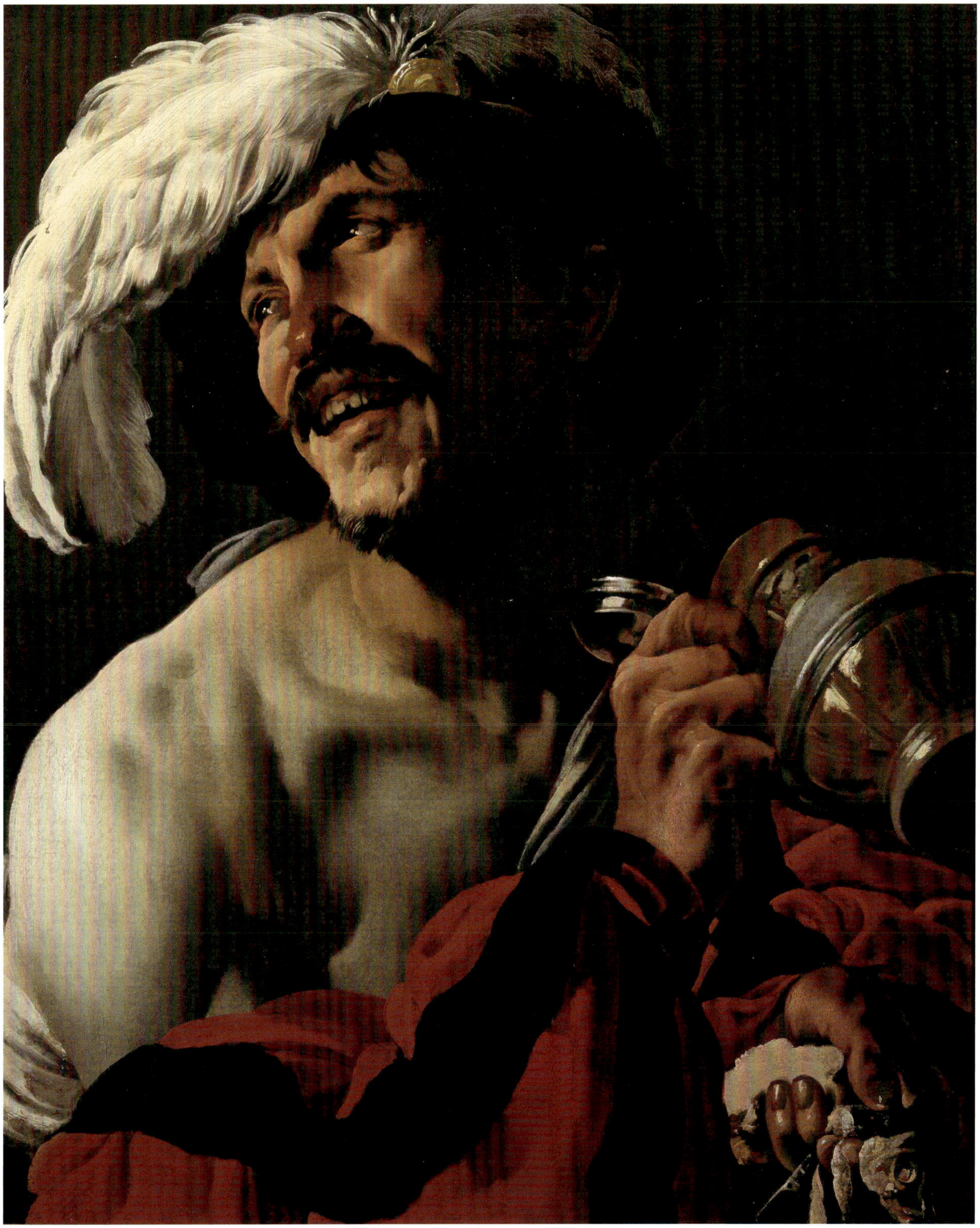

30
Hendrick ter Brugghen
The Merry Drinker, c. 1625
Centraal Museum, Utrecht

1621

Musicians

31
Dirck van Baburen
Boy with a Jew's Harp, 1621
Canvas, 65 × 52 cm
Signed and dated top right: TBaburen fecit // Ano 1621 [TB ligatured]
Centraal Museum, Utrecht, inv. 11188

32
Hendrick ter Brugghen
Fife Player, 1621
Canvas, 71.3 × 56 cm
Signed on the bonnet: HTB
Museumslandschaft Hessen Kassel, Gemäldegalerie Alte Meister, Kassel, inv. GK 179

33
Hendrick ter Brugghen
Flute Player, 1621
Canvas, 71.5 × 56 cm
Signed and dated beside the hand: HTBrugghen. Fecit 1621
Museumslandschaft Hessen Kassel, Gemäldegalerie Alte Meister, Kassel, inv. GK 180

34
Dirck van Baburen
Lute Player, 1622
Canvas, 71.2 × 58.5 cm
Signed and dated top left: Teod Babu fecit // Anno 1622
Centraal Museum, Utrecht, purchased with support from the Rembrandt Association, 1955, inv. 11481

35
Bartolomeo Manfredi
La Zingara (*The Gypsy Girl*), c. 1613/15
Canvas, 65 × 59 cm
Private collection, Courtesy Nicolas Joly Art Conseil

It would have been in the autumn of 1620, or the winter of 1621 at the latest, that Dirck van Baburen returned to Utrecht.[1] Hendrick ter Brugghen had already come back home in the autumn of 1614, and it is known that Gerard van Honthorst celebrated his return with friends and colleagues on 26 July 1620 in the Poortgen inn.[2]

It can hardly be coincidental that Baburen's first painting known to have been painted back in Utrecht is a nocturne, and the only one in his oeuvre.[3] Perhaps he wanted to show those who had remained behind that he too was able to achieve the special effect created by the use of a hidden source of artificial light, for which Honthorst had become so famous. Baburen painted a young musician who is illuminated by a smoking candle behind fluttering sheets of music (cat. 31). The ear of the sconce casts a contorted shadow on the crumpled sheet by his left arm. That is not the only thing that makes this *Boy with a Jew's Harp* so unusual. Of all the half-length musicians painted by the Caravaggisti, this is the only one who is playing that small plucked instrument. Unlike the lute, known in those days as 'the king of musical instruments', the Jew's harp was played by the common folk and was sold at fairgrounds in the 16th and 17th centuries. It consists of a small metal or wooden frame that is gripped between the teeth or lips. Mounted inside it is a loose tongue that is plucked with the fingers to make it vibrate. The oral cavity is the resonator. Variation and undertones and overtones are produced by flexing the muscles of the mouth and by breathing in and out.[4]

In 1621, the year of Baburen's *Boy with a Jew's Harp*, ter Brugghen, who had painted nothing but history pieces since his return from Italy, suddenly produced two half-length musicians (cats. 32, 33), and Abraham Bloemaert painted one (fig. 75). Those four musicians are the forerunners of almost all the other ones depicted in isolation and at half-length.[5] The origin of this new type of musician can be traced back to northern Italian painters, among them Girolamo Savoldo (c. 1480/85–after 1548) (fig. 73).[6] Caravaggio and his followers made them familiar in Rome (fig. 74).[7] Baburen had picked the subject up there and introduced it in the northern Netherlands, where it became remarkably popular, not only in Utrecht but in cities such as Haarlem and Leiden as well.

Ter Brugghen's two flute players of 1621 (cats. 32, 33) are regarded as companion pieces because of their subject, composition and common provenance, which goes back to 1768. On

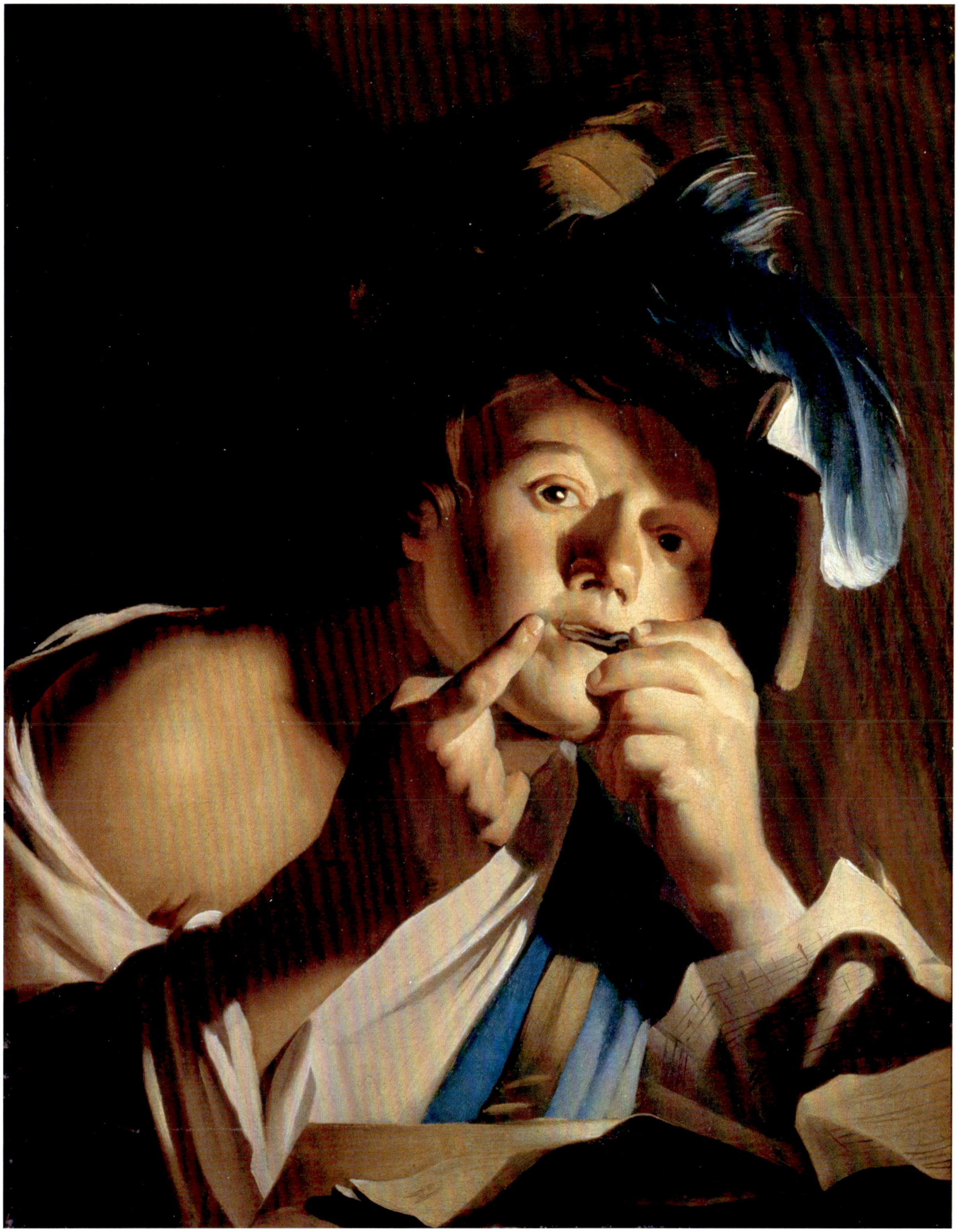

31
Dirck van Baburen
Boy with a Jew's Harp, 1621
Centraal Museum, Utrecht

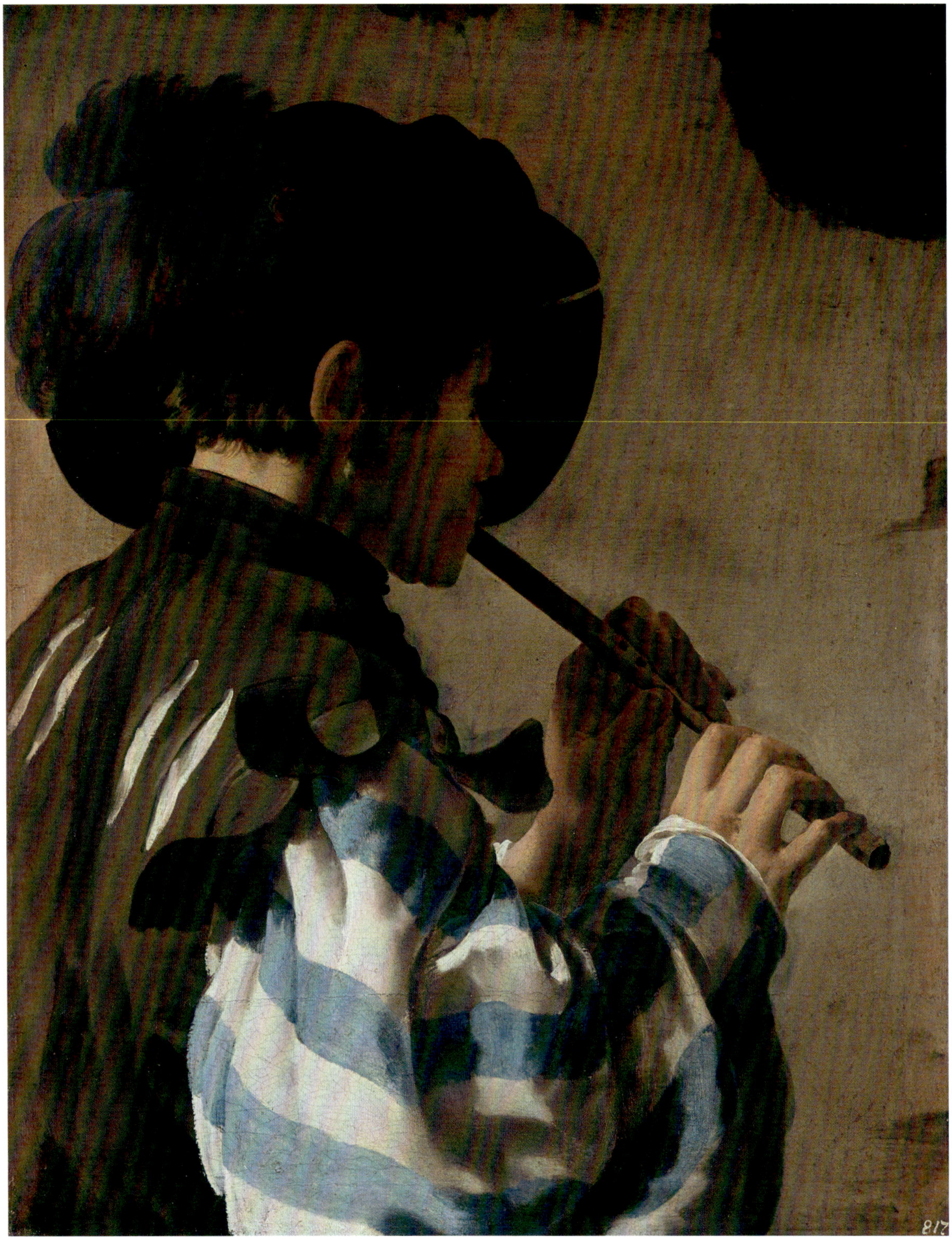

32
Hendrick ter Brugghen
Fife Player, 1621
Museumslandschaft Hessen Kassel,
Gemäldegalerie Alte Meister, Kassel

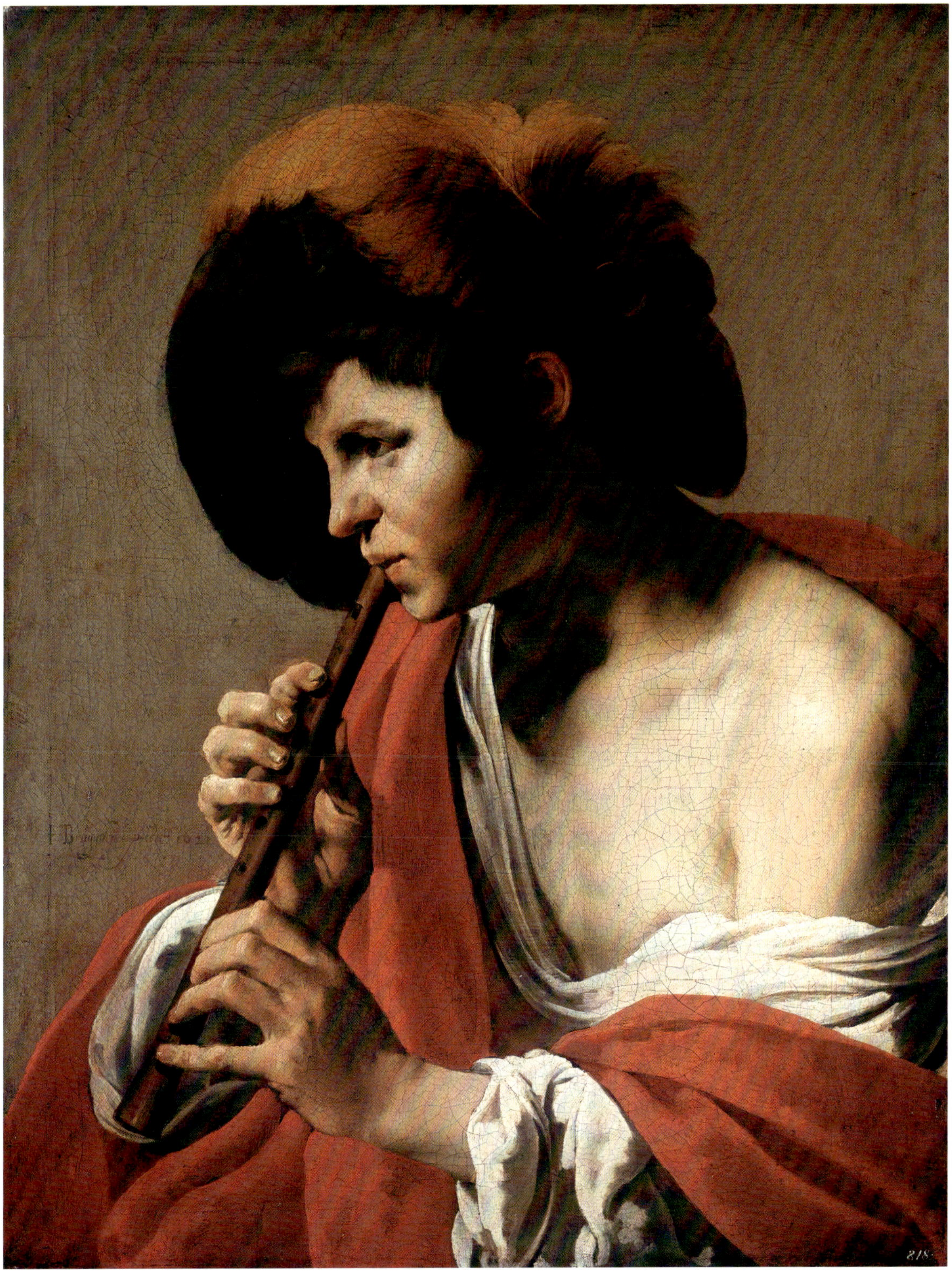

33
Hendrick ter Brugghen
Flute Player, 1621
Museumslandschaft Hessen Kassel,
Gemäldegalerie Alte Meister, Kassel

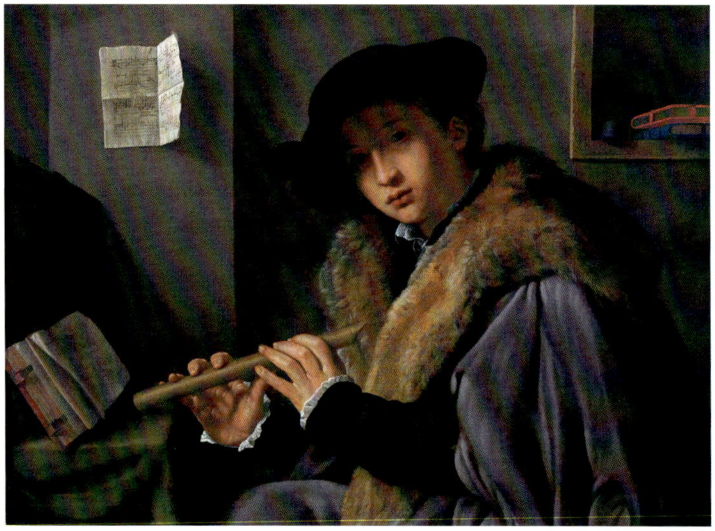

Fig. 73 Girolamo Savoldo, *Flute Player*, 1519, Pinacoteca Tosio Martinengo, Brescia

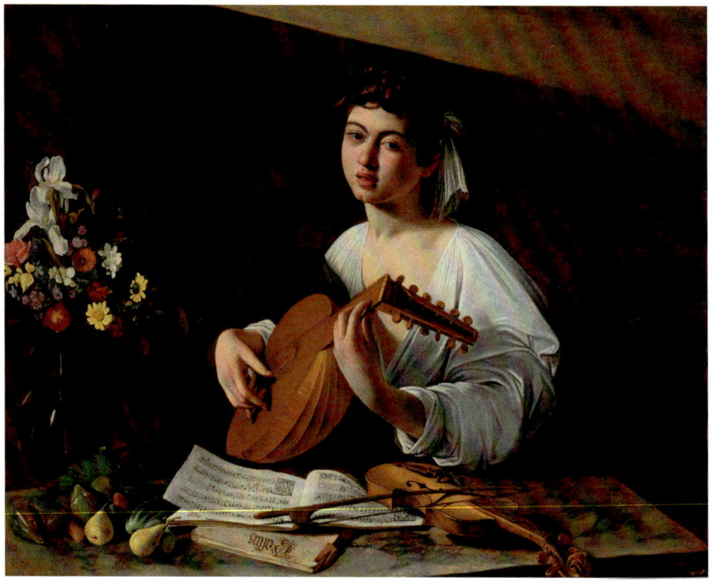

Fig. 74 Michelangelo Merisi, called Caravaggio, *Lute Player*, 1594/95, State Hermitage Museum, Saint Petersburg

closer examination, though, they are very different. The boys are not playing the same sort of flute, are wearing dissimilar clothing, have different colouration and are not occupying the same space.[8] The musician facing left is playing a recorder and is dressed in a red garment hanging off his shoulder over a white shirt. In Italian art, the recorder had been associated since time immemorial with the pastoral mode in art and poetry, which makes the boy's *all'antica* costume very fitting. His companion facing right is in theatrical Burgundian attire and is playing a short transverse flute, also called a pipe. It is an instrument with a rather piercing, high sound that contrasts with the sweet notes of the recorder. The *Flute Player* has a predominantly warm colour scheme, while ter Brugghen used cool, blue colours for the other work. It is clear from the backgrounds that they are not in the same space. The wall is smooth in the recorder scene and damaged in the one with the piper. In fact, they are each other's opposites. And although pendants they are clearly not playing together.

The *Flute Player* by Abraham Bloemaert, ter Brugghen's teacher, dates from the same year (fig. 75).[9] It is the earliest example in his oeuvre of a single half-length figure, filling almost the entire picture surface. Bloemaert, who never went to Italy, was indirectly confronted with the subject through his pupils, and with the effect of a hidden light source. He placed the young man's face slightly off centre, shifting the illuminated eye to the middle of the scene. The yellow of the doublet is reflected in the right half of the face, the neck, the hands and the plumes of the hat. The dark jug in the foreground not only acts as a *repoussoir* but also hides the source of the light.

The *Lute Player* by Dirck van Baburen (cat. 34) and his *Young Man Singing* in the Städel Museum in Frankfurt (fig. 76) date from 1622.[10] Both musicians are wearing an eye-catching, elegant bonnet adorned with a plume that is attached to the hat with a medallion. Their clothing of a striped jacket over a white undergarment can be described as *all'antica,* like the attire of ter Brugghen's *Flute Player*. In those days this archaic theatrical or rhetoricians' attire conjured up associations with people who were marginalised in society, such as gypsies and prostitutes.[11] The *Lute Player* goes a step further in that respect. His extraordinary earring, to which a cord is attached with a bow, perfects his exotic costume. In addition, his lute is battered and not looked after properly. Three of its six double strings are broken. His

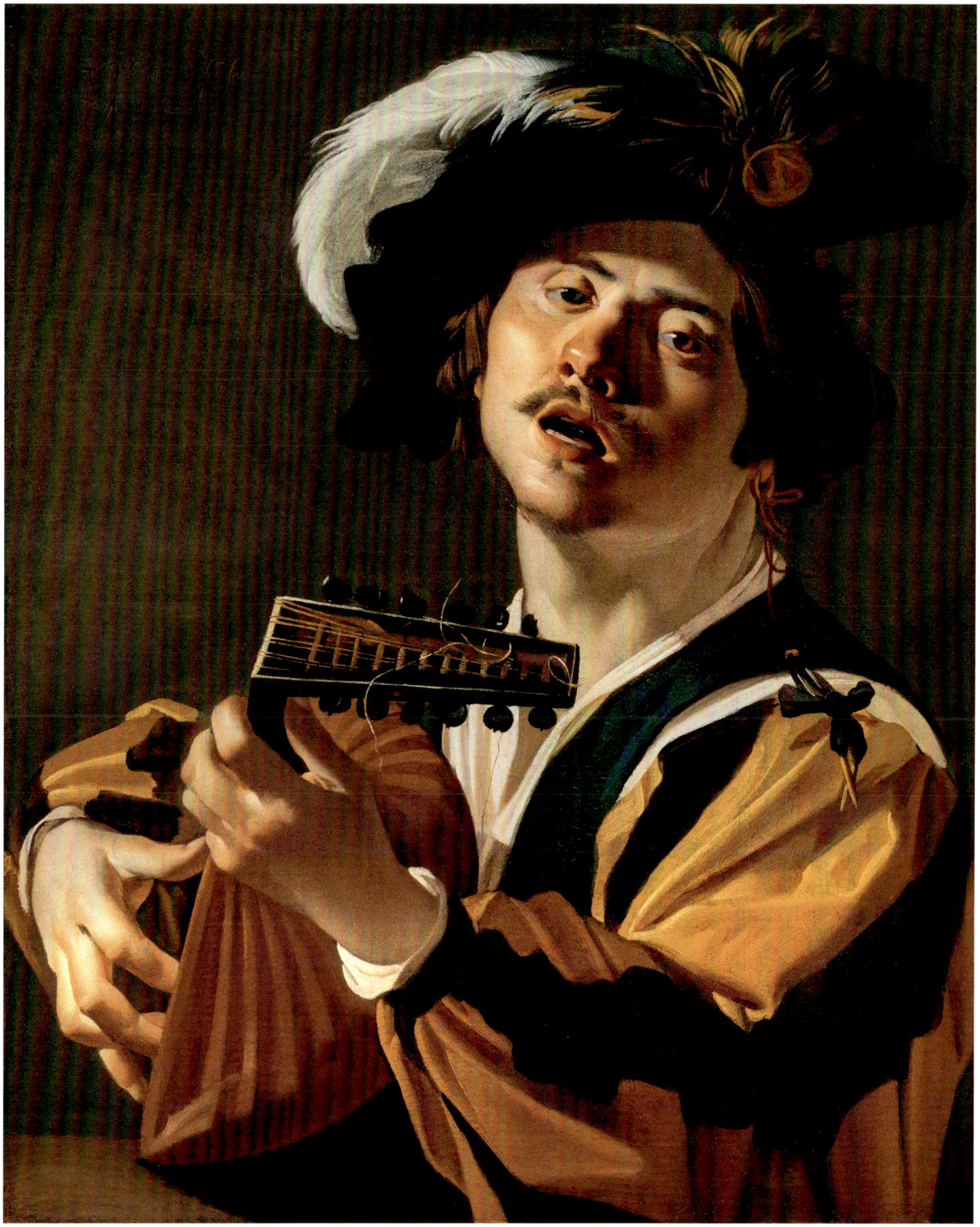

34
Dirck van Baburen
Lute Player, 1622
Centraal Museum, Utrecht

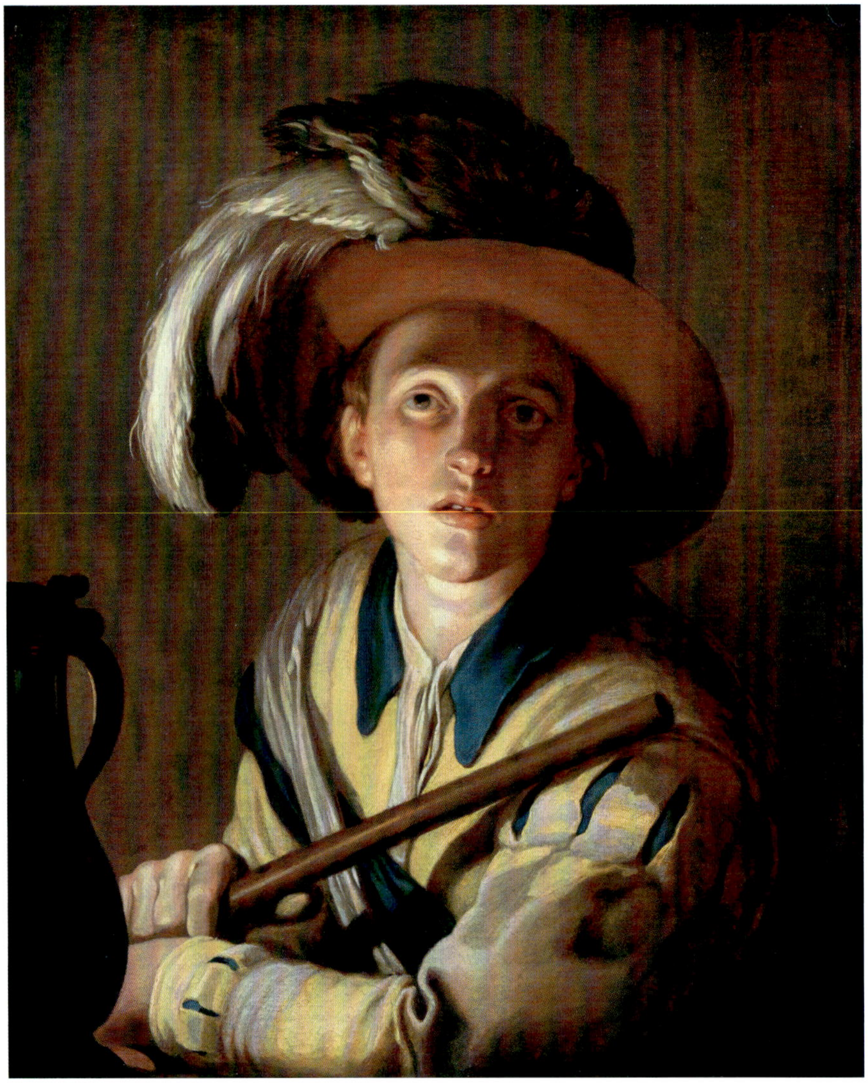

Fig. 75 Abraham Bloemaert, *Flute Player*, 1621, Centraal Museum, Utrecht

companion does not need an instrument to make music, which is why the human voice was ranked above the lute in the hierarchy. Unlike the youth playing the lute he is singing from sheet music. Baburen's *Boy with a Jew's Harp* may also have had a pendant, for in 1915 a copy was auctioned together with a *Flute Player* that is no longer known. Its pair may have been comparable to the flute player from Baburen's workshop that is now in the Gemäldegalerie in Berlin (fig. 77).[12]

Bartolomeo Manfredi's young woman with the timbrel (cat. 35) cannot be compared to the Utrecht musicians. Also known as *La Zingara* (*The Gypsy Girl*), she is holding the wooden frame with the bells in her right hand. She is looking around as if interrupting her music to look at something or someone. Manfredi had the same type of girl accompany David after his defeat of Goliath (cat. 62; detail p. 177).[13] This painting of a single figure making music is unique in his oeuvre. LMH

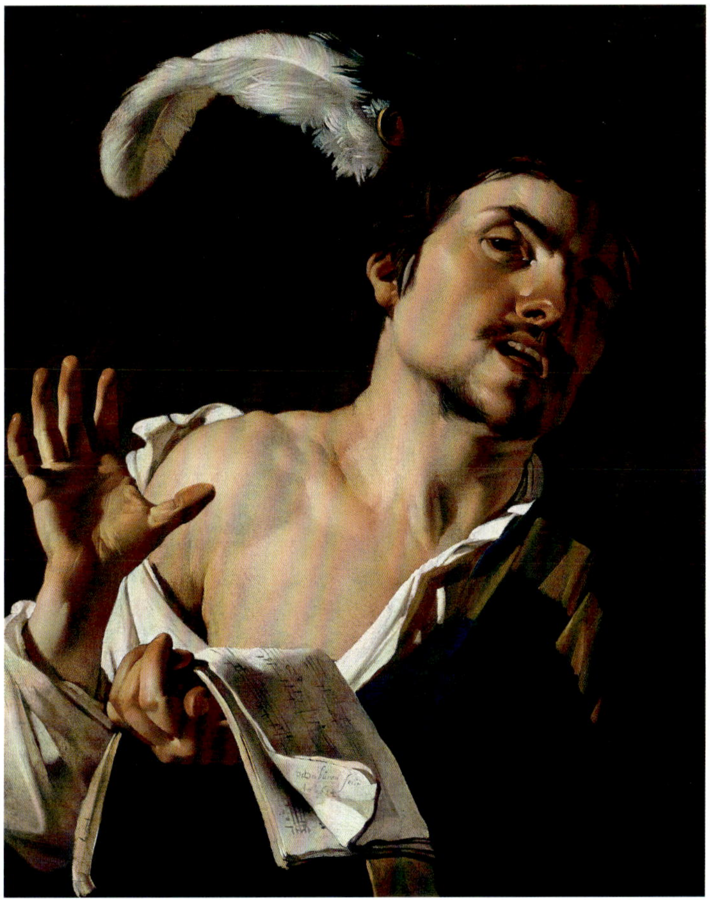

Fig. 76 Dirck van Baburen, *Young Man Singing*, 1622, Städel Museum, Frankfurt

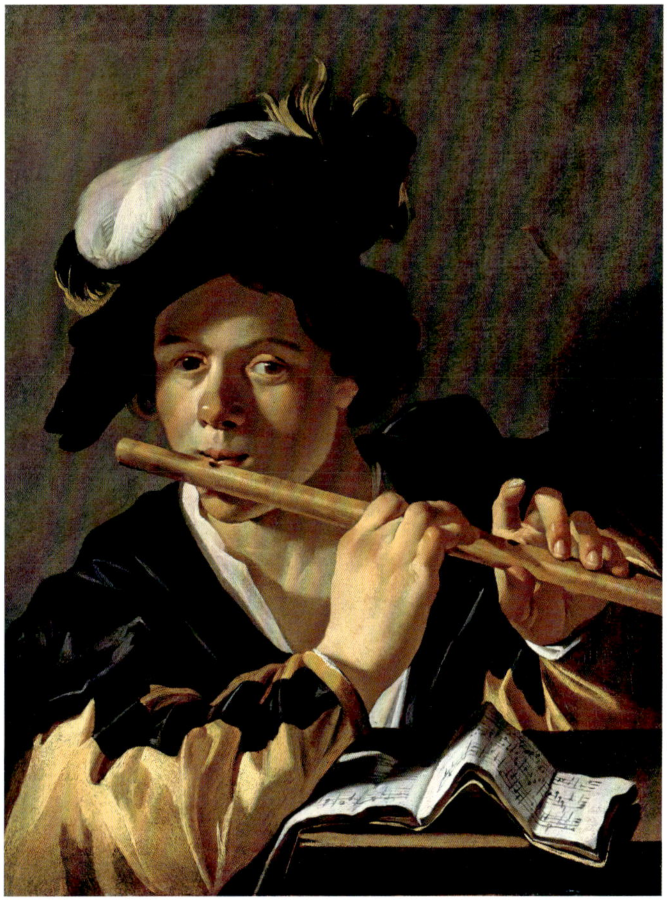

Fig 77 Dirck van Baburen (workshop), *Flute Player*, c. 1621/22, Staatliche Museen zu Berlin, Gemäldegalerie, Berlin, property of the Kaiser Friedrich Museumsverein

1 Franits 2013a, pp. 33–34.
2 Judson/Ekkart 1999, p. xxxiii and Slatkes/Franits 2007, p. 6. See also Bok 1988, p. 135, and the essay by Bok in the present publication, p. 30.
3 According to Leonard Slatkes and Wayne Franits the quality of the painting is uneven, which leads them to believe that it is a joint product of Baburen and his workshop. They cite the nose, the way in which the face was painted, and the anatomical construction of the head on the torso. See Franits 2013a, pp. 169–170, cat. BW1. Conservation in 2007 did not reveal any difference in the painting technique.
4 Ypey 1976, pp. 210–211.
5 For the subject of the flute player in Utrecht it is interesting to learn that before March 1623 there was an early 16th-century picture in the city of 'a painted head, namely a piper' ('eene geschilderde troignie, wesende eenen pijper'), which was first attributed to Correggio (c. 1494–1534), and then to Giorgione (c. 1478–1510). See Bok 1988.
6 Girolamo Savoldo, *Flute Player*, 1519, canvas, 74 × 100 cm, Pinacoteca Tosio Martinengo, Brescia.
7 Caravaggio, *Lute Player*, 1594/95, canvas, 94 × 119 cm, State Hermitage Museum, Saint Petersburg, inv. 45.
8 L.J. Slatkes in Exh. cat. Utrecht/Braunschweig 1986/87, pp. 101–102, cats. 10 and 11; Slatkes/Franits 2007, pp. 174–178, cats. A62 and A63. See also Exh. cat. Frankfurt 2009, pp. 130–131, cats. 14 and 15. For doubts about the paintings being pendants see Moiso-Diekamp 1987, pp. 169–170.
9 *Flute Player*, 1621, canvas, 69 × 57.9 cm, Centraal Museum, Utrecht, inv. 6083b.
10 *Young Man Singing*, 1622, canvas, 71 × 58.8 cm, Städel Museum, Frankfurt, inv. 2242. In 1955 the Centraal Museum bought the *Lute Player* together with its presumed companion piece, Hendrick ter Brugghen's *Merry Drinker* (cat. 30). They both came from the same 18th-century collection and had identical frames. The stretchers have labels with the numbers 4 (ter Brugghen) and 5 (Baburen). Their subjects, though, have nothing in common. The paintings are dated differently and they are not the same size. See Slatkes in Exh. cat. Utrecht/Braunschweig 1986/87, p. 186, cat. 36, and Franits 2013a, p. 137, cat. A25.
11 Exh. cat. Frankfurt 2009, pp. 140–141, cats. 19 and 20, and Franits 2013a, p. 134, cat. A24.
12 *Flute Player*, c. 1621/22, canvas, 71 × 55.4 cm, Staatliche Museen zu Berlin, Gemäldegalerie, Berlin, property of the Kaiser Friedrich Museumsverein, Kat. Nr. KFMV.291. Wayne Franits in Exh. cat. Frankfurt 2009, pp. 39–40, as attributed to Baburen; Franits 2013a, p. 178, cat. W5, as workshop.
13 See also Hartje 2004, pp. 322–323, cat. A15.

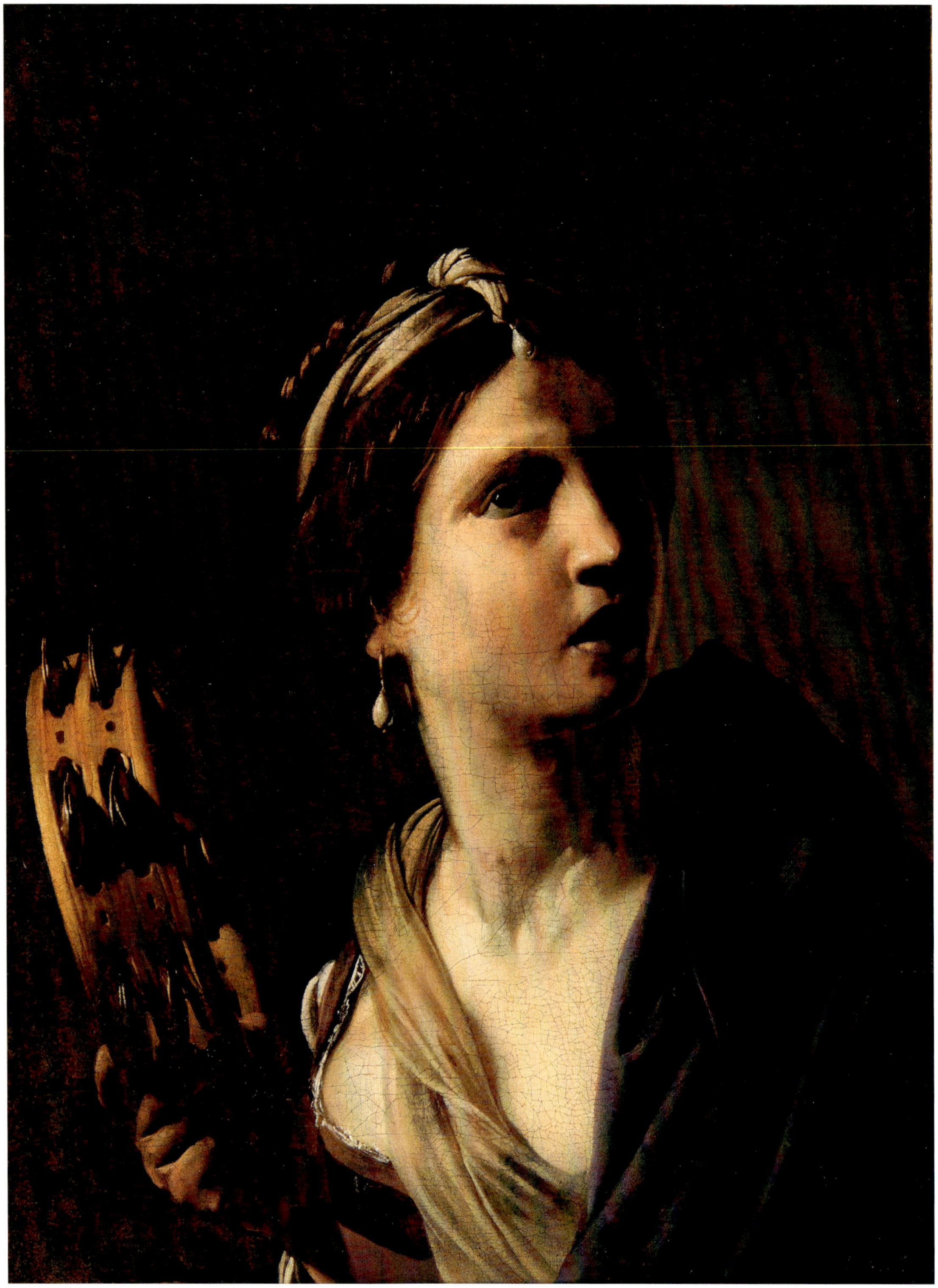

35
Bartolomeo Manfredi
La Zingara (*The Gypsy Girl*), c. 1613/15
Private collection, Courtesy Nicolas Joly Art Conseil

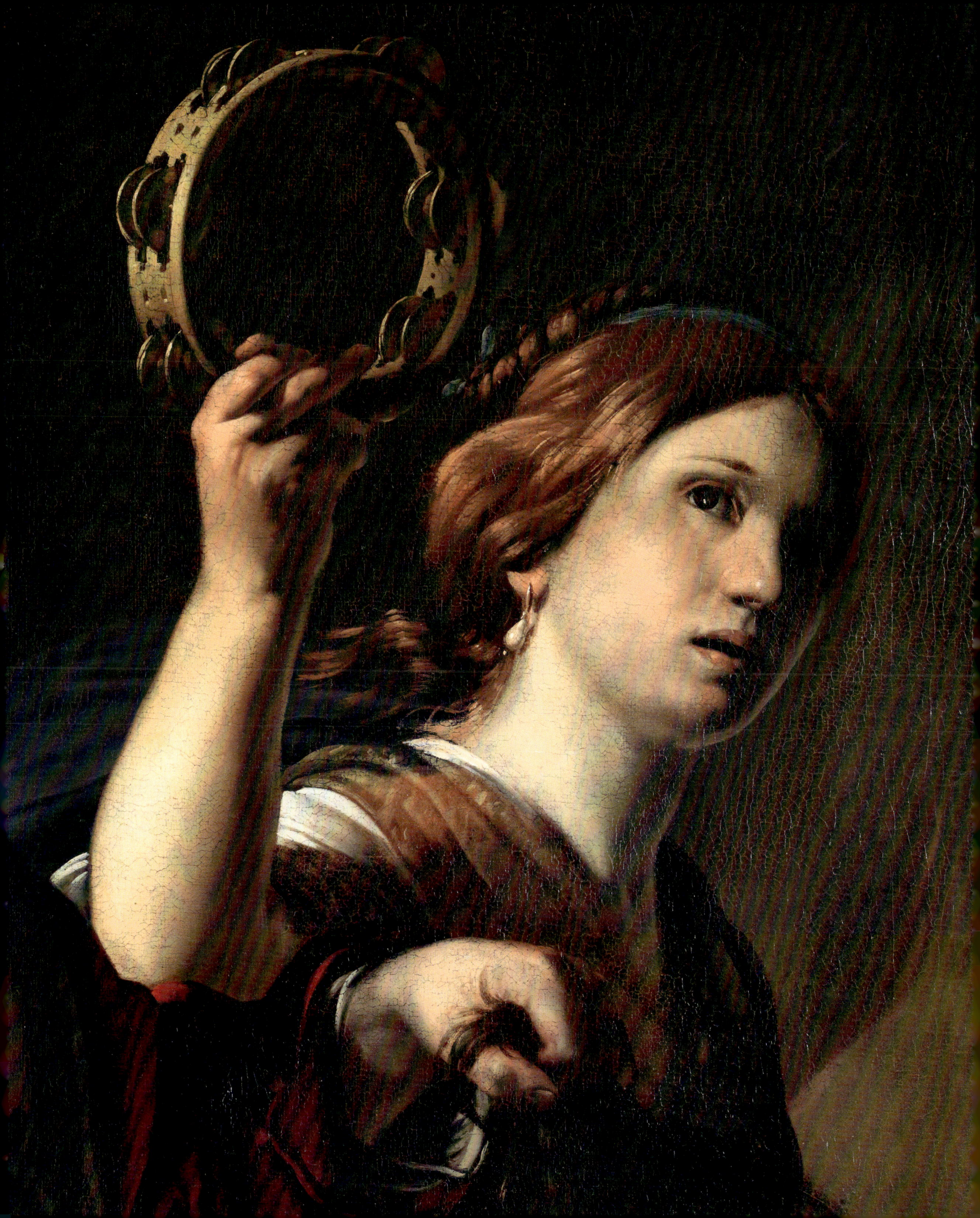

1621

The Calling of St Matthew

36
Hendrick ter Brugghen
The Calling of St Matthew, 1621
Signed and dated at the bottom centre
on the edge of table: HTBrugghen fecit. 1621
[HTB ligatured]
Canvas, 102 × 137 cm
Centraal Museum, Utrecht, acquired in 1925 with the support of the Rembrandt Association, inv. 5088

The biblical account of Matthew being called as an apostle is concise: 'As Jesus went on from there, he saw a man named Matthew sitting at the tax collector's booth. "Follow me", he told him, and Matthew got up and followed him' (Matt 9:9). The Evangelists Mark (2:14) and Luke (5:27) also relate the encounter between Christ and the publican, though they refer to him as Levi.

Ter Brugghen painted at least two versions of the subject, with the one in Utrecht (cat. 36), which is dated 1621, being the later one compared to the one in Le Havre (fig. 79), which the artist did not date.[1] Both versions draw on Caravaggio's lateral painting of the same subject, which he created between 1599 and 1600 for the Contarelli Chapel in San Luigi dei Francesi, the church of the French community in Rome (fig. 78). As early as 1565, the French Cardinal Mathieu Cointrel (Matteo Contarelli, 1519–1585) had commissioned the decoration of his burial chapel, yet its completion under the supervision of various administrators of the cardinal's estate dragged on for several decades.[2] The two lateral paintings with the Calling and the Martyrdom of the Apostle Matthew, for whom Cointrel was named, as well as the altarpiece depicting St Matthew and the Angel, were Caravaggio's first major commission for religious scenes in a space accessible to the general public. They undoubtedly held great appeal for his admirers and followers.

Ter Brugghen's first version of the subject in Le Havre, a work generally dated to the years just before 1620, demonstrates even more clearly than the Utrecht painting how thoroughly he studied Caravaggio's painting. In both cases, he inverted the composition of the original, causing Christ to approach the group including Matthew from the left. Unlike the earlier version in Le Havre, which is closer to Caravaggio's painting, the Utrecht version shows life-size, half-length figures instead of full-length figures. As a result of this and the omission of the rear-view figure of the turning young man wearing a feathered beret – who in the Le Havre version is illustrative of its closeness to Caravaggio's painting – the figures in the Utrecht version are moved closer together and closer to the picture plane, underscoring the decisive moment of the pivotal encounter.[3] The expressive play of the figures' hands, in particular, is central to the painting's theme and composition. In contrast to Caravaggio's depiction, it is clear whom

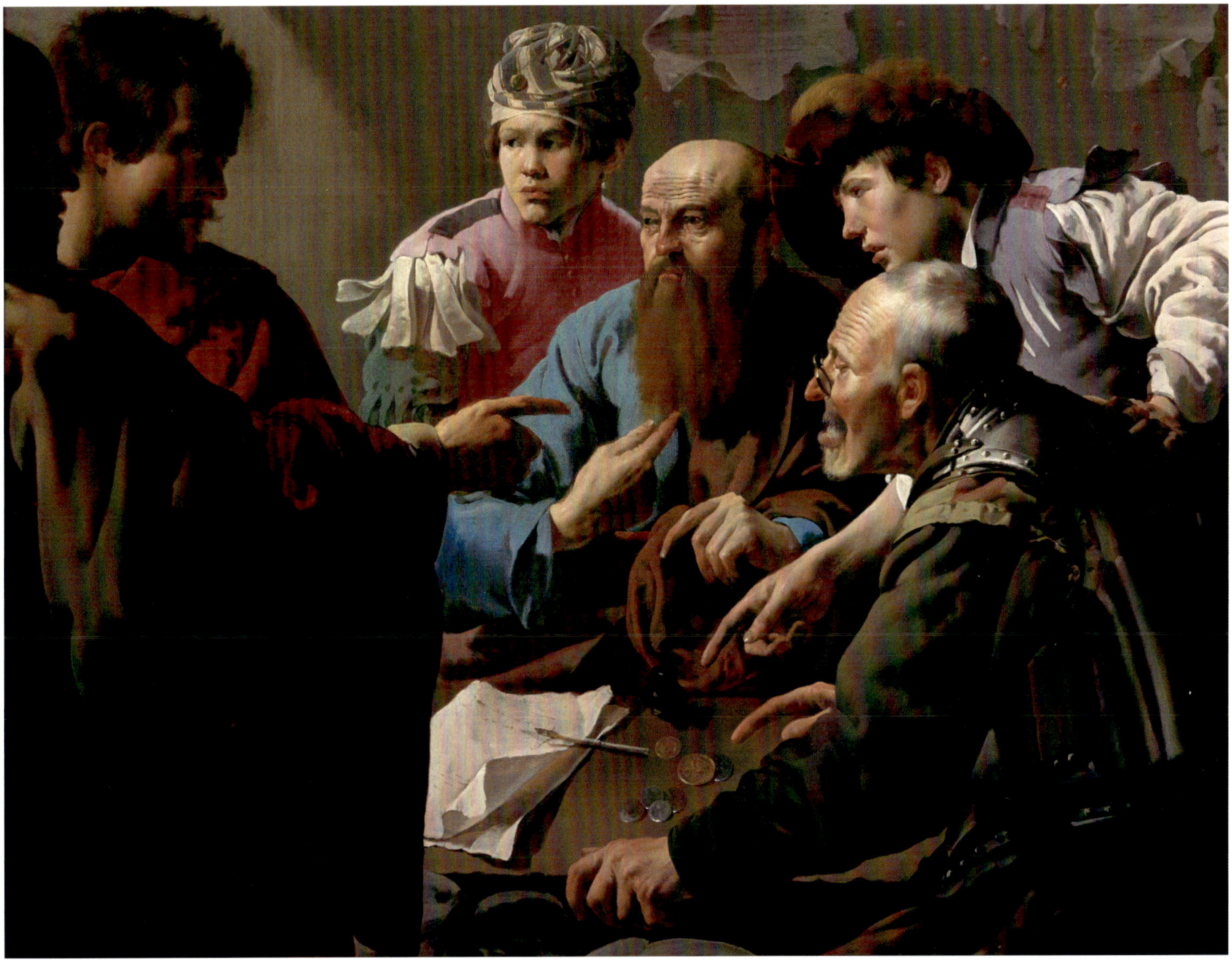

36
Hendrick ter Brugghen
The Calling of St Matthew, 1621
Centraal Museum, Utrecht

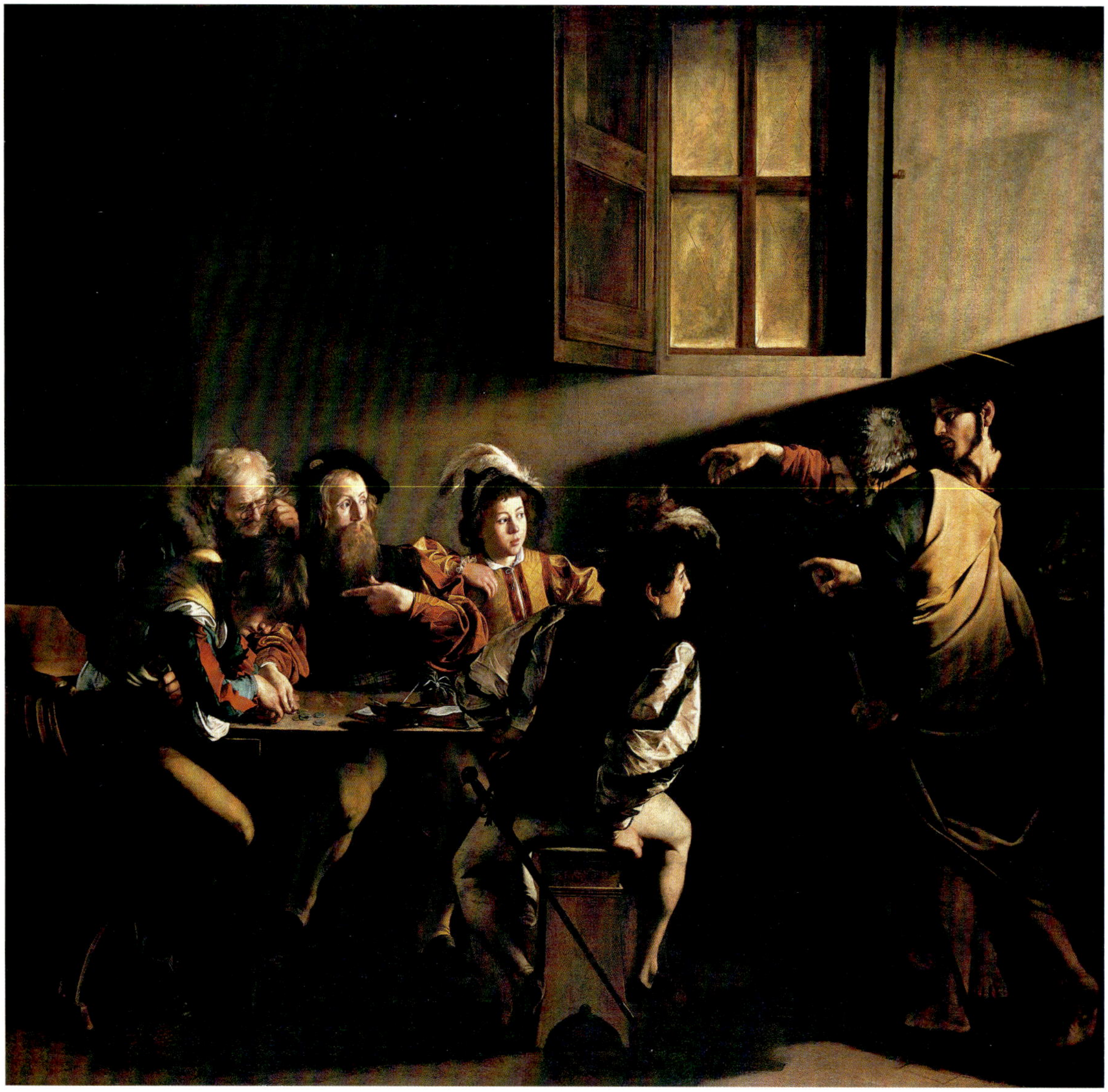

Fig. 78 Michelangelo Merisi, called Caravaggio, *The Calling of St Matthew*, 1599/1600. San Luigi dei Francesi, Contarelli Chapel, Rome

Christ calls to follow him. He addresses Matthew directly, while the latter questioningly points at himself and furrows his brow in disbelief.

Unlike Caravaggio's painting and ter Brugghen's version in Le Havre, the Utrecht version has Matthew wearing a tunic and pallium, garments typically worn by Christ and his Apostles in the iconographic tradition. Ter Brugghen thus seems to anticipate the outcome of the story: Matthew will follow Christ as his Apostle. The faces and reactions of his companions gathered around the table reflect distrust, incomprehension and ignorance. The old armour-clad man seated at the right-hand end of the table, for instance, has not yet noticed the presence of Christ and his escort. Instead he points with his right hand at the coins lying on the table in front of him, looking down at them through a pince-nez. He only pays attention to material values, and the glasses he wears – here literally and

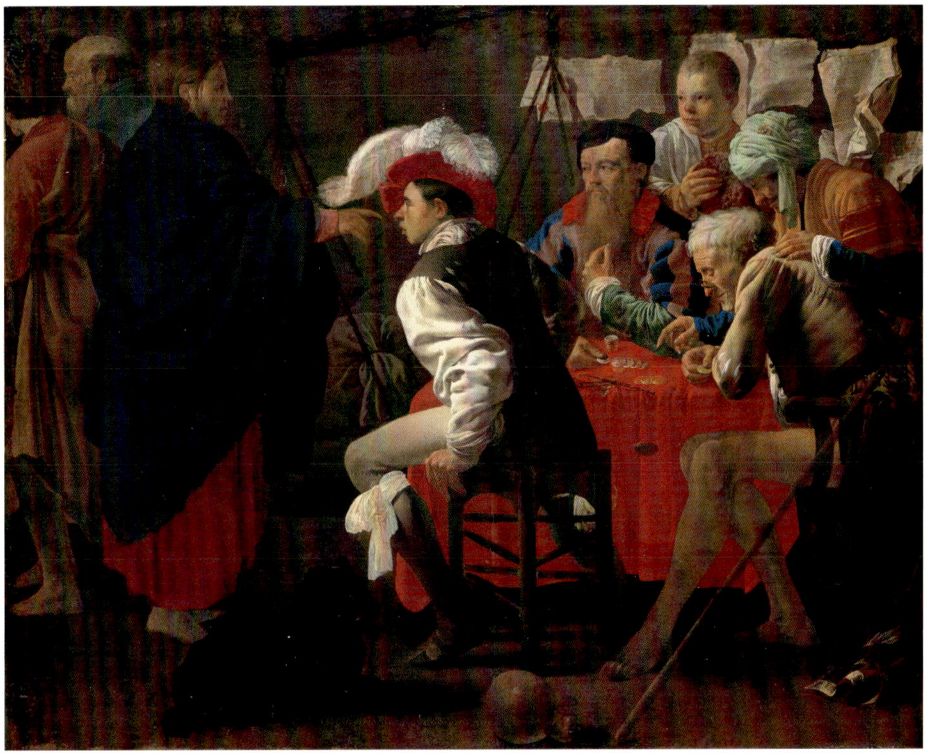

Fig. 79 Hendrick ter Brugghen, *The Calling of St Matthew*, c. 1618/19. Musée d'art moderne André Malraux, Le Havre

figuratively an allusion to the man's short-sightedness – do not save him from 'spiritual' blindness to the salvific momentousness of what is happening. He is one of a number of types of figures which ter Brugghen also repeatedly employed in different iconographic contexts. The grey-haired old man (without pince-nez), for instance, also appears in ter Brugghen's 1620 *Christ Crowned with Thorns* in Copenhagen,[4] where he is kneeling in the foreground and handing Christ the sceptre, and as a bystander (with pince-nez) in a depiction of the Doubting Thomas of c. 1622 (cat. 47).

The subject of the Calling of St Matthew was frequently depicted in 16th-century Dutch art and often associated with avarice *(avaritia)* as one of the cardinal sins.[5] The importance of northern impulses for ter Brugghen has rightly been repeatedly pointed out. In this case, the half-length and three-quarter-length figure compositions of Lucas van Leyden (1494–1533), Marinus van Reymerswaele (1490/95–c. 1567), and Jan Sanders van Hemessen (c. 1500–after 1556) are likely to have had a inspiring effect.[6]

In the Utrecht painting, ter Brugghen proves himself to be a subtle colourist. On the whole, the colouration of this work is brighter and characterised less by extreme chiaroscuro contrasts than Caravaggio's painting. Its spectrum of colours ranges from vibrant reds, browns, and greys to light green, light blue and magenta pastel shades. VM

1 For the painting in Utrecht, see Guido Jansen in Exh. cat. Utrecht/Braunschweig 1986/87, pp. 90–92, cat. 5; Cat. Utrecht 1999, vol. 2, pp. 753–756, cat. 122, and vol. 1, pp. 140–143; Slatkes/Franits 2007, pp. 123–126, cat. A34. The earlier version of the subject is in Le Havre: c. 1618/19, canvas, 152 × 195 cm, Musée d'art moderne André Malraux, inv. 77-7; see Slatkes/Franits 2007, pp. 122–123, cat. A33 (includes an extensive bibliography).

2 For the history of this commission, see Sickel 2003, pp. 89–131; and Ebert-Schifferer 2009, pp. 119–132.

3 Rüdiger Klessmann (1988, p. 59) has described the crowding of the figures and the near-complete disappearance of the background in ter Brugghen's 1621 *Calling of St Matthew* as 'horror vacui' and 'not typical of Caravaggio's art'.

4 1620, canvas, 207 × 240 cm, Statens Museum for Kunst, Copenhagen, inv. Sp365; see Slatkes/Franits 2007, pp. 98–99, cat. A13.

5 Vlam 1977.

6 See, among others, Nicolson 1958, p. 100; Vlam 1977.

1621

Christ Driving the Money Changers from the Temple

37
Dirck van Baburen
Christ Driving the Money Changers from the Temple, 1621
Signed and dated bottom left on the edge of the table: TBaburen fecit 1621 [TB ligatured]
Canvas, 158 × 206 cm
The Schorr Collection

38
Valentin de Boulogne
Christ Driving the Merchants from the Temple, c. 1618/22
Canvas, 195 × 260 cm
Gallerie Nazionali di Arte Antica di Roma, Palazzo Barberini, Rome, inv. 1261

39
Francesco Boneri, called Cecco del Caravaggio
Christ Driving the Merchants from the Temple, 1610/15
Canvas, 128 × 173 cm
Staatliche Museen zu Berlin, Gemäldegalerie, Berlin, Kat. Nr. I.447

40
Theodoor Rombouts
Christ Driving the Money Changers from the Temple, 1628/37
Canvas, 74 × 108.5 cm
Centraal Museum, Utrecht, acquired with support of BankGiro Loterij 2017, inv. 34013

Christ was furious when, immediately upon his arrival in Jerusalem, he rushed to the temple which the merchants and money changers were using as a market for their business dealings. The Gospel of John describes most vividly how Christ, armed with a whip made of cords, chased away the merchants and money changers: 'In the temple courts he found people selling cattle, sheep and doves, and others sitting at tables exchanging money. So he made a whip out of cords, and drove all from the temple courts, both sheep and cattle; he scattered the coins of the money changers and overturned their tables. To those who sold doves he said, "Get these out of here! Stop turning my Father's house into a market!"' (John 2:14–16).[1] This subject was likely particularly appealing to the artists, because it offered the opportunity to present various emotions and movement sequences.

Before turning more and more to secular subjects after his return from Rome in 1620 – probably in response to the Dutch art market – Dirck van Baburen painted mostly religious subjects upon his arrival in Utrecht. Among the first works of his Utrecht period is *Christ Driving the Money Changers from the Temple* of 1621 (cat. 37).[2] A massive fluted column in the background serves to indicate the temple architecture. In front of it, the figures are arranged in a narrow space close to the picture plane. Christ wields the whip in the air and drives a merchant in front of him who flees with a sheep wedged under his arm. He has raised his left arm to warn the money changers who are sitting at a table in the right half of the painting. Baburen captures the moment of surprise by depicting the bewilderment and incipient flurry. While the man with the money scales looks up aghast and places his hand over a heap of money to shield it, the man in the fur cap rakes the coins from the table, which in the rush fall next to his hand to the ground. At the right-hand edge, a man jumps up, startled, and instinctively reaches for his sword. Baburen placed a similar figure, reversed and with a composed demeanour, in the left foreground of his *Christ Crowned with Thorns* (cat. 41), which is dated to roughly the same time. Like the table with the dead doves on the left, it serves as a *repoussoir*, creating spatial depth and at the same time opening up the pictorial space to the viewer. The artist likely drew on Caravaggio's *Supper at Emmaus* from the Mattei collection (today in London; fig. 69) for this figure.

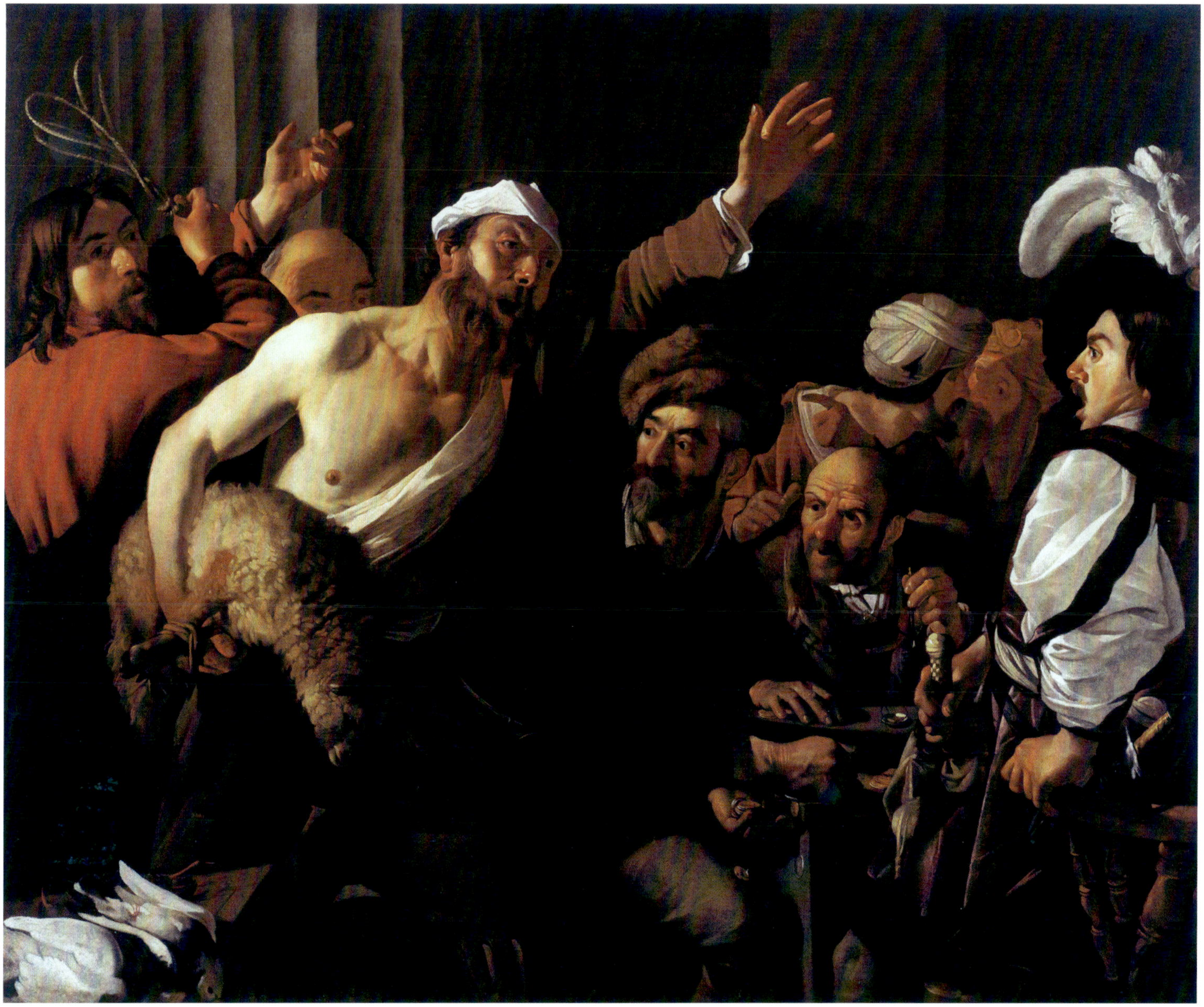

37
Dirck van Baburen
Christ Driving the Money Changers from the Temple, 1621
The Schorr Collection

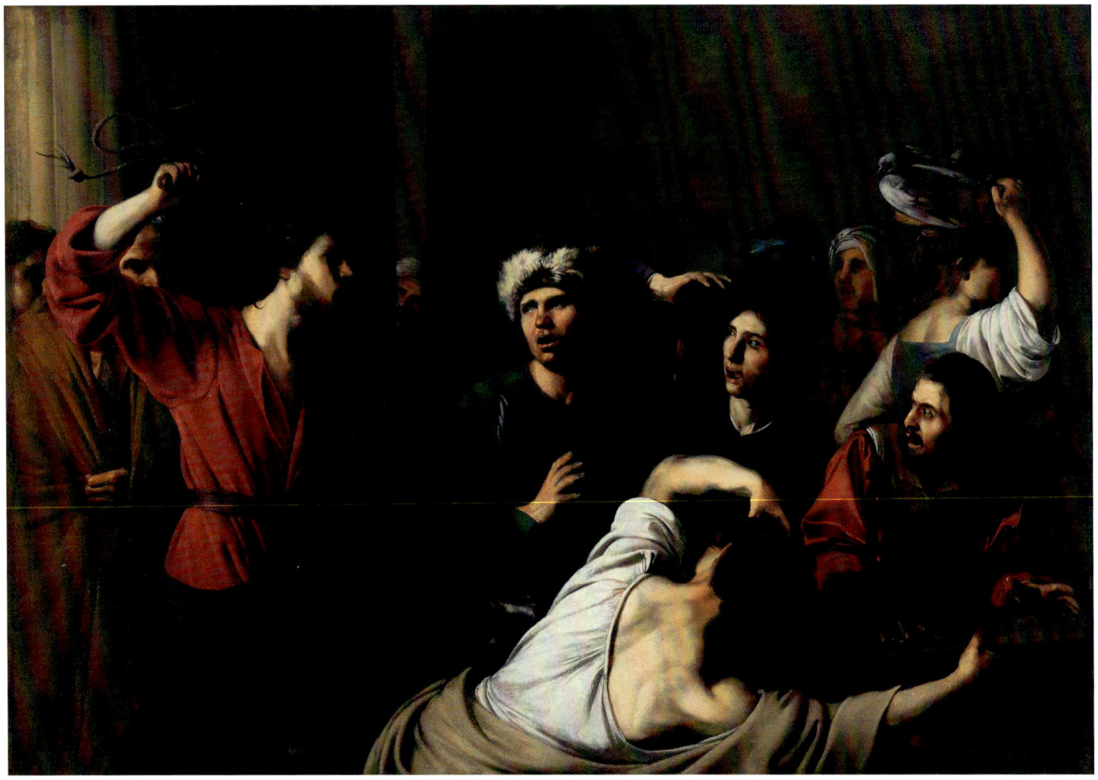

Fig. 80 Bartolomeo Manfredi, *Christ Driving the Money Changers from the Temple*, c. 1616/17, Musée des Beaux-Arts et Archéologie, Libourne

Baburen may also have been familiar with Bartolomeo Manfredi's painting *Christ Driving the Money Changers from the Temple* (fig. 80)[3] which, together with Ribera's *Denial of St Peter* (cat. 10), used to hang in the Verospi collection. As Bellori relates: 'In the house of the signori Verospi in Rome, the picture of Christ chasing the merchants from the temple can be seen, in which some very lifelike heads are portrayed, including a man who is so afraid of losing his coins that he holds his hand over them'.[4] Even this last detail mentioned by Bellori is realised by the Utrecht painter, as well as the fluted column on the far left.

Around 1618, Baburen had already explored Manfredi's compositional scheme featuring a group of men around a table on the right in a first version of the Cleansing of the Temple.[5] Accordingly, the painting is divided into two groups of figures: on the left, Christ and a fleeing merchant, and on the right, the group of money changers sitting at a table. In his second version of 1621, Baburen sticks to this basic compositional scheme.

Valentin de Boulogne may also have been familiar with Manfredi's painting in the Verospi collection. In his painting dated c. 1618/22 in Rome, he likewise depicts a female trader on the far right, who carries a basket with doves on her head (cat. 38).[6] Valentin enhances the dynamics and the fury of Christ, which cause chaos in the foreground of the picture. His right arm raised for a blow, Christ overthrows a table with his left. Two men have been knocked from their stools and fall backwards into the right and left foreground. The man in the middle who still manages to keep himself on his feet shields his head with his arms. On the right, he is joined by a group of fleeing merchants who turn around, mouths open in fear.

The figure of a fleeing boy who shouts in fear had been depicted by Caravaggio in the *Martyrdom of St Matthew* for the Contarelli chapel in San Luigi dei Francesi (fig. 17). This painting was in many ways a source of inspiration for the young artists, surely also with regard to the onlookers in the background, which can be seen in both the Baburen and Valentin paintings. It is not clear whether Valentin, like Caravaggio earlier, immortalised himself here as a spectator.[7]

The two men falling to the sides in the foreground open up the composition towards the viewer who is drawn into the action.

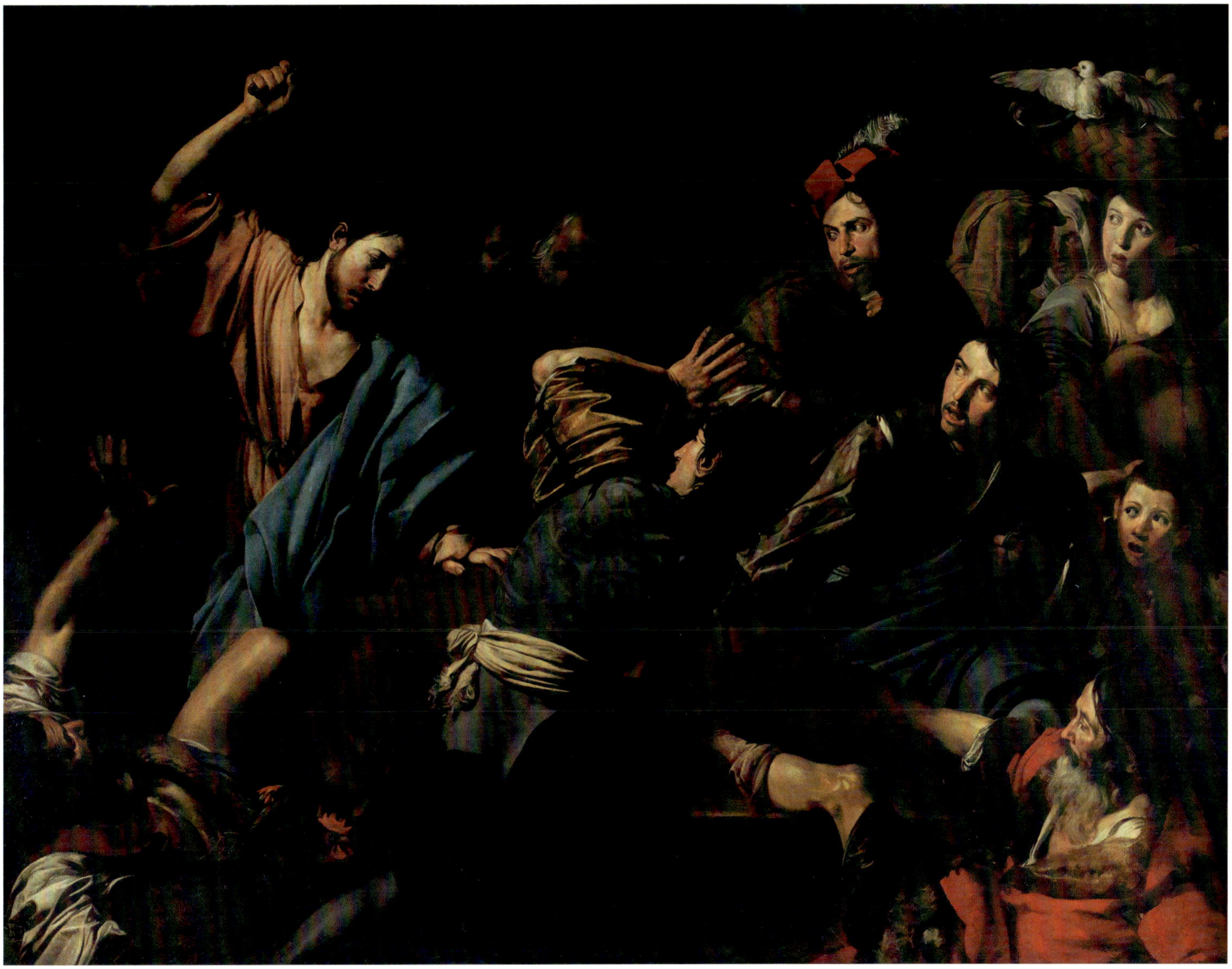

38
Valentin de Boulogne
Christ Driving the Merchants from the Temple, c. 1618/22
Gallerie Nazionali di Arte Antica di Roma, Palazzo Barberini, Rome

Francesco Boneri, also known as Cecco del Caravaggio for his connection to Caravaggio, opted for a stage-like composition in his depiction of the subject, with the interior of a temple architecture providing the setting (cat. 39).[8]

Originally, the painting was displayed at the Palazzo Giustiniani as part of the collection,[9] and based on its early date c. 1610/15, we can safely assume that Dirck van Baburen saw it there before exploring the subject himself. In terms of visual dynamic and the variety of emotions depicted, the Italian painter proves himself at least as skilful here as Valentin de Boulogne. Christ comes down the steps and sweeps his whip over the heads of the panic-stricken men. His face is distorted with rage and his eyes flash with fury. His upper body is vigorously rotated.

Total chaos and confusion prevail in the group of figures on the left. It seems as if the artist wanted to demonstrate his ability to depict various heads from all possible angles. These include the bald-headed man with a broken bowl with coins, who has fallen on the landing – a figure which may be a man from the Roman district of Ripa, who was depicted more often by the followers of Caravaggio.[10]

The dramatic action is highlighted by the light from the window at top left, which runs like a band across the image. Aside from the angry face of Christ and his hand, it hits the group where it accentuates individual parts such as faces or hands, thereby enhancing the theatricality.

Similar to Cecco del Caravaggio, Theodoor Rombouts also configures the background of his version of the subject as the architectural setting of a temple interior (cat. 40). The Antwerp-born artist was in Italy probably from 1616 until 1625. Records show he was in Rome in 1620, where he lived – like Dirck van Baburen at the time – in the parish of Sant'Andrea delle Fratte.[11]

He painted *Christ Driving the Money Changers from the Temple* only after returning to his home country. Based on the clearly visible pentimenti in the area of the arm of Christ and the woman in the background, this work is thought to be a first version or indeed a study for the painting of the same title in Antwerp[12] (fig. 81), located in Flanders in the 1660s (fig. 82).[13] This would also explain the rather drawing-like manner of painting, which in some areas is characterised by short brushstrokes, some of which are placed side-by-side like hatching. In terms of composition and colouring, however, there is little or no deviation. Unlike Cecco del Caravaggio, but similar to Valentin and Baburen, Rombouts moves the main figures close to the picture plane. The figure falling backwards in the foreground may, moreover, reference the Frenchman's painting, although the dynamics of the figures is less pronounced.

Particularly the bright, cool colours, in some cases complementary ones placed side-by-side, and the delicate fabrics of the garments, which are differentiated in terms of materiality, invoke the Flemish tradition that this work continues. SH

1 See also Matthew 21:12–13; Mark 11:15–17; Luke 19:45–46.
2 Franits 2013a, pp. 36, 110–111, cat. A16. A replica of the painting (workshop replica) is at the LWL-Museum für Kunst und Kultur in Münster: c. 1621, canvas, 156 × 195 cm, inv. 1206 LM; Franits 2013a, pp. 111–112, cat. A16W1.
3 Canvas, 162 × 244 cm, Musée des Beaux-Arts et Archéologie, Libourne, inv. D.89.1.1; Hartje 2004, pp. 304–308 (c. 1610/12); Papi 2013, pp. 171–172, cat. 33 (1616/17).
4 Bellori 1672, p. 215: 'Vedesi in casa de' Signori Verospi in Roma il quadro col Signore, che scaccia i Venditori dal Tempio, rittrattevi alcune teste naturalissime, trà quali uno, che per timore di perdere le monete vi tiene sopra la mano'.
5 *Christ Driving the Money Changers from the Temple*, c. 1618, canvas, 170 × 217 cm, private collection; Franits 2013a, pp. 95–96, cat. A5, incl. fig. p. 276.
6 Mojana 1989, pp. 68–69, cat. 8; Annick Lemoine in Exh. cat. New York/Paris 2016/17, pp. 126–128, cat. 17. Another version by Valentin de Boulogne is in the State Hermitage Museum in Saint Petersburg: *Christ Drives the Merchants from the Temple*, c. 1627/29, 192 × 266.5 cm, inv. 1214.
7 See Annick Lemoine in Exh. cat. New York/Paris 2016/17, p. 128.
8 Papi 2001, pp. 115–117, cat. 4; Gianni Papi in Exh. cat. Rome/Berlin 2001, pp. 302–303, cat. D9.
9 Danesi Squarzina 2003, vol. 1, pp. 434–435.
10 See the essay by Helen Langdon in this volume, p. 46.
11 Vodret 2011, p. 514. For Rombouts, see Papi 1998; Baldriga 2010.
12 c. 1625/37, canvas, 168 × 238.5 cm, Koninklijk Museum voor Schone Kunsten, Antwerp, inv. 801; Liesbeth Helmus in Exh. cat. Milan/Vienna 2005/06, pp. 394–395, cat. V.18.
13 Gillis van Tilborgh the Younger, *Portrait of Twelve Gentlemen in an Interior with Paintings*, 1660/69, canvas, 139 × 209.5 cm, private collection. Thanks to Liesbeth M. Helmus, who drew my attention to this picture.

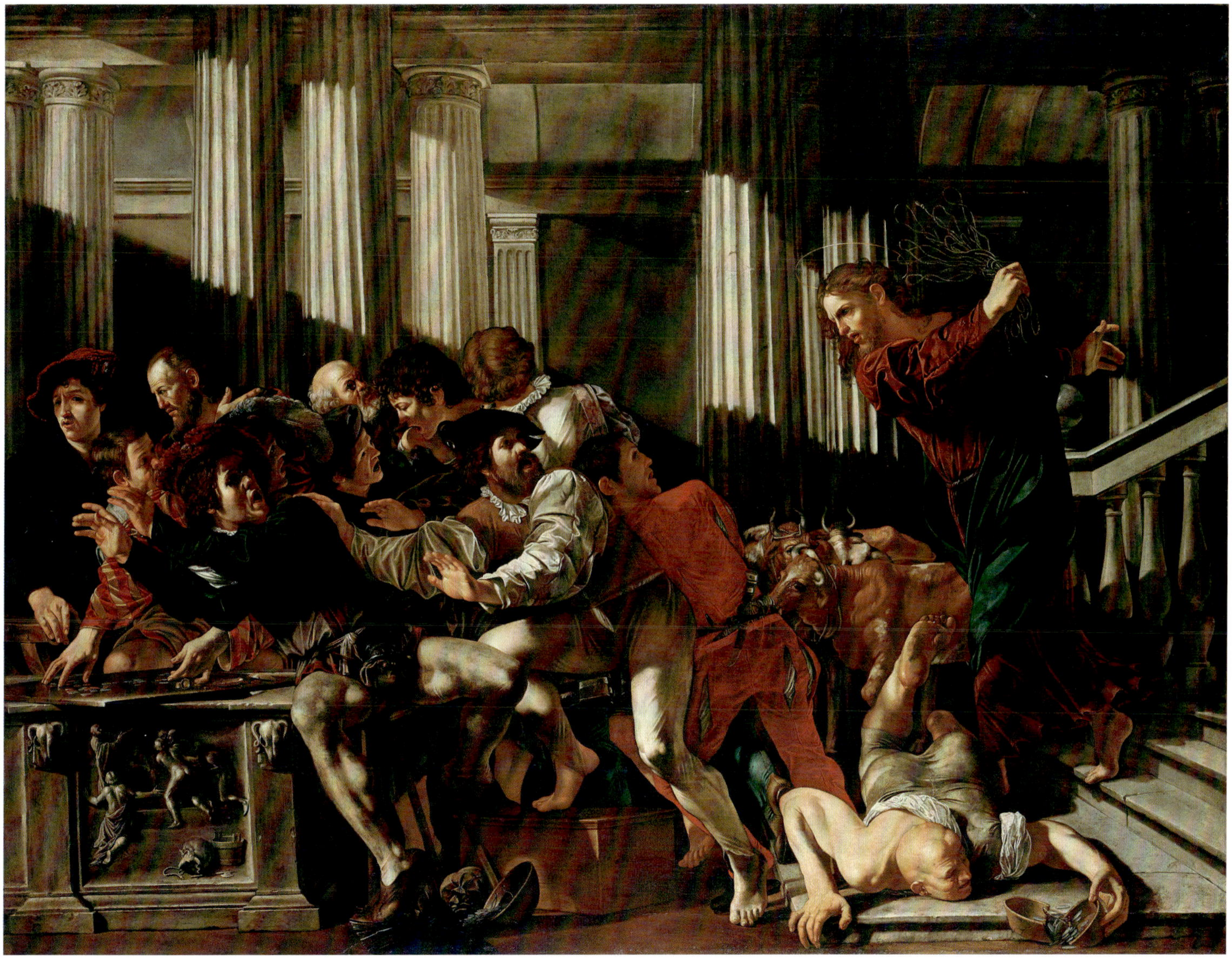

39
Francesco Boneri, called Cecco del Caravaggio
Christ Driving the Merchants from the Temple, 1610/15
Staatliche Museen zu Berlin, Gemäldegalerie, Berlin

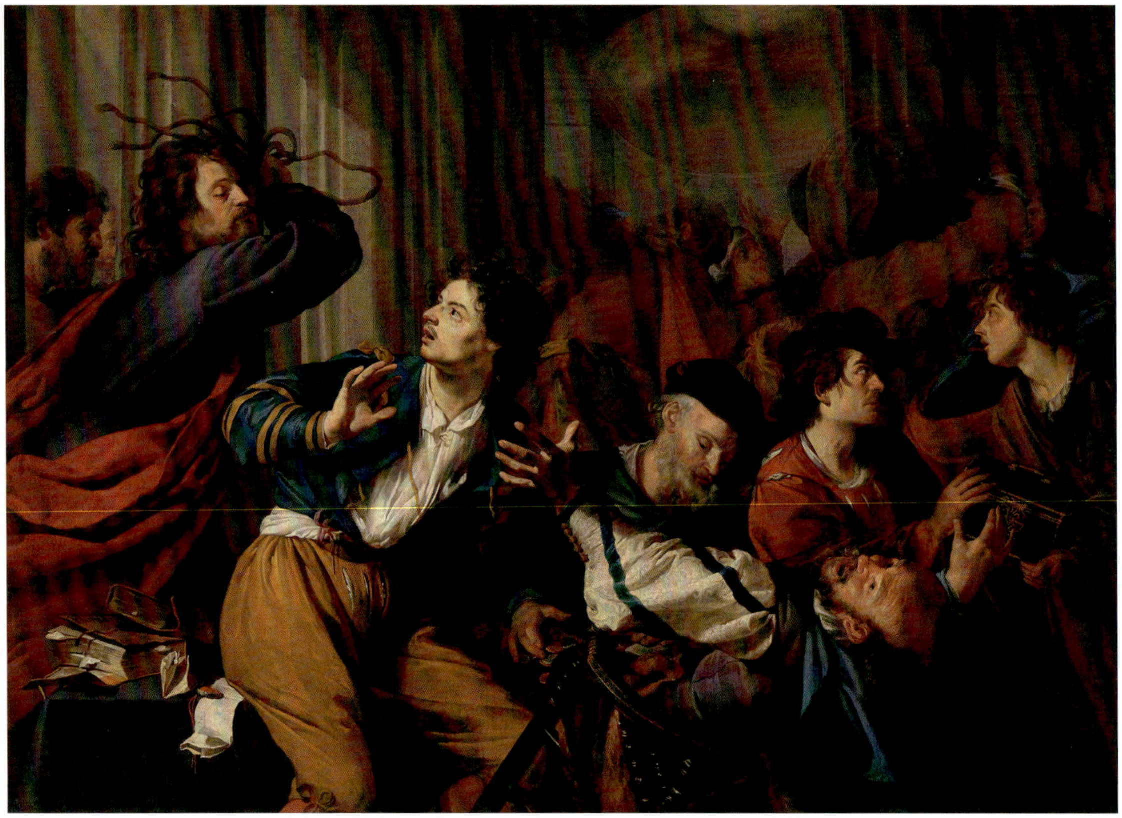

Fig. 81 Theodoor Rombouts, *Christ Driving the Money Changers from the Temple*, c. 1625/37, Koninklijk Museum voor Schone Kunsten, Antwerp

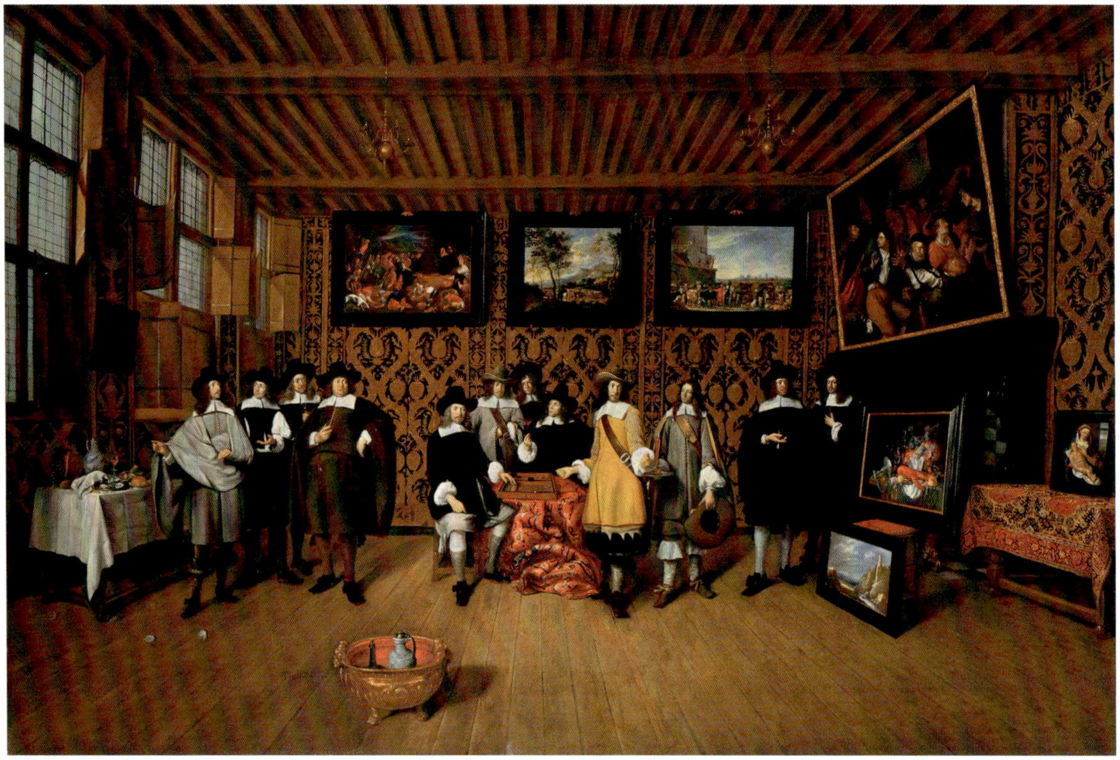

Fig. 82 Gillis van Tilborgh the Younger, *Portrait of Twelve Gentlemen in an Interior with Paintings*, 1660/69, private collection

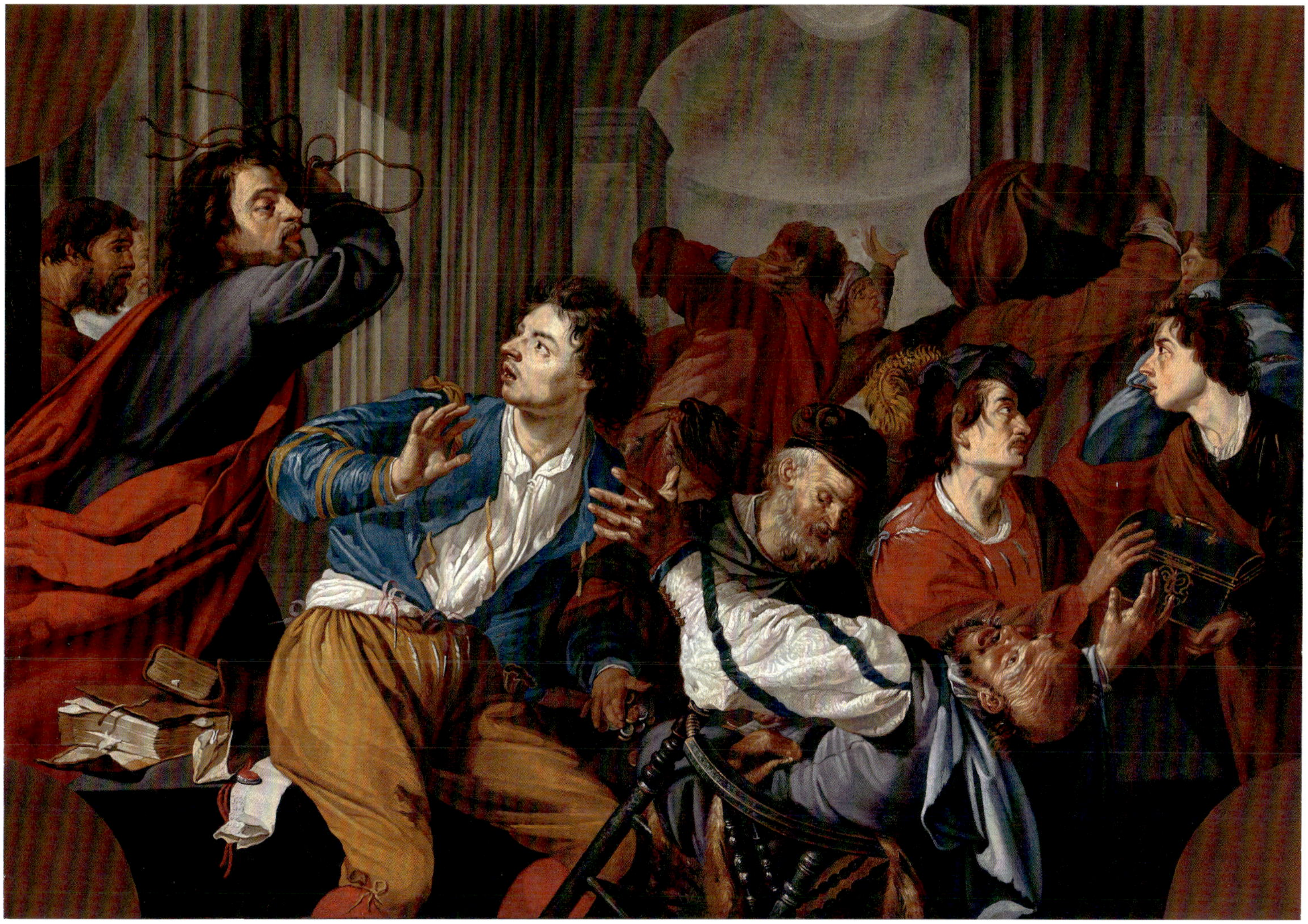

40
Theodoor Rombouts
Christ Driving the Money Changers from the Temple, 1628/37
Centraal Museum, Utrecht

c. 1621/22

The Crowning with Thorns

41
Dirck van Baburen
The Crowning with Thorns, c. 1621/22
Signed at top right: BABUREN F.
Canvas, 106 × 136 cm
Museum Catharijneconvent, Utrecht, inv. StCC s9

42
Bartolomeo Manfredi
The Crowning with Thorns, c. 1608/10
Canvas, 119 × 138.5 cm
Bayerische Staatsgemäldesammlungen, Munich,
Staatsgalerie im Neuen Schloss Schleißheim, inv. 570

43
Orazio Gentileschi
Christ Crowned with Thorns, c. 1612/15
Canvas, 119.5 × 148.5 cm
Herzog Anton Ulrich-Museum, Braunschweig,
inv. GG 805

44
Valentin de Boulogne
The Crowning with Thorns and the Mocking of Christ, c. 1627/28
Canvas, 132 × 96.3 cm
Bayerische Staatsgemäldesammlungen,
Alte Pinakothek, Munich, inv. 188

In 1621/22, shortly after his return to Utrecht, Dirck van Baburen turned twice to the subject of the Crowning with Thorns. The painting in Utrecht (cat. 41), generally identified as the second version by scholarship, is a condensation of his first version in Kansas City (fig. 83).[1] Changes were made mainly in the staffage figures on the left: in the Utrecht version, Baburen omitted the third person in the background and broke up the interaction between the two figures in front. Here, the soldier turns to Christ and the man on the far left focuses on the viewer. Both have been moved closer to the crowning scene and the image, moreover, has been cropped. This results in sharper focus on the main scene which has been moved further into the foreground. This arrangement aligns the painting even more with the Counter-Reformationist ideas of the late 16th and early 17th century in Italy, as expressed, for example, by the Bolognese archbishop Gabriele Paleotti in his *Discorso intorno alle immagini sacre e profane*, published in 1582.[2] In terms of subjects, scenes from the Passion of Christ were, in principle, suitable to elicit compassion in the viewer. As a result of Baburen's composition in the form of a semicircle open towards the front, the proximity to the action, and the gaze out of the picture, the viewer cannot avoid feeling compassion for the suffering of Christ. In this effect, Baburen's composition even surpasses Caravaggio's *The Crowning with Thorns* (fig. 84),[3] which hung in the Giustiniani Collection where Baburen and other young artists could study it. In spectacular and almost unprecedented fashion, Caravaggio had moved a few life-size figures so far into the foreground that the brutality and suffering was right before the viewer's eyes. The renown the painting enjoyed at the time is reflected in the large number of paintings of the same subject which were created from about 1608 onward by followers of Caravaggio. Characteristic of those works is the gross violence the henchmen inflict on the acquiescently lowered head of Christ with the simultaneous highlighting of the bare shoulder and neck section through subtle lighting effects.

In a total of six paintings, Bartolomeo Manfredi explored the subject particularly intensely.[4] The Munich painting (cat. 42), which is from the time around 1608/10 and thus considered an early work, is listed as 'Caravaggio' in 18th-century inventories.[5] The composition consists of just three figures. The head and torso of Christ are hunched low to the left under the force of the

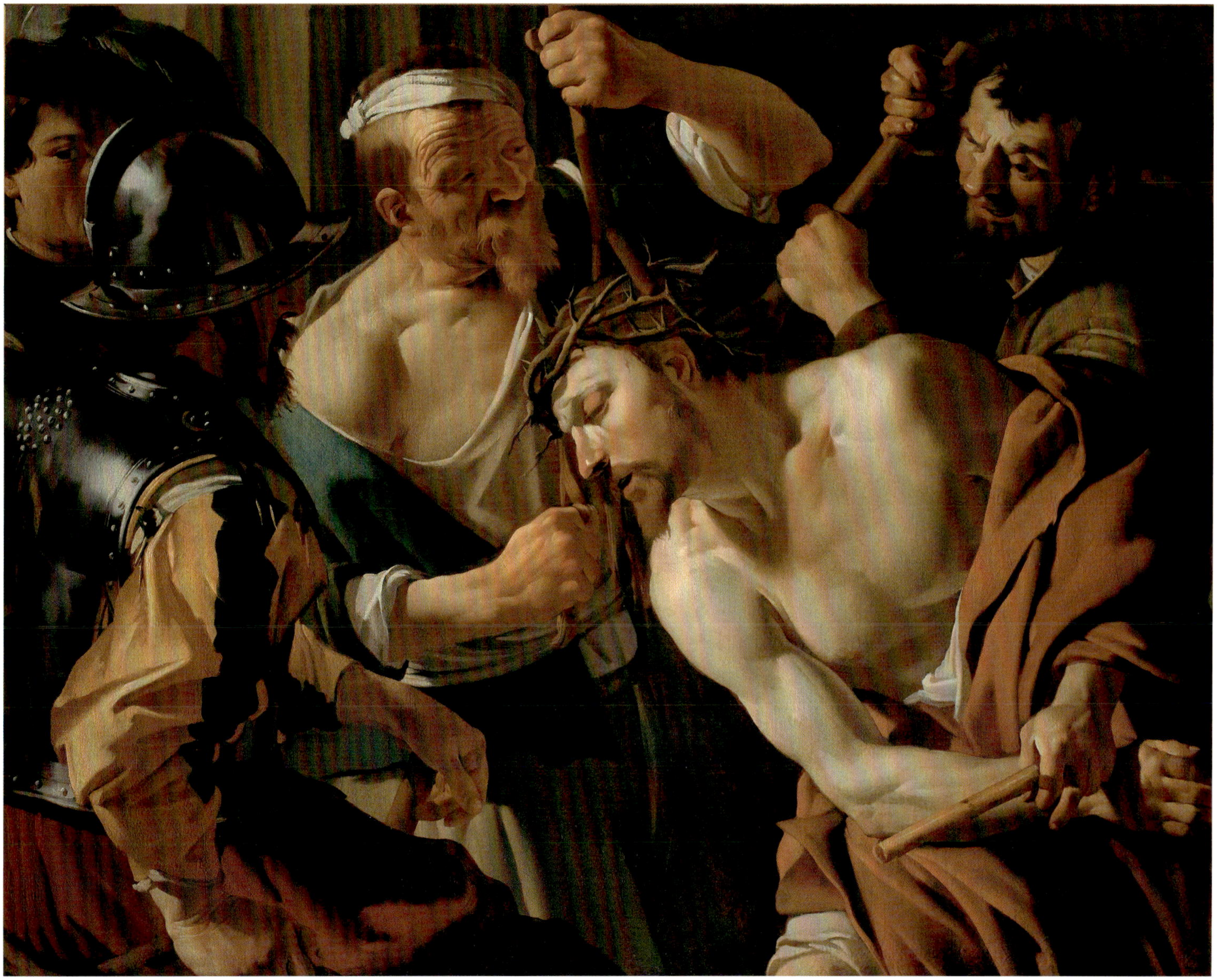

41
Dirck van Baburen
The Crowning with Thorns, c. 1621/22
Museum Catharijneconvent, Utrecht

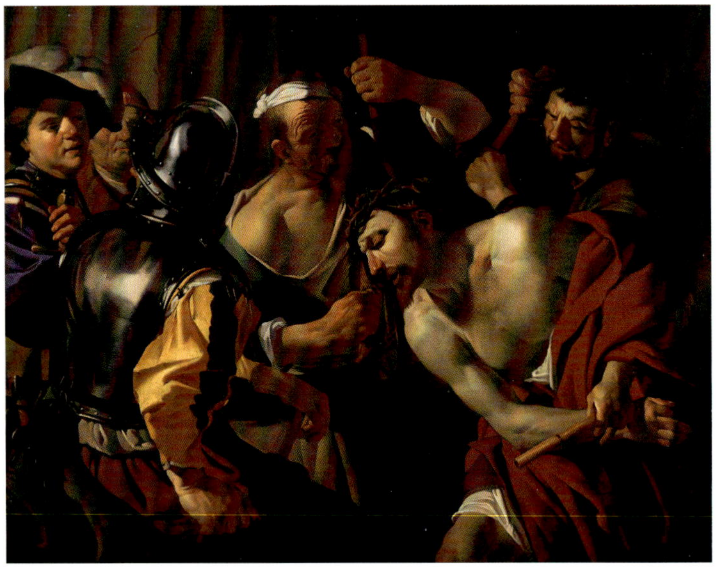

Fig. 83 Dirck van Baburen, *Christ Crowned with Thorns*, c. 1621/22, The Nelson-Atkins Museum of Art, Kansas City

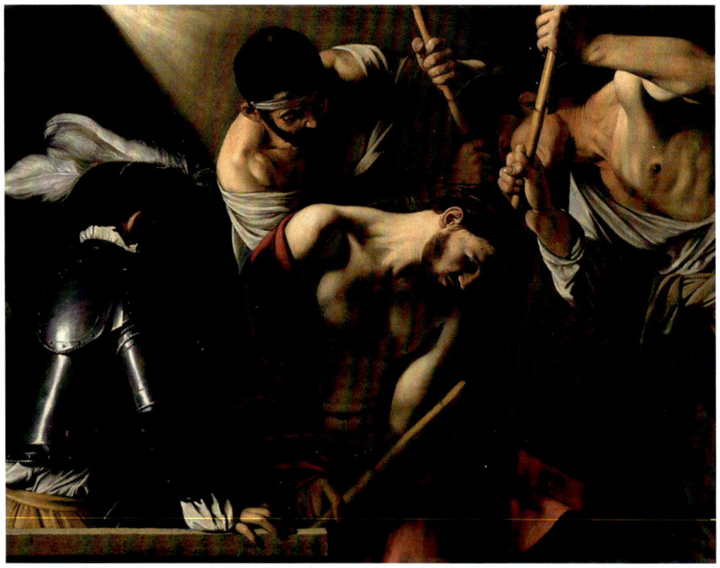

Fig. 84 Michelangelo Merisi, called Caravaggio, *The Crowning with Thorns*, 1602/03, Kunsthistorisches Museum, Gemäldegalerie, Vienna

sticks of the two henchmen. Caravaggio's elegant, beautifully curved line between the shoulder and hairline of Christ is broken up in Manfredi's painting by the accentuation of the powerful shoulder musculature, which contrasts with the humbly lowered head. The hands lie weakly on the upper leg, testament once again to the submission to his fate. Shortly afterwards, Manfredi approached the subject again: in the painting in the Uffizi he added two interacting figures on the far left (fig. 85),[6] one of which hands Christ the mock sceptre. Baburen was probably familiar with this version, as it shows compositional similarities to the painting in Kansas City (fig. 83). Not just the position of Christ indicates this, but also his posture with his hands pointing to the right. What is special is that the wrists in Baburen's Utrecht version (cat. 41) – unlike in other depictions – are not tied. In combination with Christ's strong body, this underscores once more his patience in enduring the torments.

Orazio Gentileschi's painting *Christ Crowned with Thorns* (cat. 43) very likely came from the Savelli Collection in Rome and was created around 1612/15.[7] During that period, the artist studied Caravaggio's style most intensely. The figures appear as if fitted into a display case: against a universally near-black background, they are illuminated by a bright light from the front right. The light is reflected by the bright flesh tones of the tormented Christ, which contrast with the dark complexion of the henchmen. The black backdrop not only lends the figures a raised, sculptural effect, but also makes the colours appear more vibrant. For the colour scheme, Gentileschi drew on Caravaggio's *Entombment of Christ* (cat. 22). Here, the artist chose a different moment of the Passion.[8] As 'King of the Jews', Christ is already wearing the 'royal cloak' which has been placed loosely around his hips. Now he is presented with his crown, while at the same time a cane as mock sceptre is forced into his left hand. Unique among the Caravaggesque depictions of this subject is the violent force which is used to push his head down and grab his wrist. In this regard, an etching by the Bolognese artist Annibale Carracci has been rightly cited as an additional source for Gentileschi's painting (fig. 86).[9]

A clear thematic separation between the subjects of the Crowning with Thorns and the Mocking of Christ is often difficult, as there is a tendency since the Middle Ages, especially in multi-figure depictions, to combine the two scenes.[10] Valentin de Boulogne also draws on this tradition in the Munich painting *The Crowning with Thorns and the Mocking of Christ* (cat. 44).[11] X-ray images show the overpainted portrait of a cardinal in the lower paint layer (fig. 87). The sitter is probably Cardinal Francesco Barberini for whom Valentin worked from 1627 on. Based on the portrait of the

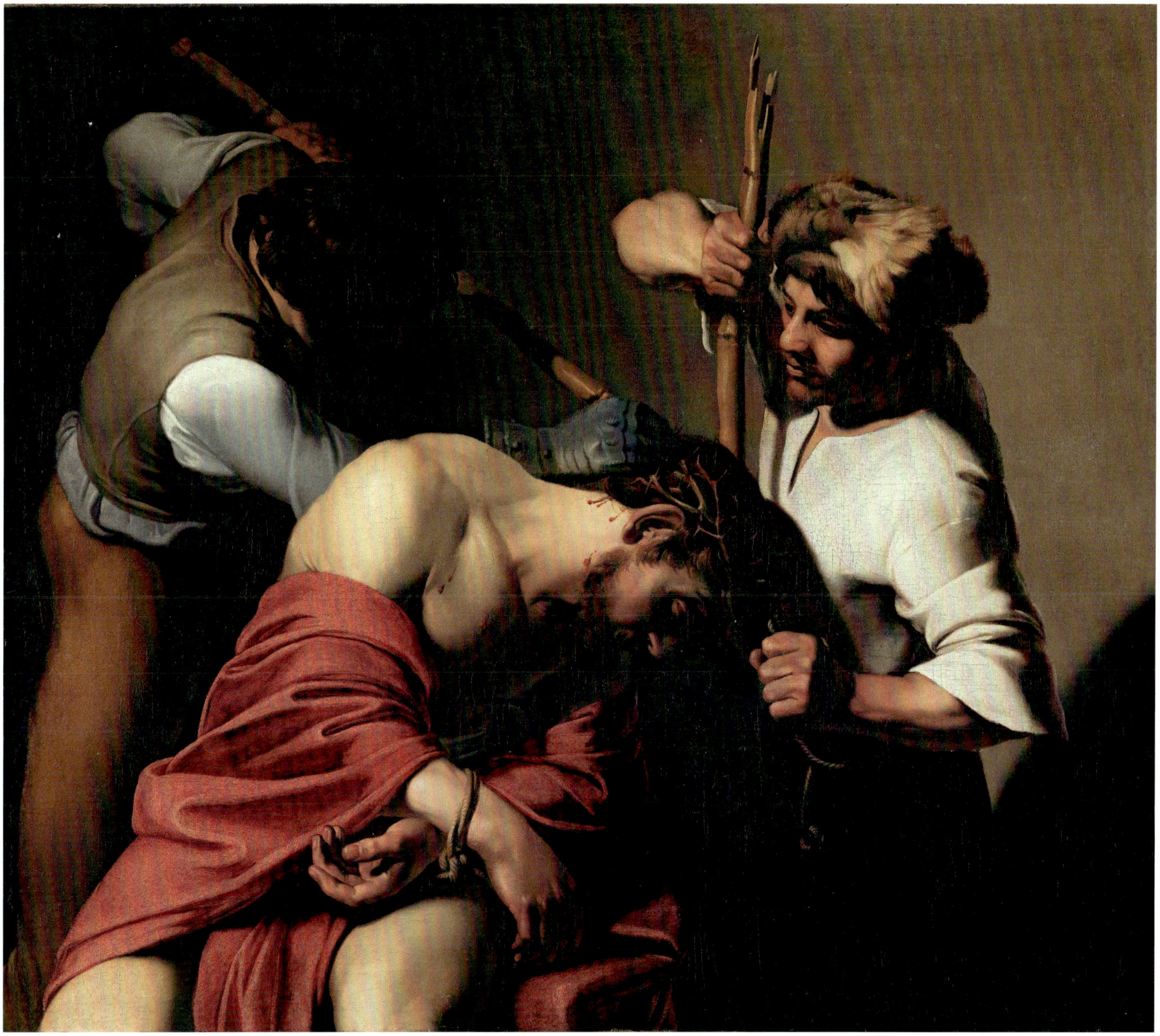

42
Bartolomeo Manfredi
The Crowning with Thorns, c. 1608/10
Bayerische Staatsgemäldesammlungen, Munich,
Staatsgalerie im Neuen Schloss Schleißheim

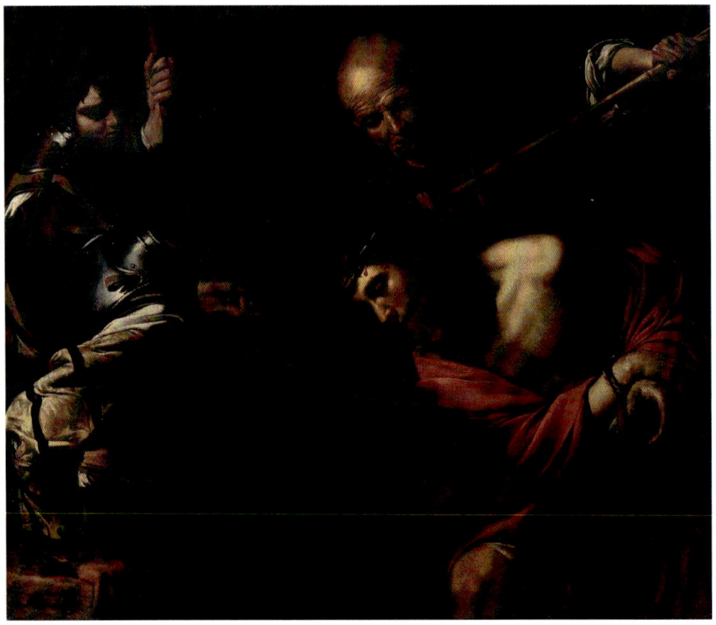

Fig. 85 Bartolomeo Manfredi, *The Mocking of Christ*, c. 1612/14, Galleria degli Uffizi, Florence

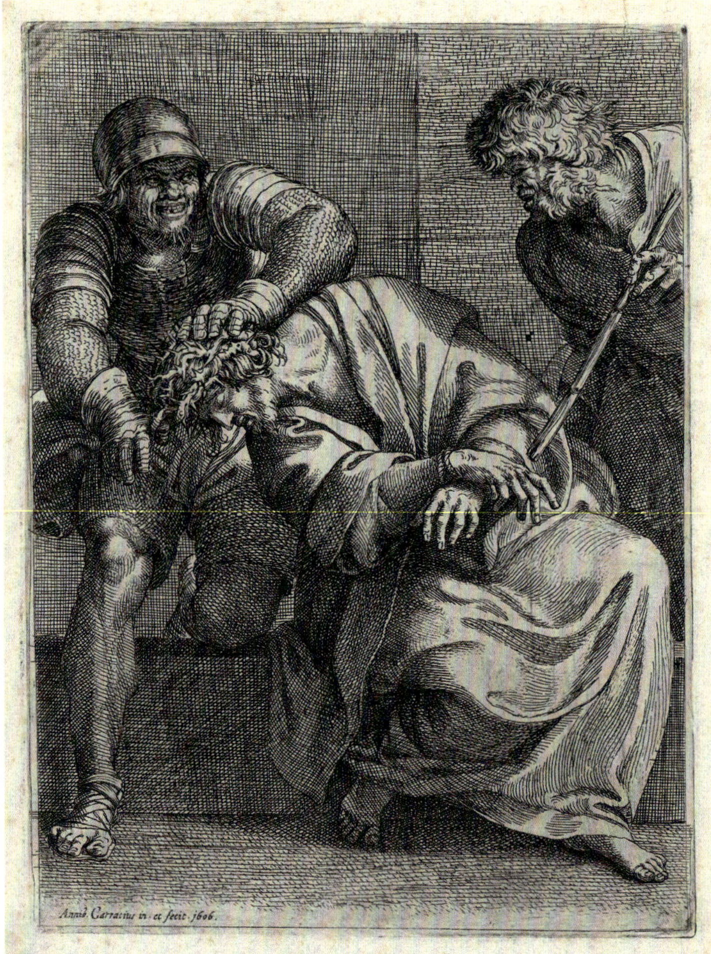

Fig. 86 Annibale Carracci, *Christ Crowned with Thorns*, 1606, The Metropolitan Museum of Art, New York, Rogers Fund 1918

cardinal and the tonality, which is consistent with the artist's late work, the painting has most recently been dated to 1627/28.[12] Chronologically, it is thus the last of a total of four paintings treating the subject by the artist.[13] Valentin chose to use a vertical format for his depiction, thus drawing on a picture format which apparently had not gained acceptance for this subject among Caravaggio's followers.[14] The source for this is probably Caravaggio's version of *Christ Crowned with Thorns*, which the latter had painted around 1604/05 for the Roman cardinal Massimo Massimi.[15] In the centre behind Christ, a henchman firmly presses the crown of thorns on him; a kneeling, mocking soldier each has been added in the front left and at the rear right. Almost imperceptibly, tears run down alongside Christ's nose, creating a silent contrast to the loudly mocking soldiers. A rather soft light compared to the other paintings falls on the scene from the front left, highlighting – aside from the armour – the shoulders, the neck and the right half of Christ's face as the brightest spots in the picture.

How very different is the orchestration of light in Baburen's painting (cat. 41): he bathes the scene in a cool, dazzling light, thereby creating high contrasts, drama and dynamics. Very much in line with Dutch pictorial tradition, his focus is, moreover, on the realistic rendering of the various materials. Especially in the area of the cuirass and helmet of the soldier, however, Baburen also visibly emulates Caravaggio's painting (fig. 84) in which the image of the shiny metal armour was also placed in the left foreground. As opposed to Caravaggio's muted colours, which create a prevailing overall impression of earthy grey and ochre tones, Baburen used a range of bright, vibrant colours and distributed them across the entire picture surface. Moreover, in depicting the henchmen in an exaggerated, almost caricature-like manner to characterise their brutality, he draws on northern European, late Gothic traditions. Baburen's interpretation and realisation of *Christ Crowned with Thorns* can be seen as representative of a distinct pictorial language which defines the works of the last years of his life in Utrecht and makes their style highly recognisable. SH

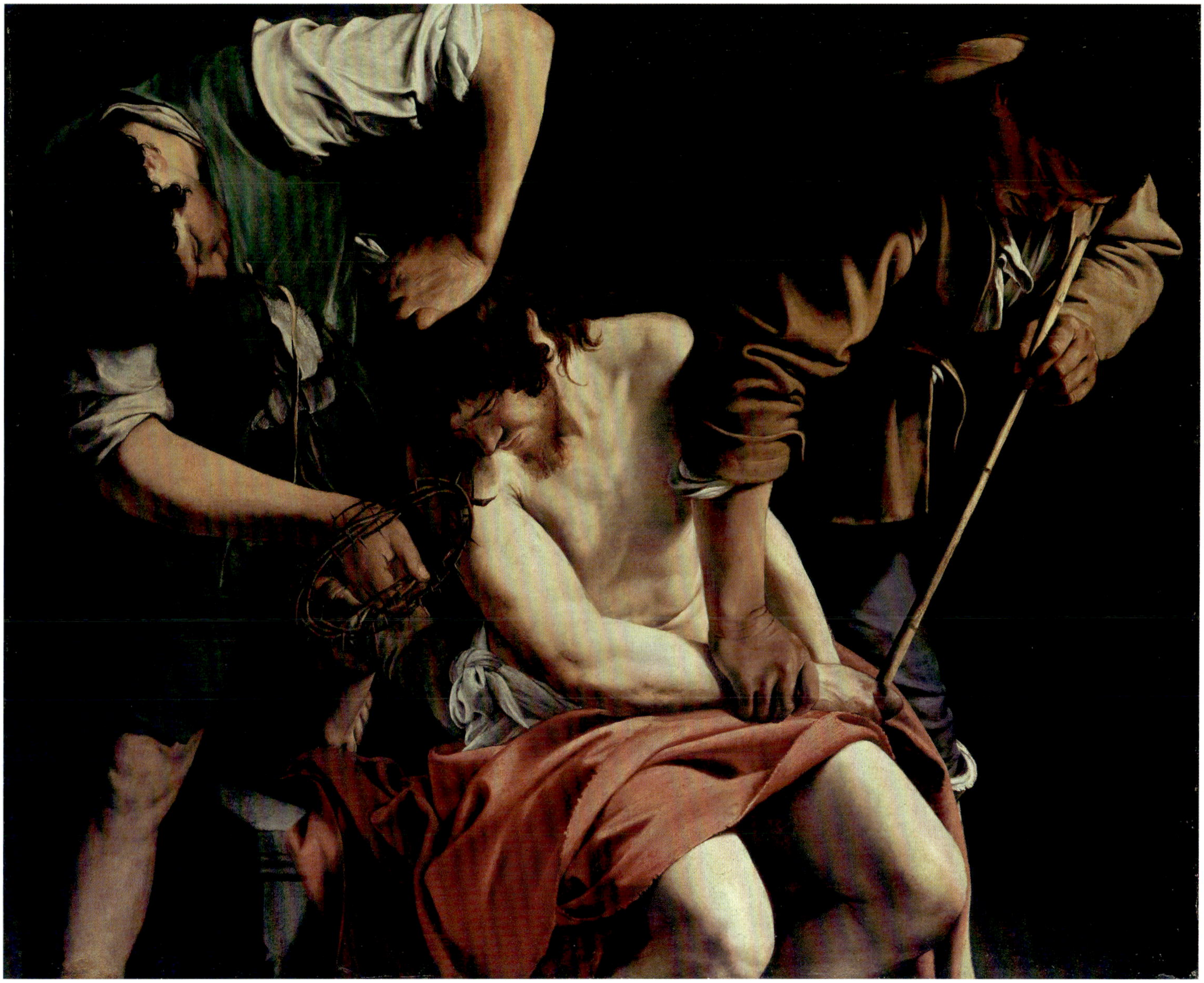

43
Orazio Gentileschi
Christ Crowned with Thorns, c. 1612/15
Herzog Anton Ulrich-Museum, Braunschweig

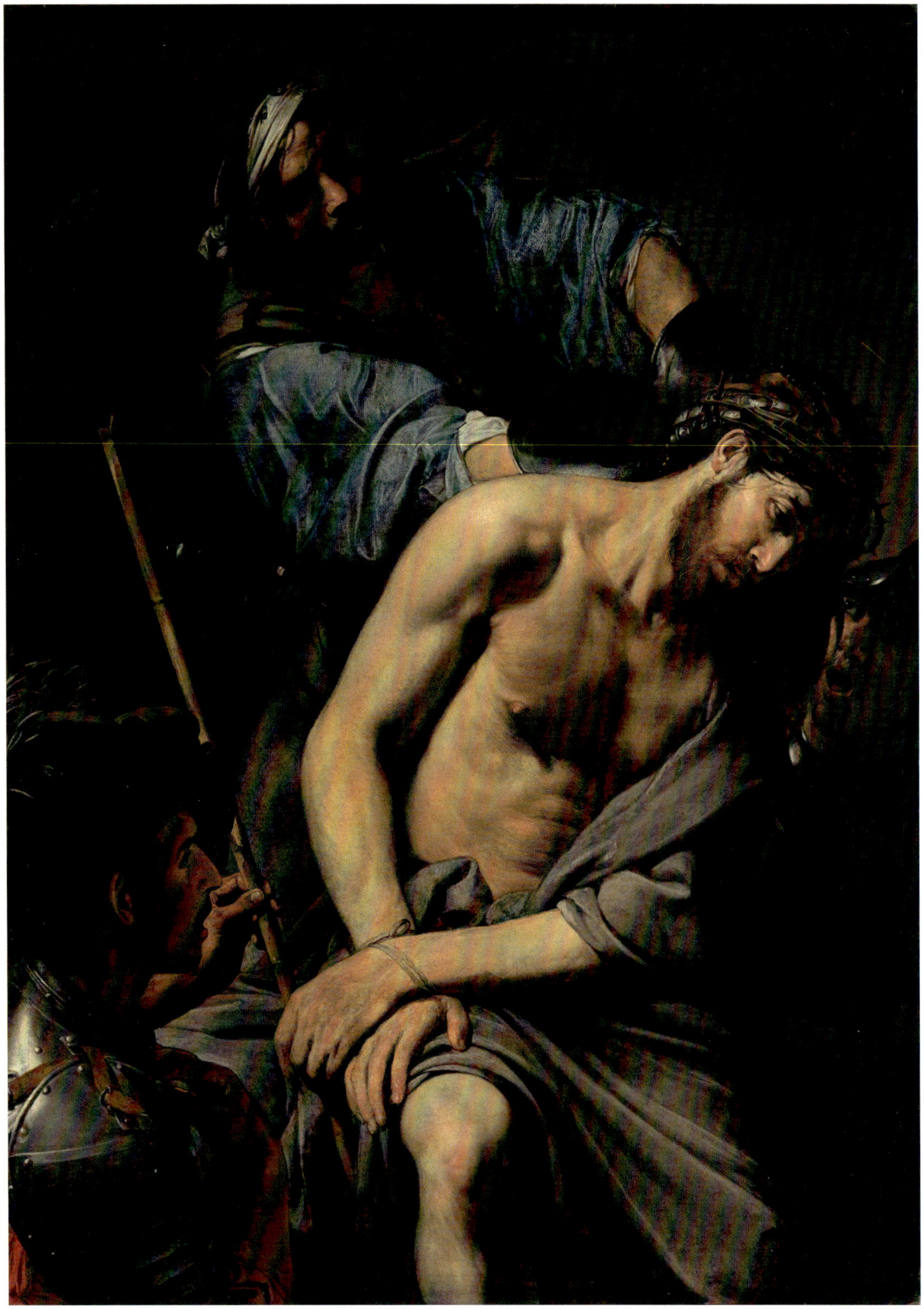

44
Valentin de Boulogne
The Crowning with Thorns and the Mocking of Christ, c. 1627/28
Bayerische Staatsgemäldesammlungen, Alte Pinakothek, Munich

1 Canvas, 130.5 × 171.1 cm, The Nelson-Atkins Museum of Art, Kansas City, inv. 84–25. For both paintings see Franits 2013a, pp. 112–115, nos. A17–A18.
2 Paleotti 1582 (2002).
3 1602/03, canvas, 127 × 166 cm, Kunsthistorisches Museum, Gemäldegalerie, inv. GG 307. Prohaska/Swoboda/Cardinali 2010, pp. 61–69.
4 For Manfredi's Crownings with Thorns and their impact, see Hartje 2004, pp. 141–160. Papi 2013, p. 173, mentions seven different versions.
5 For the first time in inv. Schleißheim 1771, no. 253. Hartje 2004, pp. 297–299, cat. A4. See for this the analysis reports of the Doerner Institut in Munich of 11 July 2017 and 19 December 2017: the beige-orange-coloured trouser leg of the figure on the left was built up with green paint; the colour scheme was modified even during the painting process. The cloak of Christ had faded badly due to the use of light-sensitive paints. In 2018, the original shade of colour was reconstructed based on the analysis findings.
6 *The Mocking of Christ*, c. 1612/14, canvas, 122 × 146 cm, Galleria degli Uffizi, Florence, inv. 1317. Hartje 2004, pp. 319–321, cat. A13; Papi 2013, pp. 173–174, cat. 36.
7 Exh. cat. Utrecht/Braunschweig 1986/87, pp. 265–267, cat. 57; Exh. cat. Rome/New York/Saint Louis 2001/02, pp. 130–133, no. 23.
8 Matthew 27:27–31; Mark 15:16–20; John 19:1–16.
9 Bissell 1981, pp. 152–153, cat. 24; Bartsch 39, no. 182.3. Exh. cat. Rome/New York/St. Louis 2001/02, p. 133. Similar violent force can be seen in Ludovico Carracci's *Christ Crowned with Thorns*, 1597/99, canvas, 221 × 147.5 cm, Pinacoteca Nazionale di Bologna, inv. 464 (previously San Girolamo, Bologna).
10 See cats. 16–18.
11 Mojana 1989, pp. 88–89, cat. 18.
12 Exh. cat. New York/Paris 2016/17, pp. 181–184, cat. 37; see Cat. Munich 2009, p. 126, and Mojana 1989, pp. 88–89, cat. 18 (1624).
13 Exh. cat. New York/Paris 2016/17, p. 95. Another painting by Valentin de Boulogne which combines the Crowning with Thorns with the Mocking is also in the collection of the Bayerische Staatsgemäldesammlungen, Munich: c. 1616/17, canvas, 173 × 241 cm, inv. 477. See the essay by Ashok Roy in this volume, pp. 91–92., fig. 47.
14 Additionally in portrait format: Valentin de Boulogne, *Christ Crowned with Thorns*, c. 1613/14, canvas, 146.4 × 106.5 cm, private collection; see most recently Exh. cat. New York/Paris 2016/17, pp. 95–97, cat. 7.
15 c. 1604/05, canvas, 125 × 178 cm, Banca Popolare di Vicenza. Ebert-Schifferer 2009, pp. 176–177.

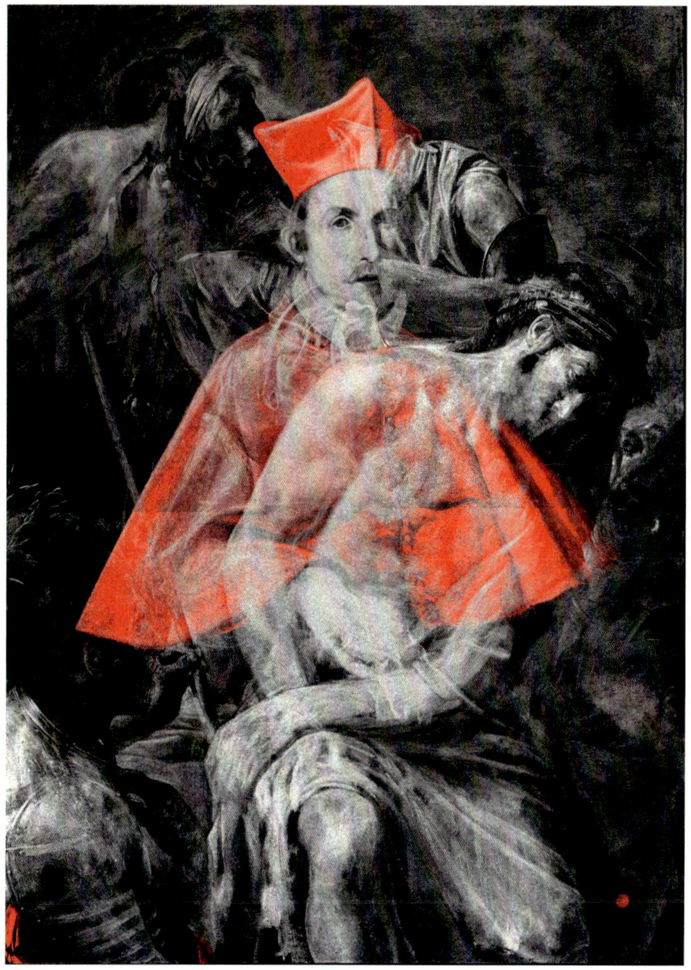

Fig. 87 Valentin de Boulogne, *The Crowning with Thorns and the Mocking of Christ* (cat. 44). Macro X-ray fluorescence scan, superposition of the element distribution images of lead (white), coming mainly from white lead, and mercury (red) from vermilion.

1622

Christ among the Doctors

45
Dirck van Baburen
Christ among the Doctors, 1622
Signed and dated right, on the edge of the table:
Teodoer de Baburen ano 1622
Canvas, 189 × 210.5 cm
Nasjonalmuseet for kunst, arkitektur og design,
Oslo, inv. 109

46
Giovanni Serodine
Christ among the Doctors, 1624/26
Canvas, 145 × 224 cm
Musée du Louvre, Paris, inv. R.F. 1983-4

A lost child who is only found three days later, safe and sound. It is a really maddening and traumatic experience for parents. It happened to Mary and Joseph. Returning from Jerusalem, where they had celebrated Passover, they discovered that the 12-year-old Jesus had not rejoined their travelling party. They returned to the city and found him in the Temple, deep in a discussion about scripture with Jewish scribes. Luke 2:42–51 describes his parents' alarm. They do not know whether to be angry or relieved. Mary asks Jesus: 'Son, why hast thou thus dealt with us? Behold, thy father and I have sought thee sorrowing'. Jesus replies with a question of his own: 'How is it that ye sought me? Wist ye not that I must be about my Father's business?'. His parents were baffled as to what he meant. Luke tells us that Jesus returned with them to Nazareth and was obedient from then on.

Mary and Joseph are missing in almost every depiction of this story. Baburen and Serodine, though, do include them, and choose a specific moment in the story. In Baburen's case (cat. 45) they are in the background, where a light vertical strip suggests that there is an opening in the rear wall. Although they are only schematic figures they are clearly recognisable. Joseph is wearing a long cloak and Mary has a blue headscarf. In Serodine's version (cat. 46), they are on the right. Joseph has wrapped a thick cloak around himself and holds a pilgrim's staff with his left hand. Mary is standing right behind him with a black scarf on her head. It is clear that they have just entered the room from the gaze of the boy with the splendid plumed bonnet, who is resting his arms on the back of a chair. In the Baburen, a boy with a large volume on his shoulder came into the room a moment ago. A second striking similarity between Baburen and Serodine is that they both emphasise Christ's sanctity, Baburen with a golden halo, the only one in his oeuvre, and Serodine with a nimbus of light. That is where the similarities end. The actual depictions could not be more different.

Baburen paints men with hands browned by the sun and dirty, calloused feet. The scribe kneeling on the right is wearing a beautiful red velvet cloak, but the man sitting on a stool across from him is naked from the waist up. Serodine, on the other hand, has a sense of decorum and has seated the three doctors in easy chairs with armrests. They are wearing costly and distinguished garb, and are quietly listening to what Christ has to say. It is clear from

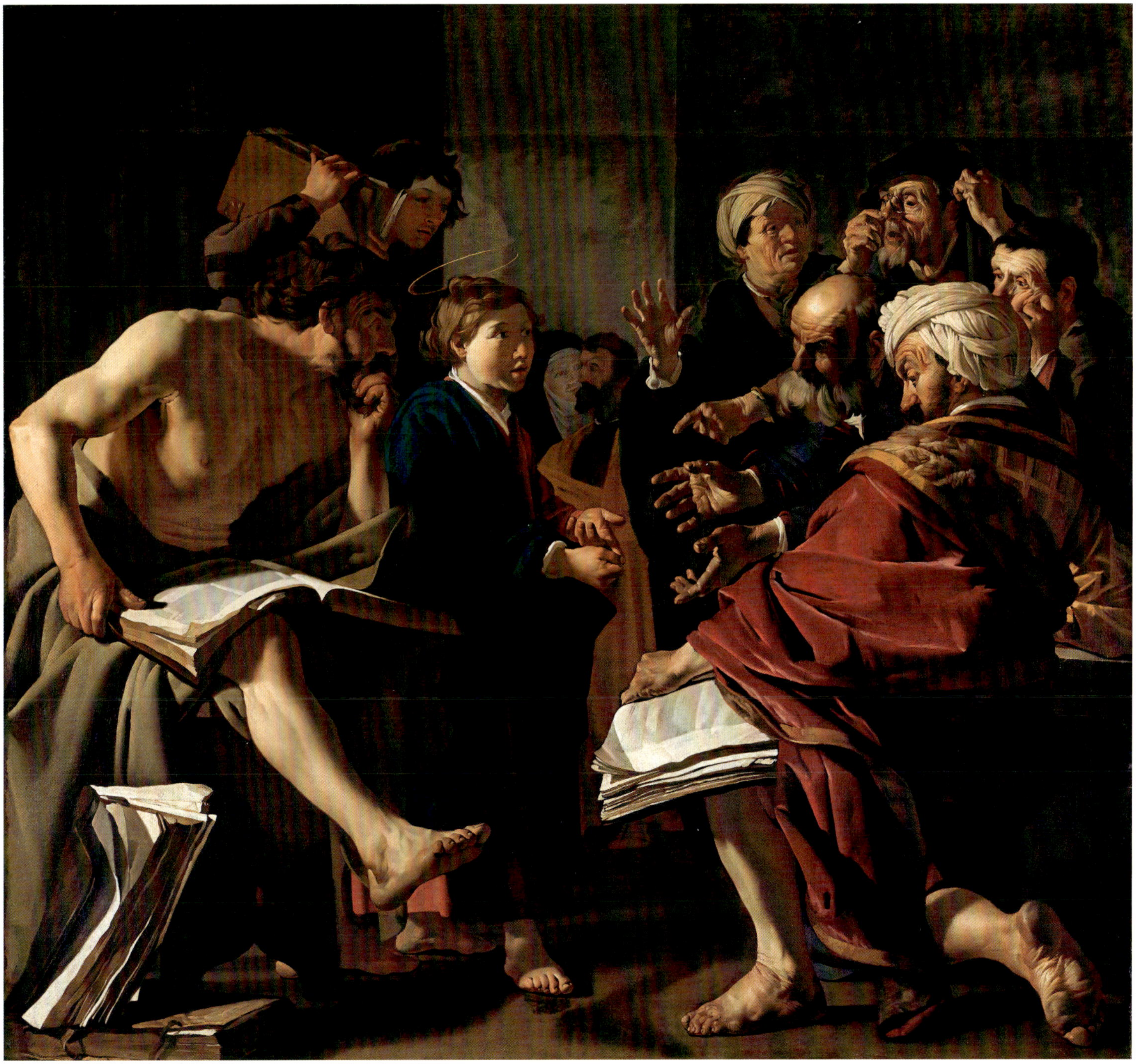

45
Dirck van Baburen
Christ among the Doctors, 1622
Nasjonalmuseet for kunst,
arkitektur og design, Oslo

the architecture that they are in the Temple. The colossal pillar on a pedestal that extends down to the top of Christ's head suggests that the building is huge. Baburen's space is indeterminate and bare. His doctors are attentive, and it is clear from their wild gestures that they are inquisitive, but also disturbed. Many hands are reaching out towards the child, creating a lively scene in which a lot is going on.

Baburen's painting originally had a horizontal format. At some stage it was enlarged with the addition of a strip 24 centimetres high at the top and with another one 2 centimetres wide on the left.[1] They give the composition room to breathe, and that was precisely the point. The Utrecht Caravaggisti often placed their figures in a confined picture surface, which later generations found too constricting.[2] However, the enlargement does spoil the original composition. The painting has never been lined, which is partly why it is in such superb condition.[3] Baburen made not a single change to the composition while he was painting it. Both the large passages and the smaller ones, and the details as well, were applied with great assurance and precision with thick, impasted paint. He modelled *alla prima*, that is to say wet in wet, with colours that he had already mixed on his palette.[4] This painting technique involves adding new paint on top of layers that are not yet dry. It is a rapid working method, but can only be done successfully by a very experienced and talented painter. It can be seen to very good effect in the still life with the large book in the left foreground.

The painting was very well received in its day, and there are no fewer than six other versions of it.[5] This is probably the one that was sold 20 years after Baburen's death on 15 March 1644 at the auction of the belongings of Boudewijn de Man of Delft, the receiver-general and director of the Dutch West India Company. It fetched 605 guldens at the sale, which was the equivalent of the annual income of a member of the middle class working in the Dutch Republic around 1640/50.[6] LMH

1 Plahter/Plahter 1999, p. 42.
2 See also cat. 23. A strip approximately 30 cm high was added at the top of Hendrick ter Brugghen's *Rich Man and Poor Lazarus*. It was folded over onto the back of the picture during the restoration of 2017/18 and is no longer visible. See also Domela Nieuwenhuis 2007, pp. 88–94.
3 Plahter/Plahter 1999, pp. 51–52. Gerard van Honthorst, *David Playing the Harp*, 1622, canvas, 81 × 65 cm, Centraal Museum, Utrecht, inv. 8670, is not lined either, and is also on its original stretcher.
4 Plahter/Plahter 1999, pp. 48–49.
5 Franits 2013a, pp. 122–124, cats. A22A1–A22R1.
6 Ibid., pp. 120–121, cat. A22.

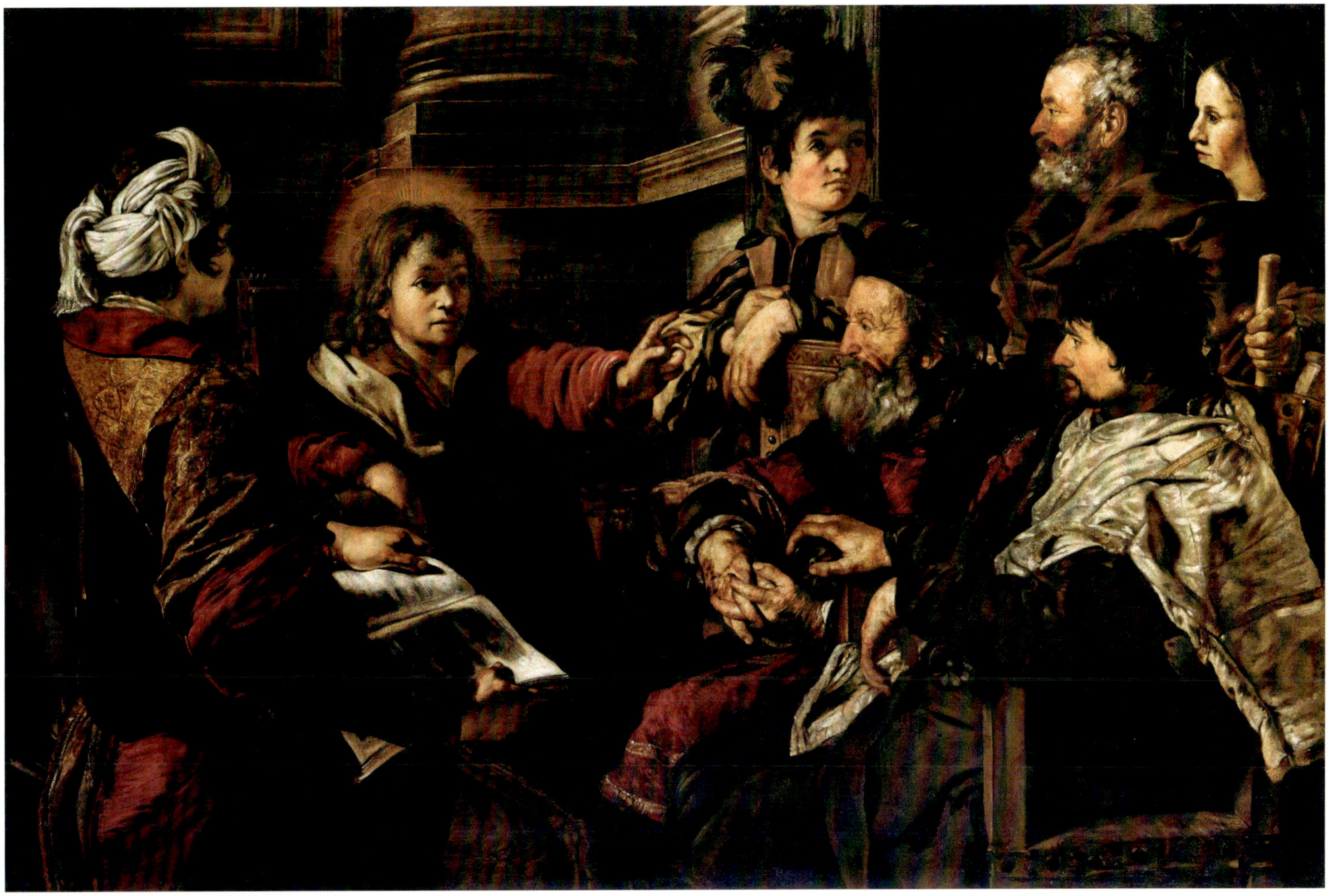

46
Giovanni Serodine
Christ among the Doctors, 1624/26
Musée du Louvre, Paris

c. 1622

The Incredulity of St Thomas

47
Hendrick ter Brugghen
The Incredulity of St Thomas, c. 1622
Canvas, 108.1 × 133.2 cm
Rijksmuseum, Amsterdam, purchased with the support of the Stichting tot Bevordering van de Belangen van het Rijksmuseum, inv. SK-A-3908

48
Michelangelo Merisi, called Caravaggio (copy after)
The Incredulity of St Thomas, 1600/25
Canvas, 108 × 146 cm
Galleria degli Uffizi, Florence, inv. 1890 no. 5807

49
Giovanni Antonio Galli (Lo Spadarino)
Christ Displaying his Wounds, c. 1625/35
Canvas, 132.2 × 97.8 cm
Perth Museum and Art Gallery, Perth and Kinross Council, Scotland, conserved with the support of the Woodmansterne Art Conservation Fund, inv. FA 192/78

The proverb 'Seeing is believing' touches not only the core of Christianity but on that of every religion. To believe is to trust in the truth of something for which there is no tangible evidence. The incredulous Thomas, who still epitomises lack of trust, goes to the heart of the doctrine of faith. Thomas does not believe that Jesus has risen from the dead, and that he has been seen alive. 'Except I shall see in his hands the print of the nails, and put my finger into the print of the nails, and thrust my hand into his side, I will not believe', said Thomas, according to John 20:24–29. Jesus provides him with that evidence eight days later, when he again appears to his disciples in a house, 'the doors being shut'. Thomas is with them this time, and Jesus turns to him and says: 'Reach hither thy finger, and behold my hands; and reach hither thy hand, and thrust it into my side: and be not faithless, but believing'. Thomas then says 'My Lord and my God', and Jesus replies: 'because thou hast seen me, thou hast believed: blessed are they that have not seen, and yet have believed'.

The focus in Hendrick ter Brugghen's painting is on the principal evidence of Thomas poking his index finger into the wound in Jesus's side (cat. 47).[1] The light falls on this central, morbid action. Thomas is leaning towards Jesus and frowns as he studies the wound closely in order to convince himself that it is real. The other three apostles, who had all believed, are keeping more of a distance. The greybeard, almost satisfied, smiles as he peers down through his pince-nez at the wound and the finger.[2] The apostle furthest away from Thomas is looking upwards, his hands folded in prayer, while his companion beside him is again looking down.[3] It is the action of the hands that unites the figures.

Ter Brugghen's painting is an interpretation of Caravaggio's *Incredulity of St Thomas* (1600/01), which was in the collection of Vincenzo Giustiniani (1564–1637) in Rome from 1606.[4] It was Caravaggio's most copied work.[5] In August 1607, on his way back from a journey though Europe, Giustiniani saw a copy of his painting in the house of Orazio del Negro in Genoa, and several other very early versions are documented, in Bologna, among other places.[6] *The Incredulity of St Thomas* in the Galleria degli Uffizi (cat. 48) is identified with the picture mentioned in 1666 in the inventory of Cardinal Carlo de' Medici (1595–1666), who died in Florence.[7]

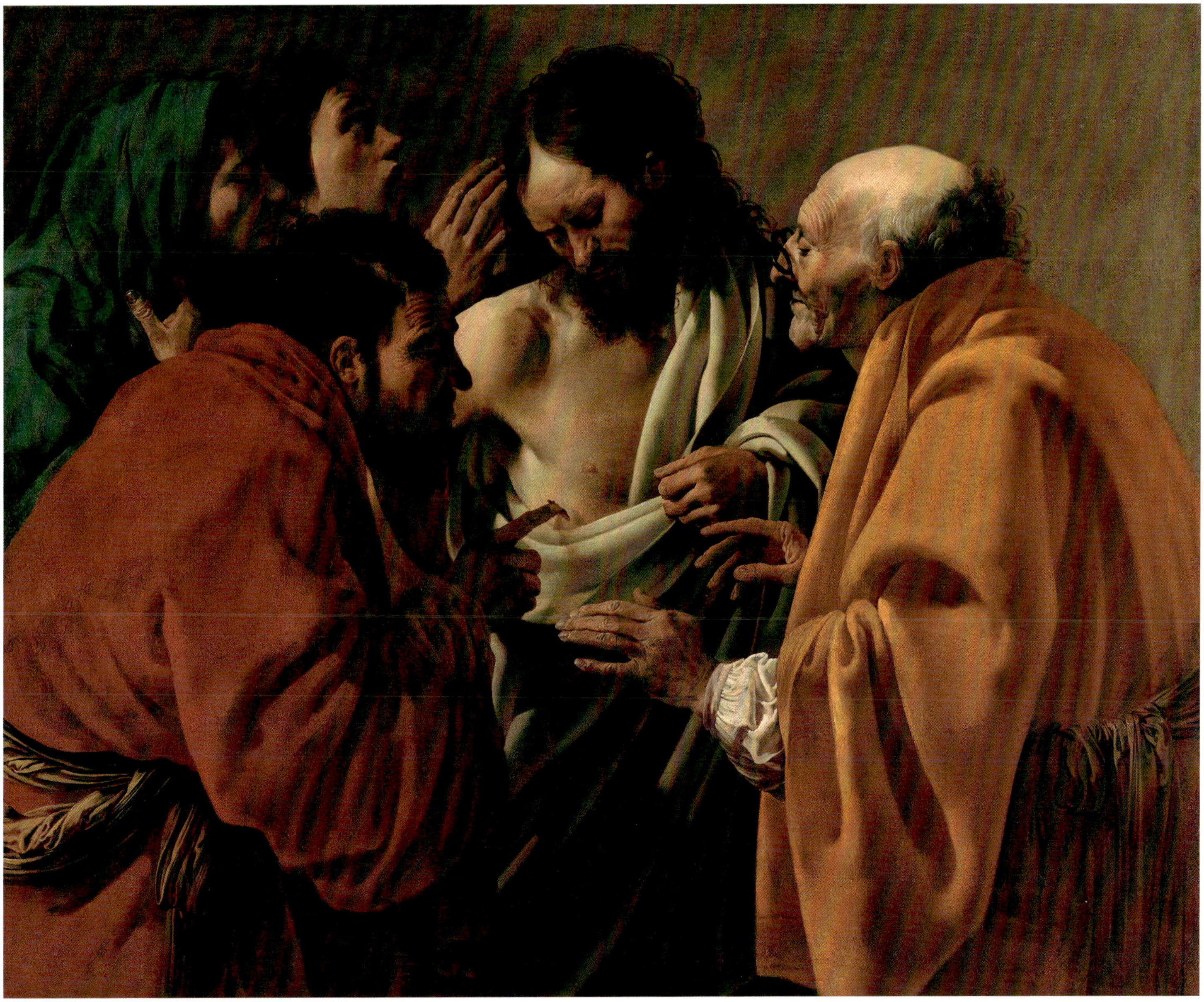

47
Hendrick ter Brugghen
The Incredulity of St Thomas, c. 1622
Rijksmuseum, Amsterdam

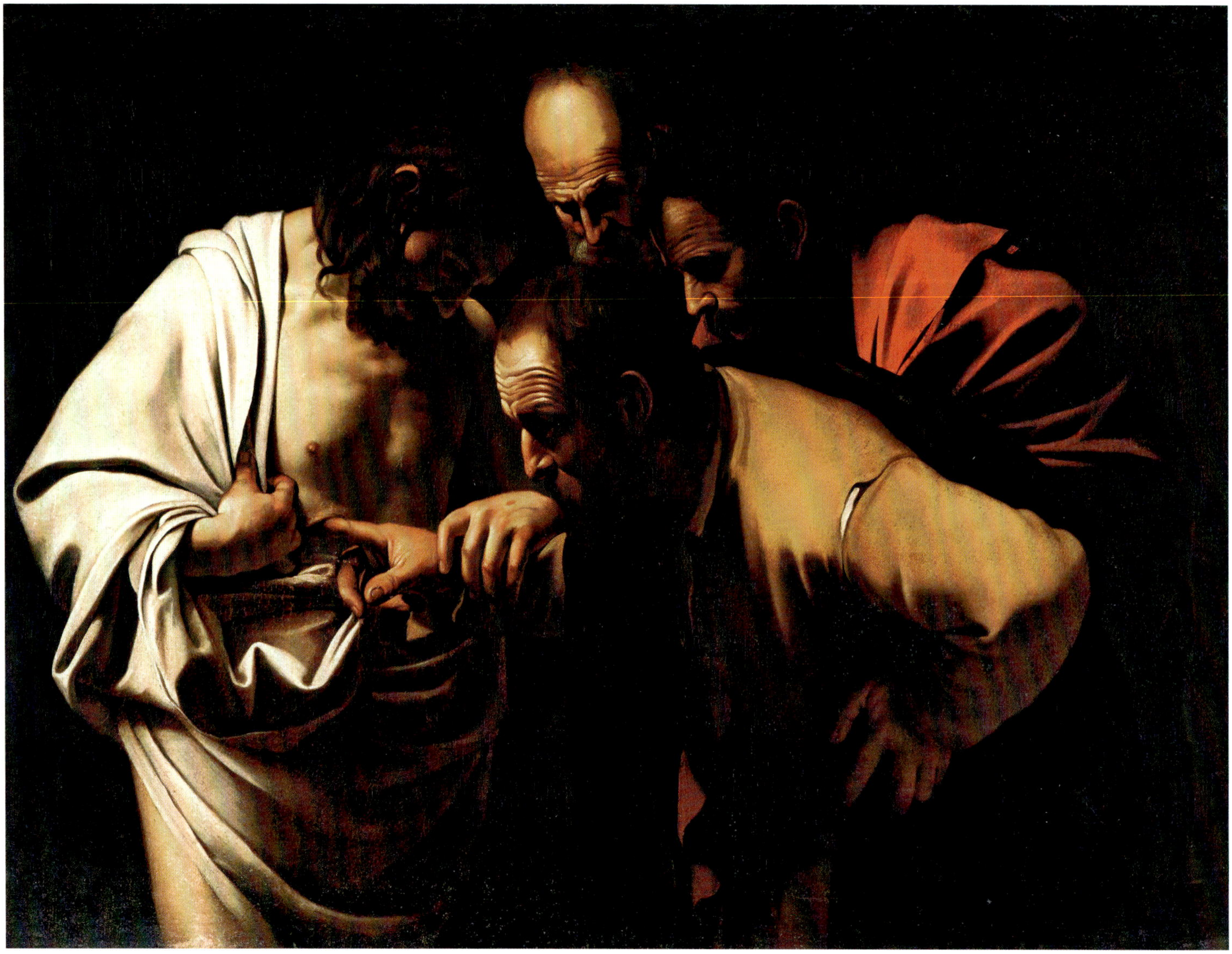

48
Michelangelo Merisi, called Caravaggio (copy after)
The Incredulity of St Thomas, 1600/25
Galleria degli Uffizi, Florence

Caravaggio's composition was revolutionary. He was the first artist to opt for a limited number of three-quarter-length figures in an indefinable space. The explicit depiction of Thomas's finger deep in the wound in Jesus's side, which was already being depicted in northern art, was new in Italy.[8] However, it was not just the innovative iconography that made this painting so popular. It was the subject, too. Thomas was a suitable role model for the faithful around 1600, for in that period, with Protestantism on the rise, a number of articles of faith were under attack, and this particular event is a testament to faith, paradoxically enough in a story about doubt.[9]

As with his *Calling of St Matthew* in Utrecht (cat. 36), which is based on Caravaggio's painting in San Luigi dei Francesi in Rome, ter Brugghen reversed the composition. All of the apostles are to the left of Jesus in the Caravaggio. With furrowed forehead, each of them is leaning forward to study Thomas's finger deep in the wound in Jesus's side, even deeper than in the ter Brugghen. The open wound is no longer bloody, but clean and smooth. It is not the wound that is at the centre of Caravaggio's composition, but Jesus's left hand gripping Thomas's wrist and guiding his hand to the wound. According to the gospel, Thomas also wanted to put his finger in the wounds left by the nails in Christ's hands. Ter Brugghen did not depict them, but Caravaggio did. Even more than with the Caravaggio, ter Brugghen's viewers can place themselves in the role of a fifth apostle taking part in the event. Against that, his composition lacks Caravaggio's symmetry, which creates a sense of quiet and fierce concentration.[10]

The powerful decision that Giovanni Antonio Galli, called Lo Spadarino, made to depict Jesus alone was highly exceptional (cat. 49).[11] The result is a monumental, almost coercive scene in which a great demand is being made of the viewer. Now we are Thomas, to whom Jesus, unasked, is giving the evidence of his Resurrection. He is spreading the side wound wide open for us with his damaged hands. His body with the white loincloth, the ends of which are draped elegantly over his arm, stands out against the dark background. Frowning, with his large brown eyes staring insistently at us and his lips slightly parted, his message is mild at the same time. Look, and believe in me, he is saying. The halo, the light around his head that proclaims his sanctity, glows around his dark hair. In this painting Jesus is no longer earthly. He has been elevated to the status of a mythical figure. LMH

1 According to Leonard J. Slatkes in Exh. cat. San Francisco/Baltimore/London 1997/98, pp. 143–145, cat. 5, and in Slatkes/Franits 2007, p. 111, cat. A21, a pentimento indicates that the finger was not originally in the wound itself. However, in the 'Technical notes' in Cat. Amsterdam 2007, pp. 92–93, cat. 37, it is stated that Thomas's hand was reserved but that the pointing finger was not.
2 It has been noted on several occasions that the figure with the pince-nez is derived from a type by Marinus van Reymerswaele. See Cat. Amsterdam 2007, pp. 92–93, cat. 37.
3 See also ibid. Seaman 2012, p. 125, identified the two figures to the left of Thomas as St John the Evangelist and the Virgin praying.
4 Caravaggio, *The Incredulity of St Thomas*, c. 1601, canvas, 107 × 146 cm. Sanssouci Palace, Potsdam, inv. 5438. Savina 2013, pp. 224–225, cat. VII, n.1.
5 Moir 1976, pp. 89–90, no. 18, mentions three prints and 27 copies, 13 of which are lost. The number of copies was raised to around 40 in 2006. See Hurttig 2014, p. 39. For the most recent and complete list see Savina 2013, pp. 224–229, no. VII. On p. 228, no. VII, n.11 is attributed to Dirck van Baburen on the basis of a black-and-white photograph, Fototeca Zeri, inv. 101814. The similarities in colouring make the influence of a print unlikely. The fact that there was already an engraving after the painting in the 17th century would have contributed to the large number of copies. Hurttig 2014, p. 39.
6 Among others, see Hurttig 2014, pp. 19–21.
7 See Gianni Papi in Exh. cat. Florence 2010, p. 126, cat. 9. Savina 2013, pp. 226–227, cat. VII, n.4; Hurttig 2014, pp. 29–30. See also Exh. cat. Düsseldorf 2006/07, pp. 258–259, cat. 42.
8 For the visual tradition of Thomas's finger or fingers in the wound, see Hurttig 2014, pp. 233–248.
9 See Benay 2014.
10 See Seaman 2012, pp. 117–149, for a theological interpretation (Protestant versus Catholic) of the modifications that ter Brugghen made to Caravaggio's version.
11 The painting was first published in Gash 2009. In Wrotham Park, Hertfordshire, there is an *Incredulity of St Thomas*, c. 1620, canvas, 114.3 × 148.6 cm, which Gianni Papi attributed to Spadarino on the basis of a photograph and was then discovered in the collection by John Gash. See Papi 2003b, p. 140, cat. 29; Gash 2015. In Exh. cat. London/Dublin/Edinburgh 2016/17, pp. 86–87, cat. 15, it is listed as Spadarino with a question mark.

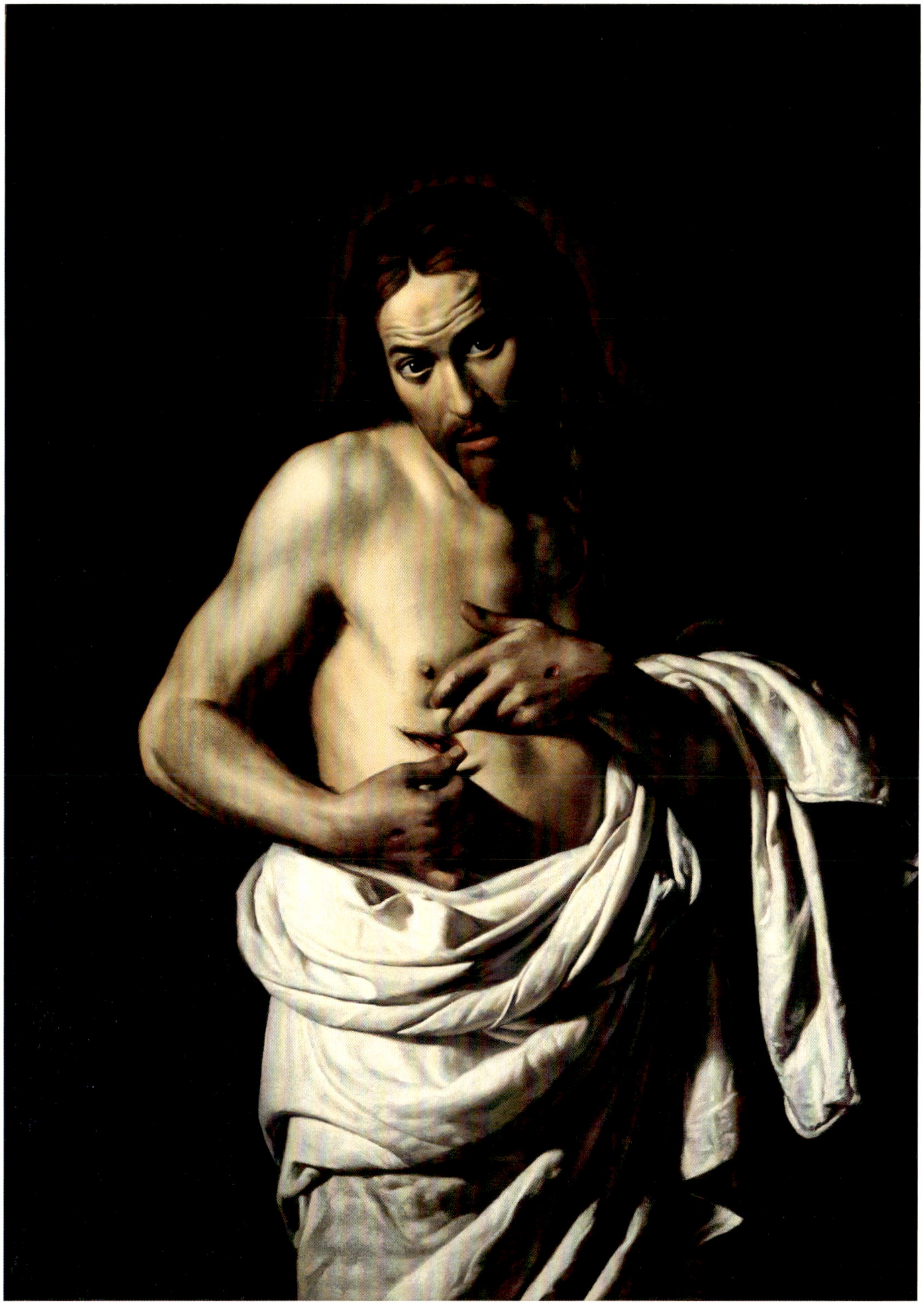

49
Giovanni Antonio Galli (Lo Spadarino)
Christ Displaying his Wounds, c. 1625/35
Perth Museum and Art Gallery,
Perth and Kinross Council, Scotland

1623

Card and Dice Players

50
Hendrick ter Brugghen
The Gamblers, 1623
Signed and dated bottom centre, to the left of the ace of spades card: HTB [f]ecit 1623
Canvas, 85.4 × 114.9 cm1
Minneapolis Institute of Art, Minneapolis, The William Hood Dunwoody Fund, inv. 60.17

51
Valentin de Boulogne
Cardsharps, c. 1614/15
Canvas, 94.5 × 137 cm
Staatliche Kunstsammlungen Dresden, Gemäldegalerie Alte Meister, Dresden, Gal.-Nr. 408
Munich only

52
Nicolas Régnier
Cardsharps and Fortune Teller, c. 1623/25
Canvas, 174 × 228 cm
Szépművészeti Múzeum, Budapest, inv. 610

53
Theodoor Rombouts
The Card Players, c. 1630
Canvas, 151.6 × 205 cm
Koninklijk Museum voor Schone Kunsten, Antwerp, inv. 358
Utrecht only

Leonard J. Slatkes, in his monograph on the painter, ranked Dirck van Baburen's *The Backgammon Players* (fig. 88) among the 'important developmental paintings of his career'.[2] Of the three authentic versions Slatkes was aware of, the one which was until recently in a private collection is regarded as the primary one. This work, which was seminal for all other depictions of the subject in Utrecht, had already been promised as a loan for the exhibition when it was destroyed by fire in February 2018.[3] In terms of painterly quality and rendition of details, as well as with regard to its preservation status – especially the vibrant colours – the work was superior to the two other paintings which are considered to be workshop replicas.[4] Based on stylistic similarities with the *Procuress* in Boston (fig. 100) and Baburen's *Christ among the Doctors* in Oslo (cat. 45), which are both signed and dated, the painting is datable to c. 1622.[5]

Baburen's soldiers are playing a game of tabula, a dice board game nowadays known as backgammon and at the time also called *tric-trac* in France, *tavola reale* in Italy, or *Puff* in Germany.[6] It was played in taverns, gaming rooms and brothels, with the German colloquial term for the latter, *Puff*, deriving from the game. Card and dice games, in particular games of chance involving high wagers which drove many an individual to ruin, led to squabbles and encouraged cheating, were harshly criticised in particular by the Church. A deck of cards was even denounced as the 'devil's prayer book'. While at the courts of Europe the game of chance for educational purposes was in keeping with social conventions, the non-aristocratic population tended to be prohibited from engaging in it.[7] But prohibitions and fines could not prevent people from playing games everywhere and that countless types of games were disseminated particularly by *landsknechts* via trade and military routes.[8]

The depiction of the subject in Caravaggesque painting goes back to Caravaggio's *Cardsharps* (fig. 89), a work created around 1595 and acquired by Cardinal Del Monte who was himself an avid card player.[9] The painting is characteristic of the early years of the young painter in Rome when he was making a name for himself with horizontal-format genre paintings featuring life-size, half-length figures. The arrangement of Baburen's figures, especially the soldier on the right whose outstretched left arm extends diagonally across the picture, may be understood as a reference to this

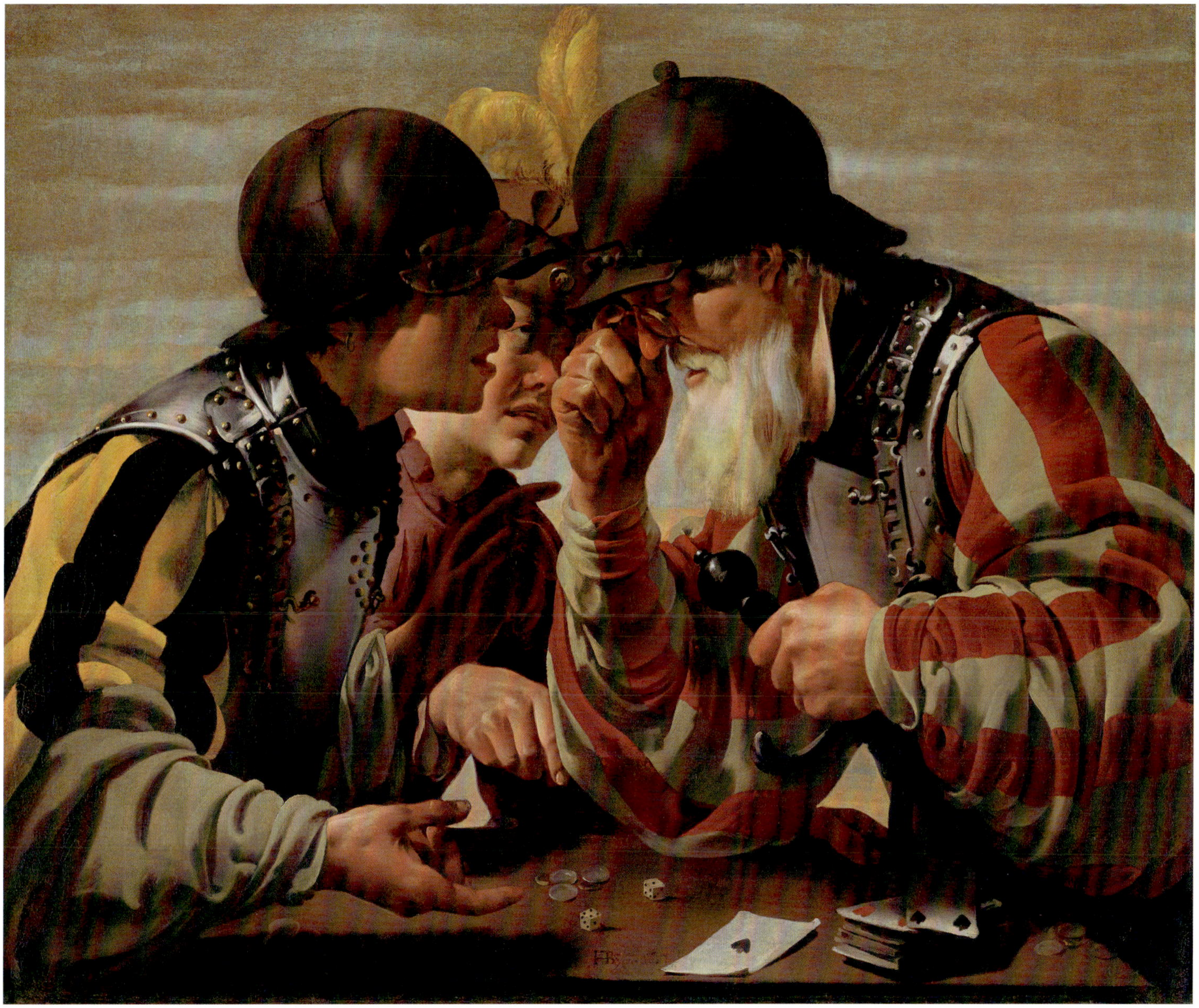

50
Hendrick ter Brugghen
The Gamblers, 1623
Minneapolis Institute of Art, Minneapolis,
The William Hood Dunwoody Fund

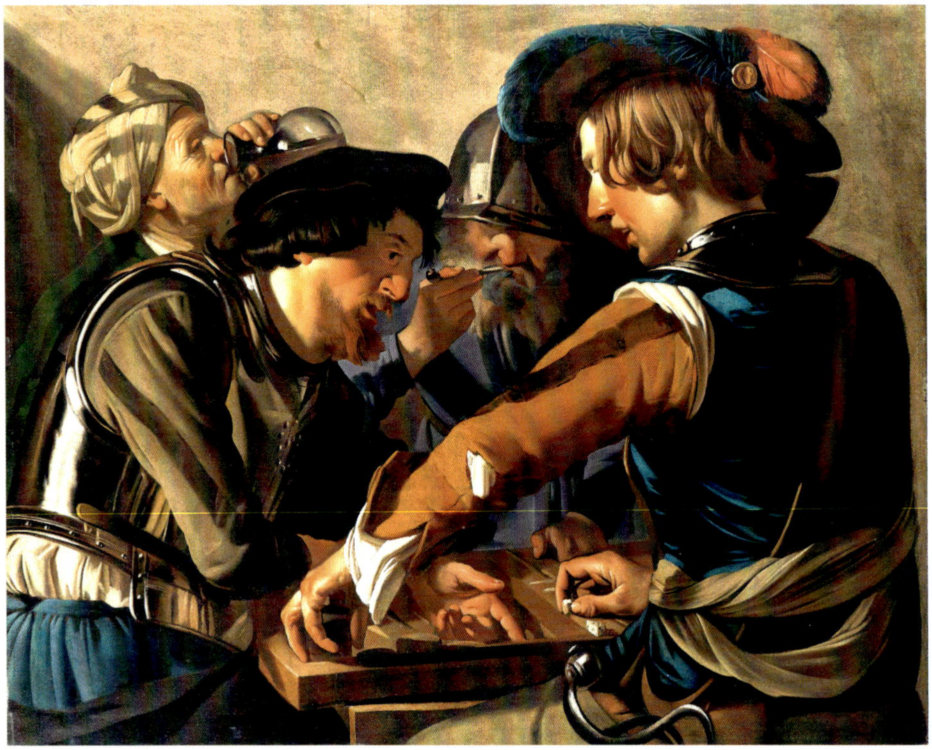

Fig. 88 Dirck van Baburen, *The Backgammon Players*, c. 1622, formerly private collection (destroyed 2018)

famous painting. Yet while Caravaggio focuses on the cheating, Baburen adds other symbols of vice to the painting, as was common in the Dutch pictorial tradition. In addition to excessive alcohol consumption – illustrated by the old woman in the background who, due to her inebriated state, is barely able to properly bring the glass white wine carafe to her mouth – smoking is denounced. The very large hand of the soldier on the left who is pointing with his finger to the game board and who, waiting for his turn, seems to be commenting on the last dice roll, may be an indication of an imminent quarrel. Like the earlier compositions of Bartolomeo Manfredi[10] and Valentin de Boulogne (cat. 51), Baburen's painting thus seems to point more emphatically than Caravaggio's to the imminent altercation between the players and, thus, to the dangerous consequences of gambling and cheating. The sword prominently placed in the picture reminds the viewer that, especially after the consumption of alcohol, injuries as a result of outbursts of rage and violence were to be expected. This reading of the painting also informs an engraved version featuring a detail of a painting by Crispijn de Passe the Elder which, as part of a series of the Four Temperaments created around 1623–1625, is titled *Irarum Causas Fugito* (Avoid the Causes of Rage).[11] The caption of the engraving *The Choleric Temparament* reads: 'A deceiver and gambler is a filthy scallywag / He drinks and gambles away his money and beats his woman'.[12]

The threat of harm as a result of gambling and cheating is also the theme of Hendrick ter Brugghen's *The Gamblers* of 1623 (cat. 50).[13] Like Baburen, his younger fellow painter, he too tightly cropped the painting, causing the almost life-size figures and the table-top running parallel to the painting's bottom edge to give the viewer the impression of being part of the action.[14] Obviously, the last dice roll sparks anger and a dispute, which leads the older soldier on the right to instinctively grab the hilt of his sword. The viewer's attention is drawn to the unusually tight constellation of the helmet-covered heads of the two players and the face of the third figure in the background, which is grazed by light coming from the side. The large, clenched hand of the older man, with which he holds his spectacles in front of his eyes to assure himself of the outcome of the dice throw, is visually associated with the heads. The play of the hands provides the viewer with additional hints as to how to read what is happening: the soldier on the left, whose eyes are completely covered by the helmet's guard, gesticulates while talking insistently to his opponent. Meanwhile,

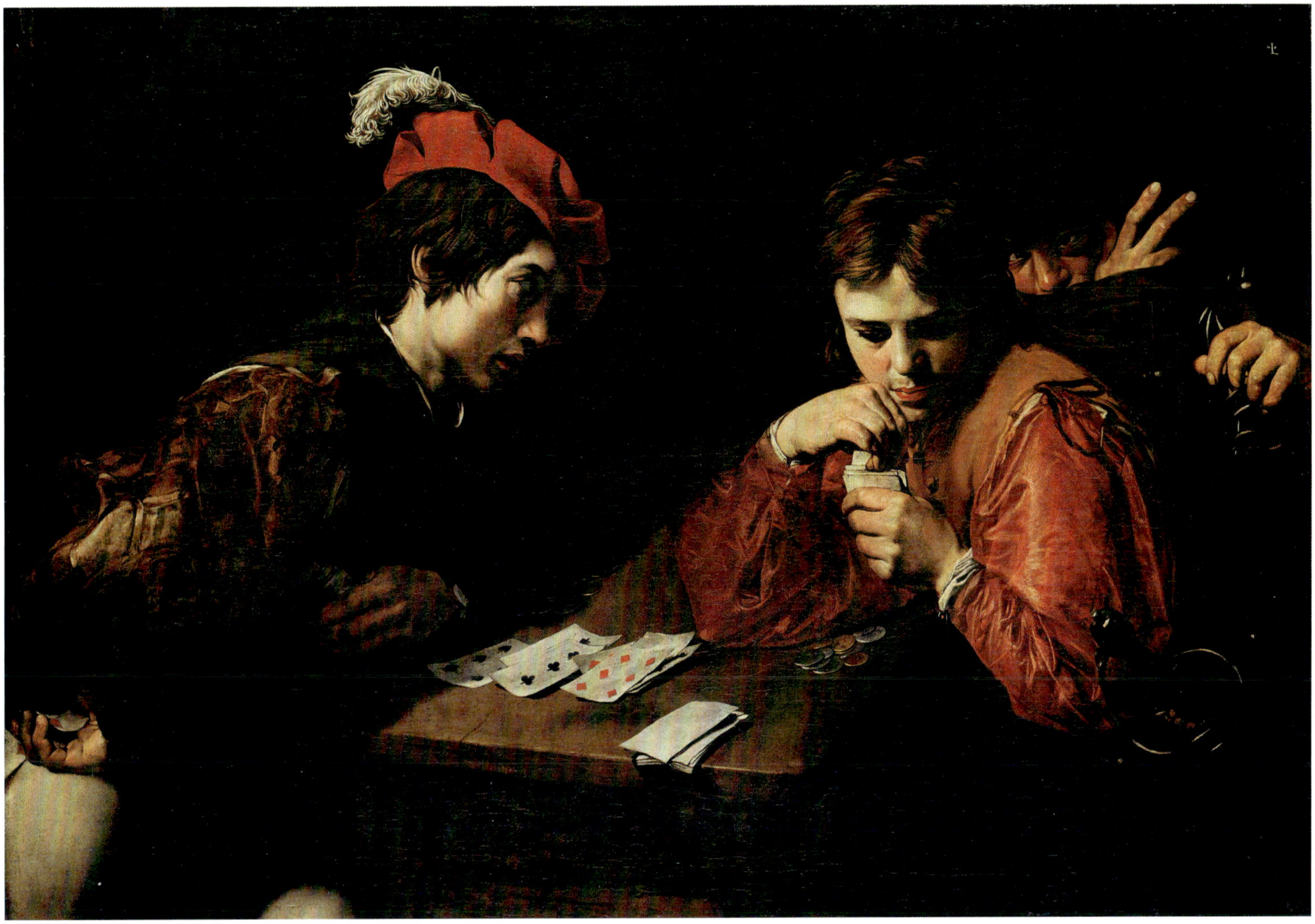

51
Valentin de Boulogne
Cardsharps, c. 1614/15
Staatliche Kunstsammlungen Dresden,
Gemäldegalerie Alte Meister, Dresden

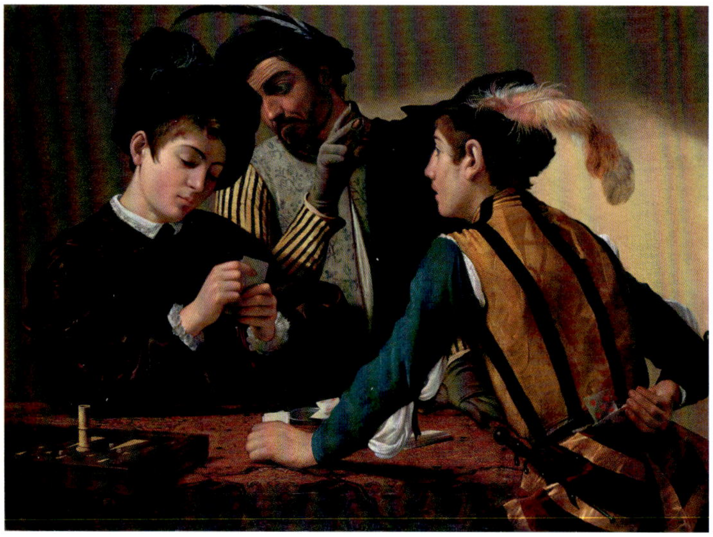

Fig. 89 Michelangelo Merisi, called Caravaggio, *The Cardsharps*, c. 1595, Kimbell Art Museum, Fort Worth

the *landsknecht* with feathered beret behind the two players points with his finger to the fallen dice and to the coins which apparently lie on the table as the stake. While he obviously takes the side of the soldier on the left, at the same time he slides his left hand inconspicuously across the table under the torso of the older, myopic player. The likely reason for the argument and, possibly, the cheating is the winning match of the numbers the dice and the hand of cards show: four and one. The spades card on top of the deck and the ace of spades, which in popular belief was associated with death, may be read as portents of harm.[15] The spectacles, traditionally a symbol of moral or spiritual blindness, inanity and deception, may serve as a hint that the older man is being cheated by the two younger ones.[16]

Some 20 years after Caravaggio's *Cardsharps*, Valentin de Boulogne addressed the subject not once but twice. Valentin painted the composition which is now kept in Dresden around 1614/15 in Rome (cat. 51).[17] It is regarded as the earlier of the two versions and was ascribed to Caravaggio as late as 1906.[18] Like Caravaggio, Valentin combines the themes of play and deception in his painting. The composition shows two young cavaliers sitting across from one another and playing cards for money at a wooden table. It is the turn of the player on the right, who is about to discard a card. Even though he holds his tightly fanned hand close to his body, an accomplice who stands behind him, emerging from the dark, reveals the value of the card to be discarded by means of finger signs to the opponent with the bright red beret and white feather. The card the opponent is hiding in his right hand behind his back, visible only to the viewer but not to the other player, also suggests that something is fishy. By allowing viewers to see the hidden card, they are implicated in the cheating and almost turned into witnesses, if not accomplices.[19] The backs of the cards are blank, rather than having patterns printed on them, as was common north of the Alps even then. This gave cardsharps the opportunity to mark individual cards with dirt streaks, so that they could recognise them. Valentin's card players are characterised by a fascinatingly nuanced colour scheme of reds and earth tones which, in combination with the controlled light on a small stage against a dark backdrop and the proximity of the viewer, reinforces the intimate and harmonious overall impression of the horizontal-format painting. In this, the painting clearly departs from Caravaggio's *Cardsharps*, which unmistakably served as a point of reference for the Frenchman. Again, the splendid sword the cheated player has close at hand, as well as a second weapon in the hands of the plotter, indicate that the loss of the game as a result of card-sharping may not end peacefully.

Like Valentin's *Cardsharps* in Dresden, Nicolas Régnier's *Cardsharps and Fortune Teller* in Budapest also originally found its way into the collection under the name of Caravaggio (cat. 52).[20] Régnier created this version of the subject around 1623/25 in Rome, before moving to Venice. It is speculated that the painting was a commission for Vincenzo Giustiniani whose collection is recorded to have included a total of nine paintings by Régnier. It may be one of the half-length groups of players painted from live models, which Joachim von Sandrart saw in the Giustiniani collection in 1628 and described.[21]

In this group of nine figures, Régnier combines pictorial subjects that Caravaggio had still treated separately in his genre paintings. This aligned the painter, who trained under Abraham Janssens in Antwerp, with the compositions of his fellow painters from northern Europe, such as Gerard van Honthorst and Valentin de Boulogne, whose dramatically lit table scenes against dark backdrops draw far more on the example of Bartolomeo Manfredi. Even if Régnier's presence in Rome is documented only from 1620 onward, it is assumed that he was there from around 1617 on.[22] According to Sandrart,[23] Régnier adopted the style of Manfredi who was even thought to have created the painting discussed here.[24] The elegant costumes, including the silvery shimmering open shoes with dark ribbon worn by the young man who has crossed his legs, resemble those of Simon Vouet.

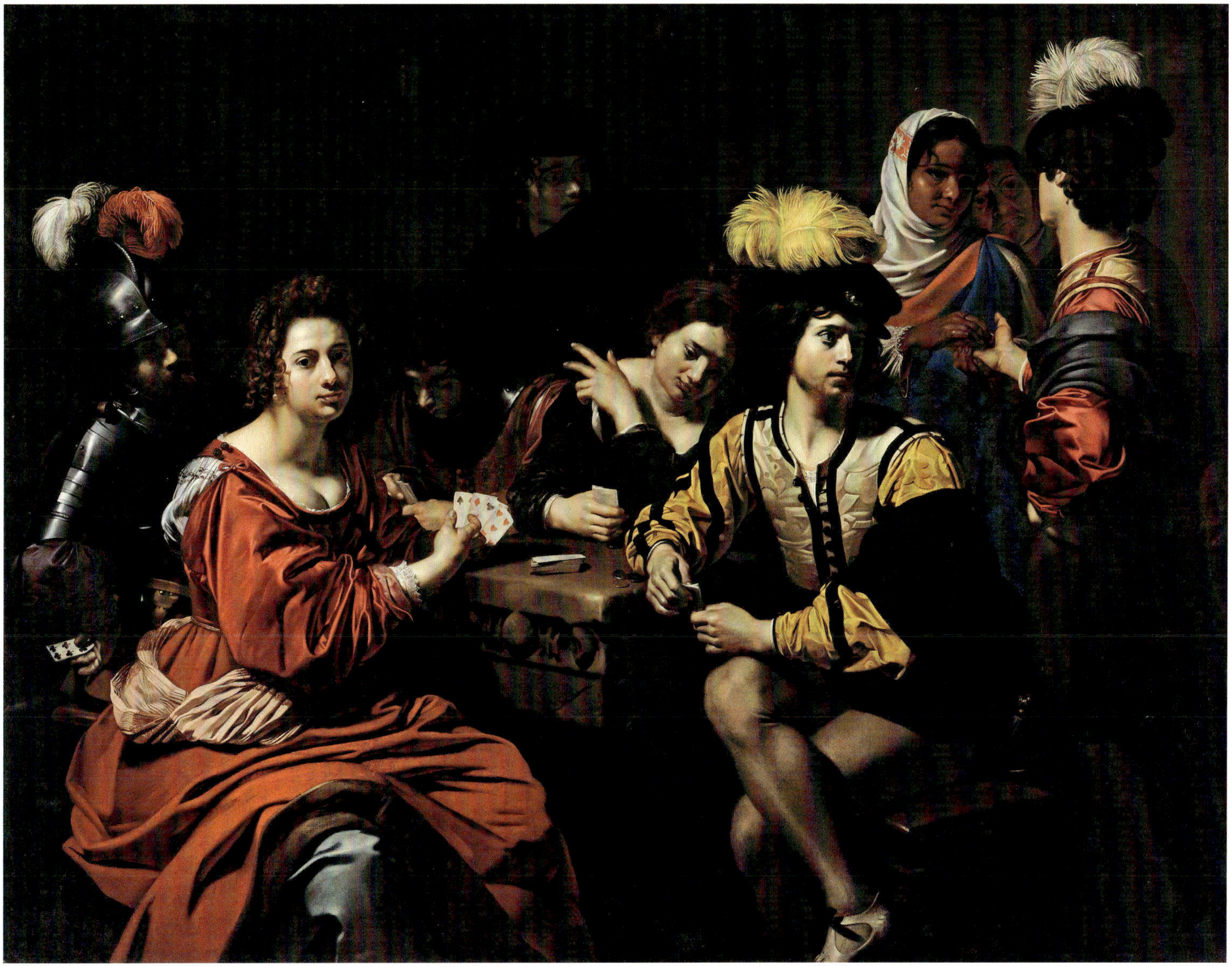

52
Nicolas Régnier
Cardsharps and Fortune Teller, c. 1623/25
Szépművészeti Múzeum, Budapest

Similar to Caravaggio and Valentin, the viewer here becomes a witness to the card-sharping: while the young lady dressed in sumptuous fabrics openly shows her hand to the audience to whom she turns, the soldier on the left peeks over her shoulder not just at her cleavage, but also at her cards, ready to play a hidden six of spades. Meanwhile, the second courtesan sitting on the opposite side of the table peers at the hand of the young nobleman with feathered hat to her left. The latter is distracted by the fortune-teller behind him and does not notice that the lady at the table next to him is using signs to reveal his hand to an accomplice emerging from the dark background.

During the 1620s and 1630s, when Caravaggism was particularly popular in the southern Netherlands, Theodoor Rombouts was among the most successful advocates of this style. Like Nicolas Régnier and Gerard Seghers, Rombouts is also said to have trained under Abraham Janssens. Working in Antwerp from 1625 onward after a roughly ten-year sojourn in Italy, the large-scale, horizontal-format genre paintings he created both as commissions and for the free market are characterised by a luminous background, sometimes with architectural elements and brilliantly colourful costumes of the figures (cat. 53). Similar to Dutch group portraits, the figures' heads are often arranged on the same level. The contrasting shades of radiant and cool blue, red, purple, white and ochre, which meet in the painting in Antwerp, are typical of Rombouts. The scene is brightly lit by a light source located outside the picture; hence we cannot speak of a night-time gathering, as in the case of the table scenes of Manfredi, Honthorst and his fellow countryman, Gerard Seghers (cat. 11). The moral reproach for passing the time in play rather than work is reinforced by the idleness depicted in broad daylight.

Common to all the scenes discussed here is the more or less obvious warning against the consequences of sinful diversions such as gambling, debauchery and indulgence in false love, and of wasting one's possessions in the process. Combined with this is the call to tame one's passions.[25] Special attention is given to gambling in the midst of unsavoury characters, loose women, gypsies and matchmakers, the outcome of which is entirely unpredictable, especially since the profitable stakes fostered cheating. Because the outcome of the game instantly decided who won and who lost, it provoked an immediate emotional response from the players. In exaggerating reality, the Caravaggesque paintings with their life-size figures, which seem close enough to touch, impressively convey this moment of tension. BE

1 Dimensions incl. the later additions (5.7 cm on the left and 5.1 cm on the right); Slatkes/Franits 2007, p. 158.
2 Slatkes 1965, pp. 75, 128. c. 1622, canvas, 96.5 × 124 cm, formerly private collection. Franits 2004, pp. 69–71; Franits 2013a, pp. 142–144, cat. A28.
3 Exhibited most recently in 2017 at the Centraal Museum, Utrecht; Exh. cat. Utrecht 2017, pp. 10, 35.
4 Volpe 1972, p. 51; Franits 2013a, p. 142.
5 *The Procuress*, 1622, canvas, 101.5 × 107.6 cm, Museum of Fine Arts, Boston, inv. 50.2721. Franits 2013a, p. 142. The 1623 *Gamblers* by Hendrick ter Brugghen (cat. 54), who turned to genre painting only after Baburen's return from Rome, is considered to be another point of reference.
6 Meier 2008, p. 78.
7 Köger 2008, p. 64; Meier 2008, pp. 89–92.
8 Feigenbaum 1996/97; Langdon 2001; Langdon 2012; Exh. cat. Montale 2013/14.
9 c. 1595, canvas, 94.2 × 130.9 cm, Kimbell Art Museum, Fort Worth, inv. AP 1987.06. For its date see Mahon 1988, p. 22. Description by Bellori 1672, p. 216. For Del Monte as a gamer, see Langdon 2012, p. 11.
10 See, for example, his *Cardplayers*, c. 1614/16, canvas, 130 × 191.5 cm, formerly Galleria degli Uffizi, Florence, no inv.; Hartje 2004, pp. 331–33, cat. A19, fig. 11 on p. 474.
11 Etching, 210 × 147 mm, British Museum, London, inv. 1877, 0609.1532.
12 'Een Tuijscher en Speelder is een vuijl Catijf / Hij drinckt en verspeelt sijn gelt en Slaet sijn Wijf.' Franits 2013a, p. 146, replica 1, fig. 52 on p. 357; Exh. cat. Utrecht 2017, pp. 11–12.
13 Slatkes/Franits 2007, pp. 158–159, cat. A50.
14 The painting's restoration showed that the canvas was enlarged at the left and right edges by a few centimetres each side. In its original dimensions, the painting's effect of proximity was thus a little stronger.
15 For the symbolic meaning of the suits of a deck of cards, see Wind 1989, pp. 16–17.
16 Exh. cat. Amsterdam 1976, p. 110.
17 Exh. cat. New York/Paris 2016/17, pp. 92–94, cat. 6.
18 Cat. Dresden 2005, vol. 1, p. 307, vol. 2, p. 560, no. 2010, c. 1615/18. Second version: *Soldiers Playing Cards and Dice (The Cheats)*, c. 1615, canvas, 121 × 152 cm, National Gallery of Art, Washington, D.C. inv. 1998.104.1.
19 Aside from Caravaggio, other painters such as Georges de La Tour used this device; see Steinhardt-Hirsch 2011, p. 167.
20 Lemoine 2007, pp. 233–234, cat. 30.
21 Sandrart 1683, p. 368, no. LXII.
22 Annick Lemoine in Exh. cat. Nantes 2017/18, pp. 38, 258.
23 Sandrart 1683, p. 368.
24 Lemoine 2007, p. 233.
25 See for this Welu 1975.

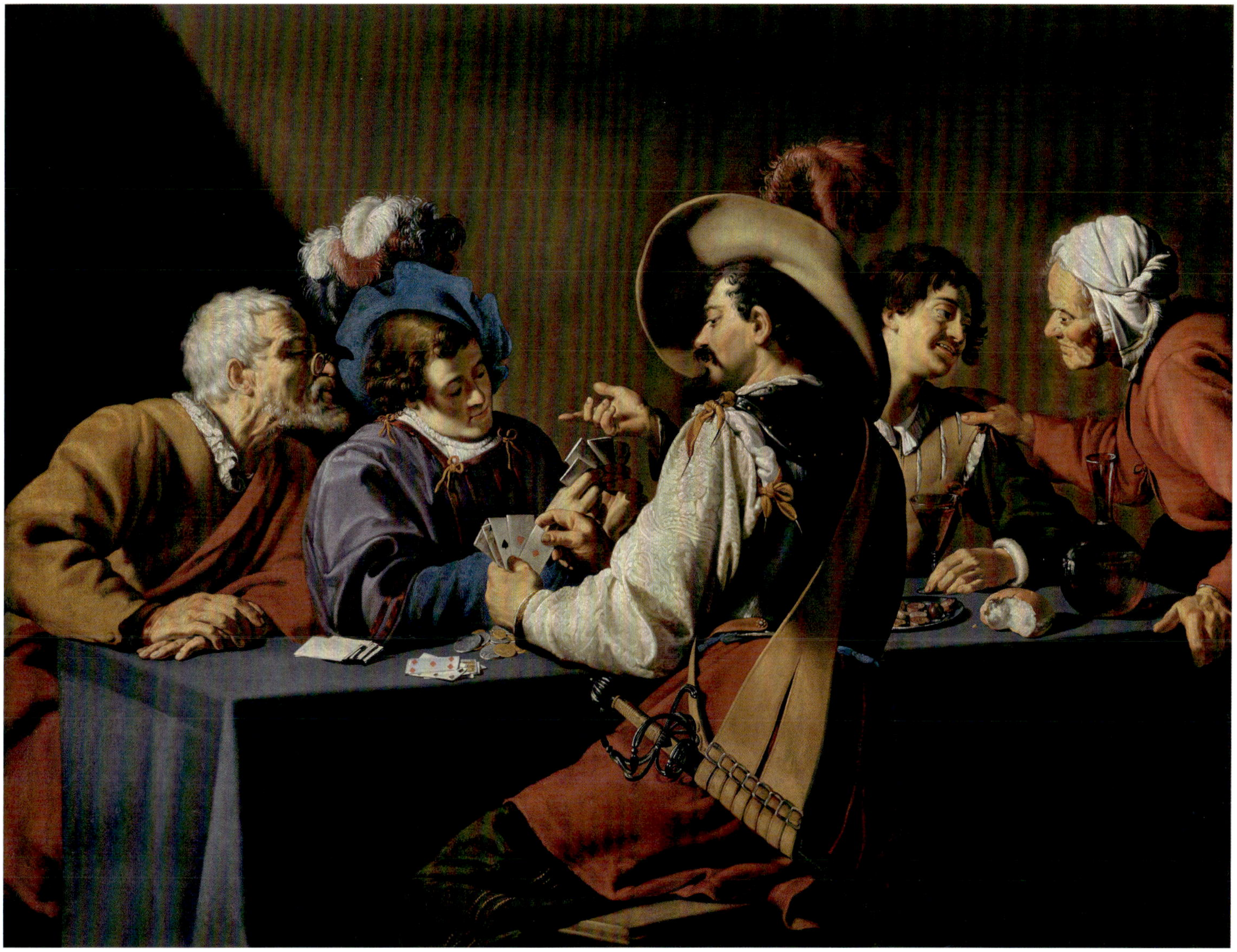

53
Theodoor Rombouts
The Card Players, c. 1630
Koninklijk Museum voor Schone Kunsten, Antwerp

1623

Prometheus

54
Dirck van Baburen
Prometheus Being Chained by Vulcan, 1623
Signed and dated bottom right: 'T.D. Baburen fecit / Ano 1623
Signed and dated bottom left, on a stone: 'Teodoor de / Babuer / fecit Ano 1623
Canvas, 201 × 182 cm
Rijksmuseum, Amsterdam, gift of J. von Loehr, Cairo, inv. SK-A-1606

During the last year of his life, Dirck van Baburen illustrated the myth of the Titan Prometheus who, after being condemned by the father of the gods, Jupiter (Zeus), was chained to a mountain in the Caucasus by Vulcan (Hephaestus) (cat. 54).[1] Each day, an eagle would feed on his liver, the organ which, in ancient times, was regarded as the seat of life. Prometheus' liver would then grow back overnight to be eaten again the next day. He received this cruel punishment for having stolen fire from the gods and given it to Man. The Prometheus legend has come down to us from various ancient authors.[2] But only the satirical stories of Lucian of Samosata and Aeschylus' tragedy *Prometheus Bound* have the young Mercury (Hermes) also present in this scene as a messenger; Baburen depicts him in the background with his winged helmet, the caduceus entwined by two snakes and a mischievous smile.

The torture of Prometheus was a frequently depicted subject especially in Italian art. In Dutch painting, by contrast, the subject is rather rare.[3] One of the best-known representations is by Peter Paul Rubens; he started working on it around 1611/12 and completed it before 1618 (fig. 90).[4] From 1618 on, this painting was in the possession of the English ambassador in The Hague, where Baburen may have seen it. Yet Baburen decided to depict the scene preceding the eagle's bloody attack: he shows the moment when Vulcan chains the Titan lying head down, on his back, to heavy stone slabs. The outstretched arms, the ghastly face with bulging eyes, and wide-open, screaming mouth convey fear and panic. Vulcan's attributes, such as the fire tongs and the forging hammer as well as the glowing furnace in the background, suggest that the scene is set in his forge.[5]

Prometheus is depicted in extreme foreshortening, a device Baburen had introduced a few years earlier in his *The Capture of Christ* (fig. 91) in the figure of the chained slave Malchus who is squirming on the ground in the face of the knife-wielding Peter.[6] In a third variation by Baburen – which, like *Prometheus Being Chained by Vulcan*, is datable around 1623 – it is the body of Marsyas that Apollo is in the process of flaying (fig. 92).[7]

As Karel van Mander noted in his *Schilder-boeck* of 1604, the prevailing opinion in Italy was that Dutch artists, rather than excelling in the painting of figures, proved their skills in the imitation

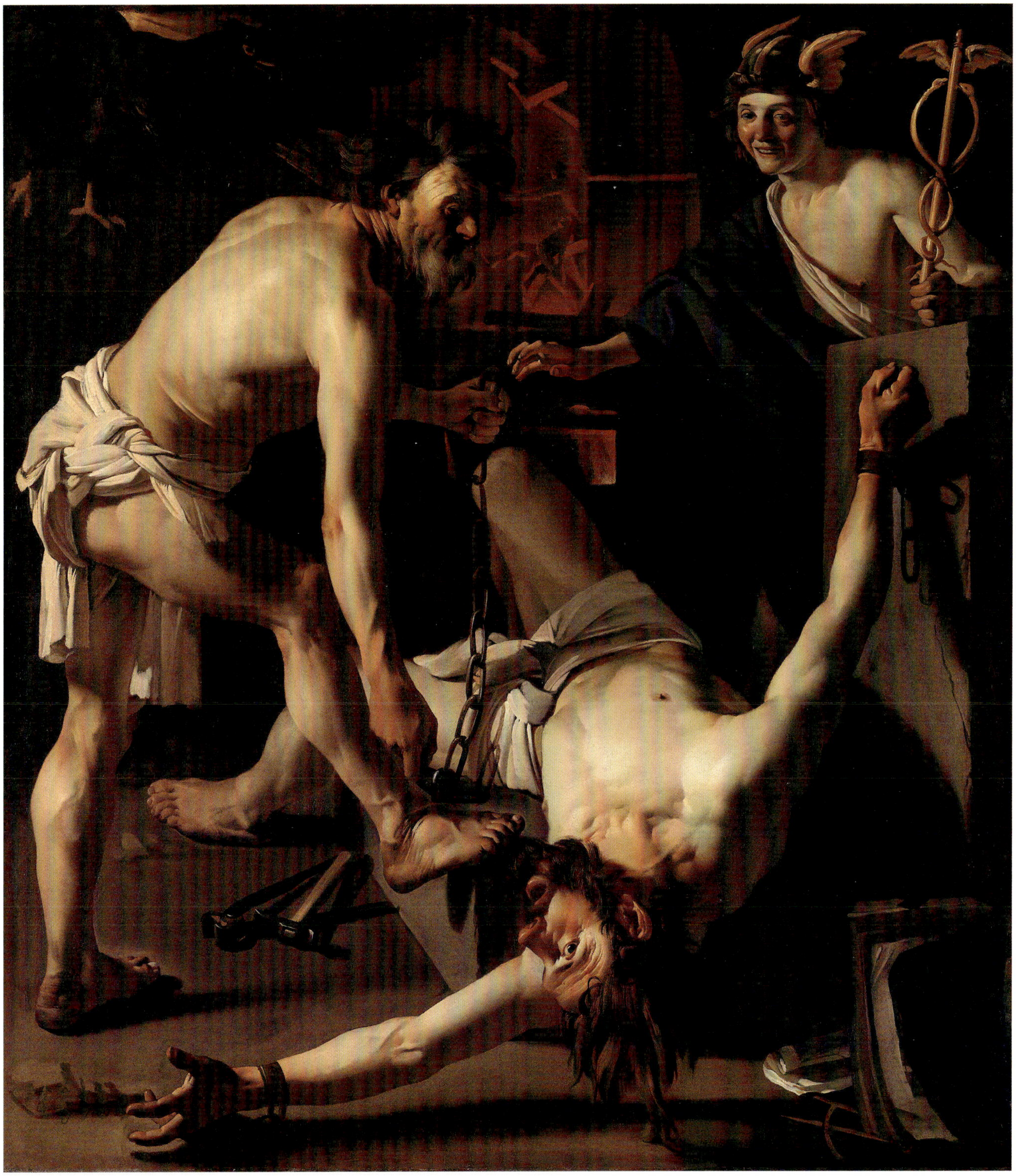

54
Dirck van Baburen
Prometheus Being Chained by Vulcan, 1623
Rijksmuseum, Amsterdam, gift of
J. von Loehr, Cairo

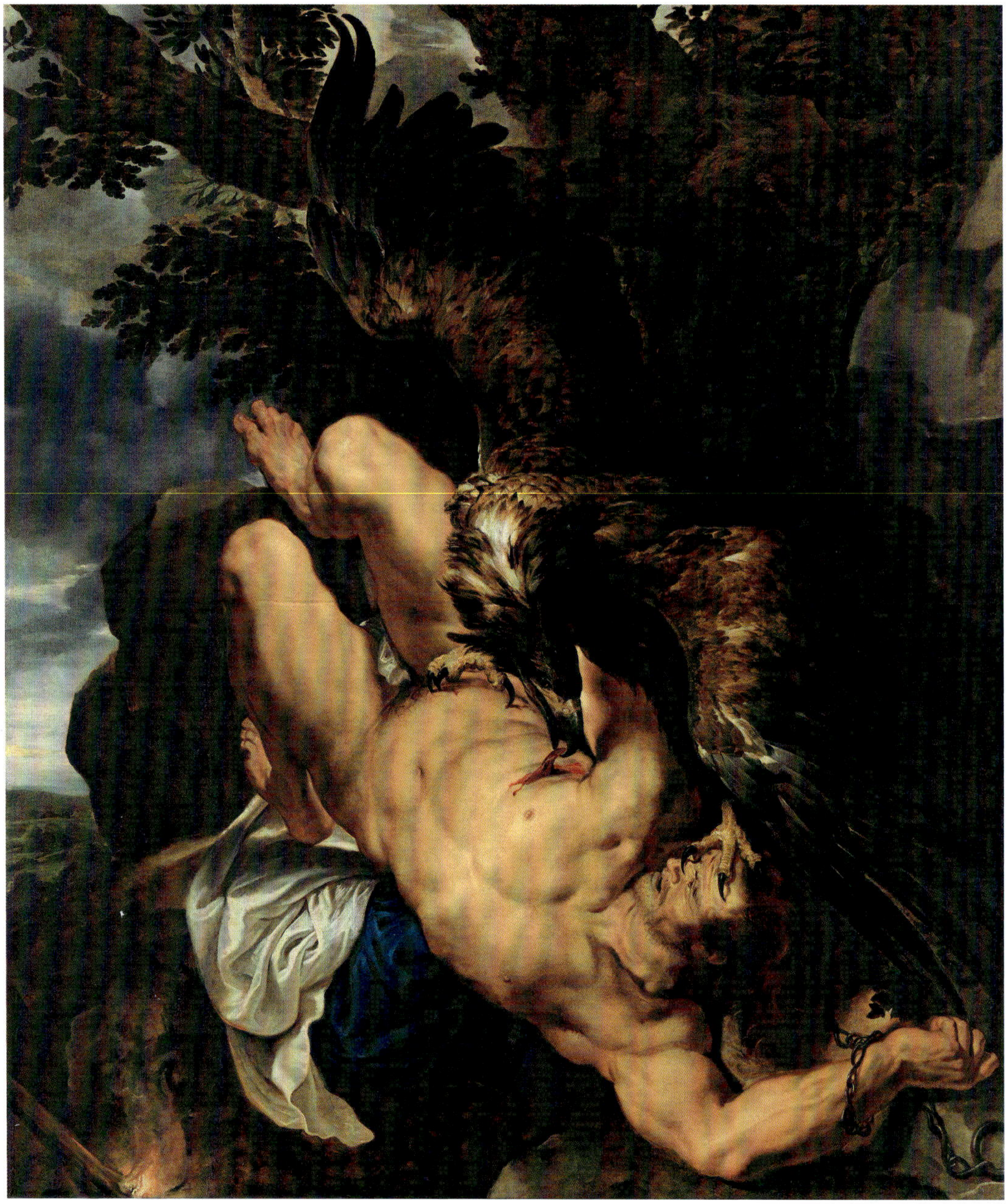

Fig. 90 Peter Paul Rubens, *Prometheus Bound*, 1611/12–before 1618, Philadelphia Museum of Art, Philadelphia, purchased with the W.P. Wilstach Fund

of nature and especially the depiction of landscapes.[8] Ever since the 16th century, Dutch artists sought to refute this prejudice, as the many examples of Dutch Mannerism show. For Baburen, as for Rubens, it may have been an incentive to choose a subject that allowed him to demonstrate his ability to depict nude, muscular and emotive bodies.

In creating such sculpturally and vividly moulded, life-size, gesticulating bodies on canvas, Baburen takes on the role of Prometheus as an artisan, a creator of figures. According to one version of the myth, Prometheus – whose name means 'forethought' – was involved in creating the first man from clay and educating him and therefore was regarded as the founder of human civilisation.

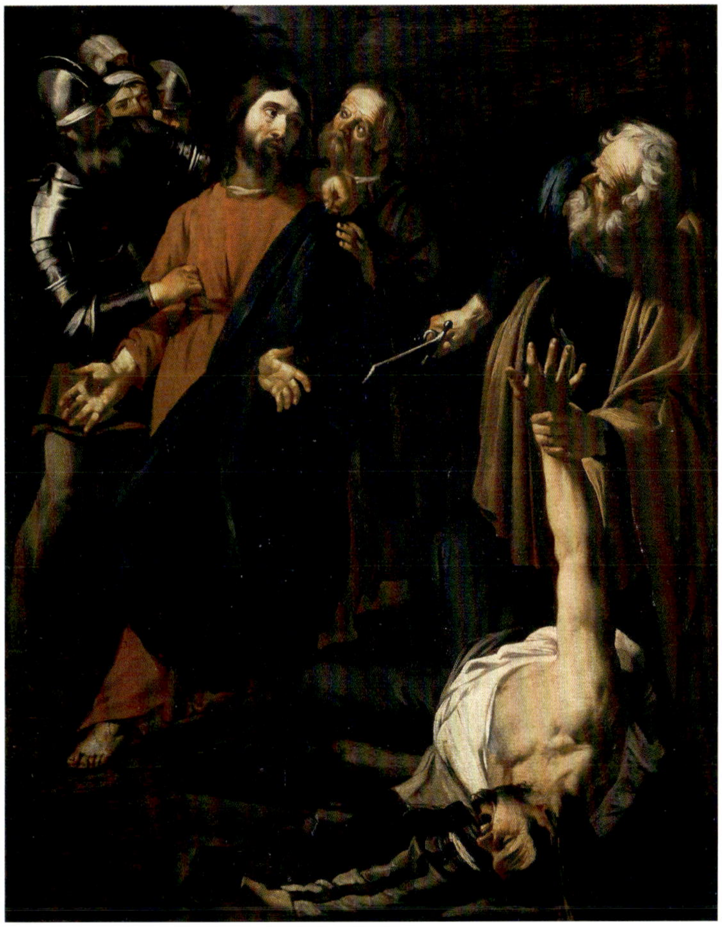

Fig. 91 Dirck van Baburen, *The Capture of Christ*, c. 1615/16, Fondazione di Studi di Storia dell'Arte Roberto Longhi, Florence

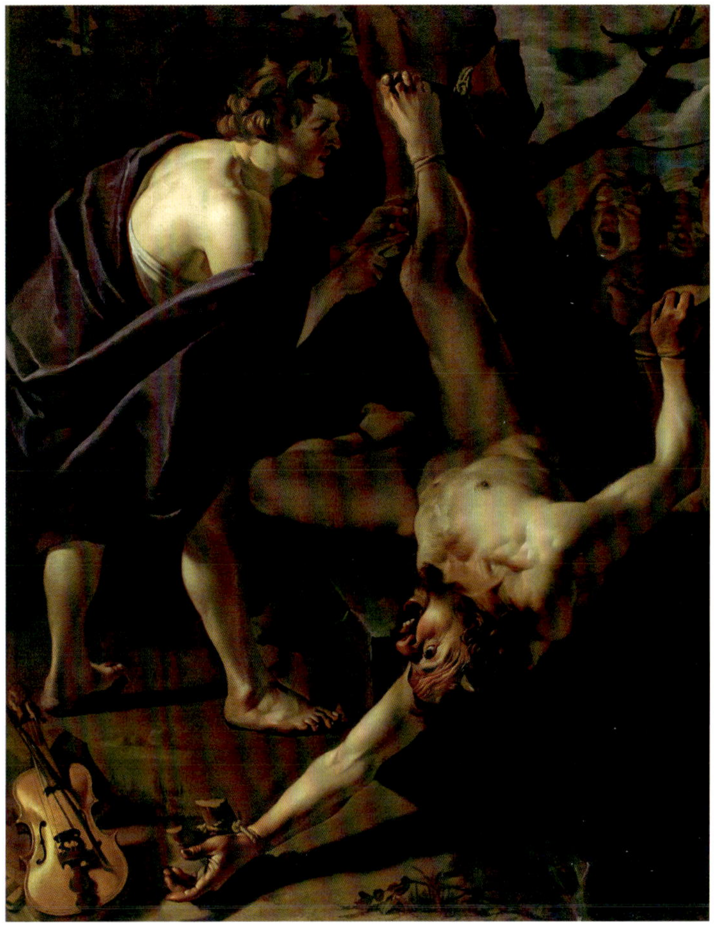

Fig. 92 Dirck van Baburen, *Apollo Flaying Marsyas (The Flaying of Marsyas)*, c. 1623, Museum of Fine Arts, Houston, Sarah Campbell Blaffer Foundation

His knowledge of the literary subject attests to Baburen's Humanistic education which set him, as an artist, apart from the craftsman.[9] This is indicated by the symbols of science – the compass, the gauge, the perspective drawing and the tome – lying next to Prometheus. The fact that the Utrecht painter signed this painting not once but twice, and used an Italianised variation of his name ('Teodoor') likely reflected a growing self-confidence. Baburen had been successful as an artist in Italy where great masters such as Titian and Raphael had also signed some of their works twice.[10] BE

1 Franits 2013a, pp. 151–154, cat. A30.
2 Hesiod, *Theogony*, 507–525; Lucian, *Dialogues of the Gods*, 1; Aeschylus, *Prometheus Bound*.
3 Among the few examples are Paulus Moreelse, *The Torture of Prometheus*, c. 1634/38, canvas, 75.5 × 62.5 cm, Centraal Museum, Utrecht, inv. 31287; and Jacob Jordaens, *Prometheus Bound*, 1642, canvas, 245 × 178 cm, Wallraf-Richartz-Museum, Cologne, inv. 1044.
4 *Prometheus Bound*, 1611/12–before 1618, canvas, 242.6 × 209.6 cm, Philadelphia Museum of Art, Philadelphia, purchased with the W.P. Wilstach Fund, inv. W1950-3-1.
5 According to Jonathan Bikker in Cat. Amsterdam 2007, vol. 1, pp. 57–60, the scene is set in the underworld (Hades).
6 c. 1615/16, canvas, 125.3 × 95 cm, Fondazione di Studi di Storia dell'Arte Roberto Longhi, Florence. Slatkes 1965, p. 101, no. A1; Franits 2013a, pp. 75–76, cat. 1.
7 *Apollo Flaying Marsyas (The Flaying of Marsyas)*, c. 1623, canvas, 192 × 160 cm, Museum of Fine Arts, Houston, Sarah Campbell Blaffer Foundation, acc. no. BF.2015.1. Franits 2013a, pp. 162–164, cat. A34.
8 Van Mander 1604, chap. 1, p. 7r.
9 For Baburen's education, see Franits 2013a, p. 4.
10 Franits 2013a, p. 152, cat. A30; Franits 2013b, pp. 9, 13, note 35. For signing habits in Dutch painting, see Van der Veen 2005, pp. 1017, and Tummers 2011, pp. 9497.

1623

David and Judith

55
Hendrick ter Brugghen
David Praised by the Israelite Women, 1623
Signed and dated at the bottom of the sheet of music: HTB rugghen 1623 [HTB in monogram]
Canvas, 81.8 × 105.4 cm
North Carolina Museum of Art, Raleigh, gift of the Samuel H. Kress Foundation, inv. GL.60.17.66

56
Michelangelo Merisi, called Caravaggio
Medusa, called *Medusa Murtola*, 1597
Canvas on panel, diameter 44.68 cm, circle diameter 48/49 cm
Signed bottom: f. michelan[gelo]
Private collection
Utrecht only

57
Simon Vouet
David and Goliath, c. 1621
Canvas, 123 × 95.5 cm
Musei di Strada Nuova – Palazzo Bianco, Genoa, inv. PB 2201

58
Jusepe de Ribera
David and Goliath, c. 1620
Canvas, 122 × 100 cm
Private collection

59
Valentin de Boulogne
David with the Head of Goliath and Two Soldiers, 1620/22
Canvas, 99 × 134 cm
Museo Nacional Thyssen-Bornemisza, Madrid, inv. 1981.16

60
Orazio Gentileschi
David and Goliath, c. 1605/07
Canvas, 185.5 × 135 cm
National Gallery of Ireland, Dublin, purchased 1936 (Lane Fund), inv. NGI.980

61
Orazio Borgianni
David and Goliath, 1609/10
Canvas, 119 × 143 cm
Real Academia de Bellas Artes de San Fernando, Madrid, inv. 93
Munich only

62
Bartolomeo Manfredi
The Triumph of David, c. 1614/16
Canvas, 128 × 97 cm
Musée du Louvre, Paris, inv. RF 1990 29

63
Orazio Gentileschi
Judith and her Maidservant with the Head of Holofernes, 1621/24
Canvas, 136.6 × 159.1 cm
Wadsworth Atheneum Museum of Art, Hartford, The Ella Gallup Sumner and Mary Catlin Sumner Collection, inv. 1949.52

64
Simon Vouet
Judith with the Head of Holofernes, c. 1620/25
Canvas, 96.8 × 73.5 cm
Bayerische Staatsgemäldesammlungen, Alte Pinakothek, Munich, inv. 2279

65
Valentin de Boulogne
Judith with the Head of Holofernes, c. 1625/28
Canvas, 97 × 74 cm
Musée des Augustins, Toulouse, inv. 2004 I 76

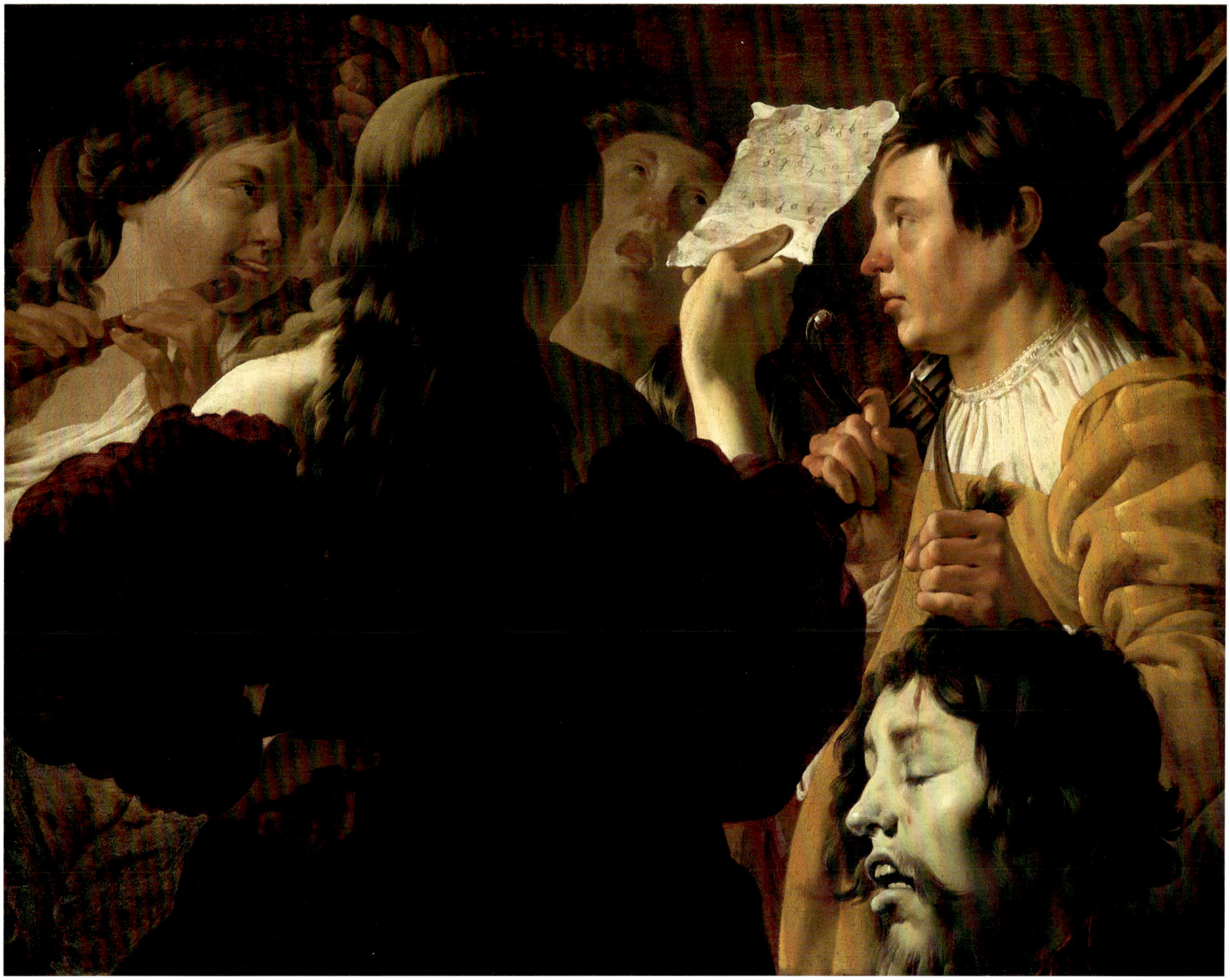

55
Hendrick ter Brugghen
David Praised by the Israelite Women, 1623
North Carolina Museum of Art, Raleigh

Scenes of beheadings, decapitated heads or both belong to the most aggressive category of iconography in painting and sculpture. Caravaggio's famous shield with the grisly head of Medusa is perhaps the most impressive example (cat. 56).[1] It is frightening not just because of the macabre expression on her face, the blood pouring out of her neck, or because of her hair of sinister, writhing snakes, but also because the myth said that you would be turned into stone if you looked into this monster's eyes. One cannot think of a better scene on a shield with which to defend oneself in battle. Scenes of the decapitation of mythological or biblical figures who symbolise evil inherently approve of the perpetrator, who is not an executioner but a respected individual who serves as a role model. Two of them are David and Judith, national heroes of the Jewish people. Brave and unflinching, they go out to do battle with the enemy. David beheaded Goliath, the fearsome champion of the Philistines, and Judith did the same to Holofernes, the commander of the Assyrian army.

1 Samuel 17 relates how David defeated the giant Goliath. The armies of the Philistines and Israelites had drawn up facing each other on the mountain slopes of the Valley of Elah. Certain that he could not be defeated, Goliath stepped forward and challenged the Israelites to choose a warrior who dared to come and fight him. The idea was that the winner of the single combat would also win the battle for his own people. Goliath is described as huge. With his scaly brass armour, helmet and leg greaves and a heavy brass shield, he was a terrifying sight, so no one volunteered to take him on. The giant ceaselessly mocked the cowardly Israelite army, until after 40 days David stepped forward. There were doubts about the suitability of the shepherd boy, who was anointed King Saul's successor by Samuel, the prophet and the Israelites' spiritual leader. It seemed inconceivable that this youth could defeat a trained, heavily armed professional fighter such as Goliath. However, as a shepherd David had killed lions and bears to protect his flock of sheep and lambs. Moreover, he was full of self-confidence, for he knew that he was strengthened by the word of God. He turned down the offer of a sword and armour, went to the river and collected five stones. Armed only with his slingshot he went out to meet the giant. The stone that he then slung at the Philistine penetrated so deep into his forehead that he dropped to the ground, and David beheaded him with the giant's own sword. As proof of his victory he took the huge head back to Jerusalem, where the women of Israel came out to greet him with singing and dancing (1 Samuel 18:6–7; cat. 20.1).

Holofernes, too, was killed with his own sword. The apocryphal Book of Judith, chapters 10–13, describes how the beautiful Jewish widow and her maidservant Abra managed to get into the Assyrian camp by claiming that they were deserters from their side. Judith then told Holofernes, the Assyrian commander, a totally bogus plan that would enable him to win the battle over her people. It took only a few days for him to fall in love with her. He invited her to come to his tent for a festive banquet, in the hope of sleeping with her afterwards. Judith, though, got him so drunk that he fell into a deep sleep. She then took his sword and with two blows cut off his head, which she put in an empty bag that her maid held open for her. They then fled and returned to Bethulia, the Jewish city that the Assyrians were besieging, where Judith showed the head as proof that Holofernes was dead. When the Assyrians discovered what had happened, they fled in confusion.

Scenes of David as a single figure with Goliath's head were extremely popular among Caravaggisti. Caravaggio used that kind of composition on at least three occasions. He painted the most famous version in Naples, shortly before his death (fig. 93).[2] He himself played the part of Goliath in the canvas, which he sent to Rome as a present for Cardinal Scipione Borghese in the hope that he would pardon him for his crimes. The tradition of concealed self-portraits originated with Giorgione, who depicted himself as David around 1510.[3] It was unique, though, for an artist to do penance and show remorse by portraying himself as Goliath, the embodiment of evil.

Caravaggio's composition is closely related to those of the Frenchman Simon Vouet (cat. 57) and the Spaniard Jusepe de Ribera (cat. 58). They are also upright knee-lengths, and they too show David holding the large sword in his right hand and the huge head in his left. One important difference, though, is that Caravaggio's David is holding Goliath's head up high and away from himself, whereas the others have the head touching David's body and resting on something. In their versions, David is looking out of the picture, almost surprised at his unlikely victory. Vouet and Ribera were contemporaries, and were both working in Rome around 1615/16. Although Ribera's *David and Goliath* dates from his Neapolitan period, the pronounced chiaroscuro contrasts hark back to his earlier Roman period.[4] The monstrous size of Goliath's head is very naturalistic. The young man's muscles are bulging from the effort of holding the gigantic, heavy sword. Vouet's David is a little chubbier and serene, and although this is one of the French artist's most Caravaggesque works it is also the most classicist of the two. Vouet added a companion

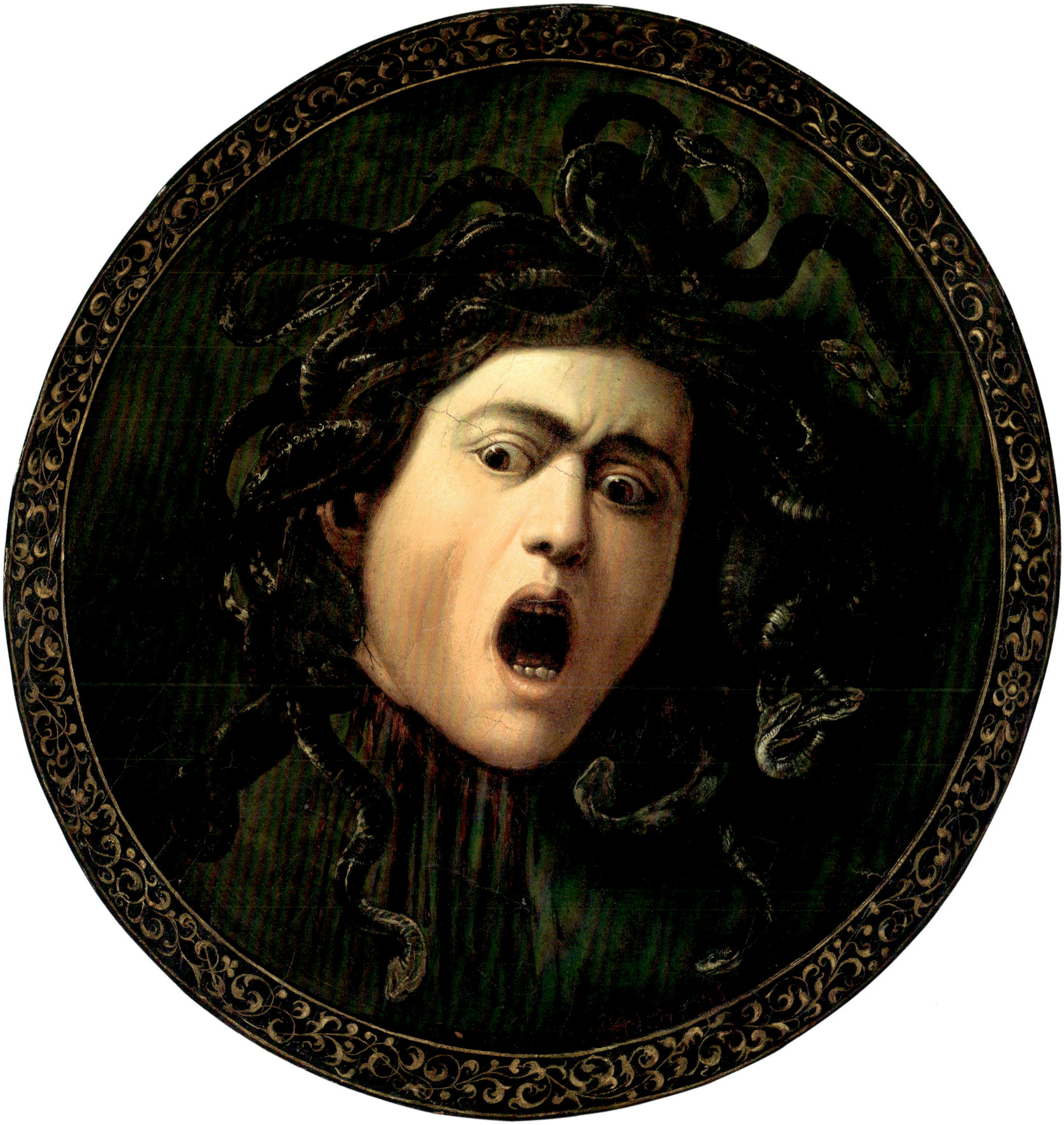

56
Michelangelo Merisi, called Caravaggio
Medusa, called *Medusa Murtola*, 1597
Private collection

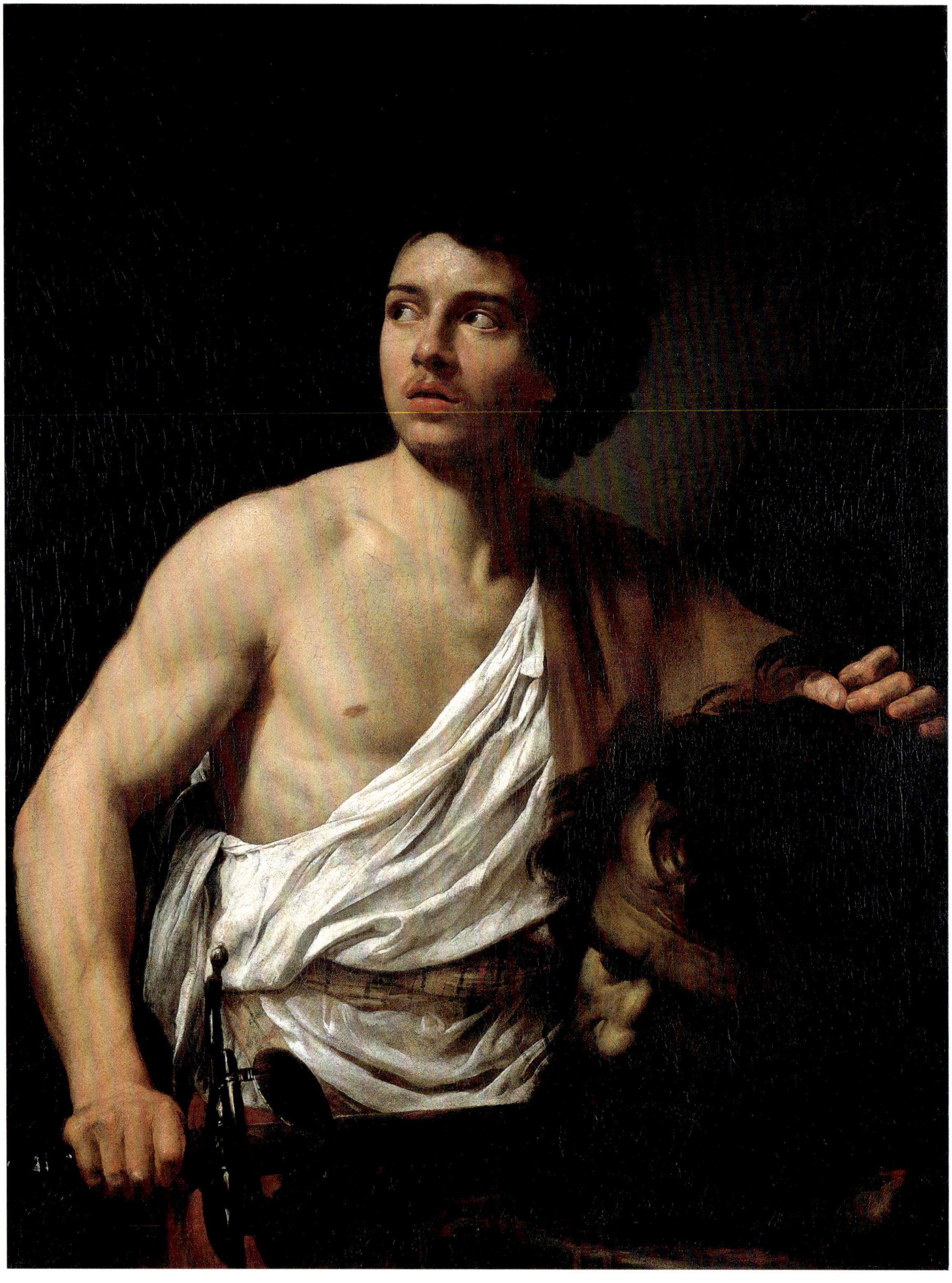

57
Simon Vouet
David and Goliath, c. 1621
Musei di Strada Nuova – Palazzo Bianco, Genoa

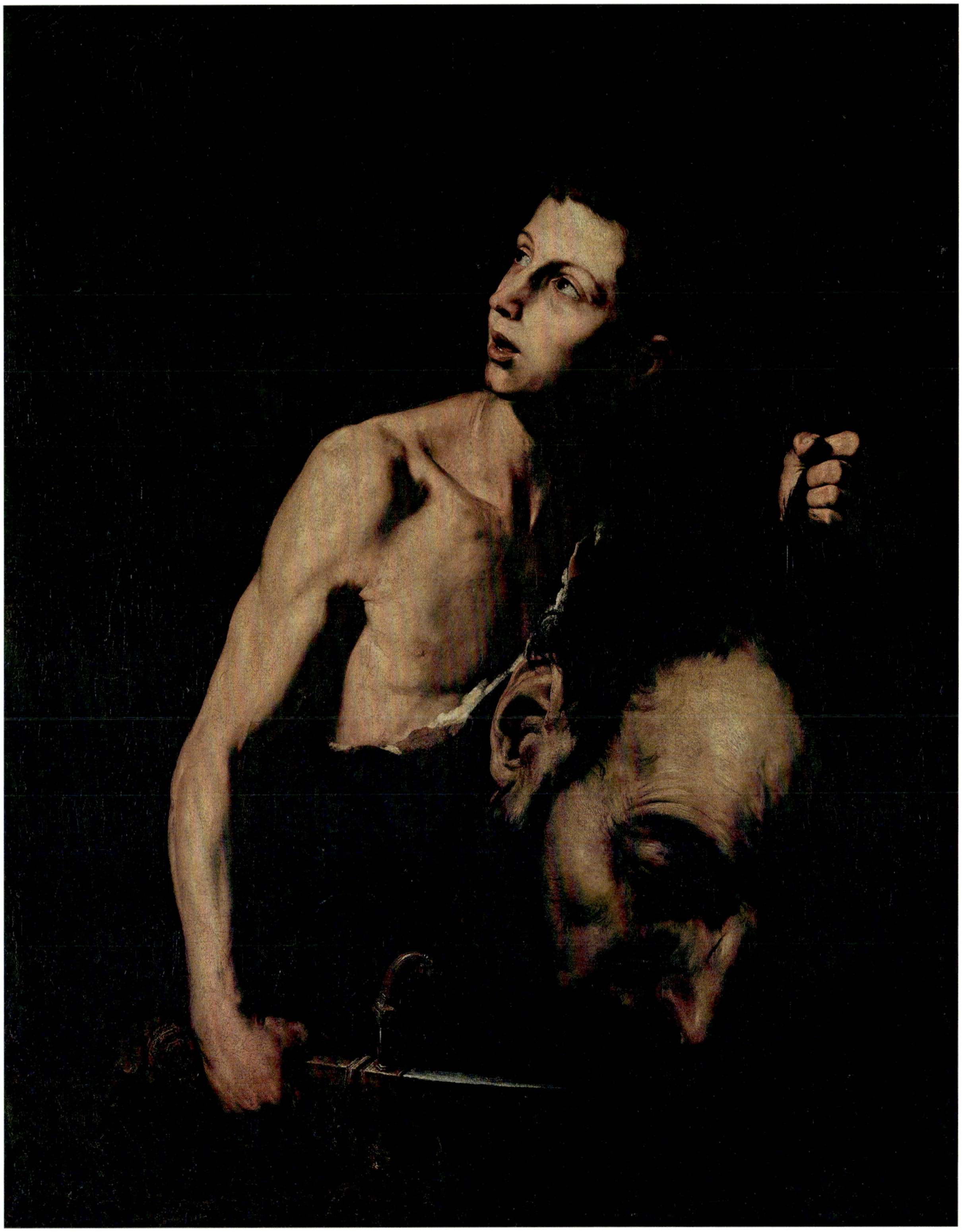

58
Jusepe de Ribera
David and Goliath, c. 1620
Private collection

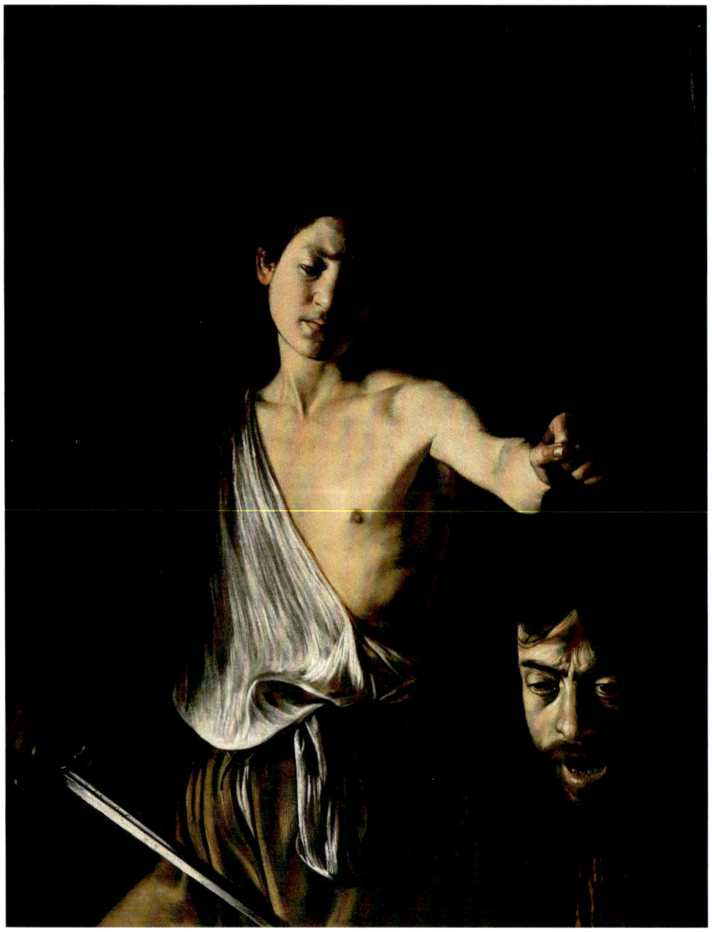

Fig. 93 Michelangelo Merisi, called Caravaggio, *David with the Head of Goliath*, 1609/10, Galleria Borghese, Rome

piece of Judith holding Holofernes' head on a balustrade in front of her as she and her maidservant look at each other. He painted the two canvases during his time in Genoa, where he was lodging with the brothers Marcantonio and Giovanni Carlo Doria. It emerges from the inventory drawn up in 1625 after the latter's death that the two pictures hung beside each other in the hall of the palazzo.[5]

The combative and beautiful David by Valentin de Boulogne is of a completely different order (cat. 59). He created an original composition by placing David between two soldiers. They are browned by the sun and are wearing contemporary armour, a plumed bonnet and a helmet. Goliath's bleeding head is lying on a stone table top between them. The pale shepherd boy, who is described as redheaded in the Bible, is bending towards us over the decapitated head, fixing us with a penetrating gaze. His slingshot is below his right hand and he is holding the sword with his left. His face is tense and concentrated, for it seems that he has just got back from the field of battle.[6]

The actual fight was also depicted by the Caravaggisti. Orazio Gentileschi painted David as an avenging angel who has raised his heavy sword high to cut off the giant's head (cat. 60). David is making eye contact with Goliath, who is lying on his back trying to ward off the blow with his huge hand.[7] Orazio Borgianni portrayed David in a murderous rage. Grim-faced, he is forcing the sword into his opponent's neck with both hands (cat. 61). Although the picture has occasionally been dismissed as comical in the later art-historical literature, the artists' biographer Giovanni Baglione called it Borgianni's masterpiece in 1641/49.[8] But all the same, how tiny David is in this showpiece compared to the gigantic, struggling Goliath.

Oddly enough, there are no such scenes of David and Goliath in the oeuvres of Dirck van Baburen, Hendrick ter Brugghen or Gerard van Honthorst. The only painting featuring David is by ter Brugghen (cat. 55).[9] In 1623 he painted the shepherd boy being serenaded by the Israelite women after his return to Jerusalem. He is unattractive, with his red nose, the sword resting on his shoulder and holding the ghastly, grey head of Goliath discoloured by death almost nonchalantly by the hair. He occupies a mere third of the painted surface. The woman with her hand on her hip, who is holding up the sheet of music for the flute player and female singer, occupies the rest. The singer has raised her eyes to heaven. In this way ter Brugghen created a remarkably original and daring composition that has nothing in common with all the other paintings illustrating this story.[10]

Bartolomeo Manfredi also painted David after his return to Jerusalem (cat. 62). His depiction is marked by an Italian elegance that is totally different from ter Brugghen's scene. The beautiful, dark-haired young man is holding Goliath's head by the hair in his left hand. His sword rests in the crook of his right elbow, with his hand supporting the blade. His only companion is a dazzlingly beautiful young woman with long, dark blonde hair. She is one of the women of Jerusalem who came out to greet David. They are walking off companionably to the rhythm of her timbrel.[11]

Judith is totally absent in the work of the Utrecht artists, but appears frequently in the work of the other Caravaggisti. Orazio Gentileschi painted Judith and Abra putting Holofernes' head

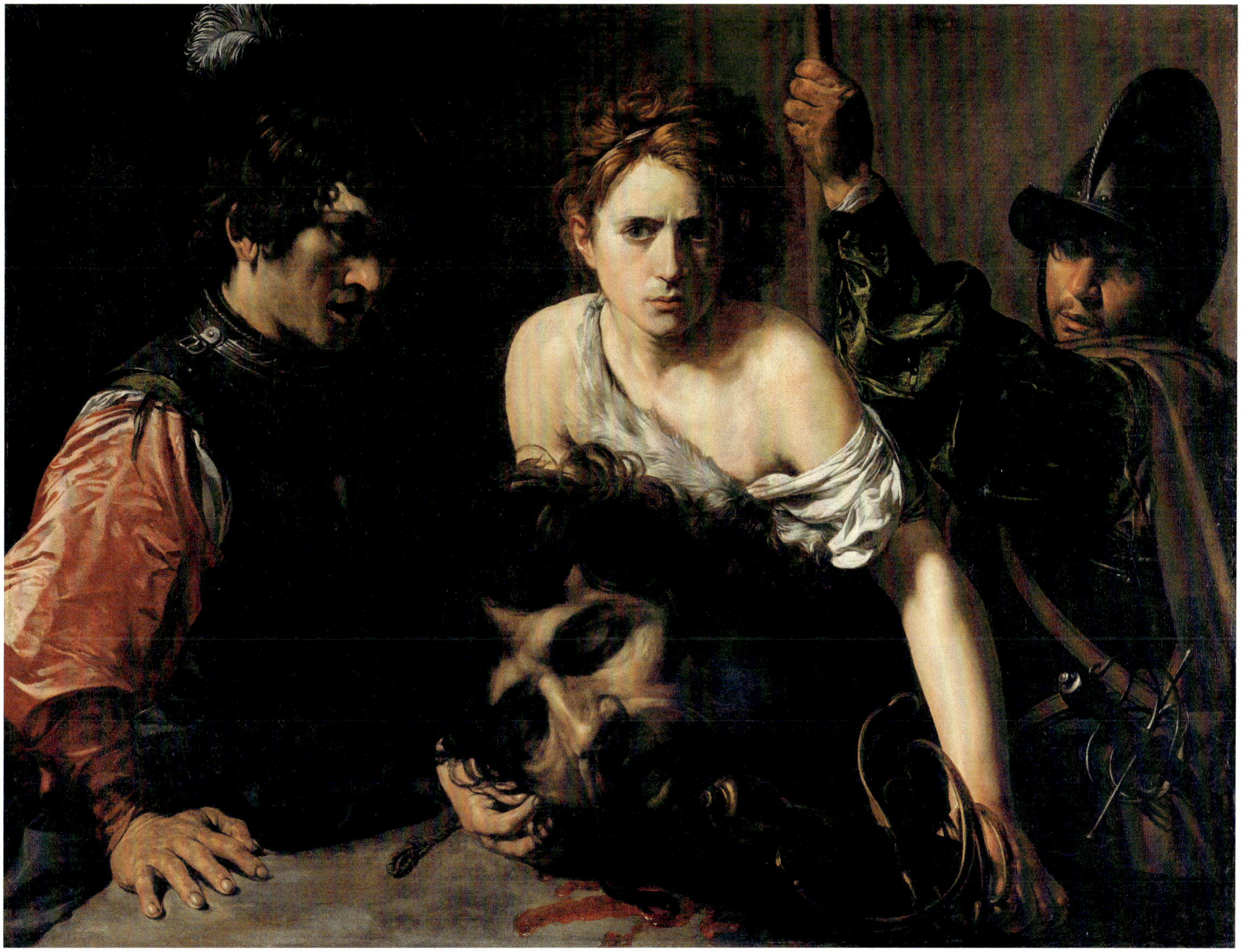

59
Valentin de Boulogne
David with the Head of Goliath and Two Soldiers, 1620/22
Museo Nacional Thyssen-Bornemisza, Madrid

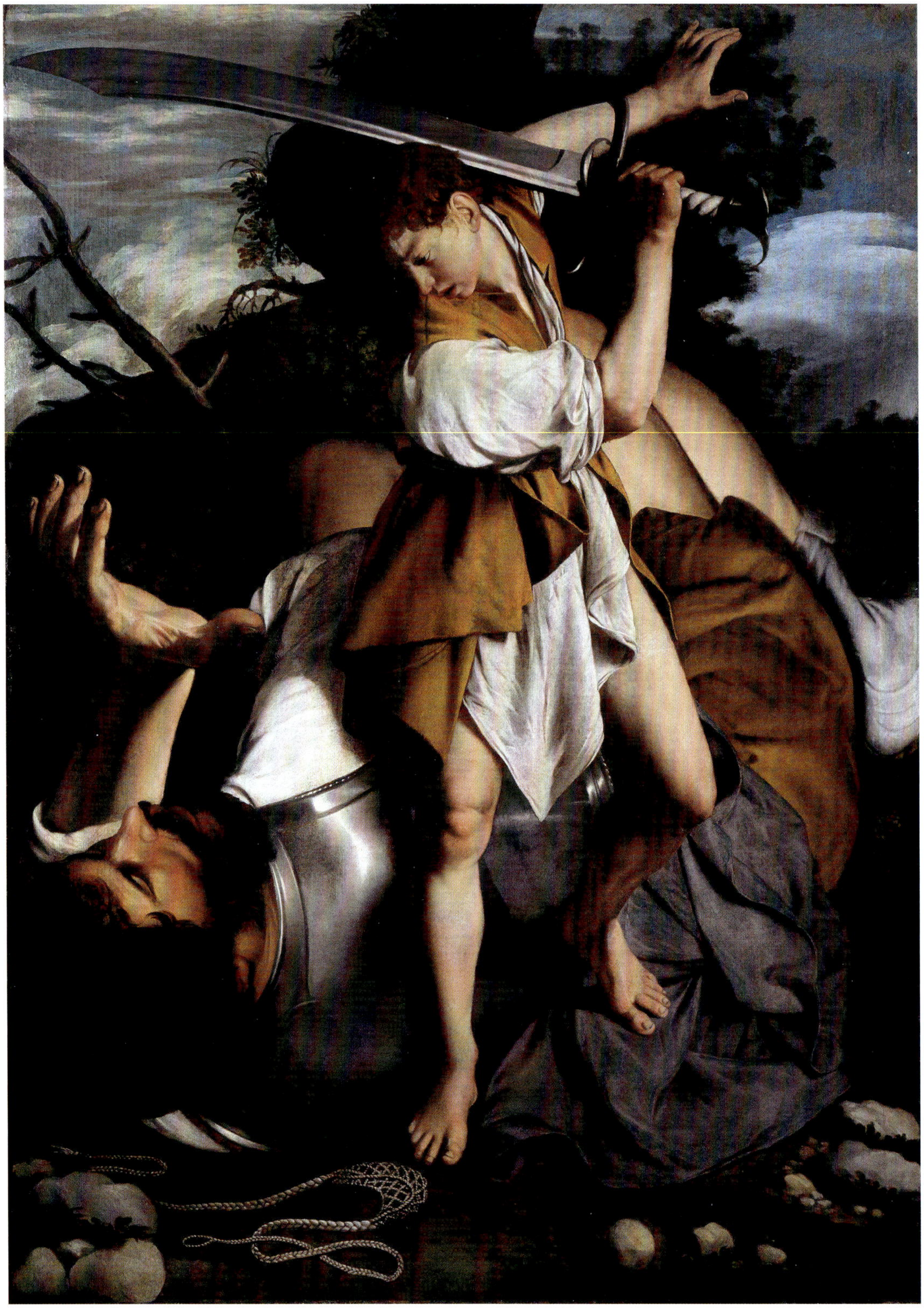

60
Orazio Gentileschi
David and Goliath, c. 1605/07
National Gallery of Ireland, Dublin

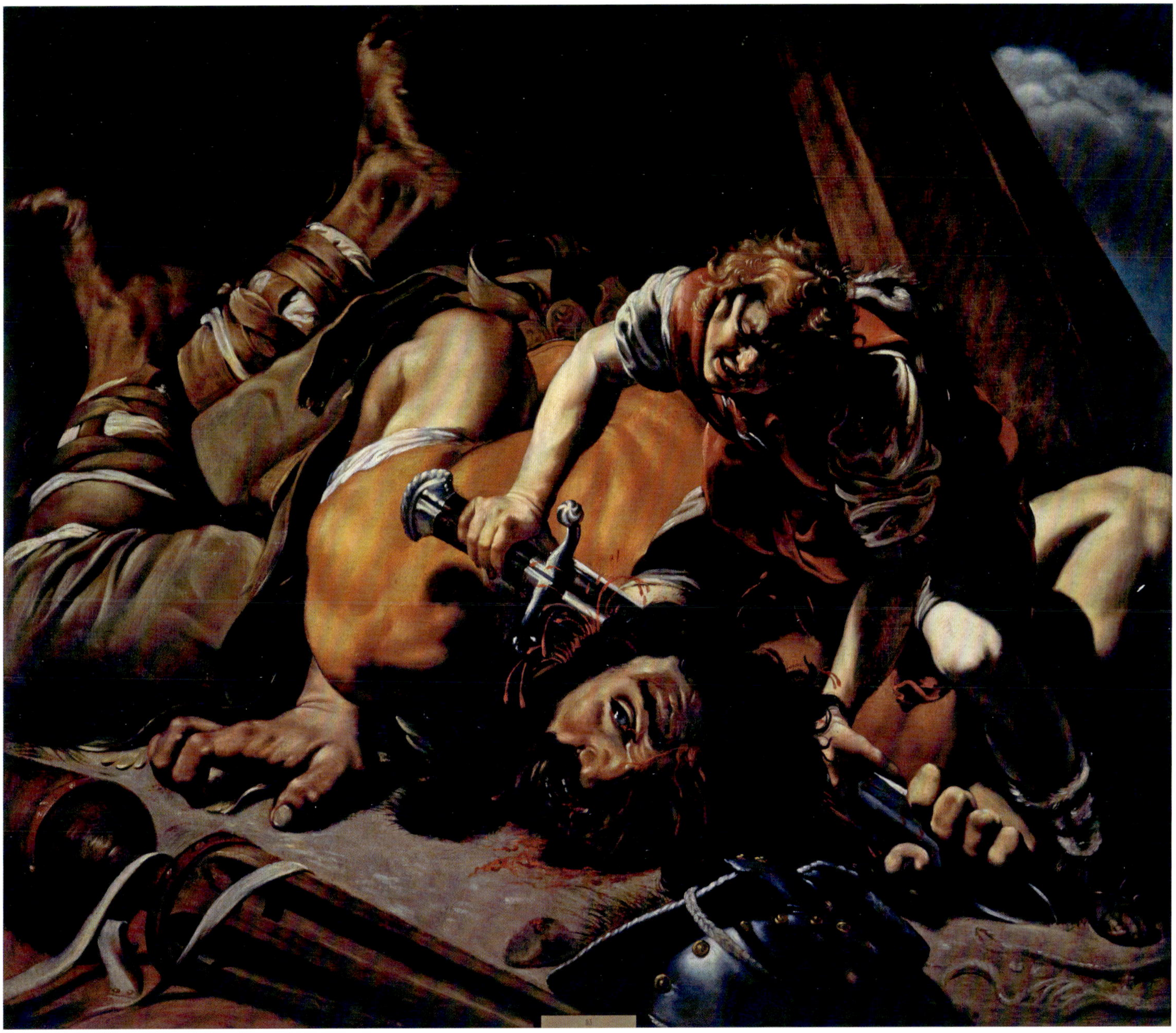

61
Orazio Borgianni
David and Goliath, 1609/10
Real Academia de Bellas Artes
de San Fernando, Madrid

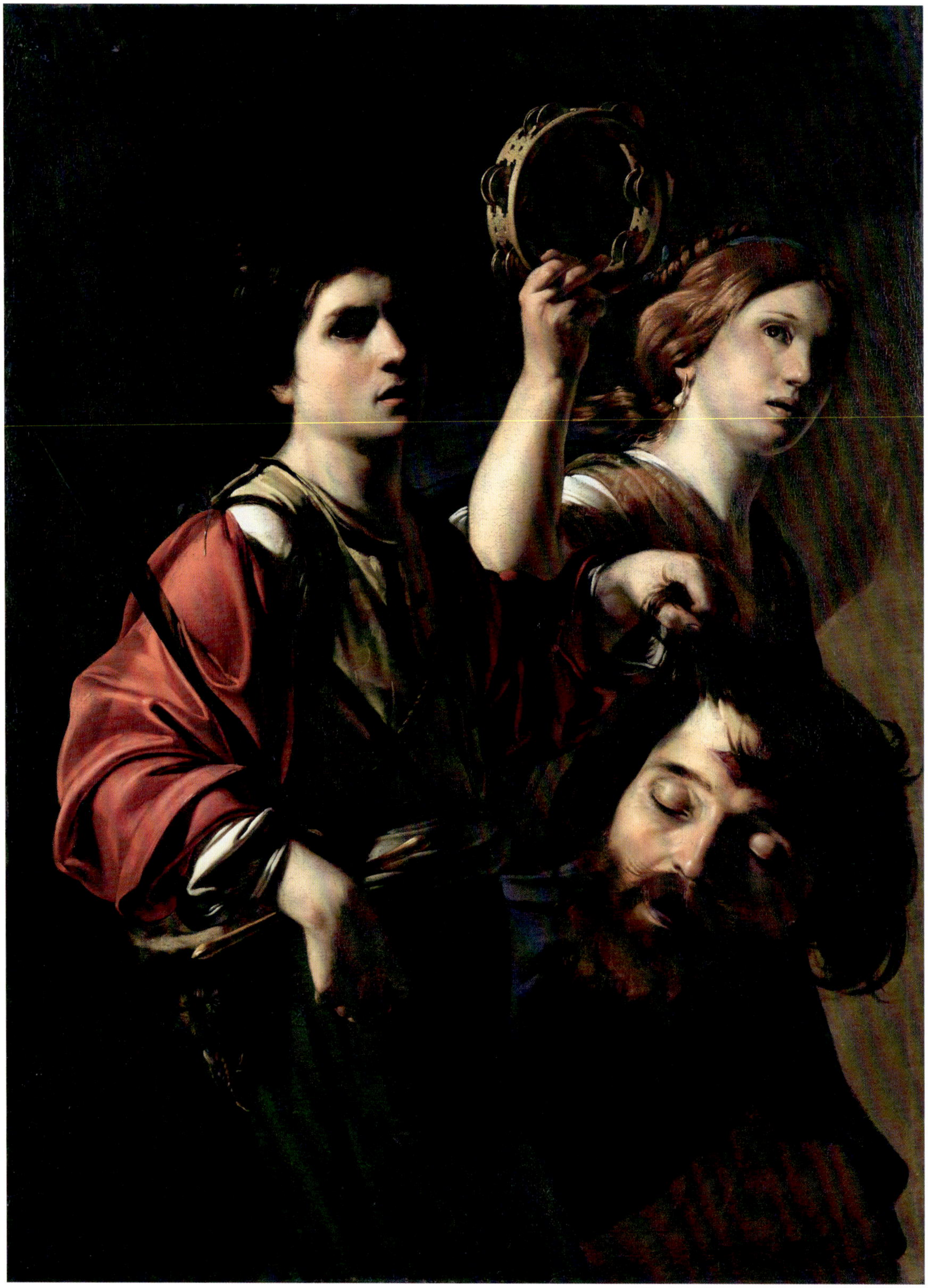

62
Bartolomeo Manfredi
The Triumph of David, c. 1614/16
Musée du Louvre, Paris

into a basket covered with a white cloth (cat. 63). Their fear of being caught is clear not only from the fact that they are looking in different directions but also from the watchful disquiet in Judith's eyes and the furrowed brow of her maidservant. The expressiveness of their faces, the superb imitation of materials, the harmonious palette and the simplicity of the composition make this an absolute masterpiece.[12] Simon Vouet and his pupil Valentin de Boulogne painted Judith as an isolated figure (cats. 64, 65). The two paintings are very similar. They are the same size, knee-lengths, and are of two attractive young women gazing out at us. They are both wearing costly blue gowns and jewellery.[13] Valentin's blonde Judith is pointing up at heaven with her right index finger as if bearing witness to God. At the same time it is a melancholy gesture of triumph, of seeking attention, as if to stress that the vital job has been done. She is holding the evidence of her victory, Holofernes' head, by the hair in her left hand while draping her wrist over the cross-guard of the sword decorated with the heads of monsters to keep it upright.[14] Vouet painted the heroine with a satisfied smile, resting her left arm on the head of her opponent. She is holding the hilt of the sword in her right hand, the blade loosely in her left hand, her little finger delicately raised.[15] It is not known whether these paintings ever had a pendant, as Simon Vouet's *David* did (cat. 57). LMH

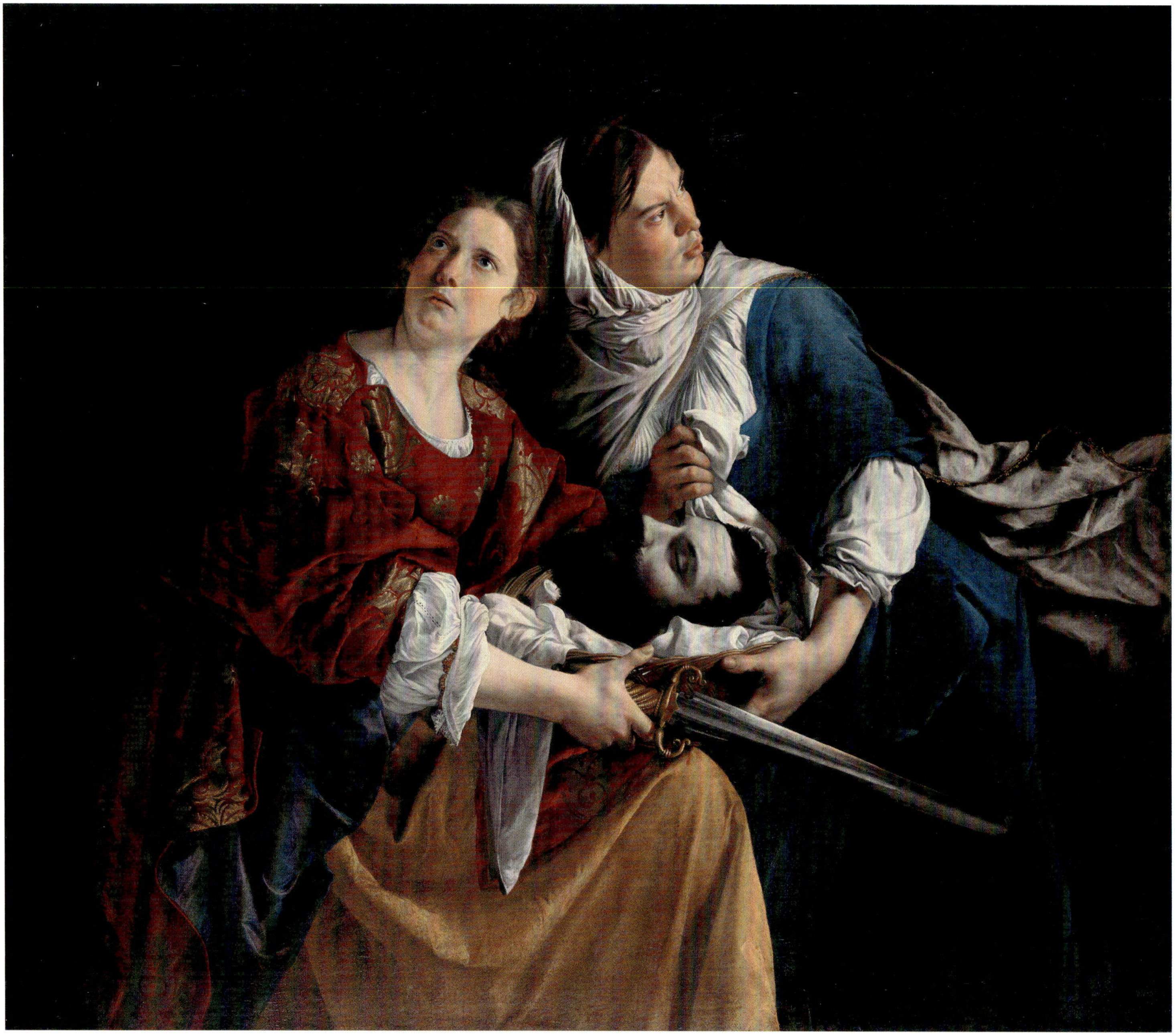

63
Orazio Gentileschi
Judith and her Maidservant with the Head of Holofernes, 1621/24
Wadsworth Atheneum Museum of Art, Hartford
The Ella Gallup Sumner and Mary Catlin Sumner Collection

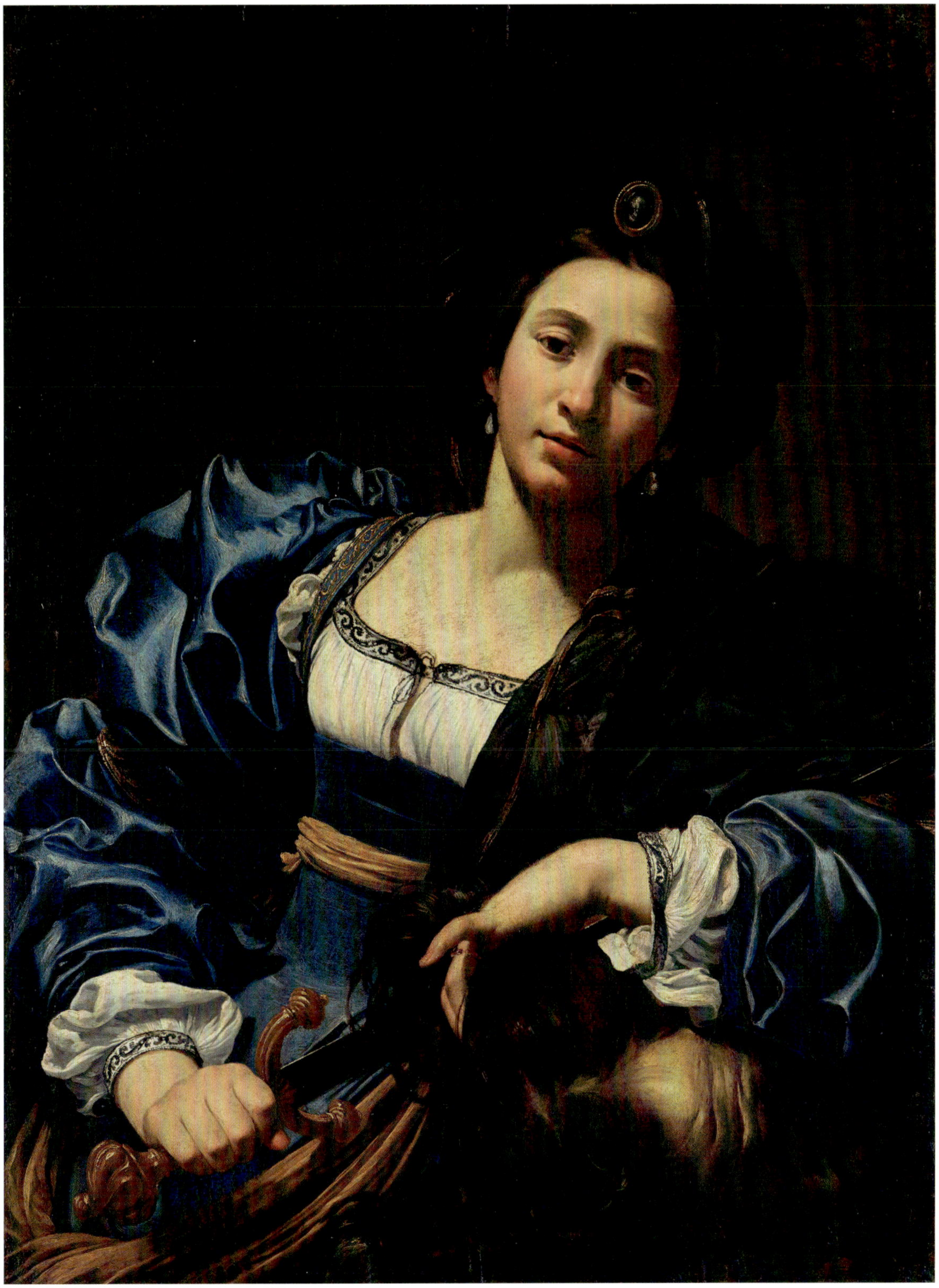

64
Simon Vouet
Judith with the Head of Holofernes, c. 1620/25
Bayerische Staatsgemäldesammlungen, Alte Pinakothek, Munich

1 On attribution and dating, see Ebert-Schifferer 2009, pp. 103–105, p. 288, cat. 60. A second version of the same theme: Caravaggio, *The Head of Medusa*, 1597/98, canvas on a poplar shield, diam. 58 cm, Galleria degli Uffizi, Florence, inv. 1351.

2 Caravaggio, *David with the Head of Goliath*, 1609/10, canvas, 125 × 101 cm, Galleria Borghese, Rome, inv. 455. The other versions are *David and Goliath*, 1598/99, canvas, 110 × 91 cm, Museo del Prado, Madrid, inv. 65; *David with the Head of Goliath*, 1606/07, panel, 95 × 116.5 cm, Kunsthistorisches Museum, Gemäldegalerie, Vienna, inv. GG 125. For Caravaggio's influence on the depiction of this subject, see Schütze 2011/12, pp. 282–291.

3 See Wenceslaus Hollar (after Giorgione, *Self-Portrait as David*, c. 1510, canvas, 52 × 43 cm (fragment), Herzog Anton Ulrich-Museum, Braunschweig, inv. GG 454), *The True Portrait of Giorgione de Castel Franco*, 1650, engraving, 228 × 195 mm, British Museum, London, inv. W,9.13. Langdon 1999, pp. 384–386, and Schütze 2009, p. 284.

4 The date is given as c. 1630 in the anonymous and undated sale catalogue of Christie's, New York. Justus Lange dates it c. 1618/19 and rightly points out that none of Ribera's other paintings owes such an obvious debt to Caravaggio's *David and Goliath* in the Galleria Borghese. Nicola Spinosa and Gabriele Finaldi date it around 1620. See Lange 2003, pp. 213–214, cat. A-30.

5 Simon Vouet, *Judith and Holofernes*, c. 1621, canvas, approx. 110 × 97, enlarged to 131 × 105 cm, private collection. In Exh. cat. Paris 1974, pp. 222–223, cat. 69, and figs. 23 and 24, this picture was wrongly described as the pendant to *St Catherine*, signed and dated 1621, in the same private collection. Both canvas, approx. 110 × 97 cm and enlarged to 131 × 105 cm. For Judith as the companion piece to David and the provenance, see Piero Boccardo in Exh. cat. Milan/Vienna 2005/06, p. 330, cat. IV.21; Adeline Collange in Exh. cat. Nantes/Besançon 2008/09, p. 132, cat. 27; Arnauld Brejon de Lavergnée in Exh. cat. Madrid 2016, p. 166, cat. 41.

6 Mojana 1989, p. 90, cat. 19; Michel Hilaire in Exh. cat. Montpellier/Toulouse/Los Angeles 2012/13, p. 188, cat. 38 (with arguments for a dating of 1620/22); Annick Lemoine in Exh. cat. Madrid 2016, p. 164, cat. 40 (as dating from around 1616/18).

7 Sergio Benedetti in Exh. cat. Milan/Vienna 2005/06, p. 188, cat. II.5; Axel Hémery in Exh. cat. Montpellier/Toulouse/Los Angeles 2012/13, p. 174, cat. 31; Laetizia Trevis in Exh. cat. London/Dublin/Edinburgh 2016/17, p. 80, cat. 13.

8 Alfonso Pérez Sánchez in Exh. cat. New York/Naples 1985, p. 102, cat. 20; Papi 1993, pp. 110–111, cat. 17; Marco Gallo in Strinati/Zuccari 2010, vol. 2, pp. 156–159, cat. VI.7. For a dating around 1607/08, see Judith W. Mann in Exh. cat. Montpellier/Toulouse/Los Angeles 2012/13, p. 114, cat. 12.

9 One possible reason for the subject's lack of popularity among the Caravaggisti is the idea that David, in line with the Council of Trent, supposedly symbolised the victory of the Catholic Church in Rome over the heretical Protestants. See Sergio Benedetti in Exh. cat. Milan/Vienna 2005/06, p. 188, cat. II.5.

10 See Slatkes/Franits 2007, pp. 81–82, cat. A5, and Bastian Eclercy in Exh. cat. Frankfurt 2009, p. 138, cat. 18.

11 The dating is according to Hartje 2004, pp. 325–326, cat. A16. Compare *La Zingara*, cat. 35. See also Maria Cristina Guardata in Exh. cat. Milan/Vienna 2005/06, p. 292, cat. IV.3, and Axel Hémery in Exh. cat. Montpellier/Toulouse/Los Angeles 2012/13, p. 174, cat. 31 (dated c. 1616/18).

12 For the bibliography on this painting see Judith W. Mann in Exh. cat. Montpellier/Toulouse/Los Angeles 2012/13, p. 122, cat. 16.

13 For both paintings, see Uppenkamp 2004, pp. 85–87.

14 Exh. cat. Paris 1974, p. 146, cat. 45; Mojana 1989, p. 164, cat. 55; and Axel Hémery in Exh. cat. Montpellier/Toulouse/Los Angeles 2012/13, p. 190, cat. 39.

15 In Loire 2011, p. 209, it is listed as workshop of Simon Vouet.

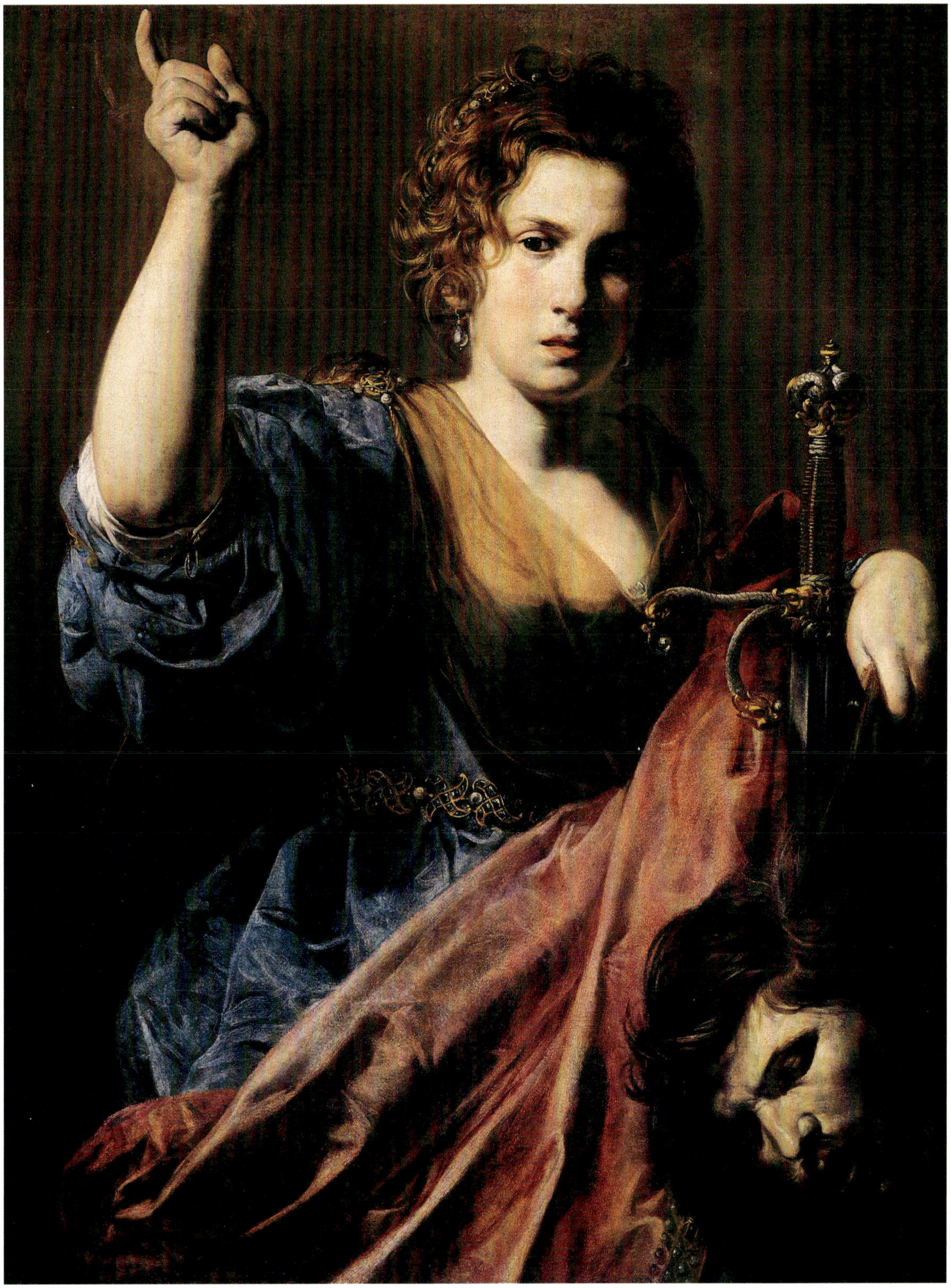

65
Valentin de Boulogne
Judith with the Head of Holofernes, c. 1625/28
Musée des Augustins, Toulouse

1623

Concerts

66

Gerard van Honthorst
The Concert, 1623
Canvas, 123.5 × 205 cm
Signed and dated top left: GHonthorst fe 1623
[GH ligatured]
National Gallery of Art, Washington, D.C., Patrons' Permanent Fund and Florian Carr Fund, inv. 2013.38.1

67

Hendrick ter Brugghen
The Concert, c. 1626/27
Canvas, 99.1 × 116.8 cm
The National Gallery, London, Bought with contributions from the National Heritage Memorial Fund, The Art Fund and the Pilgrim Trust, 1983, inv. NG 6483

After returning to his home town of Utrecht in the summer of 1620, Gerard van Honthorst created a number of genre paintings in which musicians are depicted as a single figure or as a group engaged in making music. Stylistically, they build for the most part on the candle or torch-lit night scenes he created in Rome, which had established his Europe-wide reputation (fig. 94).[1] At the same time, Honthorst created works that differed from his chiaroscuro compositions. These include the ceiling paintings inspired by Italian fresco painting, such as the fragment featuring a *Musical Group on a Balcony* of 1622 (fig. 95).[2] A similarly bright and colourful composition can be seen in his 1623 painting *The Concert* in Washington (cat. 66), which was probably created as a representative decoration for the main hall on the upper floor of Noordeinde Palace in The Hague.[3]

Honthorst dresses the merry company, including five musicians, with some festively decked out with berets and ostrich feathers, in brightly coloured and preciously iridescent cloth and groups them around a table covered with an oriental rug. The entire unspecified room is bright and evenly lit by a light source outside of the picture. The rear-view figure of a bearded string player with a bass viol depicted in partial shade in the left foreground serves as a repoussoir motif to lend the narrow stage spatial depth. As concert master, he points with his bow at a passage in the music book of the lute player, and a beat-tapping singer standing on the right at the head of the table. In the centre of the background, a smirking young man raises his glass of wine to us viewers, while at the same time admonishing us to be quiet and listen to the music. He is observed by a laughing couple on the far right, who seem to comment upon his actions with gestures.

The composition is characterised by cool hues and a variety of bright, contrasting complementary colours. Similar to his mythological, allegorical and pastoral paintings, Honthorst here combines elements of the classic, ideal style of an Annibale Carracci and the chiaroscuro effects of Caravaggio. In its bright, colourful composition the painting is reminiscent of the genre paintings Caravaggio created in the 1590s for Cardinal Del Monte in Rome. At the same time, it is related to the works of Honthorst's teacher, Abraham Bloemaert, in its use of colours.

Music played an important role for many patrons of the visual arts in Rome. Cardinal Del Monte and Marchese Giustiniani, for

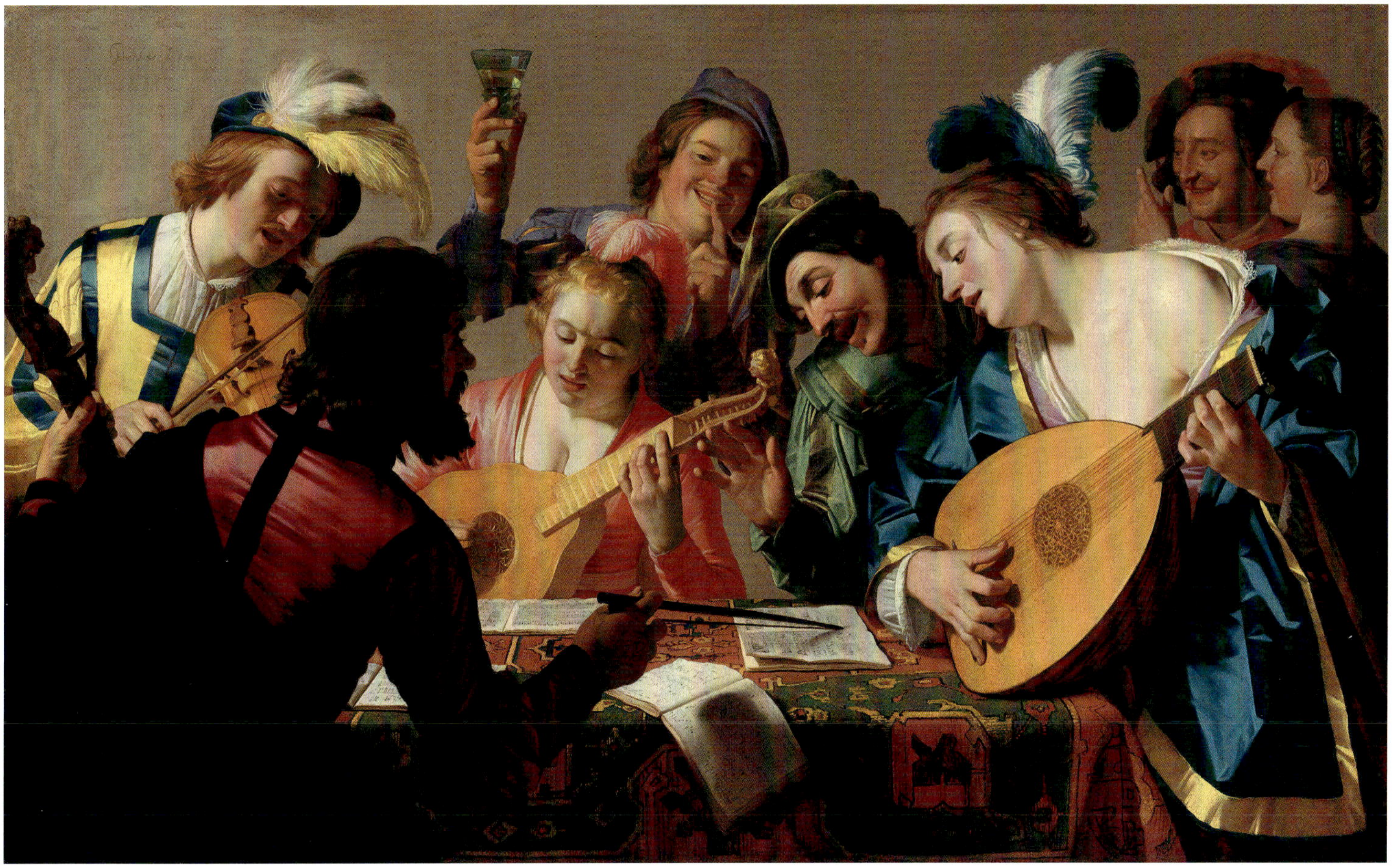

66
Gerard van Honthorst
The Concert, 1623
National Gallery of Art, Washington, D.C., Patrons' Permanent Fund and Florian Carr Fund

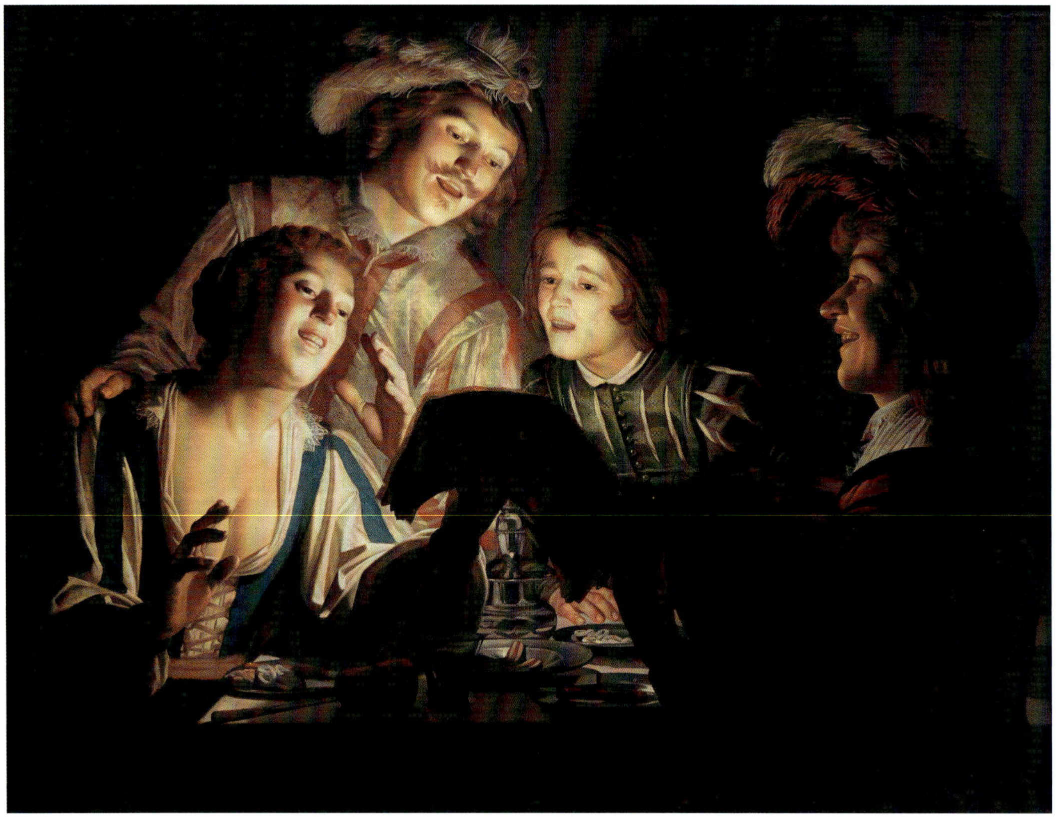

Fig. 94 Gerard van Honthorst, *Musical Group by Candlelight*, 1623, Statens Museum for Kunst, Copenhagen

example, were also among the great music lovers and patrons of their time.[4] In Utrecht, where the Musyckcamer opened in 1628 and the Collegium musicum Ultrajectinum was founded three years later, music making likewise was a regular feature of the social life of prosperous burghers.[5]

Some three years later, Hendrick ter Brugghen composed a characteristic variation of his own on the same theme (cat. 67).[6] In the light of a candle and an oil lamp hanging on the rear wall of the dark room, a lute player, a transverse flute player and a young singer join to form a musical trio. The two instrumentalists, who are shown from the back, turn towards the focused young singer who looks into an open part book and gives the beat with his raised hand. The viewer seems to surprise the intimate group through his arrival, as the two instrumentalists slightly turn without interrupting their playing. They wear wide, foreign and antiquated looking garments and headdresses which likely reminded the contemporary viewer of props of a stage play. The turban-like headgear, the red beret with a coin agrafe on the brim, and the stripe-trimmed clothes match the costumes of the courtesans, revellers, prostitutes' clients and musicians depicted in Dutch tavern and brothel scenes as well as the figures presented in the works of Caravaggio.[7]

The intimate group, which appears cohesive and absorbed in their music making, differs from most other musical groups of the Caravaggisti, which often have many more figures come together for a convivial gathering in high spirits. Rather than playing a concert for an audience, the three musicians practise the discipline of combining three musical 'voices' into a harmonious whole. The beat-tapping singer (*maet-zanger*) teaches to always strike the right balance in terms of *temperantia*, not just in music, but also in the consumption of wine and the other pleasures of life.[8]

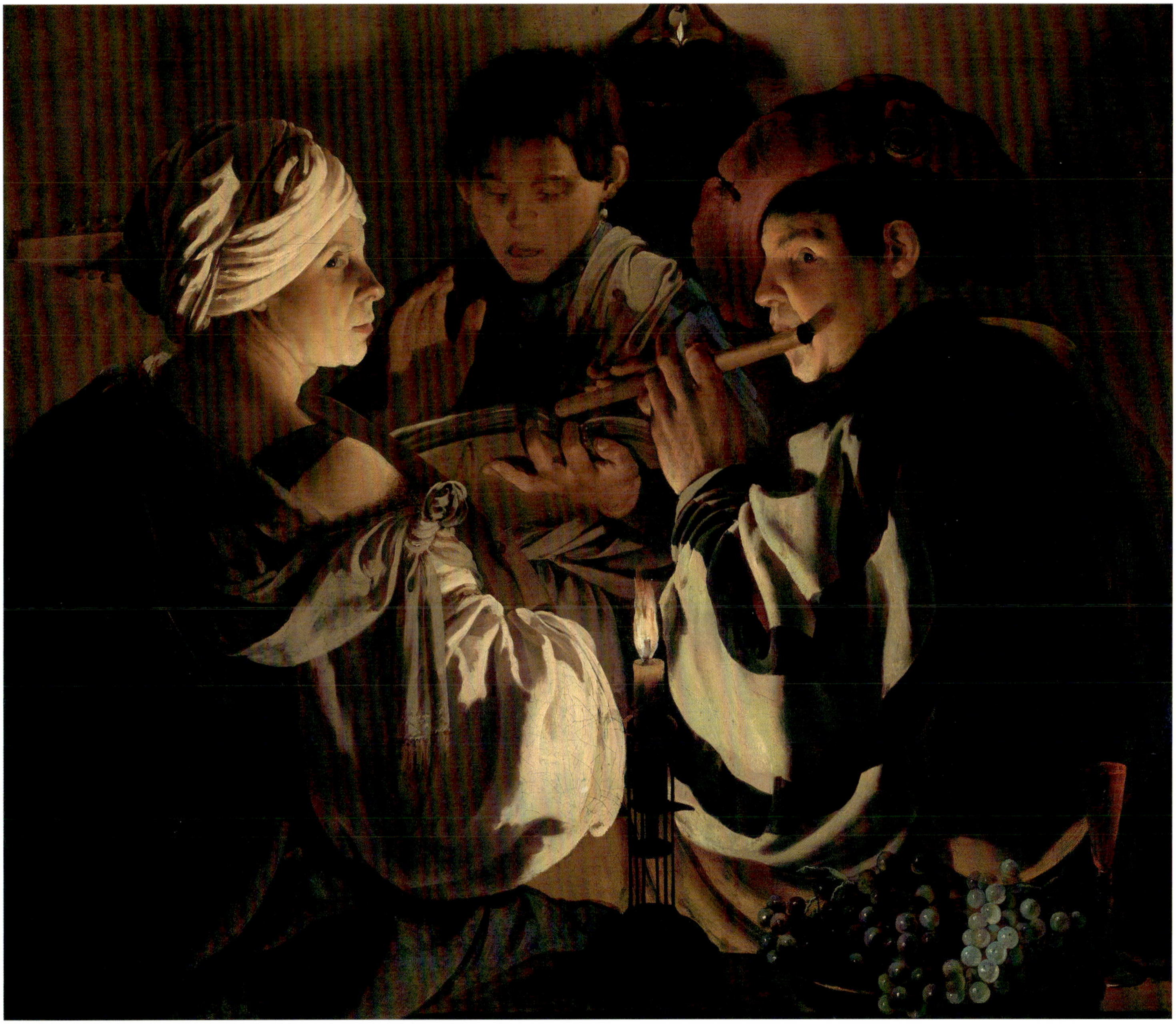

67
Hendrick ter Brugghen
The Concert, c. 1626/27
The National Gallery, London

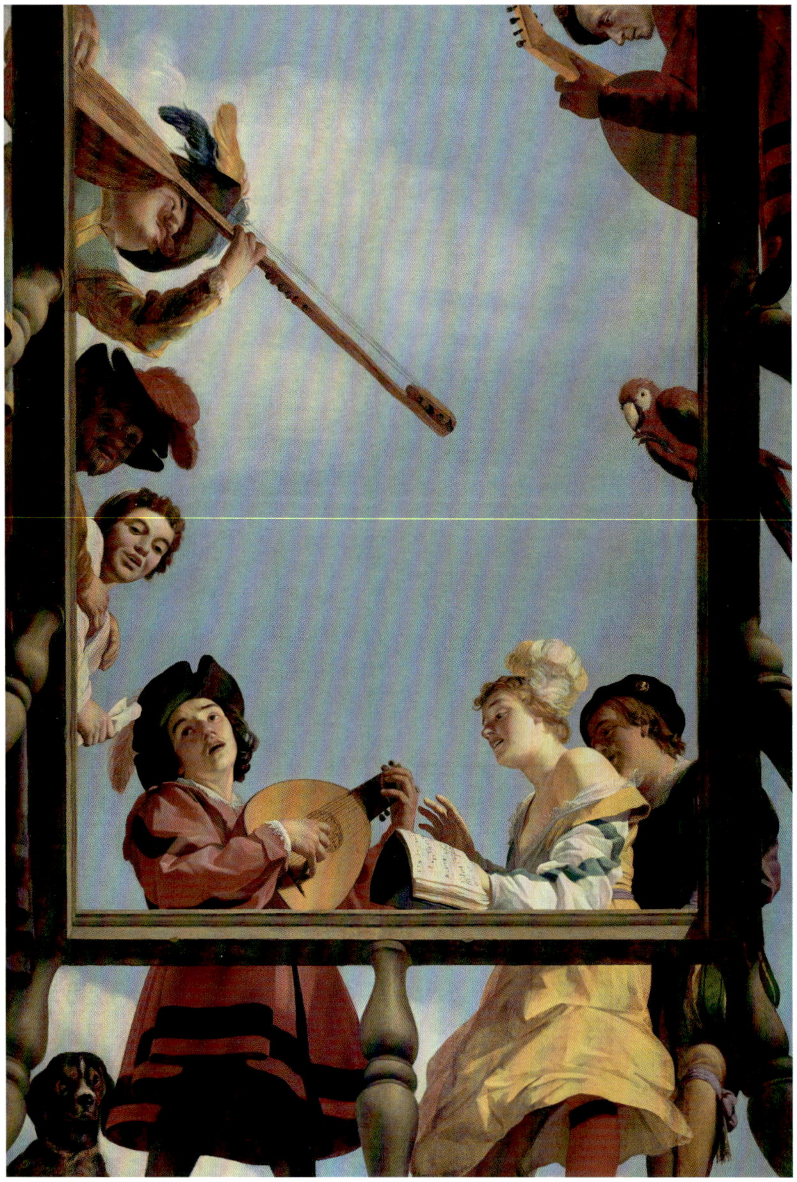

Fig. 95 Gerard van Honthorst, *Musical Group on a Balcony*, 1622, The J. Paul Getty Museum, Los Angeles

According to Leonard Joseph Slatkes, ter Brugghen drew on Caravaggio's 1597 painting *The Musicians* at the Metropolitan Museum in New York (fig. 96) in terms of both subject and form.[9] This work, which was also titled *The Concert* in the past, was listed simply as 'una musica' in the collection catalogue of Cardinal Del Monte who had commissioned it.[10] Today, it is generally interpreted as an allegory of music and love. As Slatkes noted, both artists address the hierarchy of musical sounds, in which the natural voice of the singer ranks highest, followed by the string and, lastly, the wind instruments. If we accept Slatke's proposition, ter Brugghen alludes in this gathering of young men and the young woman even more subtly than his great Italian model to the allegorical meaning.[11] Rather than Eros, it is the teasing lute player with her bared shoulder grazed by soft candlelight who here boldly points to the amorous meaning of the harmonious play. The grapes arranged in the manner of a still life and the

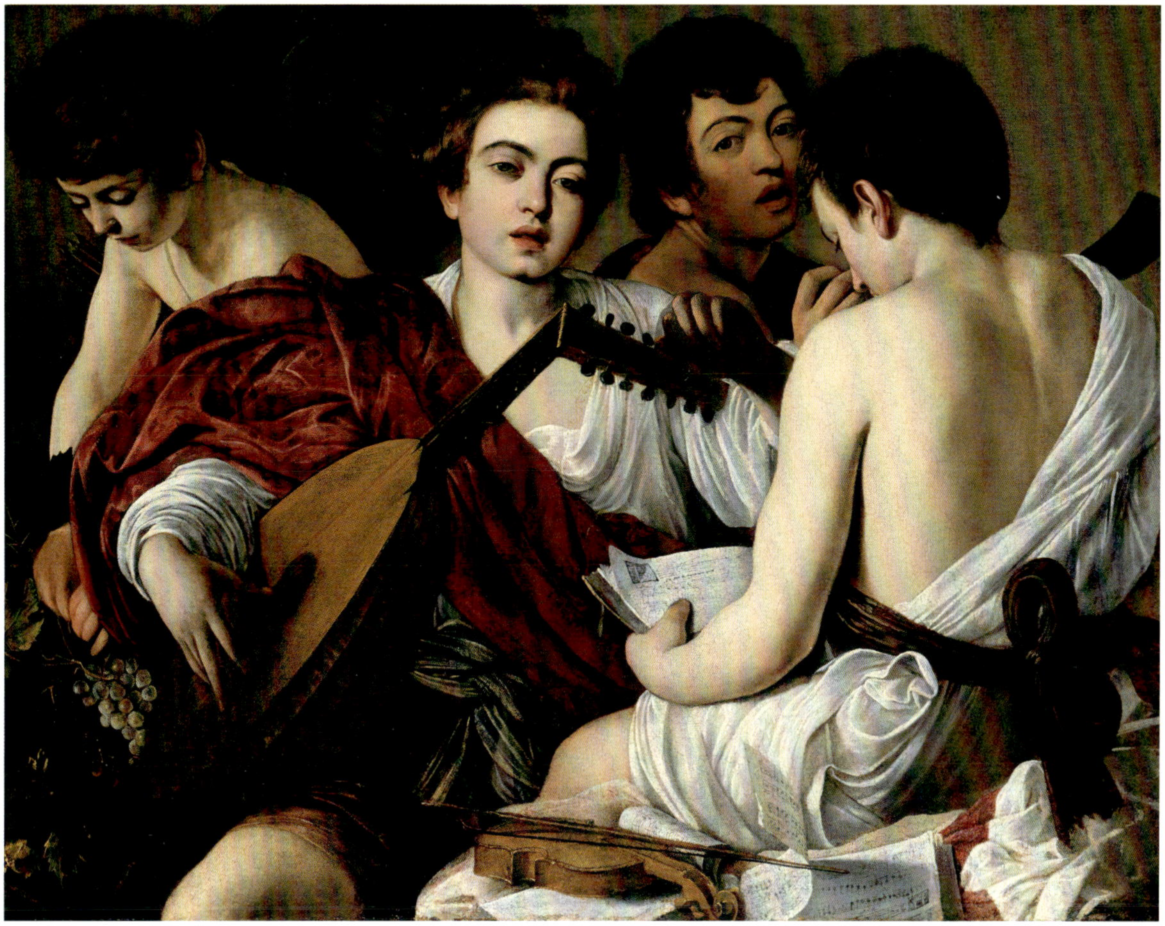

Fig. 96 Michelangelo Merisi, called Caravaggio, *The Musicians*, 1597, The Metropolitan Museum of Art, New York, Rogers Fund, 1952

Venetian red wine flute likely serve to evoke the wine's stimulating effect.[12] At the same time, this imagery may allude to the conduct of the god of wine, Bacchus, and, in doing so, warn against excessive consumption of wine. The question remains open whether the scene, in fact, represents an allegory of music and love or at the same time, as typical of the cheerful gatherings, moralisingly points to the immoral sensual pleasures.[13] Just like the group assembled at the table by Honthorst, the contemplative interaction of the musical trio allows for different readings which were to be deciphered and thereby inspire discussion among the educated viewers. BE

1 Judson 1959, pp. 61, 69, 82.
2 1622, panel, 309.9 × 216.4 cm, The J. Paul Getty Museum, Los Angeles, inv. 70.PB.34.
3 Wheelock 2015, p. 5. See also the essay by Bernd Ebert and Susanne Hoppe in this publication, p. 77.
4 Ebert-Schifferer 2012. Around 1628, Vincenzo Giustiniani personally wrote a treatise on the development of music and the practise of performance in Italia (Engl. edn. MacClintock 1961).
5 Grijp 2009, pp. 81–83; Kyrova 1994, pp. 32–34. For the importance of music and Humanistic education, see also Cavicchioli 2012, pp. 133–135.
6 Slatkes/Franits 2007, pp. 197–200, cat. A79.
7 Dekiert 2003, pp. 236, 238, and 256–272 for the roles assigned to the cast of characters.
8 See Stevens 1984 and Van Thiel 1967/68.
9 1597, canvas, 92.1 × 118.4 cm, Rogers. Fund, 1952, Acc. Nr. 52.81. Leonard J. Slatkes in Exh. cat. San Francisco/Baltimore/London 1997/98, pp. 253–254.
10 Frommel 1971, p. 35.
11 For the interpretation as an allegory of music and love, see Cats 1618.
12 This is how Cesare Ripa described it in his *Iconologia*: 'Il vino si pone perche la musica fu ritrovata per tener gli huomini allegri, come fa il vino, & ancora perche molto aiuto dà alla melodia della voce il vino buono'. Ripa 1618 (1986), p. 309.
13 For the objections to an interpretation 'in bono', see Dekiert 2003, pp. 236–239.

c. 1623

St Sebastian

68

Gerard van Honthorst
St Sebastian, c. 1623
Signed bottom left: GvHonthorst fe. [GvH ligatured]
Canvas, 101 × 117 cm
The National Gallery, London, inv. NG 4503

69

Hendrick ter Brugghen
St Sebastian Tended by Irene, 1625
Signed and dated top left, to the right of the three hands: HTBrugghen fe[cit] 1625 [HTB ligatured]
Canvas, 149 × 119.4 cm
Allen Memorial Art Museum, Oberlin College, Oberlin, Ohio; R.T. Miller, Jr. Fund, 1953, inv. 53.256

70

Nicolas Régnier
St Sebastian, c. 1624/26
Canvas, 134 × 98 cm
Staatliche Kunstsammlungen Dresden, Gemäldegalerie Alte Meister, Dresden, Gal.-Nr. 409
Munich only

71

Nicolas Régnier
St Sebastian, 1624/26
Canvas, 104.1 × 78.7 cm
The Chrysler Museum of Art, Norfolk, Virginia, gift Walter P. Chrysler, Jr., inv. 71.558
Utrecht only

Sebastian was an officer in the imperial guard of Emperor Diocletian (244–311) who was killed because of his conversion to Christianity. Jacobus da Voragine (1228/29–1298), Archbishop of Genoa, describes his martyrdom in the *Legenda Aurea (Golden Legend)*, basing his account on some very ancient Latin legends.[1] Roman soldiers bound Sebastian to a post and riddled his body with arrows. When St Irene, widow of the martyr Castulus, wanted to take his body down the following night to bury it, she discovered that he was still alive. She took him back to her house and nursed him until he had fully recovered. Sebastian now professed his faith again, but that proved fatal. He was arrested on 20 January 287 and stoned to death. His body was thrown into the Cloaca Maxima, Rome's sewer, in order to prevent any veneration of him. Sebastian then appeared in a vision to a woman called Luina and told her where his body was. She had his remains buried in the catacombs on the Via Appia, at the spot where the Basilica of San Sebastiano fuori le Mura now stands.

Jacobus da Voragine drew on another source to relate how Italy, and especially Rome, was ravaged by the plague during the brief reign of Gumbar (Ragumert), King of the Lombards (665–701). Only the foundation of an altar to St Sebastian in Pavia could bring the epidemic to a halt. One was dedicated to the saint in the Church of St Peter there, the relics for which were sent from Rome. This miracle resulted in Sebastian being invoked for protection against the plague from the 7th century onwards. The arrow, which is his attribute, is the symbol of the plague. It is written in Psalm 91 that 'Thou shalt not be afraid for the terror by night, nor for the arrow that flieth by day'. It was the arrow sowing death and destruction that God himself had fired at mankind for its sins. The fact that Sebastian survived despite being pierced by so many arrows (De Voragine says that he resembled a hedgehog) was a miracle that contributed to the belief that praying to the saint would bring about a cure.

The Dutch province of Utrecht also suffered repeated outbreaks of the Black Death. In 1621 hostilities resumed between Spain and the Dutch Republic after the end of the Twelve Years' Truce, and for the first time in years the province had to deal with Spanish incursions. A grain shortage led to high prices for food, which in turn resulted in malnutrition and disease. The mortality rate shot up at the end of June 1624, and in July three times as

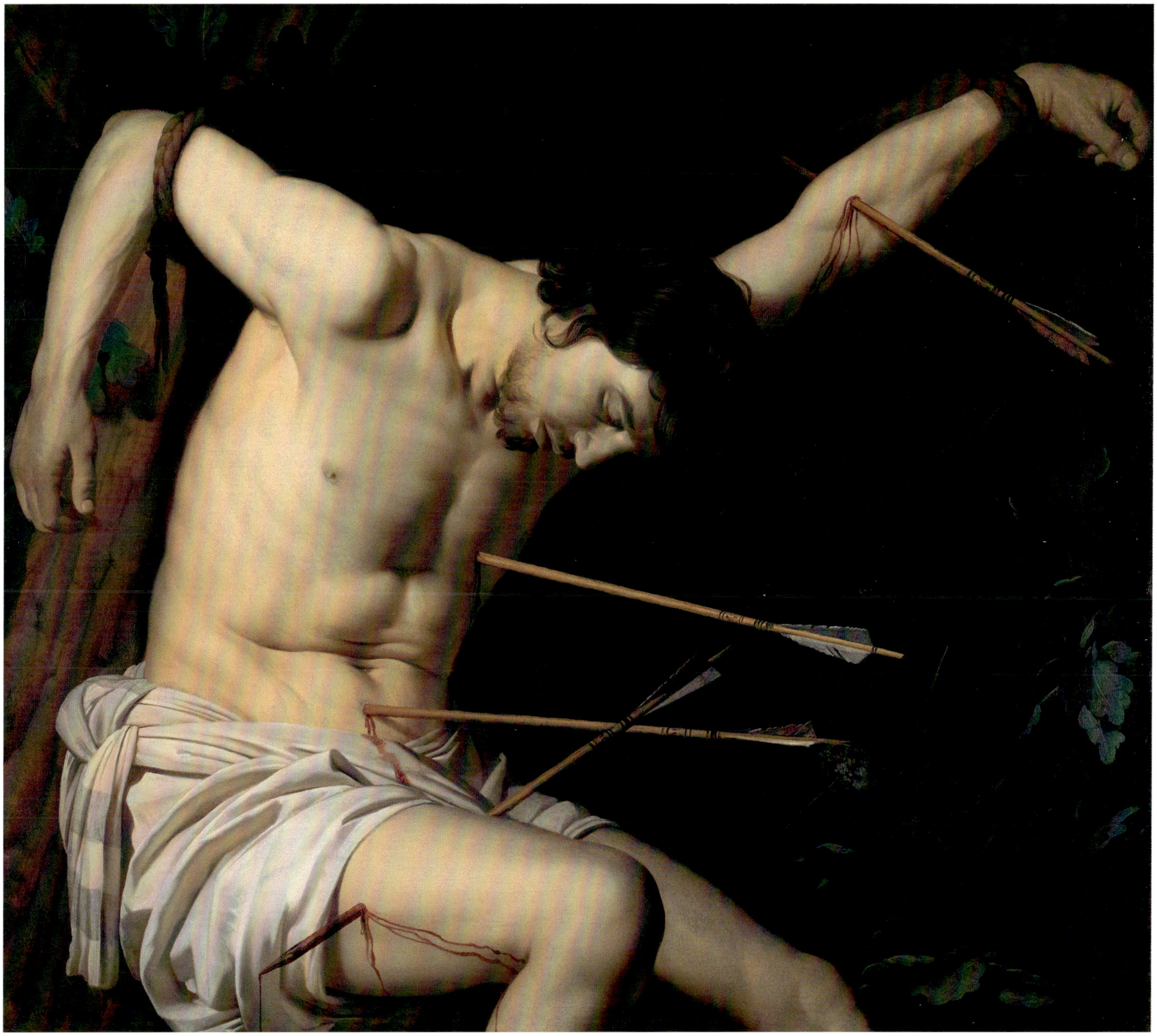

68
Gerard van Honthorst
St Sebastian, c. 1623
The National Gallery, London

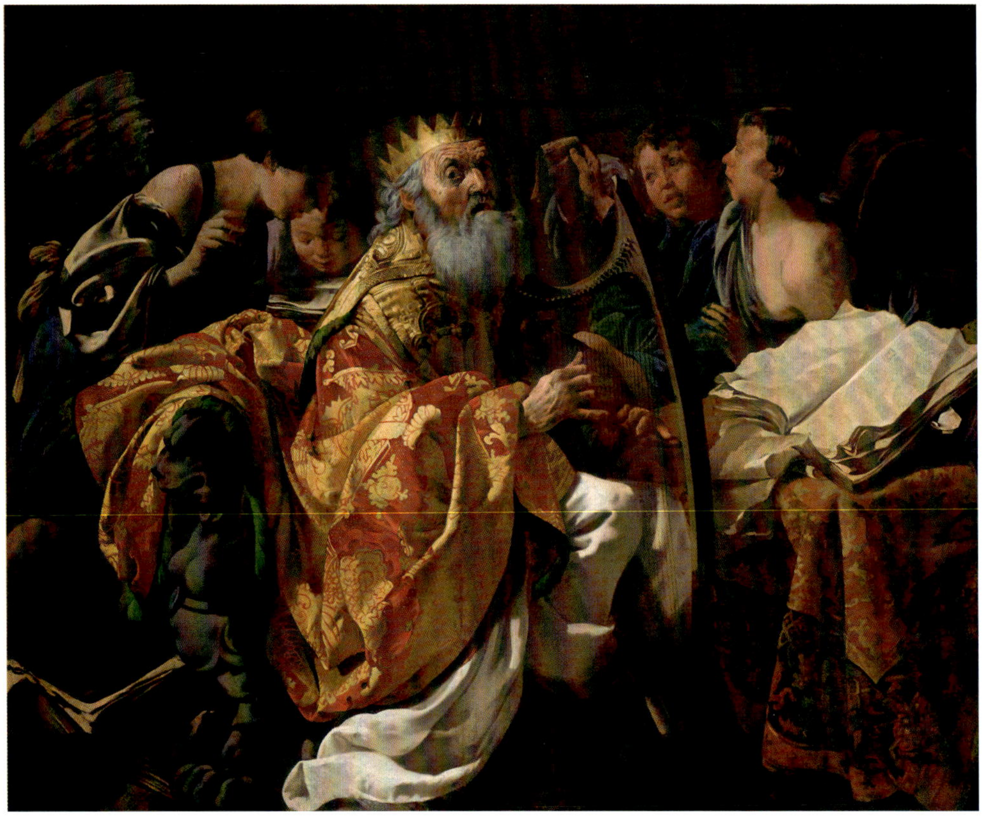

Fig. 97 Hendrick ter Brugghen, *King David Playing the Harp Surrounded by Angels*, 1628, Muzeum Narodowe, Warsaw

many people died in the city of Utrecht as in the preceding months, followed by more than 500 people in August. The many deaths were initially due to dysentery. The total number of deaths from the plague between the end of 1623 and the end of 1625 is put at 1,200 out of a total population of 30,000. The city's rulers opened the plague house on 19 August 1624.[2] It cannot be a coincidence that it was in this very period that the Utrecht Caravaggisti took to depicting Sebastian.[3]

Gerard van Honthorst's interpretation was new for the Netherlands (cat. 68). Until then Sebastian had been depicted full-length and standing upright, bound to a tree or column, as he is in the paintings by Nicolas Régnier (cats. 70, 71). In Honthorst's version he has buckled at the knees from exhaustion and pain. His head hangs heavily, and it is only the ropes binding him to the thick branches of the tree that prevent him from collapsing altogether. Four arrows have lodged in his vulnerable, beautiful, white body. One has gone through his left arm, one protrudes from his chest, another is in his stomach, and one has gone straight through his right thigh, its point dripping blood. Honthorst very ingeniously suggests the passage of time by depicting two separate streams of blood. At the moment when it hit Sebastian was standing upright, and the blood flowed down to his knee, but now that he has collapsed it is flowing down across his thigh.

Hendrick ter Brugghen shows Sebastian in a similar pose, but it is not a three-quarter length (cat. 69). The two paintings, both masterpieces by two extraordinarily talented artists, are completely different in their conception. Honthorst's solitary, suffering Sebastian is being tended lovingly by ter Brugghen's Irene and her helper.[4] The different palettes also play an important part in establishing the mood. Honthorst's is cool and bright, whereas ter Brugghen's scene is bathed in the warm glow of dawn, making it poetic and comforting. This remarkable effect and the ingenious composition make this the absolute pinnacle of ter Brugghen's art. His saint fills the picture surface. Sebastian's extended right arm stretches upwards to the bound hand in the top left corner, while the toes of his left foot touch the edge of the canvas at bottom right. The resulting diagonal is repeated in

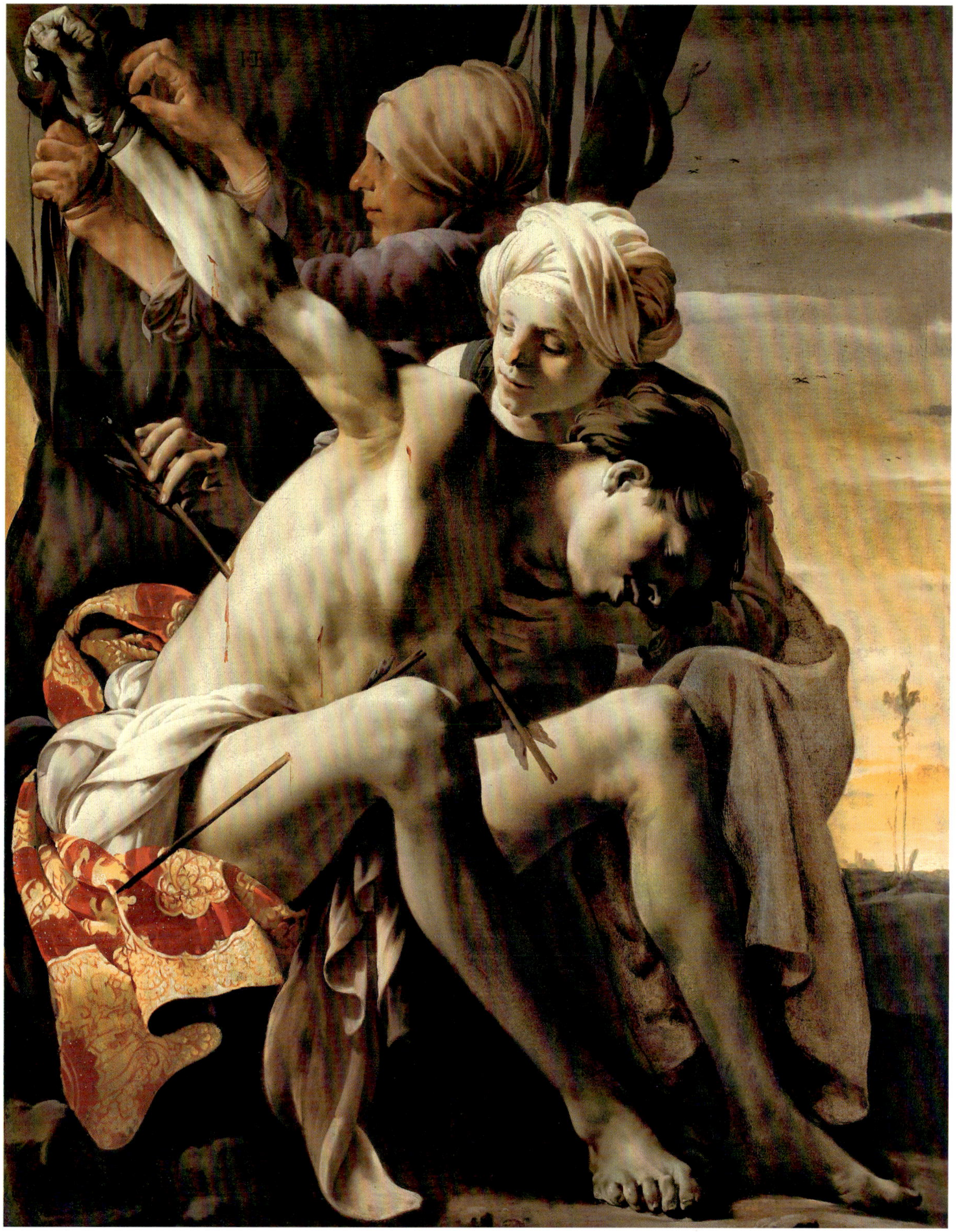

69
Hendrick ter Brugghen
St Sebastian Tended by Irene, 1625
Allen Memorial Art Museum, Oberlin College; R. T. Miller, Jr. Fund, 1953

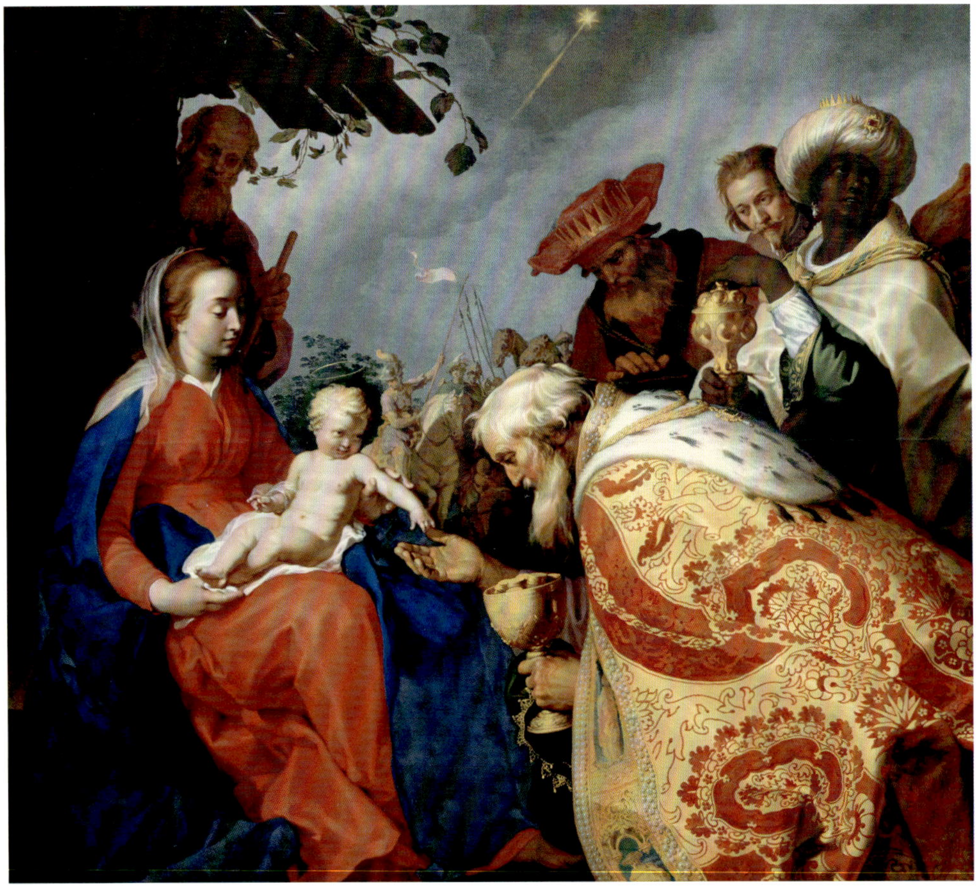

Fig. 98 Abraham Bloemaert, *The Adoration of the Magi*, 1625, Centraal Museum, Utrecht

Sebastian's drooping head, with Irene's above it in the curve of his shoulder as she carefully pulls the arrow from his back. Immediately above that is the head of her helper, who is untying the taut rope around the saint's wrist that has cut off the blood supply to his hand, turning it grey. His other arm has already been freed and hangs limply to the ground beside his left leg.

Oddly enough, little attention has been paid in the literature to the eye-catching canvas on which Sebastian is seated that is mirroring the orange–gold colour that the sun gives to the background on the right. That is why ter Brugghen added it, and he had an excuse for doing so. Irene was the widow of Castulus, who had been Diocletian's chamberlain, so she could have been very wealthy. She might have brought the costly canvas in order to lay Sebastian on it once his body had been unbound. The pattern in the canvas is comparable to the cloak in ter Brugghen's *King David Playing the Harp* (fig. 97),[5] and to Melchior's superb cope in Abraham Bloemaert's *Adoration of the Magi* (fig. 98),[6] which was also painted in 1625, like ter Brugghen's *St Sebastian*. The pomegranate pattern of Melchior's cope is closest to that of the brocade pattern of an Old Catholic chasuble (fig. 99).[7] This liturgical vestment worn by the priest at the celebration of Mass is decorated with embroidered religious scenes. Reading from the top to bottom on the front of the forked cross are the Nativity, Visitation and Annunciation, while on the back there are the Adoration of the Magi, the Presentation in the Temple, and the 12-year-old Jesus in the Temple. The chasuble is made of red velvet brocade with a pattern of flowering pomegranates, a fruit that is the Christian symbol of the Resurrection. Bloemaert, and ter Brugghen too, must have seen this chasuble or a similar one in real life, or possibly a cope of the same material, and used it as a model.

Nicolas Régnier's sensual, heroic *St Sebastian* is one of the more traditional depictions of the saint (cats. 70, 71). Régnier trained as an artist in Antwerp, and depicted the same model in different poses at least three times. All of them were painted in

Rome around 1624/26, in other words a few years after Honthorst had left.[8] The body of Régnier's Sebastian is even closer to the classical ideal of beauty than Honthorst's, with its broad shoulders and narrow waist. It is clear that painting this pale, perfect body was important to Régnier from the fact that his arrows have come from both the left and the right, leaving the front of the torso unblemished. However, the great difference between Honthorst and Régnier is the saint's pose. In Honthorst's picture he is defeated and has lost, but Régnier shows him with his face turned up to heaven, his lips slightly parted. His Sebastian is the winner; he has accepted his fate. LMH

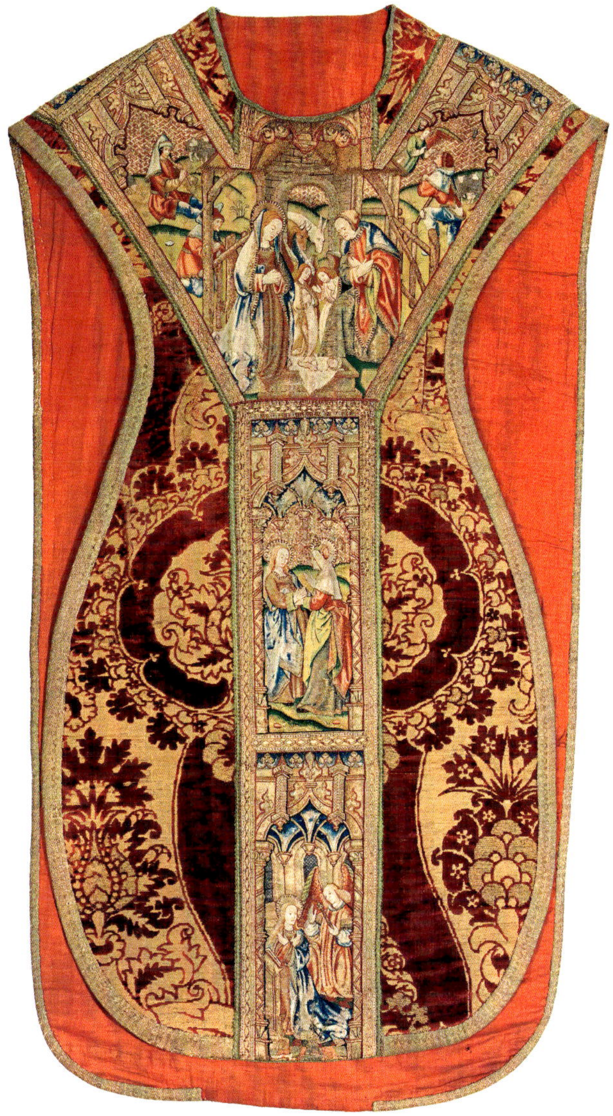

Fig. 99 Northern Netherlands chasuble, c. 1510/20, Museum Catharijneconvent, Utrecht, (on loan from Old Catholic Heritage)

1 Caxton 1900, vol. 2, pp. 232–245.
2 Rommes 1991, pp. 99–101.
3 Baburen and Jan van Bijlert painted Sebastian and Irene in the same period: Dirck van Baburen (workshop), *St Sebastian Tended by Irene*, c. 1623/24, canvas, 108 × 133.3 cm, present whereabouts unknown. Franits 2013a, p. 173, cat. W2W1. See also pp. 173–174 for replicas after this painting. Jan van Bijlert, *St Sebastian Tended by Irene*, 1624, canvas, 113 × 100 cm, Graf Harrach'sche Familiensammlung, Schloss Rohrau, Rohrau. Huys Janssen 1998, p. 107, cat. 31. For the relationship to the plague in Utrecht see also Leonard J. Slatkes in Exh. cat. San Francisco/Baltimore/London 1997/98, pp. 158–162, cat. 10, and Slatkes/Franits 2007, pp. 132–135, cat. A38.
4 See Hedquist 2017 for the introduction of Irene into the scene and the relationship between the plague in Utrecht and ter Brugghen's depiction of Sebastian.
5 Canvas, 150 × 190 cm, Muzeum Narodowe, Warsaw, inv. M.OB.529.
6 Canvas, 168.8 × 193.7 cm, Centraal Museum, Utrecht, inv. 2575.
7 Northern Netherlands, *Red Chasuble with Scenes from the Life of Christ, including the Nativity, Visitation and Annunciation*, c. 1510/20. Museum Catharijneconvent, Utrecht (on loan from Old Catholic Heritage), inv. OKM t 202. The chasuble was on display in the Centraal Museum in Utrecht for six weeks from mid-December 2011 as part of the exhibition *The Bloemaert Effect* (Exh. cat. Utrecht/Schwerin 2011/12). Slatkes/Franits 2007, p. 85, cat. A7, wrongly refer, as others before and after them do, to a similarity to the cope of David of Burgundy, which has a very different pattern. See also Hedquist 2017, pp. 21–22.
8 The same model, but here standing and with his arms tied above his head to the tree, is depicted in Nicolas Régnier, *St Sebastian*, 1624/26, canvas, 131 × 99 cm, State Hermitage Museum, Saint Petersburg. On the three paintings, see Lemoine 2007, pp. 244–245, cats. 44–46.

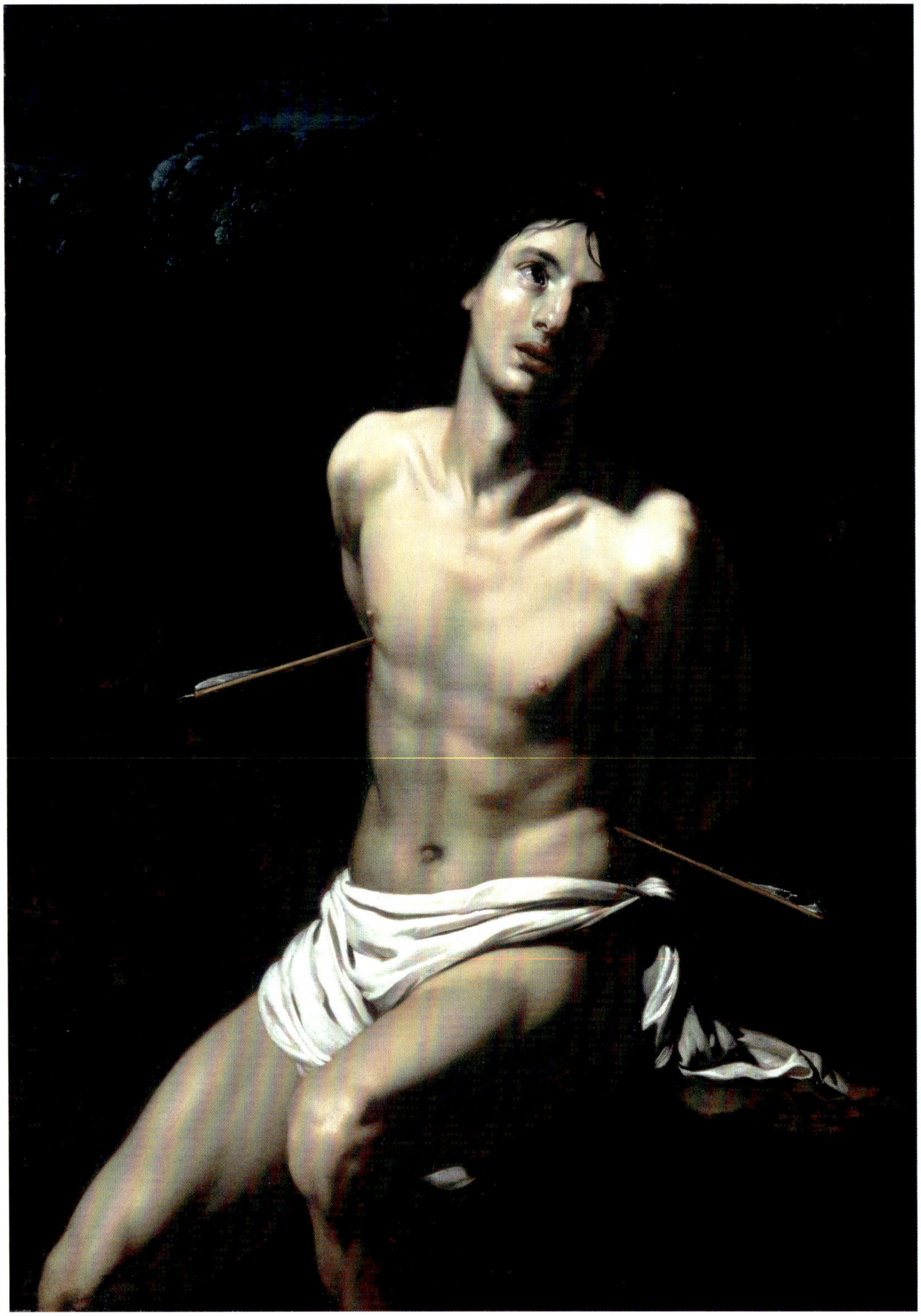

70
Nicolas Régnier
St Sebastian, c. 1624/26
Staatliche Kunstsammlungen Dresden,
Gemäldegalerie Alte Meister, Dresden

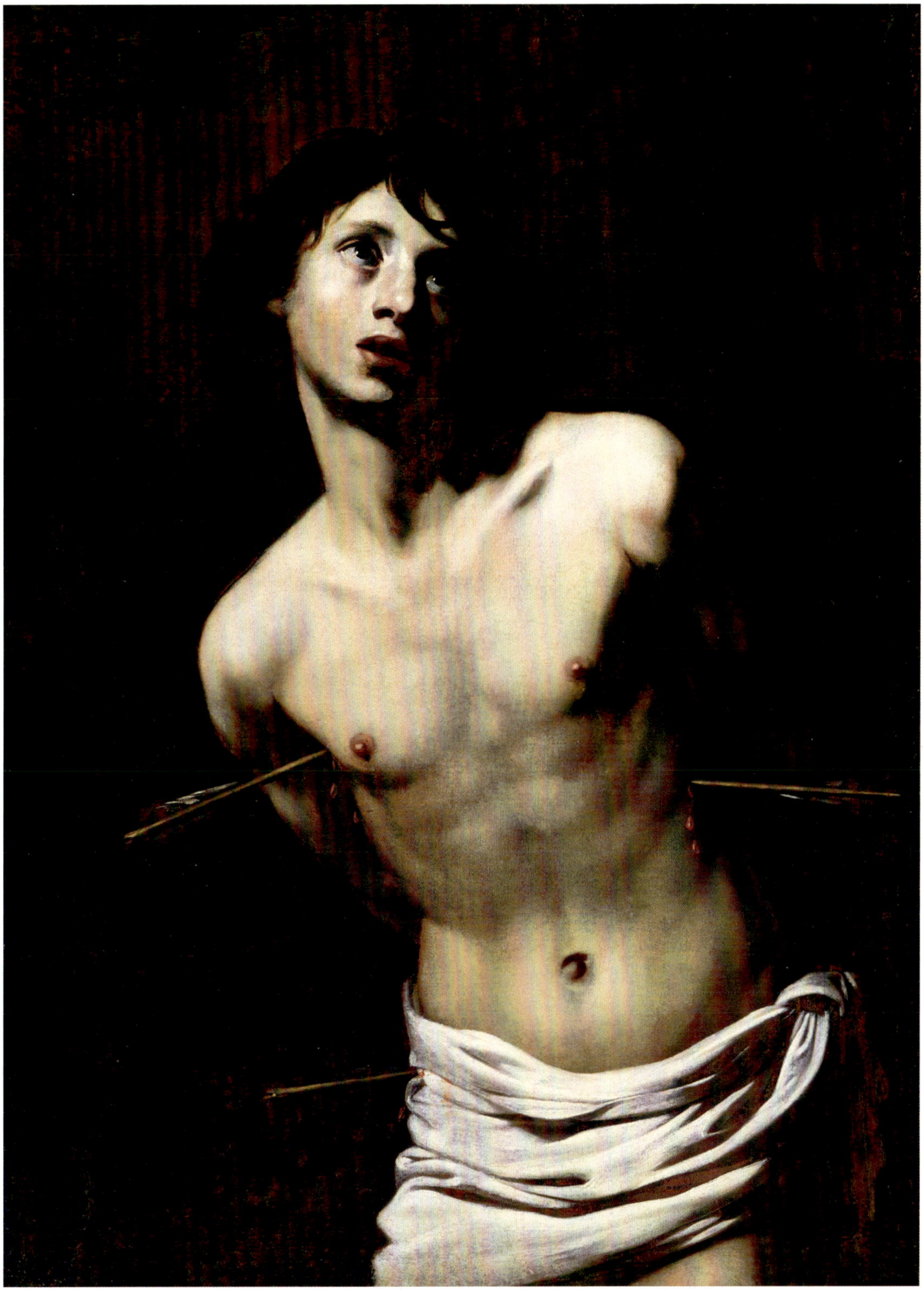

71
Nicolas Régnier
St Sebastian, 1624/26
The Chrysler Museum of Art, Norfolk, Virginia

1625

Procuress and Fortune Teller

72
Gerard van Honthorst
The Procuress, 1625
Signed at top right: GvHonthorst, fesit 1625.
[GvH ligatured]
Panel, 71 × 104 cm
Centraal Museum, Utrecht, acquired in 1951 with the support of the Rembrandt Association, inv. 10786

73
Michelangelo Merisi, called Caravaggio
The Fortune Teller, c. 1595/96
Canvas, 115 × 150 cm
Musei Capitolini, Pinacoteca Capitolina, Rome, inv. PC 131
Munich only

74
Simon Vouet
The Fortune Teller, 1617
Inscribed on reverse: AEGIPTIA · VULGO · ZINGARA · FATIVI · CERDONIS · DIVINATRIX · A · SIMOE · VOET · AD · VIVUM · DEPICTA · MCDXVII
Canvas, 95 × 135 cm
Gallerie Nazionali di Arte Antica di Roma, Palazzo Barberini, Rome, inv. 1041
Munich only

In the 16th and 17th centuries, prostitution was an inherent part of urban life in the major cities of Europe in spite of ubiquitous bans and punishments. Numerous contemporaneous travelogues and court records inform us that the trade flourished not just in Paris and London, but also and especially in Rome and Amsterdam.[1] It is therefore not surprising that the artists south and north of the Alps seized on the subject of venal love.[2]

A recurring image in this context is that of the procuress, who was traditionally depicted as an old hag with a headscarf wrapped around her head like a turban. This female figure had a high recognition value and appears in many paintings by Gerard van Honthorst (for example, cats. 28, 29).

The procuress can be seen in his eponymous painting of 1625 (cat. 72).[3] The old woman is standing behind a young gallant who turns his back to us. She leans on the back of his chair and points at the young, attractive, smiling woman sitting across from the man, who has interrupted her lute-playing. The only light source in the dark room is the candle which stands on the table between the couple and is almost entirely hidden by the man. As a result, the man's back is deeply shaded, while his silhouette is highlighted.[4] By contrast, the young woman glows in the candlelight. The light is reflected above all by the fair skin of her low-cut *décolleté* and brings out the silky sheen of the yellow gown she wears over her white, lace-trimmed bodice and tight-fitting blue corset.

The artist leaves no doubt as to the outcome of this scene: the young man has already pulled out his bulging money bag. In his right hand are coins which he offers to her. His fingers do not touch hers yet, but the shadows of the hands on the musical instrument are already joined. By means of perspectival overlap, the feather tips of their headdresses seem to boldly brush against one another, even though the table prevents them from touching.

It is surely no coincidence that one of the feathers on the young woman's hat is coloured red, matching the colour of the man's clothes. Yet another motif provides insight into the meaning of the painting. Through the man's arm we can see a wick trimmer which, on days when the wick had not yet burned down of its own accord, served to regulate the size of the candle flame. In Rome, as Honthorst was surely aware,[5] the term *cortigiana da lume* or *cortigiana da candela*[6] was a common name for a prostitute,

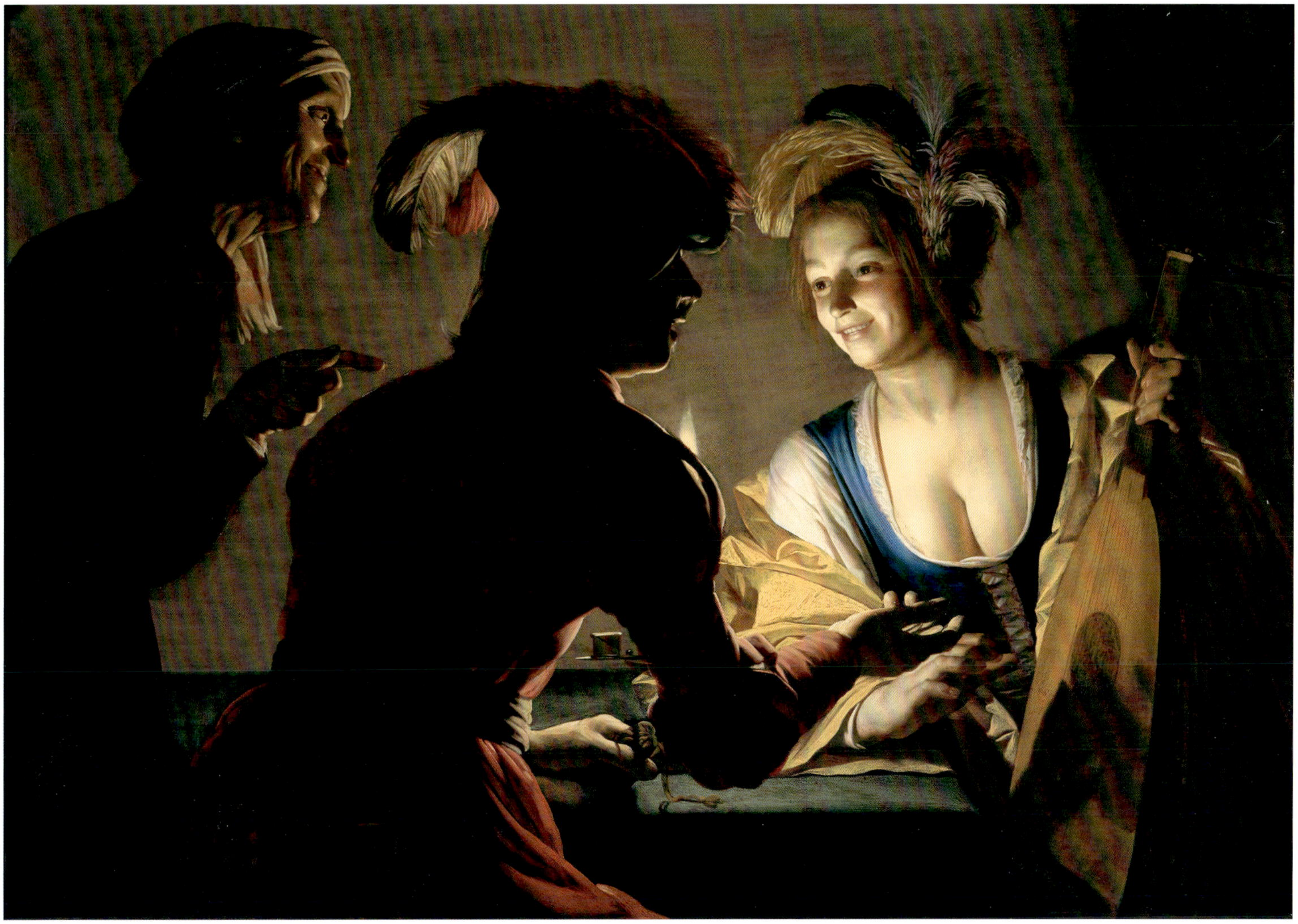

72
Gerard van Honthorst
The Procuress, 1625
Centraal Museum, Utrecht

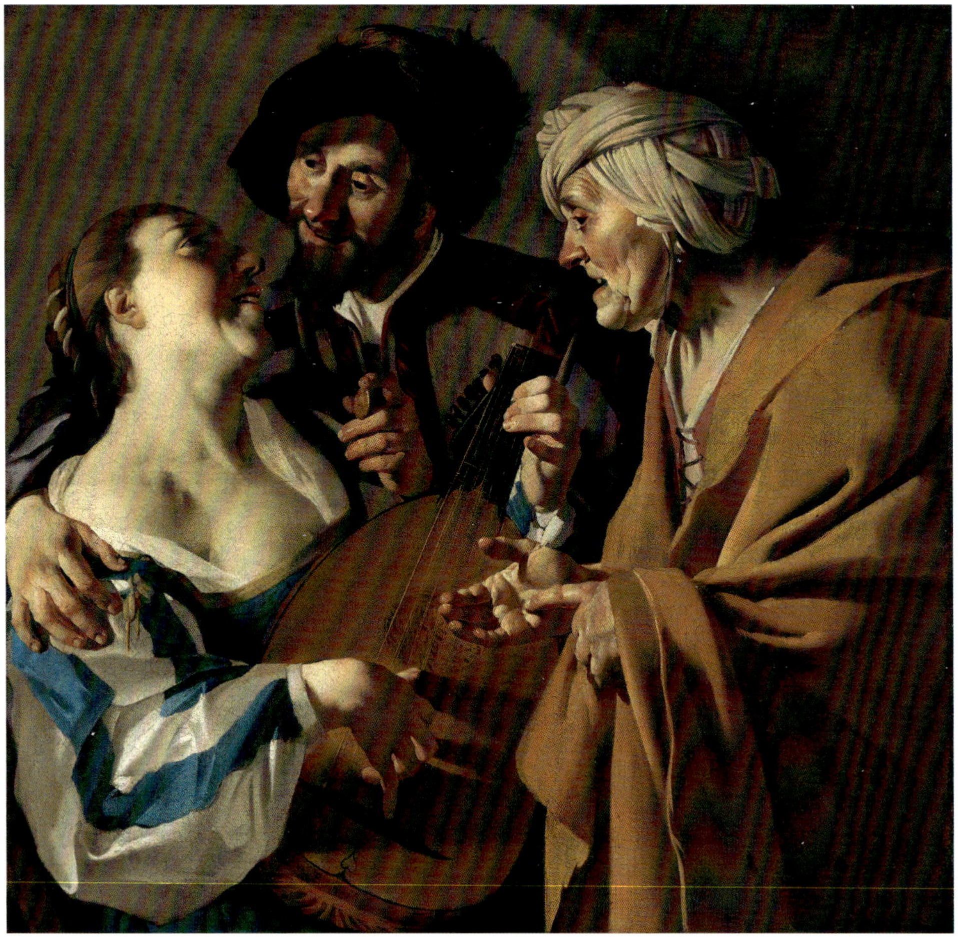

Fig. 100 Dirck van Baburen, *The Procuress*, 1622, Museum of Fine Arts, Boston, M. Theresa B. Hopkins Fund

probably because the time for a customer was measured by the length of time of a burning candle.

A painting signed and dated 1622, now in Boston, serves as evidence that in Utrecht Dirck van Baburen had already taken up the subject of the procuress earlier (fig. 100).[7] The innovations brought back from Rome, especially the extreme proximity of the half-length figures at the front of the picture, convey a greater immediacy to the viewer. Unlike in the brothel scenes of the 16th century, the focus was now no longer on the biblical theme of the prodigal son but on a staged exaggeration of reality combined with the obvious aspiration to please the senses and at the same time appeal to morality.

The starting point for this development was Caravaggio's *Fortune Teller* (cat. 73),[8] which exists in two autograph versions, created between 1594 and 1596. The paintings were bought by the papal chamberlain Gerolamo Vittrici[9] and Cardinal Del Monte. The enthusiasm for contemporary literature and the theatre likely motivated their interest in this work, as the subject depicted by Caravaggio had emerged in this context. In 1589, for instance, the comedy *La Zingana* was performed at the wedding of Cardinal Del Monte's friend Ferdinand I de' Medici and Christine of Lorraine.[10] In addition to picaresque literature and Commedia dell'arte productions, which were widespread in Italy, the *zingaresche* plays, which featured a gypsy woman as protagonist, were very popular in Rome during the carnival season. The plays which were about love, theft and deceit were performed at Roman street corners on makeshift stages or ox carts and the texts were printed in cheap booklets.[11]

In Caravaggio's composition, the half-length figures stand next to one another close to the lower edge of the picture in a

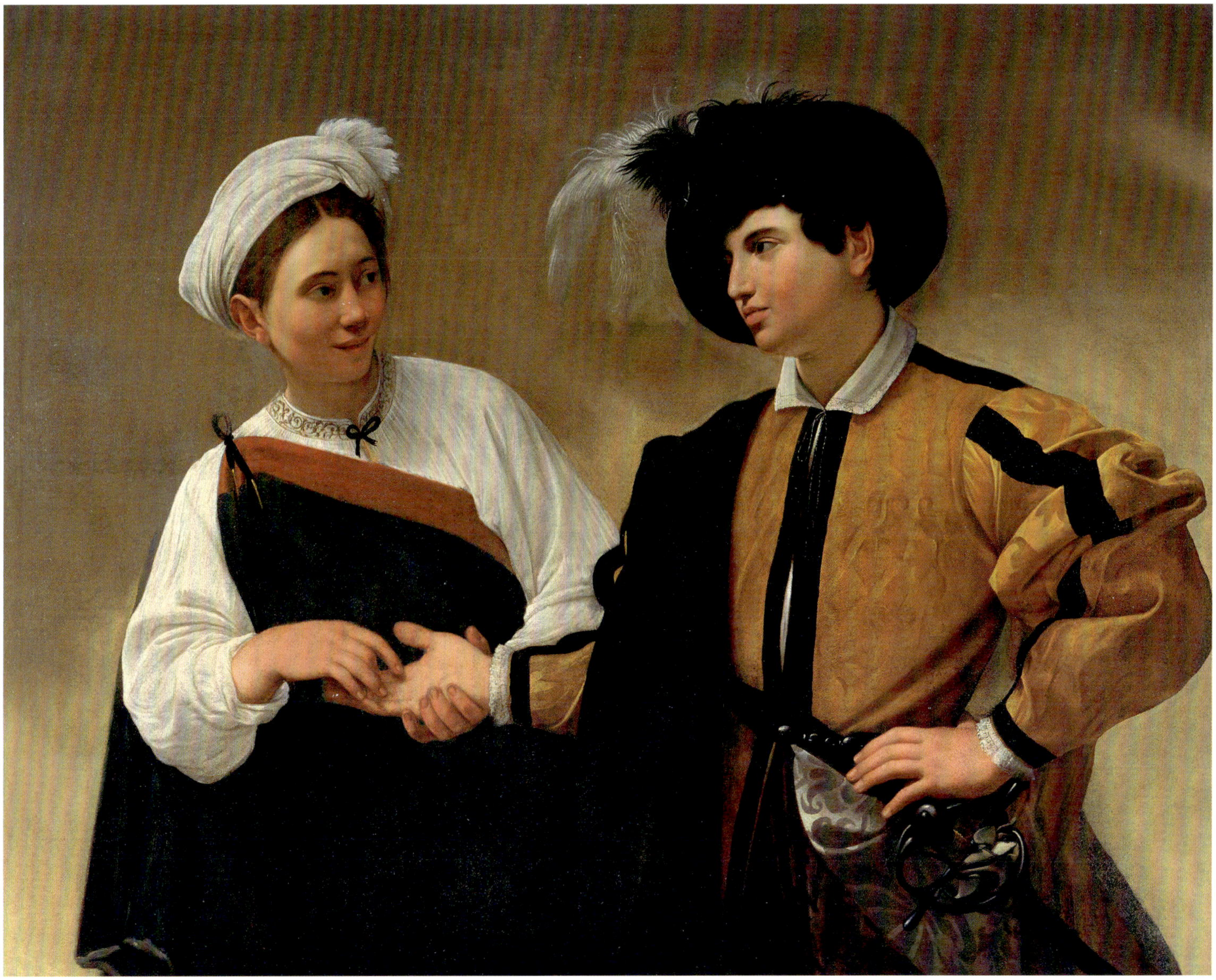

73
Michelangelo Merisi, called Caravaggio
The Fortune Teller, c. 1595/96
Musei Capitolini, Pinacoteca Capitolina, Rome

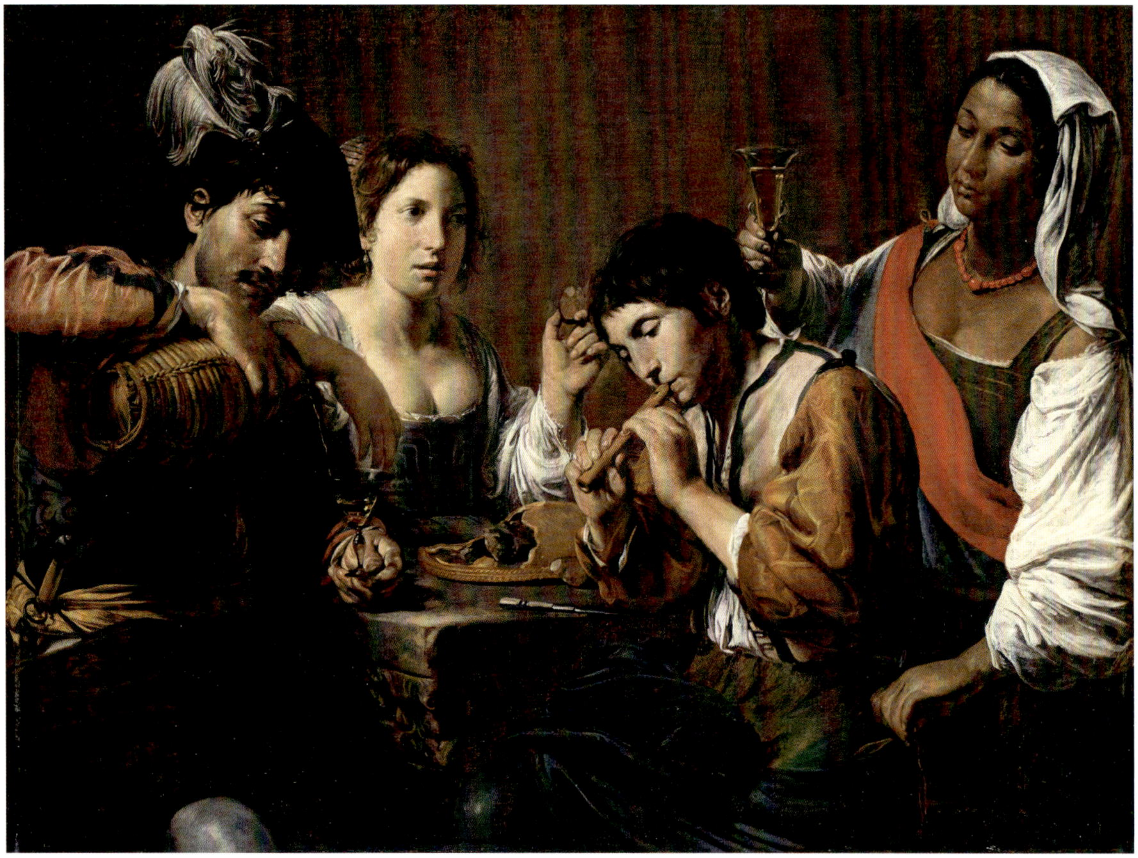

Fig. 101 Valentin de Boulogne, *Gathering in a Tavern*, c. 1625, Musée du Louvre, Paris

space lacking detail. The young woman is identified as a gypsy by her characteristic clothes with the diagonal mantle knotted on the right shoulder and the turban-like headscarf.[12] *Zingari* (gypsies) probably came to Europe at the beginning of the 15th century.[13] Believed to come from Egypt, they were also called *egiziani* (Egyptians) in Italy. Early sources already describe them as non-sedentary people who beg and steal.[14] Gypsies were especially notorious for palm-reading and they were often said to possess erotic seductive powers. In the visual arts they are usually shown surrounded by groups of people as early as the 16th century.[15] Yet until Caravaggio's visualisation, the image of a palm-reading gypsy woman had not been a subject in its own right in the art market.

Caravaggio's fortune teller wears fine, clean fabrics and thus does not reflect the reality of the late 16th century. According to the sources, gypsies were the poorest of the poor, dirty and ragged. The girl tells the young man's fortune, combined with the gesture of stroking the palm of his hand with her middle finger, which at the time was unequivocally understood as a promise of sexual intercourse.[16] But this is really just a diversionary tactic, just like her smile and her looking him in the eyes, for her middle finger is pulling the ring off his finger. Blushing with restrained desire, he returns her gaze and confidently places his left hand on his waist just above the pommel of his sword. His posture and glance convey strength and superiority, yet in his attempt to impress he fails to notice the theft. The young man will be left behind duped.

While Caravaggio approaches the subject with subtlety and charm, the paintings of the subsequent generation are bolder and simpler. This development is exemplified by Simon Vouet's 1617 painting *The Fortune Teller* (cat. 74).[17] Based on the inscription on the reverse of the canvas, Rossella Vodret was able to establish that the painting must have been in the collection of Cassiano dal Pozzo, the scholar who patronised Vouet shortly after the artist's arrival in Rome in 1613.[18] In Vouet's depiction, the confidence

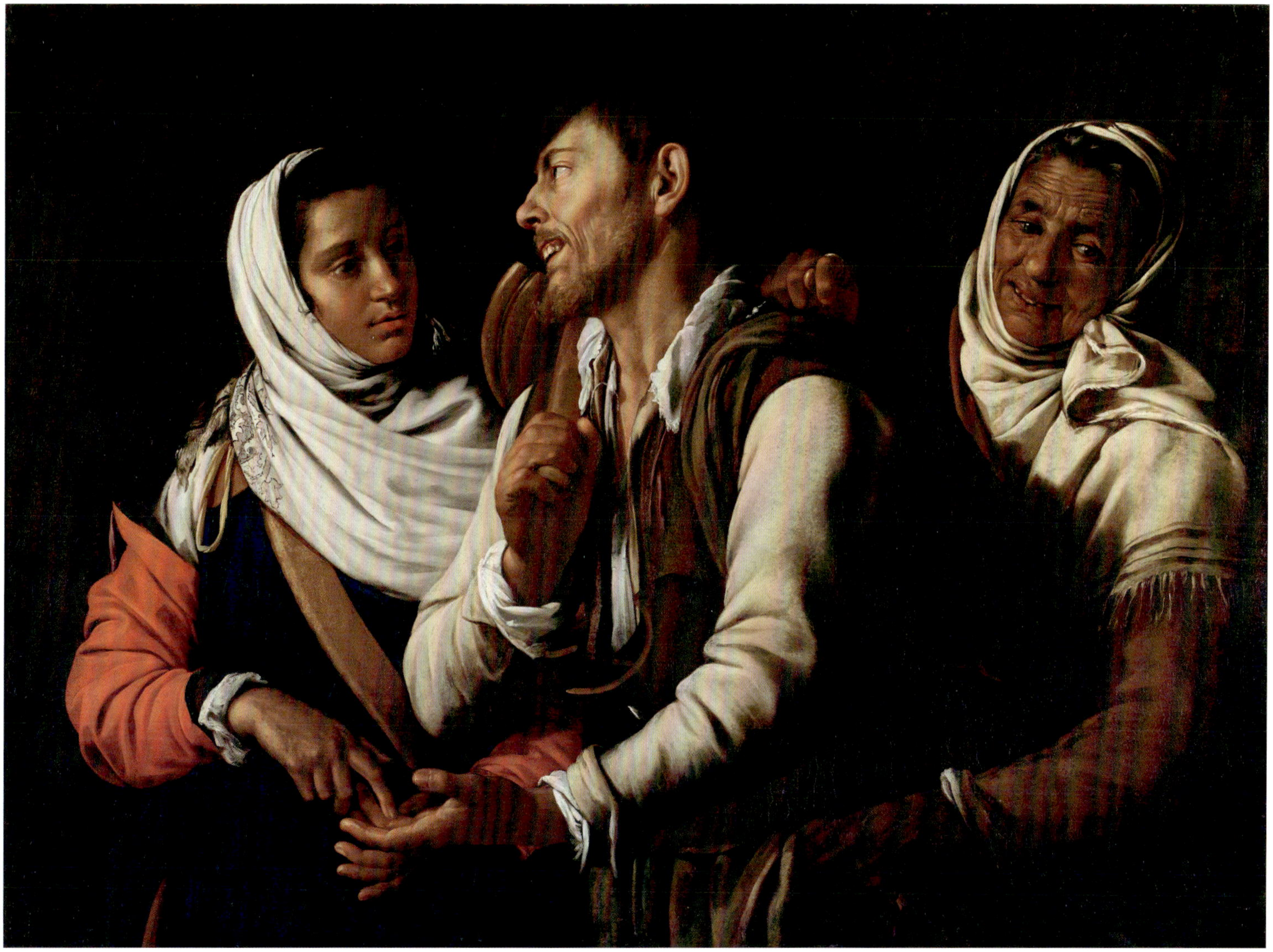

74
Simon Vouet
The Fortune Teller, 1617
Gallerie Nazionali di Arte Antica di Roma,
Palazzo Barberini, Rome

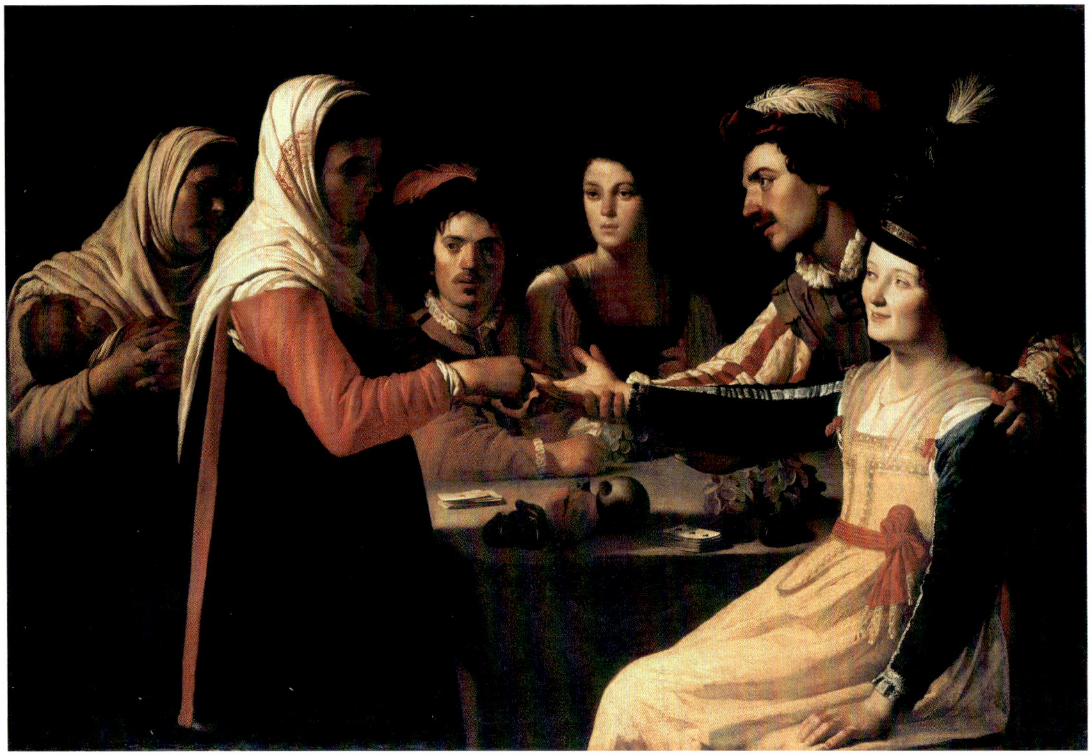

Fig. 102 Gerard van Honthorst, *The Fortune Teller*, c. 1616/17, Galleria degli Uffizi, Florence

trick is dramatised and highlighted even more due to the naïveté of the person being robbed. Vouet adds a third figure to Caravaggio's composition: While a young, pretty fortune teller distracts the simple-minded tradesman, an old gypsy woman pulls his money-bag from his trouser pocket. At the same time, she tries to make eye contact with the viewer and makes the *fica* gesture[19] to implicate him in the scam. This gesture has an obvious sexual connotation, as the thumb placed between the index and middle fingers alludes to the female sex organ. At the same time, the old woman's gesture serves to mock the oafish-looking man[20] who, perhaps hoping to be foretold an amorous adventure by the young gypsy woman, is now being robbed.

Fortune tellers were a very popular subject among Caravaggio's followers, especially in combination with groups seated at a table. These could be variously combined with merry companies, musicians and gamblers, and were often themselves depicted as the victims of robbery.[21] This development started with compositions by Bartolomeo Manfredi.[22] The function of the gypsy woman could vary. In the Budapest painting *Cardsharps and Fortune Teller* by Nicolas Régnier (cat. 52) she is placed on the right and at first glance seems to be mere staffage, yet once again she underscores the deception and impermanence of good fortune.[23] In the works of Valentin de Boulogne, which frequently feature a gypsy woman,[24] she becomes a thief and at the same time a symbol of what can happen to those who indulge in vice (fig. 101).[25] Gerard von Honthorst's *Fortune Teller*, on the other hand, shows a young couple in the foreground who are having their palms read by a gypsy woman (fig. 102).[26] What fortune the couple is hoping to be told is revealed in the figure of the old gypsy woman on the far left who holds a baby in her arms.

While the *zingari* were part of Roman everyday life, it should be noted that contemporary representations of fortune tellers did not depict the immediate reality. Based on comical features and exaggeration, there was a specific connection to picaresque tales and popular comedy, which revealed itself at a glance to the contemporary viewer. In Rome, however, the theme of prostitution visualised by procuress, whore and trick was not taken up by the local Caravaggisti. At the same time, it is noteworthy that neither Honthorst, Baburen or ter Brugghen turned to the subject of the palm-reading gypsy woman again after returning to the Netherlands. SH

1 Canosa/Colonello 1989, pp. 43–56; Van de Pol 2006; Van de Pol 2010; Martelli 2017, pp. 59–67.
2 For the representations in the Netherlands, see Van de Pol 2010, esp. pp. 9–13.
3 Judson/Ekkart 1999, pp. 227–228, cat. 292.
4 For the analysis of the light effect, see Blankert 1986/87, pp. 31–32.
5 See the essay by Helen Langdon in this volume, p. 46.
6 Canosa/Colonello 1989, p. 46; Martelli 2017, p. 59.
7 *The Procuress*, 1622, canvas, 101.5 × 107.6 cm, Museum of Fine Arts, Boston, M. Theresa B. Hopkins Fund, inv. 50.2721. Franits 2013a, pp. 125–130, cat. A23. For the dissemination of the subject, see Franits 2004, pp. 68–69.
8 Ebert-Schifferer 2009, pp. 73–78; Sergio Guarino, Marco Cardinali, and Nicola Salini in Vodret et al. 2016, pp. 130–133.
9 His painting is now in the Musée du Louvre, Paris: c. 1594, canvas, 99 × 131 cm, inv. 55. Cuzin 1977.
10 For example, Gianfranceschi 2011, p. 34.
11 Hirdt 2004; Bonfait 2008/09.
12 For the gypsies' clothing, see Moffitt 2002, pp. 133f; Etheridge 2011/12, p. 158. Hirdt plausibly points to a connection with the costumes assigned for gypsies in contemporary comedies: Hirdt 1998, p. 96.
13 In Italy, their arrival in Bologna in 1422 is documented by a source, cited by Moffitt 2002, pp. 142–143. See also generally Martelli 2017, pp. 93–114.
14 Moffitt 2002, pp. 140–142.
15 Examples cited by Cuzin 1977, pp. 16–26; Hartje 2004, p. 185; Bell/Suckow 2008.
16 Suthor 2005, pp. 126–127.
17 Vodret 1996; Exh. cat. Rome/Paris 2014/15, pp. 194–197, cat. 25.
18 Solinas 1992; Vodret 1996.
19 Lemoine 2015.
20 In a mocking sense, the gesture was at the time also frequently depicted in representations of the Mocking of Christ; see for example cat. 18.
21 For example, Bartolomeo Manfredi, *The Fortune Teller*, c. 1616/17, canvas, 122.2 × 154.4 cm, Detroit Institute of Arts, inv. 79.30; Valentin de Boulogne, *Fortune Teller with Soldiers*, c. 1618/20, canvas, 149.5 × 238.5 cm, Toledo Museum of Art, inv. 1981.53; Simon Vouet, *Fortune Teller*, c. 1620, canvas, 120 × 170.2 cm, National Gallery of Canada, Ottawa, inv. 6737.
22 Cuzin 1977, pp. 27–37; Cuzin 1980; Hartje 2004, pp. 185–210. See also cat. 35.
23 For the moral function of card and dice games, see cats. 50–53.
24 Mojana 1989, cats. 4, 31, 47, 64; Exh. cat. New York/Paris 2016/17, cats. 10, 11, 15, 24, 38, 50.
25 *Gathering in a Tavern*, c. 1625, canvas, 96 × 133 cm, Musée du Louvre, Paris, inv. 8255.
26 c. 1616/17 (Exh. cat. Florence 2015, pp. 164–165, cat. 19) and c. 1620 (Judson/Ekkart 1999, pp. 214–215, cat. 278), canvas, 137 × 204 cm, Galleria degli Uffizi, Florence, inv. 734.

1625

Rich Man and Poor Lazarus

75
Hendrick ter Brugghen
The Rich Man and the Poor Lazarus, 1625
Signed and dated bottom left: HTBrugghen fecit. 1625
[HTB ligatured]
Canvas, 168.2 × 207.3 cm
Centraal Museum, Utrecht, inv. 11241

The parable of the rich man and poor Lazarus is told in the Gospel of St Luke (Luke 16:19–31): 'Once there was a rich man who used to dress in purple and fine linen and live in great luxury every day. A beggar named Lazarus, who was covered with sores, was brought to his gate. He was always trying to satisfy his hunger with what fell from the rich man's table. Even the dogs used to come and lick his sores. One day, the beggar died and was carried away by the angels to Abraham's side. The rich man also died and was buried'. When the rich man in hell entreats Abraham to ease his agony, the latter responds that, as opposed to Lazarus, he had received blessings during his lifetime and therefore is now being tormented. Lazarus, on the other hand, is now being comforted after having received nothing but hardships. The religious, moral intent of the story is obvious: practise charity by sharing with the poor.

Brightly lit from the left in the right foreground of ter Brugghen's painting, the figure of Lazarus is seen talking to one of the rich man's servants.[1] Two dogs are about to lick his open leg wounds. Apparently, he is to be driven away from the spot. The draperies of his scanty clothing, his partly burnt skin and coarse physique with oversized extremities are characteristic of ter Brugghen and executed with the brushwork typical of him. Less prominent is the table scene in the left background, where a standing maid provides the rich man and his guests with food while turning her head towards the scene in the foreground.[2]

Technical analysis of the painting has revealed that the rich man in the background originally wore a lavishly decorated damask overcoat. The rear-view figure with feathered beret on the far left originally did not wear a headdress.[3]

The subject of the Utrecht painting is an iconographic rarity within the group of Caravaggio followers.[4] This is true not just of Utrecht. A much-discussed issue is that of possible Italian influences on this painting. Nicolson pointed to a painting by Jacopo da Ponte, called Bassano (c. 1510/15–1592) in Cleveland, which, however, shows little more than a thematic affinity.[5] Seelig views a painting of the same subject by Francesco Bassano the Younger (1549–1592) as ter Brugghen's model.[6] In it, the composition is inverted, but the sitting posture of Lazarus with the abrupt turn of the head does show a certain similarity with ter Brugghen's figure.

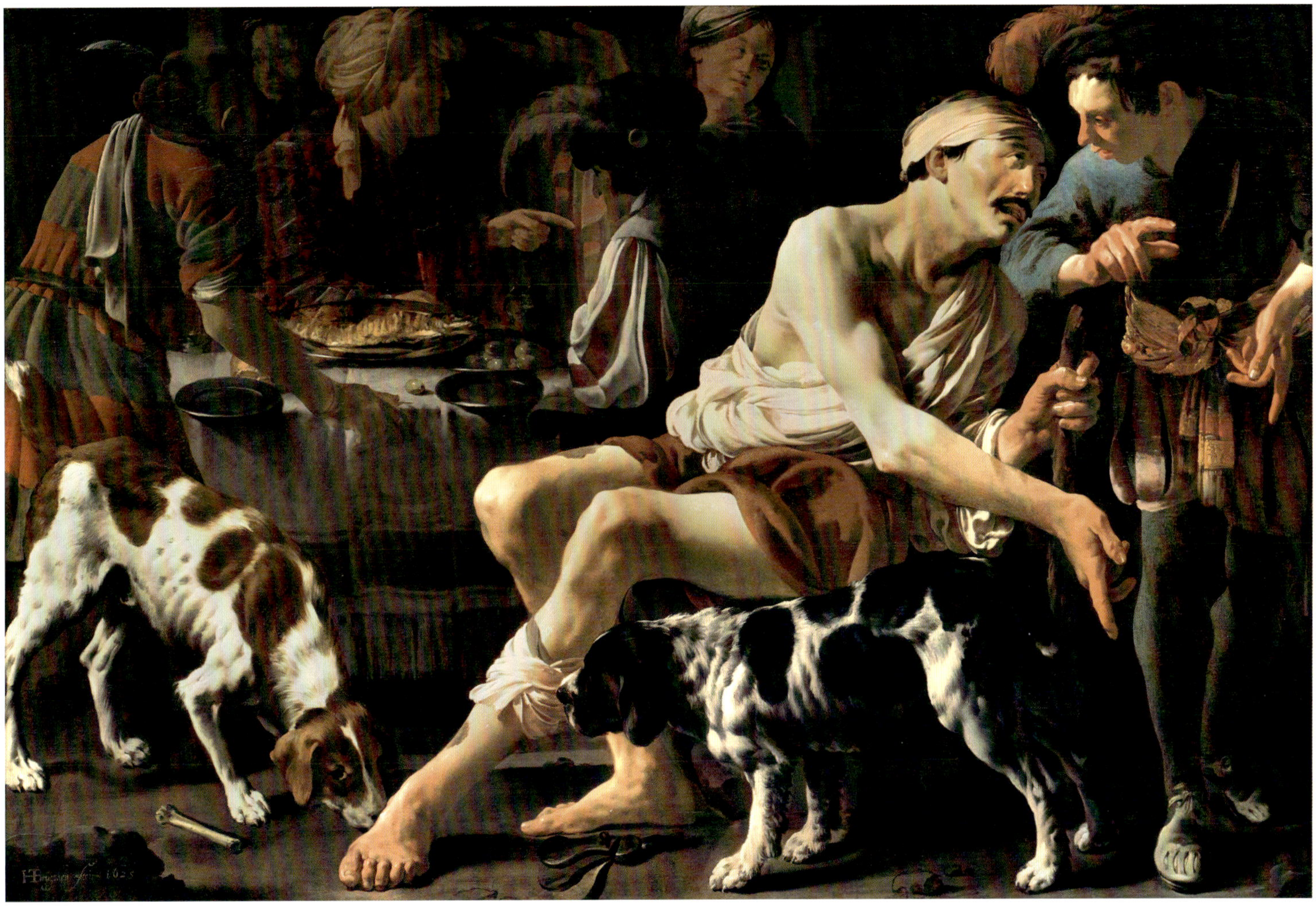

75
Hendrick ter Brugghen
The Rich Man and the Poor Lazarus, 1625
Centraal Museum, Utrecht

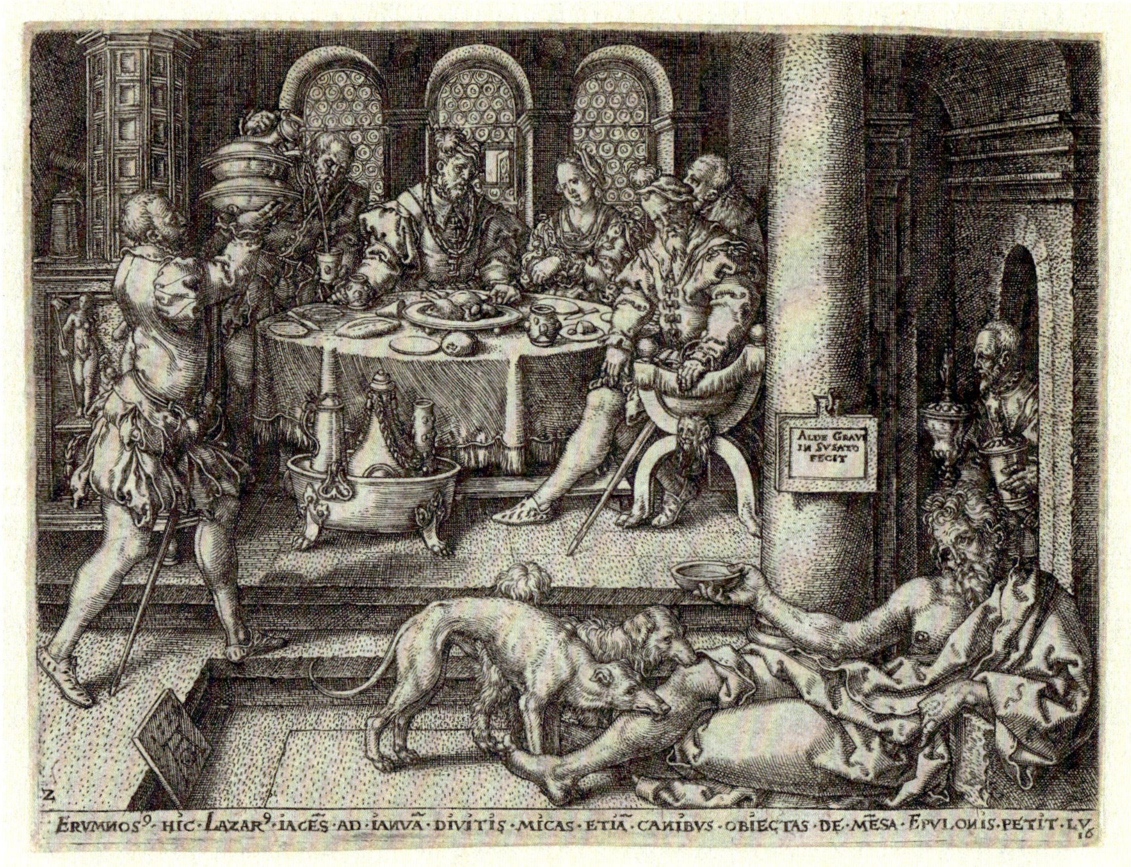

Fig. 103 Heinrich Aldegrever, *Lazarus at the Door of the Rich Man*, from the series *The Parable of Lazarus and the Rich Man*, 1554, Rijksprentenkabinet, Amsterdam, on loan from the Rijksakademie van Beeldende Kunsten

Much more likely, ter Brugghen drew, as so often, on 16th-century northern European prints. Numerous woodcuts and copperplate engravings of the same subject exist, of which one or more might have served as an inspiration for ter Brugghen. A key work in this regard is the 1554 engraving by Heinrich Aldegrever (c. 1502–1555/61; fig. 103).[7]

It remains unclear who commissioned the work which was painted long after ter Brugghen's return to Utrecht. The subject points to the worlds of charitable institutions, notably hospitals for lepers. So far, however, there is no evidence supporting the suggestion that ter Brugghen's painting may have been created for the relevant hospital in Utrecht.[8] VM

1 Slatkes/Franits 2007, p. 93, cat. A11.
2 Slatkes 1965, pp. 132–133, cat. A27, related a drawing kept at the Rijksprentenkabinet in Amsterdam, which he erroneously identified as 'Judah and Tamar' and ascribed to Dirck van Baburen, to the background scene in ter Brugghen's painting in Utrecht; see also Slatkes/Franits 2007, p. 95, note 13.
3 Domela Nieuwenhuis 2007, pp. 86–88. There Nieuwenhuis also compares the painting to two other versions of the subject, which are considered copies after ter Brugghen by Slatkes/Franits 2007, pp. 94–95, cat. R12 (canvas, 136.5 × 207 cm, St Ferdinand, Bordeaux) and R13 (panel, 127 × 157 cm, location unknown). See also Cat. Utrecht 1999, vol. 1, p. 161, incl. note 6, and vol. 2, p. 758.
4 See Guido Jansen in Exh. cat. Utrecht/Braunschweig 1987/88, p. 128; Domela Nieuwenhuis 2007, p. 83, and Slatkes/Franits 2007, pp. 93–94, cat. A11 (includes an extensive bibliography), esp. p. 94.
5 Canvas, 146 × 221 cm, Cleveland Museum of Art, Cleveland, Delia E. Holden and L.E. Holden Funds, inv. 1939; Nicolson 1958, p. 101, linked to cat. A70.
6 *Lazarus and the Rich Man*, c. 1550, canvas, 62.5 × 44 cm, Johansson Collection, Spain; see Seelig 1994, p. 15, fig. 2; Slatkes/Franits 2007, p. 423, fig. 21.
7 Domela Nieuwenhuis 2007, p. 83, incl. note 18.
8 This was first suggested by Albert Blankert, see Blankert 1982, p. 53, incl. note 42; see also Cat. Utrecht 1999, vol. 1, p. 161.

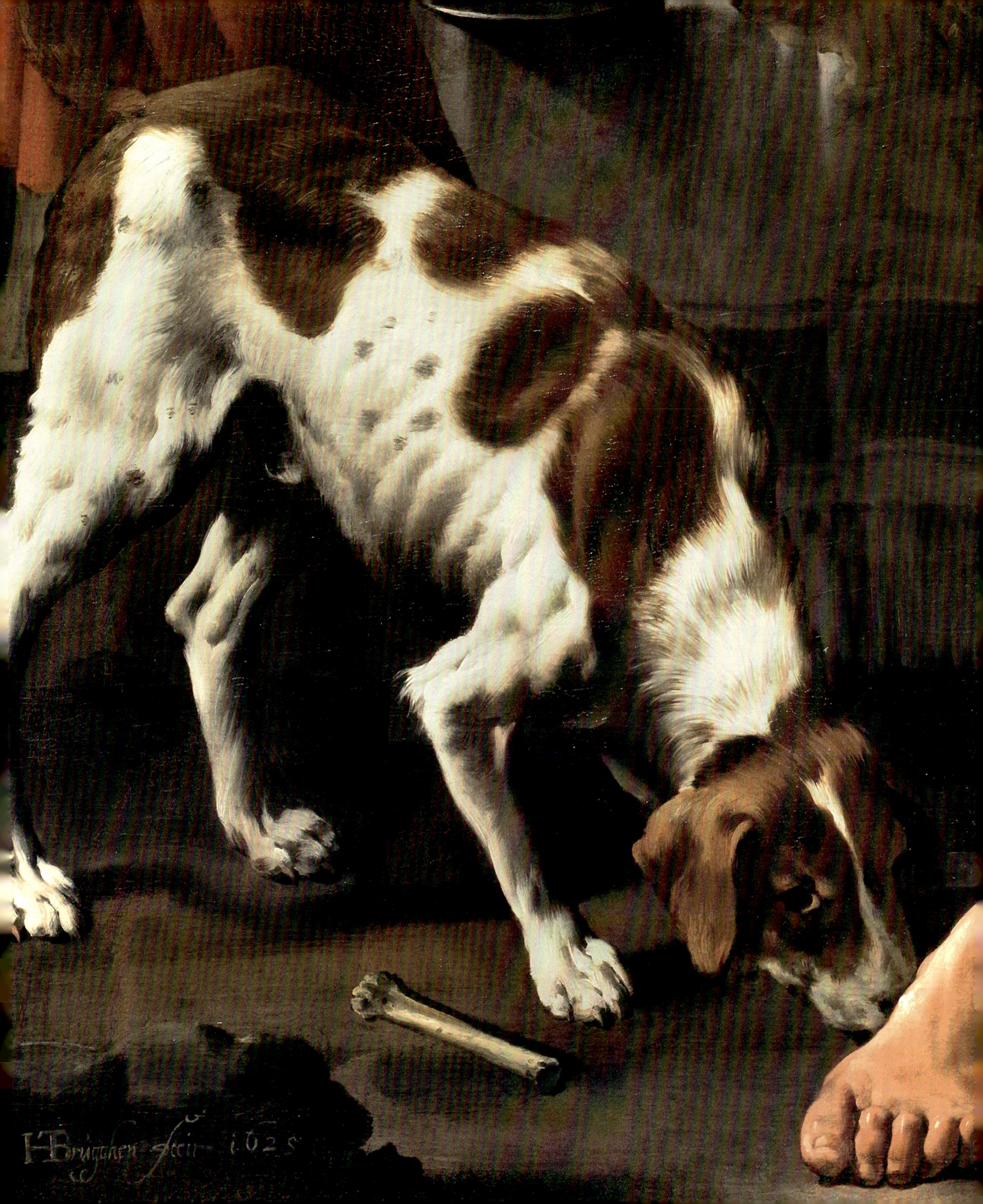
HTBrugghen fecit 1625

c. 1625

The Crucifixion

76
Hendrick ter Brugghen
The Crucifixion with the Virgin and St John, c. 1625
Signed and dated at the foot of the cross:
HTB fecit 162[?]
Canvas, 154.9 × 102.2 cm
The Metropolitan Museum of Art, New York,
Funds from various donors, 1956,
accession number 56.228
Munich only

Among the Utrecht Caravaggisti, Hendrick ter Brugghen was the only one who painted the Crucifixion of Christ (cat. 76).[1] We do not know of any painting of this subject by Caravaggio himself, and among his followers, too, only few artists did crucifixions. In most cases, those works were ecclesiastical commissions.[2]

Ter Brugghen's composition, with the cross rising in the middle and reduction of the figures to the Virgin Mary and St John the Apostle who stand beside the crucified Christ, draws on the medieval pictorial tradition as passed down by altarpieces and private devotional paintings as well as book illuminations. The horizon is set low, leaving only a small strip of ground for the figures to stand on. The flat background does not create any depth effect and evokes the gold grounds of previous centuries (fig. 104). The emaciated, scraggy body of Christ, which is sometimes compared to figures by Matthias Grünewald (1480/83–1528), is also unusual for the early 17th century.[3]

The obvious references to older styles raise questions: did ter Brugghen incorporate them to comply with the wishes of a patron, so the painting could pass for an early northern Netherlandish altarpiece to laymen?[4] Or did the artist perhaps even copy an original that was lost in the iconoclasm?[5]

In spite of the salient medieval characteristics, many factors contradict those assumptions: the scene is presented from a low-angle perspective, causing the figures of the Virgin and St John to tower monumentally. Upon closer inspection, it is clear that the empty eye sockets of the skull are directed at the viewer. The garments of the Virgin Mary and St John feature massive, baroque-style folds, and the sleeve slashed at the shoulder and upper arm of St John is in keeping with contemporary fashion. But the use of Caravaggesque visual language is nowhere more obvious than in the strong chiaroscuro contrasts and striking light effects which highlight important thematic elements such as Christ's side wound as well as the faces and hands of the Virgin and St John. Ter Brugghen shortens the distance to the depicted religious subject through the proximity to the foreground and the physical presence and emotions of the figures. He draws the viewer into the pain over Christ's sacrificial death with a realistic immediacy which would not have been conceivable in the Middle Ages.

The artist devoted special attention to the nuanced treatment of flesh tones. The body of Christ looks like a dead man's body as

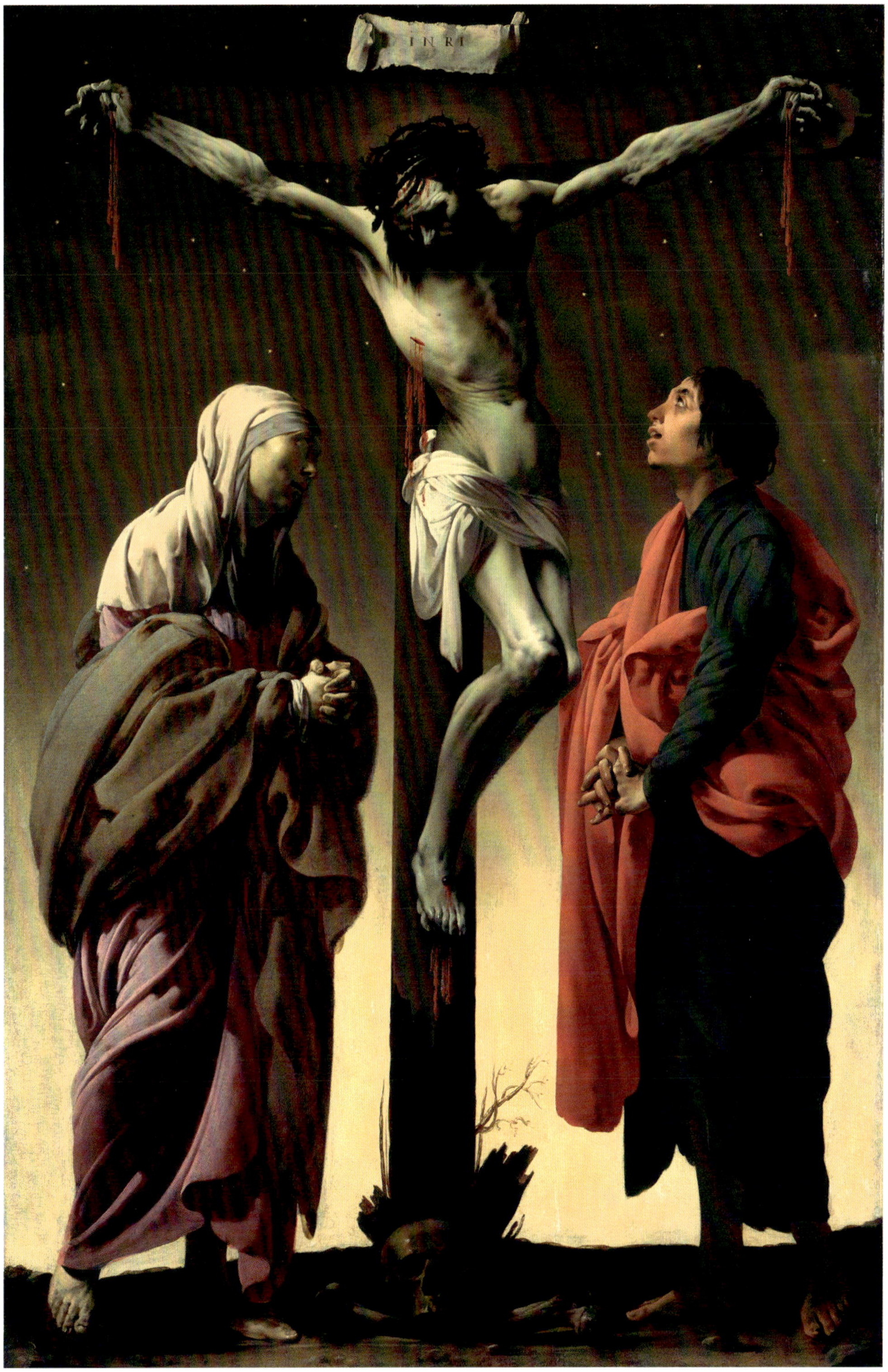

76
Hendrick ter Brugghen
The Crucifixion with the Virgin and St John, c. 1625
The Metropolitan Museum of Art, New York,
Funds from various donors, 1956

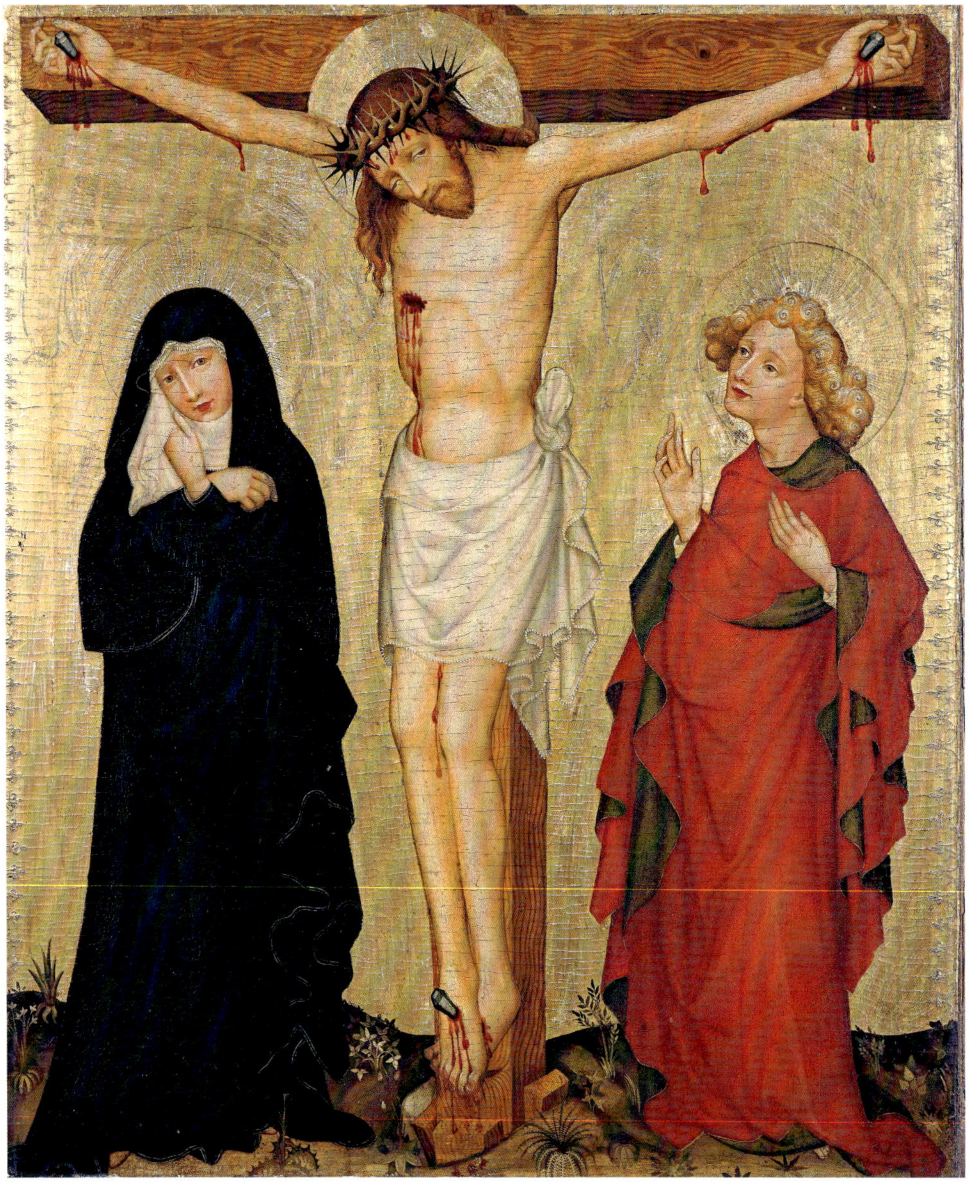

Fig. 104 Austrian/Bohemian (?), *Christ on the Cross*, c. 1400, Staatliche Museen zu Berlin, Gemäldegalerie, Berlin

a result of its grey-greenish colour. The very bright, even flesh tones of the Virgin Mary are alabaster-coloured and conformed to the ideal of beauty. St John, in turn, has a darker skin; the reddened nose as well as the more bronzed hands and feet can also be found in depictions of figures by his contemporaries, including Caravaggio (cat. 7), Ribera (cat. 25), and Baburen (cat. 54).

The orange-yellow sky above the low horizon, which darkens to a grey brown with small twinkling stars towards the top, is unusual for ter Brugghen's oeuvre and especially for Caravaggesque paintings.[6] The only other painting featuring a similarly coloured sky with a horizon set similarly low is his *Saint Sebastian Tended by Irene* in Oberlin, which is dated 1625 (cat. 69).[7]

The depiction of the Passion of Christ played an important role in the efforts of the Counter-Reformation to strengthen the faith.[8] Viscous blood prominently leaks from the wounds of Christ and is about to spill on the Virgin Mary and St John. The way it hangs down almost rope-like from his hands may be yet another echo of the Middle Ages.[9] The accentuation of the blood and Mary's gaze focusing on the side wound of Christ refer to the Eucharist which was of special significance especially in the northern Netherlands during the first decades of the 17th century.[10]

The creation of the painting is seen as related to a Catholic patron.[11] In spite of the predominant Protestantism, part of the population in Utrecht had remained Catholic.[12] Because public display of the faith was banned, it could be practised only in hidden churches, the so-called *schuilkerken*. Perhaps ter Brugghen created this painting for such a *schuilkerk*,[13] although based on its relatively small scale, a private client also cannot be ruled out.

In recent years, a second version of the subject by ter Brugghen has surfaced, which was probably created at the same time as the New York painting (fig. 105).[14] This version, while larger, condenses the pictorial content: the arm span of Christ defines the width of the picture; the life-size figures of the Virgin Mary and St John are cut off by the lower edge and depicted from the hips up. John, who has moved closer to Christ, is cut off by the right edge as well. His folded hands are at the level of Christ's feet and seem to touch them in spite of the spatial distance. Mary has tears dripping from her nose and the mood is gloomy and darkened further by the overcast sky. By intensifying the emotions in the manner of Caravaggio's art, the distance to the action is reduced even further than it is in the New York painting. Because of the focus on what is essential – mourning the death of Christ – the emotional pictorial content has an even more direct impact on the viewer.

With the New York *Crucifixion*, Hendrick ter Brugghen created a work which, based on its formal affinity with medieval art, is unique not just within his oeuvre but within Caravaggesque painting in general. SH

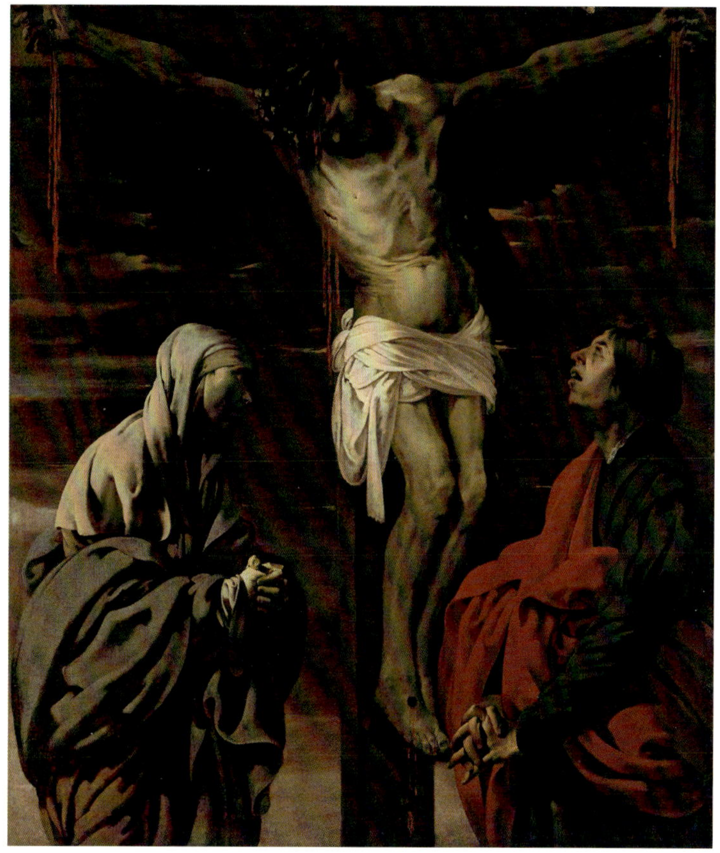

Fig. 105 Hendrick ter Brugghen, *The Crucifixion with Mary and John*, c. 1624/25, private collection

1 Virch 1958; Walter Liedtke in Cat. New York 2007, vol. 1, pp. 109–118, cat. 25; Slatkes/Franits 2007, pp. 105–107, cat. A19; Seaman 2011. A copy of the painting in St Clement's Church in Nes on the island of Ameland was destroyed by fire in 2013: Schillemans 1993, pp. 139–140, 148–149; Slatkes/Franits 2007, p. 108, cat. R22. A version by an unknown artist: *Crucifixion with Members of the Family of Adriaen Willemsz. Ploos*, after 1624, canvas, 106.2 x 80.5 cm, Centraal Museum, Utrecht, inv. 26034; Bok 1996, esp. pp. 210–213; Helmus 2007c; Slatkes/Franits 2007, pp. 108–109.

2 For example, Orazio Gentileschi, *The Crucifixion*, 1618, canvas, 368 x 210 cm, Cattedrale di San Venanzio, Fabriano; Simon Vouet, *The Crucifixion*, 1622, canvas, 375 x 225 cm, Chiesa del Gesù e dei Santi Ambrogio e Andrea, Genoa; Simon Vouet, *The Crucifixion*, 1636/37, canvas, 216 x 146 cm, Musée des Beaux-Arts, Lyon, inv. A 139. Nicolas Régnier, *Crucifixion*, 1647/49, canvas, 365 x 183 cm, Istituzioni di Ricovero e di Educazione (I. R. E), Venice, inv. I.R.E. n° 202.

3 Virch 1958, p. 224; Cat. New York 2007, vol. 1, pp. 109–110.

4 Slatkes/Franits 2007, p. 107.

5 Leonard J. Slatkes in Exh. cat. Utrecht/Braunschweig 1986/87, p. 133; Schillemans 1993.

6 For its possible meaning see Nickel 2007.

7 See also Leonard J. Slatkes in Exh. cat. Utrecht/Braunschweig 1986/87, p. 133.

8 See cats. 16–18, 41–44.

9 For the possible significance of materiality in the paintings of ter Brugghen, see Seaman 2012, esp. pp. 73–102.

10 Cat. New York 2007, vol. 1, p. 112, incl. note 20; Seaman 2011, pp. 489–492.

11 For example, Seaman 2011, pp. 494–495, 514.

12 See the essay by Marten Jan Bok in this volume, p. 24.

13 Cat. New York 2007, vol. 1, p. 109. For the historical background see also Van Eck 1993/94; Seaman 2012, pp. 49–71; Von Rosen 2015, esp. pp. 203–221.

14 c. 1624/25, canvas, 185 x 173 cm, private collection. Slatkes/Franits 2007, pp. 107–108, cat. A20; Franits 2017.

c. 1627

Esau Selling His Birthright

77
Hendrick ter Brugghen
Esau Selling His Birthright, c. 1627
Canvas, 106.7 × 138.8 cm
Signed on the base of the table: HTBrugghen fec. [HTB ligatured]
Museo Nacional Thyssen-Bornemisza, Madrid, inv. 393 (1981.16)

The Book of Genesis tells of Jacob und Esau, the twin sons of Isaac and two men of very different characters (Gen. 25:25–34): 'The boys grew up, and Esau became a skillful hunter, a man of the open country, while Jacob was content to stay at home among the tents'. Esau sells his birthright to Jacob in exchange for some lentil stew. Although he is younger than Esau, Jacob is then aided by his mother, Rebekah, who favours him over his brother, to surreptitiously receive the blessing of the firstborn from his father, Isaac.

Ter Brugghen shows the moment when Jacob offers the lentil stew to his brother who has just returned from hunting.[1] Both are depicted in profile view; between them is a table on which a candle, the scene's only light source, burns. Rebekah stands in the background on the left holding a plate with olives, and Isaac is sitting on the right.

The painting belongs to a group of works ter Brugghen created around 1626–1628, in which the effect of candlelight as an artificial source of light obviously play a central role. These works include both single-figure compositions, such as *Old Man Writing by Candlelight* in Northampton or the so-called *Melancholia* in Toronto, and multi-figure ones.[2] With regard to the painting in Madrid, it seems that an Italian source also played an essential role. A painting of the same subject by Jacopo Bassano (c. 1510/15–1592) shows a number of similarities with ter Brugghen's painting both in the arrangement of the figures and in the composition as a night scene by candlelight.[3] Different versions of the composition survive, whose attribution is unclear, even though they all seem to trace back to a prototype from the Bassano circle (fig. 106).[4] It can be safely assumed that ter Brugghen was aware of the northern Italian source, especially since his second version of the subject in Berlin, which was probably created slightly earlier, also draws on Bassano (fig. 107).[5] The biblical text does not say whether the scene took place during the day or at night. The fact that ter Brugghen, like his source, chose to depict a night scene by candlelight, thereby deviating from the iconographic tradition, is thus indicative of his work's close connection to the Bassano painting. But it is not certain whether he had access to one of the Bassano-circle versions of the subject in Utrecht, as has been suggested.[6] The subte and nuanced candlelight effects clearly attest to ter Brugghen's interest in intra-pictorial artificial light sources, which Honthorst had developed in Rome and with which he continued to impress his fellow painters after his return to Utrecht. VM

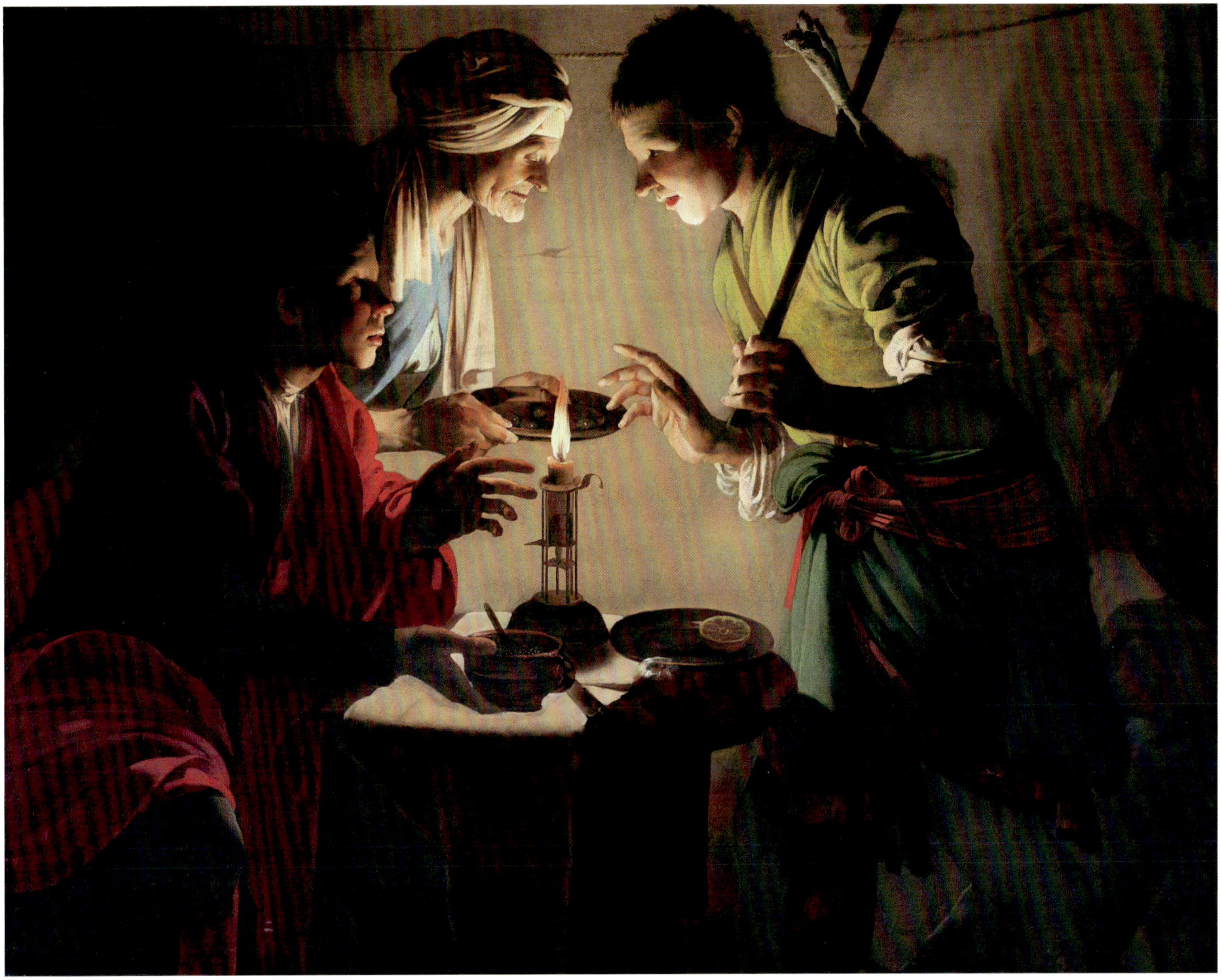

77
Hendrick ter Brugghen
Esau Selling His Birthright, c. 1627
Museo Nacional Thyssen-Bornemisza, Madrid

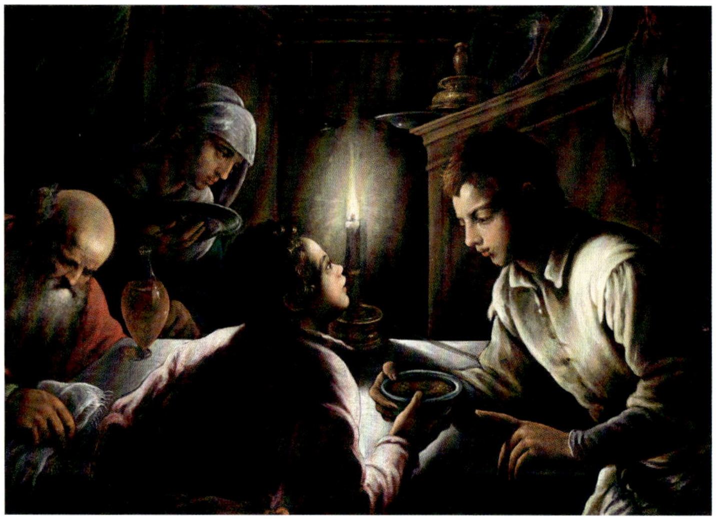

Fig. 106 Francesco Bassano the Younger (?), *Esau Selling His Birthright*, 16th century, Musée d'art et d'histoire Baron Gérard (MAHB), Bayeux

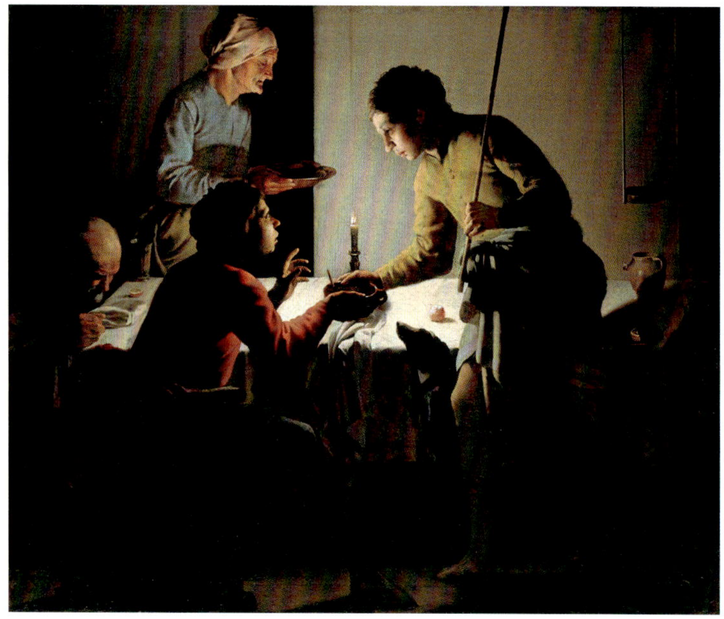

Fig. 107 Hendrick ter Brugghen, *Esau Selling His Birthright*, c. 1625/27, Staatliche Museen zu Berlin, Gemäldegalerie, Berlin

1 Slatkes/Franits 2007, pp. 76–78, cat. A2.
2 Canvas, 65.8 × 52.7 cm, Smith College Museum of Art, Northampton, inv. 1957.10; Slatkes/Franits 2007, pp. 164–165, cat. A53. Canvas, 67 × 56.5 cm, Art Gallery of Ontario, on loan from a private collection; Slatkes/Franits 2007, pp. 152–154, cat. A46. See also ter Brugghen's *The Concert* in London (cat. 67) and *The Concert* in State Hermitage Museum, Saint Petersburg, canvas, 102 × 83 cm, inv. 5599; Slatkes/Franits 2007, pp. 191–192, cat. A75. See for this also Mar Borobia in Exh. cat. Madrid 2016, pp. 146–147, cat. 32.
3 Nicolson 1960, fig. 11.
4 Francesco Bassano the Younger (?), *Esau Selling His Birthright*, 16th century, canvas, 89.5 × 128.3 cm, Musée d'art et d'histoire Baron Gérard (MAHB), Bayeux, inv. P0173. See for this Cat. Madrid 1989, pp. 508–511, cat. 121 with figs. 3, 4, as well as Slatkes/Franits 2007, p. 425, fig. 25.
5 *Esau Selling his Birthright*, c. 1625/27, canvas, 94.5 × 115.5 cm, Staatliche Museen zu Berlin, Gemäldegalerie, inv. 1982; Slatkes/Franits 2007, pp. 75–76, cat. A1.
6 As discussed by Leonard J. Slatkes in Exh. cat. Utrecht/Braunschweig 1986/87, p. 149.

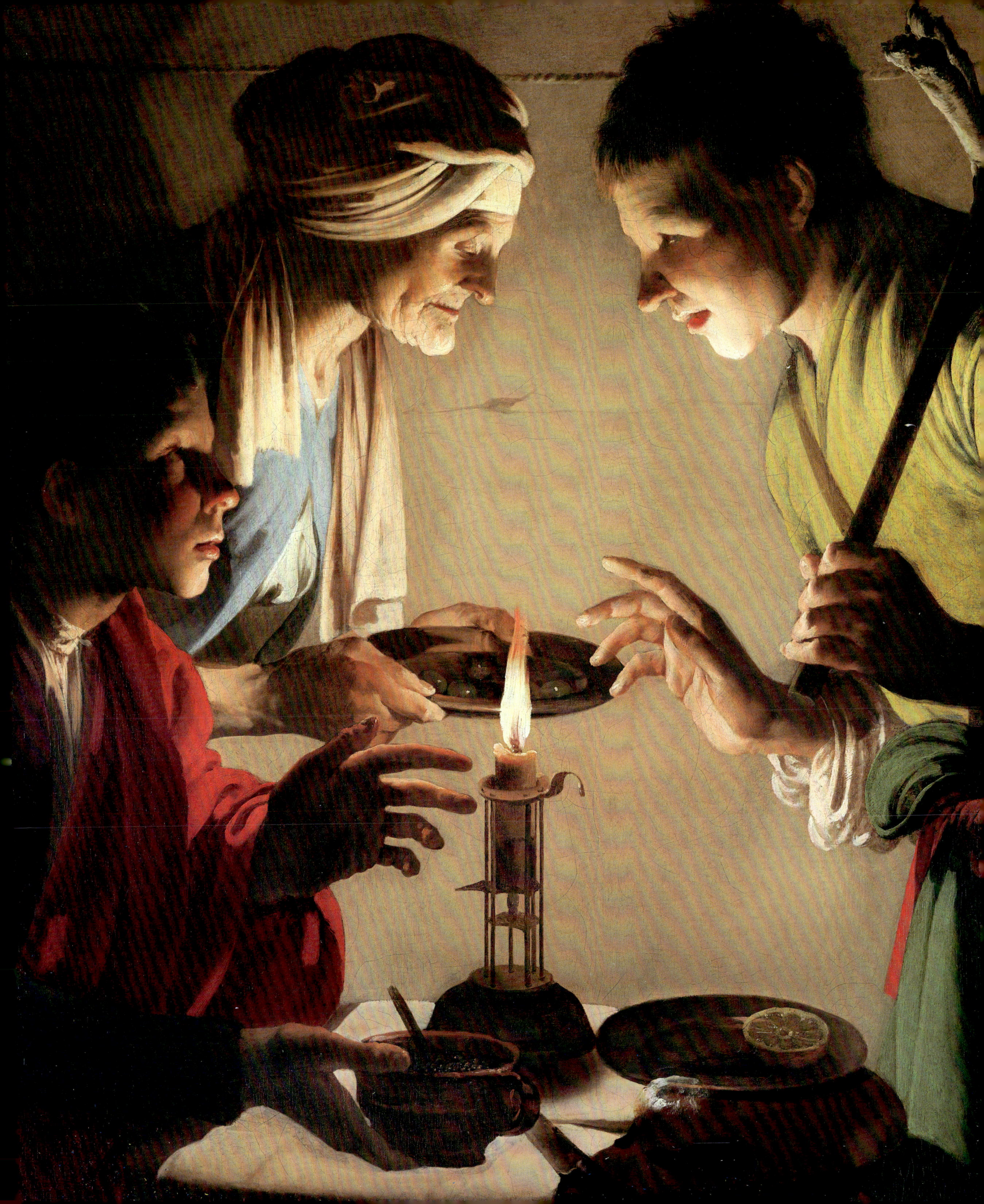

1629

The Annunciation

78
Hendrick ter Brugghen
The Annunciation, 1629
Canvas, 216.5 × 176.5 cm
Signed and dated bottom right:
HTBrugghe[n] 1629 [HTB ligatured]
Stadsmuseum De Hofstadt, Diest, inv. S11

The Annunciation, featuring life-size figures of the Archangel Gabriel and Mary, is a work ter Brugghen painted in the year of his death, 1629.[1] The painting's early provenance is uncertain. It was linked to an Annunciation by the painter, which is mentioned in a promissory note dated 18 April 1638. At the time, the painting was apparently in Deventer, in the possession of the widow of a certain Ryssen, from whom the painter Lucas Luce claimed to have bought it.[2] There are, however, good reasons to doubt this identification, as a second version of ter Brugghen's painting, which is in Kunsthaus Zürich (fig. 35), appears to be a more likely candidate based on the dimensions.[3]

The subject, format and dimensions suggest that the painting in Diest originally served as an altarpiece. Before being transferred to the museum, the painting was in the Sint-Catharinakerk (beguinage church) in Diest until 1959. When and how it had found its way there is unclear, because the relevant archive documents are lost. In general, scholarship assumes that ter Brugghen was commissioned by the Beguines, especially considering that they had already commissioned other altarpieces in 1627 and 1628, among others, from Frans Francken the Younger (1581–1642).[4] Suggestions that the departure of the Flemish Caravaggist Theodoor van Loon (1581/82–1649) to Italy in 1628 prompted the appointment of ter Brugghen seem doubtful.[5] It is noteworthy that the Beguines also owned a copy of Dirck van Baburen's *Entombment of Christ* in San Pietro in Montorio in Rome (fig. 66).[6]

The genesis of the *Annunciation* in Diest is closely related to a painting of the same subject by Jan Janssen (1590–1650) after a lost work by Dirck van Baburen (fig. 108).[7] Leonard J. Slatkes has drawn attention to various iconographic elements in ter Brugghen's painting, which are unusual in the context of an Annunciation: for example, the group of angels on clouds above the dove of the Holy Spirit, who are approaching Mary with a woven wreath. In this motif he sees the moment of the Coronation of the Virgin 'pushed back' and combined simultaneously with the incarnation. It seems at best doubtful whether the swift for winding yarn between Mary and Gabriel is, in fact, to be understood as symbolising the Cross of Christ and thus as an allusion to the Passion at the time of the incarnation of Christ.[8] Like the basket with sewing things, it may symbolise Mary's domestic virtues. According to the apocryphal Proto-Gospel of Jacob, moreover, Mary was busy

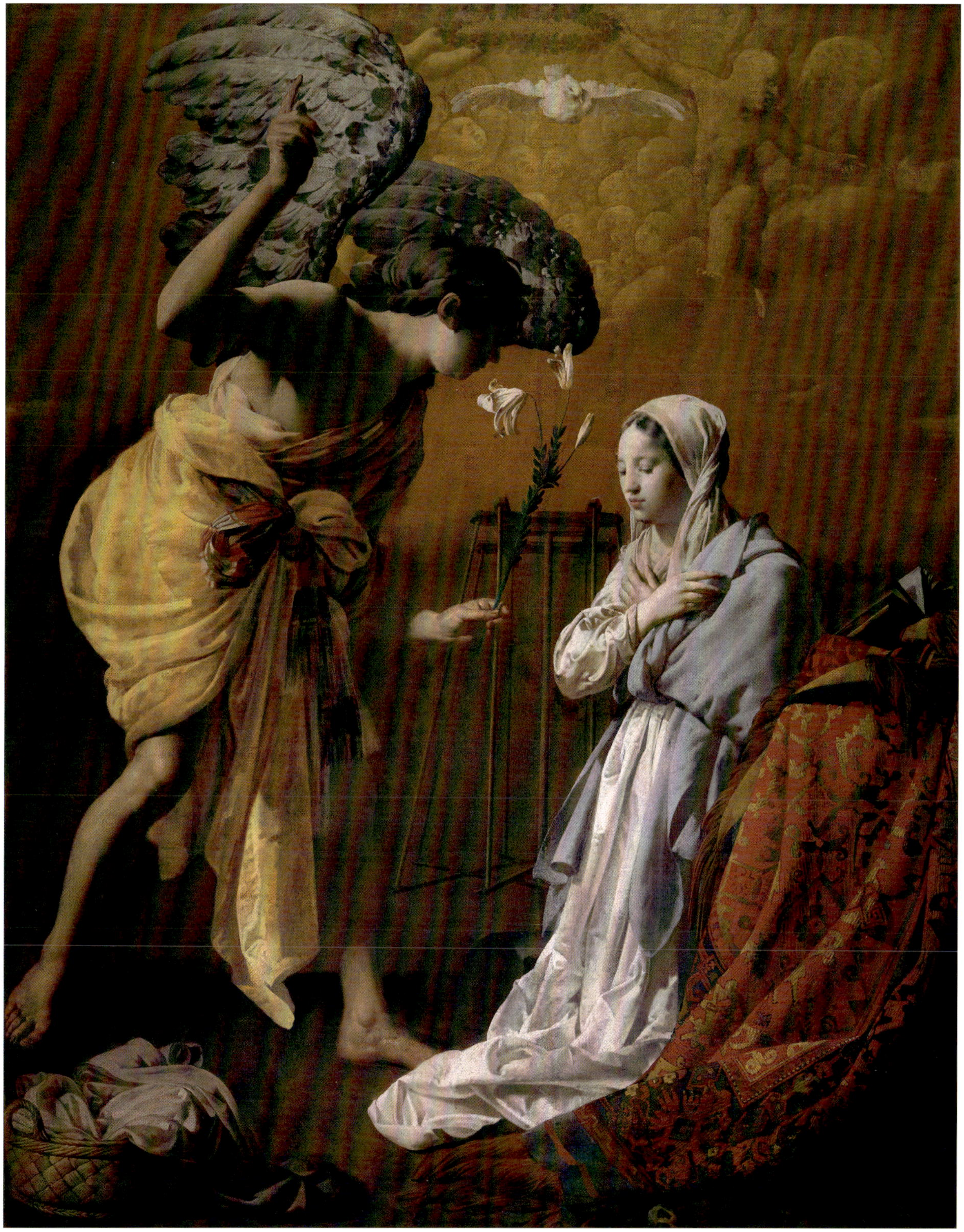

78
Hendrick ter Brugghen
The Annunciation, 1629
Stadsmuseum De Hofstadt, Diest

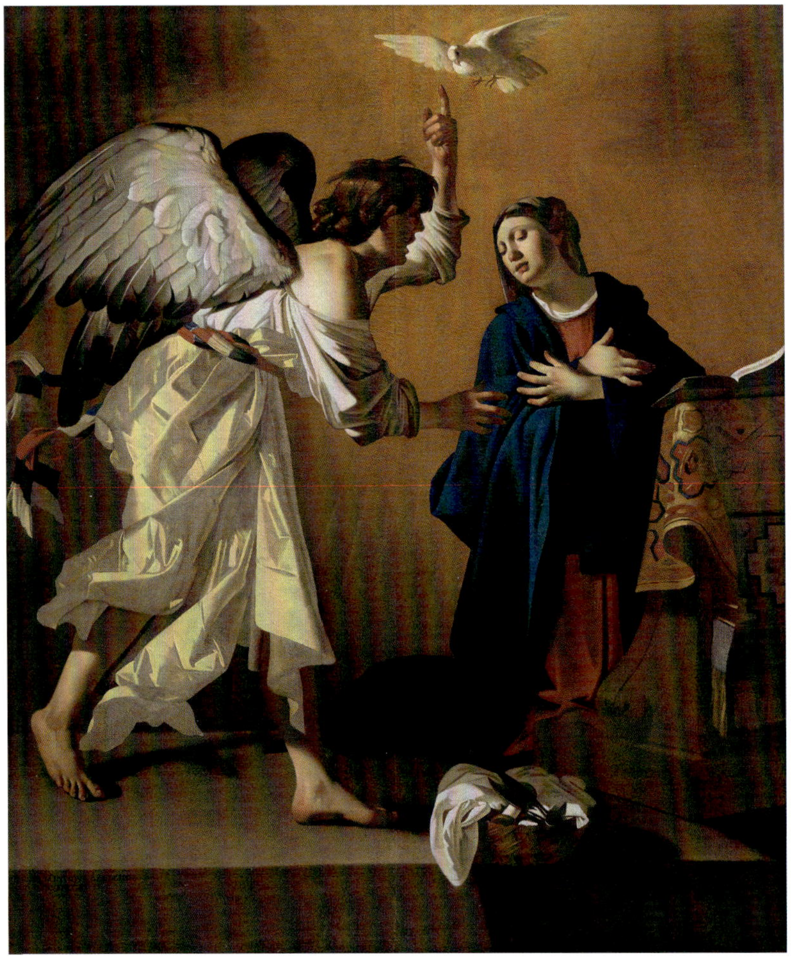

Fig. 108 Jan Janssens (after Dirck van Baburen), *The Annunciation*, c. 1621, Museum voor Schone Kunsten, Ghent

manufacturing precious fabrics (scarlet and purple) at the time of the Annunciation.[9] The dog lying on the right under the table rug may be understood in a general sense as a symbol of faithfulness, a meaning that can be traced back to Gregory the Great and Isidore of Seville.[10] VM

1 Slatkes/Franits 2007, pp. 89–91, cat. A9.
2 The document was published by Bredius 1915–1922, vol. 4, p. 1147; Nicolson 1958, p. 62, linked it to the painting in Diest. See for this most recently, Slatkes/Franits 2007, p. 89.
3 *The Annunciation*, c. 1624, canvas, 104 × 84 cm, Kunsthaus Zürich, Zürich, inv. 2010/1. See Slatkes/Franits 2007, pp. 88–89, cat. A8; Klemm 2010.
4 For a summary of the campaign to furnish the church in Diest, see most recently Von Rosen 2015, pp. 175–181.
5 See Leonard J. Slatkes in Exh. cat. Utrecht/Braunschweig 1986/87, p. 168, and Slatkes/Franits 2007, p. 90.
6 Leonard J. Slatkes in Exh. cat. Utrecht/Braunschweig 1986/87, p. 168; Franits 2013a, p. 86, cat. A3R14.
7 Nicolson 1958, p. 63, was the first to recognise the connection of both paintings and subsequently also suggest that Janssens' *Annunciation* (c. 1621, canvas, 258.5 × 220.5 cm, Museum voor Schone Kunsten, Ghent, inv. S-91) is a copy after a lost painting by Baburen (Nicolson 1979, p. 62). See for this also Leonard J. Slatkes in Exh. cat. Utrecht/Braunschweig 1986/87, p. 167, incl. note 3. By contrast, see Christopher Brown in Exh. cat. Washington/Detroit/Amsterdam 1980/81, p. 108, cat. 13; Von Rosen 2015, pp. 56–60 and 186, note 20. Both authors consider Janssens' *Annunciation* as dependent on ter Brugghen's painting in Diest.
8 See for this Leonard J. Slatkes in Exh. cat. Utrecht/Braunschweig 1986/87, p. 168; Slatkes/Franits 2007, pp. 90–91.
9 Hennecke/Schneemelcher 1968, vol. 1, p. 284.
10 See Dittrich 2004, pp. 226–245, esp. p. 227.

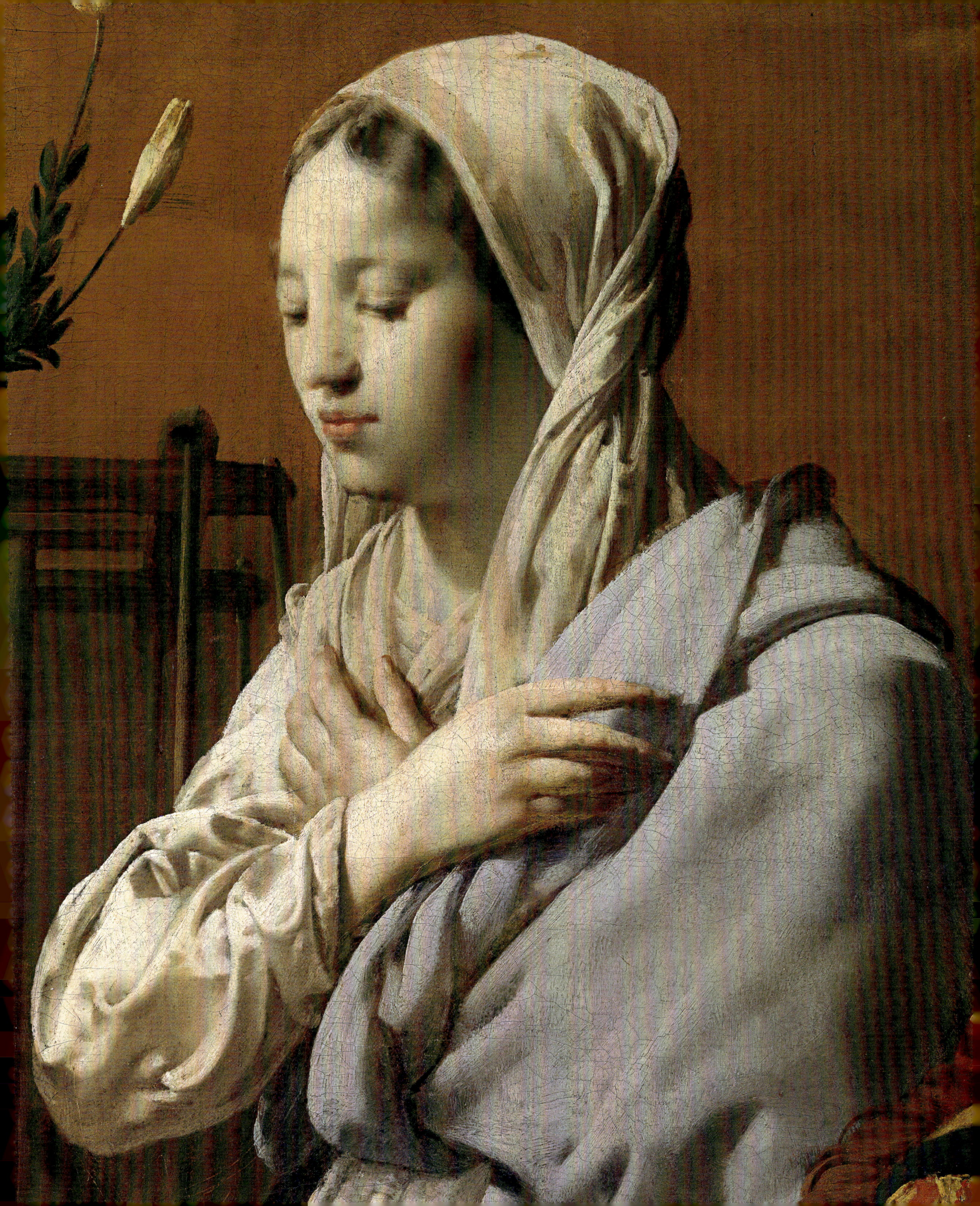

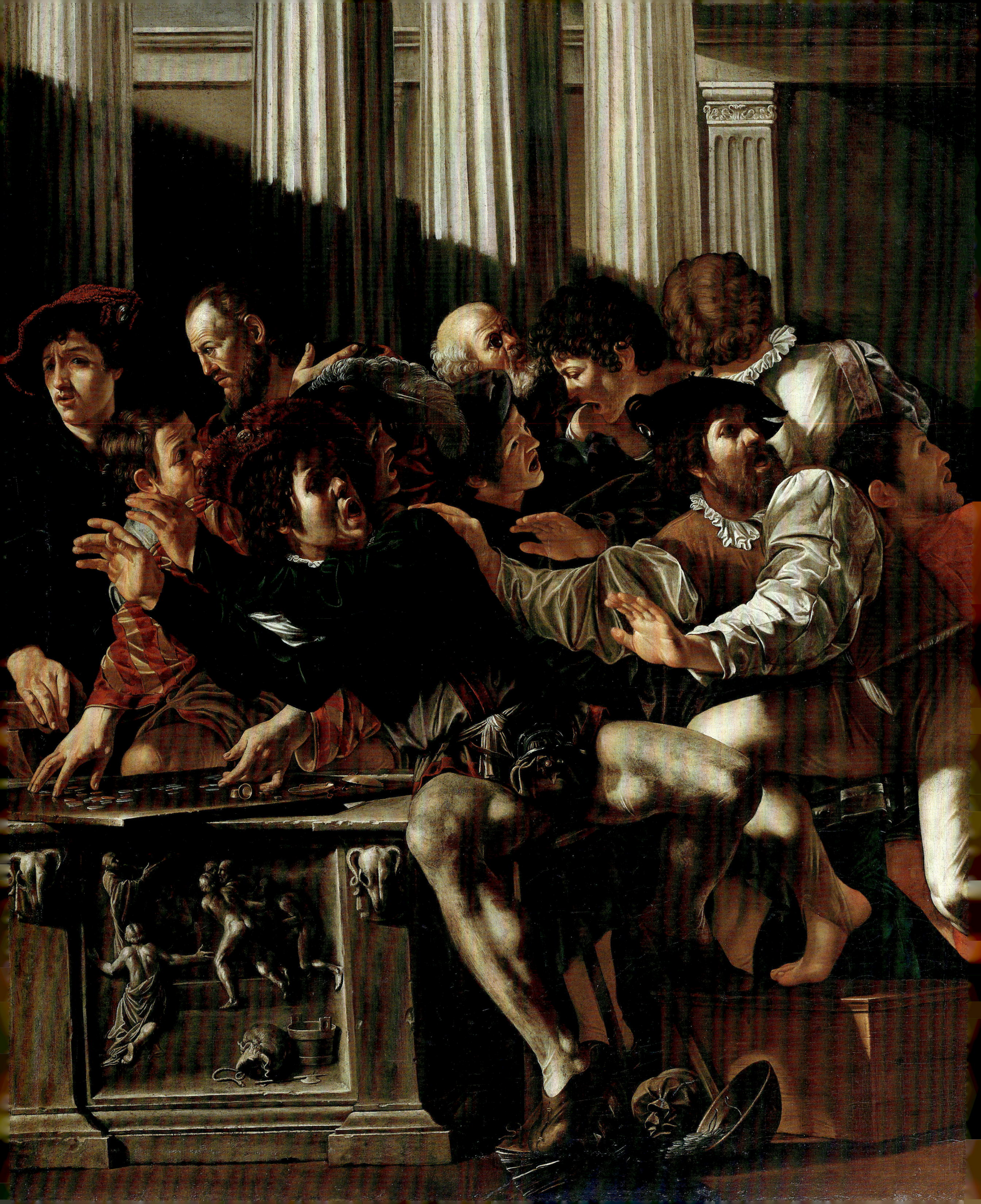

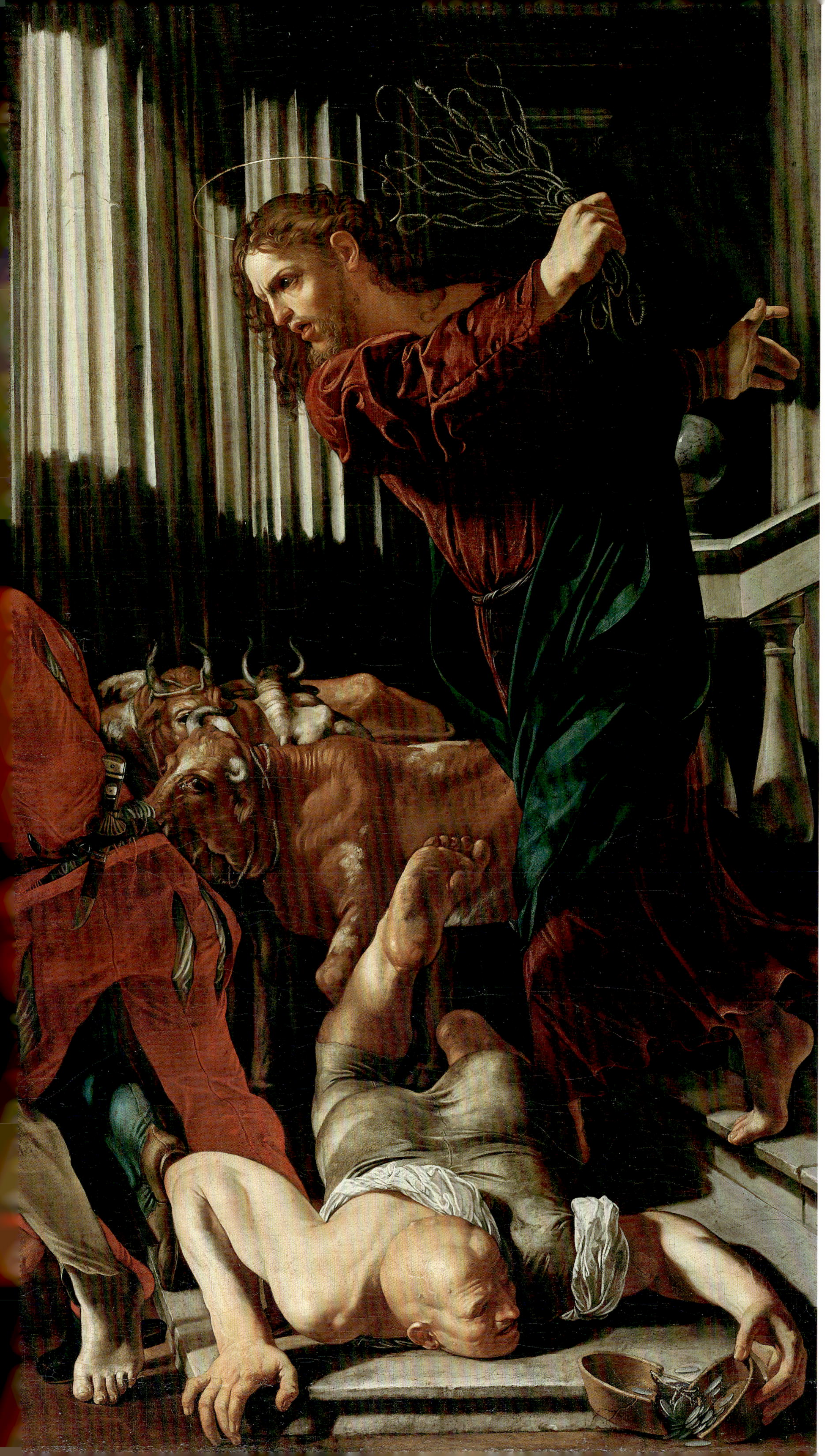

Appendices

Artist Biographies and Works Exhibited

Dirck van Baburen (c. 1592/93–1624)

Born in Wijk bij Duurstede near Utrecht in c. 1592/93, Baburen received his early artistic training from Paulus Moreelse in Utrecht. In 1611, he is listed for the last time as a member of the local painters' guild. Shortly thereafter, he travelled to Italy, where a painting in Parma, signed by him in 1615 and mentioned in historic sources, is considered the earliest evidence of his stay in Italy. In Rome, he occasionally lived together with his fellow countryman David de Haen and Nicolas Régnier. The most important commissioned works are his paintings for Pietro Cussida in the Pietà Chapel in San Pietro in Montorio. Baburen returned to Utrecht around 1620/21 and died there in 1624. During the final years of his life, he increasingly painted secular motifs, such as, for example, musicians as half-length figures.

21
The Entombment of Christ, 1617/18
Canvas, 219.4 × 139.5 cm
Centraal Museum, Utrecht

24
Christ among the Doctors, c. 1618
Canvas, 135 × 202 cm
Museo della Misericordia, Florence

31
Boy with a Jew's Harp, 1621
Canvas, 65 × 52 cm
Centraal Museum, Utrecht

34
Lute Player, 1622
Canvas, 71.2 × 58.5 cm
Centraal Museum, Utrecht

37
Christ Driving the Money Changers from the Temple, 1621
Canvas, 158 × 206 cm
The Schorr Collection

41
The Crowning with Thorns, c. 1621/22
Canvas, 106 × 136 cm
Museum Catharijneconvent, Utrecht

45
Christ among the Doctors, 1622
Canvas, 190 × 210 cm
Nasjonalmuseet for kunst, arkitektur og design, Oslo

54
Prometheus Being Chained by Vulcan, 1623
Canvas, 201 × 182 cm
Rijksmuseum, Amsterdam

Orazio Borgianni (1577/78–1616)

The son of a Florentine carpenter, Borgianni was born in Rome and was presumably trained by his brother in the art of painting. At the beginning of his training, he travelled to Sicily. Between 1598 and 1603, he stayed in Spain, where he studied the works in local collections. It remains disputed whether Borgianni also worked for the Spanish court during this time. In February 1604, he is documented in the Accademia di San Luca in Rome, where he countersigned accounts with Guido Reni. After the death of his wife, whom he had married in Spain, he moved back to Rome permanently in 1606/07, remaining there until his death in 1616. Here too, he continued to maintain intensive contacts with clients who in turn had close ties to the Spanish king. In the final years of his life, the influence of Caravaggio's painting on Borgianni's work intensified, combined with Spanish inspiration.

27
Christ among the Doctors, c. 1609
Canvas, 78.2 × 104.6 cm
Rijksmuseum, Amsterdam, on loan from the Broere Charitable Foundation

61
David and Goliath, 1609/10
Canvas, 119 × 143 cm
Real Accademia de Bellas Artes de San Fernando, Madrid

Hendrick ter Brugghen (1588–1629)

Ter Brugghen was born the son of a senior civil servant in either The Hague or Utrecht. In Utrecht, he was a student of Abraham Bloemaert. The dates and stages of his journey to Italy are not documented; it is believed that he spent time in, among others, Rome, Naples and northern Italy. In the summer of 1614, he was verifiably in Milan, together with two fellow painters who were on their way home to the Netherlands. Ter Brugghen's earliest extant painting was executed in Utrecht in 1616. That same year, he is already listed as a member of the Guild of St Luke and married Jacoba Verbeek. He lived in Utrecht until his death, with the exception of the years 1619 to 1621, during which he presumably made a second trip to Italy.

3
The Penitent St Peter, 1616
Canvas, 67.7 × 85.8 cm
Centraal Museum, Utrecht

13
The Liberation of St Peter, 1624
Canvas, 104.5 × 86.5 cm
Mauritshuis, The Hague

14
The Liberation of St Peter, 1629
Canvas, 152 × 210 cm
Staatliches Museum Schwerin, Schwerin

17
The Mocking of Christ, c. 1625
Canvas, 157 × 118.5 cm
Musée des Beaux-Arts de Rennes, Rennes, on loan from the Musée de l'Assistance Publique, Paris

30
The Merry Drinker, c. 1625
Canvas, 71.4 × 59.8 cm
Centraal Museum, Utrecht

32
Fife Player, 1621
Canvas, 71.3 × 56 cm
Museumslandschaft Hessen Kassel, Gemäldegalerie Alte Meister, Kassel

33
Flute Player, 1621
Canvas, 71.5 × 56 cm
Museumslandschaft Hessen Kassel, Gemäldegalerie Alte Meister, Kassel

36
The Calling of St Matthew, 1621
Canvas, 102 × 137 cm
Centraal Museum, Utrecht

47
The Incredulity of St Thomas, c. 1622
Canvas, 108.1 × 133.2 cm
Rijksmuseum, Amsterdam

50
The Gamblers, 1623
Canvas, 85.4 × 114.9 cm
Minneapolis Institute of Art, The William Hood Dunwoody Fund, Minneapolis

55
David Praised by the Israelite Women, 1623
Canvas, 81.8 × 105.4 cm
North Carolina Museum of Art, Raleigh

67
The Concert, c. 1626/27
Canvas, 99.1 × 116.8 cm
The National Gallery, London

69
St Sebastian Tended by Irene, 1625
Canvas, 149 × 119.4 cm
Allen Memorial Art Museum, Oberlin College, R. T. Miller, Jr. Fund, Oberlin, Ohio

75
The Rich Man and the Poor Lazarus, 1625
Canvas, 168.2 × 207.3 cm
Centraal Museum, Utrecht

76
The Crucifixion with the Virgin and St John, c. 1625
Canvas, 154.9 × 102.2 cm
The Metropolitan Museum of Art, New York, Funds from various donors, 1956

77
Esau Selling His Birthright, c. 1627
Canvas, 106.7 × 138.8 cm
Museo Nacional Thyssen-Bornemisza, Madrid

78
The Annunciation, 1629
Canvas, 216.5 × 176.5 cm
Stadsmuseum De Hofstadt, Diest

Michelangelo Merisi, called Caravaggio (1571–1610)

Born the son of Fermo Merisi of Caravaggio in Milan, Michelangelo trained there from 1584 onwards as an apprentice to Simone Peterzano. The date of his arrival in Rome is not documented. In the mid-1590s, he was taken into the household of his patron, Cardinal Francesco Maria del Monte, in the Palazzo Madama. Through Del Monte, he met Vincenzo Giustiniani, another important patron. In 1599, Caravaggio received his first public commission, the painting of the altarpieces of the Contarelli Chapel; this was followed by the side paintings in the Cerasi Chapel. From 1602/03 on, he was commissioned to paint works for the most important Roman families, including the Matteis, the Barberinis and the Borgheses. In May 1606, Caravaggio killed Ranuccio Tomassoni in a dispute, whereupon he fled to Naples. From 1607 on, he stayed in Malta, but was forced to flee from the island the following year due to a conflict and, after a one-year sojourn in Sicily, returned to Naples. On his journey back to Rome, Caravaggio died in Porto Ercole on 18 July 1610.

2
Copy after Caravaggio
The Crucifixion of St Peter, 1602/05
Canvas, 230 × 170 cm
Museo del Patriarca del Real Colegio Seminario de Corpus Christi, Valencia

7
St Jerome Meditating, 1605/06
Canvas, 145.5 × 101.5 cm
Museu de Montserrat, Montserrat

22
The Entombment of Christ, 1602/03
Canvas, 300 × 203 cm
Musei Vaticani, Pinacoteca, Città del Vaticano

48
Copy after Caravaggio
The Incredulity of St Thomas, 1600/25
Canvas, 108 × 146 cm
Galleria degli Uffizi, Florence

56
Medusa, called *Medusa Murtola*, 1597
Canvas on panel, diameter 44.68 cm, circle diameter 48/49 cm
Private collection

73
The Fortune Teller, c. 1595/96
Canvas, 115 × 150 cm
Musei Capitolini, Pinacoteca, Rome

Francesco Boneri, called Cecco del Caravaggio (c. 1588/90–after 1620)

Little is known about the life of Cecco del Caravaggio. It is believed that he came from a family of painters from Alzano Lombardo. His name presumably refers to his close relationship with Caravaggio, whom he served as a model and with whom he possibly lived in Rome in 1605. It is assumed that he accompanied Caravaggio on his flight from there to Naples. In 1613, he is mentioned among the team of painters who decorated the Villa Lante in Bagnaia. His painting of *Christ Driving the Merchants from the Temple* was in the collection of Vincenzo Giustiniani. Around 1619/20, he painted an altarpiece depicting the Resurrection of Christ for the chapel of Piero Guicciardini in Santa Felicita in Florence; the work was, however, rejected by the client and sold on the Roman art market. After 1620, all traces of the artist disappear.

39
Christ Driving the Merchants from the Temple, 1610/15
Canvas, 128 × 173 cm
Staatliche Museen zu Berlin, Gemäldegalerie, Berlin

43
Christ Crowned with Thorns, c. 1612/15
Canvas, 119.5 × 148.5 cm
Herzog Anton Ulrich-Museum, Braunschweig

60
David and Goliath, c. 1605/07
Canvas, 185.5 × 135 cm
National Gallery of Ireland, Dublin

63
Judith and her Maidservant with the Head of Holofernes, 1621/24
Canvas, 136.6 × 159.1 cm
Wadsworth Atheneum Museum of Art, The Ella Gallup Sumner and Mary Catlin Sumner Collection, Hartford

Orazio Gentileschi (1563–1639)

Born Orazio Lomi in Pisa, Orazio Gentileschi later adopted his mother's surname. Alongside his brothers Baccio and Aurelio, he presumably trained with his father, a Florentine goldsmith. From about 1575 on, he appeared in Rome as, among other roles, a collaborator in large-scale Church projects under Sixtus V. Around 1600, he met Caravaggio, whose artistic influence on Gentileschi's painting in the following years is obvious. He received commissions for altarpieces from, among others, Principe Paolo Savelli, who became his most important patron. The 1612 trial against Agostino Tassi for the rape of Gentileschi's daughter Artemisia was apparently so damaging to his reputation that Orazio moved to Genoa. In 1624, he followed the call of Maria de' Medici to Paris and, in 1626, accepted the offer of the Duke of Buckingham to live in London, where he remained until his death.

Gerard van Honthorst (1592–1656)

The son of a painter, Honthorst was born in Utrecht and trained in the workshop of Abraham Bloemaert. The year of his arrival in Rome is uncertain; the earliest document of his stay there is a drawing, dated 1616, after a painting by Caravaggio. Until his departure in 1620, he lived in the household of Benedetto and Vincenzo Giustiniani. In Rome, Honthorst received commissions from important patrons for altar and gallery paintings. Of these, his artificially lit night scenes in particular gained him notoriety, so much so that he was later nicknamed 'Gherardo delle Notti'. Back in Utrecht, he ran a large workshop with numerous students, including Joachim von Sandrart. From April to December 1628, he worked at the English court of King Charles I and was granted English citizenship in November of the same year. In the following years, his international reputation grew in aristocratic circles. In 1640, he was elected president of the Utrecht painters' guild. Honthorst died in Utrecht in 1656.

1
The Crucifixion of St Peter, 1616
Pen on paper, brown wash, 378 × 265 mm
Nasjonalmuseet for kunst, architektur og design, Oslo

9
The Denial of St Peter, c. 1616/17
Canvas, 150 × 197 cm
Musée des Beaux-Arts de Rennes, Rennes

12
The Liberation of St Peter, c. 1616/18
Canvas, 129 × 179 cm
Staatliche Museen zu Berlin, Gemäldegalerie, Berlin

16
The Mocking of Christ, c. 1617
Canvas, 146.1 × 207 cm
Los Angeles County Museum of Art, Los Angeles

19
Christ before the High Priest, c. 1617
Canvas, 272 × 183 cm
The National Gallery, London

20
The Beheading of John the Baptist, 1617/18
Canvas, 345 × 215 cm
Santa Maria della Scala, Rome

28
Merry Company with a Lute Player, c. 1619/20
Canvas, 144 × 212 cm
Galleria degli Uffizi, Florence

29
The Debauched Student, 1625
Canvas, 125 × 157 cm
Bayerische Staatsgemäldesammlungen, Alte Pinakothek, Munich

66
The Concert, 1623
Canvas, 123.5 × 205 cm
National Gallery of Art, Patrons' Permanent Fund and Florian Carr Fund, Washington, D.C.

68
St Sebastian, c. 1623
Canvas, 101 × 117 cm
The National Gallery, London

72
The Procuress, 1625
Panel, 71 × 104 cm
Centraal Museum, Utrecht

Bartolomeo Manfredi (1582–1622)
Manfredi was born in Ostiano in Northern Italy. He received his training in Milan, Cremona and Brescia. Around 1605, he moved to Rome, where he was presumably active in the workshop of Cristoforo Roncalli. In 1610, he is documented for the first time as a resident painter in Rome, where he lived until his death. He is credited with having played a leading role in the dissemination of the Caravaggesque style. Described by Joachim von Sandrart as the 'Manfrediana Methodus', his style particularly influenced young artists in the 1610s and 1620s, including the Utrecht Caravaggisti Valentin de Boulogne, Nicolas Régnier and Nicolas Tournier. Manfredi's works were also appreciated by collectors such as Vincenzo Giustiniani and the Medici family in Florence.

26
Christ among the Doctors, c. 1618
Canvas, 130 × 190 cm
Galleria degli Uffizi, Florence

35
La Zingara (The Gypsy Girl), c. 1613/15
Canvas, 65 × 59 cm
Private collection, Courtesy Nicolas Joly Art Conseil

42
The Crowning with Thorns, c. 1608/10
Canvas, 119 × 138.5 cm
Bayerische Staatsgemäldesammlungen, Munich, Staatsgalerie im Neuen Schloss Schleißheim

62
The Triumph of David, c. 1614/16
Canvas, 128 × 97 cm
Musée du Louvre, Paris

Nicolas Régnier (1591–1667)
Régnier was born in Maubeuge (then part of Flanders, today France), and received his early training with Abraham Janssens in Antwerp. Around 1616/17, he is documented in Parma and from 1620 onwards in Rome. During that year, he shared accommodation there with Dirck van Baburen and David de Haen. According to Joachim von Sandrart, Régnier was active in the workshop of Bartolomeo Manfredi, who presumably introduced him to Vincenzo Giustiniani, who appointed him as his official painter in 1622. Later, he owned his own workshop and was not only associated with the Bentvueghels but was also a member of the elite Virtuosi al Pantheon. Around 1625/26, he moved to Venice, where he stayed until the end of his life. He enjoyed notable recognition there as a foreign artist. In addition to his artistic achievements, Régnier was well known for his international contacts and his activities as a collector.

52
Cardsharps and Fortune Teller, c. 1623/25
Canvas, 174 × 228 cm
Szépművészeti Múzeum, Budapest

70
St Sebastian, c. 1624/26
Canvas, 134 × 98 cm
Staatliche Kunstsammlungen Dresden, Gemäldegalerie Alte Meister, Dresden

71
St Sebastian, 1624/26
Canvas, 104.1 × 78.7 cm
The Chrysler Museum of Art, Norfolk, Virginia

Jusepe de Ribera (1591–1652)
Also known during his lifetime as Lo Spagnoletto ('the little Spaniard'), Ribera was born in Xàtiva in the province of Valencia as the son of a shoemaker and presumably trained with Francesco Ribalta. Around 1609/10, Ribera moved to Italy, perhaps because of the economic decline of the Spanish Mediterranean region. In 1611, he stayed in Parma and from 1612 onwards in Rome. In 1613, his membership in the local Accademia di San Luca is documented. Ribera's paintings were represented in the well-known Roman collections; Vincenzo Giustiniani alone owned 13 of his works. The stylistic proximity of his early Roman works to northern European painting suggests a close exchange with young Dutch and Flemish artists. In 1616, he moved to Naples, then part of the Spanish Empire, where he lived until his death. Here, he painted, among others, a number of important works for the reigning Duke of Osuna. His workshop there enjoyed an international reputation.

4
St Peter, 1616/20
Canvas, 78 × 65 cm
Quadreria dei Girolamini, Naples

5
St Andrew, 1615/20
Canvas, 136 × 112 cm
Quadreria dei Girolamini, Naples

10
The Denial of St Peter, c. 1615/16
Canvas, 163 × 233 cm
Gallerie Nazionali di Arte Antica di Roma, Galleria Corsini, Rome

25
Christ among the Doctors, 1612/13
Canvas, 188 × 270 cm
Musée d'Art et d'Histoire de Langres, Langres

58
David and Goliath, c. 1620
Canvas, 122 × 100 cm
Private collection

Theodoor Rombouts (1597–1637)
After training with Frans Lanckvelt and Abraham Janssens in Antwerp, Rombouts travelled throughout Italy between 1616 and 1625. His stay in Rome in 1620 is documented, and he also spent time in Florence. Five years later, he became Master of the Guild of St Luke in Antwerp, where, in addition to individual Church commissions, he painted primarily secular works for private buyers and the art market. He received a large proportion of his commissions from Ghent. In the 1620s, Rombouts' style of painting, under the influence of his journey to Italy, was still marked by a strong Caravaggesque style, until around 1630, when the influence of Peter Paul Rubens became formative for him. He died in Antwerp.

40
Christ Driving the Money Changers from the Temple, 1628/37
Canvas, 74 × 108.5 cm
Centraal Museum, Utrecht

53
The Card Players, c. 1630
Canvas, 151.6 × 205 cm
Koninklijk Museum voor Schone Kunsten, Antwerp

Gerard Seghers (1591–1651)
Born in Antwerp, Seghers received his training in the local Guild of St Luke from 1603 to 1608. Before February 1613, he travelled to Italy, possibly sent by art dealers in Antwerp, with whom he maintained close relationships. In Rome, he came into contact with the local Caravaggisti and was influenced in particular by the works of Bartolomeo Manfredi. From there he travelled to Madrid in the company of the Spanish Cardinal Antonio Zapata y Cisneros, the painter Bartolomeo Cavarozzi, and Giovan Battista Crescenzi, residing there between 1617 and 1619. Around 1620, he returned to Antwerp, where he died in 1651. It is believed that he spent time in Utrecht and possibly met Gerard van Honthorst and Joachim von Sandrart there between 1624 and 1627. Commissions from the Jesuits and the city magistrates of Antwerp and Ghent strengthened his position among the highest social classes.

11
The Denial of St Peter, c. 1620/25
Canvas, 157.5 × 227.3 cm
North Carolina Museum of Art, Raleigh

Giovanni Serodine (1600–1630)
Serodine came from a family of painters in Ascona, who moved to Rome around 1595, where he was presumably born. He received his early artistic training as a stuccoist from his older brother, Giovanni Battista. The background of his education as a painter is unknown. In 1623, the brothers executed friezes together in three rooms of the Palazzo Borghese in Rome, as Giovanni had already worked there as a painter. This was followed by works in Spoleto. Among the most important of Serodine's patrons in Rome was the Mattei family, for whom he painted, among other things, a depiction of *Christ among the Doctors*. He also created altarpieces in various churches in Rome. Rumour has it that, in 1630, he was poisoned by envious fellow painters.

8
St Peter Reading, c. 1628/30
Canvas, 91 × 133.5 cm
Pinacoteca cantonale Giovanni Züst, Rancate (Mendrisio)

18
The Mocking of Christ, c. 1626
Canvas, 113 × 152 cm
Pinacoteca cantonale Giovanni Züst, Rancate (Mendrisio)

46
Christ among the Doctors, 1624/26
Canvas, 145 × 224 cm
Musée du Louvre, Paris

Giovanni Antonio Galli, called Lo Spadarino (1585–1652)
Information on the career of the native Roman and pupil of Agostino Tassi is fragmentary. In 1603, he was mentioned as a painter in the Palazzo San Marco, in the residence of Cardinal Dolfin, where he presumably met Carlo Saraceni. In 1614, he assisted Tassi in the painting of the Montalto Casino in Bagnaia and in 1616/17 in the Sala Regia of the Palazzo del Quirinale in Rome. In 1619, Spadarino, Cecco del Caravaggio and Gerard van Honthorst were commissioned to execute one panel painting each for the chapel of Piero Guicciardini in Santa Felicita in Florence. The influence of Honthorst in particular is clearly visible in Spadarino's oeuvre. From 1628 until his death, he lived near the church of Santa Maria del Popolo in Rome.

49
Christ Displaying his Wounds, c. 1625/35
Canvas, 132.2 × 97.8 cm
Perth Museum and Art Gallery, Perth and Kinross Council Scotland

Nicolas Tournier (1590–1639)
The artist was raised in Montbéliard, where his Protestant family had taken refuge from Besançon. He received his early training with his father, who was also a painter. He is known to have lived in Rome between 1619 and 1626. According to an early source, he is said to have been a student of Valentin de Boulogne.
His work was influenced in particular by Bartolomeo Manfredi, some of whose works he also copied. Little is known about his time in Rome. In 1627, Tournier returned to France. After periods spent in Narbonne and Carcassonne, he finally reached Toulouse, where he lived from 1632 until his death. Here, his large altarpieces made a significant contribution to the city's importance as one of France's main art centres.

6
St Andrew, c. 1616
Canvas, 115 × 85 cm
Private collection

23
The Entombment of Christ, 1635/38
Canvas, 314 × 166 cm
Musée des Augustins, Toulouse

Valentin de Boulogne (1591–1632)

Valentin was born in the French town of Coulommiers as the son of the painter and stained-glass artist of the same name. It was here that he presumably completed his first apprenticeship. Later, it is thought that he went to Paris or Fontainebleau for further training. He moved to Rome at a young age and spent the rest of his life there. It is not clear whether he is the artist mentioned in Rome in 1611 as 'Valentino francese', although his stay there in 1614 is documented. His oeuvre is influenced in particular by the works of Caravaggio, Bartolomeo Manfredi and Jusepe de Ribera. He maintained a long-standing artistic relationship with his fellow countryman Simon Vouet, but also sought the company of the 'fiamminghi' and was a member of the Bentvueghels. From 1627 on, Valentin's most important patron was Cardinal Francesco Barberini, for whom he painted, among other things, an altarpiece in St Peter's Basilica.

38
Christ Driving the Merchants from the Temple, c. 1618/22
Canvas, 195 × 260 cm
Gallcric Nazionali di Arte Antica di Roma, Palazzo Barberini, Rome

44
The Crowning with Thorns and the Mocking of Christ, c. 1627/28
Canvas, 132 × 96.3 cm
Bayerische Staatsgemäldesammlungen, Alte Pinakothek, Munich

51
Cardsharps, c. 1614/15
Canvas, 94.5 × 137 cm
Staatliche Kunstsammlungen Dresden, Gemäldegalerie Alte Meister, Dresden

59
David with the Head of Goliath and Two Soldiers, 1620/22
Canvas, 99 × 134 cm
Museo Nacionial Thyssen-Bornemisza, Madrid

65
Judith with the Head of Holofernes, c. 1625/28
Canvas, 97 × 74 cm
Musée des Augustins, Toulouse

Simon Vouet (1590–1649)

Simon Vouet was the son of the Parisian painter Laurent Vouet, from whom he presumably received his early training. At the age of 14, he travelled to England, returned to Paris around 1608, and moved with the entourage of the royal ambassador to Constantinople in 1611, where he painted a portrait of the sultan. He stayed in Venice between 1612 and 1613, reaching Rome the following year. Vouet was under the protectorate of the French king, which, in addition to a monthly salary, provided him with influential local contacts. He thus lived, among other places, in the households of Cardinal del Monte and the Barberini, who decisively advanced his career. From 1621 to 1622, he worked for the Doria family in Genoa; travels to other Italian cities, including Parma, Bologna and Florence, are documented. In 1624, Vouet was appointed Principe of the Accademia di San Luca. In 1627, he was summoned by Louis XIII back to Paris, where he became court painter, established a large workshop and lived until his death.

15
St Jerome and the Angel, c. 1620/21
Canvas, 144.8 × 179.8 cm
National Gallery of Art, Washington, D.C., Samuel H. Kress Collection

57
David and Goliath, c. 1621
Canvas, 123 × 95.5 cm
Musei di Strada Nuova, Palazzo Bianco, Genoa

64
Judith with the Head of Holofernes, c. 1620/25
Canvas, 96.8 × 73.5 cm
Bayerische Staatsgemäldesammlungen, Alte Pinakothek, Munich

74
The Fortune Teller, 1617
Canvas, 95 × 135 cm
Gallerie Nazionali di Arte Antica di Roma, Palazzo Barberini, Rome

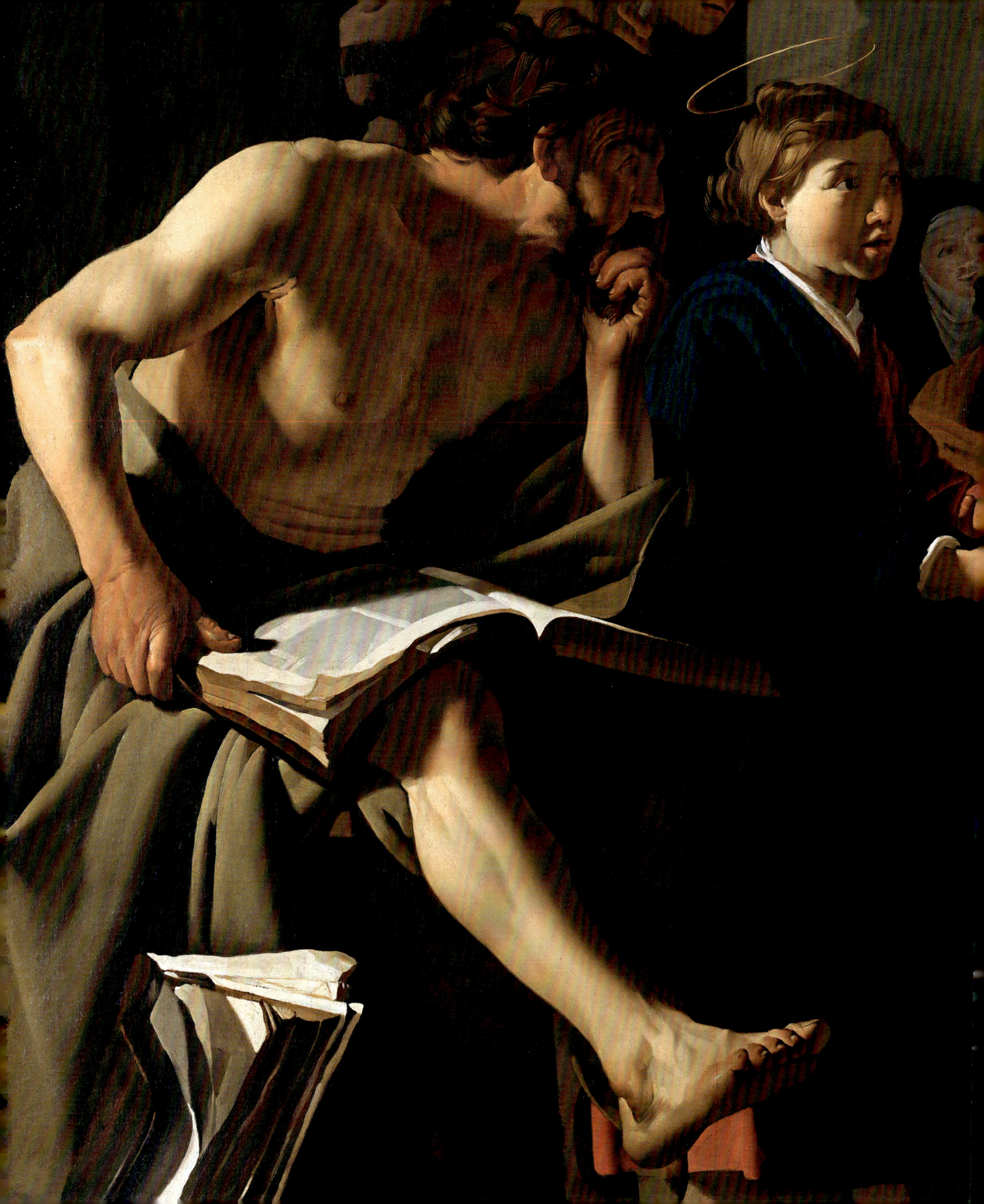

Bibliography

Ago 2006
Renata Ago. *Il gusto delle cose. Una storia degli oggetti nella Roma del Seicento*, Rome, 2006

Albach 1977
Ben Albach. *Langs kermissen en hoven. Ontstaan en kroniek van een Nederlands toneelgezelschap in de 17de eeuw*, Zutphen, 1977

Amadio 2005
Sonia Amadio. 'Artisti famosi e nomi senza opere nella parrocchia di Sant'Andrea delle Fratte, Stati delle anime I' in *Arte e immagine del papato Borghese (1605–1621)*, ed. Bruno Toscano, Beatrice Cirulli and Federica Papi, San Casciano, 2005, pp. 17–31

Aronberg Lavin 1975
Marilyn Aronberg Lavin. *Seventeenth-century Barberini Documents and Inventories of Art*, New York, 1975

Baglione 1642
Giovanni Baglione. *Le vite de' pittori, scultori et architetti dal pontificato di Gregorio XIII del 1572 in fino a' tempi di Papa Urbano Ottavo nel 1642*, Rome, 1642

Baldriga 2001
Irene Baldriga. *Vincenzo Giustinianis Persönlichkeit im Spiegel seiner Bibliothek* in Exh. cat. Rome/Berlin 2001, pp. 73–80

Baldriga 2010
Irene Baldriga. *Theodoor Rombouts (1597–1637)* in Strinati/Zuccari 2010, vol. 2, pp. 621–629

Baldriga/Treffers 2010
Irene Baldriga and Bert Treffers. *'Una maniera meravigliosamente adatta da seguire.' Percorsi caravaggeschi tra Fiandre e Olanda* in Strinati/Zuccari 2010, vol. 1, pp. 255–265

Banti 1981
Anna Banti. Vincenzo Giustiniani. *Discorso sulle arti e sui mestieri* (Raccolta di opere inedite e rare 1), Florence, 1981

Bartsch
The Illustrated Bartsch, ed. Walter L. Straus et al., 1–, New York, 1987–

Bell/Suckow 2008
Peter Bell and Dirk Suckow. 'Lebenslinien – Das Handlesemotiv und die Repräsentation von 'Zigeunern' in der Kunst des Spätmittelalters und der frühen Neuzeit' in *'Zigeuner' und Nation. Repräsentation – Inklusion – Exklusion*, ed. Herbert Uerlings and Iulia-Karin Patrut, Frankfurt a. M. et al., 2008, pp. 493–549

Bellori 1672
Giovanni Pietro Bellori. *Le vite de' pittori, scultori et architetti moderni*, Rome, 1672

Bellori 1672 (2005)
Giovan Pietro Bellori. *The Lives of the Modern Painters, Sculptors and Architects. A New Translation and Critical Edition*, ed. Hellmut Wohl and Tomaso Montanari, trans. Alice Sedgewick Wohl, New York, 2005

Bellucci/Frosinini 2012
Roberto Bellucci and Cecilia Frosinini. 'New Evaluations on Caravaggio's Methods of Underdrawing. Art Historical and Scientific Challenges' in *Caravaggio's Painting Technique.* Proceedings of the CHARISMA Workshop, ed. Marco Ciatti and Brunetto Giovanni Brunetti, Florence, 2012, pp. 51–58

Benay 2014
Erin E. Benay. 'Touching is Believing: Caravaggio's *Doubting Thomas* in Counter-Reformatory Rome' in *Caravaggio. Reflections and Refractions*, ed. Lorenzo Pericolo and David M. Stone, Farnham and Burlington, VT., 2014, pp. 59–82

Benedetti 2012
Simona Benedetti (ed.). *Architetture di Carlo Rainaldi nel quarto centenario della nascita*, Rome, 2012

Benito Domenech 1980
Fernando Benito Domenech. *Pinturas y Pintores en el Real Colegio de Corpus Christi*, Valencia, 1980

Bernardini/Mignosi Tantillo 2001
Maria Grazia Bernardini and Almamaria Mignosi Tantillo. *Caravaggio, Carracci, Maderno. La Cappella Cerasi in Santa Maria del Popolo a Roma*, Milan, 2001

Von Bernstorff 2010
Marieke von Bernstorff. *Agent und Maler als Akteure im Kunstbetrieb des frühen 17. Jahrhunderts. Giovanni Battista Crescenzi und Bartolomeo Cavarozzi* (Römische Studien der Bibliotheca Hertziana 28), Munich, 2010

Bezemer 1896
W. Bezemer. 'De magistraatsverandering te Utrecht in 1618' in *Bijdragen en Mededeelingen van het Historisch Genootschap 17*, 1896, pp. 71–106

Bieneck 1992
Dorothea Bieneck. *Gerard Seghers. 1591–1651. Leben und Werk des Antwerpener Historienmalers* (Flämische Maler im Umkreis der großen Meister 6), Lingen, 1992

Bièvre 2015
Elisabeth de Bièvre. *Dutch Art and Urban Cultures. 1200–1700*, London et al., 2015

Bilancia 2012
Fernando Bilancia. 'L'altare maggiore di Carlo Rainaldi' in Benedetti 2012, pp. 89–104

Bissell 1981
Raymond Ward Bissell. *Orazio Gentileschi and the Poetic Tradition in Caravaggesque Painting*, University Park, Pennsylvania, 1981

Bizoni 1995
Bernardo Bizoni. *Diario di Viaggio di Vincenzo Giustiniani* (Biblioteca di letteratura artistica 1), Porretta Terme, 1995

Blankert 1982
Albert Blankert. *Ferdinand Bol (1616–1680). Rembrandt's Pupil* (Aetas aurea 2), Doornspijk, 1982

Blankert 1986/87
Albert Blankert. 'Caravaggio und die nördlichen Niederlande' in Exh. cat. Utrecht/Braunschweig 1986/87, pp. 17–41

Blankert 1990
Albert Blankert. 'Onverdragelijk lelijk: het realisme van de Hollandse historieschilderkunst in de 17de eeuw' in *De eeuwwende* (Studium Generale Reeks 1), ed. André Klukhuhn, 3 vols., Utrecht 1989/90, vol. 3: *Renaissance 1600. Kunst en literatuur*, Utrecht, 1990, pp. 9–42

Blankert 1991
Albert Blankert. *A Newly Discovered Painting by Hendrick ter Brugghen*, Zwolle, 1991

Blankert 1997/98
Albert Blankert. 'Looking at Rembrandt, Past and Present' in *Rembrandt. A Genius and his Impact*, ed. Albert Blankert (Exh. cat. National Gallery of Victoria, Melbourne / National Gallery of Australia, Canberra), Zwolle, 1997, pp. 32–57

Bloemendal 2003
Jan Bloemendal (ed.). *De Utrechtse Parnas. Utrechtse Neolatijnse dichters uit de zestiende en zeventiende eeuw*, Amersfoort, 2003

Bodart 1970
Didier Bodart. *Les Peintres des Pays-Bas Meridionaux et de la principauté de Liège à Rome au XVIIème siècle* (Études d'histoire de l'art 2), 2 vols., Brussels et al., 1970

Boers 2012
Marion Boers. *De Noord-Nederlandse kunsthandel in de eerste helft van de zeventiende eeuw*, Hilversum, 2012

Bogaers 1985
Llewellyn Bogaers. 'Een kwestie van macht? De relatie tussen de wetgeving op het openbaar gedrag en de ontwikkeling van de Utrechtse stadssamenleving in de zestiende en zeventiende eeuw' in *Volkskundig Bulletin* 11, 1985, issue. 2, pp. 102–126

Bok 1988
Marten Jan Bok. 'On the Origins of the Flute Player in Utrecht Caravaggesque Painting' in Klessmann 1988, pp. 135–141

Bok 1990
Marten Jan Bok. '"Nulla dies sine linea." De opleiding van schilders in Utrecht in de eerste helft van de zeventiende eeuw' in *De Zeventiende Eeuw* 6, 1990, issue 1, pp. 58–68

Bok 1994
Marten Jan Bok. *Vraag en aanbod op de Nederlandse kunstmarkt, 1580–1700 / Supply and Demand in the Dutch Art Market, 1580–1700*, diss. University of Utrecht, 1994

Bok 1996
Marten Jan Bok. 'Laying Claims to Nobility in the Dutch Republic: Epitaphs, True and False' in *Simiolus. Netherlands Quarterly for the History of Art* 24, 1996, issue 2/3, pp. 209–226

Bok 1997/98
Marten Jan Bok. 'Artists at Work: Their Lives and Livelihood' in Exh. cat. San Francisco/Baltimore/London 1997/98, pp. 86–99, 403/404

Bok 2000
Marten Jan Bok. 'Christian von Braunschweig in den Niederlanden' in *Der Krieg in Person. Herzog Christian d. J. von Braunschweig-Lüneburg im Bildnis von Paulus Moreelse*, ed. Nils Büttner (Exh. cat. Herzog Anton Ulrich-Museum, Braunschweig), Braunschweig, 2000, pp. 14–39

Bok 2008
Marten Jan Bok. '"Schilderien te coop." Nieuwe marketingtechnieken op de Nederlandse kunstmarkt van de Gouden Eeuw' in *Thuis in de Gouden Eeuw. Kleine meesterwerken uit de SØR Rusche collectie, ed.* Martine Gosselink et al., Zwolle, 2008, pp. 9–29, 140/141

Bok 2009
Marten Jan Bok. 'Was Hendrick ter Brugghen a Melancholic?' in *Journal of Historians of Netherlandish Art* 1, 2009, URL: https://jhna.org/articles/was-hendrick-ter-brugghen-melancholic/ (accessed on 6.11.2017)

Bok 2014
Marten Jan Bok. 'De Goyer: een libertijns regentengeslacht uit Utrecht' in *Utrechtse Parentelen vóór 1650* 4, 2014, ppp. 73–171, 295–302

Bok/Kobayashi 1985
Marten Jan Bok and Yoriko Kobayashi. 'New Data on Hendrick ter Brugghen. Introduction and Family Background' in *Hoogsteder-Naumann Mercury* 1, 1985, pp. 7–34

Bok/Schwartz 1991
Marten Jan Bok and Gary Schwartz. 'Schilderen in opdracht in Holland in de 17e eeuw' in *Holland. Regionaal-historisch tijdschrift* 23, 1991, pp. 183–195

Bolten 2007
Jaap Bolten. *Abraham Bloemaert, c. 1565–1651. The Drawings*, 2 vols., Leiden, 2007

Bonfait 2008/09
Olivier Bonfait. 'Commedia dell'arte & scènes de genre caravagesques: *Les Diseuses de bonne aventure* de Simon Vouet' in Exh. cat. Nantes/Besançon 2008/09, pp. 56–65

Bonfait 2012
Olivier Bonfait. *Après Caravage. Une peinture caravagesque?*, Malakoff, 2012

Bonfait/Rousteau-Chambon 2011
Olivier Bonfait and Hélène Rousteau-Chambon. *Simon Vouet en Italie*. Actes du colloque international, 6–8 December 2008, Musée des Beaux-Arts et Archives Départementales de Nantes, Rennes, 2011

Borsi/Del Gaizo 1984
Franco Borsi and Vittorio del Gaizo. *Palazzo Madama*, 2nd edn., Rome, 1984

Borsook 1954
Eve Borsook. 'Documents Concerning the Artistic Associates of S. Maria della Scala in Rome' in *The Burlington Magazine* 96, 1954, pp. 270–275

Boyd Morris 2011
Anita Boyd Morris. 'Pictures of Debauchery: Profane Images of the Prodigal Son's Revels in Seventeenth-century Dutch Paintings' in *Dutch Crossing* 35, 2011, issue 3, pp. 213–228

Braun 1966
Hermann Braun. *Gerard und Willem van Honthorst*, Göttingen, 1966

Bredius 1915–1922
Abraham Bredius. *Künstler-Inventare. Urkunden zur Geschichte der holländischen Kunst des XVIten, XVIIten und XVIIIten Jahrhunderts* (Quellenstudien zur holländischen Geschichte 5–7, 10–14), 8 vols., The Hague, 1915–1922

Broos 1993
Ben Broos. *Intimacies & Intrigues. History Paintings in the Mauritshuis*, Ghent/The Hague, 1993

Brown 2001
Beverly Louise Brown. 'Die schwarzen Schwingen des Neids. Konkurrenz, Rivalität und Vorbild' in Exh. cat. London/Rome 2001, pp. 248–273

Brown 2002
Christopher Brown. *The Dutchness of Dutch Art*. First Golden Age Lecture, 26 September 2002 (Amsterdam Centre for Golden Age Studies), Amsterdam, 2002

Van Bueren/Van Dijk 2017
Truus van Bueren and Corinne van Dijk. *Overschilderd: van Gregoriusmis naar Bijbeltekst. De Reformatie van de Utrechtse Jacobikerk*, Hilversum, 2017

Buisman 2000
Jan Buisman. *Duizend jaar weer, wind en water in de Lage Landen*, vol. 4, 1575–1675, Franeker, 2000

Bull et al. 2013
Duncan Bull et al. 'Acquisitions. Paintings 2008–13' in *The Rijksmuseum Bulletin* 61, 2013, pp. 294–317

Van Campen 1940
Johannes Wilhelmus Canisius van Campen (ed.). *Notae quotidianae van Aernout van Buchell*, Utrecht, 1940

Canosa/Colonello 1989
Romano Canosa and Isabella Colonello. *Storia della prostituzione in Italia dal Quattrocento alla fine del Settecento*, Rome, 1989

Cappelletti 2016
Francesca Cappelletti. 'Northern Artists in Vincenzo Giustiniani's Palazzo: Living in a Baroque Palace in Rome, 1600–38' in Exh. cat. Madrid 2016, pp. 25–31

Cats 1618
Jacob Cats. *Zinne- en minne-Beelden. Emblemata, amores moresque spectantia*, Middelburg, 1618

Castro et al. 2009
Silvia Castro et al. 'Examinations of Two 17th-century Dutch Paintings with Respect to Colour Alteration and the Greyish Appearance of the Paint Layers' in *Zeitschrift für Kunsttechnologie und Konservierung* 23, 2009, issue 2, pp. 177–195

Cat. Amsterdam 2007
Dutch Paintings of the Seventeenth Century in the Rijksmuseum Amsterdam. Volume I – Artists born between 1570 and 1600, ed. Jonathan Bikker, Yvette Bruijnen and Gerdien Wuestman, 2 vols., Amsterdam, 2007

Cat. Dresden 2005
Gemäldegalerie Alte Meister Dresden. Illustriertes Gesamtverzeichnis, ed. Harald Marx, 2 vols., Cologne, 2005

Cat. London 1991
The Dutch School. 1600–1900, ed. Neil MacLaren, revised and expanded by Christopher Brown (National Gallery Catalogues), 2 vols., London, 1991

Cat. Madrid 1989
Seventeenth-Century Dutch and Flemish Painting. The Thyssen-Bornemisza Collection, by Ivan Gaskell; General Editor Simon de Pury (The Thyssen-Bornemisza collection 8), London, 1989

Cat. Munich 2009
Alte Pinakothek. Französische und spanische Malerei (catalogue of the permanent collection of the Alte Pinakothek, Munich), texts by Helge Siefert, edited by the Bayerischen Staatsgemäldesammlungen, Ostfildern, 2009

Cat. New York 2007
Dutch Paintings in The Metropolitan Museum of Art, ed. Walter Liedtke, 2 vols., New Haven, CT/London 2007

Cat. Raleigh 2009
Seventeenth-century Dutch and Flemish Paintings. Systematic Catalogue of the Collection. North Carolina Museum of Art, ed. Dennis P. Weller, Raleigh, 2009

Cat. Utrecht 1999
De verzamelingen van het Centraal Museum, vol. 5: 'Schilderkunst tot 1850' (catalogue of the permanent collection of the Centraal Museum Utrecht), ed. Liesbeth M. Helmus, 2 vols., Utrecht, 1999

Cavazzini 2004
Patrizia Cavazzini. 'La diffusione della pittura nella Roma di primo seicento: collezionisti ordinari e mercanti' in *Quaderni storici, nuova serie* 39, 2004, pp. 353–374

Cavazzini 2005
Patrizia Cavazzini. 'Artemisia and the Other Women in Agostino Tassi's Life: Attitudes to Women's Improper Sexual Behaviour in Seventeenth-century Rome' in *Artemisia Gentileschi. Taking Stock*, ed. Judith W. Mann, Turnhout, 2005, pp. 39–49

Cavazzini 2008
Patrizia Cavazzini. *Painting as Business in Early Seventeenth-century Rome*, University Park, Pennsylvania, 2008

Cavazzini 2014/15
Patrizia Cavazzini. 'Noblesse et bassesse dans la biographie des peintres de genre' in Exh. cat. Rome/Paris 2014/15, pp. 57–67

Cavazzini 2016
Patrizia Cavazzini. 'Painting could be a Cut-throat Business in 17th-century Rome' in *The Art Newspaper*, 7 October 2016

Cavazzini 2016/17
Patrizia Cavazzini. 'Success and Failure in a Violent City. Bartolomeo Manfredi, Nicolas Tournier, and Valentin de Boulogne' in Exh. cat. New York/Paris 2016/17, pp. 17–27

Cavicchioli 2012
Sonia Cavicchioli. '"Musica reservata." Indagine sui concerti dipinti nell'Italia settentrionale del Cinquecento' in Macioce/De Pascale 2012, pp. 133–147

Caxton 1900
William Caxton. *The Golden Legend or Lives of the Saints, as Englished by William Caxton*, 7 vols., London, 1900

Christiansen 2001/02
Keith Christiansen. 'The Art of Orazio Gentileschi' in Exh. cat. Rome/New York/Saint Louis 2001/02, pp. 3–37

Christiansen 2016/17
Keith Christiansen. 'Painting from Life: Valentin and the Legacy of Caravaggio' in Exh. cat. New York/Paris 2016/17, pp. 43–55

Ciatti/Lalli 2012
Marco Ciatti and Carlo Lalli. 'Caravaggio's *The Beheading of Saint John the Baptist* in Malta. Investigation into Execution, Technique, Style and Restoration' in *Caravaggio's Painting Technique*. Proceedings of the CHARISMA Workshop, ed. Marco Ciatti and Brunetto Giovanni Brunetti, Florence, 2012, pp. 11–22

Cohen 1992
Elizabeth Cohen. 'Honor and Gender in the Streets of Early Modern Rome' in *Journal of Interdisciplinary History* 22, 1992, issue 4, pp. 597–625

Cohen-Willner 1999
Saskia Cohen-Willner. 'Een schilderij van Jacopo Palma il Giovane in een vroeg zeventiende-eeuwse Amsterdamse verzameling' in *Oud Holland* 113, 1999, issue 4, pp. 175–180

Cohen-Willner 2014
Saskia Cohen-Willner. 'Between Painter and Painter Stands a Tall Mountain. Van Mander's *Italian Lives* as a Source for Instructing Artists in the *deelen der consten*' in *Art and Migration. Netherlandish Artists on the Move, 1400–1750*, ed. Frits Scholten, Joanna Woodall and Dulcia Meijers (Nederlands Kunsthistorisch Jaarboek 63), Leiden, 2014, pp. 349–383

Curti 2017/18
Francesca Curti. 'Rivalità di botteghe, rivalità di pittori: un'ipotesi per la nascita dell'inimicizia tra Caravaggio, Giovanni Baglione e Tommaso Salini' in Exh. cat. Milan, 2017/18, pp. 269–276

Cuzin 1977
Jean-Pierre Cuzin. *La Diseuse de bonne aventure de Caravage* (Les dossiers du département des peintures 13), Paris, 1977

Cuzin 1980
Jean-Pierre Cuzin. 'Manfredi's *Fortune Teller* and some Problems of the *Manfrediana Methodus*' in *Bulletin of the Detroit Institute of Arts* 58, 1980, pp. 15–25

Cuzin 1987
Jean-Pierre Cuzin. 'Manfredi e i francesi' in Exh. cat. Cremona 1987, pp. 42–49

Dandelet 1997
Thomas James Dandelet. 'Spanish Conquest and Colonization at the Center of the Old World: The Spanish Nation in Rome, 1555–1625' in *The Journal of Modern History* 69, 1997, issue 3, pp. 479–511

Dandelet 2001
Thomas James Dandelet. *Spanish Rome. 1500–1700*, New Haven, CT/London, 2001

Dandelet/Marino 2007
Thomas James Dandelet and John A. Marino. *Spain in Italy. Politics, Society, and Religion 1500–1700*, Leiden/Boston, 2007

Danesi Squarzina 1997
Silvia Danesi Squarzina. 'The Collections of Cardinal Benedetto Giustiniani – Part I' in *The Burlington Magazine* 139, 1997, pp. 766–791

Danesi Squarzina 1998
Silvia Danesi Squarzina. 'The Collections of Cardinal Benedetto Giustiniani – Part II' in *The Burlington Magazine* 140, 1998, pp. 102–118

Danesi Squarzina 2001
Silvia Danesi Squarzina. 'Benedetto, Vincenzo, Andrea: Neue Forschungsergebnisse zur Geschichte der Sammlung Giustiniani' in Exh. cat. Rome/Berlin 2001, pp. 15–45

Danesi Squarzina 2003
Silvia Danesi Squarzina. *La collezione Giustiniani*, 3 vols., Turin, 2003

Danesi Squarzina 2006
Silvia Danesi Squarzina. 'New Documents on Ribera, "Pictor in Urbe" 1612–16' in *The Burlington Magazine* 148, 2006, pp. 244–251

Danesi Squarzina/Baldriga 1995
Silvia Danesi Squarzina and Irene Baldriga (eds.). *'fiamenghi che vanno e vengono non li si puo dar regola.' Paesi Bassi e Italia fra Cinquecento e Seicento: pittura, storia e cultura degli emblemi*, Sant'Oreste, 1995

Dekiert 1999
Marcus Dekiert. '"Sic malesana meos Circe transformat honores." Der Student als Exempel der "Unberatenen Jugend" in einem Nachtstück des Gerard van Honthorst' in *Münchner Jahrbuch der bildenden Kunst* 50, 1999, pp. 147–170

Dekiert 2003
Marcus Dekiert. *Musikanten in der Malerei der niederländischen Caravaggio-Nachfolge. Vorstufen, Ikonographie und Bedeutungsgehalt der Musikszene in der niederländischen Bildkunst des 16. und 17. Jahrhunderts* (Bonner Studien zur Kunstgeschichte 17), diss. University of Bonn, Münster et al., 2003

Delumeau 1975
Jean Delumeau. *Rome au XVIe siècle*, Paris, 1975

Dittrich 2004
Sigrid Dittrich. *Lexikon der Tiersymbole. Tiere als Sinnbilder in der Malerei des 14.–17. Jahrhunderts*, Petersberg, 2004

Domela Nieuwenhuis 2001
Eric Domela Nieuwenhuis. *Paulus Moreelse (1571–1638)*, diss. University of Leiden, 2001

Domela Nieuwenhuis 2007
Eric Domela Nieuwenhuis. '*De rijke man en de arme Lazarus* door Hendrick ter Brugghen 1625' in Helmus 2007a, pp. 78–95

Drossaers/Lunsingh Scheurleer 1974–1976
S.W.A. Drossaers and Th. H. Lunsingh Scheurleer. *Inventarissen van de inboedels in de verblijven van de Oranjes en daarmede gelijk te stellen stukken 1567–1795* (Ryks Geschiedkundige Publicatiën. Grote serie 147–149), 3 vols., The Hague, 1974–1976

Dunkerton et al. 2015
Jill Dunkerton et al. (eds.). 'Titian after 1540. Technique and Style in his Later Works' in *National Gallery Technical Bulletin* 36, 2016, pp. 6–115, 124–133

Ebert-Schifferer 2009
Sybille Ebert-Schifferer. *Caravaggio. Sehen – Staunen – Glauben. Der Maler und sein Werk*, Munich, 2009

Ebert-Schifferer 2012
Sybille Ebert-Schifferer. 'Caravaggio dilettante di musica?' in Macioce/De Pascale 2012, pp. 29–39

Ebert-Schifferer 2017/18
Sybille Ebert-Schifferer. 'Amici e nemici: La rete sociale di Caravaggio' in Exh. cat. Milan 2017/18, Milan 2017, pp. 277–298

Ebert-Schifferer 2018
Sybille Ebert-Schifferer. 'Caravaggio e la luce nell'atelier' in *Lumen – Imago – Pictura. La luce nella storia dell'ottica e nella rappresentazione visiva da Giotto a Caravaggio*, ed. Sybille Ebert-Schifferer, Pietro Roccasecca and Andreas Thielemann, Rome, 2018, pp. 39–64

Van Eck 1993/94
Xander van Eck. 'From Doubt to Conviction. Clandestine Catholic Churches as Patrons of Dutch Caravaggesque Painting' in *Simiolus. Netherlands Quarterly for the History of Art* 22, 1993/94, issue 4, pp. 217–234

Van Eck 1999
Xander van Eck. 'The Artist's Religion. Paintings Commissioned for Clandestine Catholic Churches in the Northern Netherlands, 1600–1800' in *Simiolus. Netherlands Quarterly for the History of Art* 27, 1999, issue 1/2, pp. 70–94

Van Eck 2008
Xander van Eck. *Clandestine Splendor. Paintings from the Catholic Church in the Dutch Republic*, Zwolle, 2008

Ens 1602
Gaspar Ens. *Delitiae Italiae. Dat is: Eyghentlijcke beschrijvinghe wat door gantsch Italien in elcke Stadt ende plaets te zien is [...]*, Arnhem, 1602

Etheridge 2011/12
Christopher Etheridge. 'The Fortune Teller' in Exh. cat. Ottawa/Fort Worth 2011/12, pp. 156–176

Exh. cat. Amsterdam 1976
Tot lering en vermaak. Betekenissen van Hollandse genrevoorstellingen uit de zeventiende eeuw, ed. Eddy de Jongh (Exh. cat. Rijksmuseum Amsterdam), Amsterdam, 1976

Exh. cat. Berlin 2007/08
Disegno. Der Zeichner im Bild der frühen Neuzeit, ed. Hein-Thomas Schulze Altcappenberg and Michael Thimann (Exh. cat. Staatliche Museen zu Berlin, Kupferstichkabinett), Munich, 2007

Exh. cat. Cremona 1987
Dopo Caravaggio. Bartolomeo Manfredi e la manfrediana methodus, ed. Arnaud Brejon de Lavergnée (Exh. cat. Santa Maria della Pietà, Cremona), Milan, 1987

Exh. cat. Düsseldorf 2006/07
Caravaggio. Originale und Kopien im Spiegel der Forschung, ed. Jürgen Harten and Jean-Hubert Martin (Exh. cat. Museum Kunstpalast, Düsseldorf), Ostfildern, 2006

Exh. cat. Florence 2010
Caravaggio e Caravaggeschi a Firenze, ed. Gianni Papi (Exh. cat. Galleria Palatina, Palazzo Pitti and Galleria degli Uffizi, Florence), Livorno, 2010

Exh. cat. Florence 2015
Gherardo delle Notti. Quadri bizzarrissimi e cene allegre, ed. Gianni Papi (Exh. cat. Galleria degli Uffizi, Florence), Florence/Milan, 2015

Exh. cat. Frankfurt 2009
Caravaggio in Holland. Musik und Genre bei Caravaggio und den Utrechter Caravaggisten, ed. Jochen Sander, Bastian Eclercy and Gabriel Dette (Exh. cat. Städel Museum, Frankfurt), Munich, 2009

Exh. cat. Hamburg 2017
Die Geburt des Kunstmarktes. Rembrandt, Ruisdael, Van Goyen und die Künstler des Goldenen Zeitalters, ed. Franz W. Kaiser and Michael North (Exh. cat. Bucerius Kunstforum, Hamburg), Munich, 2017

Exh. cat. Lecce 2013/14
Il racconto del cielo. Capolavori dei Girolamini a Lecce, ed. Fabrizio Vona et al. (Exh. cat. Chiesa di San Francesco della Scarpa, Lecce), Naples, 2013

Exh. cat. London/Dublin/Edinburgh 2016/17
Beyond Caravaggio, ed. Letizia Treves (Exh. cat. The National Gallery, London / National Gallery of Ireland, Dublin / Scottish National Gallery, Edinburgh), London, 2016

Exh. cat. London/Rome 2001
Die Geburt des Barock, ed. Beverly Louise Brown (Exh. cat. Royal Academy of Arts, London / Palazzo Venezia, Rome), Stuttgart, 2001

Exh. cat. Madrid 2011
El joven Ribera, ed. José Milicua and Javier Portús Pérez (Exh. cat. Museo del Prado, Madrid), Madrid, 2011

Exh. cat. Madrid 2016
Caravaggio and the Painters of the North, ed. Gert Jan van der Sman (Exh. cat. Museo Thyssen-Bornemisza, Madrid), Madrid, 2016

Exh. cat. Milan 2017/18
Dentro Caravaggio, ed. Rossella Vodret (Exh. cat. Palazzo Reale, Milan), Milan, 2017

Exh. cat. Milan/Wien 2005/06
Caravaggio e l'Europa. Il movimento caravaggesco internazionale da Caravaggio a Mattia Preti, ed. Luigi Spezzaferro et al. (Exh. cat. Palazzo Reale, Milan / Liechtenstein-Museum, Vienna), Milan, 2005

Exh. cat. Montale 2013/14
Il giuoco al tempo di Caravaggio. Dipinti, giochi, testimonianze dalla fine del '500 ai primi del '700, ed. Pierluigi Carofano (Exh. cat. Villa Castello Smilea, Montale), Pontedera, 2013

Exh. cat. Montpellier/Toulouse/ Los Angeles 2012/13
Corps et Ombres: Caravage et le Caravagisme Européen, ed. Michel Hilaire and Axel Hémery (Exh. cat. Musée Fabre, Montpellier / Musée des Augustins, Toulouse / Los Angeles County Museum of Art, Los Angeles), Milan, 2012

Exh. cat. Munich 2009
Kurfürst Johann Wilhelms Bilder, ed. Reinhold Baumstark (Exh. cat. Alte Pinakothek, Munich), 3 vols., Munich, 2009

Exh. cat. Nantes 2017/18
Nicolas Régnier (v. 1588–1667), l'homme libre, ed. Sophie Lévy and Aurélien Moline (Exh. cat. Musée d'Arts de Nantes), Nantes, 2017

Exh. cat. Nantes/Besançon 2008/09
Simon Vouet (les années italiennes, 1613–1627), ed. Blandine Chavanne, Dominique Jacquot and Adeline Collange (Exh. cat. Musée des Beaux-Arts de Nantes / Musée des Beaux-Arts et d'Archéologie, Besançon), Paris, 2008

Exh. cat. New York/Naples 1985
The Age of Caravaggio, ed. Mina Gregori, Luigi Salerno and Richard E. Spear (Exh. cat. The Metropolitan Museum of Art, New York / Museo e Gallerie Nazionali di Capodimonte, Naples), New York et al., 1985

Exh. cat. New York/Paris 2016/17
Valentin de Boulogne. Beyond Caravaggio, ed. Annick Lemoine and Keith Christiansen (Exh. cat. The Metropolitan Museum of Art, New York / Musée du Louvre, Paris), New York, 2016

Exh. cat. Utrecht/Antwerpen
Caravaggio en de Nederlanden (Exh. cat. Centraal Museum, Utrecht / Koninklijk Museum voor Schone Kunsten, Antwerp), 2. vols, Utrecht, 1952

Exh. cat. Ottawa/Fort Worth 2011/12
Caravaggio and his Followers in Rome, ed. David Franklin and Sebastian Schütze (Exh. cat. National Gallery of Canada, Ottawa / Kimbell Art Museum, Fort Worth), New Haven, CT. et al., 2011

Exh. cat. Paris 1970/71
Le siècle de Rembrandt. Tableaux hollandais des collections publiques françaises, ed. Arnauld Brejon de Lavergnée (Exh. cat. Musée du Petit Palais, Paris), Paris, 1970

Exh. cat. Paris 1974
Valentin et les Caravagesques français, ed. Arnaud Brejon de Lavergnée and Jean-Pierre Cuzin (Exh. cat. Galeries Nationales d'Exposition du Grand Palais, Paris), Paris, 1974

Exh. cat. Paris 1992
Maîtres Anciens du XVIe au XVIIIe siècle, ed. Jacques Leegenhoek (Exh. cat. Société Labatut, Paris), Paris, 1992

Exh. cat. Paris 2014
Vingt-sept dessins de Gerrit van Honthorst (1592–1656), ed. Etienne Breton, Renaud Jouslin de Noray and Nicolas Schwed (Exh. cat. Saint Honoré Art Consulting, Paris) Paris, 2014

Exh. cat. Rancate 2012/13
Serodine e brezza caravaggesca sulla 'Regione dei laghi', ed. Roberto Contini and Laura Damiani Cabrini (Exh. cat. Pinacoteca cantonale Giovanni Züst, Rancate), Cinisello Balsamo, 2012

Exh. cat. Rancate 2015
Serodine nel Ticino, ed. Giovanni Agosti and Jacopo Stoppa (Exh. cat. Pinacoteca cantonale Giovanni Züst, Rancate), Milan, 2015

Exh. cat. Rennes/Strasbourg 2014/15
Ribera à Rome, autour de l'Apostolado, ed. Guillaume Kazerouni and Guillaume Kientz (Exh. cat. Musée des Beaux-Arts, Rennes / Musée des Beaux-Arts, Strasbourg), Rennes, 2015

Exh. cat. Rome 2011/12
Caravaggio's Rome. 1600–1630, ed. Rossella Vodret (Exh. cat. Museo Nazionale di Palazzo Venezia, Rome), 2 vols., Milan, 2012

Exh. cat. Rome/Berlin 2001
Caravaggio in Preussen. Die Sammlung Giustiniani und die Berliner Gemäldegalerie, ed. Silvia Danesi Squarzina (Exh. cat. Palazzo Giustiniani, Rome / Altes Museum, Berlin), Milan, 2001

Exh. cat. Rome/New York/Saint Louis 2001/02
Orazio und Artemisia Gentileschi. Father and Daughter Painters in Baroque Italy, ed. Keith Christiansen and Judith Walker Mann (Exh. cat. Museo del Palazzo di Venezia, Rome / The Metropolitan Museum of Art, New York / The Saint Louis Art Museum, Saint Louis), New York, 2001

Exh. cat. Rome/Paris 2014/15
Les Bas-fonds du baroque. La Rome du vice et de la misère, ed. Francesca Cappelletti and Anick Lemoine (Exh. cat. Académie de France, Rome / Petit Palais – Musée des Beaux-Arts de la Ville de Paris), Rome, 2014

Exh. cat. San Francisco/Baltimore/ London 1997/98
Masters of Light. Dutch Painters in Utrecht during the Golden Age, ed. Joaneath Ann Spicer and Lynn F. Orr (Exh. cat. Fine Arts Museum of San Francisco, California Palace of the Legion of Honor, San Francisco / The Walters Art Gallery, Baltimore / The National Gallery, London), New Haven, CT., 1997

Exh. cat. Toulouse 2001
Nicolas Tournier, 1590–1639. Un peintre caravagesque, ed. Axel Hémery (Exh. cat. Musée des Augustins and Musée des Beaux-Arts, Toulouse), Paris, 2001

Exh. cat. Utrecht 1980
Een schilderij centraal. De Slapende Mars van Hendrick ter Brugghen, ed. Erik de Jong (Exh. cat. Centraal Museum, Utrecht), Utrecht, 1980

Exh. cat. Utrecht 1991
Kunst uit Oud-katholieke kerken, ed. Paul Dirkse (Exh. cat. Rijksmuseum Het Catharijneconvent, Utrecht) Utrecht, 1991

Exh. cat. Utrecht 2017
Grappen en grollen. Reproductiegrafiek naar de Utrechtse caravaggisten, edited by the Centraal Museum, Utrecht (Exh. cat. Centraal Museum, Utrecht), Utrecht, 2017

Exh. cat. Utrecht/Braunschweig 1986/87
Holländische Malerei in neuem Licht. Hendrick ter Brugghen und seine Zeitgenossen, ed. Albert Blankert (Exh. cat. Centraal Museum, Utrecht / Herzog Anton Ulrich-Museum, Braunschweig), Utrecht, 1986

Exh. cat. Utrecht/Schwerin 2011/12
The Bloemaert Effect. Colour and Composition in the Golden Age, ed. Liesbeth Helmus and Gero Seelig (Exh. cat. Centraal Museum, Utrecht / Staatliches Museum, Schwerin), Petersberg, 2011

Exh. cat. Utrecht/Washington/ Houston 2015/16
Liefde en lust. De kunst van Joachim Wtewael, ed. James Clifton, Liesbeth M. Helmus and Arthur K. Wheelock, Jr. (Exh. cat. Centraal Museum, Utrecht / National Gallery of Art, Washington / Museum of Fine Arts, Houston), Washington, D.C., 2015

Exh. cat. Washington/Detroit/ Amsterdam 1980/81
God en de goden. Verhalen uit de bijbelse en klassieke oudheid door Rembrandt en zijn tijdgenoten, ed. Albert Blankert and Beatrijs Brenninkmeyer-Rooij (Exh. cat. National Gallery of Art, Washington / The Detroit Institute of Arts / Rijksmuseum, Amsterdam), The Hague, 1981

Fabbri 2005
Maria Cecilia Fabbri. 'Agli albori del collezionismo caravaggesco presso la corte medicea. Ipotesi e nuove considerazioni' in *Luce e ombra. Caravaggismo e naturalismo nella pittura toscana dei Seicento*, ed. Pierluigi Carofano, Pisa, 2005, pp. LXI–LXXVII

Falcucci 2012
Claudio Falcucci. 'Practices and Processes from the Odescalchi *Conversion of Saint Paul* to the *Adoration of the Shepherds*' in *Caravaggio's Painting Technique*. Proceedings of the CHARISMA Workshop, ed. Marco Ciatti and Brunetto Giovanni Brunetti, Florence, 2012, pp. 31–40

Fantoni/Matthews/Matthews-Grieco 2003
Marcello Fantoni, Louisa C. Matthews and Sara F. Matthews-Grieco (eds.). *The Art Market in Italy, 15th–17th Centuries. Il mercato dell'arte in Italia; secc. XV–XVII*, Modena, 2003

Farina 2014
Viviana Farina. *Al sole e all'ombra di Ribera*, Castellammare di Stabia, 2014

Federle Orr 1997/98
Lynn Federle Orr. 'Reverberations: The Impact of the Italian Sojourn on Utrecht Artists' in Exh. cat. San Francisco/Baltimore/London 1997/98, pp. 100–113

Feigenbaum 1996/97
Gail Feigenbaum. 'Gamblers, Cheats and Fortune-Tellers' in *Georges de La Tour and his World*, ed. Philip Conisbee (Exh. cat. National Gallery of Art Washington 1996/97) Washington, 1996, pp. 149–181

Feigenbaum 2014
Gail Feigenbaum (ed.). *Display of Art in the Roman Palace. 1550–1750*, Los Angeles, 2014

Fock 1979
Cornelia Willemijn Fock. 'The Princes of Orange as Patrons of Art in the Seventeenth Century' in *Apollo* 110, 1979, pp. 466–475

Fosi 2011
Irene Fosi. *Convertire lo straniero. Forestieri e Inquisizione a Roma in età moderna* (La corte dei papi 21), Rome 2011

Franits 1997
Wayne Edward J. Franits. *Looking at Seventeenth-century Dutch Art. Realism Reconsidered*, Cambridge, 1997

Franits 2004
Wayne Edward J. Franits. *Dutch Seventeenth-century Genre Painting. Its Stylistic and Thematic Evolution*, New Haven, CT et al., 2004

Franits 2009
Wayne Edward J. Franits. 'Laboratorium Utrecht. Baburen, Honthorst und Terbrugghen im künstlerischen Austausch' in Exh. cat. Frankfurt 2009, pp. 37–53

Franits 2013a
Wayne Edward J. Franits. *The Paintings of Dirck van Baburen, ca. 1592/93–1624. Catalogue raisonné*, Amsterdam, 2013

Franits 2013b
Wayne Franits. *Dirck van Baburen (Wijk bij Duurstede ca. 1592/93–1624 Utrecht). Apollo Flaying Marsyas*, New York, (privately printed booklet for Otto Naumann, Ltd.), 2013

Franits 2017
Wayne Edward J. Franits. 'Hendrick ter Brugghen's Paintings of the Crucifixion in New York and Turin and the Problem of His Early Chronology' in *Journal of Historians of Netherlandish Art* 9, 2017, issue 1, URL: https://jhna.org/articles/hendrick-ter-brugghen-crucifixion-new-york-turin-problem-early-chronology/ (accessed on 2.3.2018)

Fratarcangeli 2008
Margherita Fratarcangeli. 'La diffusione "caravaggesca" negli inventari romani del Seicento' in *Intorno a Caravaggio. Dalla formazione alla fortuna*, ed. Margherita Fratarcangeli, Rome, 2008, pp. 25–74

Friedlaender 1945
Walter Friedlaender. '*The Crucifixion of St. Peter*. Caravaggio and Reni' in *Journal of the Warburg and Courtauld Institutes* 8, 1945, pp. 152–160

Friedlaender 1955
Walter Friedlaender. *Caravaggio Studies*, Princeton, NJ, 1955

Frommel 1971
Christoph Luitpold Frommel. 'Caravaggios Frühwerk und der Kardinal Francesco Maria del Monte' in *Storia dell'arte* 9/10, 1971, pp. 5–52

Fukaya 2016
Michiko Fukaya. 'Dutch Painters in Roman Churches in the Early Seventeenth Century. *The Entombment of Christ* by Dirck van Baburen in the Context of Patronage' in *Sacred and Profane in Early Modern Art*, ed. Kayo Hirakawa (Kyoto Studies in Art History 1), Kyoto, 2016, pp. 107–128

Gage 2009
Frances Gage. 'Giulio Mancini and Artist-Amateur Relations in Seventeenth-century Roman Academies' in *The Accademia Seminars. The Accademia di San Luca in Rome, c. 1590–1635* (CASVA seminar papers 2), ed. Peter M. Lukehart, Washington D.C. et al., 2009, pp. 247–287

Gage 2012
Frances Gage. 'Illness, Invention, and Truth in Caravaggio's *Death of the Virgin*' in *Gifts in Return. Essays in Honour of Charles Dempsey*, ed. Melinda Schlitt, Toronto, 2012, pp. 337–362

Gage 2014
Frances Gage. 'Caravaggio's *Death of the Virgin*, Giulo Mancini and the Madonna Blasphemed' in *Caravaggio. Reflections and Refractions*, ed. Lorenzo Pericolo and David M. Stone (Visual Culture in Early Modernity 1), Farnham, 2014, pp. 83–104

Gallo 1997
Marco Gallo. *Orazio Borgianni. Pittore romano (1574–1616) e Francisco de Castro, Conte di Castro*, Rome, 1997

Gallo 2010a
Marco Gallo. 'Orazio Borgianni (Roma 1574–1616)' in Strinati/Zuccari 2010, vol. 2, pp. 335–343

Gallo 2010b
Marco Gallo. 'Il Maestro del Giudizio di Salomone e il giovane Ribera. Un problema ancora aperto' in Strinati/Zuccari 2010, vol. 2, pp. 483–487

Gallo 2015
Marco Gallo. 'La *Disputa di Gesù con i ravìm nel Tempio* di Orazio Borgianni. Tipologie, varianti, significati, committenti e collezionisti' in *Una vita per la storia dell'arte. Scritti in memoria di Maurizio Marini*, ed. Pietro di Loreto, Rome, 2015, pp. 167–202

Gandolfi/Zuccari 2017/18
Riccardo Gandolfi and Alessandro Zuccari. 'I primi anni di Caravaggio a Roma' in Exh. cat. Milan 2017/18, pp. 249–260

Gash 2009
John Gash. 'A Caravaggesque "Christ" in Scotland in *The Burlington Magazine* 151, 2009, pp. 682–690

Gash 2010
John Gash.'Review of *Ribera a Roma*, by Gianni Papi. – Soncino (CR). Edizioni dei Socino, 2007' in *The Burlington Magazine* 152, 2010, pp. 417–418

Gash 2015
John Gash. 'Spadarino's *Doubting Thomas* Rediscovered' in *The Burlington Magazine* 157, 2015, pp. 678–681

Gedova 2017
Polina Gedova. *Gattungsnorm und Regelbruch. Landschaftsmalerei im Diskurs der Bildgattungen. Italien ca. 1500–1650*, diss. Ludwig-Maximilians-Universität Munich, 2017

Geraerts 2015
Jaap Geraerts. *The Catholic Nobility in Utrecht and Guelders, c. 1580–1702*, diss. University College London, London, 2015

Gerson 1983
Horst Gerson. *Ausbreitung und Nachwirkung der holländischen Malerei des 17. Jahrhunderts*, 2nd edn., Amsterdam, 1983

Gianfranceschi 2011
Michela Gianfranceschi. *Le incisioni da Caravaggio e caravaggeschi. Musici, giocatori e indovine nelle scene di genere*, ed. Stefania Macioce, Rome, 2011

Gigli 1994
Giacinto Gigli. *Diario di Roma*, ed. Manilo Barberito, 2 vols., Rome, 1994

Gigli/Marchetti/Simonetta 2013
Laura Gigli. Gabriella Marchetti and Giuseppe Simonetta. 'La cappella di Pietro Cuside nella Chiesa di San Pietro in Montorio a Roma' in *Strenna dei Romanisti* 74, 2013, pp. 339–360

Grijp 2009
Louis Peter Grijp. 'Musik in Utrecht zur Zeit der Caravaggisten' in Exh. cat. Frankfurt 2009, pp. 81–93

Grilli 1994
Cecilia Grilli. 'Il committente della cappella della Pietà di San Pietro in Montorio in Roma' in *Bollettino d'arte* 79, 1994, pp. 157–164

Grilli 2005/06
Cecilia Grilli. 'Il collezionismo di Pietro Cussida a Roma e una seconda cappella della Pietà di San Pietro in Montorio' in Exh. cat. Milan/Vienna 2005/06, pp. 57–63

Hahn 1977
Sylvia Hahn. *Die Darstellung der Verleugnung und Reue Petri. Ikonographische Studie*, diss. Ludwig-Maximilians-Universität Munich, Munich, 1977

Hall 2001
Nicholas H. J. Hall. 'A Taste for Italian Art in Holland' in Exh. cat. published on the occasion of the exhibition *A Taste for Italian Art in Holland* at Hall and Knight Ltd., London/New York 2001, pp. 11–48

Hartje 2004
Nicole Hartje. *Bartolomeo Manfredi. 1582–1622. Ein Nachfolger Caravaggios und seine Europäische Wirkung. Monographie und Werkverzeichnis*, Weimar, 2004

Haskell 1963
Francis Haskell. *Patrons and Painters. A Study in the Relations between Art and Society in the Age of Baroque*, London, 1963

Hedquist 2017
Valerie Hedquist. Ter Brugghen's *Saint Sebastian Tended by Irene*' in *Journal of Historians of Netherlandish Art* 9, 2017, issue 2, URL: https://jhna.org/articles/ter-brugghen-saint-sebastian-tended-irene/ (accessed on 19.12.2017)

Van der Helm 2014
José van der Helm. 'Instructions for Learning Italian in Two Early Modern Dutch Travel Guides. *Delitiae Italiae* (1602) and *Delitiae Urbis Romae* (1625)' in *Incontri* 29, 2014, pp. 29–40

Helmus 2004
Liesbeth M. Helmus. *Stichting Victor II. The Penitent St Peter by Hendrick ter Brugghen?* 161[6], Utrecht, 2004

Helmus 2007a
Liesbeth M. Helmus. *Stichting Victor. Restauratie en natuurwetenschappelijk onderzoek in het Centraal Museum*, Utrecht, 2007

Helmus 2007b
Liesbeth M. Helmus. '*De berouwvolle Petrus* door Hendrick ter Brugghen 161[6]?' in Helmus 2007a, pp. 27–37

Helmus 2007c
Liesbeth M. Helmus. '*De kruisiging met leden van de familie van Adriaen Willemsz Ploos* naar Hendrick ter Brugghen 1624?' in Helmus 2007a, pp. 50–59

Helmus 2009
Liesbeth M. Helmus. 'Das früheste Werk Hendrick Terbrugghens. Materialtechnische Untersuchungen im Centraal Museum in Utrecht' in Exh. cat. Frankfurt 2009, pp. 55–63

Helmus 2015/16
Liesbeth M. Helmus. 'A Surprising and Diverse Life: Joachim Wtewael (1566–1638)' in Exh. cat. Utrecht/Washington/Houston 2015/16, pp. XX–XXV

Helmus/Manuth 2015
Liesbeth M. Helmus and Volker Manuth. *Utrecht & le mouvement caravagesque international*, Paris, 2015

Hémery 2015
Axel Hémery. 'Tournier (1590–1639) et Ribera (1591–1652). Une nouvelle lecture des influences artistiques sur le peintre comtois' in *Les Cahiers d'histoire de l'art* 13, 2015, pp. 7–9

Hendrix 1996
Harald Hendrix. *Kunstenaars en opdrachtgevers* (Renaissance Studies Utrecht 2), Amsterdam, 1996

Hendrix 2005
Harald Hendrix. 'Over de Italiaans-Nederlandse dichter en literatuurhistoricus T. van [der] Meijden, alias Teodoro Ameyden' in *Land van lust en weelde. Italië, Nederland en de literatuur*, ed. Jacqueline Bel (Festschrift for Ton Anbeek), Leiden, 2005, pp. 79–82

Hennecke/Schneemelcher 1968
Edgar Hennecke. *Neutestamentliche Apokryphen in deutscher Übersetzung*, ed. Wilhelm Schneemelcher, 2 vols., Tübingen, 1968

Hibbard 1983
Howard Hibbard. *Caravaggio*, New York et al., 1983

Hillegers 2017
Jasper Hillegers. 'Dirk van Baburen' in *Salomon Lilian Old Master 2018*, ed. Natasha Broad, Amsterdam, 2017, pp. 10–21

Hirdt 1998
Willi Hirdt. 'Caravaggios *Wahrsagende Zigeunerin*. Versuch einer Deutung' in *Lesen und Sehen. Aufsätze zu Literatur und Malerei in Italien und Frankreich*, ed. Birgit Tappert and Willi Jung, Tübingen, 1998, pp. 75–111

Hirdt 2004
Willi Hirdt. *Zigeunerstücke. Flugschriften Italiens zwischen 1580 und 1630* (Abhandlungen zur Sprache und Literatur 154), Bonn, 2004

Hoecker 1916
Rudolf Hoecker. *Das Lehrgedicht des Karel van Mander. Text, Übersetzung und Kommentar nebst Anhang über Manders Geschichtskonstruktion und Kunsttheorie* (Quellenstudien zur Holländischen Kunstgeschichte 8), The Hague, 1916

Van Hoogstraten 1678
Samuel van Hoogstraten. *Inleyding tot de hooge schoole der schilderkonst. Anders de zichtbaere werelt*, Rotterdam, 1678

Houck 1899
Mauritius Ernestus Houck. *Mededeelingen betreffende Gerhard ter Borch, Robert van Voerst, Pieter van Anraedt, Aleijda Wolfsen, Derck Hardensteijn en Hendrick ter Bruggen*, Zwolle, 1899

Huemer 1996
Frances Huemer. *Rubens and the Roman Circle. Studies of the First Decade* (Garland Studies in the Renaissance 5). New York et al., 1996

Hurttig 2014
Marcus Andrew Hurttig. *Caravaggios Ungläubiger Thomas. Eine ikonographische Untersuchung* (Saecula Spiritalia 48), Baden-Baden, 2014

Huys Janssen 1998
Paul Huys Janssen. *Jan van Bijlert 1597/98–1671. Catalogue raisonné* (Oculi 7), Amsterdam/Philadelphia, 1998

Inv. Schleißheim 1771
Beschreibung der Gemäelden in der churfürstlichen Residenz zu Schleißheim, verfasst worden im Jahr 1771 (copy of the original in the Hauptstaatsarchiv, Munich), Bayerische Staatsgemäldesammlungen, Library, Inv. Sch A 771/1

Janssens 2001
Sandra Janssens. 'Between Conflict and Recognition: the Bentvueghels' in *Jaarboek Koninklijk Museum voor Schone Kunsten*, Antwerp, 2001, pp. 57–85

De Jonge 1938
Caroline Henriette de Jonge. *Paulus Moreelse. Portret en genreschilder te Utrecht*, Assen, 1938

Judson 1959
Jay Richard Judson. *Gerrit van Honthorst. A Discussion of his Position in Dutch Art* (Utrechtse bijdragen tot de kunstgeschiedenis 6), The Hague, 1959

Judson 1986/87
Jay Richard Judson. 'Utrecht, Rom, Leiden' in Exh. cat. Utrecht/Braunschweig 1986/87, pp. 53–64

Judson 2000
Jay Richard Judson. *Corpus Rubenianum Ludwig Burchard*, vol. 6: 'The Passion of Christ', London/Brussels, 2000

Judson/Ekkart 1999
Jay Richard Judson and Rudolf Erik Otto Ekkart. *Gerrit van Honthorst. 1592–1656* (Aetas aurea 14), Doornspijk, 1999

Kaplan 1995
Benjamin Jacob Kaplan. *Calvinists and Libertines. Confession and Community in Utrecht, 1578–1620*, Oxford, 1995

Kaplan 2002
Benjamin Jacob Kaplan. 'Fictions of Privacy. House Chapels and the Spatial Accommodation of Religious Dissent in Early Modern Europe' in *The American Historical Review* 107, 2002, issue 4, pp. 1031–1064

Karsten 2003
Arne Karsten. *Künstler und Kardinäle. Vom Mäzenatentum römischer Kardinalnepoten im 17. Jahrhundert*, Cologne/Weimar/Vienna, 2003

Keith 2012
Larry Keith. 'Caravaggio's Painting Technique. A Brief Survey based on Paintings in the National Gallery' in *Caravaggio's Painting Technique*. Proceedings of the CHARISMA Workshop, ed. Marco Ciatti and Brunetto Giovanni Brunetti, Florence 2012, pp. 23–30

Kempers 1991
Bram Kempers. 'Opdrachtgevers, verzamelaars en kopers. Visies op kunst in Holland tijdens de Republiek' in *Holland. Regionaal-historisch tijdschrift* 23, 1991, pp. 196–209

Van Kessel/Schulte 1997
Peter van Kessel and Elisja Schulte (eds.). *Rome – Amsterdam. Two Growing Cities in Seventeenth-century Europe*, Amsterdam, 1997

Kettering 1983
Alison M. Kettering. *The Dutch Arcadia: Pastoral Art and its Audience in the Golden Age*, Totowa N.J. et al., 1983

Kirby/van Bommel/Verhecken 2014
Jo Kirby, Maarten R. van Bommel and André Verhecken. *Natural Colorants for Dyeing and Lake Pigments. Practical Recipes and their Historical Sources*, London, 2014

Klaas 2011
Jörg Klaas. *Die 'Ultramarinkrankenheit.' Studien zu Veränderungen in ultramarinhaltigen Farbschichten an Gemälden*, diss., Technische Universität Munich 2011, URL: https://mediatum.ub.tum.de/doc/982934/document.pdf (accessed on 16.4. 2018)

Klemm 2010
Christian Klemm. 'Hendrick Terbrugghen *Verkündigung Mariae*' in *Jahresbericht Kunsthaus Zürich*, Zürcher Kunstgesellschaft, Zürich, 2010, pp. 85–90

Klessmann 1988
Rüdiger Klessmann (ed.). *Hendrick ter Brugghen und die Nachfolger Caravaggios in Holland*. Beiträge eines Symposions aus Anlaß der Ausstellung Holländische Malerei in neuem Licht. Hendrick ter Brugghen und seine Zeitgenossen, Herzog Anton Ulrich-Museum, 23.–25.3.1987, Braunschweig, 1988

Köger 2008
Annette Köger. 'Spielkarten und Glücksspiel' in *Volles Risiko. Glücksspiel von der Antike bis heute*, published by the Badisches Landesmuseum Karlsruhe (Exh. cat. Badisches Landesmuseum Karlsruhe), Karlsruhe, 2008, pp. 62–67

Van Kooij 1987
Paul van Kooij. 'Ter Brugghen, Dürer and Lucas van Leyden' in *Hoogsteder-Naumann Mercury* 5, 1987, pp. 9–19

Kühn 1993
Hermann Kühn. 'Lead-Tin Yellow' in Roy 1993, pp. 83–112

Kyrova 1994
Magda Kyrova. 'Music in Seventeenth-century Dutch Painting' in *Music and Painting in the Golden Age*, ed. Edwin Buijsen and Louis Peter Grijp (Exh. cat. Hoogsteder & Hoogsteder, The Hague / Hessenhuis Museum, Antwerp), Zwolle, 1994, pp. 31–62

Labrot 1987
Gérard Labrot. *L'Image de Rome. Une arme pour la contre-réforme, 1534–1677*, Seyssel, 1987

Lammertse/Van der Veen 2017
Friso Lammertse and Jaap van der Veen. 'Der Amsterdamer Kaufmann und Kunsthändler Johannes de Renialme und sein Gemäldebestand in den Jahren 1640, 1650 und 1657' in Exh. cat. Hamburg 2017, pp. 170–191

Langdon 1999
Helen Langdon. *Caravaggio. A Life*, 2nd edn., London, 1999

Langdon 2001
Helen Langdon. 'Falschspieler, Zigeuner und Hausierer' in Exh. cat. London/Rome 2001, pp. 42–65

Langdon 2012
Helen Langdon. *Caravaggio's Cardsharps. Trickery and Illusion* (Kimbell Masterpiece Series 6), New Haven, CT/London, 2012

Lange 2003
Justus Lange. *'Opere veramente di rara naturalezza.' Studien zum Frühwerk Jusepe de Riberas mit Katalog der Gemälde bis 1626* (Kunst- und Altertumswissenschaft 2), Würzburg, 2003

Lange 2013
Justus Lange. 'Caravaggio in Cassel.' Anmerkungen zur Präsenz der Utrechter Caravaggisten in der Kasseler Gemäldegalerie' in *Patrimonia* 341, 2013, pp. 12–25

Lavin 1974
Irving Lavin. 'Divine Inspiration in Caravaggio's Two St. Matthews' in *The Art Bulletin* 56, 1974, pp. 59–81

Leeuwenberg 2008
Huib Leeuwenberg. '"Een curieus paepgen." Victor Scorel (ca. 1540–1617): kapittelvicaris, landmeter en missionaris' in *Jaarboek Oud Utrecht*, 2008, pp. 5–47

Lemoine 2000
Annick Lemoine. 'Nicolas Régnier, "peintre domestique" du marquis Giustiniani' in *Bulletin de l'Association des Historiens de l'Art Italien* 6, 2000, pp. 28–33

Lemoine 2007
Annick Lemoine. *Nicolas Régnier (alias Nicolò Renieri), ca. 1588–1667. Peintre, collectionneur et marchand d'art*, Paris, 2007

Lemoine 2015
Annick Lemoine. 'Insulter en beauté. La *pittura dal naturale* caravagesque et le geste de la *fica*' in Helmus/Manuth 2015, p. 55–67

Lincoln 2016
Matthew D. Lincoln. 'Sources for Gerrit van Honthorst's Italian Nickname' in *Notes in the History of Art* 35, 2016, issue 3, pp. 244–249

Logan 1979
Anne-Marie S. Logan. *The 'Cabinet' of the Brothers Gerard and Jan Reynst* (Verhandelingen / Koninklijke Nederlandse Akademie van Wetenschappen / Afdeling Letterkunde 99), Amsterdam, 1979

Loire 2011
Stéphane Loire. 'Simon Vouet en Italie (1612–1627). Questions d'attributions et de datations' in Bonfait/Rousteau-Chambon 2011, pp. 183–233

Lorizzo 1995
Loredana Lorizzo. 'Spiritualità carmelitana nelle opere romane del pittore olandese Gerrit van Honthorst' in Danesi Squarzina/Baldriga 1995, pp. 159–167

Lorizzo 2009
Loredana Lorizzo. 'Il marchese Vincenzo Giustiniani, Giusto Fiammingo e gli altri artisti stranieri. Un colto sodalizio nella Roma del Seicento' in *Giusto Fiammingo. La fuga del giovane nudo*, ed. Paul Smeets, Geneva, 2009, pp. 35–45

Lorizzo 2011
Loredana Lorizzo. 'Per una storia delle lotterie e delle vendite all'incanto di opere d'arte in Italia tra Cinque e Seicento' in *Fare e disfare. Studi sulla dispersione delle opere d'arte in Italia tra XVI e XIX secolo*, ed. Loredana Lorizzo, Rome, 2011, pp. 75–85

Lorizzo 2015a
Loredana Lorizzo. 'Gerrit van Honthorst a Roma. Ritratto dell'artista da giovane a confronto con la committenza' in Exh. cat. Florence 2015, pp. 91–101

Lorizzo 2015b
Loredana Lorizzo. 'Gerrit van Honthorst a Roma. Regesto documentario' in Exh. cat. Florence 2015, pp. 256–258

Lowenthal 1986
Anne Lowenthal. *Joachim Wtewael and Dutch Mannerism* (Aetas aurea 6), Doornspijk, 1986

Lugt 1936
Frits Lugt. 'Italiaansche kunstwerken in nederlandsche verzamelingen van vroeger tijden' in *Oud Holland* 53, 1936, pp. 97–135

Maccherini 1999
Michele Maccherini. 'Novità su Barolomeo Manfredi nel carteggio familiare di Giulio Mancini' in *Prospettiva* 93/94, 1999, pp. 131–141

MacClintock 1961
Carol MacClintock. 'Giustiniani's *Discorso sopra la Musica*' in *Musica Disciplina* 15, 1961, pp. 209–225

Macioce 2003
Stefania Macioce. *Michelangelo Merisi da Caravaggio. Fonti e documenti 1532–1724*, Rome, 2003

Macioce/De Pascale 2012
Stefania Macioce and Enrico De Pascale (eds.). *La musica al tempo di Caravaggio*, (conference proceedings, Biblioteca Ambrosiana, Milan, 29.9.2010), Rome, 2012

Macro 2003
Valentina Macro. 'Gli anni romani di Jusepe Ribera. Due nuovi documenti, il rapporto con i Giustiniani e una proposta attributiva' in *Decorazione e collezionismo a Roma nel Seicento. Vicende di artisti, committenti, mercanti*, ed. Francesca Cappelletti, Rome, 2003, pp. 75–80

Mahon 1951
Denis Mahon. 'Egregius in Urbe Pictor. Caravaggio Revised' in *The Burlington Magazine* 93, 1951, pp. 222–234

Mahon 1988
Denis Mahon. 'Fresh Light on Caravaggio's Earliest Period. His *Cardsharps* Recovered' in *The Burlington Magazine* 130, 1988, pp. 10–25

Malvasia 1687
Carlo Cesare Malvasia. *Felsina Pittrice. Vite de'pittori bolognesi*, 2 vols., Bologna, 1687

Mancini 1956
Giulio Mancini. *Considerazioni sulla pittura*, ed. Adriana Marucchi (Fonti e documenti inediti per la storia dell'arte 1,1), Rome, 1956

Mancini/Baglione/Bellori 2016
Giulio Mancini, Giovanni Baglione and Giovanni Pietro Bellori. *The Lives of Caravaggio*, with a Foreword by Helen Langdon, London, 2016

Van Mander 1604
Karel van Mander. *Het schilder-boeck waerin voor eerst de leerlustighe Iueght den grondt der edel vry schilderconst in verscheyden deelen wort voorghedraghen*, Haarlem, 1604

Van Mander 1604 (1973)
Karel van Mander. *Den Grondt der edel vry schilder-const*, ed. Hessel Miedema, 2 vols., Utrecht, 1973

Mannlich 1805
Johann Christian von Mannlich. *Beschreibung der Churpfalzbaierischen Gemälde – Sammlungen zu Munich und zu Schleißheim*, 3 vols., Munich, 1805

Manuth 1993/94
Volker Manuth. 'Denomination and Iconography: the Choice of Subject Matter in the Biblical Painting of the Rembrandt Circle' in *Simiolus. Netherlands Quarterly for the History of Art* 22, 1993/94, issue 4, pp. 235–252

De Marchi/Van Miegroet 2006
Neil De Marchi and Hans J. van Miegroet. *Mapping Markets for Paintings in Europe 1450–1750* (Studies in European Urban History [1100–1800] 6), Turnhout, 2006

Marangoni 1922
Matteo Marangoni. *Il Caravaggio*, Florence, 1922

Marcucci 2012
Laura Marcucci. 'Continuità e innovazione tra Girolamo e Carlo Rainaldi. S. Maria della Scala a Rom' in Benedetti 2012, pp. 66–106

Marini 2001
Maurizio Marini. *Caravaggio 'Pictor praestantissimus'. L'iter artistico completo di uno dei massimi rivoluzionari dell'arte di tutti i tempi*, Rome, 2001

Martelli 2017
Vladimyr Martelli. *Tra tolleranza ed intransigenza. Roma, il potere e le categorie marginali*, Rome, 2017

Martin 1969
Gregory Martin. *Roma Sancta*, ed. George Bruner Parks, Rome, 1969

Mazzetti di Pietralata 2012
Cecilia Mazzetti di Pietralata. 'Pale d'altare caravaggesche e committenze del partito imperiale a Roma nel Seicento: Problemi di stile e di iconografia alla prova della politica religiosa' in *La Corte en Europa: Política y Religión (Siglos XVI–XVIII)*, ed. José Martínez Millán and Manuel Rivero Rodríguez, Madrid, 2012, vol. 2, pp. 1245–1282

Mazzetti di Pietralata 2014
Cecilia Mazzetti di Pietralata. 'Gli inventari Savelli: storia e stile di una antica famiglia alla sfida della modernità nella Roma del Seicento' in *Inventari e cataloghi. Collezionismo e stili di vita negli Stati italiani di antico regime*, ed. Cinzia Maria Sicca, Pisa, 2014, pp. 107–127

Megna 2003
Tommaso Megna. 'Gherardo delle Notti a Roma. Le commissioni pubbliche, il »patronage« Giustiniani e nuovi elementi documentari' in *Decorazione e collezionismo a Roma nel Seicento. Vicende di artisti, committenti, mercanti*, ed. Francesca Cappelletti, Rome, 2003, pp. 87–100

Meier 2008
Frank Meier. 'Der Teufel schuf das Würfelspiel ... Brett- und Glücksspiele im Mittelalter' in *Glück – Zufall – Vorhersehung. Vortragsreihe der Abteilung Mediävistik des Instituts für Literaturwissenschaft im Sommersemester 2008*, ed. Simone Finkler and Burkhardt Krause, pp. 77–101, URL: http://dx.doi.org/10.5445/KSP/1000020060 (accessed on 25.4.2018)

Meijer 2000
Bert W. Meijer. 'Italian Paintings in 17th-century Holland. Art Market, Art Works and Art Collections' in *L'Europa e l'arte italiana*, ed. Max Seidel, Venice, 2000, pp. 376–417

Merlo 1987
Giuseppe Merlo. 'Ipotesi per il percorso del Manfredi' in Exh. cat. Cremona 1987, pp. 27–31

Miedema 1994–1999
Hessel Miedema (ed.). *Karel van Mander. The Lives of the Illustrious Netherlandish and German Painters*, 6 vols., Doornspijk, 1994–1999

Mijnlieff 1993
Ewoud Mijnlieff. 'Ik weet niet wat te zeggen... Italiaanse kunst in de Nederlanden 1680–1795' in *Incontri* 8, 1993, pp. 159–162

Moffitt 2002
John F. Moffitt. 'Caravaggio and the Gypsies' in *Paragone.Arte* 41/42, 2002, pp. 129–156

Moir 1972
Alfred Moir. 'Drawings after Caravaggio' in *Art Quarterly* 35, 1972, pp. 123–142

Moir 1976
Alfred Moir. *Caravaggio and His Copyists* (Monographs on Archeology and Fine Arts 31), New York, 1976

Moiso-Diekamp 1987
Cornelia Moiso-Diekamp. *Das Pendant in der holländischen Malerei des 17. Jahrhunderts* (Europäische Hochschulschriften, series 28, Kunstgeschichte = Histoire de l'art = History of art 40), Frankfurt am Main/Berne/New York, 1987

Mojana 1989
Marina Mojana. *Valentin de Boulogne*, Milan, 1989

Montias 1988
John Michael Montias. 'Art Dealers in the Seventeenth-Century Netherlands' in *Simiolus. Netherlands Quarterly for the History of Art* 18, 1988, issue 4, pp. 244–256

Mühlethaler/Thissen 1993
Bruno Mühlethaler and Jean Thissen. 'Smalt' in Roy 1993, pp. 113–130

Muller 1880
Samuel Muller. *Schilders-vereenigingen te Utrecht. Bescheiden uit het gemeente-archief*, Utrecht, 1880

Müller Hofstede 1988
Justus Müller Hofstede. 'Die Niederländer und Caravaggio. Form und Ikonographie der *lumi artificiali*' in *Sitzungsberichte / Kunstgeschichtliche Gesellschaft zu Berlin* 36, 1987/88, 1988, pp. 13–26

Neumeister 2003
Mirjam Neumeister. *Das Nachtstück mit Kunstlicht in der niederländischen Malerei und Graphik des 16. und 17. Jahrhunderts. Ikonographische und koloristische Aspekte* (Studien zur internationalen Architektur- und Kunstgeschichte 17), Petersberg, 2003

Neurdenburg 1951
Elisabeth Neurdenburg. 'De Utrechts-Haagse bouwmeesters-beeldhouwer Adriaen Fredericksz. van Oudendijck en de beelden op de poort van het Weeshuis te Buren' in *Bulletin van de Koninklijke Nederlandse Oudheidkundige*, vol. 6, 1951, issue 4, pp. 29–34

Nickel 2007
Helmut Nickel. 'The Sun, the Moon, and an Eclipse. Observations on *The Crucifixion with the Virgin and Saint John*, by Hendrick Ter Brugghen' in *Metropolitan Museum Journal* 42, 2007, pp. 121–124

Nicolaci/Gandolfi 2011
Michele Nicolaci and Riccardo Gandolfi. 'Il Caravaggio di Guido Reni. La Negazione di Pietro tra relazioni artistiche e operazioni finanziarie' in *Storia dell'arte* 130, 2011, pp. 41–64, 147–150

Nicolai 2008
Fausto Nicolai. *Mecenati a confronto. Committenza, collezionismo e mercato dell'arte nella Roma del primo Seicento. Le famiglie Massimo, Altemps, Naro e Colonna*, Rome, 2008

Nicolson 1958
Benedict Nicolson. *Hendrick Terbrugghen*, London, 1958

Nicolson 1960
Benedict Nicolson. 'Second Thoughts about Terbrugghen' in *The Burlington Magazine* 102, 1960, pp. 465–473

Nicolson 1971
Benedict Nicolson. 'Gerard Seghers and the *Denial of St Peter*' in *The Burlington Magazine* 113, 1971, pp. 304–309

Nicolson 1973
Benedict Nicolson. 'Terbrugghen since 1960' in *Album Amicorum J. G. van Gelder*, ed. Josua Bruyn and Jan Ameling Emmens, The Hague, 1973, pp. 237–241

Nicolson 1979
Benedict Nicolson. *The International Caravaggesque Movement. List of Pictures by Caravaggio and his Followers throughout Europe from 1590 to 1650*, Oxford, 1979

Nolin 2008
Heather Nolin. '"Non piacquero al Padrone." A Reexamination of Caravaggio's Cerasi Crucifixion of St. Peter' in *Rutgers Art Review* 24, 2008, pp. 41–71

North 1992
Michael North. *Kunst und Kommerz im Goldenen Zeitalter. Zur Sozialgeschichte der niederländischen Malerei des 17. Jahrhunderts*, Cologne, 1992

North 2017
Michael North. 'Der niederländische Kunstmarkt und seine Ausstrahlung in Europa' in Exh. cat. Hamburg 2017, pp. 10–17

Olde Meierink/Bakker 1997/98
Ben Olde Meierink and Angelique Bakker. 'The Utrecht Elite as Patrons and Collectors' in Exh. cat. San Francisco/Baltimore/London 1997/98, pp. 72–85

Paleotti 1582 (2002)
Gabriele Paleotti. *Discorso intorno alle immagini sacre e profane*, ed. Stefano della Torre, Vatican City, 2002

Panciroli 1600
Ottavio Panciroli. *I tesori nascosti dell'alma città di Roma*. Rome, 1600

Pampalone 2012
Antonella Pampalone. 'La lista delle Quarantore del 1597 per la festa di San Luca: nuovi documenti e precisazioni' in *L'essercitio mio è di pittore. Caravaggio e l'ambiente artistico romano*, ed. Francesca Curti, Michele di Sivo and Orietta Verdi (Roma moderna e contemporanea 19.2011,2), Rome, 2012, pp. 213–235

Papi 1990
Gianni Papi. 'Novità sul soggiorno italiano di Gerrit Honthorst' in *Paragone.Arte* 41, 1990, pp. 47–68

Papi 1993
Gianni Papi. *Orazio Borgianni*, Soncino, 1993

Papi 1998
Gianni Papi. 'Sul soggiorno fiorentino di Theodor Rombouts' in *Paragone.Arte* 49, 1998, pp. 26–38

Papi 1999
Gianni Papi. *Gherardo delle notti. Gerrit Honthorst in Italia*, Soncino, 1999

Papi 2001
Gianni Papi. *Cecco del Caravaggio*, Soncino, 2001

Papi 2002
Gianni Papi. 'Jusepe de Ribera a Roma e il Maestro del Giudizio di Salomone' in *Paragone.Arte* 53, 2002, pp. 21–43

Papi 2003a
Gianni Papi. 'Ancora su Ribera a Roma' in *Cahiers d'Historie de l'Art* 1, 2003, pp. 63–74

Papi 2003b
Gianni Papi. *Spadarino*, Soncino, 2003

Papi 2004
Gianni Papi. 'Ribera 3' in *Paragone.Arte* 55, 2004, pp. 16–21

Papi 2005/06
Gianni Papi. 'Ribera a Roma: dopo Caravaggio, una seconda rivoluzione' in Exh. cat. Milan/Vienna 2005/06, pp. 45–55

Papi 2010
Gianni Papi. 'Ancora sugli *Apostoli* di Cussida e qualche altra aggiunta al suo catalogo' in *Bulletin de l'Association des Historiens de l'Art Italien* 15/16 2009/10 (2010), pp. 7–130, 93–104

Papi 2011
Gianni Papi. 'Ribera en Roma. La revelación del genio' in Exh. cat. Madrid 2011, pp. 31–59

Papi 2013
Gianni Papi. *Bartolomeo Manfredi*, Soncino, 2013

Papi 2015
Gianni Papi. 'Gerrit van Honthorst fra Italia e Olanda' in Exh. cat. Florence 2015, pp. 32–89

Parks 1985
N. Randolph Parks. 'On Caravaggio's *Dormition of the Virgin* and its Setting' in *The Burlington Magazine* 127, 1985, pp. 438–448

Payne 1849–1852
Albert Henry Payne. *Payne's Book of Art with the Celebrated Galleries of Munich*, 3 vols., Dresden et al., 1849–1852

Peacham 1622 (1962)
Henry Peacham. 'The Compleat Gentleman. Fashioning him absolute in the most necessary & commendable Qualities concerning Minde or Bodie' in *Henry Peachman, The Complete Gentleman, The Truth of Our Times, and the Art of Living in London*, ed. Virgil B. Heltzel, Ithaca, 1962

Pericolo 2011
Lorenzo Pericolo. *Caravaggio and Pictorial Narrative. Dislocating the 'Istoria' in Early Modern Painting*, London et al., 2011

Pestilli 2017
Livio Pestilli. *Picturing the Lame in Italian Art from Antiquity to the Modern Era*, London/New York, 2017

Petrocchi 1970
Massimo Petrocchi. *Roma nel Seicento* (Storia di Roma 14), Bologna, 1970

PL
Jacques Paul Migne. *Patrologia Latina*, 217 vols., Paris, 1844–1855

Plahter/Plahter 1999
Leif Einar Plahter and Unn Simonsen Plahter. '*The Young Christ Among the Doctors* by Teodoer van Baburen. Technique and Condition of a Dutch Seventeenth-century Painting on Canvas' in *Conservare necesse est. Festskrift til Leif Einar Plahter på hans 70-årsdag. For Leif Plahter on his 70th Birthday*, ed. Erling Skaug, Oslo, 1999, pp. 42–64

Plesters 1980
Joyce Plesters. 'Tintoretto's Paintings in the National Gallery: Part II' in *National Gallery Technical Bulletin* 4, 1980, pp. 32–48

Poeschel 2014
Sabine Poeschel. *Handbuch der Ikonographie. Sakrale und profane Themen der bildenden Kunst*, Mainz, 2014

Van de Pol 2006
Lotte van de Pol. *Der Bürger und die Hure. Das sündige Gewerbe im Amsterdam der Frühen Neuzeit*, Frankfurt am Main et al., 2006

Van de Pol 2010
Lotte C. van de Pol. 'The Whore, the Bawd, and the Artist: The Reality and Imagery of Seventeenth-century Dutch Prostitution' in *Journal of Historians of Netherlandish Art* 2, 1/2, 2010, URL: https://jhna.org/wp-content/uploads/2017/08/JHNA_2.1-2_VandePol.pdf (accessed on 2.3.2018)

Pollmann 2000
Judith Pollmann. *Een andere weg naar God. De reformatie van Arnoldus Buchelius (1565–1641)*, Amsterdam, 2000

Pomponi 2011
Massimo Pomponi. 'Gli artisti presenti a Roma durante il primo trentennio del Seicento nei documenti dell'Archivio Storico del Vicariato' in Vodret 2011, pp. 107–188

Porzio/D'Alessandro 2015
Giuseppe Porzio and Domenico Antonio d'Alessandro. 'Ribera between Rome and Naples. New Documentary Evidence' in *The Burlington Magazine* 157, 2015, pp. 682–683

Prohaska 1980
Wolfgang Prohaska. 'Untersuchungen zur *Rosenkranzmadonna* Caravaggios' in *Jahrbuch der Kunsthistorischen Sammlungen in Wien* 76, 1980, pp. 111–132

Prohaska/Swoboda/Cardinali 2010
Wolfgang Prohaska, Gudrun Swoboda and Marco Cardinali. *Caravaggio und der internationale Caravaggismus* (catalogue of the collection of the Kunsthistorisches Museum, Vienna 6), Milan, 2010

Ramade 1988
Patrick Ramade. *Le Reniement de Saint Pierre* (Collections du Musée des Beaux-Arts de Rennes), Rennes, 1988

Ramon 2014
Artur Ramon. *San Jerónimo penitente de Caravaggio* (Monografies del MDM), Barcelona, 2014

Rasterhoff 2017
Claartje Rasterhoff. *Painting and Publishing as Cultural Industries. The Fabric of Creativity in the Dutch Republic. 1580–1800* (Amsterdam Studies in the Dutch Golden Age), Amsterdam, 2017

Reinders 2017
Sophie Reinders. *De mug en de kaars. Vriendenboekjes van adellijke vrouwen 1575–1640*, Nijmegen, 2017

Reinhard 1979
Wolfgang Reinhard. *Freunde und Kreaturen. 'Verflechtung' als Konzept zur Erforschung historischer Führungsgruppen: Römische Oligarchie um 1600* (Schriften der Philosophischen Fachbereiche der Universität Augsburg 14), Munich, 1979

Renger 1970
Konrad Renger. *Lockere Gesellschaft. Zur Ikonographie des Verlorenen Sohnes und von Wirtshausszenen in der niederländischen Malerei*, Berlin, 1970

Řezníček 1972
Emil Karel Josef Řezníček. 'Hont Horstiana' in *Nederlands Kunsthistorisch Jaarboek* 23, 1972, pp. 167–189

Richards 2011/12
Sandra Richards. 'Caravaggio's Roman Collectors' in Exh. cat. Ottawa/Fort Worth 2011/12, pp. 48–71

Ripa 1618 (1986)
Cesare Ripa. *Nova Iconologia*, Padua, 1618, reprint ed. Piero Buscaroli, Turin, 1986

Robertson 2008
Clare Robertson. *The Invention of Annibale Carracci* (Studi della Bibliotheca Hertziana 4), Milan, 2008

Robertson 2015
Clare Robertson. *Rome 1600. The City and the Visual Arts under Clement VIII*, New Haven, CT/London, 2015

Robinet et al. 2011
L. Robinet et al. 'Investigation of the Discoloration of Smalt Pigment in Historic Paintings by Micro-X-ray Absorption Spectroscopy at the Co K-edge' in *Analytical Chemistry* 83, 2011, issue 13, pp. 5145–5152

Roethlisberger 1993
Marcel G. Roethlisberger. *Abraham Bloemaert and his Sons. Paintings and Prints* (Aetas aurea 11), 2 vols., Doornspijk, 1993

Rommes 1991
R. Rommes. 'Op het spoor van de dood. De pest in en rond Utrecht' in *Jaarboek Oud-Utrecht*, 1991, pp. 94–120

Rommes 1998
Ronald Nicolaas Johannes Rommes. *Oost, west, Utrecht best? Driehonderd jaar migratie en migranten in de stad Utrecht (begin 16e–begin 19e eeuw)* (Amsterdamse historische reeks 38), diss. University of Amsterdam, Hilversum, 1998

Von Rosen 2015
Valeska von Rosen. *Verhandlungen in Utrecht. Ter Brugghen und die religiöse Bildsprache in den Niederlanden* (Figura 3), Göttingen, 2015

Roy 1993
Ashok Roy (ed.). *Artists' Pigments. A Handbook of their History and Characteristics*, vol. 2, Washington D.C./Oxford, 1993

Roy 2012
Ashok Roy. Caravaggio's Influence in the North' in *Caravaggio's Painting Technique*. Proceedings of the CHARISMA Workshop, ed. Marco Ciatti and Brunetto Giovanni Brunetti, Florence, 2012, pp. 85–94

Roy/Berrie 1998
Ashok Roy and Barbara Berrie. 'A New Lead-based Yellow in the Seventeenth Century' in *Painting Technique. History, Materials and Studio Practice. Contributions to the IIC Dublin Congress*, ed. Ashok Roy and Perry Smith, London, 1998, pp. 160–165

De Ruggieri 2016
Maria Beatrice De Ruggieri. 'Caravaggio's Painting Technique. Compositional Processes and Material Structures' in Vodret et al. 2016, vol. 1, pp. 89–131

Salerno 1960a
Luigi Salerno. 'The Picture Gallery of Vincenzo Giustiniani I: Introduction' in *The Burlington Magazine* 102, 1960, pp. 21–27

Salerno 1960b
Luigi Salerno. 'The Picture Gallery of Vincenzo Giustiniani II: The Inventory, Part I' in *The Burlington Magazine* 102, 1960, pp. 93–104

Salerno 1960c
Luigi Salerno. 'The Picture Gallery of Vinenzo Giustiniani III: The Inventory, Part II' in *The Burlington Magazine* 102, 1960, pp. 135–148

Salomon 2011
Xavier F. Salomon. 'The Young Ribera' in *The Burlington Magazine* 153, 2011, pp. 475–478

Sandrart 1675
Joachim von Sandrart. *Teutsche Academie der Bau- Bild- und Malerey-Künste*, Nuremberg, 1675

Sandrart 1675 (1925)
Joachim von Sandrart. *Academie der Bau-, Bild- und Mahlerey-Künste von 1675, Leben der berühmten Maler, Bildhauer und Baumeister*, ed. Arthur Rudolf Peltzer, Munich, 1925

Sandrart 1683
Joachim von Sandrart. 'Academia Picturæ eruditæ. Lateinische Ausgabe der Teutschen Academie von 1683' in Sandrart 1675 (1925), pp. 359–377

San Juan 2001
Rose Marie San Juan. *Rome. A City out of Print*, Minneapolis, MN, 2001

Sanvito 2001
Paolo Sanvito. 'Flamen und Italiener zur Zeit der Giustiniani. Kontrast zweier Kunstauffassungen' in *Jahrbuch / Stiftung Preußische Schlösser und Gärten Berlin-Brandenburg*, 2001, pp. 1–21

Savina 2013
Barbara Savina. *Caravaggio tra originali e copie. Collezionismo e mercato dell'arte a Roma nel primo Seicento*, Foligno, 2013

Van Schaik 2000
A. H. M. van Schaik. 'Een nieuwe heer en een andere leer (1528–1618)' in *'Een paradijs vol weelde.' Geschiedenis van de stad Utrecht*, ed. Renger Evert de Bruin, Utrecht, 2000, pp. 191–249

Schillemans 1992
Robert Schillemans. 'Schilderijen in Noordnederlandse katholieke kerken uit de eerste helft van de zeventiende eeuw' in *De zeventiende eeuw* 8, 1992, pp. 41–51

Schillemans 1993
Robert Schillemans. 'Over Hendrick ter Brugghen's »Kruisigingen« en de aanspraak van Adriaen Ploos op een adellijke afkomst' in *De zeventiende eeuw* 9, 1993, pp. 137–151

Von Schneider 1928
Arthur von Schneider. 'Eine Vorzeichnung Honthorsts zu der *Befreiung Petri* des Kaiser-Friedrich-Museums' in *Berliner Museen. Berichte aus den Preussischen Kunstsammlungen. Beiblatt zum Jahrbuch der Preussischen Kunstsammlungen* 49, 1928, issue 5, pp. 113–115

Schuckmann 1986
Christiaan Schuckmann. 'Did Hendrick ter Brugghen Revisit Italy? Notes from an Unknown Manuscript by Cornelis de Bie' in *Hoogsteder-Naumann Mercury* 4, 1986, pp. 7–122

Schütze 2009
Sebastian Schütze. *Caravaggio. Das vollständige Werk*, Cologne. 2009

Schütze 2011/12
Sebastian Schütze. 'Staging Religious History for Collectors and Connoisseurs' in Exh. cat. Ottawa/Fort Worth 2011/12, pp. 256–295

Schwartz 2002
Gary Schwartz. 'The Structure of Patronage Networks in Rome, The Hague and Amsterdam in the 17th Century' in *Economia e arte secc. XIII – XVIII*. Atti della 'Trentatreesima Settimana di Studi' 30.4.–4.5. 2001, ed. Simonetta Cavaciocchi (Istituto Internazionale di Storia Economica F. Datini, Prato 2; 33), Florence ,2002, pp. 567–590

Seaman 2011
Natasha Seaman. 'Materiality and the Presence of the Past in Hendrick ter Brugghen's *Crucifixion*' in *Zeitschrift für Kunstgeschichte* 74, 2011, issue 4, pp. 489–516

Seaman 2012
Natasha Therese Seaman. *The Religious Paintings of Hendrick ter Brugghen. Reinventing Christian Painting after the Reformation in Utrecht*, Farnham, 2012

Seelig 1994
Gero Seelig. 'Ter Brugghens Lazarus-Gemälde: eine Bassano-Adaption' in *Oud Holland* 108, 1994, pp. 14–16

Sickel 2001
Lothar Sickel. 'Künstlerrivalität im Schatten der Peterskuppel. Giuseppe Cesari d'Arpino und das Attentat auf Cristoforo Roncalli' in *Marburger Jahrbuch für Kunstwissenschaft* 28, 2001, pp. 159–189

Sickel 2003
Lothar Sickel. *Caravaggios Rom. Annäherung an ein dissonantes Milieu*, Emsdetten/ Berlin, 2003

Sickel 2006
Lothar Sickel. 'Zwei römische Privatsammler des frühen Seicento. Ippolito Gricciotto, Paolo Mercati und die Nachfolger Caravaggios' in *Marburger Jahrbuch für Kunstwissenschaft* 33, 2006, pp. 197–223

Slatkes 1962
Leonard Joseph Slatkes. *Dirck van Baburen, c. 1595–1624. A Dutch Painter in Utrecht and Rome*, Utrecht, 1962

Slatkes 1965
Leonard Joseph Slatkes. *Dirck van Baburen, c. 1595–1624. A Dutch Painter in Utrecht and Rome* (Orbis artium 5), Utrecht, 1965

Slatkes 1981/82
Leonard Joseph Slatkes. 'Reviewed Work. The International Caravaggesque Movement by Benedict Nicolson' in *Simiolus. Netherlands Quarterly for the History of Art* 12, 1981/82, issue 2/3, pp. 167–189

Slatkes 1988
Leonard Joseph Slatkes. 'Rethinking ter Brugghen's Early Chronology' in Klessmann 1988, pp. 77–84

Slatkes 1996
Leonard Joseph Slatkes. 'Bringing Ter Brugghen and Baburen Up-to-date' in *Bulletin du Musée National de Varsovie* 37, 1996, pp. 199–219

Slatkes/Franits 2007
Leonard Joseph Slatkes and Wayne Edward J. Franits. *The Paintings of Hendrick ter Brugghen, 1588–1629. Catalogue raisonné*, Amsterdam et al., 2007

Sluijter 1992
Eric Jan Sluijter. '"Een Schijn sonder Sijn." De Noordnederlandse schilderkunst van de 17de eeuw en de problemen van het begrip "realisme"' in *De Republiek*, ed. J. Worms (Oriëntatiecursus Cultuurwetenschappen 2), Heerlen 1992 (Open Universiteit), pp. 139–164

Sluijter 2005
Eric Jan Sluijter. 'Over "rapen" en wedijver in de Nederlandse schilderkunst van de zeventiende eeuw' in *De zeventiende eeuw* 21, 2005, pp. 267–291

Sluijter 2015/16
Eric Jan Sluijter. 'Ownership of Paintings in the Dutch Golden Age' in *Class Distinctions. Dutch Painting in the Age of Rembrandt and Vermeer, ed.* Ronni Baer (Exh. cat. Museum of Fine Arts, Boston / Nelson-Atkins Museum of Art, Kansas City), Boston, 2015, pp. 89–111

Van der Sman 2015
Gert Jan van der Sman. *I disegni di Gerrit van Honthorst* in Exh. cat. Florence 2015, pp. 102–119

Solinas 1992
Francesco Solinas. 'Ferrante Carlo, Simon Vouet et Cassiano dal Pozzo. Notes et documents inédits sur la période romaine' in *Simon Vouet*, Actes du colloque international, Galeries nationales du Grand Palais 5–7.2.1991, ed. Stéphane Loire, Paris, 1992, pp. 135–147

Spaans 1989
Joke Spaans. *Haarlem na de Reformatie. Stedelijke cultuur en kerkelijk leven, 1577–1620* (Hollandse historische reeks 11), The Hague, 1989

Spear 1982
Richard E. Spear. *Domenichino*, 2 vols., New Haven, CT, 1982

Spear 2003
Richard E. Spear. 'Scrambling for Scudi. Notes on Painters' Earnings in Early Baroque Rome' in *The Art Bulletin* 85, 2003, pp. 310–320

Spear 2012
Richard E. Spear. 'A Database of Prices Paid to Painters in Seventeenth-century Rome' in *Getty Research Journal* 2, 2010, pp. 147–150

Spear/Sohm 2010
Richard E. Spear and Philip L. Sohm. *Painting for Profit. The Economic Lives of Seventeenth-century Italian Painters*, New Haven, CT et al., 2010

Spezzaferro 2001
Luigi Spezzaferro. 'La Cappella Cerasi e il Caravaggio' in Bernardini/Mignosi Tantillo 2001, pp. 9–34

Spezzaferro/Mignosi Tantillo 2001
Luigi Spezzaferro and Almamaria Mignosi Tantillo. 'Appendice documentaria' in Bernardini/Mignosi Tantillo 2001, pp. 108–124

Steinhardt-Hirsch 2011
Claudia Steinhardt-Hirsch. 'Les Règles divines des parties. Glück und Schelmenleben in der Malerei Georges de La Tours' in *SpielKunstGlück. Die Welt als Leitlinie der Entscheidung. Beispiele aus Vergangenheit und Gegenwart in Kunst, Wissenschaft, Wirtschaft* (Grazer Edition 7), ed. Johann Konrad Eberlein, Vienna et al. 2011, pp. 165–180

Stevens 1984
Jane R. Stevens. 'Hands, Music, and Meaning in some Seventeenth-century Dutch Paintings' in *Imago Musicae* 1, 1984, pp. 75–102

Strauss/Van der Meulen 1979
Walter L. Strauss and Marjon van der Meulen. *The Rembrandt Documents*, New York, 1979

Strinati/Zuccari 2010
Claudio Strinati and Alessandro Zuccari (eds.). *I Caravaggeschi. Percorsi e protagonisti*, 2 vols., Milan, 2010

Sturm 2015
Saverio Sturm. *La 'Provincia Romana' (L'architettura dei Carmelitani scalzi in età barocca 2)*, Rome, 2015

Van Suchtelen 1991
Ariane van Suchtelen. 'Hendrik ter Brugghen's *Bacchante with an Ape*. The Painter's Working Method and Theme' in *The J. Paul Getty Museum Journal* 19, 1991, pp. 35–42

Suthor 2005
Nicola Suthor. 'Maler und Modell. Caravaggios Handleserin' in *Diskurse des Theatralen*, ed. Erika Fischer-Lichte and Christian Horn (Theatralität 7), Tübingen, 2006, pp. 123–132

Swillens 1945/46
P.T.A. Swillens. 'Rubens' bezoek aan Utrecht' in *Jaarboekje van 'Oud-Utrecht'*, 1945/46, pp. 105–125

Temminck Groll et al. 1972
Coenraad Liebrecht Temminck Groll et al. 'Utrecht in de 17e eeuw. Architectonische en stedebouwkundige aspecten' in *Jaarboek Oud-Utrecht*, 1972, pp. 115–143

Van Thiel 1967/68
Pieter J. J. van Thiel. 'Marriage Symbolism in a Musical Party by Jan Miense Molenaer' in *Simiolus. Netherlands Quarterly for the History of Art* 2, 1967/68, issue 2, pp. 91–99

Van Thiel 1971
Pieter J. J. van Thiel. 'De aanbidding der koningen en ander vroeg werk van Hendrick ter Brugghen' in *Bulletin van het Rijksmuseum* 19, 1971, pp. 91–116

Van Thiel 1988
Pieter J. J. van Thiel. 'In Quest of the Early Ter Brugghen' in Klessmann 1988, pp. 85–88

Van Thiel 1990/91
Pieter J. J. van Thiel. 'Catholic Elements in Seventeenth-century Dutch Painting, Apropos of a Children's Portrait by Thomas Keyser' in *Simiolus. Netherlands Quarterly for the History of Art* 20, 1990/91, pp. 39–62

Thielemann 2018
Andreas Thielemann. 'Glaskugeln in Wissenschaft und Kunst der frühen Neuzeit' in *Lumen – Imago – Pictura. La luce nella storia dell'ottica e nella rappresentazione visiva da Giotto a Caravaggio*, ed. Sybille Ebert-Schifferer, Pietro Roccasecca and Andreas Thielemann, Rome, 2018, pp. 65–82

Timmers 1947
Jan J. M. Timmers. *Symboliek en iconografie der Christelijke kunst*, Roermond-Maaseik, 1947

Treffers 2010
Bert Treffers. 'Dirck van Baburen e David de Haen' in Strinati/Zuccari 2010, vol. 2, pp. 287–293

Tummers 2011
Anna Tummers. *The Eye of the Connoisseur. Authenticating Paintings by Rembrandt and his Contemporaries* (Amsterdam Studies in the Dutch Golden Age), Amsterdam, 2011

Uppenkamp 2004
Bettina Uppenkamp. *Judith und Holofernes in der italienischen Malerei des Barock*, Berlin, 2004

Utrechtsch kronijkjen 1846
'Utrechtsch kronijkjen' in *Archief voor kerkelijke en wereldsche geschiedenissen, inzonderheid van Utrecht*, vol. 6, ed. Johannes Jacobus Dodt van Flensburg, Utrecht, 1846, pp. 9–222

Vannugli 1998
Antonio Vannugli. 'Orazio Borgianni, Juan de Lezcano and a *Martyrdom of St Lawrence* at Roncevalles' in *The Burlington Magazine* 140, 1998, pp. 5–15

Vannugli 2009
Antonio Vannugli. 'La collezione del segratario Juan de Lezcano. Borgianni, Caravaggio, Reni e altri nella quadreria di un funzionario spagnolo nell'Italia del primo Seicento' in *Atti della Accademia Nazionale dei Lincei* 9, 2009, issue 24, pp. 323–539

Varriano 2006
John L. Varriano. *Caravaggio. The Art of Realism*, University Park, Pennsylvania, 2006

Van Veen 1992
Hendrik Thijs van Veen. 'Uitzonderlijke verzamelingen. Italiaanse kunst en klassieke sculptuur in Nederland' in *De wereld binnen handbereik. Nederlandse kunst- en rariteitenverzamelingen, 1585–1735*, ed. Ellinoor Bergvelt and Renée Kistenmaker (Exh. cat. Amsterdams Historisch Museum), Amsterdam, 1992, pp. 102–116

Van der Veen 2002
Jaap van der Veen. 'Delftse verzamelingen in de zeventiende en eerste helft van de achtiende eeuw' in *Schatten in Delft. Burgers verzamelen. 1600–1750*, ed. Ellinoor Bergvelt and Michiel Jonker (Exh. cat. Stadelijk Museum Het Prinsenhof, Delft), Zwolle, 2002, pp. 49–89

Van der Veen 2005
Jaap van der Veen. 'By His Own Hand. The Valuation of Autograph Paintings in the 17th Century' in *A Corpus of Rembrandt Paintings*. Rembrandt Research Project Foundation, vol. 4, ed. Ernst van de Wetering et al., Dordrecht, 2005, pp. 3–44

Veldman 2001
Ilja M. Veldman. *Crispijn de Passe and his Progeny (1664–1670). A Century of Print Production* (Studies in Prints and Printmaking 3), Rotterdam, 2001

Verdi 2011
Orietta Verdi. '"So' cascato per queste strade." La città del Caravaggio' in *Caravaggio a Roma. Una vita dal vero*, ed. Eugenio Lo Sardo, Michele di Sivo and Orietta Verdi (Exh. cat. Archivio di Stato di Roma), Rome, 2011, pp. 32–45

Virch 1958
Claus Virch. 'The Crucifixion by Hendrick Terbrugghen' in *The Metropolitan Museum of Art Bulletin* 16, 1958, pp. 217–226

Vlam 1977
Grace A. H. Vlam. 'The Calling of St. Matthew in Sixteenth-century Flemish Painting' in *The Art Bulletin* 59, 1977, pp. 561–570

Vodret 1996
Rossella Vodret. 'Simon Vouet, 1617. Una "Buona Ventura" per Cassiano dal Pozzo' in *Bollettino d'arte* 98, 1996 (1997), pp. 89–94

Vodret 2011
Rossella Vodret (ed.). *Alla ricerca di 'Ghiongrat'. Studi sui libri parrocchiali romani (1600–1630)*, Rome, 2011

Vodret et al. 2016
Rossella Vodret et al. *Caravaggio. Opere a Roma: tecnica e stile*, 2 vols., Cinisello Balsamo, 2016

Vodret/Leone 2008
Rossella Vodret and Giorgio Leone (eds.). *Honthorst e il Cristo deriso della Chiesa dell'Immacolata Concezione a Roma. Studio storico-critico, tecnica di esecuzione, restauro* (I restauri della Soprintendenza per i Beni Artistici e Storici del Lazio 6), Rome, 2008

Volpe 1972
Carlo Volpe. 'Annotazioni sulla mostra caravaggesca di Cleveland' in *Paragone.Arte* 23, 1972, pp. 50–76

Van de Water 1729
Johannes van de Water. *Groot Utrechts placaatboek vervattende alle de placaten, ordonantien en edicten, der edele mogende Heeren staten ,s lands van Utrecht*, 3 vols., Utrecht, 1729

Weber 2015/16
Gregor J. M. Weber. 'Ter Brugghen's Lost Martyrdom of St. Bartholomew. What a Copy Can Tell' in *Simiolus. Netherlands Quarterly for the History of Art* 38, 2015/16, issue 4, pp. 250–259

Welu 1975
James A. Welu. '"Card Players and Merrymakers." A Moral Lesson' in *Bulletin of the Worcester Art Museum* 4, 1975, issue 3, pp. 8–16

Wethey 1964
Harold Edwin Wethey. 'Orazio Borgianni in Italy and in Spain' in *The Burlington Magazine* 106, 1964, pp. 147–159

Wheelock 2015
Arthur K. Wheelock Jr. *Gerrit van Honthorst. The Concert. 1623*, NGA Online Editions, URL: https://purl.org/nga/collection/artobject/163184 (accessed on 18.10.2017)

White 1995
Valentina White. 'Il soggiorno romano di Dirck van Baburen. La committenza e le opere' in Danesi Squarzina/Baldriga 1995, pp. 168–193

Wind 1989
Barry Wind. 'A Note on Card Symbolism in Caravaggio and his Followers' in *Paragone. Arte* 40, 1989, pp. 15–18

Witting 1916
Félix Witting. *Michelangelo da Caravaggio. Eine kunsthistorische Studie* (Zur Kunstgeschichte des Auslandes 113), Strasbourg, 1916

Ypey 1976
J. Ypey. 'Mondharpen' in *Antiek* 11, 1976, issue 3, pp. 209–231

Zicarelli 2005
Emanuela Zicarelli. 'Per un censimento degli artisti nella parrocchia di San Lorenzo in Lucina' in *Arte e immagine del papato Borghese (1605–1621)*, ed. Bruno Toscano, Beatrice Cirulli and Federica Papi, San Casciano, 2005, p. 33–48

Zuccari 2004
Alessandro Zuccari (ed.). 'San Pietro in Montorio' in *La Spagna sul Gianicolo*, vol. 1, Rome, 2004

Zuccari 2010
Alessandro Zuccari. 'Il caravaggismo a Roma. Certezze e ipotesi' in Strinati/Zuccari 2010, vol. 1, pp. 31–59

Zuccari 2016
Alessandro Zuccari. 'Observations on Iconographic and Compositional Changes in the Contarelli "Laterals"' in Vodret et al. 2016, vol. 1, pp. 211–221

Colophon

This catalogue has been published to accompany the exhibition

Utrecht, Caravaggio en Europa
Utrecht, Centraal Museum
16 December 2018 – 24 March 2019

Utrecht, Caravaggio und Europa
Munich, Bayerische Staatsgemäldesammlungen, Alte Pinakothek
17 April 2019 – 21 July 2019

Exhibition Concept
Liesbeth M. Helmus
Bernd Ebert

CENTRAAL MUSEUM

ALTE PINAKOTHEK

EXHIBITION UTRECHT

Directors
Marco Grob and Bart Rutten

Project team
Manon van den Berg – *Staff member Education & Interpretation*
Patricia Bosboom – *Staff member Marketing & Communication*
Henk Heerink – *Coordinator Technical Staff*
Liesbeth M. Helmus – *Senior Curator of Old Masters*
Maaike van Kaam – *Senior staff member Development & Sponsor Recruitment*
Kristine Kavelaars – *Senior Project Coordinator*
Martien van Liefland – *Staff member Development & Fundraising*
Manou Nonnekes – *Staff member Marketing & Communication*
Jacqueline Rutten – *Head of Public and Information*
Arthur Schoonderwal – *Head of Facilities Management*
Merel Vens – *Head of Commercial Affairs*
Marjan van Zijtveld – *Staff member Collection Management*

Exhibition Design
Marcel Schmalgemeijer

EXHIBITION MUNICH

Director General Bernhard Maaz
Head of Dutch and German Baroque Painting Bernd Ebert
Research Associate Susanne Hoppe
Assistant Patrick Kammann
Registrars Verena Rayer, Maria Espinosa
Restauration and Painting Technology Eva Ortner, Jan Schmidt, Ulrike Fischer, Johannes Engelhardt, Heike Stege, Anke Rothe, Melanie Bauernfeind, Jens Wagner
Exhibition Technicians Wolfgang Wastian, Dieter Stracke, Heino Kahrs, Diego Sanchez Villasante
Press Department Tine Nehler, Bianca Henze, Julia Kaufmann, Lucie Boucek, Max Westphal
Art Education and Visitor Services Jochen Meister, Christopher Förch, Stephanie Waldschmidt, Anke Palden
Events Barbara Siebert, Nadia Khatschi-Barnstein, Andrea Schick, Katarina Jelic, Anja Kiendl
Administration Gregor Lindermayr, Gabriele Prager, Sylvia Marx, Stephanie Niederalt
Photographic Department Haydar Koyupinar, Sibylle Forster, Nicole Wilhelms, Johannes Haslinger, Margarita Platis
Building Services Johann Strobl, Stephan Friedemann, Hermann Fronauer, Nikolaus von Killinger
Exhibition Design and Graphics designposition Büro für Gestaltung, München
Visual Communication and Social Media Kulturkonsorten, München; Google Arts & Culture, London/Berlin
Media Design Prof. Gerwin Schmidt, Büro für visuelle Gestaltung, München
Many thanks are also due to Ulrich Baur, Susanne Engelsberger, Antje Lange, Ilona von Mariassy, Johanna Mocny, Nino Nanobashvili, Sylvia Pongratz, Anna-Sophia Reichelt, Philipp Schäfer, Norbert Schölzel, Andreas Schumacher, Marlene Sichelschmidt, Jessica Vogelsang, Gerhard Wagenpfeil, Lars Zieke

CATALOGUE

Editors Bernd Ebert, Liesbeth M. Helmus
Authors Marten Jan Bok, Bernd Ebert, Liesbeth M. Helmus, Susanne Hoppe, Helen Langdon, Volker Manuth, Ashok Roy
Editing Susanne Hoppe
Picture Editors Susanne Hoppe, Patrick Kammann
Project Management Jutta Allekotte, Hirmer Publishers
Copy-editing Philippa Hurd
Translations from the German Bram Opstelten
Translations from the Dutch Michael Hoyle
Design, Typesetting and Production Sophie Friederich, Hirmer Publishers
Cover Design Gerwin Schmidt, Büro für visuelle Gestaltung, Munich
Pre-Press Reproline mediateam, Munich
Paper GardaArtMatt 150gr
Typeface Scala
Printing and Binding APPL, Aprinta Druck, Wemding

Bibliographic information published by the Deutsche Nationalbibliothek
The Deutsche Nationalbibliothek lists this publication in the Deutsche Nationalbibliografie; detailed bibliographic data is available on the Internet at http://www.dnb.de.

ISBN 978-3-7774-3132-1 (German edition)
ISBN 978-3-7774-3133-8 (English edition)
ISBN 978-3-7774-3183-3 (Dutch edition)

www.hirmerpublishers.com
www.hirmerpublishers.co.uk

The exhibition in Utrecht is sponsored by

Gemeente Utrecht
BankGiroLoterij
GIESKES·STRIJBIS FONDS
Rijksdienst voor het Cultureel Erfgoed, Ministerie van Onderwijs, Cultuur en Wetenschap
BLOCK BUSTER FONDS: BankGiroLoterij, Prins Bernhard Cultuurfonds, VSBfonds, VandenEnde Foundation
Mondriaan Fonds
VanBaaren Stichting
Turing Foundation
Ekfheinfonds
Prins Bernhard Cultuurfonds
M4 No More Boring Flooring www.m4four.com
PHILIPS

The exhibition in Munich is sponsored by

EvS Ernst von Siemens Kunststiftung
Finanzgruppe
Sparkassen-Kulturfonds des Deutschen Sparkassen- und Giroverbandes
Bayerische Sparkassenstiftung
Stadtsparkasse München
Kingdom of the Netherlands
Kulturstiftung der Länder

Picture Credits

Abingdon Alamy Stock Photo / Jozef Sedmak: p. 66
Abingdon Alamy Stock Photo / The Picture Art Collection: p. 132r
Amsterdam Rijksmuseum: pp. 32, 57, 71, 88, 108r, 203, 217
Amsterdam Rijksmuseum / on loan from the Broere Charitable Foundation: pp. 157, 159
Amsterdam Rijksmuseum / on loan from the Rijksakademie van Beeldenden Kunsten: p. 260
Antwerp Royal Museum of Fine Arts © www.lukasweb.be – Art in Flanders vzw: pp. 96/97, 215 / Hugo Maertens: p. 188t
Belgium private collection: p. 210
Berlin bpk / Alinari Archives / Alinari: p. 45
Berlin bpk / Alinari Archives / Magliani, Mauro for Alinari: pp. 100l, 226
Berlin bpk / Gemäldegalerie, SMB / Jörg P. Anders: pp. 60l, 69, 123, 126, 268r / Christoph Schmidt: p. 264
Berlin bpk / Gemäldegalerie, SMB, property of the Kaiser Friedrich Museumsverein / Jörg P. Anders: p. 175r
Berlin bpk / Kassel, Museumslandschaft Hessen Kassel: pp. 170, 171
Berlin bpk / Kimbell Art Museum / Art Resource, NY: p. 212
Berlin bpk / RMN – Grand Palais / Benoît Touchard: p. 268l / Franck Raux: p. 254 / Michel Urtado: p. 177, 201, 230
Berlin bpk / Scala: pp. 42, 59r, 100r, 149, 180, 204, 253
Berlin bpk / Scala – courtesy of the Ministero Beni e Att. Culturali: pp. 87, 108l, 155, 161, 164r, 194l, 256
Berlin bpk / Staatliche Kunstsammlungen Dresden: p. 124 / Hans-Peter Klut: p. 211, 248
Berlin bpk / Staatliches Museum Schwerin / Gabriele Bröcker: p. 127
Berlin Bridgeman Images / photo © Christie's Images: p. 134
Berlin Bridgeman Images / The Art Institute of Chicago, IL, USA / Through prior acquisition of the George F. Harding Fund: p. 56
Berlin Bridgeman Images / Musée des Beaux-Arts André Malraux, Le Havre, France: p. 181
Berlin Bridgeman Images / North Carolina Museum of Art, Raleigh, USA: pp. 121, 221
Berlin Bridgeman Images / Palazzo Farnese, Rome, Italy: p. 48
Berlin © Staatliche Museen zu Berlin, Gemäldegalerie / Christoph Schmidt: pp. 187, 274/275
Boston © [2017] Museum of Fine Arts: p. 252
Braunschweig Herzog Anton Ulrich Museum, Kunstmuseum des Landes Niedersachsen, Museumsfotograf: pp. 118, 195
Brescia Pinacoteca Tosio Martinengo Brescia, on loan from the Unicredit Art Collection: p. 172l
Brussels © Royal Museums of Fine Arts of Belgium / photos: J. Geleyns: p. 58
Budapest © Szépművészeti Múzeum – Museum of Fine Arts Budapest: p. 213
Cambridge Imaging Department © President and Fellows of Harvard College: pp. 64, 68
Copenhagen Statens Museum for Kunst, National Gallery of Denmark, photo: Jakob Skou-Hansen: p. 238
Diest De Hofstadt Municipal Museum Diest: pp. 271, 273
Doornspijk from: Judson/Ekkart 1999 (fig. III): p. 116
Dublin © National Gallery of Ireland: pp. 70, 228
Florence © Firenze, Fondazione di Studi di Storia dell'Arte Roberto Longhi: p. 219l
Florence Misericordia di Firenze (fondata nel 1244): p. 153
Frankfurt © Städel Museum – ARTOTHEK: p. 175l
France private collection: p. 106
Genoa Museo dell'Accademia Ligustica di Belle Arti: p. 140
Genoa © Musei di Strada Nuova: p. 224
Ghent Museum voor Schone Kunsten, © www.lukasweb.be – Art in Flanders vzw: p. 272
Grenoble Ville de Grenoble / Musée de Grenoble – J.L. Lacroix: p. 162
Haarlem Teylers Museum: p. 28
Hartford Allen Phillips\Hartford, Wadsworth Atheneum: p. 232
Houston Museum of Fine Arts: p. 219r
Kansas City The Nelson-Atkins Museum of Art, photo: Jamison Miller: p. 192l
Kassel Museumslandschaft Hessen Kassel, Gemäldegalerie Alte Meister: p. 33
Langres Coll. Musées de Langres, © S. Riandet: p. 154
Libourne Jean-Christophe Garcia © Musée des beaux-arts de Libourne: p. 184
London Courtesy of Robilant+Voena: p. 165
London Schorr Collection: p. 183
London © The National Gallery: pp. 1, 139, 164l, 239, 243
London © The National Gallery / photo: Ashok Roy: p. 90
Los Angeles County Museum of Art, photo: Museum Associates / LACMA: pp. 18/19, 131
Los Angeles Digital image courtesy of the Getty's Open Content Program: pp. 132l, 240
Madrid Colomer Collection: p. 225
Madrid Museo de la Real Academia de Bellas Artes de San Fernando: p. 229
Madrid Museo Nacional Thyssen-Bornemisza: pp. 85, 227, 267, 269
Mainz © GDKE_Landesmuseum Mainz (Ursula Rudischer): p. 75
Minneapolis Minneapolis Institute of Art: pp. 117, 209
Modena Ministero dei Beni e delle Attività Culturali e del Turismo – Archivio Fotografico delle Gallerie Estensi – photo: Carlo Vannini: p. 166
Montserrat Museu de Montserrat: pp. 10, 112
Munich Bayerische Staatsgemäldesammlungen: pp. 47, 76, 77, 80, 83, 91, 163, 193, 196, 233 (Haydar Koyupinar, Sibylle Forster, Nicole Wilhelms, Margarita Platis, Johannes Haslinger)
Munich © Doerner Institut: p. 197
Naples Ministero per i Beni e le attività culturali e del turismo – Fototeca del Polo Museale della Campania: pp. 107, 109
New York Sotheby's / private collection: pp. 31, 188b
New York The Metropolitan Museum of Art: pp. 40/41, 44r, 86, 145, 194r, 241, 263
Norfolk Chrysler Museum of Art, Norfolk, Virginia: p. 249
Oberlin Allen Memorial Art Museum, Oberlin College: p. 245
Oslo Nasjonalmuseet for kunst, arkitektur og design: pp. 99, 199, 282
Ottawa National Gallery of Canada: p. 59l
Padua Mauro Magliani: p. 223
Paris C2RMF / Philippe Salinson: p. 133.
Paris Bibliothèque nationale de France: pp. 54/55
Paris private collection: p. 110
Paris private collection, Courtesy Nicolas Joly Art Conseil: p. 176
Perth Courtesy of Perth Museum and Art Gallery, Perth and Kinross Council Scotland: p. 207
Philadelphia Philadelphia Museum of Art: p. 218
Pommersfelden Kunstsammlungen Graf von Schönborn: p. 136
Rancate (Mendrisio), Cantone Ticino, Svizzera, Pinacoteca cantonale Giovanni Züst, photos: Roberto Pellegrini: pp. 6/7, 113, 137
Rennes © Jean-Manuel Salingue – Musée des beaux-arts de Rennes – 2018: pp. 2/3, 115
Rome Alessandro Vasari: pp. 92, 143
Rome Bibliotheca Hertziana – Max-Planck-Institute for Art History, Rome: p. 67
Rome German Archaeological Institute, Rome, Library: p. 53
Rome Gallerie Nazionali di Arte Antica di Roma: p. 185, 255 / Bibliotheca Hertziana – Max-Planck-Institute for Art History, Rome, photo: Enrico Fontolan: p. 119
Rome Sovrintendenza Capitolina ai Beni Culturali, Museo di Roma, Archivio Iconografico: pp. 36, 39, 43
Rotterdam Museum Boijmans Van Beuningen / Studio Tromp, Rotterdam: p. 24
Saint Petersburg Courtesy of The State Hermitage Museum, Saint Petersburg, Russia: pp. 120, 172r
Santiago de Compostela © Jesús Madriñán: p. 148
The Hague Mauritshuis: pp. 60r, 125
Toulouse Musée des Augustins, photo: Daniel Martin: pp. 150, 151, 235
Utrecht Centraal Museum: pp. 4, 169, 174, 189, 246 / Ernst Moritz: pp. 27, 34, 50, 105, 147, 167, 173, 179, 259, 261 / Tom Haartsen: p. 251
Utrecht Het Utrechts Archief: pp. 20, 22/23, 25, 26
Utrecht Museum Catharijneconvent: pp. 12, 89, 191, 247
Valencia Museo del Patriarca, Real Colegio Seminario de Corpus Christi de Valencia: p. 101
Vienna Albertina: pp. 82, 135
Vienna KHM-Museumsverband: p. 192r
Warsaw © Copyright by Ligier Piotr/Muzeum Narodowe w Warszawie: p. 244
Washington, D.C. National Gallery of Art: p. 44l, 129, 237
Zürich © Kunsthaus Zürich: p. 73

It has not been possible to identify the image rights holders in every case. Legitimate claims will of course be compensated according to the usual regulations. All other images are taken from the authors' archives.

Front and back cover
Hendrick ter Brugghen, *St Sebastian Tended by Irene* (detail), 1625, © Allen Memorial Art Museum, Oberlin College Oberlin, Ohio; R. T. Miller, Jr. Fund, 1953